# The Remuneration Handbook

International Second Edition

# Endorsements

Those of us who have been involved in the publication of the recent SID Remuneration Committee Guide appreciate the importance and complexities of remuneration. Remuneration is a sophisticated tool that has the ability to drive behaviour - both positive and negative - and outcomes. Effective approaches to remuneration require knowledge of finance, accounting, statistics, psychology, governance and labour law, as well as the human resource domains such as performance management and career planning. Certainly, in this book, Fermin Diez has brought the needed multidisciplinary perspective that incorporates the various elements of compensation in a holistic, practical and detailed manner. While the book is clearly a reference handbook for human resource practitioners, it is also one for boards, especially for Remuneration Committee members who need to delve into the intricacies of remuneration strategies, models, and their mechanics.

*Willie Cheng, Chairman, Singapore Institute of Directors*

The knowledge and insights shared in this book are testament to Mark and Fermin's commitment to ensuring that organisational success is achieved through ethical reward practices that drive sustainable individual and business performance. Their passion for the development and advancement of reward professionals and practices has already led to the implementation of impactful and cost-effective reward strategies in many organisations. I therefore highly recommend this book to anyone who is serious about developing and executing a total reward strategy that focuses people on achieving their objectives in a way that benefits all stakeholders.

*Lindiwe Sebesho, President (2015 – 2016), South African Reward Association (SARA)*

Remuneration is more than just compensation for services rendered by individuals to organisations; it's a psychological tool to foster psychological ownership and work engagement, and to retain top talent. In this International Edition of the *Remuneration Handbook*, Mark Bussin and Fermin Diez capture not only the practical realities, challenges and management of REM within the corporate reality, but emphasise the psychological impact thereof on the retention of top talent. This book carries my highest recommendation for all those wanting to streamline, benchmark and manage remuneration more effectively within the private and public sectors.

*Llewellyn E. Van Zyl, Associate Professor in the Programme of Industrial Psychology, School of Behavioural Sciences, Faculty of Humanities, North-West University*

If you were searching for an authority with a deep and wide knowledge of the principles and dynamics of remuneration, you would be looking for Dr. Mark Bussin. Having worked closely with him over the past 15 years, I can confidently say that Mark is one of a select few people who have a highly strategic, yet very practical, understanding of the role remuneration plays in the lives of employers, employees and society at large. This handbook distils and explains that vast body of knowledge and experience Mark has acquired.

*Alan Hosking, Executive Editor & Publisher: HR Future, Osgard Media*

This work offers a one-stop shop that not only provides insight on remuneration as a strategic tool in the execution of organisational goals, but is also a demonstration of the fundamentals necessary to achieve compatibility between human engagement and expended effort. It deals with the organisational capability to master the demands of a competitive market environment in acknowledging and rewarding talent. This International edition of *The Remuneration Handbook* is bound to become a landmark work that shows how to develop and manage remuneration as an organisational practice. Not only does it touch on the basics of remuneration, but it also sheds light on the processes involved in getting it right. It is a journey from the traditional approach to the most up-to-date minute detail of what remuneration entails. It furthermore offers an overview of the governance that is necessary to get it right. The adoption and application of the content will assist practitioners and organisations to envision, design, develop and implement a remuneration strategy that has the potential to address most of the uncertainties that surface every time the issue of remuneration is brought to the table. It is a comprehensive source to be consulted in managing expectations about remuneration.

*Prof. Frans Maloa, Department of Industrial and Organisational Psychology, College of Economic and Management Sciences, University of South Africa*

In this edition of his book, Mark has once again demonstrated why he is probably the best this country and the continent has to offer with regards to thought leadership and people development on matters related to total rewards and recognition, and their impact on both business and employee performance. Mark has managed to bring simplicity to the complex world of remuneration by clearly "joining-the-dots" between organisational culture, strategy/plans through different business cycles, setting individual objectives and targets, and managing and rewarding team and individual performance. The tools provided in this book are practical for ease of use by both remuneration and HR experts to support line managers in managing their businesses. Given the current shareholder/stakeholder activism on total rewards, this guide on the Remuneration Committee's mandates, roles and responsibilities addresses the missing but critical link of governance and monitoring requirements – a useful tool for boards of companies.

*Kgabo Moabelo, Past Executive Vice President: People and Organisational Effectiveness, Gold Fields*

Dr. Mark Bussin's name is synonymous with global remuneration trends across a number of sectors. We at DBSA have been using Dr. Bussin's sound advice and counsel throughout the years at all levels. We have been able to drive a long-term sustainable compensation strategy by working with him.

I recommend that all companies going through any kind of transformation engage Dr. Bussin on all matters of remuneration.

*Ms Dolores Mashishi, Group Executive: Corporate Services, The Development Bank of Southern Africa*

The earlier edition of *The Remuneration Handbook* demystified the mechanics of remuneration. It made the subject more appealing to the HR practitioner who had in the past moved away from this subject as it was perceived as too technical for the layman. In this new International Edition, Mark and Fermin manage to simplify the area with great insight. The good thing about this book is it now contextualises remuneration in such a way that we all want to do it according to the book. I am even tempted to say it's like the law on remuneration matters. What a relief to all of us in the People Management domain. The new edition has gone even further to make organisations experts in these matters. I see that even line managers who are not traditionally trained in these matters have developed a huge interest in applying some of the messages HR has been preaching for some time. It is indeed helping us to do what is right for both the employees and the organisation. It is a fantastic reference book with technically sound content. Well done – I love having it on my desk daily.

*Obadiah Khwinana, Business Executive at Auditor General of South Africa*

The International Edition of the *Remuneration Handbook* is the definitive text for remuneration practice. The book has been updated with the latest global trends and developments in this evolving and growing specialised field of human resource reward practice. We believe that it is no coincidence that reward has become one of the strongest performance areas in the SABPP audits conducted against the National HR Standards. This book is playing a significant role in elevating reward practice to national, continental and international standards of excellence. All reward and human resource managers, as well as top and senior management teams and indeed remuneration committee members, should read and apply this text to further improve remuneration governance and practice

*The late Marius Meyer, Senior Lecturer in HR Management, Department of Industrial Psychology, Stellenbosch University*

Bussin and Diez, two leaders in the field, have produced a remarkably detailed and comprehensive handbook on compensation. It is a giant work filled with rich detail on how modern organisations organize pay systems. If one had the energy, she could read it cover to cover and be up to speed quickly on the profession. It can also be used as a wonderful reference work to check in on a dizzying set of compensation issues. I'll be recommending it to my students and colleagues in the profession.

*Professor Joseph Rich, Director of the Institute for Compensation Studies, and Kenneth Kahn, Dean of the School of Industrial and Labor Relations at Cornell University*

To be an effective professional in the field of compensation and benefits takes many years of experience. Fermin Diez and Mark Bussin are two highly accomplished "pracademics" that have successfully managed to distill their collective many years of experience into this *Remuneration Handbook*. The key feature of the book is the emphasis it has on the broad practical application of the concepts presented, yet always staying close to the research foundations on which these principles rest. For both experienced professionals as well as those new to the field, this is a reference book to keep close at hand. Its rare to find a book that addresses your day to day questions in a simple yet comprehensive way.

*Ashwani Dahiya, Global Chief Talent Officer & Head of Corporate HR, Cipla*

It is rare to find someone who has the unique experience that Dr. Mark Bussin provides in this most important area of remuneration and related topics - his input is both strategic and relevant. Together with that, Mark is able to look at your unique situation and provide solutions to real world problems that are both practical and implementable.

*Eileen Wilton, CEO Gijima*

First published in 2017 (International Edition).
Second updated edition in 2021 (International Edition).

ISBN: 978-1-86922-891-0 (Printed)
eISBN: 978-1-86922-892-7 (PDF eBook)
eISBN: 978-1-86922-893-4 (Epub)
eISBN: 978-1-86922-894-1 (Mobi)

Published by KR Publishing
P O Box 3954
Randburg
2125
Republic of South Africa

Tel: (011) 706-6009
Fax: (011) 706-1127
E-mail: orders@knowres.co.za
Website: www.kr.co.za

Printed and bound: HartWood Digital Printing, 243 Alexandra Avenue, Halfway House, Midrand
Typesetting, layout and design: Cia Joubert, cia@knowres.co.za
Cover design: Sean Sequeira, idDigital, sean@iddigital.co.za
Editing: Adrienne Pretorius, pretorii@mweb.co.za
Proofreading: Jill Bishop, jill.bishop@absamail.co.za
Project management: Cia Joubert, cia@knowres.co.za
Index created with TExtract/www.Texyz.com

# The Remuneration Handbook

A practical and informative handbook for
managing reward and recognition

**International Second Edition**

**DR. MARK BUSSIN & DR. FERMIN DIEZ**

kr
publishing

2021

# Acknowledgements

We share many common passions: a good bottle of red wine, loud rock'n'roll and how remuneration affects everyone in one way or another. Although we are from – and live in – different parts of the world, we find that many of the issues we face transcend frontiers, and when the opportunity to collaborate emerged, we both jumped at it with glee.

This book would not have been published without the extensive contributions from many very dedicated people.

A number of people were instrumental mentors in setting the base right. Thank you to Martin Westcott, Jon Cole, Naomi Brehm, Adele Slotar, Charlie Rogers and Robin Ferracone for teaching and sharing their knowledge.

Thank you to the contributors of the relevant chapters.

Many more of our colleagues, clients and students have inspired us and challenged our thinking – thank you to all.

To Knowledge Resources, thank you for co-ordinating the production and marketing of this book.

A special thank you to Chris Blair for his insight.

A great thank you to Marina, Daniel, Kate, Genna, James, Augusto and Su-Yen for your inspiration and patience.

Dr. Mark Bussin and Dr. Fermin Diez
Johannesburg and Singapore, 2021

# Foreword

by Professor Margie Sutherland

Remuneration is a driver of organisational strategy, operational performance, employee commitment, job satisfaction and retention. It is thus a key element of performance management and as such needs to be deeply understood. It is simultaneously a highly complex field – half an art and half a science – needing deep understanding to inform the myriad decisions and trade-offs one has to make when making reward decisions. The outcomes of these decisions have the potential to be either positive or negative for individuals, teams and organisations. Remuneration is never neutral. This book will assist students and managers of remuneration to maximise the return on employee costs, which in many firms account for more than 50 percent of operating costs. In order to maximise the return on investment, the remuneration system must be defendable, efficient and effective. Remuneration intersects with many domains in organisational life: budgeting, cost control, annual reporting, human behaviour, process efficiency, marketing, market research, communication practices both internal and external, as well as productivity. It has its own lexicon which needs to be mastered.

The current range of legislative, corporate and organisational reporting demands; the often critical media reportage and exposés; stakeholder pressure for moral corporate governance; and demands for greater transparency increase the need for this book. Remuneration management is a difficult skill that needs to be mastered as part of the career capital of human resource managers who are serious about their own futures and credibility. All executives who serve on, or aspire to serve on, boards of directors and remuneration committees need a sound body of knowledge of remuneration practices to influence the success of the organisations they serve. This book provides the base for acquiring the knowledge skills and world view necessary for accountable leadership.

Remuneration has additional layers of complexity stemming from high GINI coefficients, over-supply of unskilled labour, under-supply of skilled and executive talent, and the presence of many expatriate managers. These factors lead to steep pay slopes unknown in more developed economies. There is a concomitant under-supply of remuneration experts and thus remuneration management should be a career of choice and point of differentiation for managers within the human capital domain globally. The insights in this book need to be put to good use and will provide the springboard for career and organisational success.

Mark Bussin and Fermin Diez have consistently contributed to the development of a host of human resource managers and remuneration experts via their corporate and consulting experience, wise counsel, writings, and hundreds of lectures, TV and radio interviews. They have upskilled a generation of remuneration professionals, helped define the field of practice, and made a significant contribution to the national level of excellence in the field.

As a young postgraduate student, Mark was given an article to read on "Super-leadership", in which he learned that to rise to great heights, one has to give away all that one knows to as many people as possible. This he has done tirelessly. He has informed the remuneration skills, knowledge and world view of thousands of individuals and organisations. Fermin has also felt this urge to develop more and better professionals in the HR field, as evidenced by his nearly 30 years of teaching and writing. His view of HR as "Implementing Business Strategy Through People" permeates much of this book. It is a great pleasure to see the fruits of their careers made available to a wide audience in this well-written, usable and value-adding handbook.

Professor Margie Sutherland
Gordon Institute of Business Science
University of Pretoria

# Table of contents

# About the authors

## Dr Mark Bussin

Mark is the Chairperson of 21st Century, a specialist reward and remuneration consultancy. He has HR, reward and remuneration experience across all industry sectors, and is viewed as a thought leader in the HR, reward and remuneration arena. He serves on and advises numerous Boards and Remuneration Committees on Executive Remuneration. Mark holds a Doctorate in Commerce. He has published or presented over 350 articles and papers, and has received awards for his outstanding articles in this field. He has appeared on television and radio, and in the press, giving expert views on remuneration. Mark is a guest lecturer at several universities and supervises Masters' and Doctoral theses in the Reward area. He is a past President of SARA (South African Reward Association) and a past Commissioner for the remuneration of Public Office-Bearers in the Presidency. Mark tutors reward and finance modules for WorldatWork globally.

Mark enjoys flying Cessnas and loves his family time.

Mark can be contacted at: drbussin@mweb.co.za or visit his website: www.drbussin.com or on mobile number +27829010055.

## Dr Fermin Diez

Fermin has had a life-long commitment to the development of people and the HR profession. He has nearly 40 years of experience in human resources, which includes public sector, consulting, corporate and academic roles in 40 countries in all continents.

He is the Deputy CEO at Singapore's National Council for Social Service as well as its Group Director for Human Capital Development. As a consultant Fermin has worked with major HR consultancies Mercer, Towers Watson and Deloitte. Most recently he was the Talent Business Leader for Asia, Middle East and Africa at Mercer. He has advised multinationals, local companies and public sector organisations across various industries, at the Board and C-Suite levels. He also led the team that advised on the review of the pay programme for political appointees in Singapore. As a Human Resources leader, he has been Regional Head of HR for two large MNCs in Asia Pacific and in Latin America: PepsiCo and Freescale. In his academic career, he is an Adjunct Professor at both Singapore Management University (SMU) and Nanyang Technological University (NTU). Fermin has also previously taught Business Policy and Strategic Planning in Latin American universities. His current area of research is the comparative effectiveness of various pay schemes. He has co-authored two other books: *Human Capital and Global Business Strategy* and *Fundamentals of HR Analytics*.

Fermin obtained his Doctorate from Singapore Management University, his MBA from the Wharton School, University of Pennsylvania and his undergraduate degree in Psychology from the University of Michigan. He is certified by SHRM as a Senior Professional of Human Resources (SPHR). He is also a CCP (Certified Remuneration Professional) from WorldatWork. He is a former member of the Global WorldatWork Board of Directors, and a current member of the Global Advisory Council there. Fermin has served on the Taylor's Education Group Board, on the JurongHealth Board, and on the National University Health System where he was on the Human Resources Committee. Previously he was on the Singapore Management University Business School Advisory Board, and on the Children's Cancer Foundation Board. He is a regular speaker at regional and global fora (Rio de Janeiro, New York, Miami, Philadelphia, Hong Kong, Singapore, London, Brussels, etc.) and is a frequent commentator in the media including CNA, CNN and Reuters. He is also a fellow of the Singapore Institute of Directors and a Master Professional of the Institute of HR Professionals, where he is Dean of Education and Chairman of the Assessments Committee.

Fermin enjoys playing his guitars and travelling with his wife and children.

He can be reached via email at fermin@fermindiez.com or mobile phone +65 9819-3425.

# List of contributors

The following contributors are true experts and have developed world-class methodologies in remuneration. They are thought leaders who are highly regarded by peers and clients alike.

**Chris Blair** is CEO of 21st Century Pay Solutions group. He has consulted nationally and internationally to several hundred organisations. Email: cblair@21century.co.za

**Craig France** is a Chartered Accountant and Executive Consultant. He is a thought leader in the area of incentive schemes and sales commission schemes. Email: craigfrance@21century.co.za

**Craig Raath** is an Executive Director responsible for Sales and Marketing and is a thought leader in the area of Employee Engagement. Email: craath@21century.co.za

**Tamaryn Loots** is a Payroll and Legislation Specialist at VIP Payroll. Email: tamarynl@vippayroll.co.za

**Dr. Lukas de Swart** has moved from top management positions in large corporates to consulting. He is a thought leader in Reward, Project Management and Processes. Email: lukas.deswardt@vodamail.co.za

**Morag Phillips** is an Executive Director and is responsible for human resource management. She runs the Survey Benchmarking division and electronic products. Email: mphillips@21century.co.za

**Dr. Ronél Nienaber** is one of the leading HR and Reward practitioners in Africa and has held some of the largest jobs in Reward and HR Management in South Africa. She is a founder, past president and EXCO member of the South African Reward Association. Email: ronel.nienaber@sasol.co.za

**Tom Farmer** runs his own consulting firm Freelance Total Rewards in South East Asia. He has also held senior roles at Intercontinental Hotels, Mercer and Hewitt, and is a frequent instructor for WorldatWork. Email: tfarmer@freelancetotalrewards.com.

**Samir Bedi** is a partner at EY in Singapore, specialising in Human Capital Consulting. He also teaches Remuneration at Singapore Management University. Email: Samir.bedi@sg.ey.com

**Shai Ganu** is a Partner at Mercer, responsible for the Talent business across Asia, covering the Information Solutions, Management Consulting and Board Advisory portfolios. He is an author, speaker, board member, university lecturer, and renowned expert in Executive Remuneration. Email: shai.ganu@mercer.com

**Rosaline Koo** is the founder and CEO of CXA, one of the fastest growing start-ups in Asia and one that is disrupting the market of Employee Benefits thanks to its innovative approaches. Email: rosaline@cxagroup.com.

# About this book

This book is aimed at helping current and future HR practitioners, remuneration professionals and business leaders understand the complex subject of Remuneration. Our aim is to define how to design and apply Total Rewards models in order to provide value to their organisations through improving this key area of the Employee Value Proposition.

The area of Rewards is increasingly important for business, HR and remuneration leaders as the VUCA world we live in faces dramatic demographic shifts, sustained market growth globalisation, and cultural and generational differences that are causing many organisations to re-think the way they engage with their people. Pay may not be the only part of the Employee Value Proposition (EVP) today that helps to attract, retain and engage talent, but it is clearly important. Properly designed pay programmes can create value, but pay plans that do not consider local culture and practices will likely fail or fall short of expectations are of limited real value, and can even create discord in the organisation.

The key features of the book you are holding include:

- A detailed explanation as to why one size does not fit all when it comes to deploying remuneration programmes;
- A look at Sales Remuneration, Benefits, Payroll issues, Executive Pay, Director's Pay and Governance – subjects that are not often included in books of this nature; and
- An overview of culture matters in developing pay programmes.

One of the main features of our book is the blend of academic rigour coupled with practical advice to illustrate the points we make. We include examples/cases where one of the authors or collaborators has had a direct hand in implementing the strategy or concepts explained in the book.

Our aim was to create a document which can serve practitioners in the field as well as educators in University programmes focused on HR Management:

- To provide insights on the power of pay programmes in organisations;
- To share helpful considerations for more holistic pay programme design and implementation;
- To provide remuneration practitioners and HR professionals, both current and future, with helpful frameworks and essential ideas for their success; and
- To create a strong text for use by HR students in undergraduate and graduate programmes as well as a reference guide for practitioners.

We made some improvements to this second edition, including updated every chapter and made additions to the areas of Job Evaluation, Pay Structures and Performance Appraisals. We also completely updated the last chapter on Future Trends. Finally, we devoted more attention to the areas of governance and executive remuneration.

The book is organised as follows:

Chapter 1 provides a broad overview of the role of pay with regards implementing strategy through people. It also introduces the total rewards model that we follow in the understanding of how rewards operate.

Chapters 2 through 8 deal with all aspects of setting up a Base Pay programme. We also include a chapter on Performance Management.

Chapters 9 and 10 deal with two practical issues for Remuneration professionals: Total Pay Packages and Payroll.

Chapters 11 through 15 are all about Incentives, including Sales Remuneration and Executive Pay.

Chapter 16 is about Benefits, the next part of the Total Rewards model.

Chapters 17 and 18 talk about the last part of the total Rewards model: Retention, Engagement and Recognition.

Chapter 19 deals with the complex issue of Expatriate Remuneration.

Chapters 20 and 21 focus on rewarding Directors, including a look at Governance issues which are a big topic of discussion globally.

Finally, Chapter 22 looks into the future of the Remuneration arena.

Where relevant, each chapter includes one or more practical examples to illustrate the theory. All chapters end with a summary and key questions for consideration. We also include a thorough bibliography which can be used for suggested readings.

One final note: although we believe the terms "Remuneration" and "Compensation" to be interchangeable, we acknowledge that in the US, Canada and South America, "Compensation" is preferred, while the UK, Australia, NZ, and most of Africa prefer "Remuneration". American multi-nationals in Asia seem to have infiltrated the term "Compensation". As we both prefer the term "Remuneration", we have made every attempt to use it consistently throughout the book.

We trust you will find this handbook a useful tool to learn about the different aspects of Remuneration and as a reference guide for years to come.

# Acronyms used

| | | | |
|---|---|---|---|
| AO | Advanced operational | LTO | Labour turnover |
| BCG | Boston Consulting Group | NEDs | Non-executive diretors |
| BPR | Business process re-engineering | PAYE | Pay as you earn |
| BS | Bonus schemes | PPP | Pay Progression Policy |
| C&B | Compensation & Benefits | PRP | Performance-related pay |
| CBP | Competency-based pay | PS | Profit-sharing |
| CEO | Chief executive officer | RemCos | Remuneration committee |
| CGT | Capital gains tax | RI | Rolling incentives |
| CLC | Corporate Leadership Council | SaaS | Software-as-a-Service |
| COL | Cost of living | SARA | South African Reward |
| COLA | Cost of living allowance | | Association |
| CR | Compa-ratio | SARS | South African Revenue |
| CS | Commission schemes | | Service |
| CST | Critical success targets | SBP | Skills-based pay |
| DDI | Development Dimensions | SEISs | Share-based Executive |
| | International | | Incentive Schemes |
| EIM | Enterprise incentive management | SS | Share schemes |
| EPS | Earnings per share | SST | Stratified Systems Theory |
| ESS | Employee Self Service | STIs | Short-term incentives |
| EVA | Economic value added | TGP | Total guaranteed package |
| EVP | Employee Value Proposition | TR | Total reward |
| EXCO | Executive Committee | TSR | Total shareholder return |
| FMCG | Fast Moving Consumer Goods | UIF | Unemployment Insurance |
| GDP | Gross domestic product | | Fund |
| GP | Guaranteed pay | UQ | Upper quartile |
| GS | Gain-sharing | VAS | Value-add schemes |
| HD | Highest decile | VBM | Value-based management |
| HR | Human resources | VP | Variable pay |
| IME | Internationally-mobile expatriate | | |
| JE | Job evaluation | | |
| KPAs | Key performance areas | | |
| LD | Lowest decile | | |
| LLB | Legum Baccalaureus (degree in law) | | |
| LMA | Local market approach | | |
| LQ | Lower quartile | | |
| LRA | Labour Relations Act | | |
| LTIs | Long-term incentives | | |

# CHAPTER 1

# Organisation Strategy and Reward Policy

## 1.1 Introduction

The main purpose of the Human Resources (HR) function of an organisation is to help implement the business strategy through its people.[1] The need for the remuneration policy, strategy and systems to underpin business strategy has never been greater. Our organisations have been downsized, right-sized, subjected to business process re-engineering (BPR) and transformed, to enable them to compete in today's volatile, uncertain, complex and ambiguous (VUCA) world. Unfortunately, our pay systems have not always responded to these and often lag behind in organisation transformation.

This book is a practical guide that can be followed so that the remuneration policy and strategy can effectively "catch up" with the business strategy. It is the remuneration policy and strategy that underpin business strategy, and not the other way around. There is no such thing as the "best" policy or strategy, only the one that best drives the human resources (HR) and business strategies.

Strategy is about making the right choices for any particular situation or circumstance. In different situations or circumstances, one might choose a different strategy.

## 1.2 Context

Traditionally, pay systems were aimed at ensuring conformity by rewarding seniority and attendance. However, to implement their business strategies, organisations today seek to encourage employees to be customer-centric, highly responsive, committed to quality, efficient, innovative, focused, culturally sensitive and effective.

Reward programmes are increasingly used to attract, retain and motivate employees.[2] Well-designed remuneration systems play a strategic role by promoting organisational success in highly competitive markets in which technological change constantly influences how employees perform their jobs.[3] Indeed, some go so far as to argue that there are strong links between remuneration system design and organisational performance.[4]

---

1   Thomas, Smith & Diez, 2013.

2   Ibid.

3   Martocchio, 1998; Bussin, 2015b.

4   Greenhill, 1988; Modise, 1993; Rodgers, 1999; Rynes & Gerhart, 2000; Van der Vyver & Bussin, 2013; Young, 2002.

Milkovich and Newman[5] provide a powerful analogy of the impact of pay. When the supertanker Exxon Valdez ran aground in Alaska, fast action was required to rescue wildlife from the spreading oil. For $20 an hour, local members of an Eskimo tribe were hired to care for stranded whales, cleaning and feeding them until they could be released. When the temporary, highly-paid jobs were no longer available, the Eskimos went back to their usual occupation – hunting the whales. The point is that money matters. It matters what is paid and how it is paid.

There are many examples of pay systems that have gone wrong, and unhitching an organisation from them is difficult. To alleviate this, more information is needed to understand the impact of pay policy changes on organisations. In its simplest form, remuneration policy has positive and negative effects on organisations. One needs an appreciation of which remuneration policy changes have had the greatest positive and negative impacts on organisations over the past three years. There is solid evidence that remuneration decisions affect business performance.[6] Strategic differences do matter, and organisations need to be informed when making these choices. We hope that readers of this book will gain a better understanding of the impact of business strategy on remuneration policy decisions.

The collapse of major companies and the media scrutiny of pay practices in prominent companies has led to an urgent need for additional information on which to base decisions and a heightened requirement for shareholders to be more active in the influencing of these key decisions.

## 1.3 Organisation strategy

To get the remuneration strategy right, HR professionals need to really understand the business well and how it competes for customers, revenue and profits. There are many different strategy models, and an organisation can use any one of them that works for it. Here we will discuss three different ways of looking at organisational strategy.

### 1.3.1 Competitive strategy

Organisations typically place primary focus on one of three areas:

- Operational excellence: a price/cost-based strategy that can include a combination of price, quality, dependability and ease of purchase, minimising waste and rewarding efficiency.
- Product/service leadership: an innovation-based strategy that focuses on product development and market exploitation, creating the best products, generating more/better ideas and commercialising them faster than their competitors.
- Customer intimacy: a solutions-based strategy that focuses on creating results for carefully selected customers by building bonds to meet or exceed custom needs in order to build loyalty.

---

5   Milkovich & Newman, 2014.

6   Bussin & Huysamen, 2003; Gerhart, 2000.

Each of these strategies attract a different type of underpinning reward strategy.[7] Operational excellence, for example, could mean a focus on productivity gain sharing, whilst product or service leadership may require a workplace that supports creative thinking.

## 1.3.2 Market positioning

Where the organisation is positioned in the Boston Consulting Group's (BCG) matrix has a bearing on the remuneration mix. Earnings potential may be different if there are different business units in different quadrants (see Figure 1.1).

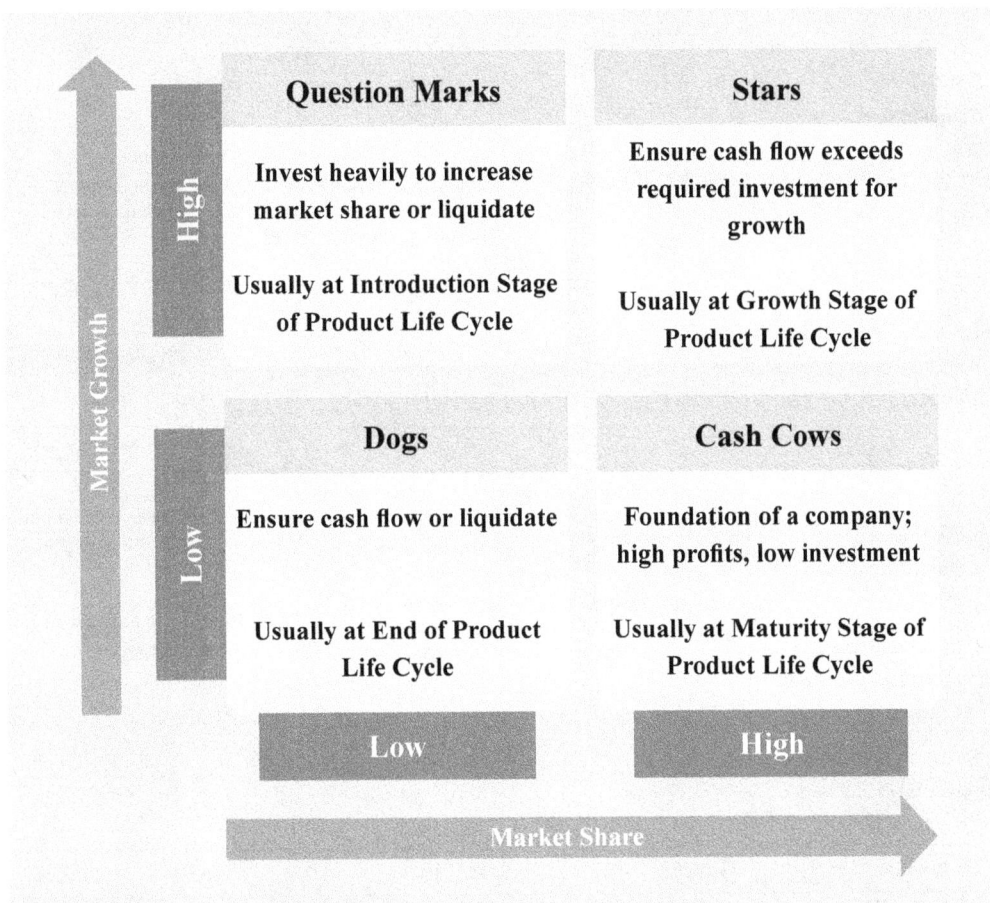

*Figure 1.1: BCG matrix*

## 1.3.3 Business life cycle

Where the organisation is in its business life cycle has a significant impact on the Remuneration Strategy adopted. Figure 1.2 shows an example of Industry or Business Growth, while Table

---

7    Bussin & Huysamen, 2003.

1.1 shows the most appropriate Remuneration Strategy for each. Depending on where the organisation is on the curve, the remuneration strategy may be different. The biggest impact is on the remuneration mix (relationship between fixed and variable pay).

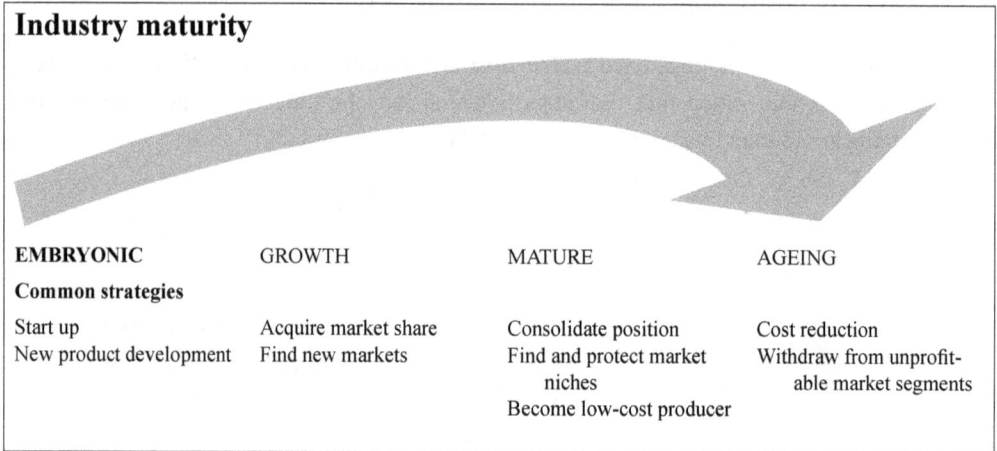

**Industry maturity**

| EMBRYONIC | GROWTH | MATURE | AGEING |
|---|---|---|---|
| **Common strategies** | | | |
| Start up | Acquire market share | Consolidate position | Cost reduction |
| New product development | Find new markets | Find and protect market niches | Withdraw from unprofit-able market segments |
| | | Become low-cost producer | |

*Figure 1.2: Business life cycle*

*Table 1.1: Industry growth rate and remuneration strategy*

| Common approaches to remuneration | | | |
|---|---|---|---|
| Less emphasis on salary, benefits and perks<br><br>Attention to share options and long-term incentives<br><br>Stress on non-financial rewards (excitement of the new venture) | Continued emphasis on long-term incentives with increasing attention | Cost attention focused on keeping salary and perks competitive<br><br>Reduced concern for long-term incentives<br><br>Bonuses oriented to productivity improvement | Benefits and salary are king.<br><br>Very little attention given to long-term growth- oriented incentives |
| Embryonic | Growth | Mature | Ageing |
| Start up<br><br>New product development | Acquire market share<br><br>Find new markets | Consolidate position.<br><br>Find and protect market niches<br><br>Become low-cost producer | Cost reduction<br><br>Withdraw from unprofitable market segments |

## 1.4    Organisational characteristics

When developing a pay strategy, HR professionals must consider a number of components that can enhance or compromise a remuneration plan.

Organisations rarely, if ever, have a remuneration plan devoted solely to one of these components. Companies use a mix of all aspects but choose to emphasise the components that best suit their corporate culture and business strategy.

The following are key components in remuneration's role in business strategy:

- **Organisation Structure:** Is the corporation hierarchical or does it maintain relatively few employee levels?
- **Organisational Culture:** Does management focus on efficiency and maintenance of the status quo, or does it encourage innovation and creativity?
- **Competitive Positioning:** Does the organisation intend to maintain or expand its market share?
- **External Environment:** How does the organisation's remuneration plan compare to remuneration of competitors? What are the internal/external demographics of the workforce? How do current employees view the remuneration system?
- **Policy Administration:** Is the organisation highly centralised or decentralised? How does the organisation communicate management    decisions and corporate policy to its workforce?

### 1.4.1    Organisational structure

The structure of an organisation is derived directly from the corporate strategy and culture, and reflects the influence of the corporation's competitive positioning and management philosophy. It has great influence on remuneration plan administration. Organisations generally maintain either a hierarchical or a flat structure.

*Hierarchical structure*

In this type of structure, we will find many levels of employees with relatively small differentials between them. The many levels create high job specificity, which will drive many elements of the remuneration strategy design. The structure is commonly found in unionised manufacturing environments. Remuneration often plays a support role in these cases, with the following characteristics:

- High base salary to aid in long-term employee retention.
- Little emphasis on performance incentives to promote stable environment.
- Skills-based pay possible to increase flexibility and efficiency of workforce.
- Use of non-monetary rewards for recognition purposes only.
- Emphasis on traditional benefits

### *Flat structure*

Under a flat structure, we will normally find relatively few employee levels with large differentials between levels. This type of structure requires greater workforce flexibility, which influences the design of rewards strategies. It is typical of research and development-oriented industries. Remuneration often plays a change-agent role, with the following characteristics:

- Low base salary due to low cash flow
- Emphasis on organisation, unit and individual incentive pay to create a dynamic, competitive environment
- Use of non-monetary rewards as performance incentives
- Emphasis on flexible and non-traditional benefits

## 1.4.2    Organisational culture

The culture is largely reflective of the organisation's competitive positioning and has significant implications concerning organisational structure. Generally, organisations attempting to expand their market share promote a risk-taking spirit to complement an aggressive vision. Conversely, companies focusing on market share maintenance are more risk averse, relying upon established norms.

### *Risk-taking*

In a risk taking culture, it is normal to find a measure of high financial risk due to an aggressive market approach. This often leads to reduced cash flow due to investment into new products and/or markets, which requires a flexible workforce and low job specificity. Remuneration will tend to have the following characteristics:

- Low base salary due to low cash flow.
- Emphasis on organisation, unit and individual incentive pay to create a dynamic, competitive environment.
- Use of non-monetary rewards as performance incentives.
- Emphasis on flexible and non-traditional benefits.

### *Risk adverse*

In a risk adverse culture, the emphasis is on consistency and loyalty, which requires adherence to established policies, relying on traditional norms and values. These cultures are usually described as highly paternalistic. In this environment, remuneration would have these characteristics:

- High base salary to aid in long-term employee retention.
- Little emphasis on performance incentives to promote a stable environment.
- Skills-based pay sometimes used to increase the flexibility and efficiency of the workforce.
- Use of non-monetary rewards for recognition purposes only.
- Emphasis on traditional benefits

### 1.4.3 Competitive positioning

Competitive positioning refers to an organisation's competitive outlook and the central vision driving the business strategy. In its simplest form, a business philosophy seeks either to expand or maintain market share.

*Expansion*

This is similar to the risk-taking culture above, where one would find high financial risk due to an aggressive market approach. This often leads to reduced cash flow due to investment into new products and/or markets, which requires a flexible workforce and low job specificity. Remuneration will tend to have the following characteristics:

- Low base salary due to low cash flow.
- Emphasis on organisation, unit and individual incentive pay to create a dynamic, competitive environment.
- Use of non-monetary rewards as performance incentives.
- Emphasis on flexible and non-traditional benefits.

*Maintenance*

With this business strategy, we normally find a stable environment due to a conservative market approach. Often it is accompanied by a relatively high cash flow, high job specificity and formalised rules and functions. Remuneration will tend to have the following characteristics:

- High base salary to aid in long-term employee retention.
- Little emphasis on performance incentives to promote a stable environment.
- Use of non-monetary rewards for recognition purposes only.
- Emphasis on traditional benefits.
- Skills-based pay possible to increase the flexibility and efficiency of the workforce.

### 1.4.4 External environment

The external environment represents influences on remuneration plan design that are largely uncontrolled by HR professionals. The two uncontrollable variables are workforce demographics and competitor remuneration. Demographics – the age, tenure and diversity of a company's workforce – play a large role in whether a conservative or aggressive remuneration programme will succeed.

*Homogeneous*

A homogenous workforce tends to be relatively older with long tenured employees. It is often dominated by a single type of employee. Remuneration will tend to have the following characteristics:

- Conservative approach.
- High base salary to aid in long-term employee retention.
- Little emphasis on performance incentives to promote a stable environment.
- Use of non-monetary rewards for recognition purposes.
- Emphasis on traditional benefits, especially retirement-oriented programmes.
- Often provides elder-care benefits.

### Diverse

In contrast, a diverse workforce will be relatively younger with shorter tenures. Remuneration in this case will tend to have the following characteristics:

- Aggressive approach.
- Low base salary due to low cash flow.
- Emphasis on company, unit and individual incentive pay to create a dynamic, competitive environment.
- Use of non-monetary rewards as performance incentives.
- Emphasis on flexible and non-traditional benefits to accommodate a younger workforce.
- Often provides child-care benefits.

## 1.4.5   Policy administration

The main objectives concerning the administration of remuneration are to promote both a feeling of ownership and fairness. These goals are greatly influenced by both the level of centralisation and the openness of communication within the organisation.

### Centralised

In a centralised environment, there is generally limited communication. However, little communication is necessary due to acceptance of established norms, values and policies, and there is often a sense of fairness due to an internally consistent delivery. Thus, there is little difficulty communicating about the remuneration plan due to its simplicity. Remuneration in these cases will tend to have the following characteristics:

- High base salary to aid in long-term employee retention.
- Little emphasis on performance incentives to promote a stable environment.
- Use of non-monetary rewards for recognition purposes only.
- Emphasis on traditional benefits.

### Decentralised

In a decentralised environment, there is generally a trusting atmosphere with open communication, which promotes a sense of ownership as individual business units make remuneration decisions. Communication is necessary to explain the complex nature of remuneration plans. Remuneration in this case will tend to have the following characteristics:

- Low base salary due to low cash flow.
- Emphasis on organisational, unit and individual incentive pay.
- Use of non-monetary rewards as performance incentives.
- Emphasis on flexible and non-traditional benefits.

## 1.5 Reward strategy

Once an organisation adopts a total reward framework, the next step is to design an overall rewards strategy and practices that support the achievement of the business strategy. For example, an organisation that relies heavily on the expertise and customer knowledge of its employees may choose to emphasise retention over performance, and thus offer employees flexibility to choose from the different components included in the framework and within the overall remuneration strategy and policy, at the same total cost for the employer. The total reward framework allows for the design of different, employee-initiated reward profiles. For example, in recognition of superior performance, employees may prefer to attend an international conference instead of receiving five extra days' leave, or take a 10 percent reduction in salary in return for working five hours fewer per week (that is, working 4.5 days instead of five full days).

Although total flexibility in reward offerings may be appealing to many employees, the reality is that for large and medium-sized organisations today, it is very difficult (although technologically possible) to administer thousands of different reward profiles on the basis of unique individual preferences. The administration and governance burden would be onerous (although some day this cost may come down). A way some companies have of overcoming this difficulty is to segment the workforce. Workforce segmentation stems from marketing methodologies where customers are segmented in order to develop more effective marketing strategies.[8] Reward profiles are different types of rewards clustered according to the needs of different employee segments. In this way, the reward needs and attitudes of the different employee segments are determined and responded to without creating an unmanageable administration burden.[9] Reward profiles for different segments of employees are more manageable than thousands of different individual reward profiles.

For most organisations, the cost associated with salaries, incentives, benefits and perks is the largest expense on their income statement, from 50 to 65 percent.[10] However, organisations offer the same reward package to all employees without differentiating according to individual preferences.[11] This means that organisations are offering benefits, perks, incentives and other types of rewards to employees at huge expense, but receive limited return on their investment, as the offering may not align to employees' specific needs.[12] A recent trend that has emerged

---

8    Du Toit, Erasmus & Strydom, 2007.

9    Gross & Edelsten, 2006.

10   Gerhart & Rynes, 2003; Milkovich & Newman, 2014.

11   Menefee & Murphy, 2004; Moore & Bussin, 2009.

12   Thornton, 2008; Schlechter, Faught & Bussin, 2014.

is that reward preferences are predictable according to different generations. Giancola[13] states, however, that there is a closer correlation between "stage in life cycle" and reward preferences than between different generations and reward preferences per se. Therefore, younger people generally have a greater need for additional leave to attend to family responsibilities, and older workers are less inspired by career aspirations. These preferences are not necessarily linked to respective generational profiles. Demographic factors such as age are therefore important in analysing reward preferences.[14]

This view was confirmed in a study conducted by global consulting house Willis Towers Watson, where younger respondents preferred bonuses of all types as well as flexible schedules compared to older respondents, who also indicated a greater preference for retirement plans compared to younger workers.[15]

Attitudes towards reward programmes are changing. Employers realise today that remuneration is no longer used only as a currency in exchange for effort, time and skill, and reward programmes are increasingly used to attract, retain and motivate employees.[16] It has also been proven that, where reward processes have been linked to key performance drivers in an organisation, employee morale, retention, engagement and productivity have significantly improved. Furthermore, governance and compliance with organisational policies and regulatory requirements are enhanced.[17] This confirms that although there appears to be a need for more flexible reward programmes aligned to employee needs, these programmes should still be governed by policies, guidelines and frameworks, and should not lead to total flexibility at the expense of regulation.

## 1.6   Multi-dimensional construct of reward

The reward arena is fertile ground for confusion. The same term can have different meanings, derived from different situations and contexts. It is therefore important to clarify a few related terms on the basis of the most widely used interpretations. Some elements of a reward system are described as follows:

- Policies provide guidelines on managing rewards and include, for example, comparison to market, internal equity versus external equity, the composition of the total reward offering, the role of line managers in decision-making, governance concerning pay decisions, and transparency.
- Practices or systems provide for financial and non-financial rewards and outcomes (for example increases) that can be either performance- or non-performance-orientated.

---

13   Giancola, 2008.
14   Bussin, 2015b.
15   Menefee & Murphy, 2004.
16   Gross & Friedman, 2007.
17   Corsello, 2006.

- Processes are concerned with reward, for example, evaluating the relative size of jobs (job evaluation) and assessing individual performance (performance management).
- Procedures are followed in order to maintain the reward system and to ensure that it operates efficiently and flexibly and provides value for money.
- Reward criteria refer to the bases upon which organisations determine and distribute rewards.
- Reward strategy sets out what the organisation intends to do in the longer term, for example, to develop and implement reward policies, practices and processes to support the achievement of business goals and meet individual needs.[18]

The reward strategy of an organisation therefore informs all employees of the direction the organisation wishes to take on reward management, as well as the types of rewards that are offered to support the accomplishment of the organisational strategy.[19] The strategy provides a well-reasoned and actionable framework for developing reward policies, practices and processes. It further differentiates the components of total rewards and is based on the needs and values of the organisation and its employees. The reward strategy ensures that the organisation is directing its reward investments appropriately to achieve the greatest business impact.[20]

Effective reward strategies positively influence employee behaviour by incorporating extrinsic and intrinsic motivators. Employees receive tangible and intangible rewards in return for their performance, while making a meaningful contribution to the organisation. As the organisation succeeds, so does the employee, and vice versa.[21]

The total reward framework evolves from the organisation's reward strategy. "Total reward" is defined as the combination of all types of rewards, including financial and non-financial, indirect as well as direct, intrinsic and extrinsic, which are made available to employees. The concept of total rewards therefore combines what are referred to as "transactional rewards" (tangible rewards, including pay and benefits) and "relational rewards" (referring to intangible rewards such as learning and development, recognition and status, and challenging work).[22]

There are a number of different total reward models described by several authors.[23] Although these models differ in the detail of the content covered, the key features in all are similar. WorldatWork, the largest global not-for-profit professional association dedicated to knowledge leadership in total rewards, defines total rewards as containing six core reward categories, which are illustrated in the following model (see Figure 1.3):

---

18  Armstrong, 2014; Milkovich & Newman, 1999; Gross & Friedman, 2007; Chiang, 2005.

19  Henderson, 2003.

20  Armstrong, 2014; Gross & Edelsten, 2006.

21  Martin, 2004.

22  Armstrong, 2014:629; Milkovich & Newman, 2014:7.

23  WorldatWork, 2007; Armstrong, 2014; Armstrong & Thompson, 2005; CLC, 2002c; Mercer Human Resources Consultants, 2007; Gross & Friedman, 2007; Zingheim & Schuster, 2007; Towers Perrin, 2006.

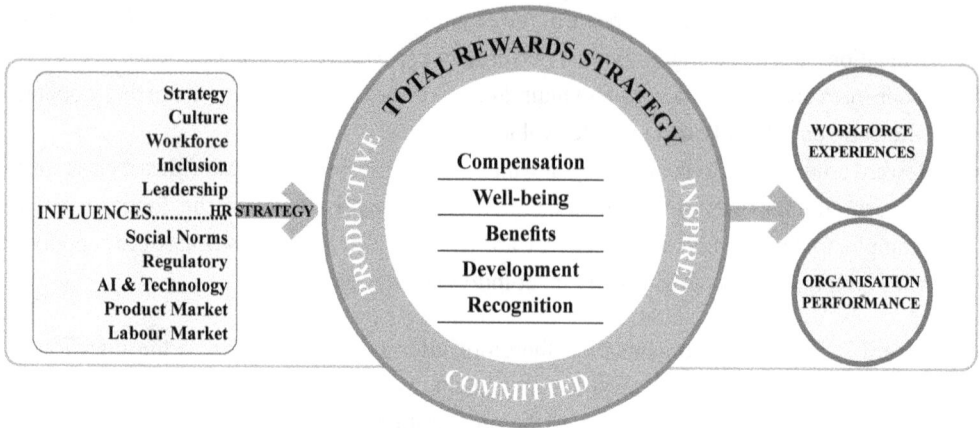

*Figure 1.3: WorldatWork's total rewards model[24]*

The five elements of total rewards that collectively define an organisation's strategy to attract, motivate, retain and engage employees are:

- **Compensation (also known as remuneration in some parts of the world): Pay** provided by an employer to its employees for services rendered (i.e. time, effort and skill). This includes both fixed and variable pay tied to performance levels. Note that **Performance Management** is included as part of compensation. We define it as the alignment of organisational, team and individual efforts toward the achievement of business goals and organisational success. Performance management includes establishing expectations, skill demonstration, assessment, feedback and continuous improvement.[25]

- **Well-being:** A specific set of organisational practices, policies and programmes, plus a philosophy that actively supports efforts to help employees achieve success at both work and home.

- **Benefits:** Programmes an employer uses to supplement the cash compensation employees receive. These health, income protection, savings and retirement programmes provide security for employees and their families.

- **Development:** Provides the opportunity and tools for employees to advance their skills and competencies in both their short- and long-term careers.

- **Recognition:** Either formal or informal programmes that acknowledge or give special attention to employee actions, efforts, behaviour or performance and support business strategy by reinforcing behaviours (e.g. extraordinary accomplishments) that contribute to organisational success.

Just a note for clarity: "compensation" is frequently used in America, but in other countries, such as Australia, New Zealand, Africa and Europe aren't countries and those in Asia, typically the word "remuneration" is used. Where America refers to compensation committees

---

24  WorldatWork, 2020.

25  Ochurub, Bussin & Goosen, 2012.

(CompComms), other countries refer to remuneration committees (RemCos). These terms are often used interchangeably in this book.

It is useful to note, however, that the elements of the Total Rewards model are often included as part of a description of an organisation's employee value proposition (EVP), which explains the at times interchangeable use of the terms EVP and total rewards in the literature and in the Human Resources community.

Armstrong and Brown[26] combine transactional and relational rewards in their description of total reward, as per the following table. The following table illustrates the model presented by Armstrong & Brown:[27]

*Table 1.2: Armstrong and Brown's total rewards model*

| Transactional rewards | Base pay | Total remuneration | Total reward |
| --- | --- | --- | --- |
| | Contingent pay | | |
| | Employee benefits | | |
| Relational rewards | Learning and development | Non-financial/intrinsic rewards | |
| | The work experience | | |

The models proposed by WorldatWork[28] and Armstrong & Brown[29] are similar, with the exception that "performance and recognition" are not explicitly stated by the latter; they state "the work experience" as a specific component of total rewards, a term which is not included in the WorldatWork[30] model. It is, however, clear from the literature that the terms "work-home (life) balance", "work-life quality" and "workplace quality" are sometimes used interchangeably further expand their model by categorising rewards as transactional and relational rewards and extrinsic and intrinsic rewards.[31]

Zingheim and Schuster[32] offer a more cryptic view of total rewards, and categorise the different types of rewards as follows:

- Total pay.
- Performance management and management of people.
- Total rewards other than pay.

According to this model, work-life balance and learning and development are included in the component "total rewards other than pay". The category of performance management and

26  Armstrong & Brown, 2006:22.

27  Armstrong & Brown, 2006:22.

28  WorldatWork, 2020.

29  Armstrong & Brown, 2006.

30  WorldatWork, 2020.

31  CCOHS, 2002; Lawler, Nadler & Camman, 1980; Moen, 2000; Armstrong & Brown, 2006.

32  Zingheim & Schuster, 2007.

management of people primarily deals with the performance management of people, while pay, benefits, recognition and fairness are elements contributing to the "total pay" category of the model. It is interesting to note that the concept of "fairness", which essentially refers to employee values and is typically contained in the reward philosophy[33], is introduced as a component of this total reward model.

Mercer Human Resources Consultancy defines total rewards as consisting of three main categories, namely pay, benefits and career.[34] Work-life balance is included under "benefits", while "employment stability" and "nature of work" are introduced under the "career" component. However, according to Black[35] and CLC[36], employment and organisational stability form part of the organisation's EVP and not the total rewards model.

Although there appear to be differing opinions around the nomenclature used in the reward categories, the inherent meanings of the different categories are not too dissimilar. In analysing the components which underlie the categories, authors appear to have similar views around the inclusion of core types of financial and non-financial rewards, but differ in terms of where these are categorised.[37] There also appear to be differing views around the inclusion of components which are, according to some literature, more related to EVP and not directly with total rewards. In understanding the reward preferences of employees, the components that underlie the respective categories will be included in the reward questionnaire. The extent to which there are different beliefs around the value of the respective components and categories are illustrated by a study undertaken by Gunkel[38] on reward preferences of three sets of employees working for one organisation, but located in China, Japan, USA and Germany. The study reflects distinct differences in reward preferences and reward motivators between employees in the different countries. The reward categories used in this study included:

- Earnings and achievement.
- Family-related rewards.
- Fringe benefits.
- Recognition.
- Training, responsibilities and use of skills.
- Work environment.

Chinese employees found informal recognition significantly more motivating than expected in comparison with the German sample, which found this type of reward significantly non-motivating. The German employees viewed the organisation's car scheme significantly more

33  CLC, 1999b.
34  Gross & Friedman, 2007.
35  Black, 2008.
36  CLC, 2007a.
37  Schlechter, Thompson & Bussin, 2015.
38  Gunkel, 2006.

motivating, in contrast with the Japanese employees, who found this type of reward non-motivating. The Japanese employees of the study found "improvements in working conditions" to be a motivating reward in comparison to the United States employees, who found it to be non-motivating. This study illustrates the differences in reward preferences and motivators of employees working for the same organisation but in different geographic locations. The results support research conducted by Hofstede[39], which confirmed the need for reward practices to be tailored according to cultural differences. It can be deduced from these studies that there is a need for differentiation in reward offerings for different employees, and also across different countries and cultures.

However, Gerhart and Rynes[40] stated that, "Money is the crucial incentive because, as a medium of exchange, it is the most instrumental. No other incentive or motivational technique comes even close to money with respect to its instrumental value". The value of earnings or salary in the total reward framework should therefore never be underestimated.

A study conducted by Sibson & Organisation in collaboration with WorldatWork in 2000 reflected no difference in the need for cash rewards between older and younger workers – all respondents indicated an equal need for financial remuneration.[41] A study conducted by Willis Towers Watson in 2003, however, reported opposite findings, where reward preferences differed according to different age groups.[42] The reward preferences for different employee segments, supported by the studies of CLC[43] and Gunkel, Hofstede and Furnham[44], prove a need for more uniquely tailored reward offerings, over and above a cash offering.

Finally, Stein believes, "Too often our workplaces are stress factories with huge and unnecessary losses of productivity. We need to stop and look at how important work is in people's lives. By paying more attention to the emotional aspects of the workplace, we can make the work experience much more meaningful. The organisations that get this right are the ones that will compete successfully in the global workplace".[45]

The needs of employees are an important consideration in designing the total reward strategy. Understanding employees' reward preferences will therefore influence the reward strategy and in turn the total rewards framework.[46] Menefee and Murphy[47] corroborate this belief: "The

---

39  Chiang, 2005.

40  Gerhart & Rynes, 2003:48.

41  Giancola, 2008.

42  Menefee & Murphy, 2004.

43  CLC, 2002a.

44  Gunkel, 2006; Chiang, 2005; Furnham, 2003.

45  Stein, 2007.

46  Giancola, 2008; Nienaber, Bussin & Henn, 2011; Bussin & Toerien, 2015; Snelgar, Renard & Venter, 2013.

47  Menefee & Murphy, 2004:16.

employee value rankings of the monetary and non-monetary rewards provide a blueprint for total reward packages offered to employees."

Different parts of the total rewards model may appeal to different employees due to individual preferences. Note that these individual preferences may change over time as life circumstances change for the employee (marriage, children, mortgage, retirement, etc.).

The total rewards strategy and framework are integral parts of an organisation's EVP.[48] In designing the framework, the components offered by competitor organisations should be considered, as should the value that employees attach to the respective components.[49] A sound reward framework positively influences the EVP, enhances the employer brand, and builds the organisation's reputation as an "Employer of Choice" for current and prospective employees.[50] There is no one-size-fits-all; it is up to employers to understand the business strategy, the preferences of their employees and the characteristics of the markets within which they operate, and to use this information to develop 'a best fit' total reward model for their organisation.

## 1.7    Remuneration strategy

There are several methods that can be used to assist organisations to develop a remuneration strategy. The most common methods are linked below and should be used in conjunction with each other.

### 1.7.1    The strategy process

Figure 1.4 below shows the strategy process from business strategy filtering down to remuneration strategy, and some of the strategic choices that need to be made. This is a useful guide to setting compensation strategy.

---

48   CLC, 2005a.

49   Harris & Clements, 2007.

50   Corsello, 2006; Smit, Stanz & Bussin, 2015.

**Vision**
↓
**Mission**
↓
**Strategic objectives**
↓
**Functional/operational strategy and objectives**
↓
**HR strategy**

| ER strategy | Reward strategy | Talent strategy | People strategy |

Low base salaries ................................................................ High base salaries

Internal equity .................................................................... External equity

Few perks ........................................................................... Many perks

Standard fixed package ...................................................... Flexible package

No incentives ..................................................................... Many incentives

No employment security ..................................................... High employment security

Hierarchical........................................................................ Flatter structures

Individual pay .................................................................... Team pay

Pay for input....................................................................... Pay for output

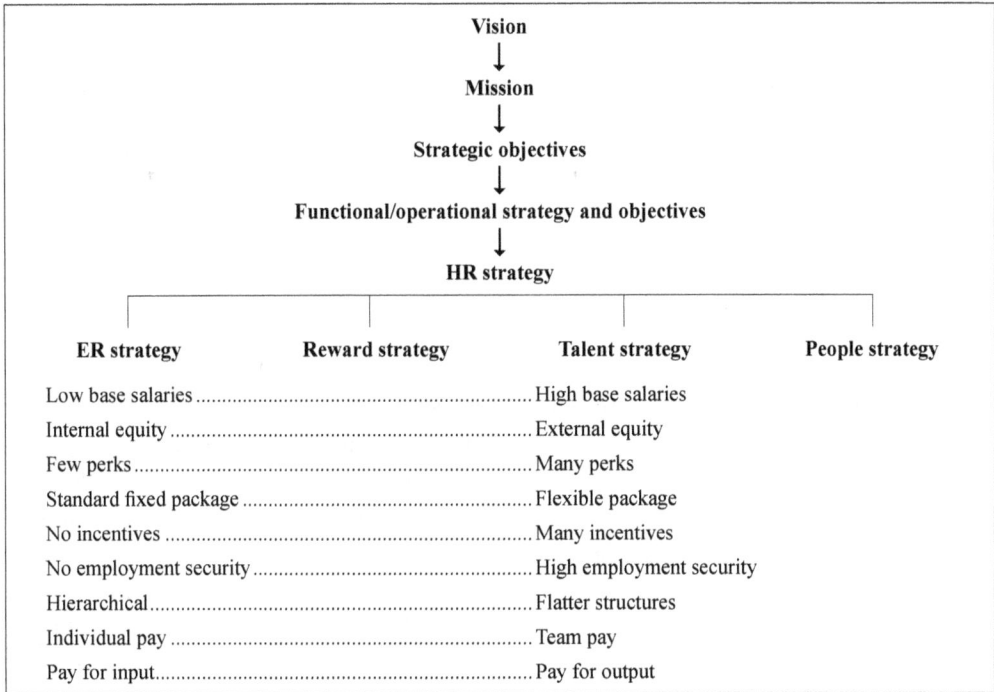

*Figure 1.4: The strategic process*

## 1.7.2 The pay continuum

Figure 1.5 shows the pay continuum, which may assist with the design of a remuneration strategy. There is no right or wrong answer, just a much better strategy than that used by competitors. The way to use this model is to assess at which stage your organisation is predominantly, and where it would like to be. The strategy involves closing this gap.

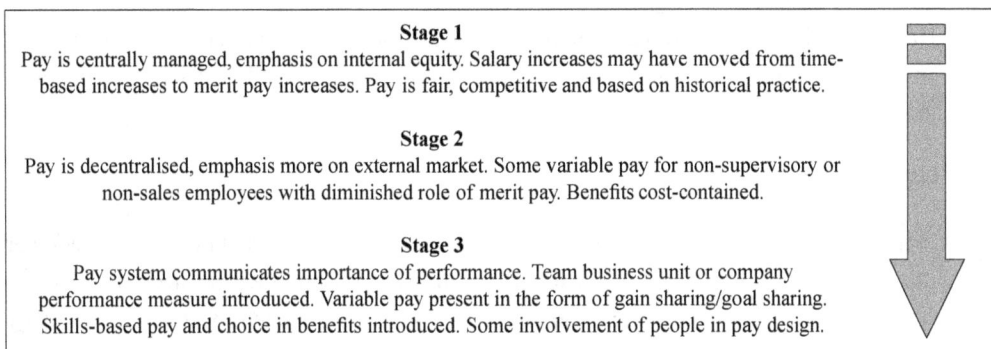

**Stage 1**
Pay is centrally managed, emphasis on internal equity. Salary increases may have moved from time-based increases to merit pay increases. Pay is fair, competitive and based on historical practice.

**Stage 2**
Pay is decentralised, emphasis more on external market. Some variable pay for non-supervisory or non-sales employees with diminished role of merit pay. Benefits cost-contained.

**Stage 3**
Pay system communicates importance of performance. Team business unit or company performance measure introduced. Variable pay present in the form of gain sharing/goal sharing. Skills-based pay and choice in benefits introduced. Some involvement of people in pay design.

*Figure 1.5: The pay continuum*

### 1.7.3 The planning process

A strategic remuneration plan must support the organisation's objectives. The plan should include:

- Base pay.
- Short- and long-term incentives.
- Fringe benefits.
- Growth opportunities.
- Recognition.

The remuneration plan helps to ensure that the remuneration system will support the organisation's long- and short-term objectives without overlap (there should not be more than one pay plan driving the same objectives). Not all the tools from Toolkit 1: Sample Remuneration Policy and Philosophy should be used, only those that will give you a return on pay investment and best underpin and support the business strategy.

The ultimate objectives of these plans are to ensure that the organisation attracts and retains the right employees and that it motivates them to do those things that support the business plan. Recognition for outstanding achievement is also an important part of the process. The steps involved are:

- **Step 1:** Identify business objectives.
  Use the business plan as a reference.

- **Step 2:** Assess the current remuneration system.
  Evaluate how well it supports the objectives of the business. Identify any gaps and any areas that are over-funded.

- **Step 3:** Develop pay strategy.
  This closes the gaps identified in Step 2 and forms the basis of the remuneration strategy. The remuneration philosophy is then updated accordingly and aligned with the business strategy.

*Your business plan (Step 1)*

Let's assume that organisation X's strategy is "to transform its business and increase shareholder value through growth". Implicit in this is that everything Organisation X does needs to be world class, including the support systems, and especially the remuneration system. The strategy includes three key themes:

- Increase return on investment.
- Optimise cash generation.
- Grow knowledge and skills base.

These themes are articulated through the strategies and the initiatives associated with them, which may be refined from time to time as the business develops. This is one of the most compelling reasons to review the remuneration planning process regularly.

The measures of Organisation X's strategy are currently expressed as strategic targets and performance goals. These are:

- Return on shareholders' funds.
- Return on capital employed.
- Cash generation.
- Employee knowledge and skills growth.

Given the above, it is necessary to re-evaluate the current remuneration system regularly, within the context of the HR strategy, and, if there are any gaps in alignment, work out strategies to close the gaps.

### Remuneration planning chart (Step 2)

The remuneration planning chart (Table 1.3) will be updated annually as the business strategy is enhanced. Alignment of the pay system follows thereafter. The purpose of the chart is to gauge the extent to which the current pay system underpins the business strategy.

The framework has the key elements of the business strategy on the horizontal axis and the key remuneration drivers on the vertical axis. The chart is then completed using the following symbols:

- √ Current system by itself cannot produce the desired objectives.
- √√ Current system produces the desired objectives.
- P Indicates the proposed strengthening of the pay strategy.
- X Current system works against achieving the objectives.

Ideally, the business objectives should be well supported by the symbol √√, indicating that the current system produces the desired result. Where there is not enough support, the remuneration system should be strengthened.

*Table 1.3: The remuneration planning chart*

| | Attract | Retain | Motivate (Achievement of strategic goals) | | | | | Projects | |
| --- | --- | --- | --- | --- | --- | --- | --- | --- | --- |
| | | | Shareholder returns | Cash | Leveraging knowledge | Other 1 | Other 2 | | |
| Base pay/package | | | | | | | | | |
| PRP | | | | | | | | | |
| Executive bonus scheme | | | | | | | | | |
| Share option scheme | | | | | | | | | |
| Car scheme | | | | | | | | | |
| Retirement | | | | | | | | | |
| Medical aid | | | | | | | | | |
| 1. Bonus scheme to include cash and knowledge | | | | | | | | | |
| 2. Develop equitable pay grade solutions | | | | | | | | | |
| 3. Convert executives to full total package | | | | | | | | | |
| 4. Develop project bonus scheme | | | | | | | | | |
| 5. Review long-term incentive scheme | | | | | | | | | |
| 6. Share allocation model | | | | | | | | | |

## Develop reward strategy (Step 3)

To strengthen the alignment with the business strategy, the following amendments should be considered:

- **Include cash generation and knowledge leveraging.**
  To drive the strategic goals, include objectives in the bonus scheme that underpin cash generation options after knowledge leveraging.
- **Develop equitable pay and pay grade solutions.**
  Develop a defensible pay grade system that is equitable, both internally and laterally.
- **Convert executives to full total package.**
  This will give employees more flexibility in their pay packages.
- **Benchmarking** with other companies in similar sectors and markets will provide you with information on what is most prevalent in the industry.

- **Develop "project" bonus schemes.**
  If culturally suited and in alignment with what is typically provided in the sector and location, incentives for project assignments should be tailored for each project.[51]
- **Review or develop long-term incentive schemes.**
  Encourage long-term thinking when taking business decisions and reinforce the drive to instil the "knowledge-based" management style. An incentive plan that rolls over for three years will be developed for senior executives to strengthen retention capabilities. This may be an add-on, or it may replace the current share scheme.
- **Design a defensible allocation model for long-term incentives.**
  Defensible remuneration systems are increasingly important, and where supported by market data and legislation, should include the allocation of long-term incentives for eligible employees. A defensible methodology will be developed.
- **Award schemes.**
  These are generally performance-related (overall financial performance, productivity, product or service quality) or for specific goals or skills acquired. Awards are competitive in nature; there will be winners.

The last step in any planning process is to evaluate if the plan achieved the intended results. Strategic planning of remuneration allows an organisation to focus on its strategic objectives and develop a comprehensive remuneration plan to underpin it, considering base pay, short and long-term incentives, fringe benefits, growth opportunities and recognition.

An evaluation of the impact of compensation on business outcomes helps to ensure that the remuneration system supports the organisation's long and short-term objectives without overlap, i.e. more than one pay plan driving the same objectives.

Not all the criteria mentioned in this chapter should be used; organisations can focus on only those that give a return on its remuneration investment and best underpin the business strategy.

To do so, the organisation can describe the objective(s) for each plan that was implemented, as it was originally defined: What behaviours, results, or outcomes were expected to be achieved, within which population(s), over what time frame?

At the end of the specified time frame (or at a convenient interim point), the organisation should measure to what extent the remuneration plan achieved the desired objective(s). For example, if the organisation wanted to use the annual bonus plan to increase employee awareness of financial objectives and share with managers and above in the organisation's success, at the end of the period it can evaluate the degree to which this population effectively understands the organisation's financials and the amount of profit that was shared with this group.

---

51  Van der Merwe & Bussin, 2005.

## 1.8 Key trends

Many organisations want to know what is happening locally and internationally as input to their strategy and policy processes. Figure 1.6 below gives a breakdown of current key reward trends.

| FROM: | | TO: |
|---|---|---|
| **PAY** | | |
| • Traditional add-on | → | Total package |
| • Fixed pay | → | Variable pay |
| • Little or no shareholding | → | Bigger stake in business |
| • Board decides | → | Non-executive remuneration committees |
| • Board disclosure | → | More disclosure |
| • One size fits all | → | Best fit approach with flexibility in terms of preferences |
| **PERFORMANCE MANAGEMENT** | | |
| • Activities | → | Outputs/results |
| • Executive bonus | → | Workforce bonus |
| **WORK** | | |
| • Duty sheet, rigid work | → | Flexible, adaptive |
| • Job descriptions | → | Role descriptions |
| • Guaranteed employment | → | Staying relevant, contract |
| • Hierarchical structure | → | Broader bands |

*Figure 1.6: Current key compensation trends*

## 1.9 Remuneration policy

A remuneration policy should cover at least the following headings:

- Statement of intent
- Purpose
- Application and scope
- Document control and versions
- Links to performance and talent management
- Communication and the extent of transparency allowed

Disclosure of individual salaries is generally protected by law. Some companies do, however, disclose pay scales and remuneration guidelines. An exception may be directors' salaries, a performance bonus scheme, and long-term incentives, which are disclosed as part of the remuneration policy in the annual financial statements and regulated by the listing authorities.

The following are normally disclosed in the annual financial statements:

- Remuneration mix.
- Philosophy of guaranteed pay (GP).
- Philosophy and details of variable pay (VP) plans.
- Comparative benchmarking.
- Annual remuneration reviews – how are these determined.
- Remuneration committee members and role of the committee.

See Toolkit 1: Sample Remuneration Policy and Philosophy for an example of a remuneration policy.

## 1.10 Conclusion

In this opening chapter we covered the various elements of a remuneration policy and several frameworks on how to set a remuneration strategy. The important point is that the remuneration policy and strategy need to underpin the HR and organisation strategy, as depicted in Figure 1.7below. The figure illustrates how to link total remuneration to the business strategy.

The next chapter, dealing with job roles and competence, could be seen as the "foundation" of the remuneration "house".

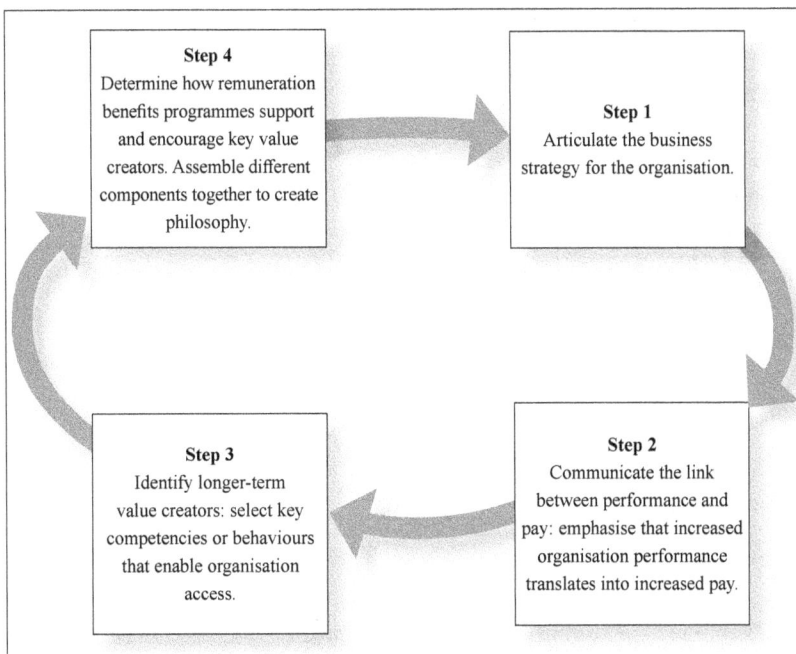

| **Step 4** Determine how remuneration benefits programmes support and encourage key value creators. Assemble different components together to create philosophy. | **Step 1** Articulate the business strategy for the organisation. |
| **Step 3** Identify longer-term value creators: select key competencies or behaviours that enable organisation access. | **Step 2** Communicate the link between performance and pay: emphasise that increased organisation performance translates into increased pay. |

*Figure 1.7: Linking total remuneration and business strategy*

> ## Case study: Netflix
>
> By all accounts, Netflix is a very successful company and poised to become the first global television provider. In a 124-page PowerPoint deck,[52] they explain their culture, with a deep complement of how their HR policies (including compensation) support their business strategy. Created with the help of Patty McCord, who at the time was the company's Chief of Talent, the deck is Netflix's CEO Reed Hastings' presentation to employees in which he details how he hires, fires and rewards employees.
>
> In far more than a nutshell, the deck explains that for Netflix to continue to grow as fast and as profitably as possible, it can only do so with "A" players as employees. In order for "A" players to join Netflix and maintain a high level of performance, the company has to pay "whatever it takes", give freedom to managers to do so, but also provide "a generous severance" to those who no longer fit the company. Among other things, Netflix has an open vacation and an open expense account policy (take/spend as much as is necessary).
>
> After you have read the deck and the article, you should be able to answer the following questions:
>
> 1. What is Netflix's business strategy?
> 2. To accomplish their strategy, what kind of people do they need to hire? Define an "A" player in terms of Talent.
> 3. Can you identify the key elements in their Remuneration Strategy that allows Netflix to attract, retain and motivate the "A" players they seek? Is it sustainable?
> 4. Can you also identify other HR policies that help find and keep "A" players?
> 5. Would any of these policies work well by themselves?[53]

## 1.11 Summary

A remuneration policy and strategy should be designed to underpin the HR and business strategy. There are many different reward models. Organisations should select the best model for their organisation and write the remuneration policy around it. A key consideration when setting a remuneration strategy is the industry maturity curve, because the remuneration mix differs according to what stage the product or organisation is in. Every organisation should have a remuneration policy and remuneration committee to ensure good corporate governance.

## 1.12 Self-evaluation questions

1. Describe any rewards model and the elements therein.
2. Describe the remuneration strategy process.
3. Describe the most common remuneration approaches for each stage of industry maturity.
4. Describe key trends to be considered when designing a remuneration strategy.

---

52  Hastings, 2009.

53  McCord, 2014.

## 1.13 Exercise

Your company had a great year and thus you were able to secure 15% more budget; how would you spend it and why? Assume all starts at Stage 2 and 50%.

| | Current | New | Reasons |
|---|---|---|---|
| Base pay | | | |
| Cash award | | | |
| Annual incentives | | | |
| Long term incentives | | | |
| Perks (e.g. cars) | | | |
| Benefits | | | |
| More training | | | |
| More staff | | | |
| Work-life balance programmes | | | |
| Others (specify) | | | |

# CHAPTER 2

# Job Roles and Competence

## 2.1 Overview

In this chapter, we discuss how job roles and competence may be seen as the "foundations" of remuneration practice.

### 2.1.1 What is a job description?

A job description is the accurate, realistic, current picture of what tasks make up a job. It outlines the job's location, purpose, responsibilities, authority levels and supervisory relationships, as well as the interrelationships between the job and others in the same area. It serves as a dynamic document which takes account of organisational change, is unambiguous, and can be understood and interpreted similarly by both the incumbent, his or her supervisor, and other potential users such as the HR Department. It does not include incidental or trivial tasks.

### 2.1.2 What is a role description?

Role descriptions refer to broader aspects of behaviour, for example, working flexibility, working with others, interrelated tasks, and styles of management. They describe the part to be played by individuals in fulfilling their job requirements. Often they incorporate the results of skills or competence analysis and sometimes performance standards.

For example, a job may be to water the garden. A role or output would be maintaining a healthy garden (a role or output is broader than a job).

## 2.2 Terminology

A job consists of a collection of duties and responsibilities which can be further divided into specific tasks and even further into task elements. Table 2.1 below summarises the terms used in the process of writing job descriptions.

*Table 2.1: Terminology for job descriptions*

| Term | Definition | Example: Executive secretary |
|------|-----------|------------------------------|
| Task elements | These are the smallest work elements | Inserting a piece of paper into a printer |
| Tasks | Task elements combine to form a task with a defined outcome | Typing the minutes of a particular meeting |

| Term | Definition | Example: Executive secretary |
|------|-----------|------------------------------|
| Duties | Specific requirements of the job | Maintaining a record of those minutes from a series of meetings |
| Responsibilities | What the employee is held accountable for | Having accountability for the recording, typing, dissemination and maintenance of the records |
| Position | Where there are enough duties and responsibilities to require the employment of a worker, a position exists | Executive secretary to the MD versus the executive secretary job |
| Job | Where more than one worker is employed in the same or similar position(s), a job exists | When two workers are employed as secretaries and their duties and responsibilities are the same, there are two secretarial positions but only one secretarial job |
| Occupation | Jobs common to many separate organisations | Many organisations employ secretaries, therefore it is an occupation |
| Work team | A work group or team exists when a worker interacts with others to produce a component of a product or service for sale or consumption | The sales team headed by the sales manager of which the executive secretary is a member |
| Job analysis | The process of determining and defining the content of jobs | Job analysis of the executive secretary job |
| Job description | The description of a job as a result of job analysis | Executive secretary job description |
| Role description | A broader look at the job description | Provision of administrative support |
| Competence | The skills, attitude and behaviour required | Proficient provision of administrative support |

## 2.3    Uses for job descriptions

This topic highlights the specific purposes of the job description writing process. The goal of this topic is to assist the reader to use the process within an organisation.

Job descriptions are valuable sources of information for recruitment, performance appraisal, career pathing and the development of training programmes, as well as the implementation and ongoing maintenance of a job evaluation system.

The writing of job descriptions provides a unique opportunity to study the organisation. The organisation will have an opportunity to determine key areas of responsibility, levels of authority and accountability, reporting relationships, lines of communication, spans of control, job design, staffing levels and anomalies.

Motivations for carrying out a job description writing process are to enable:

- Job evaluation – the information on which the job will be graded.
- Creation of the information needed for organisational review.
- Detailed information for recruitment.
- Development of job procedures and performance standards.
- Development of a framework for performance and progress reviews.
- Detailed information for the development of skills, training programmes, career pathing, and manpower planning.
- Development of specific plans for individual induction training.
- To assist with an assessment of how competent the incumbents are in relation to the requirements of the job.

## 2.4    Factors influencing jobs

Two types of factors influence jobs, namely non-discretionary for the individual, and variable and discretionary for the individual.

Factors which are non-discretionary for the individual include:

- Organisation: structure and policy.
- Legal requirements.
- Division of labour.
- Design of equipment.
- Physical arrangement.
- Methods, procedures, traditional practices.
- Job standards.
- Work environment.

Factors which are variable and discretionary for the individual, and may have to be further developed if possible, include:

- Skills
- Experience
- Personality
- Performance.

The analysis and job description writing process is often conducted by supervisors, job incumbents, Human Resource specialists, outside consultants, or a combination of the above. The best results come from directly involving supervisors and incumbents. Involvement of key participants implies that each job description will be simple, clear and based on accurate information. This can be ensured by establishing what is expected from employees. Before being signed off as correct, the accuracy of the description should be agreed on by the:

- Supervisor
- Employee
- Head of department, and, where appropriate
- Trade union, if appropriate.

It is not the role of the employer or trade union to "sign off" the job description; it is management's role. If the incumbent refuses to sign the job description, it is still valid.

There are certain skills required for writing job descriptions. The individuals or groups chosen to do the analysis should possess the following skills:

- Good interpersonal skills.
- Good writing skills.
- Knowledge of how the organisation functions.
- An inquisitive and analytical nature.
- Objectivity in their business dealings.

One does not have to be an expert at doing the job; one has to know how to write a job description. For example, a football team or boxer's coach does not necessarily have to be young and fit and a first league player – they have to know how to coach. It is therefore quite feasible for a good job description writer to write the job description of an astronaut, for example, by careful interviewing.

## 2.5   Planning and preparation for job description writing

As the longest and most vulnerable in terms of time loss, the job writing phase should be carefully planned. A project manager should be appointed to make the following decisions:

- How many job descriptions should be written?
- How many job analysts are needed to complete the task in time to allow for the grading committee to be trained, all jobs to be graded, and the pay review (if there is one) to be completed?

The timetable must allow for a "job description writing course" to train nominated job analysts where necessary. The project managers should also help the job analysts to plan their writing programme. Although competent job analysts should be versatile and capable of writing any job description, it is good practice for them to start with a training course, or to have an understanding of the work already. The following requirements should be discussed with the relevant supervisors:

- Selection of employees to be interviewed.
- Competence of employees to be interviewed.
- Interviews to be conducted as "one-on-one", with a small group of employees in the same job or with the employee and a shop steward (if appropriate).
- Provision of an interview room.
- An opportunity to observe the incumbent in operation (if necessary).
- Gathering previous job descriptions and other information to facilitate the analysis.

It is often more expedient to interview the managers regarding the job in their department and writing the job descriptions directly from this interview. Follow these tips to ensure effective planning of the job description writing process:

- Asking for an organogram of the division or department in advance helps with understanding the big picture; it makes it easier to get a feel for when incumbents inadvertently include the duties of their manager in their own job descriptions.
- The programme should progress from lower level jobs upwards. This enables analysts to work on easier jobs first, gaining confidence for the writing of more complex descriptions, and allows a clearer view of the organisation's operations and hierarchy.
- Details of the interview are to be properly recorded. If it is not possible to interview all employees, make it clear that representatives of certain job categories were chosen.
- Monitor the quality and checking process for each job description. All completed descriptions should be signed off by the employees, supervisor, shop steward where appropriate, and head of department.
- Discuss the reproduction of job descriptions for the grading committee. Some organisations choose to grade their jobs internally and set up a grading committee for this purpose. Each member of the grading committee requires a copy of the job description when doing the grading.

## 2.6 Understanding a typical job description form

The following headings and tips will help in documenting a job or role that can be used for nearly all systems of job evaluation. (See also Toolkit 3: Sample Job Description Form.)

### 2.6.1 Primary purpose of the job

In one sentence, the primary purpose of the job tells us why the job exists. This should be unique to this job and not generic so that it fits other jobs in the organisation.

### 2.6.2    Major task headings

Major task headings should match the headings in Section 5 of Toolkit 3, which detail the key performance areas. These are the major outputs of the job.

### 2.6.3    Adverse working conditions

This is important for recruitment or special monetary allowances that may need to be paid. For example, working near a furnace, or frequent travelling and the need to spend nights away, may be considered adverse working conditions.

### 2.6.4    Other special requirements

This refers to special skills or competencies that may be required in a job.

### 2.6.5    Salient information/parameters of the work environment

This is useful for showing parameters such as budget size, sales, units serviced, billing, turnover, tonnes per annum, and so on. This also gives one a feel for the size of a job. For example, one may get sales representatives selling 100,000 units per month and others selling 5,000 units per month – the parameters would be totally different in each of these cases.

### 2.6.6    Detailed description

The detailed description should match the headings in Section 2 of Toolkit 3, which lists the key performance areas (KPAs).

### 2.6.7    Job specification

This is a requirement set by the organisation, to be completed by senior management.

## 2.7    The job description interview

Table 2.2 below sets out guidelines which can be used when conducting interviews.

While conducting an interview, it is important to bear the following in mind:

- Do not ask leading questions, but probe for clarification.
- Continually try to establish whether you have enough information. You will need to describe the skills and knowledge required, the nature of supervision given, typical decisions taken, and the pressures involved in the job.
- Do not question the validity of the interviewee's comments; the manager will.
- Do not get influenced by the incumbent's performance or competence to fulfil the role.

- When the interviewee has described a specific task area, repeat the important points to ensure complete understanding and that the facts are correctly recorded, and to reassure him or her of your continued understanding and interest.
- Finish the interview with a summary of the entire job and explain the process which will result in the completed job description.

*Table 2.2: Guidelines for conducting interviews*

| Step | Action |
|------|--------|
| 1 | Meet with incumbent. |
| 2 | Explain the purpose of the interview and put incumbent at ease. |
| 3 | Complete administrative detail. |
| 4 | Complete background information. |
| 5 | Conduct interview using job description form as an interview guide and for notes during interview. Alternatively, use a structured questionnaire. |
| 6 | Determine the purpose of the job by asking the question, "Why does the job exist?" |
| 7 | Ask for an outline of the job by doing the following:<br>• Probe, question and direct interview.<br>• Do NOT dominate or use leading questions. |
| 8 | Find out and understand how each task is done, how often it is done and how long it takes. |
| 9 | Recap:<br>• after each task; and<br>• at the end of the interview. |
| 10 | Decide whether or not you have enough information to present a lucid description for another reader and for the purpose of grading. |
| 11 | Tell the incumbent that he or she will be able to check the draft and the final copy. |

### 2.7.1   Interview techniques

Encourage the interviewee to express his or her views freely and honestly. Develop a relaxed atmosphere of trust to ensure open communication. Ask questions that will help you to decide how the job's decisions are made and what the employee is responsible for.

### 2.7.2   Emphasis while interviewing

The most important factor in interviewing is curiosity. Often the employee has never had to tell someone else about how his or her job is done and will sometimes have difficulty detailing his or her full range of tasks and responsibilities. Interest shown – or lack of it – will make all the difference as to how the interviewees feel about themselves and about job evaluation, and how freely they provide information.

Don't make assumptions about tasks which are or are not done. The employee may decide not to mention "trivialities". Always ask how, why and how often things are done, and what equipment, tools and resources are used.

### 2.7.3    Four golden rules of interviews

Here are four golden rules which should be followed for guidance when interviewing:

- **Let the interviewee do the talking.** Use further questions only to probe, control and lead on to the next topic. A common fault is for the interviewer to work too hard, talk too much, or lose control of the interview.
- **Use silences.** Resist the temptation to fill silence; allow the interviewee time to think and reply.
- **Observe body language.** Watch non-verbal behaviour. Part of an interviewer's skill is to see, interpret and use the messages that are conveyed through posture and gestures.
- **Create an encouraging, interested atmosphere.** Use facial expressions, eye contact, tone of voice, uh-huh noises, and head nods. Body posture can be used to relax or intensify the atmosphere.

### 2.7.4    Dealing with difficult interviewees

People are not always easy to interview; the interviewer often has to help the employee describe his or her job. Behaviour must be correctly diagnosed, and appropriate tactics should be adopted. Table 2.3 below illustrates common remedies for popular interview problems.

## 2.8    Writing the job description

When writing job descriptions, the following guidelines can be used:

- Write the job description immediately after the interview, using the job description writing form. (See Toolkit 3: Sample Job Description Form.)
- List tasks in chronological sequence for lower-level jobs or in order of importance for higher-level jobs.
- For a concise and uniform style:
  - Use point form.
  - Start every sentence with action verbs.
  - Use an agreed format for organisational design.
  - Talk in the present tense.
- Examples:
  - Use exact terms, such as "3", NOT "a few".
  - Use job titles rather than names.
  - Do not include the duties of others in your job description.
  - Write up the job description as soon as possible after the interview.

- Level cutters: These serve to clearly demarcate the difference between two adjacent job levels for job evaluation purposes. For example:
  - Entry Level Engineer: Participates in project teams
  - Engineer: Leads one or more sub-teams within projects
  - Sr. Engineer: Leads a project or several small projects
  - Engineering Manager: Leads multiple projects

| Problem | Common symptoms | Useful remedies |
|---------|-----------------|-----------------|
| **The nervous interviewee** | Tense, awkward, aggressive or over-formal behaviour | <ul><li>Adopt a relaxed manner and posture.</li><li>Introduce humour if possible.</li><li>Concentrate on the interviewee's interests, successes and safe, easy topics.</li><li>Chat about any common interests or work situations until the interviewee is more at ease.</li><li>Ask open-ended questions.</li></ul> |

*Table 2.3: Remedies for interview problems*

| Problem | Common symptoms | Useful remedies |
|---------|-----------------|-----------------|
| **Interviewees who talk too little** | An interviewee who talks too much in an attempt to compensate | <ul><li>Ask easy, open-ended questions.</li><li>Wait for answers.</li><li>Use silences.</li><li>Give encouraging responses to replies.</li><li>Use "tell me more about" questions.</li></ul> |
| **Interviewees who talk too much** | Much talking, but little valid information | <ul><li>Ask more specific, closed questions.</li><li>Make frequent but smooth interruptions.</li><li>Conduct the interview with more formality and fewer inviting responses.</li></ul> |
| **Bombastic interviewees** | The interviewee overstates the job, due either to insecurity or with the intention of manipulating the system | <ul><li>Resist the temptation to deflate.</li><li>Probe for precise details, giving credit where it is due.</li></ul> |
| **Interviewees who play the wrong role** | The interviewee asks all questions, queries the need for job evaluation, and perhaps talks against it, indulges in irrelevant personal confidences, and so on. | <ul><li>Use a friendly, information-giving but organisational approach to gain control of the situation.</li></ul> |

## 2.9  Checking and obtaining commitment to a job description

Table 2.4 below illustrates different steps which can be taken to ensure commitment to the job description.

*Table 2.4: Steps for obtaining commitment*

| Step | Action |
| --- | --- |
| 1 | Interview incumbent. |
| 2 | Check details with supervisor. |
| 3 | Ensure agreement between incumbent and supervisor. |
| 4 | Draft the job description. |
| 5 | Check the draft job. |
| 6 | Check description with incumbent, supervisor, shop steward and head of department. |
| 7 | Get the job description typed up. |
| 8 | Have the job description signed by the incumbent, supervisor, shop steward, and head of department. |

The incumbent signs only to acknowledge that he or she has seen the job description. He or she does not sign it to "approve" the job description – the manager does that.

The job description form has many uses and forms part of the "foundation" of the remuneration "house". It needs to be updated every time there is a change in the job. If there is a more than 20 percent change in the job content and complexity, it should be submitted to the grading committee (this is explained in the next chapter) to see if there is a grade implication.

Long job descriptions do not lead to higher grades, and short job descriptions do not lead to lower grades. It is the complexity of the job that determines the grade. The next chapter looks at job evaluation.

## 2.10  Summary

Job descriptions are the foundation of remuneration. They provide key information for job grading, which in turn leads to a pay scale and short- and long-term incentives. Job descriptions should be approximately three to four pages in length and should cover the primary purpose of the job, the key performance areas and job specifications. Job descriptions should be an accurate and current description of what incumbents are currently doing.

## 2.11 Self-evaluation questions

1.  What is the difference between a job description and a role description?
2.  What are the key elements that go into a job description?
3.  What are the golden rules for interviews?
4.  Name some guidelines for writing the job description.

## 2.12 Exercise

Find a job description on the internet. See, for example, the one below from Hiring.Monster. com.[1]

1.  How many of the elements described in section 2.6 can you find in this description?
2.  What is missing?
3.  How would you improve upon it?

## Accounting Supervisor

**Job Responsibilities:**

Secures financial operations by monitoring and approving financial processing, reporting, and auditing; supervising staff.

**Job Duties:**

- Accomplishes accounting human resource objectives by selecting, orienting, training, assigning, scheduling, coaching, counselling, and disciplining employees; communicating job expectations; planning, monitoring, appraising job contributions; recommending compensation actions; adhering to policies and procedures.
- Meets accounting operational standards by contributing financial information to strategic plans and reviews; implementing production, productivity, quality, and customer-service standards; resolving problems; identifying system improvements.
- Meets accounting financial standards by providing accounting department annual budget information; monitoring expenditures; identifying variances; implementing corrective actions.
- Maintains cash flow by monitoring bank balances and cash requirements; investing excess funds.
- Approves cash disbursements by verifying check amounts against invoices, authorizing checks and wire transfers.
- Approves ledger entries by auditing transactions.

---

1    Monster, 2020.

- Renews business insurance by scheduling values including personal and real property, vehicles, computers, equipment, media, and accounts receivable.
- Supports annual audit by providing information and answers to auditors.
- Reports 401k savings by distributing and explaining quarterly election forms.
- Verifies employee benefit invoices by verifying coverage and costs.
- Protects organisation's value by keeping information confidential.
- Maintains financial security by adhering to internal controls.
- Updates job knowledge by participating in educational opportunities; reading professional publications; maintaining personal networks; participating in professional organisations.
- Accomplishes accounting and organisation mission by completing related results as needed.

**Skills and Qualifications:**

Accounting, Supervision, Benefits Administration, Audit, Managing Processes, Reporting Research Results, Quality Management, Corporate Finance, Developing Budgets, Attention to Detail, General Math Skills

# CHAPTER 3

# Job Evaluation

## 3.1 Introduction

Job evaluation is the systematic and objective process of comparing one job to another within an organisation to arrive at different job levels or a "pecking order". It does so without looking at individual characteristics, personality or performance.

Individual abilities and efforts may be taken into account and reflected in the employee's earnings, but this is entirely different from the grading of the job. Job evaluation grades the job, not the person. Neither individual effort nor labour market conditions are taken into account when conducting the grading.

There are two broad stages to negotiate during the process of job evaluation:

- **Stage 1:** Only the job is graded in its current state. This is not an idealistic future job and we must pretend that there are no incumbents. Always consider competence in evaluating the role; not 'what could go wrong'.
- **Stage 2:** After the job has been graded, we look at individuals in the job and decide where to place them on the pay scale.

## 3.2 The need for job evaluation

When an organisation is first formed, the owner or manager knows exactly what tasks are performed in every job, what person is required to fill that post, and how much to pay this person. If necessary, this "pay policy" can be justified to employees. In addition, the employee usually has a one-on-one relationship with the manager and negotiation around the remuneration issue is informal and sometimes frequent.

As the organisation grows it becomes more structured, which enables the owner, manager or management team to control it. Various sections are created. Sectional managers become responsible for the hiring, firing and remuneration levels of staff. The changing perception of management and the varied priorities between section managers lead to discrepancies in pay rates between divisions and even between jobs with similar skills. A variety of pay rates may exist for a number of reasons, including the following:

- There is little co-ordination of pay rates.
- There is no logical basis for the pay structure.
- There are constant demands for parity, and general dissatisfaction.

Assessment and comparison are related to job content. Although job evaluation helps to determine relative pay levels, the pay levels for particular jobs and individual earnings remain organisational policy decisions based on internal and external factors.

Most countries have legislation around pay equity or equal pay for work of equal value. Having a job evaluation system goes a long way to comply with this type of legislation because one can more easily explain why certain categories of employees earn commensurate amounts of pay.

## 3.3 When should job evaluation be used?

Job evaluation can be used in the following circumstances:

- A variety of pay rates exist for variety of reasons.
- Similar jobs are rewarded on different levels.
- There are demands for parity.
- There is little co-ordination of pay rates.
- There is no logical basis for pay rates.
- "Job values" are confused with "person values".
- Organisational structure reviews are required.
- Development of career paths is required.

Job evaluation should be applied in situations where discrepancies are seen in interdepartmental hierarchies regarding job values. It should also be applied where salaries and wages are not equitably distributed.

## 3.4 Terminology

### Definition of job evaluation

Job evaluation is the systematic and objective process of comparing one job to another within an organisation without looking at individual characteristics, personality or performance.

### Definition of terms relating to job evaluation

Job evaluation depends on understanding, acceptability and objectivity. To aid understanding, it is necessary to define the terms commonly used. Table 3.1 below lists these definitions.

## 3.5 Why job evaluation?

This topic focuses on the need for job evaluation within an organisation, specifically, job evaluation as a means of:

- Facilitating the evolution of the organisation.
- Helping management and employees see how different jobs relate to each other.
- Plotting career paths through the hierarchy.
- Assisting with skills development within the workplace.
- Conducting a detailed analysis of wage and skills gaps for providing a common language and defined point of reference for negotiation and collective bargaining.

*Table 3.1: Definition of terms relating to job evaluation*

| Term | Definition |
|---|---|
| **Job analysis** | The process of examining the content of a job; breaking it down into its tasks, functions, minor functions, processes, operations and elements |
| **Job description** | The description of a job as a result of a job analysis |
| **Job evaluation** | The whole process put together |
| **Job grading** | The ranking or assigning of levels to jobs as a result of a job analysis |
| **Job specification** | The qualifications, experience and personal qualities required by the job-holder (mainly used for recruitment) |
| **Wage and salary structures** | The assignment of a monetary value to each grade, based on:<br><br>• Affordability.<br>• Market norms and rates.<br>• Employee representation negotiations.<br>• Economic environment and indicators. |

### 3.5.1   Evolution of remuneration systems

As companies grow from being owner managed, more formal systems need to be implemented that "explain" why employees should earn what they earn. Job evaluation and salary structures provide the cornerstone for the explanation.

### 3.5.2   Job description and job evaluation

During the process of job evaluation, we ask questions about the tasks being performed in a particular job, the relationship of jobs to each other, overlapping job content, and responsibility. The content provided in the job descriptions can be effectively used for job design and job enrichment programmes. Job evaluation systems have to be flexible to accommodate the changing, dynamic environments within the market as well as in the organisation.

### 3.5.3   Job evaluation and organisational design

Job evaluation can be a logical follow through in support of organisational design. Many of the problems that inhibit the effectiveness of organisations have to do with job or role perceptions.

Sorting out problems of job definition and relativities can often dispose of the root cause. It is often easier to see career paths which facilitate skills development, especially under the job family modelling or career path approach.

### 3.5.4 Detailed analysis of actual salary structure

Job evaluation and salary structures provide useful data for analysing an organisation's pay slope, pay ratios, pay ranges and overlap. There are legislative requirements asking companies for this type of data, thus some kind of job evaluation system is needed in order to fulfil submission requirements.

### 3.5.5 Popular misconceptions

The following misconceptions need to be overcome:

- "Everyone will get a big increase."
- "The new hierarchy will be very different and difficult to recognise."
- "There will be many changes in status."
- "Some people will have their pay reduced."
- "Job evaluation solves all problems."
- "We don't need job descriptions."

## 3.6 Benefits of job evaluation systems

Benefits of job evaluation systems include the provision of a logical graded hierarchy and pay structure. In this way, inequalities are reduced, and management and employees are able to see how different jobs relate to one another. Job evaluation provides a way to regain control over salary and wage administration, ensuring a consistent rationale for pay structures. Wage and salary administration are seen to be fair, and a detailed analysis of wage and skills gaps becomes possible. In addition, negotiation and collective bargaining are made easier by using a common language or defined point of reference. Compliance with legislation for those countries that have pay equity legislation is a considerable advantage.

## 3.7 Understanding the organisation structure

Benefits which accrue from job descriptions and the process of writing them provide an opportunity to study the organisational structure and to identify anomalies, since the job analyst has to understand fully how each job is structured. The following must be noted by the job analyst:

- Key areas of responsibility.
- Levels of authority and accountability.

- Reporting relationships.
- Spans of control.
- Lines of communication.
- Job design.
- Resourcing levels.

## 3.8. Information for recruitment

Benefits which will accrue from job descriptions and the process of writing them are detailed information for recruitment, specifically for:

- Developing the job specification.
- Planning the interview.
- Meaningful advertising.
- Providing prospective employees with details of what is required in the job.
- Meaningful induction training.

## 3.9 Additional benefits

Further benefits which accrue from job descriptions and the process of writing them are that they supply:

- A basis for job procedures and performance standards.
- A framework for performance and progress review.
- Detailed information for career pathing and resource planning.
- Detailed information for the development of training programmes.

They also assist the organisation to comply with legislation that requires organisations to justify differences in pay.

## 3.10 Job evaluation process

This topic outlines the two broad stages in the process of job evaluation. These stages are shown in Table 3.2.

*Table 3.2: Two broad stages in job evaluation*

| Stage | Description | Outcomes |
|-------|-------------|----------|
| 1 | The job, not the individual – job descriptions and job grading | Job or role descriptions and a grade |
| 2 | The individual in the job – development of salary structures | A salary structure |

### 3.10.1 Evaluation of person versus job

It is important to understand that it is the job itself that is to be evaluated and not the person in the job. Job evaluation is an impersonal process in Stage 1, and takes no account of the quality, performance, or effort that a person brings to the job. It is only in the development of the salary or remuneration structure at Stage 2 that one can take personal qualities, characteristics of the person in the job, performance, and effort into account.

The current wage or salary structure in an organisation is often another source of bias in Stage 1. Consciously or unconsciously, we tend to construct a hierarchy of jobs in our own minds based on what we know of the existing wage or salary structure. The grading committee must continually be reminded that it is "the job and not the person" which is important, and that current wage or salary levels are irrelevant to the grading process.

### 3.10.2 Internal versus external factors

Assessment and comparison concern job content, not the value of a job to the organisation. Although job evaluation is used to determine relative pay levels, pay levels for particular jobs and individual earnings remain organisational policy decisions based upon internal and external factors. Internal equity and external equity features are used to compile the salary structure. Figure 3.1 below shows a typical salary structure.

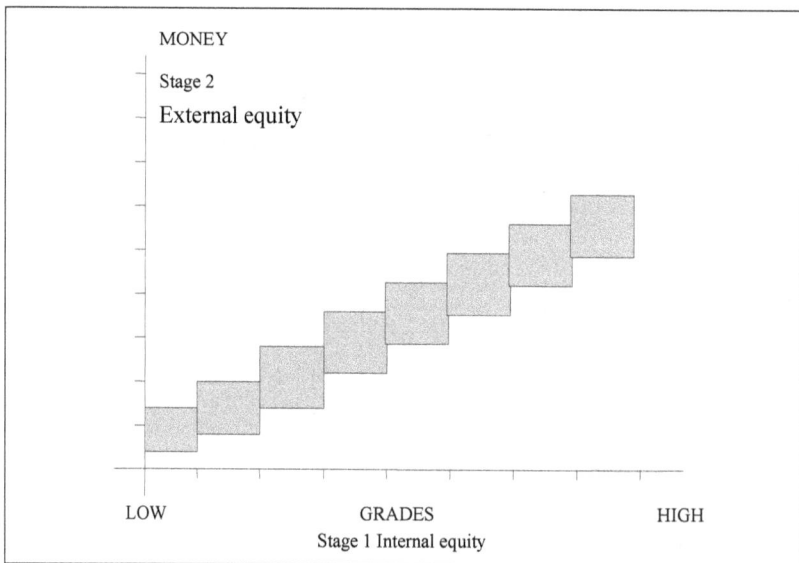

*Figure 3.1: Salary structure showing Stage 1 and Stage 2*

## 3.11   Job descriptions and job grading (Stage 1)

The processes of developing job descriptions and conducting job grading are set out in Table 3.3 below.

*Table 3.3: Job descriptions and job grading: Stage 1*

| Step | Description | Outcomes |
|------|-------------|----------|
| 1. | Selection of a job evaluation system | A justification of why system was chosen |
| 2. | Selling the concept and the system to management and employees | Communication documents |
| 3. | Designing the job description forms in accordance with organisation requirements | Job or role description forms |
| 4. | Deciding on how and how many job descriptions are to be written | A list of jobs or roles to be written |
| 5. | Training the people who will write job descriptions | Competent job or role description writers |
| 6. | Monitoring the quality of job descriptions | Quality descriptions |
| 7. | Training the grading committee | Trained grading committee |
| 8. | Grading the jobs | All jobs or roles graded |
| 9. | Training an auditing committee and auditing the jobs | Trained audit committee and audited jobs |

This process is inflexible. One must observe the grading rules if the system is to retain its credibility. To enable the grading committee to grade jobs objectively, job descriptions must be written. Most systems of job evaluation require job descriptions if gradings are to be justified.

### 3.11.1 Salary structure (Stage 2)

This is a separate process, with seven steps which are outlined in Table 3.4.

*Table 3.4: Salary structure process: Stage 2*

| Step | Description | Outcomes |
|------|-------------|----------|
| 1. | Wage and salary structuring, benefits and incentives | Defensible salary structure |
| 2. | Checking conditions of service | Alignment of conditions of service and grades |
| 3. | Develop plan to implement | Implementation plan |
| 4. | Implementation | |

| Step | Description | Outcomes |
|------|-------------|----------|
| 5. | Designing the maintenance system | Often computerised |
| 6. | Explain the system | Communication document |
| 7. | Compile procedures manual | Procedures manual |

## 3.11.2 Comparing Stages 1 and 2

The two stages can be compared as shown in Table 3.5.

*Table 3.5: Comparison of the two stages*

| Comparing | Stage 1 | Stage 2 |
|-----------|---------|---------|
| Flexibility | Inflexible; the grading rules must be applied. | Flexible; individuals can be paid anywhere along the pay scale in line with the organisation pay progression policy. |
| What is taken into account | Looks at the job, not the person performing the job, grade the job and not the person. | Takes account of personal qualities and characteristics of person in job. |
| Personal or impersonal | Impersonal | Personal. |
| What is important | Observe grading rules. | Quality, competence, performance, and scarcity of skill and effort are taken into account. |

To implement this, management should pay special attention to the following guidelines:

- Be committed to the programme and the motives for carrying it out.
- State belief in justice and fairness.
- State that no-one will have their basic pay reduced.
- Reiterate that it is the job that is to be evaluated and not the person.
- Explain the method simply.
- Ensure appropriate participation.

## 3.12 Why job evaluation systems fail

In most cases, where a system collapses, it is not because of the system itself, but is usually due to one of the following factors:

- Weak initial implementation.
- Weak top management support.

- Lack of employee participation and support.
- The upgrading of jobs without a corresponding change of job content.
- Inadequate administrative support.
- Lack of communication.
- System is not managed.
- Job descriptions are not reviewed and re-graded as jobs change.
- New employees and managers are not educated on the system.
- No cross-correlation of other similar jobs in the organisation leading to inconsistency.
- Lack of transparency.

A job should be re-graded only if there is an appropriate or noticeable change in job responsibilities or in the organisational structure. Resist the temptation to upgrade the job merely so that the person can be paid more. Greater flexibility must be built into the salary structure. Upgrading without a corresponding change in job content is the major cause of the collapse of job evaluation systems.

## 3.13   Choice of a job evaluation system

All currently popular systems produce similar and workable hierarchies. The criteria for the choice of a system are the following:

- The Chief Executive understands the system and is committed to it.
- Everyone, including the people at the lowest level in the organisation, understands and accepts the system.
- The system is defensible.
- Updating and maintaining the system is not an administrative burden.
- The system is flexible and can accommodate all types if grading systems including broad-banding.
- The system is user-friendly and supports the culture of the organisation.

Remember that there is no such thing as a good or bad job evaluation system. They all do the same thing – rank job descriptions relative to one another. Previous studies have shown a 0,94 correlation between all systems of job evaluation.[1]

## 3.14.   Categorisation of job evaluation systems

It is the corruption of a system that makes it seem poor or inappropriate, making maximum participation and commitment essential. Job evaluation systems can be categorised according to the below:

---

1   Bussin, 2015.

- The basis or method of comparison:
  - ○ Comparing job against job.
  - ○ Comparing job against some scale.
- The means or method of analysis used:
  - ○ Considering the entire job.
  - ○ Considering job elements or factors.

Table 3.6 summarises the various approaches to the categorisation of job evaluation systems.

*Table 3.6: Summary of approaches to the categorisation of job evaluation systems*

| Basis or method of comparison | | Means or method of analysis | |
|---|---|---|---|
| | | **Consider job elements or factors** | **Consider entire job** |
| **Basis or method of comparison** | Comparing job against job | Factor comparison, for example, Hay, Mercer's IPE | Ranking, internal benchmarking, paired comparisons, market pricing |
| | Comparing job against some scale | Points methods, for example, Peromnes, JE Manager, EQUATE, JE Paterson Points | Classification methods, for example, Stratified Systems Theory (SST), Paterson, TASK |

## 3.15 Points to remember when evaluating jobs

When evaluating jobs, remember the following:

- There is no such thing as a scientific method of job evaluation. Although scientific principles and processes may have been used in the development of certain methods, in practice they are all systematic approaches to the establishment of the hierarchy of jobs in an organisation.
- Virtually all job evaluation methods used world-wide do the same thing: rank the relative worth of one job to another and produce nearly identical hierarchies.
- Each method has advantages and disadvantages. Organisations should select the best suited according to their requirements, but realise that good implementation and ongoing management are more important than the system chosen.

### 3.15.1 Consistency

Toolkit 4: *Common Systems of Job Evaluation* sets out a brief description of the factors of some of the job evaluations systems used and an approximate cross-correlation table between them.

Because there is no such thing as a scientific system of job evaluation and because all methods are systematic approaches to grading jobs, the grading committee should be a standing committee, as there are often ongoing appeals to re-evaluate when job content changes and to evaluate new jobs.

### 3.15.2 Flexibility of the system

The job evaluation system must be flexible and grow with the organisation's needs. If it is perceived to be a dynamic, living system, it can even become a motivational influence. There should be procedures for updating job descriptions and subsequent re-evaluation.

## 3.16   Job evaluation: Frequently asked questions and sample answers

Table 3.7 illustrates commonly asked questions from employees about the job evaluation process, and some possible answers to these queries.

*Table 3.7: Commonly asked questions and possible answers*

| Commonly Asked Questions | Possible Answers |
|---|---|
| Am I being evaluated? | Definitely not. The job is being graded regardless of incumbent. |
| What method of job evaluation are we using? | The XYZ method, which is one of the most commonly used systems. It has the following features … |
| Who will be doing the job grading? | An objective outside consultant or grading committee will receive the job description, with no name on the job description, and apply the grading rules to arrive at an accurate grade. |
| When are jobs graded? | Jobs are graded whenever there is a significant change in job content, or for new jobs. |
| Will the company pay me more money as a result of the job evaluation? | No. Job evaluation is a process of ranking the relative worth of one job to another. If the job is upgraded, a higher pay scale will apply, but it does not automatically guarantee a pay increase. |
| Will job evaluation solve problems I have with my manager? | Not likely. It does not solve all problems and does not replace good management and leadership. |
| Why are we implementing job evaluation, then? | The organisation needs to have a defensible rationale for developing pay structures to ensure that similar jobs have the same pay range. It is also used to support recruitment processes, organisation design and facilitating external comparisons of job and pay levels. |

| Commonly Asked Questions | Possible Answers |
|---|---|
| Can I see my grade? | Yes, you will be told your grade and it will be explained to you (depending on the organisational policy). |
| Can I see another person's grade? | No, we respect the individual's right to privacy regarding their remuneration and grade. |
| What if I do not understand why I am on a particular grade? | First ask your manager or head of department to explain it to you. If there is still uncertainty, speak to the HR manager. |
| Is there going to be any training? | If there is a need, there will be annual refresher courses on how the system works. |
| Does the Executive Committee support the principles of job evaluation, and are they committed to its fair application? | Yes. EXCO is committed to the fair application of job evaluation. To this end, an objective, external consultant will be used to ensure the integrity of the system, either to audit results or to evaluate jobs. |
| Will my job description and grade put me in a "box" and stifle my creativity? | No, you can be as creative as you can and want. If your role changes because of it, we can re-write your job description to include these changes and re-evaluate the job to determine if your pay grade should also change. |
| Is job evaluation causing too much hierarchy and one-to-one reporting? | Job evaluation per se does not cause this; changes in the organisation design do. |

## 3.17 Summary

Job evaluation is the systematic and objective process of comparing one job to another within an organisation to arrive at different job levels. It does so without looking at individual characteristics, personality or performance. All job evaluation systems do the same thing, i.e. rank jobs according to complexity of work. Job evaluation systems assist with equal pay for work of equal value considerations. Many organisations have started to outsource the grading of their job descriptions to keep it professional and impartial. Job evaluation fails when jobs are upgraded without a corresponding change of job content. Job evaluation systems need to be maintained and audits should be done every few years to secure the integrity of the system. Make sure that all the leaders have a good understanding of the system you have chosen.

## 3.18 Self-evaluation questions

1. What is the definition of job evaluation?
2. Why do organisations need job evaluation?
3. Why do job evaluation systems fail?
4. What are the key factors to take into account when choosing a job evaluation system?

5.    What are the main factors to remember when evaluating jobs?

## 3.19    Exercise

Have a look at the Job Evaluation Point-Factor System below:[2]

1.    Can you identify the compensable factors?
2.    What can you say about the relative weight of each of the factors?
3.    Do you agree that the factors should be weighed this way? Why or why not? How would you weigh them and why?
4.    How many levels do you think can be created with this point-factor system? Explain.
5.    Do you think this is a good way to determine how much a job is worth? Is your answer in relative terms or in absolute terms?

There are 5 major factors that encapsulate the Paterson derived grading theory. These are:

| Skill | Effort | Responsibility |
|---|---|---|
| Knowledge and Skills (KS) | Problem Solving (PS) | Judgement (J) |
| | | Accountability (A) |
| | | Impact (I) |

### Points to Grade Table

| Points | Grade | Level Description | Paterson Equivalent | Occupational Levels |
|---|---|---|---|---|
| 33 - 35 | 7 | Global Corporate Governance | G | Global executive |
| 28 - 32 | 6 | Strategic Intent | F | Top management |
| 23 -27 | 5 | Strategy Execution/Senior Management/Senior Professional/ Specialist | E | Senior management |
| 18 - 22 | 4 | Tactical Management/ Professional | D | Professionally qualified and experienced specialists and mid-management |
| 13 -17 | 3 | Advanced Operational/ Supervisory | C | Skilled technical and academically qualified workers, junior management, supervisors, foremen, and superintendents |
| 8 -12 | 2 | Operational | B | Semi-skilled and discretionary decision making |
| 5 -7 | 1 | Primary | A | Unskilled and defined decision making |

---

2    21st Century Pay Solutions, 2021.

# CHAPTER 4

## Setting Pay Levels

### 4.1  Why use market surveys?

There are many reasons that organisations use market surveys, but the most common reasons are to:

- Put pay scales to the job grades.
- Compare pay and benefits for equivalent jobs in other organisations.
- Track pay increases and market movements in pay.
- Provide input into one's remuneration strategy and policy.

The data often helps an organisation to achieve the following:

- Set entry rates or new graduate starting salaries.
- Verify salary structures or make appropriate changes.
- Identify positions that need to be paid differently than the rate for the grade (such as a Corporate Lawyer).
- Assess typical salary increases required for the salary structure as a whole, or by grade or by position.
- Keep informed of benefits being offered.
- Review all the components of the total reward mix: guaranteed pay vs. variable pay (for example, incentives or shares), as well as non-cash engagement elements.
- Assess the slope, pay ranges and overlap of the pay structure.

### 4.2  Statistics commonly used in surveys

Salary surveys are designed to tell us about annual fixed and variable pay levels at a given point in time. Such surveys are relatively simple to understand, but before picking one up, users should be familiar with some statistical terms and aware of some of the hidden pitfalls. In this section we cover some of the basic statistics and tools required to analyse the data.

#### 4.2.1  Measures of central tendency

To understand salary surveys fully, a little statistical knowledge is needed. Few specialists, when faced with an array of salary figures, could easily identify the relevant information. For this reason, survey data are usually reduced to a central tendency figure. A central tendency is defined as a point within a group of data which is central to the group and around which other values are distributed.

There are three different types of central tendency – the mean, the median and the mode. Most salary surveys use at least one of these to give some idea of the middle or "typical" salary for a job. The three terms are defined as shown below.

### 4.2.1.1 Mean

The arithmetic mean, which is most commonly referred to as the average, is simply the sum of the individual figures divided by the number of items. The mean salary for these five figures – 150,000, 130,000, 120,000, 110,000, and 100,000 – is 122,000. This is the total sum of 610,000 divided by five. The mean is influenced (skewed) by any number that is an outlier. In other words, an average can drop or increase if a very low or high value is included in the data set. For instance, if we replace the number 150,000 for a new number 190,000, the new mean would be 130,000.

### 4.2.1.2 Median

The median is the middle number of a particular range placed in rank order. The median salary of the five figures above is 120,000, found simply by arranging the numbers in the following order – 150,000, 130,000, 120,000, 110,000, 100,000. When there is an even number of salaries, the median is the average of the two middle figures. The median is not influenced by outliers, so changing the 150,000 figure to 190,000 has no bearing on the median, which remains at 120,000.

### 4.2.1.3 Mode

The mode is the most frequent figure found in the data set; that is, the salary received by most in the sample. If 12 staff members received 110,000, five received 100,000 and 10 received 120,000, the mode is 110,000 as 12 individuals received this salary as compared to five and 10 for the other two.

### 4.2.1.4 Weighting

In some cases, more accurate statistical procedures, such as weighted averages, are adopted to give a more representative picture. Weighting is used when there are large numbers of employees or data are skewed towards one or more larger organisations. Consider, for example, the mean average salary of the following employees:

*Table 4.1: Average vs. weighted average*

| | (A)<br>Salary | (B)<br>Number of Employees | (C)<br>Total |
|---|---|---|---|
| Company A | 8,500 | 25 | 212,500 |
| Company B | 9,000 | 30 | 270,000 |
| Company C | 9,500 | 35 | 332,500 |
| Company D | 10,000 | 40 | 400,000 |
| Company E | 12,000 | 50 | 600,000 |
| Total | 49,000 | 180 | 1,815,000 |
| Average | 9,800.00 | Weighted average | 10,083.33 |

To calculate the weighted average, each salary is multiplied by the number of employees receiving that salary to give total pay for each rate (A x B = C). This results in a grand total of 1,815,000, which is divided by all the employees, 180, to give a weighted mean average of 10,083.33. This contrasts with the simple mean average of 9,800, which is found when each individual salary is added to give 49,000 and then divided by the number of participating companies (five).

### 4.2.1.5 Using Central Tendencies

Although there are three types of measures of central tendency, the mode is rarely used; in practice, most surveys concentrate on the mean and median. Given that salary distributions are usually positively skewed (for an explanation of what this means, see section 4.2.2 below), for survey users there is often a conflict between which is the best measure to adopt. Both the mean and the median have their uses and limitations, but in the end, it depends on the purpose of the survey.

The mean is readily understood, and employees often feel it is fair to be paid the average salary. In addition, using averages has some practical advantages, e.g. they can be used as the basis for further calculations, whereas medians cannot. It is relatively simple to combine separate averages to find a mean for a whole sample. On the other hand, it is often argued that the median is a more representative figure because it reduces the impact of the more extreme higher salaries. Many organisations also prefer to use the median, along with the inter-quartile range (the range between the 75th percentile and the 25th percentile; see section 4.2.2.1 below), as the basis for salary comparison, because it says more about the distribution of pay levels. Always be sure to ascertain if the survey is reporting medians or means, although they often report both.

The preferred trend is to reference a survey that includes all relevant data of a full population of employees, rather than skewing the results by excluding certain data or making assumptions with it. From a user point of view, the important element is to ensure that you are familiar with the methodology of the survey you are using to make decisions; for instance, if the survey includes averages instead of weighted averages, the survey provider should make this clear to the user.

## 4.2.2 Measures of the Distribution of Salaries

In themselves, averages do not always give a full picture and many practitioners are equally interested in the distribution of salaries. The relationship between the averages, however, can indicate the pattern of distribution. In statistics, a data range can be illustrated by a distribution curve. When the figures are symmetrically dispersed around the mean, the result is a bell-shaped curve. Under such circumstances, the mean and the median are closely aligned.

When the mean and the median diverge, the distribution curve is "skewed" to the left (positive) or the right (negative), as illustrated in Figure 4.1. For salary distributions, it is common for the mean to be higher than the median, indicating that there are always a few high salaries pulling up the average. Salary distribution curves are therefore usually positively skewed.

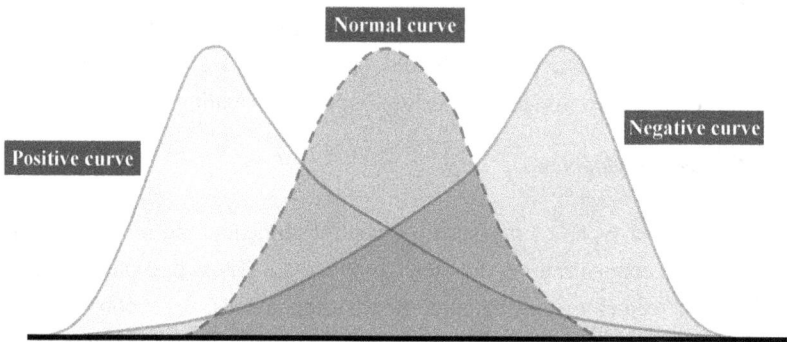

*Figure 4.1: Bell-shaped and positively skewed curves*

### 4.2.2.1 Quartiles, deciles and percentiles

A common way of looking at salary distribution is to divide data ranges around the median by using quartiles or deciles. Just as the median cuts the distribution of a group of salaries into two equal parts, data can also be broken down into quarters and tenths. Quartiles divide data into four equal parts and deciles into ten, and both are found in a similar way to that in which the median is found. The term "percentile" is used when referring to any such division of the data set.

- The upper quartile (UQ) or 75th percentile cuts off the top quarter of the distribution.
- The lower quartile (LQ) or 25th percentile cuts off the lower quarter.
- The highest decile (HD) or 90th percentile cuts off the top tenth.
- The lowest decile (LD) or 10th percentile cuts off the bottom tenth.

Note that the 60<sup>th</sup> percentile is the point where 60% of the data are below and 40% above. It is not the 50<sup>th</sup> percentile plus 10%, which is a common mistake made by inexperienced practitioners. We will revisit this concept again in the next chapter.

## 4.3 Definitions used in surveys

Alongside an understanding of what the various statistical measures are conveying, a clear definition of what is being surveyed is also essential. The meaning of basic salary or total earnings or total package may seem obvious, but a close inspection of surveys from different providers soon shows that these terms are often used in different ways. For this reason, a robust survey will always provide definitions of the terms used, and the diligent user should always check them before analysing the data, especially if you are working with several countries and several salary survey providers.

The definitions can be represented as shown in Table 4.2. However, it is important to note that there are many variations to represent remuneration data in salary surveys and one needs to be sure to be comparing apples with apples if one has offices and divisions in different countries and is using salary surveys from different vendors.

*Table 4.2: Structuring remuneration – example*

a.  *Base Salary*

+ Allowances
= *b. Total Fixed Pay*

+   Annual Incentives
= *c.  Total Cash* (b + Annual Incentives)

+   Long-Term Incentives
= *d.  Total Compensation* (c + LTI)

Life/Health Plans
+   Pension/CPF Contribution
+   Other Benefits
= e.   *Total Benefits* (Sum of three above)

f.   *Total Package* (d + e)

### 4.3.1 Base salary

This is typically the monthly salary paid, multiplied by the number of months of guaranteed salary. Note that this number is not always 12, as many countries – and companies – have different policies around this.

### 4.3.2 Allowances

This usually refers to the annualised guaranteed cash – or near cash – allowances made to employees that are not included in other calculations such as bonuses, salary increases, etc. In some countries these can be paid in the form of food vouchers, transportation vouchers, salary packaging, Christmas bonuses, etc.

### 4.3.3 Total fixed pay

Based Salary plus Allowances. Also sometimes referred to as Total Guaranteed Pay.

### 4.3.4 Annual incentives

The analysed value of short-term incentives, sales incentives/commissions, profit-sharing or other annual (or more frequent) incentive awards.

### 4.3.5 Total cash

Total Fixed Pay plus the Annual Incentives.

### 4.3.5 Long-term incentives

The annualised value of any incentive awards with longer than a one-year horizon. For share-based incentives, these are valued using Black-Scholes, binomial or a similarly accepted methodology.

### 4.3.6. Total compensation

Total cash plus the long-term incentives.

### 4.3.7 Benefits

Information on benefit provision is relatively straightforward, although it should be made clear at what job or salary level particular benefits are available. Many salary surveys collect at least some information on benefits, although few details are given about how they operate. For more extensive information, it is necessary to consult a specialised benefit survey. The benefits structures vary across countries and organisations, thus it is important to clarify the specific components the survey is reporting on, in order to have a relevant comparison. For instance, in one country, a car benefit may be included as an allowance, and in another as a benefit. Table 4.3 shows an example of the calculation of benefits.

*Table 4.3: Calculation of benefits*

| |
|---|
| Organisation car and car allowance costs are either based on actual cost or estimated from standard AA (Automobile Association) rates indicating fixed and running costs for the identified vehicle. |
| Pension or provident fund and medical/healthcare is based on the employer's contribution. If a survey reports on total guaranteed package, then the retirement fund and healthcare benefits may be reporting the total contribution per benefit. |
| Housing benefit is based on the actual monetary amount of the benefit offered. |
| In the case of a subsidised home loan, the cost is the difference between the interest rate charged by the organisation and the commercial interest rate the employee would have paid had they borrowed from a bank. |
| Club fees, professional fees or subscriptions are based on the actual cost of these benefits. |
| In the case of low-cost loans, the cost is the difference between the interest rate charged by the organisation and the interest rate the employee would have paid if they had borrowed from a commercial lender (similar to a housing loan). |
| Other benefits (for example, cell phone allowance or computer allowance) are based on the actual or estimated cost. |

### 4.3.8 Total package

The total amount of direct compensation plus the annualised value of all benefits.

### 4.3.9 Other common definitions found in salary surveys

- **Comparative ratio.** The common usage of this term, namely the comparative ratio or "compa-ratio", is the actual organisation salary divided by the internal salary reference point (or midpoint; see next chapter for more details) for the appropriate position. Typically expressed as: ".9 compa-ratio" for a person who is paid 10% below the midpoint.
- **Market ratio.** This is the same as above, except compared to the market reference point. Note that, customarily, this is multiplied by 100, so that one would say: "90% of market" for a person who is paid 10% below the market reference point (e.g. median).
- **Modal grade.** This is the most common grade for the specific position in the market.

## 4.4 Regional and organisation variables

Salary information is sometimes analysed according to a number of different variables such as location, industry and organisation size, which can make a considerable difference to salary levels. A small manufacturing organisation in a tourism area, or one in a rural area, for example, would not expect to pay the same as a merchant bank in the city, whether the salary in question is for a finance director or for a filing clerk. Once again, clear definitions of each variable should be provided in every survey.

There is a strong correlation between executive salaries and organisation size. Surveys may use several indicators of organisation size, but the most common are annual sales turnover (revenue), asset value, net profit, and the number of employees. Complexity measures include the number of core businesses in the organisation, the number of regions, organisation structure and the number of countries in which the organisation operates. In general, the bigger the organisation becomes, the higher the salaries become. Pinpoint accuracy in measuring size is not necessary because surveys usually analyse salaries within a range of organisation sizes.

## 4.5   Job matching

A salary survey will stand or fall by how well the jobs were matched with one another. Depending on various factors, but typically the level in the organisation, it adds to the validity of the market comparison when jobs are matched as far as possible to:

- Industry.
- Sector – private or public.
- Location.
- Size of organisation (for example, revenue, net profit, number of employees, asset value).
- Range of responsibilities.
- Job size and complexity or level in the organisation.

On the last point, there are several levels of accuracy of job matching, and depending on the need, each has its use.

### 4.5.1   Benchmark jobs

These are jobs commonly found in your industry and used in compensation surveys. It is common to find that only about 50% of all jobs in an organisation will be benchmark jobs in published surveys, and perhaps as high as 70% in club surveys. When matching, a good standard is when at least 70% of your organisation's job corresponds to the content described in the survey's benchmark job.

### 4.5.2   Job or role title only

This is suitable only when there is no deviation from the title or from what one would expect in the job, otherwise this can be very misleading.

### 4.5.3   Summary description of role and reporting line

This is typically used in most salary surveys. It allows thumbnail-sketch job matching and alleviates major discrepancies.

### 4.5.4  Capsule job or role description

This is often used in club surveys (see Section 4.6), and may comprise 100 to 300 words, showing reporting lines, authority levels, and sometimes qualifications and experience.

### 4.5.5  Complete job or role descriptions

This method leaves little room for error and is used when considering only a few positions that require a high degree of accuracy.

### 4.5.6  Job evaluation

This is often used in conjunction with the above methods and ensures that jobs of similar size and complexity are compared.

## 4.6  Who is surveyed?

Organisations usually participate in salary surveys to benchmark against organisations similar to them in all or some of the following characteristics:

- Size and structure.
- Industry type (products, services).
- Geographic location.
- Revenue/income size.
- Required job skills.

The key methods of obtaining required data, with implications, advantages and disadvantages, are shown in Table 4.4 below.

## 4.7  Club surveys

Some organisations or industry groups form "survey circles" or "clubs" and, on an agreed basis, share salary and benefit information. The following series of checklists may be helpful to those considering starting a salary club.

*Table 4.4: How to obtain data*

| Method | Cost | Time | Reliability & validity | Confidentiality | Detail? |
|---|---|---|---|---|---|
| Published Printed | Low | Annual publication | High reliability; validity = 3 months old – 9 months old | High | Some |
| Published web-based | Low | Immediate | High reliability; Always valid | High | Some |
| Customised survey | High | 6 – 8 weeks | High | High | Yes |
| Shared industry survey | Low | 6 – 8 weeks | High | High | Yes |
| Free information/network | No costs | Fast | Low | Low | No |

## 4.7.1 Membership criteria (or "Who Should I Compare Against?")

Which companies are eligible for membership? Are they all:

- In the same business, that is, competitors?
- Of similar size and type, for example, all "blue chip"?
- In the same locality?
- Of similar parentage, for example, all subsidiaries of Japanese multinationals?
- Are separate parts of the same organisation allowed to participate or is only aggregate data accepted?
- How are decentralised companies treated?
- Is there a minimum and maximum number of participants?
- Who decides on requests to join the club? Who is "qualified" to do so? Do existing members have a veto?
- Is membership restricted to companies that can provide data on a specified minimum number of jobs?
- Is it possible to expel club members if they transgress club rules?

The core criteria here is to consider to whom you may lose employees, and from whom you would recruit.

## 4.7.2 Collecting the data

- Who collects the data? One of the members, a combination of members, a consultant?
- How frequently will the survey be conducted? Annually, every two years, semi-annually?
- How can accurate job matching be ensured? By using summary job descriptions, personal visits to participants to discuss differences in job scope and other problems, and a regular "audit" of job matching?

- How is the information collected? By email/internet questionnaire or personal visit?
- What data are required? Basic actual salaries of individuals in post, salary ranges, bonus payments, other cash additions to pay, details of benefits such as pensions, cars, medical insurance?
- Is the survey "open" or "closed"? In other words, are participants able to identify the salaries paid by other members?
- Are all grades of employees to be included in the one survey, or will separate surveys cover different groups of staff?
- Is a 100 percent response rate expected?
- What sanctions can the club impose if members fail to provide data?

### 4.7.3 Analysing and presenting the results

- Are actual salaries and salary ranges listed by the organisation in rank order, using a simple number code?
- What statistical analyses are produced from the aggregate data? Averages, medians, quartiles and inter-quartile ranges (if the samples are large enough)? Should these relate to individual salaries, organisation averages or medians, or salary range midpoints?
- Are any significance or correlation tests done on the statistical results?
- How can the results of the club survey be compared with general data on salaries from commercial surveys, for example?
- Are club members charged a fee to cover the cost of analysing the results and producing the survey report?

### 4.7.4. Considerations before deciding to conduct a survey

Before deciding to conduct a survey, consider the following:

- Time.
- Costs.
- Usefulness of data.
- Survey purpose.

Ensure that you also take account of hidden concerns such as confidentiality, or the difficulty in persuading peer organisations to participate.

When you receive a report, consider:

- Participants and sample size.
- Definitions of remuneration components.
- Job matching and statistical methodology.
- Data validation and "trimming".

- Date of validity.
- The interpretation and analysis.

Always remember that…

- The market does not move equally year-on-year.
- More specifically, the market for each job/job family does not move equally year-on-year or in tandem with other jobs/job families.
- An average is not a reliable reflection – the median is a more robust view.
- Data should not be weighted or smoothed – unless identified in the report.
- The biggest organisation does not necessarily pay the most.
- Carefully choose your comparator group.
- You do not need to pay more when the business is in a more profitable position – go back to your strategy!

## 4.8   Published surveys

There are several providers of published surveys, and many of the larger organisations are now participating in international surveys. The following checklist may be useful in evaluating the published surveys:

- What is the core competence of the producers of the survey?
- What is the survey based on, and what data are incorporated into the survey?
- Is there a participant list, and are the participants comparable?
- What data collection method was used, and how reliable was it?
- Which methods of job matching were used?
- From what date are the data valid, and how often is the survey published?
- What statistical methods are used? Are there quality controls for the data and reports?
- What presentation format is used, and what statistics, graphs or pie charts are shown?
- Is there a different survey for general staff and top executives? If so, what methodologies were used for job matching?
- Are pay increase predictions included in the survey?
- Is there information on benefits, incentives, allowances, salary administration policies, and future trends?
- What is the cost of the survey, and what is the value proposition of the consultancy?
- How easy is the survey to use and administer?
- What is the reputation of the survey provider?
- Why was the survey produced?
- What are the statistical tools and checks used?

For an example of an online published survey visit www.rewardonline.co.za.

## 4.9 Other sources of pay data

In the absence of salary surveys, there are other, often less accurate, sources of salary data. Common sources of this data are set out below:

- Associations and societies.
- Some associations survey their members' salaries and produce results for just that discipline, for example, chemical engineers.
- Personnel and recruitment agencies. This may be a useful source of data for specific functions, for example secretaries, although they are only surveying those incumbents currently in the job market.
- Internal searches.
- Newspaper/online advertisements and job sites.
- Government institutions and economic desks.

These sources may give a very broad overview of salaries, however careful consideration must be given to the accuracy of job matching, and it is often necessary to validate this against a club or published survey.

Organisations should have a policy for all managers to follow when they are presented with threats of resignations over salaries, especially if employees only have these alternative sources of data to make their claim. Most organisations will not make a counter-offer until they have comprehensively researched the salaries for themselves.

## 4.10 Layout of information

The results of remuneration surveys can be presented in several different ways. The tables below are examples of some of the possibilities.

*Table 4.5: Sample layout of published survey – benefits*

| | Benefit | Percentage who receive benefit | Lower quartile | Median | Upper quartile | Average cost |
|---|---|---|---|---|---|---|
| C | General bonus | | | | | |
| A | Performance/Incentive Bonus/Commission | | | | | |
| S | Entertainment allowance | | | | | |
| H | Car allowance/Expenses | | | | | |
| NON | Organisation car | | | | | |

| | Benefit | Percentage who receive benefit | Lower quartile | Median | Upper quartile | Average cost |
|---|---|---|---|---|---|---|
| C | Accommodation/House subsidy | | | | | |
| A | Pension or provident fund contribution | | | | | |
| S | Medical aid contribution | | | | | |
| H | Other benefits | | | | | |
| | **Total average cost: cash and non-cash benefits** | | | | | |

*Table 4.6: Sample layout of a club survey: Guaranteed package by participant*

| | Organisation | | | | | |
|---|---|---|---|---|---|---|
| **Position** | **A** | **B** | **C** | **D** | **E** | **F** |
| Financial controller/manager | | | | | | |
| Financial accountant | | | | | | |
| Financial assistant | | | | | | |
| T manager | | | | | | |
| HR manager | | | | | | |
| HR co-ordinator | | | | | | |
| Recruiting co-ordinator | | | | | | |
| Senior PA or assistant to executive | | | | | | |
| Junior PA or assistant to manager | | | | | | |
| Graphics manager | | | | | | |
| Graphics co-ordinator | | | | | | |
| Information services researcher | | | | | | |
| Messenger or driver | | | | | | |

*Table 4.7: Sample of survey data*

| Market refinement | Career stream | Position class | Base salary number of organisation | Base salary number of observation | Base salary perc25 | Base salary mean | Base salary median | Base salary perc75 |
|---|---|---|---|---|---|---|---|---|
| Food & restaurant combined | Executive | 56 | 9 | 19 | 187,569 | 224,782 | 219,286 | 257,742 |
| Food & restaurant combined | Executive | 57 | 11 | 21 | 203,090 | 244,600 | 238,166 | 282,833 |
| Food & restaurant combined | Executive | 58 | 12 | 60 | 219,897 | 266,165 | 258,671 | 310,366 |
| Food & restaurant combined | Executive | 59 | 9 | 17 | 238,094 | 289,632 | 280,942 | 340,579 |
| Food & restaurant combined | Executive | 60 | 10 | 28 | 257,796 | 315,168 | 305,130 | 373,733 |
| Food & restaurant combined | Executive | 61 | 3 | 8 | 279,130 | 342,955 | 331,401 | 410,115 |
| Food & restaurant combined | Executive | 62 | 8 | 11 | 302,228 | 373,191 | 359,933 | 450,039 |
| Food & restaurant combined | Executive | 63 | 7 | 17 | 327,238 | 406,094 | 390,922 | 493,849 |
| Food & restaurant combined | Executive | 64 | 5 | 13 | 354,318 | 441,898 | 424,579 | 541,923 |
| Food & restaurant combined | Executive | 65 | 4 | 6 | 383,638 | 480,858 | 461,134 | 594,678 |
| Food & restaurant combined | Executive | 66 | 5 | 5 | 414,385 | 523,253 | 500,836 | 652,568 |

## 4.11 Guidelines on selecting comparators

There have been many practical lessons learnt over the years. Some of the more important ones relating to developing a "comparator cut" of a general market survey are set out below:

- Once you have sufficient participants in the survey, the information becomes repetitive and does not alter materially if you get more participants. This starts at around eight comparators and flattens out around 16 to 20 participants.
- You will always find an exception or two, and most people have almost certainly heard only of the higher exception.
- If you have a sticky situation with a particular job's benchmark, don't go to war on a benchmark done only on title, grade and capsule job description. In this instance, one needs a more comprehensive appreciation of the job and perhaps a personal visit to the comparator organisation.
- For key positions, always use more than one method of comparing the jobs to the market and try comparing the job to several markets.
- Find a robust "peg" for the CEO – it gives a good anchor.

- Select comparators for different reasons. Find ones that are not necessarily only in your industry sector, or find ones more applicable to you, where there may be some similarity in the following features:
    - Complexity and type – for example, single or multiple products processes, capital or labour intensive.
    - Market or customer – who do you compete with for share of purse?
    - Organisation structure – for example, another organisation with two large, dominant divisions.
    - Location of business – for example, hotels, banks and mobile phone companies operate throughout the world.
    - Ownership structure – for example, global owners or family-owned listings.
    - Geographic location – it is often wiser to compare with organisations in the region, even though they are not in your industry sector.
    - Competing for the same resources or customers. Your competitors for talent are often the ones with a similar operating or business model.

Using these metrics opens the debate of which job below deserves to be paid more – the executive in charge of A or the executive in charge of B? (A is labour intensive, and B is capital intensive.)

- A employs 10,000 full time staff and makes a profit of 1 million.
- B employs 500 full time staff and makes a profit of 25 million.

There are compelling arguments for both A and B. The main point is that there are many considerations and variables. In this case, only two are presented. It is not a simple matter, and a lot of passion is spent on convincing the other party on the complexity of one's situation.

It is important to have a good feel for who one's competitors and comparators are. Selecting the comparators should be done against agreed criteria. Use several different criteria and be sure to understand exactly what the job entails.

## 4.12 Summary

Pay levels are set for grades and for specific positions in an organisation. In small businesses, the pay level is set by the owner and his or her gut feel of fair pay. As an organisation grows, it requires more sophisticated market and salary surveys which are usually run by consultants. Surveys reflect the various percentiles of remuneration, as well as the different elements of remuneration, including base pay, benefits, short-term incentives and sometimes long-term incentives. The most important thing to get right is accurately matching the job to the salary survey job. A 70 percent match is considered good. Selecting comparator organisations is very important and the organisations need to be of similar size and complexity to your own organisation. Lastly, remember to consider that the components of pay that are being reported on should be relevant – total package versus total package!

## 4.13  Self-evaluation questions

1.  Why do organisations use market salary surveys?
2.  Name four main components of remuneration.
3.  What is a club survey?
4.  What information is typically shown in salary surveys?
5.  What are the key determinants of setting executive pay?
6.  How does one select comparator organisations?
7.  What cautions should you look out for in a survey?

## 4.14  Exercise

Your CEO has heard your pleas and has agreed to give you 10% additional budget to improve the total remuneration of your employees. Would you quickly decide to give everyone a 10% salary increase? Or a higher increase only to specific groups? Would you improve the benefits and/or perks? Or the amount of retention pay given? How about additional spend on training? Or in recognition programmes? Would work-life balance play a part in your plans to spend this windfall amount?

Provide a detailed rationale on how you would allocate these monies and why.

# CHAPTER 5

# Salary Structures

## 5.1 What is a salary structure?

A salary structure comprises salary grades or levels that have salary ranges attached to them. These salary structures are derived from market information and internal job hierarchies, and an organisation typically uses a market reference point for the midpoint of their salary scale, e.g. the market median/50th percentile, the 75th percentile, or some other percentile that best suits its rewards strategy. The market reference point chosen will depend on the role of base pay in the total rewards strategy. Organisations that wish to attract employees based mostly on their level of pay may want to use a higher percentile. Others that have a more balanced approach between pay, professional development and career opportunities may opt for a lower target percentile to have funds available to invest in other elements of total rewards to attract, retain and motivate staff.

## 5.2 Why organisations have salary structures

Job grades and salary structures provide defensible systems and procedures for implementing the pay policy in a consistent way. The purpose of a salary structure is to provide guidelines as to which salary scale and grade each employee is on; it provides a logical framework upon which to base remuneration decisions. The application is shown in Table 5.1 below.

Ultimately, the organisation is looking for a salary structure that is equitable from both an external and internal perspective.

*Table 5.1: Possible applications of a salary structure*

| Instance | Application |
|---|---|
| **Recruitment** | Managers can grade the job and offer a salary in the salary range (according to the remuneration policy). |
| **Performance** | Employees who demonstrate sustained superior performance could move through the salary scales more quickly. |
| **Competence and skill demonstration** | Some remuneration policies have a progression policy that allows individuals who apply relevant competence and skill to move up the salary scales more quickly. |
| **Business needs or scarcity of skill** | The business imperative is particularly applicable during transformation of organisations. This, together with scarcity of some skills, sometimes leads to "anomalies" in the salary structure, but these are defensible. |

## 5.3    Features of well-designed salary structures

The features of well-designed salary structures are set out below and could serve as a checklist when designing salary structures for your organisation:

- The salary structure supports the remuneration, HR and business strategies.
- The principles of internal and external equity are upheld.
- Grades and levels reflect the organisation and work design.
- Logical metrics are used when determining the number of grades, salary scale range and width, slope, overlap, differentials and when best practice has been considered.
- Are flexible enough to respond to internal and external pressures.
- Allow superior performance to be rewarded.
- Ensure consistent decision-making and application of the remuneration philosophy.
- Implementation is not disruptive or costly.
- Clearly show career movement, pay opportunities and career ladders.
- Have appropriate stakeholder buy-in.
- Are legally defensible.
- Are affordable, yet competitive.

One of the most difficult challenges in salary structure design is getting the balance right between affordability and competitiveness. To do this, one size may not fit all, and *best fit* is more important than best practice.

## 5.4    What influences the design of salary structures?

Not all salary structures are the same; organisations compete by differentiating their salary structures. Factors most likely to influence your structure are:

- Supply and demand – the market rate for the job or grade. This may vary by country/market.
- Cost of living.
- The financial position of the organisation or industry.
- Management decisions – policy.
- Trade unions and collective bargaining agreements in place.
- The current salary/wage structure.
- The number of grades from top to bottom.
- Target market percentile as determined by the remuneration strategy.

Consider the following before designing a salary structure:

- Strategic issues such as:
    - Whether the structure is able to support an organisation's business strategy.
    - Compatibility with total reward design strategy (including base pay, variable pay and other elements in the total remuneration and employee experience strategies).

- ○ Guaranteed pay to variable pay ratio.
- Competitive practices – specifically, external equity and the organisation's stated comparative position to the market (i.e. median, upper quartile etc.), as per the remuneration strategy.
- The organisation's job and workplace design approach to produce internal equity.
- Administrative policies of the organisation.
- Funds available.

## 5.5 Developing a salary structure

This section outlines the key considerations in the design and development of salary structures. It focuses on internal and external equity as the main anchors.

### 5.5.1 Internal equity

In Chapter 3 we explained that internal equity starts with a job evaluation process to determine the relative value assigned to different jobs within an organisation. Jobs are arranged into a job worth hierarchy and those with a similar relative value are then grouped into salary grades. In addition, internal equity assesses how reasonable these grades are and how they link to market levels of pay for the job, as we discussed in Chapter 4. Internal equity can be examined on two levels, namely horizontally (between departments) and vertically (within one department).

Internal equity is a key consideration in developing salary structures not only within a job family, but also among various job families that have common job grades. Without a grade structure it is difficult to create a salary structure, as there is nothing upon which to "anchor" the salary ranges.

### 5.5.2 External competitiveness

This is the second consideration in the design of a salary structure. The focus in this area is on external equity and is based on an organisation's need to compete in a free market for products and services, as well as for talent. Part of this competition for talent involves the management of labour costs – ensuring that the labour force is neither overpaid (leading to a higher cost than necessary for the organisation to provide/produce its product/service) nor underpaid (possibly leading to a high turnover or labour unrest which could harm productivity). Pay mix is important as all components of the remuneration package must be added together to get a holistic comparison to the market. In simple terms, external competitiveness speaks to the organisation's ability to attract and retain the key talent it needs to be successful.

Low turnover or a lack of competitors for labour is not an indicator of a lack of competitiveness in an industry or that the remuneration system is working perfectly in the organisation, since turnover could be present – or absent – for a number of different non-pay related reasons.[1]

---

1    Schlechter, Syce & Bussin, 2015.

To avoid having the organisation's employees leave to move to other organisations motivated by higher pay elsewhere, and to be able to attract possible candidates from competitors for talent, reliable remuneration data regarding these organisations should be obtained via salary surveys (see Chapter 4). It is essential for an organisation's human resource strategy to be tied directly to the data gathered on any defined competition.

## 5.6   Designing an effective salary structure

Follow the steps below to ensure that you have taken account of internal equity and external competitiveness when designing your salary structure.

Steps one to three are based on the assumption that the organisation is using a point-factor job evaluation plan. Steps four onwards are the same for both point-factor and classification systems. Complete these steps to design the salary structure. Note that steps one to five are related to determining internal equity and steps six to ten are used to establish external competitiveness.

As a general guideline, as the job level increases, the reliance on external data (as opposed to internal considerations) also increases.

*Table 5.2: Steps to designing an effective salary structure*

| | Step | Action |
|---|---|---|
| Internal relativity | 1. | Review overall point differentials. |
| | 2. | Rank order jobs by total evaluation points. |
| | 3. | Develop job groupings. |
| | 4. | Develop preliminary point bands. |
| | 5. | Check intra-family and supervisory relationships. |
| External relativity | 6. | Incorporate market data. |
| | 7. | Review market inconsistencies. |
| | 8. | Smooth out grade midpoints. |
| | 9. | Review differences between midpoints and market references. |
| | 10. | Resolve inconsistencies between internal and external equity. |

Table 5.3 below contains a detailed breakdown of the salary structuring procedure along with a focus on key issues and questions to ask. These steps are detailed in the table below. We will talk about calculating the salary structure in Section 5.8 below.

*Table 5.3: Salary structuring procedure*

| Action | Explanation | Key issue | Key questions to ask |
|---|---|---|---|
| **Review overall point differentials** | Review all job evaluation points to see if any job evaluations stand out from the group. During this step, make any points changes necessary to reflect the internal value of the job. | Do any job evaluations appear to be "out of place" either vertically or horizontally? | • Do the evaluators fully understand their jobs?<br>• Is the job description or questionnaire complete?<br>• Is the job being compared to the correct peer group?<br>• Is the rater evaluating the job or the person? |
| **Rank order of jobs by total number of evaluation points** | Rank all jobs in ascending or descending order. | Does the hierarchy of positions make intuitive sense? | • Does the hierarchy reflect the differences in functions of the various positions?<br>• Has the position been overrated or underrated?<br>• Do the differences in points reflect the degrees of difference between positions? |
| **Develop job groupings** | To develop groupings, look for break points. Ensure that the levels identified are compatible with the number of levels in the organisation. | How to develop job groupings that are meaningful and not contrived. | • Where are the natural break points?<br>• How many levels should there be to accommodate levels within the<br>• organisation? |
| **Develop preliminary point bands** | Salary-grade point bands (ranges) can be developed as either absolute point spreads or percentage-based point spreads across a range. | Determining the width of each point band (salary range per grade/level). | • Wider point bands will require fewer grades and will group a larger number of jobs together. Related questions to ask include:<br>  ◦ Is this in line with the organisation's corporate policy?<br>  ◦ Are jobs with similar skill, effort and responsibility being grouped together? |

| Action | Explanation | Key issue | Key questions to ask |
|---|---|---|---|
| **Check intra-family and supervisory relationships** | This last step in the internal equity process focuses on checking the evaluations to ensure that they represent all levels and reporting relationships within the organisation. Ensure that you determine if jobs of similar skill, effort and responsibility are within the same salary level. Check that dissimilar jobs are not placed within the same level and that subordinate/supervisor positions are not placed in the same grade. | Peer and subordinate/ superior relationships. | • Are there enough levels between supervisor and subordinate positions?<br>• Do the set levels accurately reflect levels within job families? |
| **Incorporate market data** | Use the preliminary data gained in steps four and five. Add market data to identify differences between the way that the organisation and the market value particular jobs. | How to obtain the best fit between internal evaluation and market value. | • Are the market numbers reliable?<br>• Are the job matches appropriate?<br>• How many open grades are needed to meet future needs?<br>• Is it possible to keep the market comparisons current? |
| **Review market inconsistencies** | The organisation must now decide the importance of the internal values that have been placed in its positions. It must also decide whether the organisation can afford to pay differently from the market. Can the organisation risk the internal integrity of the remuneration programme by relying more heavily on the market value of these positions? | The organisation must decide whether it can accept the salary structure with varying percentages between its midpoints. | • Is the number of grades selected still accepted?<br>• Can the differences between the midpoints be smoothed without affecting the integrity of the market competitiveness?<br>• How important is it to be aligned to the market? |

| Action | Explanation | Key issue | Key questions to ask |
|---|---|---|---|
| **Smooth out grade midpoints** | In this step, a decision must be made about where it is most important to be most competitive and where the most payroll money is at stake. At this point, you must test to see which midpoint-to-midpoint percentage increment is most logical to use. | The organisation must decide whether there is an ideal midpoint-to-midpoint percentage spread. | • Is smoothing out always necessary or desirable?<br>• At what point is it advisable to stop the smoothing-out process so that the salaries generated are competitive, but the payroll monies are not used ineffectively or irresponsibly? |
| **Review differences between midpoints and market references** | Any large differences between proposed midpoints and individual job market benchmarks must be identified. | The organisation must determine the percentage factors to be used in order to smooth the midpoints. | • Which jobs have a greater need to be competitively paid?<br>• Can a job be underpaid without affecting the organisation's ability to attract and retain employees?<br>• Can the organisation afford the financial implications of overpaying some jobs? |
| **Resolve inconsistencies between internal and external equity** | Note that most organisations are willing to accept pay levels that are within 20% of the competitive market. To manage inconsistencies and decide what adjustments to make in balancing internal values and external competitiveness, the organisation must take into account its corporate culture and ability to pay. | The organisation must determine what is more important, internal or external equity. | • What is the organisation's culture?<br>• What is the organisation's stance on the consistent treatment of its employees?<br>• Is there a high turnover in the organisation?<br>• Is it in a strategically important job family? |

The result of the above procedure is a structure which shows how each evaluated position relates to each other job internally and how they relate to the market.

## 5.7   Terminology

This section provides definitions and explanations for terms that are commonly used in reference to salary structures. The following definitions are essential for the understanding and application of salary structures in the workplace. These are summarised in Table 5.4 and explained in greater detail below.

*Table 5.4: Definitions of salary structure terms*

| Term | Definition |
|---|---|
| Salary structure | Refers to the pay scales attached to grades and the way in which these scales are structured; their range, their slope overlap, differentials and market positioning. |
| Salary ranges | Refers to the width of the salary scale, that is, the distance between minimum and maximum pay for each grade. It is usually measured in terms of the percentage above and below each midpoint, or the full range from minimum to maximum salary scale point. |
| Salary overlaps | The extent to which the maximum of the lower grade overlaps with the minimum of the next higher grade. It is dependent on both the salary range and the salary slope. |
| Salary slopes | The steepness or angle of the salary curve. The percentage difference between the pay for one grade and another. Provides a useful tool for measuring and comparing salary slopes. |
| Salary ratio | The ratio between the CEO's pay and the lowest pay. The highest salary divided by the lowest salary. |

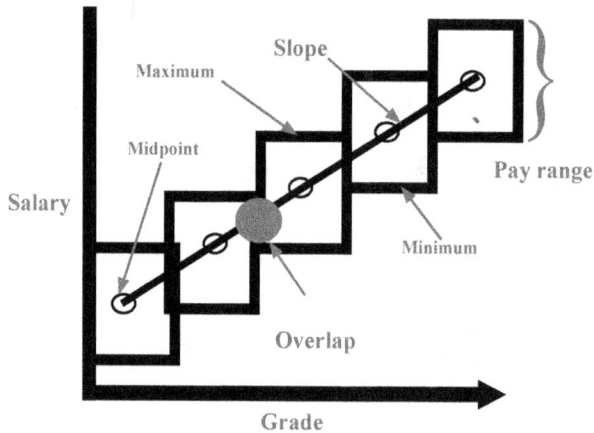

*Figure 5.1: Key components of a salary structure*

### 5.7.1 Components of a salary range

The above diagram (Figure 5.1) reflects the key components and decision points in the design of a salary structure. These components and decisions are explained below.

A salary range often has the following components: a minimum value, maximum value, and midpoint or central value. A market reference point is used as the start point for the salary scale design, and is typically used at the midpoint of the scale. In the example below, we note that there are many decisions to be considered, one of which is which market point to reference. The two examples in Table 5.5 below illustrate two different structures built around two different market reference points: Example one uses the 50th percentile whereas Example 2 uses the 25th percentile. Note that the difference to the minimum and maximum from the midpoint are generated by the lower and upper guides, although these should, as much as possible, be related to the market data.

*Table 5.5: Examples of use of market reference points*

| Paterson | Market total guaranteed package | | | | |
| --- | --- | --- | --- | --- | --- |
| | 10th | 25th | 50th | 75th | 90th |
| D1 | 286,727 | 337,917 | 391,480 | 453,999 | 502,632 |

| | Paterson | Proposed pay scale | | | |
| --- | --- | --- | --- | --- | --- |
| | | Lower guide | | Midpoint | | Upper guide |
| Example 1 | D1 | -13% | | 391,480 | | +15% |
| Example 2 | D1 | 293,988 | | 337,917 | | 388,605 |

Once the midpoint is selected, the next steps are to build the range around the midpoint.

## 5.7.2 Calculation of a salary range

The difference between the maximum and the minimum value in the salary spread is the "range spread" or height of the range. This is normally expressed as a percentage of the difference between the minimum and the maximum divided by the minimum. In the example below, the maximum of the range is 90,000 and the minimum is 60,000.

*Example of a salary range calculation*

$$\frac{\text{Maximum} - \text{Minimum}}{\text{Minimum}} = \frac{90,000 - 60,000}{60,000} = 50\%$$

### 5.7.3 Calculation of the midpoint spread

Calculation of the spread on either side of the midpoint can be done using the following formulae:

$$\frac{\text{Minimum} - \text{Midpoint}}{\text{Midpoint}} \quad \text{and} \quad \frac{\text{Maximum} - \text{Midpoint}}{\text{Midpoint}}$$

*Example of midpoint spread calculation*

Following the same example, where the maximum is 90,000 and the minimum is 60,000, the midpoint is 75,000. The spread on either point of the midpoint is therefore equal in percentage terms on either side of the midpoint, and is calculated using the midpoint as denominator, as follows:

$$\frac{60,000 - 75,000 = -20\%}{75,000} \quad \text{and} \quad \frac{90,000 - 75,000 = 20\%}{75,000}$$

### 5.7.4 The question of uniformity

In the example above, the range spread is 50%; the spread does not have to be uniform throughout the salary structure. Variations in range spreads are influenced by the level and sophistication of skills required for a given position. For example, entry level positions with skills that can be quickly mastered usually have narrower salary range than supervisory, managerial or high-level expert/technical positions. That is because there is no point is paying more than a 10-15% premium for a skill that can be easily replaced at a lower cost.

In general, the longer an individual is expected to stay in a job grade, the greater the range spread should be. Thus, for professional entry level jobs, where incumbents are expected to progress quickly to the next level, range spreads can be 30-40%, whereas for senior level jobs (e.g. those reporting to the CEO) that may never progress beyond their current role to the next level role, the salary range would need to be large enough to accommodate 10 or more years of the incumbent being in the same job. In this case, salary ranges of more than 60%, even beyond 100%, are not unusual. The higher salary ranges are typical in more broad-banded structures that have fewer numbers of levels/grades. We discuss broad-bands in the next chapter.

### 5.7.5 Ranges for different job levels

The following are typical range spreads for different job levels found in an organisation.

*Table 5.6: Typical range spreads by various job levels*

| Percentage spread* | Typical job levels |
|---|---|
| 20–40% | Lower level service, production and maintenance |
| 30–50% | Clerical, technical, specialist |
| 40–60% | Higher level professional, middle management |
| 60% and over | Higher level managerial, executive and expert technical |

When choosing a salary range spread, note that this number will determine the maximum and minimum salaries for that grade. As the spread gets larger, maximums increase and minimums decrease, with midpoints remaining constant. When minimums are too low, the organisation will be forced to pay the employee a higher amount in the range to remain competitive. Further, this narrows the position's long-term earning potential. In turn, a high maximum may provide higher long-term earning opportunities which are costlier than is required for the organisation to be competitive.

### 5.7.6 What is a midpoint?

A salary range midpoint is an essential element in salary management. It is often used as a reference point or "target". The midpoint is typically set to equal the market reference point (market median, 75th percentile on another point chosen by the organisation to suit its total rewards strategy). However, it is important to note that the market reference point on which midpoints are estimated may differ by level in the organisation as well as by job family. For instance, an organisation may target the market third quartile for scarce or business critical job families.

### 5.7.7 Compa-ratio

The compa-ratio (short for "comparative ratio") is an important tool for managing remuneration costs. An individual compa-ratio expresses the relationship between the incumbent's salary and the midpoint. Compa-ratios can be calculated for individuals, job families, departments or the organisation as a whole using the formula:

$$\frac{\text{Incumbent/job family/department/organisation salary}}{\text{Midpoint(s)}}$$

A market compa-ratio follow the same logic, except that is calculated directly with the market reference point (median, 75th percentile, etc.) as the denominator. It is a common convention that compa-ratios are calculated without multiplying by 100 (as in the formula above), however, market compa-ratios are multiplied by 100. Thus, if someone is paid at the midpoint of the salary grade, his or her compa-ratio would be 1.0, whereas the same person, if they are paid at the market reference point, we would say their compa-ratio is 100% of market. A compa-ratio of .9 would mean the person is paid 10% below the midpoint, while a compa-ratio of 110% would mean that the person is paid 10% above the market reference.

Most organisations aim to have compa-ratio of close to 1.00 to their salary grade midpoints for competent performers with a good track record. Individual compa-ratios can vary according to how long the individual has worked in a job, previous work experience, scarcity of skills and job performance, depending on the criteria that the organisation use for their pay progression.

Organisations must be able to justify their current compa-ratio at individual, team and organisation wide level. Overall, the compa-ratio (like other parts of the remuneration strategy) should be aligned to the overall goals and objectives of the organisation.

## 5.7.8 Range penetration

Another method to use for tracking an organisation's remuneration system is to view an employee's salary in relation to the total salary range. This is know as termed range penetration. Range penetration is calculated using an incumbent's salary and the minimum and maximum values in the salary range.

### Formula for calculating range penetration

The formula for calculating range penetration is shown below. Assuming a person makes 85,000, using the minimum and maximum from the examples above we can calculate their range penetration as follows:

$$\text{Range penetration} = \frac{(\text{Incumbent salary--Range minimum})}{(\text{Range maximum} - \text{Range minimum})} \times 100$$

$$\text{Example:} \quad \frac{(85{,}000 - 60{,}000)}{(90{,}000 - 60{,}000)} \times 100 = 83{,}3\%$$

Range penetration is not reliant on the midpoint, a single number. Instead, range penetration refers to how far into a range a particular individual's salary has penetrated. As it does not rely on the midpoint, it is often used in broad-banded structures.

## 5.7.9 Midpoint progression (Slope)

Midpoint progressions are the percentage difference between salary grade midpoints. Salary slopes are often viewed as the steepness or angle of the salary curve. The midpoint progression provides a useful tool for measuring and comparing salary slopes. On the assumption that there is an equal increase in responsibility between each grade and the next one in an organisation, the "ideal" salary slope should have an equal percentage increase in salary between each grade and the next.

Generally speaking, the larger the midpoint progression, the steeper the slope of the curve. This could be because there are fewer number of grades within a salary structure, or because the market difference between entry level jobs and senior level jobs is very high. By contrast, a smaller midpoint progression may be due to a larger number of salary grades within the pay structure, or to a lower difference between entry level and senior level pay levels.

There are several ways to calculate midpoint progression: regression, present-value/future-value and average of market pay. We explain each of these below:

### Regression analysis

This approach helps to align market rates more closely with organisation policy. This is done by carrying out a simple regression of job evaluation points (x-variable) against market data (y-variable) to develop salary structures.

### Present-value/future-value formula

This formula may be used to determine the percentage between midpoints, assuming that you know the number of grades and the highest and lowest midpoints. The formula is as follows:

$$PV = FV \, (1 + i)^n$$

Where:     PV = Present Value (midpoint of lowest salary grade) FV = Future Value (midpoint of highest salary grade)

n = Total number of desired grade *intervals* (one less than the total number of grades in the structure)

i = Percentage difference between midpoints

### Average of market pay rate

This method for developing midpoints and resulting midpoint progressions uses the average of the market pay rate for different jobs within the benchmark job groupings. The resulting midpoint progression would have varying percentage differences between midpoints, reflecting patterns in the market.

### When progressions are not constant

The salary structure of an organisation does not have to have constant percentage progressions, and it is unlikely to happen if midpoints are tracked to market at each grade/level. When this occurs, promotional increases may be uneven and sometimes difficult to administer. If the percentage difference between midpoints is too high, this could result in costly promotional increases. If, on the other hand, it is relatively low, the result could be salary compression problems between supervisory and subordinate posts, and difficulty in matching promotions with the appropriate compensatory rewards.

An alternative may be to reference market data only at the top and bottom of your scale, and to create an exponential progression across the levels between the two anchor points. Note that the risk here is to test that your salary structure may look robust from a midpoint progression point of view, but may lose track to the market which may not mirror the same progression.

### 5.7.10   Salary grade overlaps

It is normal for the minimum and maximum value of a grade to fall into the adjacent range. The width of the range and the midpoint differentials determines the amount of overlap between adjacent grades. Grade overlap is significant when midpoint differentials are small and range spreads are large, but they are small when range spreads are small and midpoint differentials are large.

When using a pay for performance system, grade overlap allows high performers in lower salary ranges with a longer time within a grade to be paid more than a relatively new (or lower) performer in a higher salary range. In other words, salary grade overlaps support pay-for-performance and career progression strategies in organisations.

Despite the benefits, too much overlap limits the difference between midpoints, which then limits the earning potential of the staff and may cause pay compression problems between supervisors and subordinates.

*Formula for calculating overlap*

The formula for calculating overlap is:

$$\frac{(\text{Maximum of lower grade} - \text{Minimum of higher grade})}{(\text{Maximum of higher grade} - \text{Minimum of higher grade})} \times 100$$

A typical overlap is 30% to 50%.

## 5.8   Plotting the curve

The process to calculate and plot a salary curve involves several steps, which are described below. Note that the explanation below assumes that readers are able to use Excel to do simple regressions.

### 5.8.1 Which market reference point to use

We have discussed earlier that salary surveys usually provide data in quartiles, and that the organisation must decide which market reference point best suits its total rewards strategy. This process is straightforward if the organisation chooses to use the median or the 75th percentile, as the data are usually provided as such in the surveys. However, if the organisation chooses, for instance, the 40th percentile or the 62.5th percentile, the process is slightly more complicated, as these data points are not in the survey. A way to approximate these are to extrapolate between the nearest lower and higher percentiles provided. For example, to calculate the 40th percentile, one could take the difference between the 25th percentile and the 50th percentile salary figures, divide this number by 25 (the number of percentage points difference between the 25th and the 50th percentiles), multiply times 15 (the number of percentage points between the lower end – that is the 25th percentile – and the desired 40th percentile), and add this number to the 25th percentile.

To illustrate this, assume the 25th percentile in the salary survey is 60,000 and the 50th percentile is 100,000. The approximation to the 40th percentile would be {[(100,000 - 60,000) / (50 - 25)] * (40 - 25)} + 60,000 = <u>84,000</u>. It is important to note that this is only an approximation, as we do not have the raw data to estimate percentiles accurately.

A similar process can be used to approximate any percentile.

### 5.8.2 Start with total compensation and work backwards

Salary structures are usually calculated in terms of monthly base salary, as this is the figure we will most generally use to communicate salary offers, promotions, increases, etc. However, using the base salary number in the survey does not take into account variable pay or other differences in the policies of the organisations participating in the survey. In practice, companies want to match total compensation, not just the base salary. Thus, best practice regarding the calculation of a salary structure is to use the total compensation number from the market survey data, and back out the organisation's pay policies to arrive at an own base salary number. For example, let's assume the organisation has a policy to pay 13th month salaries, one additional month of allowances between food and transportation vouchers, and a target variable pay policy of 20% (equivalent to 2.5 months of base salary). The process would involve using the total compensation number at the reference point (following the example above, let us use the 50th percentile of 100,000), divide this by 16.5 months of pay (12 months base, 1 month for the 13th month, 1 month for allowances and 2.5 months for variable pay at target) and arrive at the estimated market base salary at the 50th percentile.

Hence, 100,000/16.5 = <u>6,060.60</u> estimated monthly base salary at market median.

### 5.8.3   Ageing of data/salary structure philosophy

The market data in a survey are typically expressed as of a specific date, often June 30th or similar. However, the data will be used for the structure that will be implemented for the next year, perhaps starting on the following April 1st. A number that survey vendors often provide is the estimated salary movement for the next year. Let's assume the dates for survey data validity and salary structure implementation are as above, and that the estimated salary movement for the next year is 6%. To make the survey data useful, we need to age it to the date when it will be needed. In simple terms, we would take the estimated monthly base salary we calculated above, and age it by the prorated number of months from the survey date until the structure implementation date. In our example that would be nine months between the two dates, so we divide the 6% estimated movement by 12 months in a year and multiply by the nine months interval we need.

Thus, (6/12) * 9 = 4.5%. We would need to age the data by 4.5%. In other words, our number above becomes 6,060.60 * 1.045 = 6,333.33.

However, we would be placing the salary structure to be the same as the market at the beginning of the year. In other words, since salaries are estimated to keep moving at the rate of 6% during the year, we would be lagging the market the whole year, and by the end of the year our structure would be out of phase with the market by 6% (94% of market). When we age data to the beginning of the structure period, we call this a *lag structure philosophy*.

To have a *lead structure philosophy*, we age the data to the end of the structure period (let's assume the structure is to stay in place for a year). This would mean ageing by 21 months (from date of survey to end of effectiveness of structure in March 31st of the subsequent year). Following the formula above that would be (6/12) * 21 = 10.5%, and our new estimated base salary at market median, aged to the end of the structure period, would be 6,060.60 * 1.105 = 6,696.96.

The lag structure philosophy may keep the organisation at risk of losing staff, and yet the lead structure philosophy may prove too costly. Some organisations thus choose a middle-of-the-road approach, which is the *lead-lag structure philosophy*. In this case, the data are aged to the middle of the salary structure validity period, thus leading the market for half the year and lagging for the other half. This approach balances risk and costs. In our example, we would age the data by a total of 15 months as such: (6/12) * 15 = 7.5%, and our new estimated base salary at market median, aged to the middle of the structure period, would be 6,060.60 * 1.075 = 6,515.15.

### 5.8.4   Calculate full structure

To calculate the salary structure midpoints, we do a simple regression of the salary grades (x-variable) against the estimated salaries by grade (according to the methodology described above). The number of grades and widths/ranges would be as determined according to your remuneration strategy and policy. Assume number of ranges and height of ranges are set following the principles set in Section 5.6. Use all the modified data points from the survey.

When calculating the best regression model in Excel, use the graph option and pick scatterplot with no lines. To draw the trendlines, ideally test various options. As salaries are often increased in percentages, it is more likely that the salary slope will be exponential rather than a straight slope. However, it is advisable to test all the curves; the best one will the one with the highest coefficient of determination ($r^2$). In Excel, right-click on the trendline, and in the menu that opens, click on format trendline and then click on the options to display the formula and the $r^2$. This will allow for this information to be shown on your graph. Once you have determined which trendline option best suits the data, use the formula linked to that option to calculate the midpoints for each salary grade (plug each salary grade into the x-variable portion of the formula). The result will be the midpoint for that grade. Figure 5.2 shows an example of calculated curves using all the percentile data. Often you may want to plot only two or three of these to show how the market behaves.

Note that the same methodology can be used to estimate the salary curve for the organisation. Simply replace the market data for internal data by grade. It is often useful to plot the internal line in the same graph to have a visual comparison against the market data.

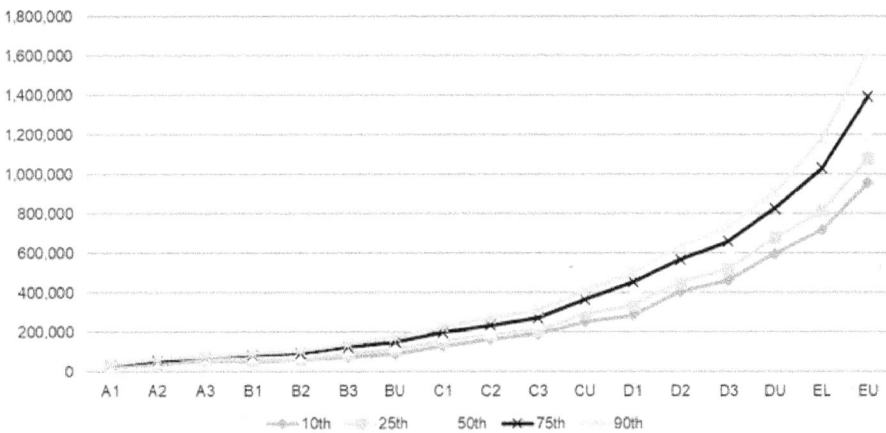

*Figure 5.2: Regression of estimated market salary data pay by salary grade*

Once the midpoints are calculated, you can also calculate the minimum and maximum for each grade. If you already know the percentage above and below the midpoint where these points lie, then use these. If you only know the range spread (or your desired range spread), you can use the following formulae to calculate minimum and maximum.

$$Minimum = \{Midpoint/[1+(Range\ Spread/2)]\}$$

$$Maximum - Minimum * (1 + Range\ Spread)$$

The resulting salary structure may look like the one shown below in Table 5.7.

Table 5.7: Example of a salary structure

| | Proposed Pay Range | | | | |
|---|---|---|---|---|---|
| Grade | Minimum | Midpoint | Maximum | % Midpoint progression | % Range spread |
| 1 | 17777.53 | 21341.568 | 24888.536 | 12.61% | 40 |
| 2 | 20020.07 | 24033.693 | 28028.092 | 12.61% | 40 |
| 3 | 22545.49 | 27065.415 | 31563.687 | 12.61% | 40 |
| 4 | 24383.66 | 30479.572 | 36575.487 | 12.61% | 50 |
| 5 | 27459.53 | 34324.408 | 41189.289 | 12.61% | 50 |
| 6 | 30923.4 | 38654.249 | 46385.099 | 12.61% | 50 |
| 7 | 33518.31 | 43530.276 | 53629.3 | 12.61% | 60 |
| 8 | 37746.47 | 49021.388 | 60394.35 | 12.61% | 60 |
| 9 | 42507.98 | 55205.175 | 68012.776 | | 60 |

## 5.9 Different salary structures: Applications

It is not essential for organisations to have only one salary structure for their staff. Since the salary structure must match the overall business strategy and be aligned to the market, management may choose to have more than one salary structure, or to have only one but applied in different ways to different roles, to fit the various specific needs of the business.

To illustrate the dynamics of adjusting the salary structure to a specific need, it is useful to examine the difference between the structure adopted for clerical/blue collar jobs versus technical and professional jobs. Different supply and demand forces in the labour market govern each group. This could result in different salary structures being seen for different groups of jobs. The same could be said for sales roles. More to the point, if an organisation has specific roles that are hard to find (e.g. cybersecurity expert), they may opt to put in place a separate salary structure for these scarce roles.

Having said this, as far as possible, organisations attempt to keep this process simple, and a unified salary structure that suits the entire organisation is usually the preferred approach, rather than having many salary structures to manage and explain.

## 5.10    Salary progression policy guidelines

Moving through the job grades is relatively well understood. Most know that as the job gets more complex, the job grade will increase. Employees often ask how they can move up the salary scale for their job grade.  This is called salary progression, and an organisation would typically define this as part of their remuneration strategy.

Where an organisation has a robust performance management system, salary scale progression should be based on individual performance and other criteria as set out in the salary progression policy. These other criteria are often linked to the acquisition of relevant skills and competencies. Salary progression is also affected by the number of salary grades, span of each salary grade and levels of hierarchy within the structure.

## 5.11    Placement of incumbents in the salary scale

Salary scale placement addresses the following issues:

- Where to place a new employee on the salary scale.
- Where to place an employee who has been promoted.
- Where to place employees with differing skills.

Set out below are some guidelines that organisations can use to determine the basis by which employees may move through the salary scale range.

### 5.11.1   Based on performance and capabilities

Employees are placed, based on their performance and capabilities, at the relevant scale level as follows:

- Between lower guide and midpoint of salary scale: the employee meets some of the job requirements but requires further development.  Some evidence exists of the employee's past performance.  Further training and experience are required to fully meet the job requirements.
- Mid-point of salary scale: the employee fully meets the job requirements. Evidence exists that the employee's performance meets the requirements of the job.
- Above midpoint to upper guide of salary scale: the employee exceeds the job requirements. The employee's performance/experience/track record exceeds the requirements set. Tangible evidence exists of the employee's past performance achievements exceeding the expectations for the job.

## 5.11.2  New appointments

When starting in a new position/promotion/upgrade an employee may be appointed as follows:

- Between minimum and lower guide of salary scale: the newly appointed employee meets some of the job requirements but requires further development. Some evidence exists of the newly appointed employee's performance from their CV and past references. Further training and experience are required to become fully competent.
- Mid-point of salary scale: the newly appointed employee fully meets the job requirements based on their CV and past references.
- Above midpoint of salary scale: the newly appointed employee exceeds the job requirements. Evidence of the newly appointed employee's past performance/experience/track record exceeds the requirements set. Tangible evidence, beyond what is written on their CV, exists to attest to the employee's past achievements.

Table 5.8 below sets out another approach to the movement through salary scales.

*Table 5.8: Example of an approach to the movement through salary scales*

---

**Recruitment level (Q1)**

- Recruitment level for entry into a job.
- Minimum entry qualification and competencies as inherently required by a job.
- Basic understanding of the specified functional area.
- Extensive training and development requirements.
- Potential to acquire competencies for the full scope of the job.

**Development level (Q2)**

- Basic understanding of policies, directives and procedures applicable to the job.
- Able to function without assistance on common/usual assignments.
- Can operate with assistance on unusual/uncommon assignments.
- Narrow range of knowledge, skills and application.
- Basic knowledge of theoretical elements applicable to the job.
- Basic knowledge and understanding of fundamental and /or widely used methods.
- Basic core competence requirements are known and understood.
- Can interpret key indicators within own environment and recommend appropriate actions.
- Information/decisions that need to be shared with outside parties are reviewed by superior prior to release.
- Functions within clearly specified guidelines.
- Training and development required to meet the requirements of proficiency.

---

*Proficiency level (Q3)*

- Meets all requirements as set in the basic level.
- Declared proficient in a specified role-mastery of full scope of job.
- Fully accountable and functions independently in terms of day-to-day tasks.
- Can give guidance/assistance to other colleagues regarding processes, tasks, policies and directives.
- Can identify and interpret elements and their relationship without supervision/assistance.
- Superior's functional input required only as a sounding board for tasks at hand.
- Identifies, analyses and interprets information and/or situations and makes useable/workable recommendations.
- Good understanding of bigger scenario.
- Accredited, certified, authorised, etc. for the performance of tasks of own duties.
- Performs well on tasks of a single function and additional projects of an atypical nature.
- Proactive in development of own role/function.
- Recognised as a credible advisor in own function/role.
- Good theoretical and/or practical exposure in own role.
- Can represent a function or discipline with full knowledge and skill.
- Good understanding of customer base and requirements.
- Can develop short- and medium-term plans.

*Advanced and/or specialist level (Q4)*

- Meets all requirements as set in the proficient level.
- Competent and acknowledged as an expert within own job.
- Provides useable solutions (proactive exploration) based on a wide frame of reference.
- Can development short-, medium- and long-term plans.
- Knowledge and skill influence strategic direction of own role and can provide inputs beyond own functional area.
- Ability to establish new and own methods or systems – innovative.
- Can establish information networks impacting on own role, job and functions.
- In-depth knowledge of own function and its relationship with other functions.
- Own work is accepted with or without minor alterations by the recipient.
- Opinion leader/subject matter expert in own area.

## 5.12   Implementation of salary structures: A checklist

The following sample checklist will assist with the process of designing and implementing a salary structure.

| Item | Yes | No |
|------|-----|-----|
| • Job grading is complete, and grades are signed off.<br>• Market salary scales are available for each grade.<br>• Individual salaries are available for each grade.<br>• Organisation remuneration policy and strategy is available and gives guidance on design issues such as:<br><br>    ○ market stance;<br>    ○ guaranteed pay/variable pay philosophy;<br>    ○ performance, contribution and competence pay stance;<br>    ○ pay progression principles;<br>    ○ range, slope, overlap philosophy; and<br>    ○ cost-benefit analysis of several options is done.<br><br>• There is an implementation project plan covering:<br><br>    ○ timing;<br>    ○ communication plan;<br>    ○ dealing with anomalies (upgrades, downgrades, salaries above and below the proposed salary scales); and<br>    ○ stakeholder presentations complete (for example, Remuneration Committee, EXCO, and trade union).<br><br>• Policy and procedure documents have been written. | | |

## 5.13   Conclusion

The design of salary structures must be done purposefully to achieve the desired balance of internal equity with external competitiveness. Although it is not an exact science, despite all the numbers and formulae shown above, there needs to be a robust and rigorous approach which can be easily explained and defended to all stakeholders.

Having considered these principles and elements of best practice, it is important to design a structure of best fit that allows your organisation to:

• Showcase its unique value proposition and identity.
• Highlight that money is not the only value you offer to employees.
• Indicate the role that salaries have in your total reward offering.
• Accept that benchmarks are not a rule.
• Internalise that salary surveys are the beginning of the process, not the end point.

## 5.14  Summary

A salary structure comprises a job grade and commensurate salary scales linked to each grade. The key architecture of salary structures refers to salary ranges, salary overlap, salary slope and midpoint progression. The purpose of salary structures is to assist line managers so that they know where to appoint staff so that staff performing work of similar value, are paid similarly. The salary ranges come from market benchmarking and salary surveys and need to be kept competitive in accordance with the market. Well-designed salary structures assist in attracting, motivating and retaining staff.

## 5.15  Self-evaluation questions

1.  Why do organisations have salary structures?
2.  What are the key features of a well-designed salary structure?
3.  What is the formula for salary ranges?
4.  What is a salary progression policy?
5.  What is a gap ratio?

## 5.16  Exercise

1.  Use the data below to calculate a salary structure using a straight line
2.  Re-calculate the salary structure using different types of lines (Power, exponential, etc.)
3.  Which type of line provided the best model? Which one would you implement? Explain.

| Job title | Salary grade | Job evaluation points | Market median |
|---|---|---|---|
| Customer service manager | 9 | 386 | 60,600 |
| Senior drafter | 8 | 303 | 47,600 |
| Customer service supervisor | 7 | 288 | 45,200 |
| Drafter | 7 | 264 | 39,000 |
| Senior computer operator | 6 | 248 | 39,000 |
| Offset press operator ii | 5 | 220 | 34,500 |
| Administrative assistant | 5 | 218 | 34,700 |
| Executive secretary | 5 | 214 | 34,100 |
| Maintenance plumber | 5 | 211 | 33,300 |
| Computer operator ii | 4 | 200 | 33,100 |
| Bookkeeper | 4 | 195 | 30,600 |
| Senior secretary | 4 | 192 | 30,200 |

| Job title | Salary grade | Job evaluation points | Market median |
|-----------|:---:|:---:|:---:|
| Customer service representative | 4 | 190 | 29,800 |
| Computer operator | 4 | 190 | 27,500 |
| Offset press operator i | 3 | 178 | 28,000 |
| Secretary | 3 | 174 | 26,700 |
| Maintenance painter | 3 | 168 | 27,300 |
| Clerk typist | 2 | 162 | 24,100 |
| Groundskeeper | 1 | 142 | 21,400 |
| Mail clerk | 1 | 140 | 22,000 |

# CHAPTER 6

# Broad-banding

## 6.1 What is broad-banding?

Broad-banding can be summarised in the following way: what would have been three, four or five salary ranges in a traditional salary structure are combined and treated as a single, broad-band. The main logic behind the adoption of broad-banding is simple, namely that it attempts to mirror the organisational hierarchy which has evolved primarily to flatter structures. Typically, one job reporting to another would not fall within one band, however with flatter structures, the continuous hunt for "promotion" to the next salary level has also played an important role in the creation of broad-bands. These allow more flexibility in terms of the ability to pay people more even if they remain within the same salary grade.[1]

Compared to a conventional salary structure, broad-band structures have fewer salary bands and broader minimum to maximum spreads. Broad-bands feature a few, relatively wide pay ranges that retain many characteristics found in conventional salary administration processes. This is shown diagrammatically in Figure 6.1.

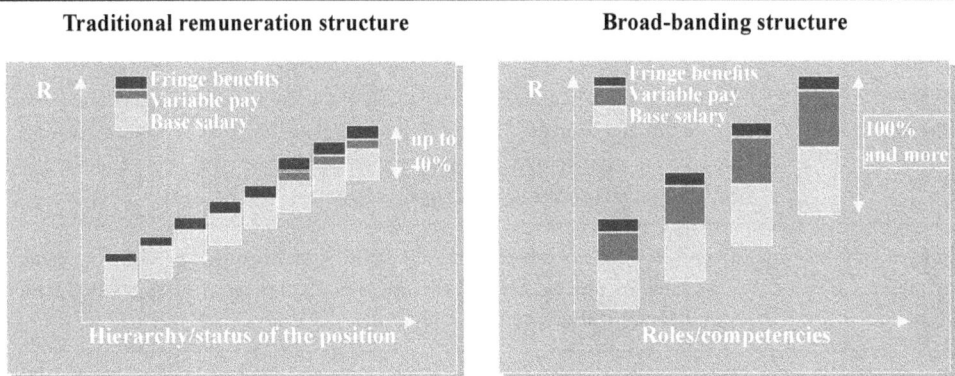

| Traditional remuneration structure | Broad-banding structure |
|---|---|
| • Many, but narrow salary bands | • Fewer, but broad salary bands |
| • Little difference between minimum and maximum salary within a salary band (between 20% and 40%) | • Big difference between minimum and maximum salary within a salary band (between 50% and 100%) |
| • Little variable payment (up to 20% of base salary), only for top management | • High variable payment (up to 100% of the base salary), for all employees |
| • Fringe benefits and further qualification programmes are a matter of course | • Emphasis on the value of fringe benefits and qualification programmes |

*Figure 6.1: Traditional versus broad-band structures*

---

1    Nzukuma & Bussin, 2011.

## 6.2   Reasons for implementing broad-banding

### 6.2.1   Goals of broad-banding

Companies adopt broad-banding for the reasons shown in Table 6.1 below. With the advent of agile organisations, this will become even more prevalent. A broad-banded structure accommodates teams in an easier way than strict traditional structures do.

*Table 6.1: Goals of broad-banding*

| Goal | Specifics |
|---|---|
| Improve competitive advantage | Broad-bands enable the organisation to break down the conventional hierarchy and thereby emulate the characteristics of their smaller competitors, namely:<br><br>• quickness/nimbleness;<br>• more flexibility to manage pay without having to promote staff;<br>• creativity;<br>• increased employee involvement; and<br>• willingness to embrace risk. |
| Support a new climate or culture | Broad-bands support cultures that promote customer-centric values. Specifically, employees are less internally focused and instead are focused more outside the organisation on their customer base and the competitive challenges of the market. |
| Support de-layering initiatives | Reducing the number of job levels results in management having increased spans of control and decreased ability to provide close supervision to their increased numbers of direct reports. As a result, the detail-orientated conventional salary administrative process must change. |
| Suggest new ways of integrating activities | Less-structured organisations are likely to view work as a process that can be performed by process teams that work laterally through the organisation rather than functional teams that work vertically. |
| Promote a broad view of work | Broad-bands provide employees with the opportunity to create their own jobs. The focus is therefore on value-add. Employees become less focused on grade and the tasks included in the job description and more focused on identifying the critical needs of the organisation and trying to ensure that these needs are met. |
| De-emphasise an incremental view of career development | Broad-bands provide the opportunity for employees to use the whole organisation for their development opportunities. Employees no longer have to concentrate simply on "working up" within their functional areas, because they can see how lateral, cross-functional development opportunities could help them create their own careers and increase their impact on the organisation. |

### 6.2.2 Competitive forces

There are a number of competitive forces facing organisations in the global business arena that have necessitated the implementation of broad-banding. For instance, there is an increased need for technical knowledge in jobs, which will require organisations to focus on technical mastery and not just the administrative size of the role, to determine how much to pay individuals.

Another trend is an increased need for nimbleness and flexibility and less hierarchy, necessitating the need for flatter structures.

Other trends pushing towards the adoption of flatter organisational structures, and thus broad-bands, are a reduction in trade barriers, increased capacity and capability of information and computer technology, increases in buying power, globalisation and global integration (decline of sovereignty) – including increased access to capital markets and information/media.

This is set to continue unabated and, in some senses, the Covid-19 pandemic catapulted all types of organisations into the fourth industrial revolution in a matter of months. To accommodate the new way of work, many organisations have abandoned their traditional structures for broad-bands.

### 6.2.3 The need to become world-class

World-class organisations are those organisations that are able to respond more effectively to the business challenges they face in a way that is better than that of their competitors. To compete globally, an organisation must not only do business internationally, but must also have a corporate culture and value system that allows it to move its resources anywhere in the world to achieve the greatest competitive advantage. The strategic intent of world-class organisations is to concentrate on delivering the highest-quality product or service to the most profitable world markets at the lowest cost under changing market and competitive conditions. The focus is therefore on the client or customer, which translates into profitability.

Internally, two essentials for the organisation to achieve this objective are the right structure and a highly qualified workforce. These goals are supported by broad-banding.

## 6.3 Implementation of the broad-banding strategy

The implementation of broad-banding requires careful thought and planning. In the absence of careful planning, costs can run away from you. Set out below are some guidelines that could serve as checklists for your implementation. Please indulge us if the rest of this chapter is checklist orientated; we have found them to be invaluable when embarking on this journey.

### 6.3.1 Essentials for pre-implementation design

It is essential to take account of the following when preparing for implementation:

- It should have Board sign-off, but definitely EXCO sign-off.
- Plan around it taking six to 24 months for complete implementation and it continuously requires re-enforcing.
- Should ideally be done for the whole business, but usually starts in one area (biggest win area).

### 6.3.2 Overall process

The overall process to implement broad-banding is shown in Table 6.2.

*Table 6.2: Process of implementing broad-banding*

| Stage | Description | Detail |
|---|---|---|
| 1. | Assess the readiness of the organisation (one to three months) | Focus on the existing remuneration system's strengths and weaknesses to see whether broad-banding is required. Formal readiness assessment often includes interviews with line management, employee focus groups and diagnostic attitude surveys. |
| 2. | Design a broad-banding framework (three to six months) | During this stage, the cross-functional organisation design team will establish the parameters of the broad-banding system, typically on the basis of the organisation's levels of work, including:<br><br>• band criteria;<br>• number of bands;<br>• position or role assignments;<br>• band ranges; and<br>• pay delivery systems. |
| 3. | Develop a communications strategy and training plan This stage can run concurrently with Stage 2 (one to three months) | The design team must work in close association with communication and training experts to develop an appropriate strategy. Factors to consider are the following:<br><br>• Estimate anticipated demand for training – can current facilities deliver?<br>• Plans must be developed – who goes first?<br>• What rate of development is required?<br>• How will you manage expectations?<br>• Are expectations high, unrealistic or unreasonable?<br>• Long-term costs – are they worth it? |

| Stage | Description | Detail |
|-------|-------------|--------|
| 4. | Test and implement the programme (one to three months for testing) | This stage involves a final test of the design, communication and training approaches using focus groups and training simulations. Responses should be used to modify the programme design.<br>*Note:* Design team members must be active in assessment and roll-out. |
| 5. | Assess the new programme (one to three months, should be repeated) | This stage must take place six to 18 months after implementation. The design team and/or HR staff should evaluate the programme against the design objectives established in Stage 1. |

### 6.3.3 Steps for implementation

To implement a broad-banding programme, the steps shown in Table 6.3 have proven to be successful.

*Table 6.3: Steps for broad-band implementation*

| Step | Action |
|------|--------|
| 1 | Form a steering or work committee of legitimate participants. |
| 2 | Develop a business case for proposed changes. This should answer the questions:<br>• Why broad-banding?<br>• What will it achieve?<br>• What costs are involved? |
| 3 | Complete a job analysis and work-design process. |
| 4 | Develop the reward and pay system. |
| 5 | Calculate actual cost implications of the programme. |
| 6 | Develop policy guidelines. These should include questions related to issues such as:<br>• eligibility;<br>• who goes first; and<br>• rules of the game. |
| 7 | Develop training manuals. |
| 8 | Implement the programme. |
| 9 | Evaluate and track changes. |

It is essential that the person controlling the process communicates throughout and has a sponsor (at senior management level) and a champion (usually the head of HR). Remember to put a system in place that evaluates the success of the implementation year on year.

## 6.4 Paradigm shifts: new versus traditional business models

Broad-banding represents a change of paradigm from traditional business models to new organisational structures designed to support a move to customer-centric businesses. This is reflected in all areas of the organisation.

Traditionally, the criteria for better increases or better remuneration within an organisation are: conformity, seniority, attendance, inflation, and longevity. In these cases, there is a mismatch between conventional remuneration programmes and business needs.

Greater focus on the customer demands a greater degree of teamwork (less pass-around), extensive training (anchored by problem-solving, competence, product knowledge) and a greater willingness and ability to think up and down the organisational value chain. This additional need for teamwork and flexibility puts pressure on a traditional graded structure, which tends to be more rigid around working within job-families (silos) to seek promotions.

The customer-driven approach requires the organisation to "delight" the customer. This entails:

- Little or no pass around.
- Quick decisions and solutions to problems.
- First-time right response.
- Problem-solving at source.
- Good product knowledge.

The old and new organisational pay paradigms are compared in Table 6.4; the broad-banding response to these paradigms are shown in the last column. It must make business sense to implement broad-banding and it should drive the business strategy.

*Table 6.4: Changing pay paradigms*

| Conventional pay programmes | Customer-centric business needs | Broad-banding programmes |
|---|---|---|
| Hierarchy; graduations | Flat, delayered structure | Fewer levels |
| Control managers and employees | Control by managers and employees | Empowerment; ownership |
| Job-focused | Team-focused | Fewer labels; person-based pay |
| Slow, bureaucratic | Adaptive; mobility required | Reinforcement for horizontal or lateral development |
| Policy-based; structured | Flexible; decentralised | Less structure; fewer rules |
| Driven by internal equity | External focus | Market-driven pay |

## 6.5    The mechanics of broad-banding

The structures of traditional grades versus broad-bands are set out below. Some of the key decisions to be made include the following:

- Deciding on the number of broad-bands.
- Range characteristics and the role of market data.
- Pay delivery.
- Movement through the broad-bands.
- Pay progression within the broad-band.
- Achieving best value for money and cost control.

### 6.5.1  Deciding on the number of broad-bands

This is nearly always dictated by the work design and the number of levels in the organisational hierarchy which support and underpin the work design. For instance, a traditional organisation with several hierarchical layers that is moving to a new structure with only the following layers:

- Business unit manager
- Business area manager
- Section manager
- Unit supervisor
- Team leader
- Team member

You may wish to consider transitioning to a broad-banding structure with six levels, corresponding to the six roles listed above.

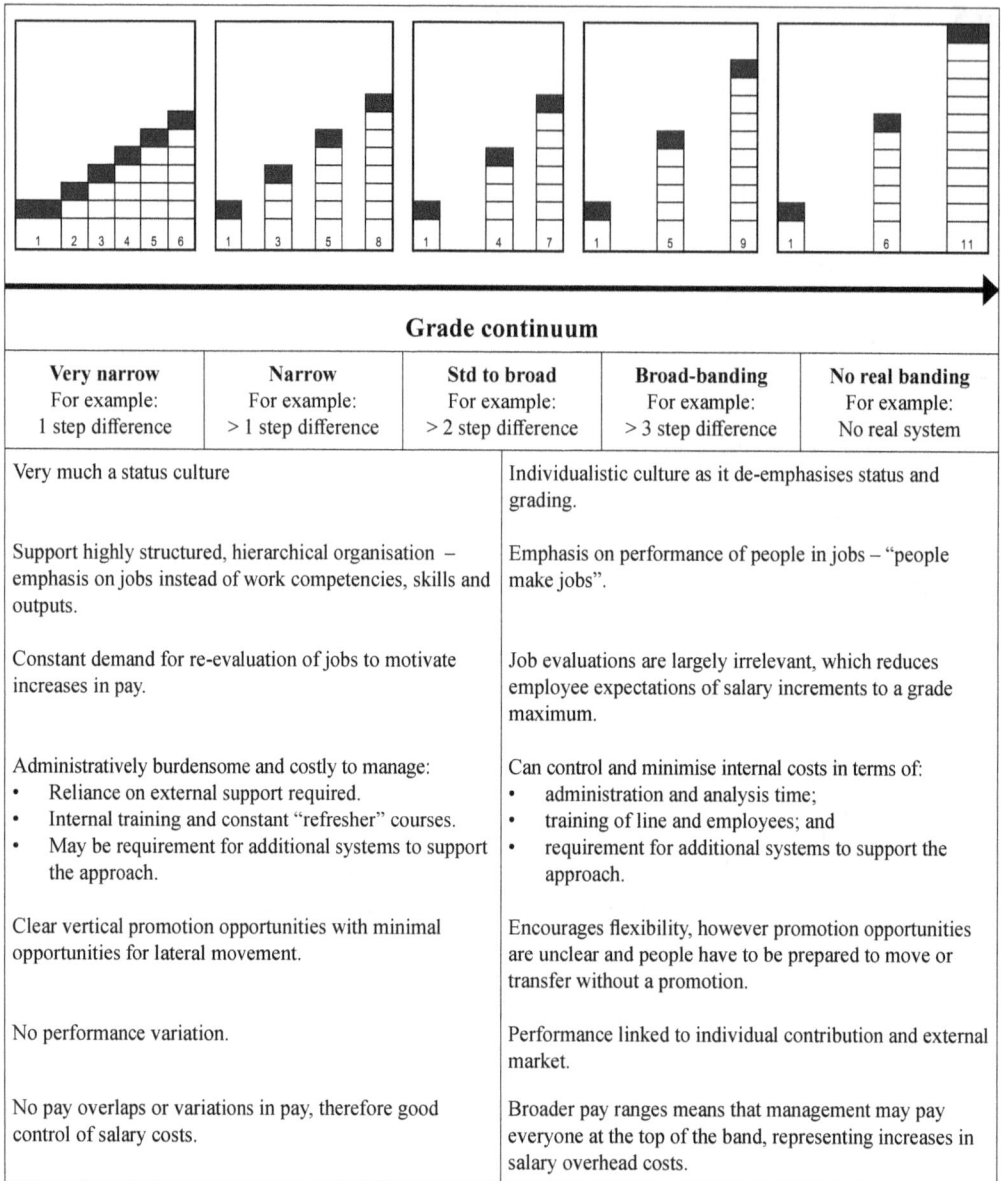

| | | | | |
|---|---|---|---|---|
| 1 2 3 4 5 6 | 1   3   5   8 | 1   4   7 | 1   5   9 | 1   6   11 |

**Grade continuum**

| Very narrow | Narrow | Std to broad | Broad-banding | No real banding |
|---|---|---|---|---|
| For example: | For example: | For example: | For example: | For example: |
| 1 step difference | > 1 step difference | > 2 step difference | > 3 step difference | No real system |

| | |
|---|---|
| Very much a status culture | Individualistic culture as it de-emphasises status and grading. |
| Support highly structured, hierarchical organisation – emphasis on jobs instead of work competencies, skills and outputs. | Emphasis on performance of people in jobs – "people make jobs". |
| Constant demand for re-evaluation of jobs to motivate increases in pay. | Job evaluations are largely irrelevant, which reduces employee expectations of salary increments to a grade maximum. |
| Administratively burdensome and costly to manage:<br>• Reliance on external support required.<br>• Internal training and constant "refresher" courses.<br>• May be requirement for additional systems to support the approach. | Can control and minimise internal costs in terms of:<br>• administration and analysis time;<br>• training of line and employees; and<br>• requirement for additional systems to support the approach. |
| Clear vertical promotion opportunities with minimal opportunities for lateral movement. | Encourages flexibility, however promotion opportunities are unclear and people have to be prepared to move or transfer without a promotion. |
| No performance variation. | Performance linked to individual contribution and external market. |
| No pay overlaps or variations in pay, therefore good control of salary costs. | Broader pay ranges means that management may pay everyone at the top of the band, representing increases in salary overhead costs. |

*Figure 6.2: Broad-banding Continuum*
*Source: Feinberg[2]*

Feinberg[3] helps us understand the continuum from too many broad-banding levels to too few (see Figure 6.2 above). On the one extreme, too few levels make for narrow bands which are not too different than traditional salary grades, while few bands mean there is no real system in place. The "sweet spot" seems to be where three traditional grades are subsumed under one broad-band.

2    Feinberg, 2009.

3    Ibid.

As stated earlier, broad-banding is not a strategy on its own, but is used to underpin customer-centric business strategies or flatter organisational design structures.

### 6.5.2 Range characteristics and the role of market data

Table 6.5 sets out some of the differences between typical traditional graded structures and typical broad-band structures. It also highlights how market data are used within the context of broad-banding.

*Table 6.5: Comparison of traditional versus broad-band structures*

| Aspect | Traditional graded structures | Broad-band structures |
|---|---|---|
| Number of levels | 15 to 26 | 6 to 12 |
| Pay scale width (minimum to maximum for a grade or band) | 30% to 100% | 50% to 300% |
| Pay overlap between grades or bands | 10% to 30% | 20% to 40% |
| Career development | Moving up grades | Typically horizontal (bigger projects, stores, lines, shafts, cases, and so on) |
| Typical main focus | Job grading | Competence and performance |
| Pay delivery | Job grade, competence and performance<br><br>Focus on job | Mostly competence and performance or both<br><br>Focus on person |
| System mostly controlled by | HR function | Line management |
| Market data | By grade is typically adequate unless position is scarce, demanding a premium | By position or job family becomes necessary |
| Band descriptions | By grade or specific job title | By roles or level of work (Stratified Systems Theory (SST)) |
| Job evaluation | In forefront and important | In the background as an administrative tool |
| Cost control | By policing | By empowerment |

## 6.6 Job family design

Broad-banding is often supported by the introduction of job family design. This helps with "pegs" within broad pay scales. A job family is a series of jobs which are involved in work of the same nature but require different levels of skill, responsibility and competencies for each job level. The term "job family" describes the key factors which differentiate one level from the next. For example, a personal assistant or secretarial job family may look as in Table 6.6.

*Table 6.6: Example of a personal assistant or secretarial job family*

| Level | Job | Responsibility |
|-------|-----|----------------|
| 4 | Personal assistant to Chief Executive | Responsible for performing secretarial duties for the Chief Executive of a confidential nature, often liaising with key stakeholders |
| 3 | Executive secretary | Responsible for performing secretarial duties for one or more executive managers |
| 2 | Senior secretary | Responsible for performing secretarial duties for one or more senior managers |
| 1 | Junior secretary | Responsible for performing secretarial duties for one or more managers |

An entry-level junior secretary would be one who has recently graduated from school, who has little experience, whose skills are being developed, and who would be given responsibilities at a lower level than compared to, say, a senior secretary who has greater relevant job experience. On the other hand, a personal assistant would be someone with many years of experience, whose skills and competencies are exemplary and who completes the job duties of a high-level assistant. The "value" of a position within this job family would therefore vary widely based on the individual's experience, competencies, and level of responsibility.

A pictorial example of an engineering job family showing the split or dual career path between the technical track and managerial track is shown in Figure 6.3.

## 6.6.1 Defining levels within a job family

Defining levels within a job family includes:

- Determining the advantages and disadvantages of a job family approach for your organisation and the benefits, if implemented, to your organisation.
- Determining the number of job families required, which is typically between five and ten.
- Describing the nature of work to be undertaken in each job family.
- Establishing the different levels of work in each family based on job evaluation, or alternatively each level can be defined in terms of accountability and competencies which are required to carry out work at this level.

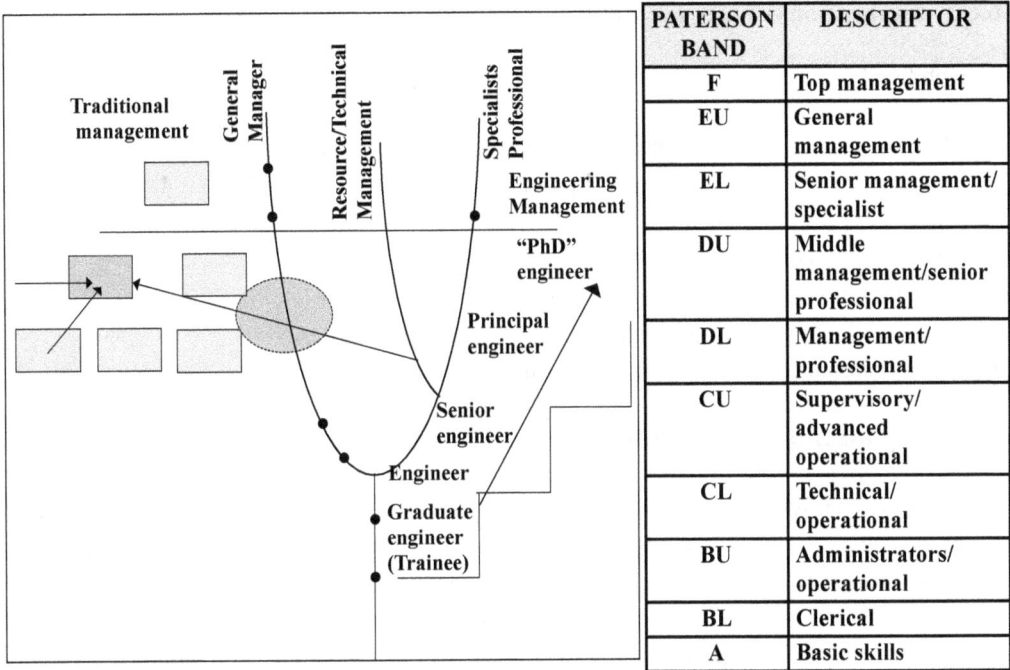

| PATERSON BAND | DESCRIPTOR |
|---|---|
| F | Top management |
| EU | General management |
| EL | Senior management/ specialist |
| DU | Middle management/senior professional |
| DL | Management/ professional |
| CU | Supervisory/ advanced operational |
| CL | Technical/ operational |
| BU | Administrators/ operational |
| BL | Clerical |
| A | Basic skills |

*Figure 6.3: Engineering dual career path*

## 6.6.2  Reasons for implementing a job families approach

There are several reasons for implementing a job families approach:

- Supports de-layered, flatter structures, thereby reducing the need for structured job evaluation.
- Provides job clarity, as accountabilities of role are clearly defined.
- Defines what good performance looks like in all of these work activities.
- Provides a transparent and straightforward basis for job evaluation through the identification
- of levels of work.
- Provides a straightforward link to the external pay market (job family structures are market
- driven, and information from relevant salary surveys will need to be collated).
- Outlines succession and career path planning (provides clear definitions for career paths within job families, across job families, and even diagonally to other job families).

Employees in a job family are also empowered, because promotions focus on individual performance, development and training, based on the competencies required for each level of work.

### 6.6.3 Implications of this approach

The job family approach:

- Improves competencies of the workforce through better selection and placement.
- Increases training and development participation.
- Increases retention of competent employees.
- Improves individual performance and contribution.
- Provides flexibility to line managers in staffing decisions.
- Provides flexibility to line managers when assigning job duties.
- May make salary management functional or job family-specific.

## 6.7   Pay administration under broad-banding

The competencies and experience of individuals at each defined level of work is an important factor in creating "value" for an organisation. In order to cater for this, the remuneration policy of the business should provide a means of relating "value" to experience, the required level of work competencies, and individual performance. Depending on the culture of the business (for example, the level of transparency), it also provides a basis for employees to compare possible progress in the organisation with what they believe they could achieve elsewhere.

This can be achieved through the use of an experience- or competency-based salary progression curve, which is aimed at relating salaries over a fairly long-term period to the increased competencies and experience of the individual concerned (in conjunction with their performance). This process can be used for professional staff whose starting salary is linked to the market rate for their qualifications, for example, with a newly qualified accountant, the system will assume that when individuals have finished professional training, they will develop within their disciplines at some standard rate or rates as a result of their experience in the field. It also assumes that because of the nature of their work, they are using their professional expertise to deal with a range of problems in which the results cannot be directly quantified and where responsibilities are related primarily to the capacity of the individual concerned.

For illustrative purposes, a single rate progression curve is shown in Figure 6.4. As mentioned earlier, the salary would be determined by reference to a salary survey which indicates market rate for this type of professional work at varying work and achievement levels. For example:

- The first degree equates to a market rate of 150,000.
- An honours degree equates to a market rate of 160,000.
- A qualified professional equates to a market rate of 180,000.

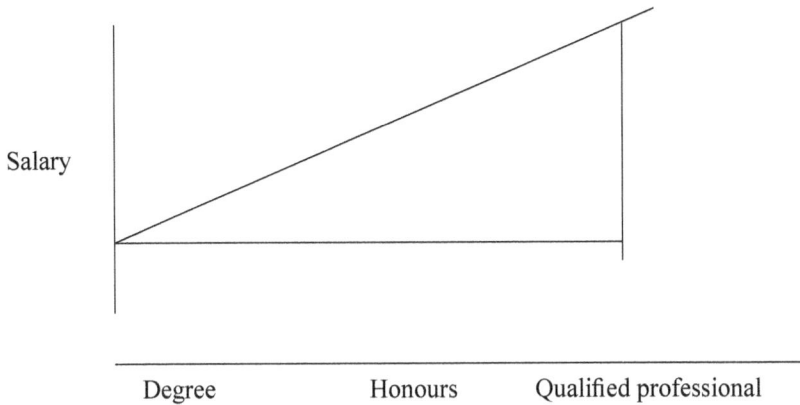

*Figure 6.4: Single rate progression curve*

The pay administration process would also be performance-based, which would mean that individuals with lower qualifications should have the opportunity of catching up or overtaking those with higher qualifications, based on their performance. The progression curve should be flexible and provide scope to advance people according to their contribution to the business.

Movement through the broad-band, for example, from primary to operational to advanced operational, is usually dictated by the particular grading rules being used, as well as by the Pay Progression Policy (PPP). The most commonly used criteria for the PPP for individuals are:

- Performance.
- Track record and experience.
- Market scarcity.

Managers under a broad-banding approach would need to be trained and empowered to manage salary increase decisions. With no reference point and a broader band, salaries can potentially increase much more. The control lies in training extensively and budgeting tightly.

## 6.8    Potential Results of Broad-banding

Broad-banding offers some very important benefits to the organisation. Not least of these is the ability that the programme provides to overcome the shortcomings of conventional pay systems in the light of today's business needs. In addition, the programme provides benefits associated with the strategic goals of the organisation, its development goals and its structure.

The current business environment provides a number of serious challenges to conventional pay systems. Potential beneficial results of broad-banding are:

- Improved customer service.
- Increased productivity (unit costs reduced).
- Increased job flexibility.
- Better understanding of the value chain.
- Improvements for teamwork.
- Improved quality.
- Enhanced competitiveness.
- Forced transformation.
- An easing of lateral job changes.
- Improved flexibility in pay structure.
- Support of organisational change.
- Payment for skills and performance.
- Benefits relating to the development of people, which include:
    o improved front-line employee decision-making;
    o promoting skills upliftment; and
    o increased competence.

Broad-banding has specific implications for the structure of an organisation, specifically: de-layering of the enterprise, reducing differences in hierarchy, an empowered workforce, and a flatter structure.

## 6.9    Essentials for implementation of broad-banding

Essentials for the successful implementation of a broad-banding programme are:

- The establishment of the link between broad-banding and the organisation's business strategy.
- Involvement of line management.
- Correct selection of employees.
- Broad-banding becomes part of the overall remuneration strategy.
- Consideration and promotion of critical success factors in the organisation.
- Taking into account all relevant remuneration issues.
- Heeding lessons learnt by forerunner companies.

### 6.9.1  Link to Business Strategy

For broad-banding programmes to succeed, they must be linked to the organisation's business strategy. This will ensure that broad-banding supports transformation, creates flexibility and problem-solving ability, enhances quality, results in quick turnaround times, fosters teamwork, empowers business units and divisions, and supports restructuring.

### 6.9.2 Involvement of line management

Management are essential to redesign the job or work, decide on the skills density thereof, decide on the rate of progression through skills matrices, and in turn, control or decide on their pay costs, within the agreed system. This results in more effective redesign and (re)deployment, which leads to continuous improvement, greater efficiency and improved productivity and, in turn has a positive impact on the bottom line.

### 6.9.3 Selection of employees

The following are essential for the selection of employees in the new structure:

- Develop criteria for selection of employees.
- Ensure compliance with all relevant labour legislation, and the organisation's own agreement with stakeholders, for example recognition agreements and organisation values.
- Develop a meticulous and thorough communication strategy.
- Train managers to counsel, retrench and communicate retrenchment benefits.
- Ensure that a defined strategy is in place for when selected employees are on extended training.

### 6.9.4 Incorporation into the remuneration strategy

Broad-banding should be included into the overall remuneration strategy. This implies the integration of performance appraisals, merit increases, grading, incentive pay, promotions, and pay reviews.

### 6.9.5 Factors that favour successful application

The critical success factors identified through experience are:

- If there is no business case, don't implement broad-banding.
- It is critical not to de-layer too quickly.
- Broad-banding is tied to other strategies such as work (re)design and career development.
- The presence of an executive sponsor on the board is essential.
- The presence of a full-time champion is essential.
- The establishment of a legitimate steering committee is essential.
- A change management strategy must already be in place.
- There must be a way to "replace" sub-grades that are "lost" through incompetence or poor performance.
- There needs to be a thorough understanding of the implications of broad-banding on the organisation's remuneration system, namely: larger pay ranges, the need to modify the fringe benefits policy, new pricing of skills, and an almost certain initial increase in the

salary bill.
- The job design must be robust.
- Intensified efforts must be made to train the organisation leadership.
- Employees' resistance to change must be recognised.
- There must be recognition that future structures require an investment in training.
- The strategy must begin with job design and training plans. These can then be followed by pay solutions.
- Management must be willing to go with an 80 percent solution, if necessary.

It is important to keep in mind that expectations will probably be high, and change management will be indispensable.

## 6.10 Readiness matrix example

Table 6.7 sets out an example of a "readiness matrix" for implementing broad-banding. It should be adapted to your organisation and completed by the leadership team.

*Table 6.7: "Readiness matrix" for implementing broad-banding*

| Criteria | Division 1 | Division 2 | Division 3 |
|---|---|---|---|
| • Executive commitment<br>• Work processes dependent on teams<br>• Broader roles; flexibility in work assignments<br>• High trust level<br>• Investing in employees<br>• Urgency; desire for change<br>• Organisation enthusiasm for broad-banding<br>• Performance management<br>• Career development<br>• Communication<br>• Training<br>• Link of pay and performance<br>• Managerial skill set | | | |
| Overall rating | | | |

## 6.11 Practical toolkit to prepare for broad-banding

Toolkit 5: *Preparation for Broad-banding* should assist you in preparing for the implementation of broad-banding. Adapt it to suit the needs of your organisation.

## 6.12 Summary

Broad-banding occurs when one combines several narrow grades into one broad-band. The reason organisations implement broad-banding is to create bigger steps between levels of work. This changes the intense focus of minute and incremental changes to the job description to step-change value-add behaviour. Commensurately, the pay scales are much wider and one needs to implement good pay progression policies to replace the sub-grades that are lost. It creates better understanding of the work value chain and customers experience less "pass-around". Broad-banding is driven mostly by work design.

## 6.13 Self-evaluation questions

1. Describe in your own words what is meant by broad-banding.
2. Name three reasons for implementing broad-banding.
3. What is a key consideration when deciding on the number of broad-bands?
4. Name five differences between a traditional structure and a broad-band structure.
5. What are the potential results of broad-banding?
6. How would you know if an organisation is ready to implement broad-banding?

# CHAPTER 7

## Competence and Skills-based Pay

Whilst not very common approaches, there may be a resurgence in interest in implementing these approaches to remuneration. The reason for the increased interest is that the new way of working has put a lot of pressure on job evaluation. This is an alternative to job evaluation that requires serious consideration.

### 7.1    Definitions, reasons and objectives of competency-based pay (CBP)

Competencies are the combination of observable and measurable skill, knowledge, performance behaviours and personal attributes that contribute to enhanced employee performance and organisational success. A competency-based reward system recognises what people accomplish at work rather than rewarding the acquisition of additional knowledge or skills.

Core competencies:

- Communicate to employees the behaviour patterns that distinguish good from poor performance.
- Allow the organisation to create a competitive advantage by differentiating itself in the marketplace.
- Enable the organisation to achieve its goals and objectives.

Some major objectives of CBP systems are to:

- Shift the focus from enhancing pay via job evaluation to application of competence.
- Emphasise what the organisation is prepared to pay for.
- Replace with competency milestones the sub-grades that are lost when implementing broad-banding.
- Lift the skills base of employees in a relatively short space of time (up to three years).
- Improve the "return on salary spend" by enhancing productivity and quality.
- Relate pay to demonstrated competence (sometimes translated as improved performance).
- Add value and predict success.
- Align reward and core values.
- Develop a culture of learning, growth and continuous improvement.

An organisation should be very clear about why it wants to implement CBP before embarking on the restructuring process.

## 7.2 The mechanics of CBP

There are numerous variations in the mechanics and application of CBP, however two main variations have developed which are described below:

- Organisation-wide generic competencies.
- Job family-specific competencies.

### 7.2.1 Organisation-wide generic competencies

Table 7.1 below is an example of a typical CBP application.

*Table 7.1: Sample competency-based table*

| Not applicable | Least skilled | | Not a strength | | Appropriate skill level | | A strength | | An exceptional skill | |
|---|---|---|---|---|---|---|---|---|---|---|
| N | 1 | 2 | 3 | 4 | 5 | 6 | 7 | 8 | 9 | 10 |

| Customer service | | Business and individual skills |
|---|---|---|
| Treats customers as business partners | | Demonstrates broad business knowledge and skills |
| Identifies, understands and responds appropriately to needs of customers | | Acts to add value to the business |
| Presents ideas simply and clearly | | Recognises problems and identifies underlying causes |
| Listens actively to internal and external customers | | Makes timely decisions |
| Solicits and provides constructive, honest feedback | | Coaches and develops others |
| Keeps others informed | | Is trustworthy, open and honest |
| Balances requests with business requirements | | Visualises the present and future, and develops strategies to get there |

| Teamwork | | Evaluation scale | |
|---|---|---|---|
| Supports team goals | | N | Not applicable or not observed. |
| Puts interest of team ahead of self | | 1–2 | Least skilled. The individual consistently fails to reach behaviour and skill expectations in this area. |
| Builds consensus and shares relevant information | | 3–4 | Not a strength. The individual meets some behaviour and skill expectations in this area but sometimes falls short. |
| Recognises and respects the contributions and needs of each individual | | 5–6 | Appropriate skill level. This individual meets the majority of the behaviour and skills expectations in this area for the job. There is generally a positive perspective toward responsibilities. |
| Actively seeks involvement or uses input from people with different perspectives | | | |
| Builds and maintains productive working relationships | | 7–8 | A strength. This individual meets most and exceeds some of the behaviour and skill expectations in this area. |
| Treats others, such as protected group members, fairly | | 9–10 | An exceptional skill. This individual consistently exceeds behaviour and skill expectations in this area. |

## 7.2.2 Job family-specific competencies

These are normally written up for each job family to show career progression or milestones. They often replace sub-grades that are lost in the broad-banding process. This type of competency process is more strongly associated with broad-banding than the organisation-wide generic competencies. Table 7.2 below shows a typical application. Each broad-band typically has the descriptions shown in the table.

*Table 7.2: Typical contribution milestones in a broad-band*

| Milestone 4 | Shapes | • Provides strategic leadership<br>• Promotes growth and development<br>• Identifies and sponsors others |
|---|---|---|
| Milestone 3 | Guides | • Shares own expertise<br>• Develops, mentors and coaches<br>• Deals with those outside the organisation |
| Milestone 2 | Applies | • Demonstrates full competence/mastery in area of own work<br>• Makes significant contribution to work team<br>• Is independent, a problem-solver and/or decision-maker, works without significant direction |
| Milestone 1 | Learns | • Learns activities or tasks associated with own work/role<br>• Learns to work and co-operate with colleagues<br>• Depends on others for instructions, guidance and direction |

### 7.2.3  Link to pay

In both cases, as one scores higher and moves through the milestones, the pay increases. In the organisation-wide example, pay is typically tied to once-off bonuses, while in the job family example, pay is linked to and included in guaranteed remuneration.

## 7.3  Competency-based reward systems

For the most part, using competencies in reward systems is a fairly new practice, and some novel approaches have emerged. It is quite difficult to summarise the variety of approaches currently being utilised or pilot-tested. It is possible, however, to identify how the approaches vary and the series of choices we face in developing a competency-based pay system.

### 7.3.1  Determining the starting point for the pay decision

As in the design of any remuneration system, an organisation must first identify what it fundamentally wants to remunerate – the job, the role, the person, or a combination thereof.

- **Job:** This is the narrowly-defined, relatively static cluster of duties and responsibilities in which the individual is employed (for example, remuneration analyst, senior remuneration analyst, recruiter, and senior recruiter).
- **Role:** This is a more dynamic cluster of frequently changing duties and responsibilities requiring broadly similar types of knowledge, skills, and abilities (for example, human resources professional).
- **Person:** This refers to the cluster of attributes possessed by the individual, regardless of position assignment.

Recently, a number of companies and consulting organisations have positioned competencies as an approach to paying for the person rather than the job. While competency-based systems can be an effective mechanism for managing person-based pay, most systems still maintain the job as the fundamental basis for defining value. Competencies displayed together with actual performance against objectives are often used as a way of determining the individual's value in the job.

In today's environment, more organisations are looking to broad-bands as the vehicle for managing pay. However, we have found competency-based systems that utilise traditional ranges, wide ranges, and broad-bands, which are defined respectively as follows:

- **Traditional ranges:** A large number of grades (approximately 18) with relatively narrow spreads from minimum to maximum (e.g. 40 percent to 60% percent)
- **Wide ranges:** A somewhat smaller number of grades or bands (11 to 15) with range spreads of 70 percent to 100 percent

- **Broad-bands:** Typically four to eight bands representing significant career changes, with range spreads in excess of 100 percent at the top end.

Nothing about competency-based pay would necessarily dictate one approach over another. One must consider how work is organised, the hierarchical structure of jobs within the organisation, the nature of career development, and other factors.

### 7.3.2  Which pay decisions should competencies influence?

Competencies can influence pay decisions through a number of mechanisms. Competencies can influence:

- **Pay opportunity** by influencing the grade or band to which the individual, role, or job is assigned.
- **Pay increase decisions** by influencing the overall performance assessment.
- **Incentive pay decisions** by either determining or influencing the incentive payment calculation.

While the use of competencies to influence pay decisions is becoming more widespread, it is seldom the case where pay decisions are determined exclusively by competencies. More often than not, competencies are used together with other factors to determine appropriate pay.

### 7.3.3  Should we reward competency level or competency growth?

To the extent that the decision is made to use competencies to influence the base pay decision, organisations must decide whether to reward for competency level or competency growth.

In one method of paying for competency level, a target or standard level of competency is established for an individual, role, or job. The individual's actual competencies are assessed relative to this standard, and a gap is determined. An individual whose competency level is lower than the target level should be paid less than the target rate of pay for the job. By contrast, an individual whose competency level is higher than the target level should be paid more. Successfully implementing this approach requires:

- A fairly high level of precision in the assessment tool to differentiate level differences.
- A high level of trust in the evaluators/assessors.
- Patience, since experience suggests that changes in competency levels require significant development time.

Another method of paying for competency level is simply to use competencies to place individuals into a zone of a pay range. For example, the individuals who are highest in competencies would be paid at the top of the range.

With respect to rewarding the competency growth, we have found that organisations base their salary increase decisions on either change in level of competency over a specified period of time or achievement of some specific competency development goal. This requires a detailed and regular competency assessment approach which is often discarded due to its labour intensity. It is further important to only link pay decisions to competencies displayed and not acquired.

### 7.3.4 How should the organisation provide rewards for results?

Organisations paying for competencies are sometimes concerned that individuals will lose their focus on results or performance, but it's not an either/or proposition. Many organisations reward both competencies and results, although the mechanisms for doing this vary from organisation to organisation.

Some organisations choose to determine salary increases using both results or performance and competency growth, as illustrated below. In this case, individuals can receive large salary increases only by increasing their competencies and delivering results. Failure to succeed in one or the other area would result in a smaller increase. Table 7.3 illustrates how to achieve this.

*Table 7.3: Rewarding results and competency growth*

| Rewarding results and competency growth | | | |
|---|---|---|---|
| Performance | Competency Growth | | |
| | Below | Meets | Exceeds |
| Exceeds | 3% | 12% | 15% |
| Meets | 3% | 6% | 9% |
| Below | 0% | 0% | 0% |

Competencies are relatively enduring and, once acquired, are unlikely to disappear or lose value. It makes sense to reward competency development with a form of remuneration that is likewise enduring – base pay. By contrast, results have a temporary quality. Exceptional results in one quarter could be followed by average results the next. Therefore, it makes sense to reward results with a temporary, non-enduring form of remuneration – bonus.

Set out below is a comparative table between "pure" versions (not combinations) of PBP and CBP to assist in selecting the most appropriate system. One is not "better" than the other; they achieve different things. Both of these approaches require human assessment. This in turn places incredible pressure on the need for robust systems and defensible assessment techniques – especially if it is linked to pay.

*Table 7.4: Comparison of mechanics of PBP and CBP*

| Performance-based pay | Competency-based pay |
|---|---|
| 1. What work is done (results). | 1. How work is done (behaviour). |
| 2. Looks backwards (pays for results already achieved). | 2. Looks forwards (competency predicts success). |
| 3. Pay decisions are usually made by comparing results against targets. | 3. Pay decisions are based on assessing competencies displayed. |
| 4. Targets may change from year to year. | 4. Competence profiles often stay the same for many years. |
| 5. Facilitates integration of individual, team and organisation objectives. | 5. Facilitates integration of core, generic and individual competence. |

*Source: Armstrong & Murlis[1]*

## 7.4 Skills-based pay

### 7.4.1 Understanding the definitions, reasons and objectives

Skills-based pay (SBP) is often used interchangeably with competence-based pay, but there are some crucial differences. Skill is often described as the part of the iceberg you can see, even though it forms part of competence. It is therefore easier to assess and link to rewards as it is more tangible and often related to a demonstrable technical skill. More often than not, it is applied to manual workers, artisans and clerical workers.

SBP is not a new concept and has long been used in the trades and accounting, engineering and legal professions. Wherever there is a progression of skill acquisition related to an increase in pay, this is a form of skills-based pay.

### 7.4.2 The mechanics of skills-based pay

There are two main forms of SBP, namely:

- Acquiring points which add up to form pay bands.
- Moving through skill blocks or modules or clusters of skills (often associated with broad-banding).

#### 7.4.2.1 Points model

In the points model, all the tasks or skills that need doing are assigned points. These points often differ depending on how easy or difficult the tasks are, for example, easy = 1 point, difficult = 5 points. As one acquires points, one earns more money:

---

1    Armstrong & Murlis, 2004.

| Starting salary | = | 5,000 |
|---|---|---|
| 1 to 10 points | = | plus 10% |
| 11 to 20 points | = | plus 10% |
| 21 to 30 points | = | plus 10% |
| 31 to 40 points | = | plus 10% |

The salary for a person who possesses all the skills required for that particular part of the value chain can sometimes be around 50 to 100 percent of starting salary.

These models require one to move through skill blocks or clusters often associated with broad-banding, as shown in Figure 7.1 below:

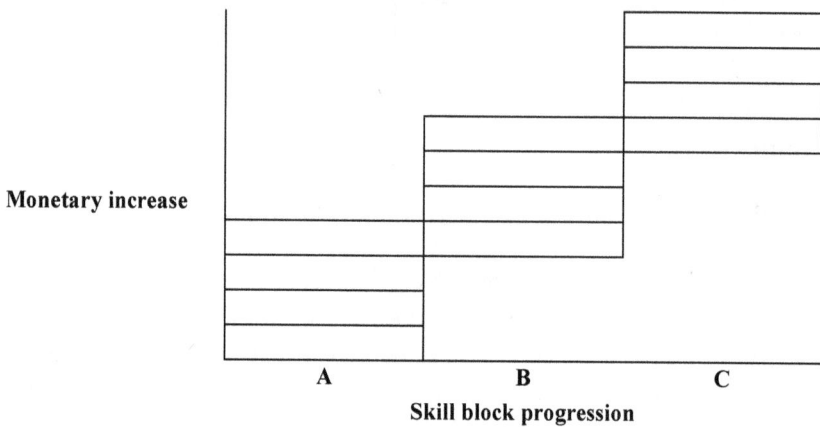

*Figure 7.1: Skills block progression*

The job grades forming the broad-bands provide for internal and external equity benchmarking. This provides a means of comparison between departments. Extensive training is usually required for SBP and if possible, there should be accreditation, enabling portability of skills.

## 7.5. Critical success factors: Integration of performance-based pay, CBP and SBP

Intertwining these programmes into a cohesive whole requires addressing many critical success factors. One way of describing these is that there should be an evolution towards this end, which requires many interfaces, for example with leadership style, work design and team roles. The following Table 7.5 (adapted from Productivity Development/CWE) demonstrates this.

*Table 7.5: High-performance organisation continuum*

| High-performance organisation continuum | | | | |
|---|---|---|---|---|
| **Traditional** | **Enlightened** | **Multi-skilling** | **Self-sufficient** | **Self-managed** |
| Supervisor organised | Supervisor requires input, provides options but still makes final decision | Supervisor and employees make decisions together | Team regularly engages in decision-making with leadership | Self-managed teams responsible for work process |
| | Basic skills training provided | Employees receive some technical and team skills training | Team engaged in multi-skilling and continuous improvement | Training conducted regularly |
| | | Supervisor ultimately responsible for work | Meaningful coaching and development provided | Remuneration tied directly to performance |

The transition process often takes years. The table below indicates progress through the years.

*Table 7.6: The transition process*

| The transition process | | | |
|---|---|---|---|
| **Design element** | **Day one** | **Day two** | **Day three** |
| **Team roles** | **Multi-skilling** | **Self-sustaining** | **Self-managed** |
| **Job or work design** | Minimum number of classifications. | Training for traditional jobs to service associate. | Fully-fledged service associate role. |
| **Remuneration** | Broad pay bands for each job. | Team-based component introduced. | Mature team-based pay plan. |
| **Variable pay** | Simple centre-wide milestone plan for reaching key targets – quality, time, attendance. | Team-based component introduced. | Mature team-based component introduced. |
| **Skills** | Begin cross-training immediately on basic skills. Begin social skills training in groups. Inform people of joining on future vision. | Continue cross-training. Begin training on support skills. | Team supports itself in all ways. |

| The transition process | | | |
|---|---|---|---|
| **Design element** | **Day one** | **Day two** | **Day three** |
| **Team roles** | **Multi-skilling** | **Self-sustaining** | **Self-managed** |
| **Measurement** | Existing facility-level metrics. | Transition to standardised metrics at the team level. | Full-blown team level measurement managed system. |
| **Management system** | "Team leader" provides guidance and direction to a specific team. | Begin transition to team-based decision-making with support from team leader. | Team leader provides support to self-managed teams. |

The skills requirements, decision-making processes and communication styles are shown in the table below.

*Table 7.7: Work-design continuum*

| **Dimension** | **Traditional** | **Enlightened** | **Multi-skilling** | **Self-sustaining** | **Self-managed** |
|---|---|---|---|---|---|
| **Skill requirements and job scope** | Narrowly-defined single-skill jobs | Minimal back-up skills in support of narrowly-defined jobs | Emphasis on back-up skills | Multi-skilled labour force for floor operations only | Diverse and multi-skilled |
| **Types of supervision and team involvement** | Top-down decision-making | Minimal input to decision process by lower levels in the hierarchy | Process improvement teams make recommendations to management | Teams involved in the decision-making process | Totally team-based work units collaborate on decisions |
| **Communication** | Information about the business provided by management on a need-to-know basis | Some information available if any individual asks the manager | Management holds periodic "update" meetings | Team members gather and share information as needed | Team members are responsible for sharing business information on a scheduled basis |

An example of a reward continuum is shown in the table below. It needs to be amended to suit each organisation's requirements.

*Table 7.8: Reward continuum*

| Dimension | Traditional | Enlightened | Multi-skilling | Self- sustaining | Self-managed |
|---|---|---|---|---|---|
| Base pay | Informational "raises" on individual basis | Time-based general increases | Merit pay programme with pay increases each year based on personal performance | Pay-for-skills or competencies forms part of pay for lower level employees only | Pay-for-skills or competencies forms part of pay for entire organisation |
| Variable pay (team component) | For top executives | For managers and above | In addition, for selected individual contributors | In addition, for lower level employees | Across the board variable pay programme |
| Variable pay (individual component) | Discretionary | Based only on personal quantitative results | Add qualitative factors related to final success | Add qualitative factors related to customer satisfaction and team success | Completely integrate with team component |
| Recognition (cash and non-cash) | Little or no recognition for outstanding individual or group achievements | Ad hoc recognition by top management | Supervisors may nominate individuals for recognition awards; final decision made by senior management | Team input and recognition award process | Teams provide recognition for own members |

Many believe that moving along these continua enhances employee engagement. In turn, engaged employees generally perform better and are less likely to leave the organisation. They are also more likely to innovate, which is often what puts great organisations ahead of their competitors.

## 7.6 Summary

Competency-based pay is uncommon and usually applies when there is an assessment system in place. Competencies are linked to behaviours expected of employees and managers in the organisation, according to their hierarchical level and functional job family. Pay is managed by linking remuneration to the competencies individuals possess in line with the role they are currently filling. Skill-based pay is associated with the types of observable expertise in the performance of tasks. Pay is managed by increasing remuneration in line with mastery of additional skills. The purpose of these types of pay programmes is to reward the individual for the acquisition and use of additional skills and competencies, and thus becoming more valuable to the organisation.

## 7.7   Self-evaluation questions

1.   Describe what is meant by skills-based pay.
2.   How would you measure the acquisition of skills?
3.   Should you pay when skills are acquired, or when they are used?
4.   What is the difference between performance-related pay and competency-based pay?
5.   How would you measure skill acquisition?
6.   How should you pay individuals whose competencies exceed those required by the job?

## 7.8   Exercise

Your company has decided to move away from job evaluations and "paying for the job" to a new system based on paying for skills. In such a system, how would you:

1.   Identify and recognise high performers?
2.   Decide whom to promote among several internal candidates?
3.   Allocate bonus pools to various teams and individuals?
4.   Identify and address low performers?
5.   Ensure high levels of performance and engagement?

# CHAPTER 8

# Individual Performance and Base Pay

## 8.1 Definitions, reasons for and objectives of performance-related pay

Performance-related pay (PRP) is pay that varies depending on individual, team or organisation performance. This section focuses on individual PRP. In later chapters we take up the notion of team and organisational rewards (variable pay and choosing the right incentive scheme). PRP which applies to individuals is associated with salary structures, grades and a performance and/or competence rating. This differs from incentive schemes, which are team- or organisation-based, as these schemes are normally formula driven and the payments are once-off. In individual PRP schemes, a managerial rating often translates into the size of a pay increase relative to the "purse" that is available. The differences between team and individual PRP can be summarised as shown in Table 8.1 below.

*Table 8.1: Individual PRP versus team PRP*

| Individual PRP | Team PRP |
|---|---|
| 1. Usually associated with managerial assessment of performance and/or competence<br>2. Payment is often in the form of a pay increase and is pensionable<br>3. Payments are mostly annual | 1. Typically formula driven<br>2. Payments are usually once-off and are not pensionable<br>3. Payments can vary from monthly to every three years |

Companies implement PRP for a variety of different reasons, but the most common objectives are to strengthen the relationship between performance and reward, drive organisation strategy implementation to the individual level, retain top performers by rewarding them for sustained superior performance, send a clear message to non-performers (which is usually accompanied by counselling and/or training), instil a performance culture into the organisation, facilitate and necessitate performance contracting (resulting in performance reviews and assessments), link the salary and wage bill to the fortunes of the business, and differentiate reward levels in a defensible manner. Research conducted by several major international organisations show that those organisations that have well developed PRP and performance management systems (PMS) outperform their competitors on almost every measure.

## 8.2 The mechanics of PRP

PRP is mostly driven by a PMS involving a way to measure and rate the performance of each individual, where a higher performance appraisal rating leads to a bigger pay increase.

## 8.2.1 Categories of performance management systems

The main categories of PMS are summarised in Table 8.2 below. There are other possible systems, some of which form subsets of these main categories.

*Table 8.2: Main categories of performance management systems*

| Type of system | Brief description |
|---|---|
| **Traditional** | Usually have 10 to 20 pre-determined factors which are generic and apply to all positions. These are rated by the manager on a rating scale, for example, 1 to 5 or 1 to 10. |
| **Output driven** | Individual outputs or outcomes are agreed on each year and are position-specific. Rating is usually on a "hit-or-miss" basis, whether the outcome has been achieved or not, and is typically rated by the customer (internal or external). |
| **360°** | Also has pre-determined factors which are generic and apply to all positions. The rating, however, is done by subordinates, peers and managers. These systems are often computer-based to cope with the administrative requirements of several raters. |
| **Balanced Scorecard** | Measures are devised typically for companies or SBUs, under the four main headings of financial, customers, learning and growth, and internal business processes. These can then be cascaded down to departments and individuals. |

## 8.2.2 Examples of performance management systems

Well-written outputs and performance indicators take the "pain" out of the dreaded performance assessment process. With this approach, one should just rate if the output was achieved or not. This is a bit like landing a plane – one can either land a plane, or one can't. There is no mark, such as 57 percent, for landing planes.

An example of an output-driven performance contract follows.

*Table 8.3: Output-driven performance contract*

| Outputs/deliverable | Conditions/quality requirements | How will we know/ indicators | Who has input? | Delivered by/to customer |
|---|---|---|---|---|
| 1. Total package and tax structuring of packages implemented | • Legal<br>• Payroll can handle it | Board sign-off and implemented | Auditor and Tax Manager | 28 February to Board or Finance Director |

| Outputs/deliverable | Conditions/quality requirements | How will we know/ indicators | Who has input? | Delivered by/to customer |
|---|---|---|---|---|
| 2. Performance management system implemented | • Controlled and owned by line managers<br>• Process developed and manuals provided<br>• All managers undergo training<br>• Easy to use | Board sign-off and implemented | Line Managers and Consultants | 30th June to Operations Director |
| 3. Debtors days reduced to 45 days | • Debtors days reduced from 60 to 45<br>• Process developed and in place<br>• All debtors' clerks undergo training<br>• No customer complaints | Management accounts | Finance Manager and Debtors Clerk | 30th June to Finance Director |
| 4. New finance system implemented to track EVA | • Compatible with current system in place<br>• "Real time" queries can be done | CEO sign-off and implemented | IT Manager, Finance Director and CEO | 31 December to CEO |

### 8.2.3  Setting targets

The key in performance management is not the forms or the process used, but rather the setting of targets and then tracking if they are being achieved. Performance management is the way in which organisations monitor and assess how employees are performing. The assessment of performance is then used in the PRP to link pay to performance.

To set targets appropriately and derive maximum benefit from PRP, it is necessary to set out clear objectives with quantifiable performance targets. This way employees can best understand what it is they are expected to do. Proper target setting (often called Key Performance Indicators, or KPIs) will help with the following:

• Ensure that employee contributions support the business objectives.
• Communicate to employees what is truly important.
• Develop standards to measure the expected and achieved quantity and quality of work.
• Identify problem areas early.
• Identify ways to make the business run more efficiently and effectively.
• Monitor the success of the business.

There are many tools and frameworks that can be used to develop KPIs, monitor performance and support the achievement of improved performance in terms of cost, quality, timeliness, resources, customer satisfaction and employee skills/competencies/behaviours. Some of these are: Six Sigma, Business Process Reengineering (BPR), Business Excellence, ISO Standards for Quality Management, The Big Picture, EFQM (European Foundation for Quality Management) and Kaizen Blitz. All of these can be used in the context of, say, Balanced Scorecards, or any other type of PMS.

The standard process starts with setting goals at the top of the organisation and then "cascading" these down the hierarchy, so that if each member of the team that reports to any one supervisor achieves their objectives, then the supervisor will have achieved his or her objectives as well. Typically this process can be done across several levels in the organisation, although the goals in the lowest levels tend to be by team as it becomes difficult to differentiate individual performance.

A common approach to target setting follows the acronym "SMART": Specific, Measurable, Achievable, Relevant and Time-bound.

- Specific means that they are clearly understood.
- Measurable means they are easy to track, and also to determine minimum levels of acceptable performance as well as levels of excellent performance.
- Relevant means that the objectives are set in areas of the business related to the supervisor's goals and that employees can influence.
- Time-bound means clarity is provided around the deadlines against which the KPIs will be measured.

We have left out "Achievable" as this is an aspect of goal setting which merits greater attention. Research on goals[1] supports the S-M-A-R-T approach to target setting with a caveat: the "A", which normally stands for "Achievable", really stands for "Amazingly Difficult" or "Almost Impossible". In other words, KPIs are more likely to be achieved if we set "stretch targets" for employees.

### 8.2.4 Application of reward or merit matrices

Once we have scores for each individual, or for the team (often at lower levels), reward or merit matrices are applied to the scores. An example of a one-dimensional matrix is shown in Table 8.4 below.

---

1    Locke & Latham, 1990.

*Table 8.4: One-dimensional merit matrix*

| Scale point | Performance description | Reward implication |
|---|---|---|
| 5 | Far exceeds job requirements. The employee's performance is visibly outstanding on a sustained basis and far exceeds the requirements set. Tangible evidence exists of the employee's ongoing achievements. | Deserving of a special reward or merit increase. |
| 4 | Exceeds job requirements. The employee's performance exceeds the requirements set. Tangible evidence exists of the employee's achievements. | Should receive an above-average increase. |
| 3 | Meets job requirements. The employee's performance meets the requirements set. | Deserving of the percentage increment top management sets for the organisation in general. |
| 2 | Meets some job requirements. Requires further development. The employee's performance does not yet meet all of the requirements set. Some evidence exists of the employee's competence. | Should receive a restricted increase, lower than the average increase. |
| 1 | Below job requirements. The employee's performance is below the standard requirements set. Little or no evidence exists of the employee's competence. | An increase should not be given, or only a very small one. |

Naturally, it could be very costly to the organisation if nearly all employees scored a five. For this to be the case, there would probably be an unusual circumstance surrounding this level of all-round outstanding performance. It would be more usual for the scores to be somewhat evenly distributed among the five-point scales. The table below serves only as a guideline to be used with respect to how many people should fall into each category. Top management may allow deviations from this in line with exceptional or unusual circumstances, especially if a specific department has done particularly well. This may or may not be the case for each department.

*Table 8.5: Performance rating distribution guidelines*

| Description | Desired distribution |
|---|---|
| Far exceeds job requirements (5) | Up to 10% |
| Exceeds job requirements (4) | Around 25% |
| Meets job requirements (3) | Around 50% |
| Meets some job requirements (2) | Around 10% |
| Below job requirements (1) | Less than 5% |

It cannot be over-stressed that this is merely management information and is to be used as a guideline to "normalise" the ratings provided to different employees by different raters who are considered to be more or less lenient. If one is using software, the actual distribution is calculated for the organisation and this can be compared to the desired distribution. It is then possible to identify different types and quality of consistency among raters by specific departments.

Note that many companies choose to make these guidelines compulsory ("The Forced Curve"). Much has been written on this topic alone. Suffice it to say that it is a major source of employee discontent. A recent trend, started by several high-tech companies in Silicon Valley such as Microsoft and Google, and echoed by professional service firms such as Deloitte and Accenture, is to move away from forced curves, or ratings altogether.[2] As a general rule, companies have used ratings to differentiate performers, however this differentiation is more readily apparent when the goals are set such that only the top performers achieve them (the "stretch targets" that were mentioned earlier). This was the approach used for many years by CEO Jack Welch at GE. Many other companies, on the other hand, have adopted the "Curve" as a way to compensate for inconsistent KPI setting across the company. Thus, forced ranking is used to try to "normalise" the ratings when the measuring yardstick is inherently defective. As a consequence, many employees who believe they met, or even exceeded, their targets, are "forced" down to make up for the fact that their objectives were probably easier than those of another person in a different function. This built-in perceived unfairness (e.g. I exceeded my targets and still only got an average rating"), coupled with insufficient information (e.g. who was the recipient of the higher rating and how was their performance better?") is the source of most employee discontent.

The companies that are trying to move away from this system are approaching it from a variety of angles. Some are willing to "Pay for Development" instead, emphasising growth as a way to achieve higher remuneration and using the performance appraisal as an opportunity to coach employees in their skill and competency acquisition. Others may be simply "changing the labels" or making adjustments to the process, as they find it hard to move away from a pay-for-performance model. As is often the case, any change in an HR policy affects the culture as well as other HR policies, meaning to say that companies wanting to change their performance appraisal programme must keep in mind the implications it will have on other parts of the organisation.

Recently there have been a number of reports and articles challenging the use of rating scales, specifically, forced rankings and performance ratings. Some have gone as far as to pronounce "ratings are dead". The downside of performance ratings – numeric or degree scales – are that they can be demotivating, subjective and limited. This may be true, but it is more about HOW ratings are used, rather than the ratings themselves, that is a problem.

---

2    See "Reinventing Performance Appraisals", Marcus Buckingham and Asley Goodall, Harvard Business Review, April 2015

As Rock and Jones[3] point out, many large companies have moved away from a simple rating system towards newer ways of differentiating performance. These researchers found that social threats and rewards, like sense of status or fairness, activate intense reaction networks in the brain. This explains the intense reactions people have toward being assessed on a rating scale, which focuses the brain on the rating rather than the message.

Rock and Jones[4] note that the trend to move away from traditional performance ratings is increasing and that there are clear signs of success associated with this move. They describe four main reasons why the trend is gaining in momentum and showing such success:

1.  **The changing nature of work** – annual performance reviews do not take into account the collaborative team-based approach to work where people are involved in multiple teams, often spread around the world. The assessment of performance often involves matrix partners or team leaders who are not the direct line manager of the individual. In addition, goals often do not last for a full year in the new fast-paced world of work. Goals may need to be set weekly or monthly and they may change. Annual reviews are not agile enough to enable this type of performance.

2.  **The need for better collaboration** – forced rankings have been shown to hamper collaboration. With many people competing for the top 15% of the rating scale, they stop working as a team and may even try to sabotage or undermine one another.

3.  **The need to attract and keep talent** – development is usually formally included in performance reviews. When performance reviews are scheduled once or twice a year, development is only discussed in these sessions. Research has shown that when ratings are removed, managers speak to their employees about development more regularly, promoting engagement and development, leading to greater attraction and retention of talent.

4.  **The need to develop people faster** – when ratings are removed, people tend to have more frequent dialogues which are characterised by openness. Conversations are moving from the justification of past performance toward more future-oriented growth and development.

There has been a large amount of hype about the 'death of performance ratings', with companies like Accenture, Microsoft and Adobe publicly announcing that they have scrapped the use of formal ratings. The question is whether this radical approach is sustainable and suitable for all. Research conducted by the Corporate Executive Board (CEB) suggests that it is not as simple or as universal a solution as one might think.

---

3   Rock & Jones, 2015.

4   Ibid.

## Why did Accenture stop using performance ratings?

In a bold move, especially for a company managing hundreds of thousands of people, Accenture recently 'revolutionised' and revamped its performance management process. In 2015, Accenture announced it would stop 90% of the traditional performance management processes that it said took up too much time, and were hated by managers and employees alike. But was the change as revolutionary as it seems?

From the headlines, it seemed Accenture was scrapping performance management totally – which is not completely accurate. In the past Accenture's performance management system prescribed that each employee be reviewed once a year using a set performance review process and specific documents. This process was time consuming and tended to focus on the paperwork rather than the person and performance. The process of performance management had not been adapted to the workplace or ways of work; for a company that worked on multiple, ever-changing, fast-paced activities, a static annual review was not appropriate.

It was nearly impossible to effectively manage and measure performance at one point in the year when most employees worked across multiple projects, with multiple people during the course of the year.

Accenture took the decision to retain performance management, but to measure and review performance more appropriately. They decided to conduct more frequent reviews following assignments/projects, and also to do so with less bureaucracy. This makes a lot more sense for a fast-paced, agile firm.

Accenture also took a decision to scrap their performance rating system of forced ranking. In its place a system was introduced where each employee is rated against their own expectations and performance goals.

The philosophy of performance management at Accenture has changed to one characterised by development and 'instant' feedback and review as described by the CEO:

> *Performance management is extraordinarily important to get people to their very best. Do you feel good in your role? If yes, that's the perfect time for you to experiment with something new, to get out of your comfort zone. This willingness to learn is probably the most important thing for leaders of today and tomorrow.*

Performance is an ongoing activity. It's every day, after any client interaction or business interaction or corporate interaction. It's much more fluid. People want to know on an ongoing basis, am I doing right? Am I moving in the right direction? Do you think I'm progressing? Nobody's going to wait for an annual cycle to get that feedback. Now it's all about instant performance management.[5]

Although most of the focus in the media has been on Accenture eliminating performance ratings, what is perhaps more instructive is their decision to adopt a developmental framework with frequent reviews and feedback.

CEB surveyed nearly 10,000 employees in their 2016 Pay for Performance Employee Survey. These employees were from across the globe, spanning 18 countries, and from a representative sample of industries and organisational sizes. They found that in companies where performance ratings had been eliminated, there was an initial period of "euphoria" where employee morale

---

5    Cunningham, 2015.

was boosted, but that post this period, reality set in leading to discontent. Employees became unhappy as they were unable to understand the philosophies behind pay and performance systems without the visible symbol of a rating. Employee engagement scores dropped 6% while performance dropped by 10%, largely due to managers' inability to manage talent effectively without ratings.

Getting rid of performance ratings can only be effective when managers have the skills to have difficult conversations, are able to guide conversations about pay without a rating to "tie it to", and can communicate clear and effective expectations. This requires a significant investment in manager upskilling and coaching, and even then success is not guaranteed.

So, what's the bottom line? Should performance ratings stay or go? The elimination of ratings in isolation is likely to do more damage than good. A sustainable change in approach which promotes a developmental underpinning to the entire field of performance management is a far better option. It is clear that the key levers of a successful performance management system include:

- Effective and agile goal setting.
- Regular feedback from managers both formally and informally.
- A constructive, forward-looking approach grounded in development where the manager is a coach and not an assessor.
- Multi-source feedback including feedback from the manager, peers and stakeholders.
- Elimination of forced ranking.

There are companies where performance ratings may have been successfully eliminated, but these companies are the exception, not the norm, and they have invested heavily in the coaching and upskilling of managers. For most, there is definitely still a place for performance ratings. As CEB very clearly states: do not get side-tracked by the ratings debate. Rather focus on manager development and enhancing the overall performance management system.

---

### Don't kill ratings off just yet … the Facebook experience

Facebook has discovered that when an assessment of performance is required, as it ultimately must be in all companies, it is how the assessment is made and not the rating itself that makes the difference. Even when ratings are supposedly eliminated and not written down, they are still made in "people's heads". When there is no rating to support an assessment, you run the risk that employees will find the assessment even more subjective as the criteria and scoring become vague.

Goler, Gale & Grant[6] conducted a survey in their organisation – Facebook – and found that 87% of people wanted to keep performance ratings. Despite their downside, the authors said their benefits should always be considered:

---

6    Goler, Gale & Grant, 2016.

- Fairness – employees want performance management to be fair, and many believe you need ratings to show the fairness. Employees are less likely to be disappointed with a lower reward or poor assessment if it is based on a rating. This is only the case though, if people see the process as fair.
- Transparency – employees want to be told how their contributions are seen in the organisation; they want to know how well they are performing. This could be done without ratings, but it is not always easy for managers to have the discussion without ratings.
- Development – Goler and her colleagues argue that when ratings are not used, the time spent on performance management decreases. They also argue that performance ratings and reviews should focus on development, and that when one is receiving a lot of information as an employee, ratings help contextualise and make meaning of that information.

The authors say:

> At Facebook we are trying to build a culture in which people approach ratings with curiosity and a learning orientation. When our senior leaders receive performance evaluations, they often share the feedback with their teams, normalizing the fact that even people who consistently deliver strong results sometimes have lapses.

In countries that have equal pay for work of equal value legislation, one definitely needs a performance score if one wants to differentiate pay. On balance, the honeymoon period of throwing out ratings is over and most organisations have reverted back to using some form of rating system.

## 8.2.5 Annual salary adjustments

The suggested steps and considerations in this procedure are the following:

- KPI achievement is assessed and weighted for their level of priority.
- Individual ratings are completed for all employees at least two months before the increment date.
- A summary of rating scores is prepared (at least one month before the increment date).
- A salary increase percentage is determined for the organisation as a whole (usually based on how far from the market benchmark are the organisation's midpoints, coupled with the expected market movement, filtered by the organisation's ability to pay).
- This percentage is allocated to the staff who meet the requirements set and who fall in the middle of the salary range for their grades.
- Suitable higher and lower percentages are calculated for employees who exceed requirements and are undergoing development to ensure that sufficient differentiation as well as the desired total salary cost increase is achieved.
- Lower increases will apply in the case of employees who have not met job requirements.
- Flexibility will be allowed by top management in determining final increments, especially in cases of very high and very low ratings, as well as in allowing for rounding off of salary figures.

- Adjustment of salary anomalies and gaps will be built into final increments after due consultation with salary survey data and discussion with departmental heads.

The following table is an example of a possible guideline as to how the procedure could be followed, assuming an overall organisational annual salary increase percentage of 5 percent.

*Table 8.6: Simple merit increase guidelines*

| Performance Rating | Percentage Increase |
|:---:|:---:|
| 5 | 8% to 10% |
| 4 | 6 to 8% |
| 3 | 4 to 6% |
| 2 | 2 to 4% |
| 1 | 0% |

The following remuneration review guidelines are suggested to assist with the implementation of the review:

- In addition to the above salary adjustment guidelines, it is important to remember that there may be a market premium on certain scarce skills in a particular area as well as on high-performing equity appointments.
- Employees who are not considered for salary increases, such as new appointments, should not be included in the review base. Employees who as a result of poor performance will not be awarded an increase must, however, be included.
- Earnings on equity dimensions must be monitored to ensure that an earnings gap, if any, is addressed and not widened. It is suggested that department heads complete a compa-ratio analysis (see "How to Apply the Concept of Compa-ratio" below) before and after the review by race, gender, seniority and any other demographic variable of interest.
- It is recommended that the salaries of employees are positioned across the full spectrum of the salary scale. Employees who are below the minimum of the salary grade ("red circle") and above the maximum of the grade ("green circle") should be listed separately and commented on.

### 8.2.6  How to apply the concept compa-ratio to PRP

Compa-ratio (CR) is an abbreviation of "comparative ratio". The CR shows the relative position of the employee in the pay range. For example, if the employee is earning 8,000 and the midpoint is 10,000, the CR is .80 (the salary is divided by the midpoint of the range).

Industry guidelines or norms suggest that a CR of less than .80 is low and that there is a risk of losing the employee. Above 1.20 CR typically indicates that the employee has a scarce skill or that the person has consistently been an excellent performer over many years and is thus remunerated above the norm.

### 8.2.7 Two-dimensional merit matrices

A more sophisticated merit matrix has two dimensions. It shows not only the performance score, but also where an individual is located on the salary range or CR. Below is an example of a two-dimensional performance matrix. The percentage increase to be granted is reflected in the middle of the matrix.

*Table 8.7: Two-dimensional merit matrix*

| Position in Range | Performance rating | | | | |
|---|---|---|---|---|---|
| | 1 | 2 | 3 | 4 | 5 |
| Fourth Quartile (CR 1.11-1.20) | 0% | 0% | 3% | 6% | 9% |
| Third Quartile (CR 1.01-1.10) | 0% | 1% | 4% | 7% | 10% |
| Second Quartile (CR .91-1.00) | 0% | 2% | 5% | 8% | 11% |
| First Quartile (CR .80-.90) | 0% | 3% | 6% | 9% | 12% |

A matrix like this accelerates pay increases for top performers who are being paid at the lower end of the pay scale (or have a CR lower than 1.00). It decelerates poor performers' pay increases if they are at the top of the pay scale (or have a CR over 1.00).

### 8.2.8 How to calculate a two-dimensional merit matrix

There are several ways in which to calculate the percentages of increase for each cell of Table 8.7. To do so, there are several specific decisions to be made:

- **What is the available salary budget?** As indicated earlier, this is usually based on how far from the market benchmark the organisation's midpoints are, coupled with the expected market salary movement, filtered by the organisation's ability to pay. Typically, it is number negotiated with the Finance Department during the annual organisational budget exercise.
- **How much higher (or lower) should an increase be for the next level of performance?** In other words, for two people currently doing the same job and paid the same amount, if one of them receives a rating of '3' and the other a rating of '4', how much higher should the increase for the higher rated employee be? This is a judgement call, usually tempered by how much the highest salary increase would be, and by providing that much, would

it affect the "reasonableness" of the increase to average employees in the middle of the salary range? Table 8.6 has a difference of 3% for each level of performance, and a highest possible increase of 12%.

- **How much higher (or lower) should an increase be for the next level of position in range?** Here the question is similar: If two employees are doing the same job and receiving the same performance rating, but one of them is currently paid in the second quartile and the other in the third quartile, what should the difference in the percentage of increase be for each? Similar considerations about the highest salary increase and how it would affect the average increase apply here as well. Table 8.6 has a 1% difference due to position in range. Note that if your current pay system is lacking equity, you may want to consider making this aspect weigh more.

One way to calculate these matrices is to use last year's performance ratings for each employee, with their current salary and applying the intended budget, and the differences by performance and position in range determined. Another way to do it is to use the % distribution for all performance ratings (e.g. what % of employees were rated 5, etc.), and the % distribution for all positions in range (e.g. what % of employees are paid in the fourth quartile, etc.). By multiplying the percentages across the rows and columns of the matrix (e.g. the % of people rated 5 and paid in the fourth quartile is equal to the % of people rated 5 times the % of people paid in the fourth quartile), you can estimate the percentage of people that would correspond to each cell. This number can then be multiplied times the expected salary increase per cell, as estimated previously, and by adding all the cells you will obtain an estimate of how much the overall salary increase would be if you follow the estimated increases. If the initial table exceeds (or falls short) of the expected budget, you can make adjustments in several ways:

- Change the expected increase for the middle of the table (performance rating 3 and second quartile in Table 8.6) and adjust the rest of the cells according to the differences determined by performance and position in range.
- Change the percentage difference for performance.
- Change the percentage difference for position in range.
- Manually adjust specific cells (for instance, in Table 8.6 you can decide that all those with a performance rating of 2 and currently paid in the third or fourth quartile should get no increase).
- Some combination of all of the above.

This process is one of trial and error. Keep working on your table until you are satisfied that it will do what you intend for it to do: reward good performers and help correct any pay equity imbalances.

Remember that the promotion increase budget, as well as the budget for new hires, must be addressed separately.

### 8.2.9 Should non-KPI related aspects of performance management be included in PRP?

There is an ongoing debate about whether or not to link some aspects of the PMS (especially 360-degree) to rewards. In Table 8.8 below we summarise the common reasons for first implementing a developmental-only process and initially avoid the link of development to pay. The most common practice is to initially implement non-KPI related aspects of performance management focusing on development first and, over time and if warranted, then link it to pay.

## 8.3 Critical success factors for PRP

Strengthening the link between performance and pay is a global trend. Some of the critical success factors discussed below may seem obvious but serve as a useful checklist.

### 8.3.1 Readiness

The following questions must be asked to ensure that the organisation is ready to implement PRP:

- Will it fit our culture and support the organisation?
- Are the top executives, and especially the CEO, driving it?
- Has enough time been allowed for thorough communication and training on the new system?
- Are employees receptive to the process?
- Will managers "own" the process?
- Are there enough resources (HR and/or consultants) to implement and do the training?

*Table 8.8: Reasons to avoid linking development aspects of PMS to rewards*

| | |
|---|---|
| **New rules** | Receiving feedback from multiple sources changes the rules for success. It takes employees a while to get used to the "new rules". |
| **Competencies** | The competencies used for 360-degree feedback are new and different from classic evaluation criteria. Employees need the opportunity to become familiar with these new expectations before they impact performance and pay decisions. |
| **Training** | Participants need to be trained in performance-appraisal systems. A one-time use of 360-degree feedback as a developmental process gives everyone training in providing feedback as well as receiving it from others. |
| **Experience** | Using 360-degree feedback for development only gives everyone experiential learning in the process. Experience is likely to reduce participant anxiety substantially. |
| **Refinement** | A first project never seems to be perfect. Participant assessment from an initial process can yield insight into which design features to change or refine. |
| **Low risk** | Receiving feedback from multiple sources when the results do not impact on pay lowers employee perceptions of the "riskiness" of the new process. |

| Validation | Process validation occurs when value and credibility are established among participating employees. |
|---|---|
| Gaming | When participating employees have less at stake, they are more likely to provide honest feedback without trying to "beat" the system in their favour. |

### 8.3.2 Appropriateness of the system

It is necessary to ask the following questions to ensure that the PMS can be understood and administered:

- Do we have a robust system with good measures?
- Does our system support and drive our business strategy?
- Has the link to pay been clearly explained?
- Is the system administration process well designed?
- Does the system allow flexibility, especially in the link to reward?

### 8.3.3 Support and maintenance

It is absolutely essential to be able to answer in the affirmative the following questions regarding support and maintenance:

- Is there someone who will co-ordinate the implementation and drive it?
- Can the system be institutionalised, allowing for continuous improvements to be made to the system from year to year?

There is no single best PMS or performance management method, and often we allow the "filling out of the forms" to hijack the process. It is more important to institutionalise the process and have meaningful performance discussions than to let a statement or rating on a piece of paper detract from the performance review. Leaders must not use the paper as a crutch – it is an aid to what we are trying to do.

## 8.4 Summary

Performance-related pay is pay that varies depending on individual, team or organisation performance. It is often underpinned by a performance management system and market salary survey data. It usually applies to individuals when it comes to the annual salary adjustment. Organisations work out the incumbent's compa-ratio and give them a pay increase according to their individual performance and where they are paid relative to the market. The purpose of individual performance-related pay is to reward the individual for better results.

## 8.5 Self-evaluation questions

1. What is the difference between individual and team performance-related pay?
2. Describe a common performance-rating scale.
3. What is a compa-ratio?
4. Name two common elements of a merit matrix.
5. What is the difference between performance-related pay and competency-based pay?

## 8.6 Exercise

1. Calculate a merit increase table with the following data:

| Performance Rating | Proportion in Category | | Position in Range | Proportion in Category | | Salary Increase Budget |
|---|---|---|---|---|---|---|
| Outstanding | 15% | | 1st Quartile | 35% | | 5.5% |
| Exceeds Expectations | 45% | | 2nd Quartile | 25% | | |
| Meets Expectation | 35% | | 3rd Quartile | 24% | | |
| Below Expectations | 5% | | 4th Quartile | 16% | | |
| Unsatisfactory | 0% | | | | | |

2. Be sure to indicate:

   a) How much more (or less) to pay for position in range differences.
   b) How much more (or less) to pay for differences in performance rating.
   c) Which combinations of position in range and performance should not receive any increase.

# CHAPTER 9

## Allowances As a Component of Total Fixed Pay

### 9.1 Why allowances and how do they fit into total packages?

In Chapter 4 we reviewed how the total package is structured. In Chapters 5 through 7 we discussed various aspects around basic salary. In this chapter we will address allowances and how to include them as part of the overall remuneration strategy. Figure 9.1 illustrates this concept.

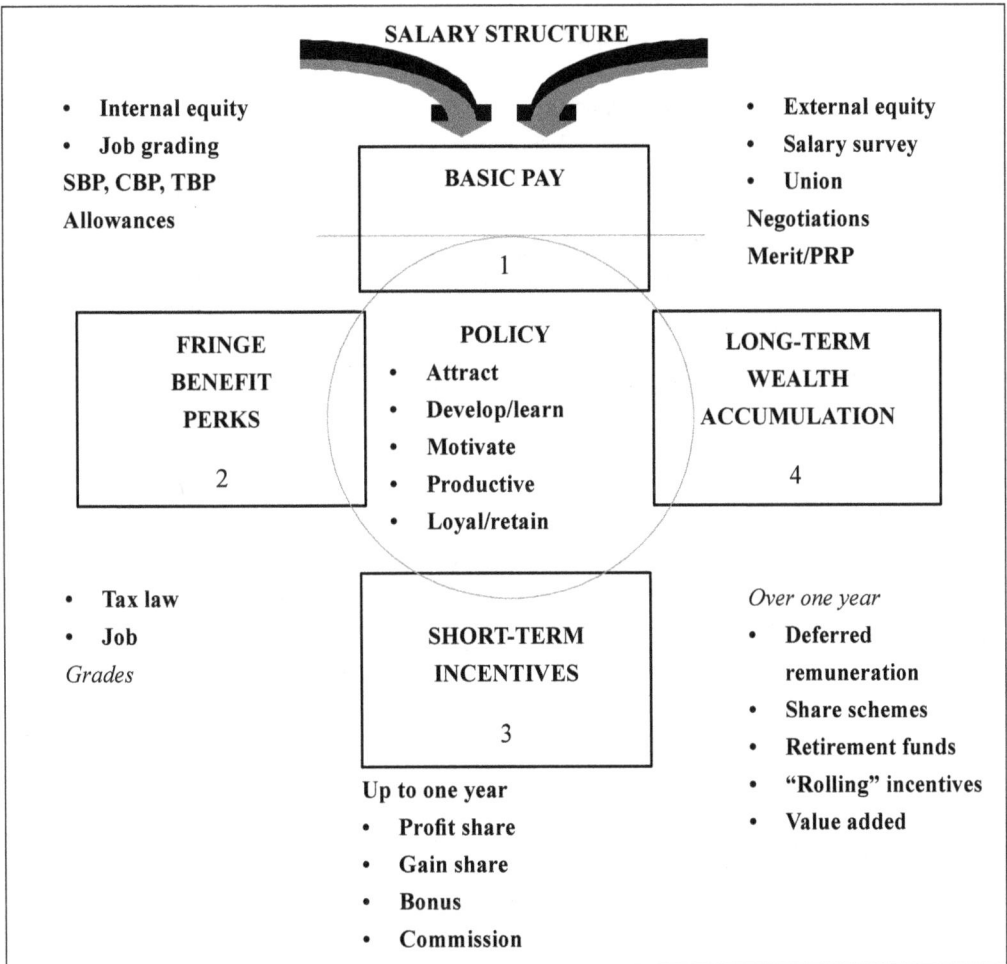

*Figure 9.1: Main pay components of a remuneration model*

Numbers 1 and 2 are part of guaranteed remuneration and, when combined, conform fixed pay. Numbers 3 and 4 are variable pay; the trend is to hold numbers 1 and 2 steady, while leveraging numbers 3 and 4.

Allowances are generally used by companies to provide benefits to all employees that do not vary by pay level or pay amount (e.g. food vouchers, transportation vouchers, etc.), or that have a tax advantage (e.g. in some jurisdictions, cars or housing provided by the organisation are not taxed). One other reason why allowances and other emoluments are commonly used is that the amounts paid do not count towards statutory benefits, overtime and other basic-salary related calculations – including bonuses, severances or merit increases.

## 9.2    What does fixed pay mean?

Fixed pay (guaranteed cost of employment) is often confused with total cost to organisation. The following concepts are defined in table 9.2 below:

| **Basic Salary** |
| --- |
| + Allowances (travelling/entertainment/subsistence/PC/telephone) |
| + Guaranteed annual bonuses (13th cheque/Christmas bonus) |
| + Other fixed emoluments (car/housing provided by the organisation) |
| + Inconvenience pay (overtime/standby/shift) |
| = **Total Fixed Pay** |
| + Short-term incentives (performance bonuses/commissions) |
| = **Total Cash** |
| + Long-term incentives (shares) |
| = **Total Compensation** |
| + Employer contribution to medical/retirement/group life benefits |
| + Employer contribution to statutory benefits |
| = **Total Package (Total Cost to Organisation)** |

*Figure 9.2: Elements of total rewards*

## 9.3 Why the trend?

Many organisations are moving to administering total fixed pay as a whole, rather than separating basic pay from allowances. This is in line with current global remuneration trends. There are several good reasons and advantages to manage fixed pay in this way:

- Greater flexibility to manage fixed pay.
- Easier to structure fixed pay packages in accordance with individual needs.
- Fixed and known guaranteed employment costs – no hidden extras.
- Better positioned to attract and retain high quality staff.
- More equitable and defensible approach to remuneration.
- Simplified and accurate market comparisons and benchmarking.
- True worth known to and understood by employees.
- Simplified cost control and costing.
- Improved potential to create direct links between performance and pay.
- Achievement of internal equity.
- Safety in the event of a tax audit.

The next section describes how the total fixed pay packaging approach works and gives broad tax guidelines. This should not be construed as tax advice.

## 9.4 How the total fixed pay packaging approach works

The items that are included in total fixed pay are all payments and benefits of a fixed and regular nature that are subject to exact valuation. Employees are fully entitled to such payments and benefits.

Employers have a moral obligation to ensure that employees are covered for health risks and emergencies and are saving for retirement. These obligations are easily met by making membership on the medical schemes and retirement funds compulsory. Exceptions would include being a registered dependant on a spouse's medical scheme.

In the following paragraphs we discuss some key points around fixed pay packaging.

### 9.4.1 Negotiations

Where trade unions are recognised, any changes to conditions of employment must be negotiated with the trade unions. Sometimes organisations are subject to regulation through bargaining councils, which means that their remuneration practices are prescribed by industry-specific needs. It is likely that a negotiation regarding total fixed pay packaging would be analysed in detail.

### 9.4.2 Guaranteed 13th cheque

The 13th cheque is usually guaranteed and paid annually. Where a pro rata bonus is forfeited on resignation, people can plan their departure in such a way that they can still receive the maximum benefit. The incorporation of the 13th cheque in the total fixed pay package should therefore not result in an extra cost to the organisation. Accrued bonuses are paid out on conversion.

### 9.4.3 Medical aid membership

Where medical aid contributions are subsidised, those employees who are not members of the medical aid do not benefit from such subsidies. These benefits are usually equalised when converting to total fixed pay packages.

The member is responsible for the full contributions payable to the medical aid fund. Employers should therefore ensure that the medical aid fund rules reflect the total contribution payable by each member. In a total fixed pay package structure, an employee may request that the employer pay the full contribution on his or her behalf. The full contribution would then be allocated as the relevant package component. The employee therefore also carries the full cost of contribution increases, which are sometimes higher than wage inflation and eat into the disposable net salary.

Employee benefit schemes exist to support employer remuneration structures. The trend in the market is to offer flexibility of choice and not to subscribe to one scheme only. However, in some industries (e.g. mining), an in-house medical aid is mostly prevalent.

### 9.4.4 Retirement fund contributions

Pensionable earnings (retirement funding income) are defined in terms of the rules of the fund. In countries where pension plans are prevalent, the trend is to express retirement funding income as a factor of the total remuneration package. The market norm ranges from 40 to 70 percent.

The conversion to packages need not impact the employer contributions, as the current actual employer contributions are deemed equitable and are usually incorporated into total fixed pay packages.

Once converted, retirement funding income could be an option within a range, for example, between 50 percent and 100 percent of total package. As the future contributions would be one of the package components based on the individual's choice, flexibility would not result in any additional cost to the organisation.

Insured risks (death and disability cover) are often offered separately from retirement benefits. A commonly used approach is to negotiate flexible levels of cover with the underwriters and to offer members the option of choosing the level most suitable to them. The costs of the selected benefits are allocated as a relevant package component.

### 9.4.5  Car allowances

Where car allowances are paid, organisations will often distinguish between employment cost and operational or business expenses. The fixed cost of acquiring a motor vehicle is considered to be part of the total fixed cost of employment. The use of a motor vehicle for business purposes results in a business expense that is reimbursed. Car allowances are typically dependent on the local market practice and not necessarily a guaranteed benefit. The benefit is usually linked to an advantageous tax treatment in the specific country. Many tax authorities do not accept the principle of standard allowances based on job grade. Transportation allowances may be paid only to those individuals who are expected to use their own vehicles for business purposes. In these cases, the amount that should be allocated as the travelling allowance should be based on the cost and the use of the vehicle. Individuals are therefore required to justify the values of their travel allowances before the amount is accepted. This situation results in organisations deciding to not provide a car but rather a car allowance, which even if taxable, offers shelter from adding it to basic salary and thus having this amount be part of other calculations like severance payments, annual bonuses or merit increases.

### 9.4.6  Business travel reimbursements

Most companies reimburse actual business kilometres travelled. The market differentiates between staff with car allowances and those without. The trend is to reimburse staff without car allowances at a higher rate than that payable to staff qualifying for a car allowance.

The reasons for differentiation are:

- Those not receiving car allowances need to be reimbursed for both fixed and variable costs, whereas the total packages of car allowance recipients are deemed to be inclusive of the fixed cost components.
- The rate applicable to car allowance recipients is partly taxed during the year but qualifies for a business cost deduction at the end of the tax year.

### 9.4.7  Tool-of-trade vehicles

The market recognises the need for tool-of-trade (pool) vehicles for individuals who are required to travel extensively for business. The tool-of-trade vehicle is treated as an operational or business cost. In this way employment costs remain equitable, while operating costs are recorded separately. Incidental private use of the vehicle does not necessarily comprise a fringe benefit. Certain requirements may be applicable in various tax environments.

### 9.4.8 Organisation cars vs. motor vehicle allowances

The debate on organisation cars versus motor vehicle allowances is long standing among compensation professionals. Many individuals express opinions that promote one or the other. The bottom line is that the benefits derived from either option are linked to the costs and usage of the vehicle.

Depending on the tax provisions in each country, the car allowance seems to be less targeted than the organisation car, making the car allowance more beneficial for most users. However, both organisation car and car allowance have a right of existence.

As a general rule, the organisation car seems to be more beneficial in cases of relatively low business use, irrespective of the value of the vehicle. Where the price of the vehicle exceeds the maximum (it often changes each year), the organisation car seems more beneficial, even in cases of higher business use. The organisation car should not be overlooked by deskbound staff and executives.

The trend in the market is to re-introduce "new generation" organisation cars as a fixed pay package option wherever the tax rules are beneficial. To overcome the asset, cost and risk debate, employers enter into agreements with car rental companies, which ensure that the total related costs are allocated as one of the total fixed pay package components. The principle is that the individual bears the full consequence of his or her choices.

### 9.4.9 Benefit values

Benefit values are defined independently from retirement funding income. There is sometimes a need to calculate payments such as overtime, inconvenience pay and certain statutory contributions using an equitable value lower than the remuneration package. Benefit values are often defined as a fixed percentage of remuneration packages, which is applicable to all. These values can be as low as 8 percent to as high as 70 percent, depending on the specific market.

### 9.4.10 Severance pay

The amount and calculation of severance pay, including the value of leave on termination of service for whatever reason, varies considerably from one country to the next. In some cases it is not regulated at all (e.g. Singapore), and companies adopt a "market practice" or "organisation policy" approach. In other countries it is very regulated and enforced (e.g. Mexico, South Africa). In these cases, severance calculations follow specific procedures and methodologies for calculation and payout.

### 9.4.11 Accumulated leave

Accrued leave should be capped at current values prior to the conversion to fixed pay packages. Any further accumulation should be limited to the value of the leave at the time of accumulation. The current accrual could be reduced to more acceptable levels by encouraging employees to take long outstanding leave. Alternatively, employees could be encouraged to convert the accumulated leave to cash, depending on the cash flow position of the organisation.

Inequities are usually confined to housing benefits and employer contributions to medical aid schemes. If equity were to be improved on conversion, it would result in an increase in the current cost of employment. If these issues are not addressed, it will restrict equity on conversion.

## 9.5    Fixed pay package structuring options

Structuring of remuneration packages means that employees are allowed to choose the package components that suit their lifestyles from time to time. Although the same options are available to all, the relevance of the item to the position the individual may hold should be used as the basis for the selection and approval thereof.

Employers need not take on any risks when offering flexibility. Employers are generally also agents of their relevant tax authorities and have to satisfy the principal that any structure is justified, based on an individual's duties. For instance, travelling allowance can be granted to an employee only if a car is required to do their work.

The choice of items making up the annual package will be subject to tax in accordance with local tax legislation. Any changes in the legislation involving additional taxes to be paid will not be the responsibility of the employer.

The following options can be considered when structuring a fixed pay package.

### 9.5.1  Organisation car

An employee may choose the use of a motor vehicle in lieu of pay. The portion of the individual's remuneration package that will be allocated to the provision of an organisation car will be subject to an agreement between the employer and the employee.

The private use of an organisation-provided vehicle allocated to an employee results in a taxable benefit. The organisation car fringe benefit value is based on the original cost of the vehicle (excluding finance charges, interest and value-added tax).

For each month during which the employee is entitled to use the vehicle for private purposes, the organisation car fringe benefit value will be a percentage of the value of the vehicle. If the employee has the use of more than one motor vehicle during the same period, the value of the second or successive vehicles must be calculated at a higher percentage.

If the employer acquired the vehicle 12 months or more before the date on which the employee is granted the use of the vehicle, a depreciation allowance must be deducted from the cost of the vehicle. The depreciation allowance is calculated on the reducing balance method at the specific rate for each completed period of 12 months, calculated from the date on which the employer acquired such vehicle to the date on which the employee was first granted the use of the vehicle.

### 9.5.2  Motor vehicle allowance

Motor vehicle allowances may be granted only to individuals who are required to travel for business purposes. The portion of the fixed pay package that may be allocated as a motor vehicle allowance is subject to an agreement between the employer and the employee.

The motor vehicle allowance covers only the fixed costs of the motor vehicle. The number of business kilometres travelled should be reimbursed at rates determined by the employer from time to time. Such reimbursements comprise a variable allowance, which is payable in addition to the total package.

Some tax authorities do not limit the amount payable as a travelling allowance but will apply a "reasonableness" test. The amount payable should be reasonable compared to the position and responsibilities of the recipient and should be preferably based on the cost and use of the vehicle.

The travelling allowance is tax-deductible in the hands of the employer, while some or all of the fixed and variable allowance is subject to employees' tax. The employee is sometimes allowed a deduction for "business purposes" on assessment.

### 9.5.3  Employer contributions to medical benefits

Contributions and benefits are determined by the organisation and may vary from time to time. Changes in the contributions are the responsibility of the employee. If the employee requests the employer to pay the full medical benefit contribution, which is included in the total package, some or all of such contribution will be taxable as a fringe benefit in the hands of the member, depending on the local tax regulations. The full contribution is often tax-deductible on the side of the employer.

### 9.5.4  Employer contributions to retirement fund

Contribution percentages are also determined by the organisation and may vary from time to time. Contributions are based on an amount agreed between the employer and the employee. The organisation pays the contributions in terms of the rules of the fund. The total contribution is included in the total package.

Employee contributions to pension funds are usually tax deductible to the individual (within certain limits). Employee contributions to provident funds may or may not be tax-deductible to the individual, depending on the local tax regulations.

The combined employer contributions to health insurance and retirement funding (pension and provident fund) are normally tax-deductible to the employer, although in some cases only up to a specified percentage of pensionable income.

### 9.5.5 Annual cash lump sum

An employee could choose to have a portion of his or her cash paid out in a lump sum. The amount to be paid as a lump sum, and the date of payment thereof, are subject to an agreement between the organisation and the employee.

The cash lump sum is tax-deductible to the employer, while the full amount is subject to employees' tax, which may be withheld monthly in equal instalments or withheld in full on the payment date, according to local tax regulations.

Most employers prefer to accrue the cash lump sum on a monthly basis. The monthly accrual is declared as income and taxed accordingly. This eliminates the risks associated with provisions spread across more than one tax year.

### 9.5.6 Cash

There is no concept of "basic salary" in a total fixed pay package. The balance of the total fixed pay package not allocated to one of the components above will constitute the cash component, which is payable monthly in equal instalments. The cash component is a tax-deductible expense to the employer, while the full amount constitutes taxable income to employees.

Further options that some employers allow as package components include professional subscriptions, personal computer, personal telephone, home office, deferred remuneration, and additional voluntary leave. Depending on the way in which they are offered, some of these components may contain elements of risk, and care should be exercised to not fall afoul of the local tax authorities, as the organisation may be found liable.

## 9.6    A typical process

### 9.6.1  Phase 1: Design and development phase

*Evaluation*

- Review the HR and remuneration principles, policies and practices.
- Evaluate the current optional benefits, conditions of employment, employee benefits and all relevant pay scales, where applicable.
- Recommend changes, if and where necessary.

*Cost implications*

- Verify the most recent payroll and pay-related data.
- Determine the current total cost to the organisation.
- Quantify the impact of changes on the total cost to the organisation, if any.
- Recommend the total fixed pay package structure most suitable to the organisation.
- Obtain management approval.

*Documentation*

- Draft a proposed remuneration policy and employment contract that is most suitable for the organisation.
- Draft a letter to individuals regarding the changes and the implementation thereof.
- Prepare presentation and communication material.

### 9.6.2  Phase 2: Implementation phase

*Communication/Package structuring*

- Distribute individual letters.
- Conduct information sessions.
- Consult with and advise individuals on the structuring of their fixed pay packages.
- Ensure that individual options are correctly exercised, recorded and processed.

## 9.7    Do's and don'ts in the total fixed pay package approach

The following lessons have been learnt over many years of experience and serve as a useful guide:

- Make sufficient resources available during the investigation and preparation phases.
- Do not change if you do not understand the implications and consequences.
- Get expert advice if necessary.

- Include all fixed and regular items that can be accurately quantified in the all-inclusive package.
- Keep variable items, business reimbursements and statutory contributions outside the all-inclusive package.
- Go for full equity and face the reality of reasonable equity costs on conversion.
- If the cost of inequities cannot be absorbed on conversion, phase it in over three to five years, or at least have a strategy to address internal equity over time.
- Do not ignore inequities. They will not disappear on conversion.
- Consult and communicate well.
- Give individuals enough time to grasp the implications of the change.
- Ensure that individuals understand the advantages and benefits but also the risks and responsibilities that accompany a conversion to all-inclusive packages.
- Assist individuals with the structuring of their packages. Specialists and/or a software package may add tremendous value.
- Do not underestimate the high value of freedom of choice for the individual.
- Record and communicate annual amounts in line with the market.
- Round off annual all-inclusive packages on conversion and with each increase.
- Decide, and communicate, how the organisation will grant increases: will they be based on the total all-inclusive package in line with movements in the labour market? If so, note that the percentage will be lower than a percentage based on basic salary because of the items included on conversion; an 8 percent increase in basic salary may equate to a 6.8 percent increase in total package.
- Do not accept responsibility for increases in former components of the total package, such as increases in health plan contributions. The market will discount such factors.
- Do not re-define who should be allowed which options. The job requirements should be clear on this.
- Do not repeat tax or labour law in the remuneration policy as these often change.
- Make sure that all systems (Payroll and HR) as well as all documentation (conversion letters, employment letters, HR policies, guidelines and fund rules) correctly reflect and support the all-inclusive package concept.

The next section provides some guidance on the use of an amendment to software for the total package approach.

## 9.8    Suggestions on software use

Payroll and HR systems will require once-off changes on conversion. Once the system is in place, maintenance is simple. Most payroll systems can accommodate the all-inclusive package concept with relative ease and little change. If not, consider changing your payroll or payroll administrator.

If you acquire a software package as a tool to assist individuals with the structuring of their packages, ensure that it caters for all your needs. Models available in Excel can be customised for this purpose. A good model includes the individual's annual remuneration agreement, monthly advice, monthly taxable pay calculation, annual tax assessment, and all related details. Models often need to be customised to suit an organisation's particular needs.

## 9.9    Role of HR business partners

The total fixed pay package approach impacts on nearly all aspects of the HR cycle and value chain. Ensure that the remuneration manager empowers all the role players, especially the HR business partners, to talk knowledgeably about the concept.

Linking remuneration to the HR function allows for an integrated service to the business and greater focus on its strategies. Among the advantages of linking remuneration to the Human Resources function are the following:

- Integrated systems.
- Increased data integrity.
- Improved information availability.
- Improved response time.
- Increased flexibility and ease of change to meet business needs.
- Developed staff through increased complexity and variety of tasks.
- Improved teamwork – there is a close working relationship between payroll administrators and HR consultants.
- Effective one-stop employee pay and benefits service and information centre.
- Enhanced employee education and communication.
- Improved customer service and satisfaction.

## 9.10   Ongoing maintenance of the system

Total fixed pay all-inclusive packages will not replace the current review cycles or requirements. Review dates will be the same as in the past (unless any changes are communicated on conversion).

Employers find that systems are easier to use and maintain after the conversion. This is due to one standard reward system being used for all.

Employees have the right to restructure their packages every time their circumstances warrant such restructuring (for example, when buying a new car, changing jobs, being transferred or promoted, or receiving an interim increase). Once an individual has decided on the new split of his or her package, a new remuneration agreement will be prepared and recorded. Packages cannot be restructured retrospectively. Once an individual has made his or her choice, it is binding until changed, following one or more of the events above.

It is the employers' responsibility to keep track of and stay in line with labour and related law changes. All systems must correctly reflect the policies and applicable law at any point in time.

In due course, this approach will lead organisations to consider more flexible fixed pay approaches, in line with the current trend of flexible benefits (see Chapter 16).

## 9.11  Summary

Total fixed pay packaging is a remuneration approach that adds basic pay and the cost of allowances and other emoluments together to form a single fixed pay number. Organisations implement it to make their administration processes much easier and to maximise existing tax provisions. The advantage for the individual is that it provides some flexibility on how the package is paid to him or her, a concept called "my-pay-my-way".

## 9.12  Self-evaluation questions

1.  What are allowances? And emoluments?
2.  Describe in your own words what "total fixed pay package" means.
3.  Why do organisations want to offer total fixed pay packages?
4.  Describe the two main phases of implementing total fixed pay packages.
5.  Name some lessons learnt when moving to a total fixed pay package approach.
6.  What should stay out of the total fixed pay package?

# CHAPTER 10

## Payroll

### 10.1 Payroll management

The importance of the payroll department has long been underestimated and undervalued. The interaction of the payroll department with other departments in the organisation is vital to ensuring the accuracy and integrity of the payroll. Line managers should ensure the timeous and accurate submission of payroll input. Top management buy-in to payroll processes and deadlines is also an important factor in the successful functioning of any payroll department.

Calculating the cost of incorrect or inaccurate payroll processing emphasises the importance of payroll controls. What additional cost does the company have to carry if extra overtime hours are incorrectly processed on a regular basis? What is the cost of leave provision if the processor fails to process one leave day per year for every employee?

Payroll should not just be seen as a means to process input and pay employees. It should be used as a management tool. The setup of payroll parameters is important in the management of input and desired output results. Reporting on historical data in order to do trend analyses can assist greatly in decision-making in terms of future remuneration policies. Effective reporting is also a useful budgeting tool. Payroll interfaces to third-party software, which includes interfacing to accounting and HR management systems, are becoming more important.

### 10.2 The role of the payroll department

The payroll and HR departments are inter-related and operate in close contact. The HR department formulates the personnel policies and manpower planning, whereas the payroll department sees to the implementation and maintenance of the payroll and related functions. The role of the payroll administrator within an organisation is varied and dependent on the size and type of the organisation. In a big organisation, for example, the payroll department will be responsible for payroll-related duties only, while HR will be responsible for the maintenance of leave and personnel information and remuneration.

With a small organisation, the information is often of a much smaller volume, so that it is more than possible for the payroll department to handle both the HR and payroll-related functions. Some organisations pair the payroll function with a financial role, such as a bookkeeper. Integration of processes between the payroll, HR and finance departments is important to ensure that all relevant timelines are adhered to and all deadlines are met.

## 10.3  The payroll, HR and benefits manager's role

The payroll, HR and benefits manager's role is to ensure that a total remuneration and reward framework is in place to promote a fair and consistent reward experience in the company or group. This role provides high-level consultation and advice to a number of stakeholders and is responsible for the annual increase process, annual bonus process, new remuneration programmes or changes to existing ones, incentive plans, and retention plans.

Typical payroll, benefit and other tasks that need to be fulfilled are:

- Ensuring that legislation and statutory requirements are translated correctly into the payroll setup, which includes input documentation, calculations, reporting and exports.
- Ensuring the correct implementation of remuneration policies and procedures, as well as employee contract specifications in the payroll.
- Performing an internal audit to ensure that all internal processes are being adhered to.
- Facilitating the internal and external audit process.
- Entering into and updating service level agreements with payroll and service providers.
- Aligning input documentation with input requirements, ensuring that the necessary checks are in place to control data input and conducting checks on the payroll before signing it off for month end. It is vitally important that data integrity is maintained in the payroll environment.
- Ensuring the involvement of different parties in the sign-off process to ensure data integrity.
- Balancing the signed-off payroll to net salary payments, third party payments, reports and exports.
- Ensuring that proper backup procedures are in place. Statutory requirements generally require data to be kept for a specific time period.
- Managing staff members, such as administrators and data capturers.
- Building relationships with third parties, such as retirement fund administrators, trustees and software and service suppliers.
- Ensuring that staff is trained to maintain a professional and compliant payroll department.
- Accepting responsibility for communicating information to the organisation with regard to payroll-related and statutory changes affecting employees.
- Analysing data to assist with analysis, forecasting and budgeting.
- Assisting in pay level/job grade management and performance management.
- Reconciling payroll data records with cash flowing through the income statement.
- Accepting responsibility for ensuring correct payments and submission of reports and files to statutory bodies.
- Drafting and updating of the remuneration and reward framework.
- Interacting with and managing payroll and benefit employees.

## 10.4  Items affecting payroll administration

### *10.4.1  Legislation and policy*

There are numerous items affecting the proper administration of a payroll in each country. The most important is the legislation regulating payroll administration. Examples of relevant legislation include:

- Basic Conditions of Employment.
- Compensation for Occupational Injuries and Diseases.
- Employment Equity Act.
- Income (Payroll) Tax.
- Labour Relations.
- Occupational Health and Safety.
- Skills Development.
- Unemployment Insurance.

Another document that has an influence on payroll is company policy. A company policy document contains all the policies and procedures applicable to a particular company. It will therefore vary from company to company. These policies and procedures are decided on and formulated by the management of each individual company. A company's policy needs to function within the framework of legislation, while payroll in turn functions within the boundaries set by the company policy and legislation as shown in Figure 10.1.

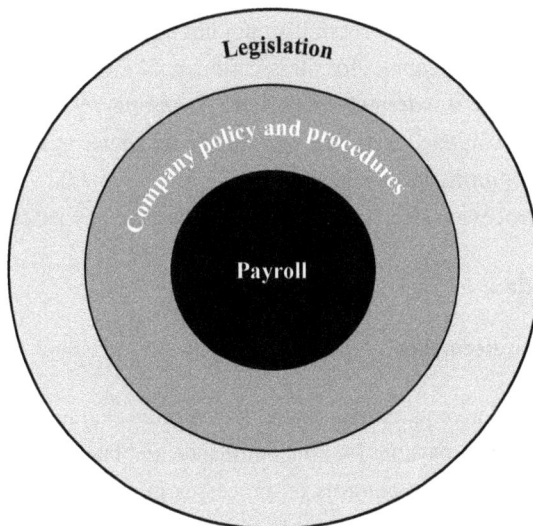

*Figure 10.1: Interdependence of payroll, company policy and legislation*

### 10.4.2   Confidentiality

Confidentiality is specifically addressed in legislation which refers to "preservation of privacy". This states that you may not disclose any information which you have obtained in the course of your duties concerning the financial affairs of any other person, although, there may be exceptions.

A payroll administrator may, for example, be contacted by a retail store chain that wants to check an employee's credit references. If the store wants to know what the employee's earnings are, ask what amount he or she gave them and confirm it or refer them to a credit bureau. Do not give the amount yourself.

A payroll administrator should always keep the principle of confidentiality in mind. You should regard all financial information as confidential. Even particulars such as an employee's marital status and age should be treated as confidential.

Other considerations include the following:

- Do not print payslips or other reports to a printer to which everyone has access. This is especially important if your payroll is installed on a network where you may print to different printers.
- Do not leave payslips, reports or any other confidential information lying in your office when you leave the office. The office door should preferably be locked when you leave.
- Do not give any unnecessary particulars concerning employees or the company to people over the phone.
- It is recommended that the payroll administrator has an office of his or her own, or that there is at least a lockable filing cabinet for filing confidential information.
- The layout of the office is extremely important. If your payroll is processed electronically, the screen must be positioned in such a way that people entering the office will not be able to see confidential information on the screen.
- Payrolls that are processed electronically must be restricted by passwords.

## 10.5  Payroll trends

### 10.5.1   Legislation requirements

The complexity of legislation requirements makes it ever more challenging to ensure a compliant payroll. Penalties and interest payable for noncompliance and late payments to statutory bodies make it essential to maintain tight controls on processes in order not to escalate payroll costs unnecessarily.

Statutory bodies are moving towards electronic submission and integration of data. The information burden associated with these requirements, as well as file layout requirements and validation of data that needs to be performed, makes it essential to make use of payroll software and service providers that will enable the seamless submission of records and integration with these systems.

### *10.5.2* **Centralised payrolls**

Companies are continually searching for more efficient processes through standardisation and centralisation. One way to achieve this is to centralise payroll operations and move away from disparate or decentralised payroll operations. Centralisation is a great cost-saving initiative and, at the same time, a very challenging process.

A first step in centralising payroll processes is to review existing policies and procedures. Analysing current requirements will give a clear indication of future expectations and it also provides the opportunity to analyse resource requirements in the centralised environment. Understanding how current decentralised processes relate to each other is imperative in the centralisation exercise. This is especially important in global operations, where different country requirements need to be combined into centralised processes.

The cost of centralisation should be weighed up against the cost of maintaining a decentralised payroll. The practical implementation of processes, as well as the cost of statutory compliance, should be considered in this process. Auditing, information and security requirements may differ between geographical areas in which the company might operate. It could be challenging establishing realistic and workable policies and procedures to ensure compliance on the one hand, and internal efficiency on the other.

A great benefit of a centralised payroll is the agility it gives the company in terms of reporting. Since data are consolidated, it makes it much easier to access and analyse than trying to combine different data sources. Performing remuneration cost analysis and administration of leave is much easier in a consolidated environment. Direct comparisons can be done with real-time data, and it is always ensured that the "same" data are used in comparisons, monitoring and budgeting. There are also advantages to having a combined database in terms of auditing requirements.

Centralising your payroll activities can lead to cost reductions in the long term. Although the capital outlay for software acquisition, licence fees, and initial IT infrastructure costs to maintain a large payroll environment may be costly, reduced payroll personnel, training and support costs will ensure lower payroll overheads in the long term. Some multi-national payrolls working across different locations with different tax requirements and time zones are often regionalised.

## 10.6  Integration of payroll and HR databases

Payroll and HR databases carry a vast amount of duplicate information. In addition, certain payroll information is used in the determination of values required by reports sent to statutory bodies as required.

Sharing a database means that no duplicate entry of data are required, and no interfacing or integration of data are required. Entering duplicate information into different databases may lead to data integrity issues, and also requires more manpower hours. Where an interface is provided between the payroll and HR databases, data may not be available in real time on either system, resulting in outdated information. Controls also need to be in place to ensure that data are loaded in the correct location, in order to prevent data loss.

A consideration when determining which system to use is not necessarily whether it provides an integrated database, but whether it provides the ability to interface with other software providers. The ability to interface and integrate with other software providers will enable you to select the software package that is best suited to your needs and requirements, even if it means purchasing systems from different providers. Integration between these chosen systems, which cater for specific needs and requirements, will provide a total solution to the user which far exceeds the benefits of having a single database from a single software provider. The effectiveness of the workflow capabilities of the interface is also a consideration to keep in mind, as this is a determining factor in how flexible processes can be.

A further consideration regarding integrated systems is that processes and procedures of the payroll and HR departments need to be aligned more closely, since these departments are now working on the same data at the same time. The processes, from recruitment through to third party, interfacing at month-end, need to be aligned to ensure data integrity.

## 10.7  Web-based solutions

The introduction of hosted software and service offerings has caused a shift in both development and usage of software. Software-as-a-Service (SaaS) is a great option for businesses that lack the financial and technical resources to implement, customise and maintain in-house software and IT infrastructure. The main benefits of making use of hosted applications are decreased IT costs; having access to the software and data anytime, anywhere; and the software provider ensuring safe and secure data hosting. In addition, implementation, maintenance and training costs are kept to a minimum.

Support queries are aided by having access (permission granted) to actual client data. This leads to more efficient support and reduced support time. In addition, updates, enhancements and bug fixes can be made on a regular basis and without user intervention. Regular updating of software also leads to faster learning by the user and simplified customer support.

## 10.8 Payroll services

### 10.8.1 Payroll outsourcing

Companies are under constant pressure to do more with less – to reduce costs but also provide better service. Market trends have indicated that outsourced payrolls are highly cost effective, especially for smaller businesses that cannot afford a payroll department or dedicated payroll personnel. In certain circumstances, an outsourcing solution might not be more cost effective when directly translating the cost of an internal appointment compared to the outsourcing cost. One has to take into consideration the whole value proposition, especially where industry knowledge and survey information are part of the outsourced solution.

Outsourcing helps payroll and HR professionals to free themselves from routine tasks to enable them to take part in strategic processes. The following benefits are experienced:

- **Reduction in needed company resources:** Generally, a single resource or employee is needed as main payroll contact to enable the successful operation of an outsourced payroll. Payroll management is a time-consuming activity, so with this burden removed, other employees can be redeployed to focus on core business activities.
- **Reduction in payroll associated maintenance costs:** The outsourcing department employs only highly efficient and trained individuals who have in-depth theoretical and practical payroll and payroll product knowledge. All maintenance is to be performed by these employees and therefore no external parties are needed to carry out system changes at high hourly rates.
- **Payroll is delivered accurately and on time:** Human capital is an employer's greatest asset. It is therefore of the utmost importance to ensure that confidence and faith are instilled in all levels of the company to ensure a highly satisfied and trusting workforce. This can be achieved by supplying employees with a stable and trustworthy payroll. The outsourcing service provider should also ensure that the payroll is kept in line with the latest statutory requirements and therefore out of the watchful eye of tax and labour authorities.
- **Company expansion:** Outsourcing your payroll gives you better scope for expansion of your company without employing additional payroll staff to deal with the growing business.
- **Training:** Training costs are drastically reduced as the detailed knowledge required for maintaining a statutory compliant payroll is retained within the scope of the outsourcing service.
- **Staff turnover and continuity:** It is often extremely difficult to replace key resources in a company's payroll environment. The outsourced solution will provide the client with a trouble-free continuous management system by means of which the problem is passed to the outsourcing service provider.

- **Security and technology:** Data security is of the utmost importance in a payroll environment, and it is extremely important for the service provider to comply with very stringent standards and requirements. All data are protected against piracy and intrusion by making use of cutting-edge safety technology and user-access control.

Typical value-added services provided by outsourced service providers include a needs analysis to tailor the service solution to the requirements of each client. High-level reviews of remuneration structures are done to ensure compliance with current legislation and statutory requirements. Leave administration forms part of most standard payroll outsourcing solutions. The preparation of payslips and the payment of employee salaries and third-party payments can be handled as part of the service. Reporting and submission of statutory reports are essential components of an outsourcing service solution.

### 10.8.2    Employee self-service

Employee self-service (ESS) is usually a web-based application which integrates with payroll and HR software packages either uni- or bi-directionally. ESS empowers staff to maintain their personal details, change benefit options, apply for leave and training, and view information such as their personal development plan, pay slips and all deductions in a paperless environment. It also gives line managers the ability to maintain and view employee details even when out of the office.

In the ever-changing environment of managing staff, ESS applications have proven to be an asset. Advantages to the employer with the implementation of an ESS application include the reduction of labour-intensive capturing of data into payroll, and HR transactions and details. Employees now have the ability to view and update certain information themselves, which is managed by a workflow system in order to authorise the updating of the information into applicable applications. This workflow system also aids in tracking the submission of requests such as leave and training.

Processes such as leave management can be controlled more closely, providing up-to-date leave information and provisioning information at any time.

Making use of an ESS application reduces printing and distribution costs, as relevant information is available to employees online. A history of payslip and tax and other deductions is available to employees, reducing queries to the payroll and HR departments.

## 10.9  Summary

Payroll has become more complex in many countries because of the many different currencies, pay regulations, allowances and tax systems, yet in some countries it is becoming far easier because everyone is moving towards a straight cash package. Accuracy and legal compliance are key considerations when running the payroll. The extent of confidentiality needs to be carefully set out in the remuneration policy. A growing trend is the integration of the payroll and HR software packages, with the inclusion of employee self-service (ESS) and the outsourcing of payroll responsibilities.

## 10.10  Self-evaluation questions

1. What should you do to enhance confidentiality of the payroll?
2. Name some payroll trends.
3. Should the payroll and HR database be integrated?
4. Describe what is meant by employee self-service.

# CHAPTER 11

## Team-based Pay

### 11.1 Types of teams

Team-based pay schemes provide financial rewards to individual employees working within formally established teams with shared objectives. Payments under the scheme depend on team performance and they can be shared equally among team members, or distribution can vary between individuals. The payment can be made in the form of a bonus or lump sum which might not be pensionable, or can be a consolidated part of salary and pensionable.

Generally speaking, there are three types of teams: parallel, project and work. The members of parallel teams, project teams and work teams are interdependent and work on a common task, although they may or may not be from the same organisational unit.

#### 11.1.1 Parallel teams

Parallel teams supplement the regular organisational structure and perform problem-solving and improvement-oriented tasks. Parallel teams usually contribute useful ideas about how to improve quality and productivity. Examples of parallel teams are problem-solving teams, quality circles, quality improvement teams, and employee participation teams. These improvement-oriented teams are called parallel teams because participating employees are taken out of their regular organisations and placed in separate team structures with different operating procedures and objectives. Parallel teams usually meet regularly (each week or two) and follow a defined problem-solving or quality-improvement process. Employees are trained in the use of these processes and make recommendations that are considered by the management hierarchy. Typically, no change results unless management approves the recommendations.

#### 11.1.2 Project teams

Project teams involve a diverse group of knowledge workers, such as design engineers, process engineers, programmers and marketing managers. They are brought together to conduct projects for a defined but typically extended period of time. These knowledge workers apply their disparate specialities to develop innovations and fulfil customer requirements. Examples of project teams are new product development teams, information systems teams and new factory design teams. Project teams are assigned unique, uncertain tasks and are expected to innovate. Their products are usually identifiable, but measurement may be difficult because the value of the unique output may not be known for a long time after the work is completed. Project teams usually have broad mandates and considerable authority. They are assigned the responsibility of making key decisions within broad strategic parameters. Project teams need    to respond to the requirements of their sponsors and customers for their work. Therefore, they balance the need for independent thinking with responsiveness to key stakeholders and make sure that appropriate external communication occurs. Finally, project teams are structures that disband once projects are completed.

### 11.1.3 Work teams

Work teams are responsible for producing a product or providing a service; they are self-contained identifiable work units that control the processes involved in transforming inputs into measurable outputs. They are performing units in which members report through the team and are responsible for the group's performance. Work teams are found most frequently in manufacturing settings, but this design is applicable to any situation in which people are interdependent and can be collectively responsible for a product or service. Examples include production, assembly, administrative support, insurance processing, customer sales and service, and management teams. For work team members to take responsibility for the team's performance, they must feel in control of the work processes and make key decisions about how the work is done. The degree of management responsibility placed in the group varies significantly. Typically, work teams control how the task is performed, but not what is performed. Management sets performance and quality standards.

## 11.2   Parallel teams and pay

Because parallel teams are an extra, they have the fewest implications for the reward system in an organisation. They are an add-on and, as such, can potentially be supported by add-on reward systems. Rewards can and should be used to motivate effective problem-solving. Membership is not usually an issue because individuals are already members of the organisation and are released from their regular, often less interesting, work to participate in problem-solving activities.

A relatively wide variety of approaches can be used to reward parallel teams for the effectiveness of their problem-solving work. Gain-sharing works particularly well when it is combined with problem-solving groups, open financial-information systems and participative decision-making. A major motivational weakness with gain-sharing plans is that the line of sight between a suggestion and the size of a bonus is weak.

| | |
|---|---|
| ***Example of gain-sharing*** | |
| A typical formula is: | |
| Share in the improvement on the formula | Output |
| | Input |

The sharing debate should start at 50:50 between employees and the organisation, but this can differ, depending on whether the organisation is capital-intensive or labour-intensive.

---

*Example*

1. The formula could be:
   Sales income/Salary costs and raw materials + other controllable costs

2. In numbers it could be: 10m/5m = 2

3. The numbers are usually taken from what happened the previous year, and one shares in improvements to the ratio.

4. Sharing takes place when:

   - Output grows and input stays constant (15m/5m = 3m).
   - Output stays constant and input reduces (10m/3.33m = 3m).
   - Output increases and input decreases (12m/4m = 3m).

---

In all cases, there is an improvement of one, and this would be shared 50:50 between employees and employer.

## 11.3  Project teams and pay

The use of project teams presents a particularly interesting challenge for reward systems. They often require a reward system that is specifically designed to support them. The obvious first choice for motivating a group is a reward system that establishes metrics for successful group performance and sets rewards that are tied to the accomplishments of the group. It is also desirable to have the rewards distributed at the time the group completes its project. One alternative to rewarding group performance at the end of each project is to rely on a gain-sharing plan or a collective pay-for-performance system that covers a total organisational unit. This may be the preferred alternative to rewarding individual teams when, in fact, the teams' activities have a major impact on the effectiveness of the unit, and it is difficult to measure the effectiveness of each team. It also may be a preferred alternative if project teams are in existence for short periods of time.

Sometimes it is necessary and desirable to focus on individual performance in a project team environment. The best approach is to measure the contributions of individuals to the team's effectiveness and to measure each individual's performance at the completion of each project. Individual ratings can be modified by the success of the overall project. In many cases, peer ratings, as well as customer satisfaction ratings, need to be used. Peer ratings are particularly critical because, in most project teams, peers are in the best position to assess the contribution of team members.

In many respects, skills-based pay fits a project-based organisation better than job-based pay. In a true project-based organisation, often it is not clear what an individual's job is. What must be clear are the skills the individual has. Often, the critical organisational effectiveness issue is developing the right skills mix so projects can be staffed with individuals who are competent to execute them.

Attainment of skill or competence is not enough, however – it must lead to increased performance and results. Combining the two, competence and performance, into one milestone alleviates the debate about whether to pay for skills held or skills needed. This is illustrated in Figure 11.1 below.

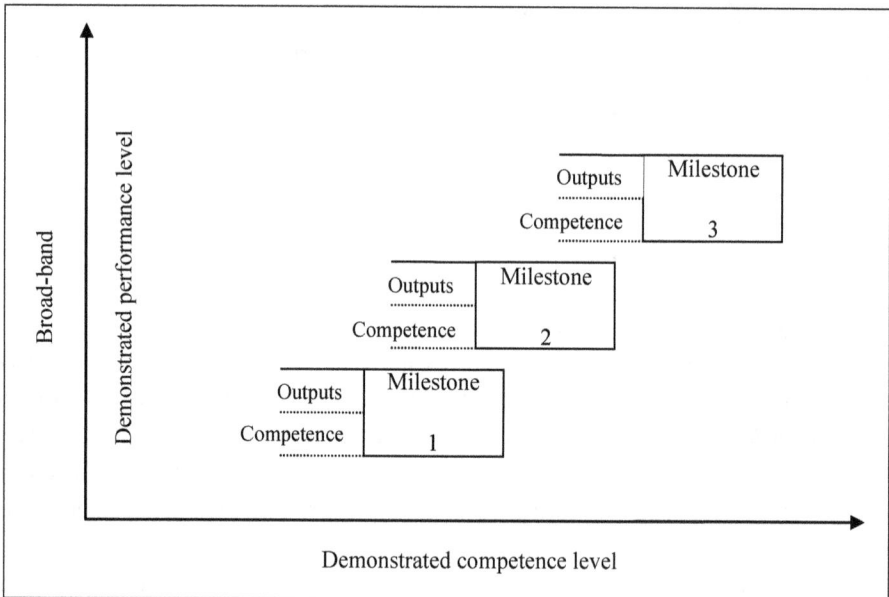

*Figure 11.1: Paying for combined milestones*

## 11.4  Work teams and pay

The use of work teams requires a fundamental shift in reward practices. Traditional reward practices are designed to support individual job performance through individual pay-for-performance systems and job-based remuneration. Neither of these practices fits the requirements of work teams.

The most effective way to motivate team performance is to establish objectives and metrics for successful team performance, and link rewards to team success. There are three ways of rewarding performance at the team level. First, rewards can be tied to team performance through the use of a merit-pay system based on team performance appraisals. Second, special awards can be given to teams to recognise outstanding performance. Third, rewards can be given to teams by using gain-sharing plans.

Merit pay in the form of salary increases or bonuses can be distributed to a team based upon the results of a team performance appraisal. For performance appraisal to work for teams, there must be clear and explicit objectives, accepted measures, and feedback about team performance. Team performance appraisals provide opportunities for teams to conduct self-appraisals and obtain customer evaluations. This data can be used to assist managers in the determination of team ratings.

### 11.4.1   Option 1

If team members are not highly interdependent, then it may make sense to combine team and individual merit pay. A bonus pool can be created based on team performance, with the amounts divided among members based on individual performance. For this not to be divisive, it is critical that the manager solicit input from team members about the relative contributions of individual members. It is more effective if team members assess team performance before individual performance, because team performance sets the framework for individual performance. Individuals will perform better if team members support one another, understand all the components of the team task, and have the opportunity to develop multiple skills.

### 11.4.2   Option 2

The second way of linking pay to team performance is through the use of special award or recognition programmes. Programmes of this type reward exceptional performance after it has occurred. Special awards should be used only to recognise special team achievements. Because work teams perform ongoing and repeated work to produce products or services, performance that meets the requirements of customers should happen regularly, but extraordinary performance will be rare.

### 11.4.3   Option 3

Gain-sharing is the third major approach that can be used to provide rewards for team performance. Gain-sharing requires the work unit covered to be relatively autonomous, responsible for a measurable output, and comprised of members who are interdependent. Gain-sharing is particularly well suited to the participative nature of work teams. It provides motivation for work teams to monitor their performance and learn about leverage points for improving performance. Gain-sharing can help work teams identify ways to improve their performance continuously.

In general, an organisation composed of work teams needs to make sure the pay-for-performance systems it has in place motivate team performance. This can be done by the design of the right mix of team-level and organisational-level pay-for-performance systems. The more that work teams stand alone as performing units, the more rewards should be focused at the team level. The greater the interdependencies between work teams and functional groups, and among different work teams, the more the pay-for-performance systems should operate at the organisational level.

Skills-based pay is well suited to work teams and is used most commonly in team environments. Skills-based pay should be designed to motivate team members to be cross-trained and become multi-skilled. Skills-based pay should also be used to encourage team members to learn vertical skills that are applicable to work normally performed by managers. This learning is critical if a team is to operate in a self-managing manner and not just as a traditional work group.

---

### Example of team-based pay

A work line at a flour mill business looked like this:

| Job 1 | Job 2 | Job 3 | Job 4 |
|-------|-------|-------|-------|
| Job 5 | Job 6 | | |

---

The van driver found that he was missing his time slots for delivery. This meant great inconvenience, not only to the driver, but the business was also losing out through the inefficiencies of the van returning with undelivered flour. The problem encountered was that other people in the work line did not want to assist the van driver as it was not in their job description, and there was no additional remuneration for the work done. The job descriptions were rigid, with many job titles and grades, and teamwork and co-operation were at an all-time low.

### The solution?

All the old job descriptions were discarded in favour of a work domain description, which gave the description of the entire work line rather than each task along it. The result was as follows:

---

There were six different job titles for six different jobs. They were as follows:

Work domain description

- **Flour loader:** Flour was poured from the milling machine into a sack. When it reached the 100kg mark, this person stopped the machine and passed it on to the next job.
- **Finisher:** An industrial sewing machine was used to seal off the flour bags before they were passed on to the trolley packer.
- **Trolley packer:** Flour bags were taken on a trolley to the waiting van to be loaded.
- **Flour packer:** This person loaded bags onto the van.
- **Van assistant:** This worker helped with loading and offloading the van.
- **Van driver:** The van driver was responsible for the safe delivery of the bags of flour.

---

Added to this, a remuneration pool of 30,000 per month was given to the team to split as they saw fit. The team decided that everyone should receive the same, except for the driver, who received a little more. This encouraged them to multi-skill, and ultimately, they could all work up and down the work line. Teamwork was greatly enhanced through this process.

When one of the six workers retired, the others were encouraged to recruit their own fellow work line member. On asking if the pool amount would change if no one was recruited, the answer was that it would not. The workers then decided not to recruit the new person and instead worked the line with five people.

A summary of these approaches to team-based pay is shown in Table 11.1.

*Table 11.1: How pay systems fit with teams*

| Pay system | Type of team | | |
|---|---|---|---|
| | **Work team** | **Project team** | **Parallel team** |
| Skills-based pay | ✓ | ✓ | |
| Job-based pay | | | ✓ |
| Individual merit pay | | | ✓ |
| Gain-sharing | | | ✓ |
| Recognition schemes | | | ✓ |
| Team- or unit-level reward | ✓ | ✓ | |

## 11.5  Best practice guidelines

- **Do not rely on peer group pressure to deal with "freeloaders".** Handle individual performance issues effectively and swiftly.
- Ensure that if you have teamwork and team pay, there is an **adequate system for individuals to develop themselves** and to advance their careers. Make sure the individual development dimension is not lost.
- **Team performance indicators** which may be suitable in the design of a team bonus scheme (probably using a combination of factors) include:
  - Quantity of work done by the team.
  - Cost effectiveness or value for money indicators.
  - Customer/client satisfaction surveys.
  - Level or value of sales.
  - Speed and/or accuracy of work.
  - Staff development indices (e.g. levels of skills, staff retention and staff turnover).

When team bonuses are used, they should be paid on top of a fair level of basic pay. It is not advisable to make more than about 15-20 percent of an individual's total earnings depend on team performance, as the pressure on individuals will be too immense and may prove counterproductive.

The aspects of team performance which are measured for this purpose must be those over which team members have adequate control or influence. If people can control only how the work is done and not the amount of work, then bonus criteria should reflect quality standards rather than quantity of work.

The distribution of payments to the team needs careful handling, otherwise everyone will receive the same. There must be some open and apparent reason for an uneven distribution.

Consider very carefully whether team-based pay is right for your organisation. Research has shown that team incentives work in environments where there is interdependence.[1] Understanding the key attributes of effective teams is easy. Cultivating their attributes in your organisation may be quite different. While there is no magic pill to solve this dilemma, a rewards and recognition programme can go a long way to achieving tangible results.

## 11.6  Why teams sometimes fail

Although team-based pay is critical to the success of teamwork in the workplace, many teams fail regardless of the pay system. Some common reasons why some teams fail to meet expectations are:

- Unclear goals.
- Changing objectives.
- Lack of accountability.
- Lack of management support.
- Lack of role clarity.
- Ineffective leadership.
- Low priority of team.
- No team-based pay.

Teams do not usually fail because the individual skills are inadequate, nor because they do not enshrine the virtues of customer satisfaction, quality and so forth. Teams often fail when people in them do not feel safe going after their own stated goals. In other words, individuals do not know what they are trying to achieve with their team.

Organisations establish bonuses to motivate people, but bonuses do not motivate when they are automatic or guaranteed. Teams will not carry out business objectives if doing so puts them or their jobs at risk.

---

1    Diez, 2018.

## 11.7  What makes a good team?

All successful teams demonstrate the same fundamental features, such as:

- Strong and effective leadership.
- Clear objectives.
- The ability to make informed decisions.
- The ability to act quickly on these decisions.
- Free communication.
- The requisite skills and techniques to fulfil the project at hand.
- Clear targets for the team to work toward.

The next section explores various team-based pay plans.

## 11.8  Different types of team incentive plans

Building successful teams requires the delicate balance of remunerating individual efforts as well as team efforts. The pay-for-performance plans may be divided into four main areas:

- Individual-based plans.
- Team-based plans.
- Business area- or department-wide pay-for-performance plans.
- Corporation-wide pay-for-performance plans.

Picking the right plan gives an organisation a competitive advantage. A brief description of each type of plan is set out below.

### 11.8.1  Individual-based plans

- Individual-based plans are the most widely used pay-for-performance plans.
- Of the individual-based plans commonly used, merit pay is by far the most popular; its use is almost universal.
- Merit pay consists of an increase in base pay, normally given once a year.
- Supervisors' ratings of employees' performance are typically used to determine the amount of merit pay granted.
- Once a merit pay increase is given to an employee, it remains a part of that employee's base salary for the rest of his or her tenure with the organisation.
- In addition to merit pay, another fairly common individual incentive is the annual bonus.
- This is also based on the ratings of supervisors, although often measured against pre-set targets.
- Payments of these bonuses are usually in cash.

### 11.8.2   Team-based plans

- Team-based plans normally reward all team members equally, based on group outcomes.
- These outcomes are often measured objectively against pre-set team targets.
- The criteria for defining a desirable outcome may be broad or narrow.
- Payments to team members may be made in the form of a cash bonus or in the form of non-cash rewards such as trips, time off, or luxury items.

### 11.8.3   Business area- or department-wide pay-for-performance plans

- Performance plans in this category normally reward all team members equally, based on group outcomes.
- These outcomes may be measured objectively or subjectively.
- The criteria for defining a desirable outcome may be broad or narrow.
- Payments to team members may be made in the form of a cash bonus or in the form of non-cash rewards such as trips, time off, or luxury items.

### 11.8.4   Corporation-wide pay-for-performance plans

- These performance plans reward all employees based on the entire corporation's performance.
- The most widely used programmes of this kind are profit-sharing or share schemes.
- Profit-sharing is a corporate-wide pay-for-performance plan that uses a formula to allocate a portion of declared profits to employees.
- Typically, profit distributions under a profit-sharing plan are in the form of a cash bonus and are not added to salary.

## 11.9   Design considerations

The basic elements of an incentive plan are:

- Purpose and objectives.
- Eligibility to receive incentives.
- Participation.
- Alignment of team and organisational goals.
- Funding.
- Measurement.
- Timing (shorter time between payoffs is better because it raises motivation).
- Administration.
- Unhitching.
- Arbitration.
- Evaluation of whether or not the plan needs to be changed.

The elements form the headings of the incentive scheme rules. The rules need to be transparent and easily available for all to see.

## 11.10 Performance measurement

Perhaps as important as a good team-based remuneration programme is the ability to measure the performance of a team. One cannot pay for performance until one knows what the measurements are. The first step is to identify the measures, then link them to the appraisal, before linking the appraisal to remuneration.

Finding the right things to measure is critical. The measurement must be something that the team has control over and something that has the potential to add value to the business. The following African saying illustrates the point: "Don't tell me how many flowers you visited; tell me how much honey you produced." The honey is the accomplishment; the valuable result. Visiting the flowers is just the process. The number of flowers visited is measurable, but it's the wrong measure.

Not all measures can be quantified. Sometimes numbers are not appropriate and verifiable, and descriptive measures are needed instead.

## 11.11 Rewarding top performers

How awards are presented to top performers is just as important as the awards themselves. Below are some useful thoughts to consider:

- The right awards presenter must be selected. That does not mean you need a celebrity or even the CEO. The person in the organisation with the highest rank who knows the employees personally and knows what they have accomplished is a very suitable choice.
- If feasible, an audience of the employees' peers should be assembled for the presentation. This yields a dual advantage. It is an effective way to recognise the award winners, and it will build pride in the organisation in other employees as well.
- Stress the employees' performance and highlight their personal contributions. Be specific and note the positive effects of what these employees have done to earn their awards.
- Include a few anecdotes and a brief history to show how the employees' achievements tie to the organisation's culture and values.
- Thank employees sincerely. The best way to make a memorable impact is to offer a simple thank you, said with obvious gratitude.

## 11.12   Pay – The final frontier

When you get to the point of determining team-based pay, address the following questions:

- How should individual performance be factored into pay decisions?
- How much of a bonus is the correct amount?
- Should team members be paid different bonuses?
- Will the incremental pay be enough to boost performance, or will we end up spending more without achieving more?

If there is any formula for success at team-based pay, it is this: design the teams well first, and make sure the organisation's culture supports them. Then, and only then, worry about how to pay them. Figure 11.2 shows an example of a team-based pay performance matrix.

| Team (Highest ranking to lowest ranking) | Average performance | Individual increase/ incentive |
|---|---|---|
| Team 1 |  | **Team 1** |
|  | 7% | Top 8 – 9% |
|  |  | Middle 7% |
|  |  | Bottom 5% |
| Team 8 |  | **Team 8** |
|  | 4% | Top 6% |
|  |  | Middle 4% |
|  |  | Bottom 2% |
| Team 16 |  | **Team 16** |
|  | 0% | All 0% |

*Figure 11.2: An example of a team-based pay performance matrix*

## 11.13   Advantages and disadvantages of various incentive schemes

**Gain-sharing** is a system whereby money or resources that are saved by a team are returned, in some degree, to the team. Gain-sharing, which is in used in a great number of companies around the world, links people's pay with organisational success. The easiest gain-sharing plan to set up is an organisation-wide or location-wide system. It is harder to measure the success of most kinds of teams in money, although design, research, quality improvement and problem-solving teams are exceptions.

**Profit-sharing** is better known and more widely spread than gain-sharing, perhaps because the idea is simpler. Every year or quarter, a portion of the profit achieved is paid to employees based on corporate or division-wide performance. The problem is that profit is a single, organisation-wide measure, thus the line of sight for low-level employees is poor.

**Employee ownership** plans go by such names as share option plans, share purchase plans, and employee share ownership plans. However, although the concept of ownership is great, line of sight as to how each individual or team's work influences share price is poor for most employees.

The key to supporting teams in any form is moving knowledge, information, power and rewards downwards in the organisation, essentially overcoming a hierarchical structure that generally does not support team operation.

**Non-financial rewards/recognition schemes**. Few team leaders have a laundry basket of financial favours to hand out to deserving team members, but there are still many no-cost or low-cost ways to keep team members involved and willing to perform. Some ideas are:

- Establish a prize.
- Get team members involved.
- You may not get rich, but you can be famous!
- Praise in print.
- Meet the boss.
- Share the spotlight.
- Treat team members to a free lunch.
- Lavish team members with attention.

Napoleon said one could not pay a soldier enough to go into battle, but he would die for a yellow ribbon.

## 11.14 Some final thoughts on teams and pay

### 11.14.1 Enhancing teamwork

- Select a leader who is well liked and respected by the other team members. The leader should be motivated and enthusiastic about the focus of the team.
- Recruit team members from different units and different levels.
- Be sure that each team has a common goal and definitive strategies to help them accomplish that goal. Each team member must know what is expected of him or her.
- Establish a method for each team to communicate its status and activities to the rest of the organisation.
- Develop a system to reward each team and stick to it. It should include both individual and team incentives.

There is no silver bullet, but there have been some interesting lessons learnt about rewarding teams over the years.

- A cash award has to be generous enough to get team members' attention.
- Team bonuses can be linked to milestones, such as bringing in a project on time and on budget.
- A milestone bonus must be vested when earned – but you may decide against paying it out right away. This encourages teams to keep moving forward and not to view the milestone as an end point.
- Consider letting the team members divide up the bonus pool.
- Cash awards are manageable when people in an organisation participate in only one or two teams.
- Give employees a choice. Non-cash awards can be just as effective as cash awards.
- Offering a choice does not require you to use a catalogue. The key is offering employees the choice. Consider developing a menu of rewards, for example, movie tickets, dinner, paying for a specialist service, or a parking space.
- Combine cash and non-cash awards. This ensures that employees receive a tangible reward as well as the intangible "pat on the back" from the "Big Boss".

Remuneration is a key component of team-based reward systems. There needs to be a fine balance between rewarding individual contributions in teams and the team effort as a whole. Team rewards should be based on the achievement of team goals that are very closely aligned with the overall organisational strategy and goals.

## 11.15  Summary

A growing international trend is to harness the strength of teamwork. Well-functioning teams deserve great rewards and team-based pay needs to be seen to be fair. Team-based pay is often a function of rewarding milestones, competence and outputs. Key design considerations are whether to reward the team members equally or whether to differentiate performance within a team. How about letting the team decide which it is?

## 11.16  Self-evaluation questions

- Name the main types of teams.
- What are the key pay considerations for project teams?
- What are some of the best-practice guidelines for teams?
- What makes a team good?
- How can you enhance teamwork?

**Side Bar**

How much of the total incentive received by each individual should come from corporate results? Or should incentives be tied more to teams? Or to individuals?

The Finance function is generally inclined towards increasing the percentage of variable pay, based on overall corporate results. The logic is fairly straightforward: if the company has additional profits to spare, then there will be enough money to share. And if results are not positive, then there is no need to pay additional money, thus reducing financial risk. From an HR perspective, many practitioners would rather err on the side of more money being paid, more fixed pay and more incentives tied to individual performance, as this way each individual has clear line of sight between their efforts and the payout received. How then to reconcile these two extremes?

One rule of thumb is that the higher up the role being addressed is in the organisation, the more variable pay should be used, and the more of it that should be tied to corporate results. This allows to keep pace with the principle of line of sight while at the same time increasing variable pay tied to company results. Graphically it would look like this:

**Illustrative: Percentage of incentives from company/individual results, by level**

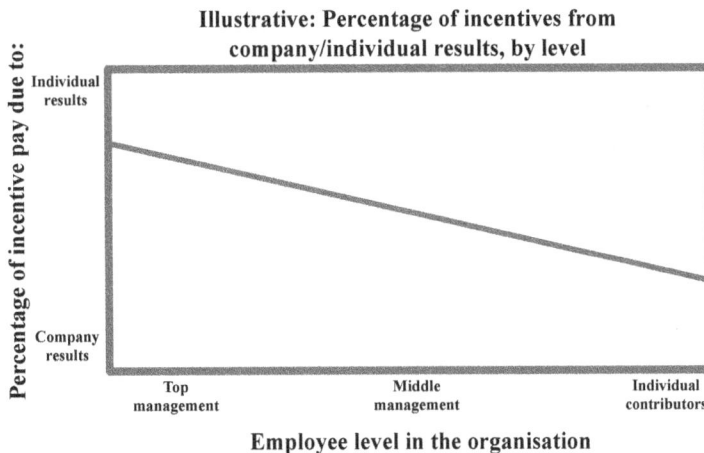

**Employee level in the organisation**

# CHAPTER 12

## Variable Pay and Incentive Schemes

This chapter describes the various types of variable pay systems and incentive schemes available for general employees. The next two chapters go into detail on what we introduce in this chapter. Sales force schemes and Executive Pay programmes are treated elsewhere in the book.

### 12.1 Variable pay and incentive schemes

The most common forms of variable rewards are normally described under the headings of short-term incentives (STIs) and long-term incentives (LTIs). There are many different definitions for these but, broadly speaking, they can be grouped as per the sections below:

#### 12.1.1 Short-term incentives (STIs)

These are incentive schemes that reward superior performance over a period of up to one year. Typically they reward what happened last year and look backwards. The main examples of STIs are:

- Profit-sharing (PS).
- Gain-sharing (GS).
- Bonus schemes (BS).
- Commission schemes (CS).

#### 12.1.2 Long-term incentives (LTIs)

These are incentive schemes that look into the future and reward superior performance over more than one year. Typical examples are:

- Rolling incentives (RI).
- Value-add schemes (VAS).
- Share schemes (SS).

Organisations should use both STIs and LTIs in their remuneration mix.[1] The primary purpose of this is that it encourages the long-term viability of the organisation and executives are encouraged not to "fleece" the organisation for short-term gains, because they would have too much to lose in the long-term..[2] A well-designed total earnings scheme should prevent this from happening.

---

1  Begbie, Bussin & Schurink, 2011; Malambe & Bussin, 2013.

2  Grigoriadis & Bussin, 2007.

## 12.2 Difference between variable pay and "Pay at Risk"

With the concept of "pay at risk", guaranteed pay is put at risk. In other words, you may not be entitled to your total package if you do not achieve certain hurdles. Thereafter you can earn your market-related package, and on top of that, variable pay is applied.[3] This is shown in Figure 12.1.

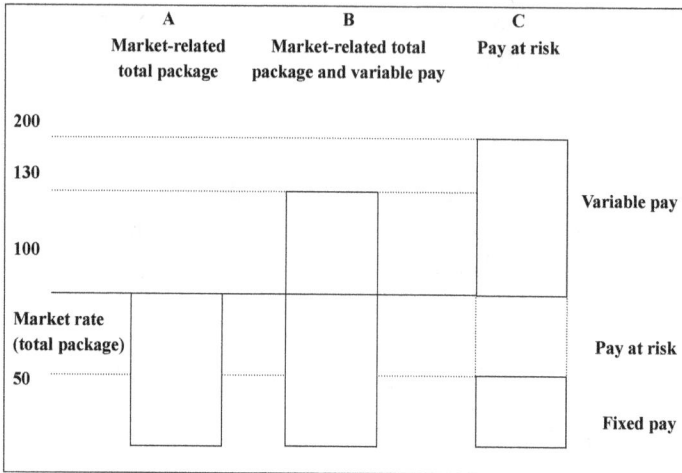

*Figure 12.1: The link between variable pay, fixed pay and pay at risk*

Most organisations around the globe go for option B, whereas in the United States of America, option C has considerable attraction. In our experience, if companies wanted to move towards option C, they would have to give a three- or four-to-one potential payback ratio to persuade participants to give up their fixed pay. It is, of course, easier to implement in "start-up" companies, or with new lines where there is no precedent. In tough economic times, rather than give up current fixed pay, the annual increase can be sacrificed and put at risk for variable pay.

## 12.3 Why implement variable pay?

More and more companies are implementing incentive and bonus schemes. Set out below are some guidelines on selecting an incentive scheme and some of the critical success factors for implementation. Most organisations implement incentive schemes in order to:

- Incite superior individual, team and organisation performance.
- Align with shareholder thinking (agency theory).
- Share some of the wealth created in the organisation.
- Tie the onerous salary bill to the fortunes of the organisation.
- Reward participants for a job well done.
- Drive organisation strategy.

---

3    Sibangilizwe, Bussin & de Swardt, 2013.

- Create more shareholder wealth.

The type of scheme implemented depends largely on what the reason is for wanting to implement the scheme. It also affects the scheme design, principles, measures used, and targets set.[4] It is a widely-held view that there is no one best type of scheme – the scheme has to be designed to drive the behaviour you want. There are, however, vast bodies of research which show that organisations that have financial incentive schemes outperform those which do not.[5]

## 12.4 The business case for incentives and good rewards

Offering top salaries and attractive incentives to staff is the quickest, surest way for an organisation to become profitable, according to a survey conducted in the United States of America.[6]

The comprehensive cross-industry survey study found that investing to attract and keep top sales, marketing and customer service professionals can add more than $40m to a typical $1bn business unit's bottom line. The survey put the potential payback for financial rewards and incentives at $13m. Other investments related to creating a high-performance organisation could add another $27m, including, for example, attracting and retaining "stars" ($10m) and developing selling and service skills ($9.5m).

Sales and marketing remuneration above industry averages were closely related to higher profits in every industry studied. The survey sampled the views of about 500 executives from more than 250 companies such as chemicals, communications, electronics and high technology, forest products, pharmaceuticals and retailing.

For the 21 capabilities with a particularly high effect on organisation profits across industries, it was determined that even moderate improvements could result in additional pre-tax profits of $40m to $50m a year for a typical $1bn business unit. A fully-fledged, multi-pronged approach to driving world-class performance with these 21 capabilities could boost pre-tax profits by $120m to $140m a year. Technology skills ranked among the top value-adding skills in all industries studied. Many capabilities fuelled by technology help groups gain knowledge of customers, convert it into insight, and implement plans based on that insight.[7] Bu using technology to collect and analyse data, then sharing information gained with everyone in the organisation, profits could be lifted by another $12m.

This research takes the guesswork out of where CEOs should put their investment dollars. It starts and finishes with people and the technology that enables them to understand their customers better and to convert that knowledge into tangible results.

---

4   Malambe & Bussin, 2013.

5   Diez, 2018.

6   Business Day, 2000.

7   Begbie, Bussin & Schurink, 2011.

| The 21 highest profit-driving capabilities (m) | |
| --- | --- |
| Incentivising/Rewarding people | 13 |
| Customer services | 13 |
| Turning customer info into insight | 12 |
| Attracting/retaining people | 10 |
| Building selling/service skills | 9.5 |
| Strong value propositions | 9 |
| Partner/alliance investment | 9 |
| eCRM | 8 |
| Sales planning | 7.5 |
| Key account management | 6 |
| Advertising | 5.5 |
| Customer retention/acquisition | 5.5 |
| Managing product and service mix | 5 |
| Promotion | 5 |
| Ability to change the organisation | 5 |
| Measuring profitability | 4.5 |
| New products/services | 3.5 |
| Channel management | 3 |
| Segmentation | 2.5 |
| Building service culture | 2 |
| Brand management | 1.5 |

*Figure 12.2: Profit-driving capabilities*
*Source: Business Day[8]*

## 12.5 Implementation considerations

Implementing variable pay stands a better chance of succeeding if one uses the following headings to guide thinking:

- Purpose of the scheme.
- Scope and eligibility.
- Measures and targets.
- Funding the scheme.
- Sharing ratios between employees and company/shareholders.
- Payment cycle.
- Administration details.

---

8    Business Day, 2000.

- Unhitching.
- Clawback clauses.
- Dispute resolution.

### 12.5.1  Is your organisation ready?

Variable pay has been around for a very long time and is here to stay. Ask the following questions to determine whether or not your organisation is ready to implement a variable pay programme:

- Does the business have substantial control over its performance?
- Have most of the major structural changes or system improvements been completed so that an effort to develop a new pay programme will not be perceived as a waste of time or overwhelming?
- Do clear, reliable measures support the existing strategy and long-term goals of the business?
- Is feedback on actual performance versus desired performance processed to employees in an effective manner?
- Do employees understand the measures and know what actions will lead to improvements?
- Are the current base pay levels internally equitable and externally competitive?
- Do the managers of the business consistently demonstrate leadership skills?
- Is the culture of the group characterised by trust, mutual respect, and a willingness to work toward common goals?
- Does the programme have a sponsor and a champion?

## 12.6  Design considerations

The relationship between guaranteed pay (GP) and variable pay (VP) is known as the remuneration mix. A comparison of the application of remuneration mix across the following variables is shown in the figures and tables below.

- Level in the organisation.
- The stage in the organisation's life cycle.
- Industry.
- Country/Region.

### 12.6.1  Level in the organisation

Figure 12.3 shows how guaranteed pay and variable pay can be applied in relation to job level.

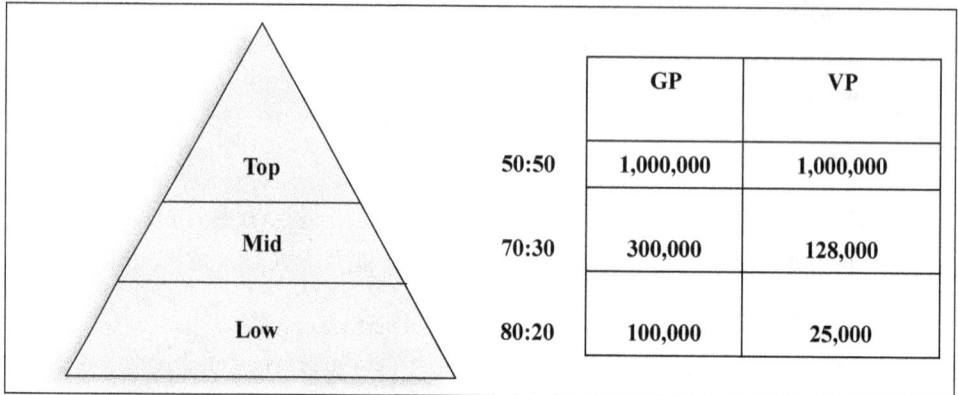

| | GP | VP |
|---|---|---|
| **Top** 50:50 | 1,000,000 | 1,000,000 |
| **Mid** 70:30 | 300,000 | 128,000 |
| **Low** 80:20 | 100,000 | 25,000 |

*Figure 12.3: Remuneration mix by level*

## 12.6.2   Life cycle of the organisation

The way that guaranteed pay and variable pay are balanced within an organisation should be linked to the organisation's stage in its life cycle.

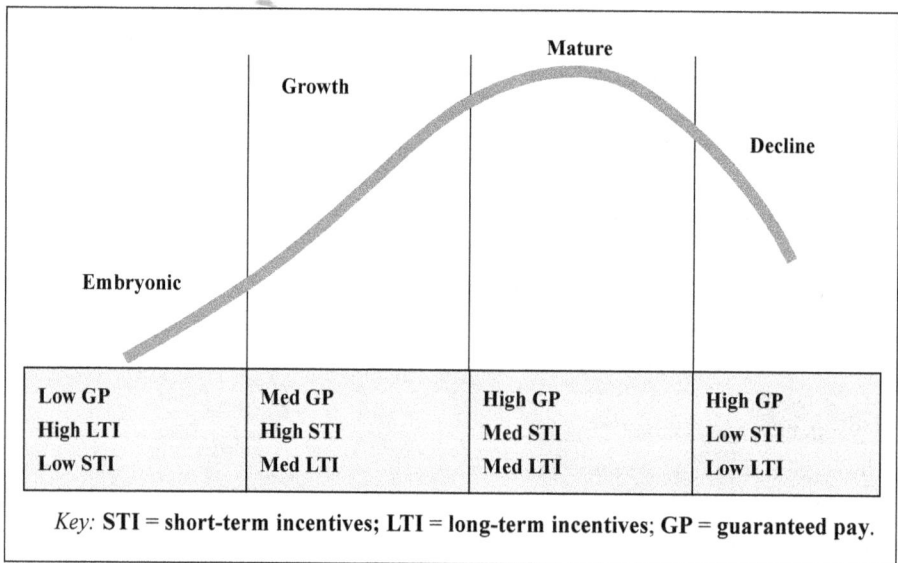

| Low GP | Med GP | High GP | High GP |
|---|---|---|---|
| High LTI | High STI | Med STI | Low STI |
| Low STI | Med LTI | Med LTI | Low LTI |

*Key:* **STI** = short-term incentives; **LTI** = long-term incentives; **GP** = guaranteed pay.

*Figure 12.4: Remuneration mix by organisation life cycle*

## 12.6.3   Comparisons by industry or job

Table 12.1 shows a comparison between the remuneration mix for different jobs and industries.

| GP : VP Ratio | Examples of jobs |
|---|---|
| High GP : Low VP 85 : 15 | • Clerks<br>• Accountants<br>• Parastatal<br>• Government |
| Low GP : High VP 50 : 50 | • Merchant bankers<br>• Treasury<br>• Sales clerks<br>• Dealers<br>• Stockbrokers |

*Figure 12.5: Remuneration mix by job and industry*

### 12.6.4 Comparing ratios by country/region

The typical remuneration mix for CEOs may differ from country to country. An example is shown in Table 12.1.

*Table 12.1: Typical remuneration mix for ceos by region*

| Country | GP | VP |
|---|---|---|
| Africa | 100 | 70 |
| Asia | 100 | 100 |
| United Kingdom | 100 | 120 |
| United States | 100 | 300 |

In countries where inflation is a concern, or where budget forecasts are seldom accurate, GP is preferred over VP. One size does not fit all.

## 12.7 Incentive scheme design and framework

To design the incentive scheme and framework, assess whether the following apply:

- Business objectives of the group as a whole include:
  - Quantitative measures.
  - Usually, financial measures.
  - The same for the whole organisation.
- Strategic objectives of the function, division or department include the following features:
  - Qualitative or quantitative measures.
  - Drivers of the business strategy.
  - Different for each region or function.

- The organisation chooses the percentage weighting for each.
- The same framework applies to the whole organisation.

## 12.8 Design process

Figure 12.6 is a useful step-by-step guide to incentive design and can also be used for change management and communication purposes.

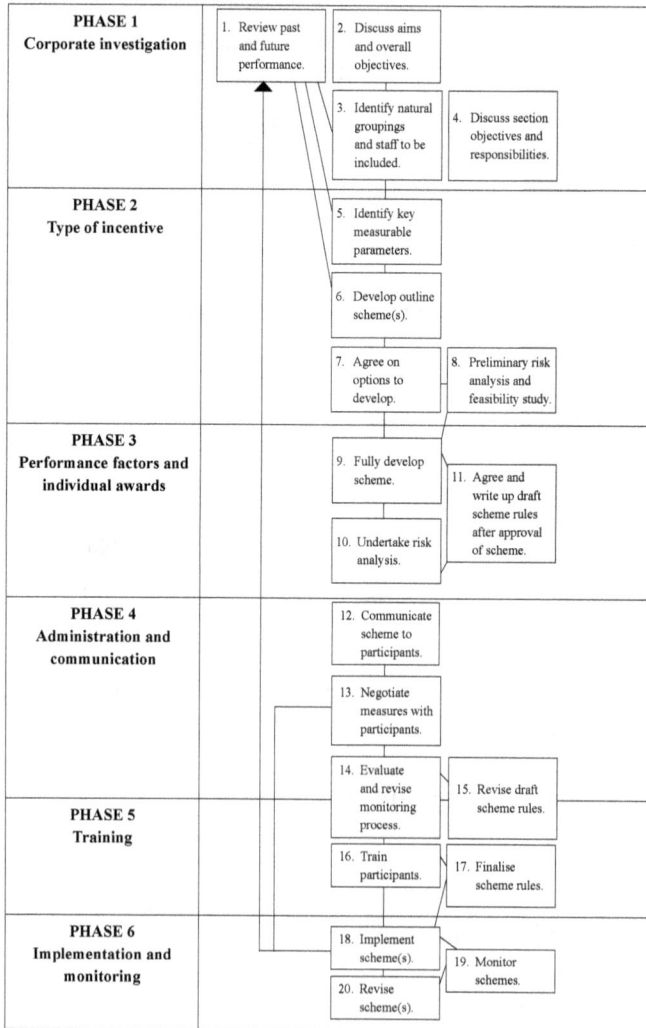

| PHASE 1 Corporate investigation | 1. Review past and future performance. | 2. Discuss aims and overall objectives. | |
|---|---|---|---|
| | | 3. Identify natural groupings and staff to be included. | 4. Discuss section objectives and responsibilities. |
| PHASE 2 Type of incentive | | 5. Identify key measurable parameters. | |
| | | 6. Develop outline scheme(s). | |
| | | 7. Agree on options to develop. | 8. Preliminary risk analysis and feasibility study. |
| PHASE 3 Performance factors and individual awards | | 9. Fully develop scheme. | 11. Agree and write up draft scheme rules after approval of scheme. |
| | | 10. Undertake risk analysis. | |
| PHASE 4 Administration and communication | | 12. Communicate scheme to participants. | |
| | | 13. Negotiate measures with participants. | |
| | | 14. Evaluate and revise monitoring process. | 15. Revise draft scheme rules. |
| PHASE 5 Training | | 16. Train participants. | 17. Finalise scheme rules. |
| PHASE 6 Implementation and monitoring | | 18. Implement scheme(s). | 19. Monitor schemes. |
| | | 20. Revise scheme(s). | |

*Figure 12.6: Incentive scheme design process*

*What works for your organisation?*

The good news about short-term incentive plan design is that the possibilities are endless and the potential for creativity is unlimited. There are more than 25 different methods that can be used for determining incentive awards, so there is no single right answer. The real challenge, therefore, is to select a design process that works well for a given organisation at a given time/period.

## 12.9  Goals for the incentive schemes

Incentive schemes are vital for an organisation because they:

- Establish competitive earnings opportunities.
- Attract and retain high-calibre staff.
- Allow competitiveness in the marketplace.
- Reinforce divisional and corporate goals.
- Encourage exceptional performance.
- Are linked to overall strategies.

## 12.10  Non-negotiable principles for effective incentives

To be effective, incentives must:

- Impact on the bottom line.
- Support and drive organisational objectives.
- Be objective.
- Be measurable.
- Have stretch goals or objectives that are accepted or agreed upon by participants.
- Be communicated.
- Be consistent.
- Have rules.
- Have payouts which are meaningful.

## 12.11 Choice of scheme

The type of scheme chosen must align with employees' line of sight. Some schemes are more appropriate than others for the various levels in a business. In our experience, the best schemes for each level are shown in Figure 12.7.

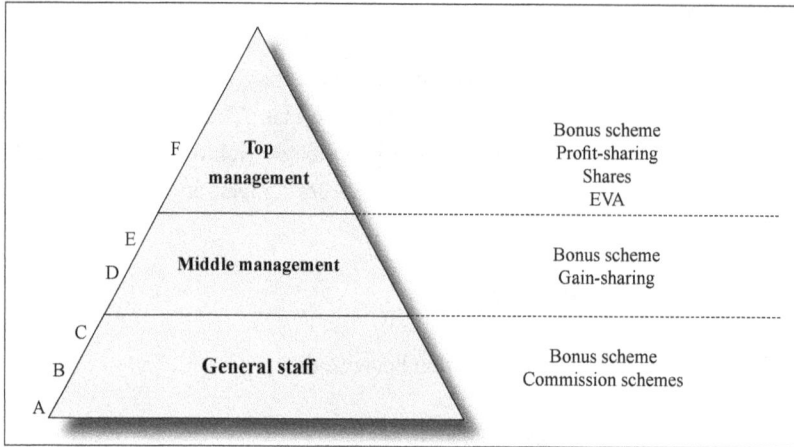

*Figure 12.7: Appropriate incentive scheme by level*

An example of how an organisation can structure their incentive schemes is shown in Figure 12.8. The ranges are typically 50 percent on either side of the average.

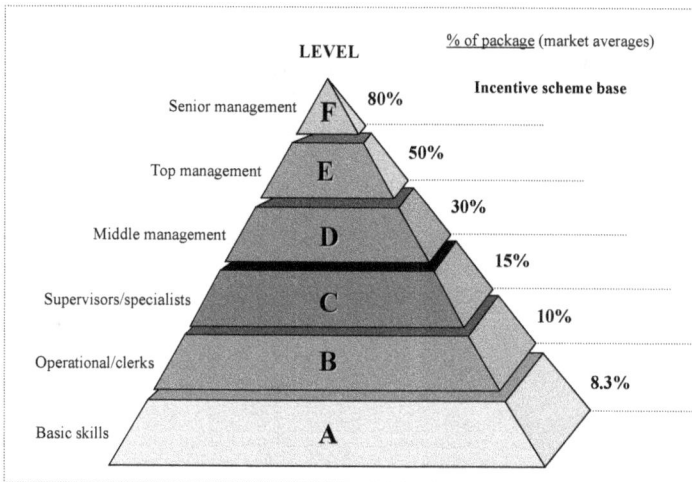

*Figure 12.8: Example of an incentive scheme as a percentage of total guaranteed package*

## 12.12   Size of the incentive award

### 12.12.1 Guidelines

The organisation's total remuneration strategy should drive the size of the award in that it should state:

- How much of the total remuneration is derived from short-term incentives.
- What level of short-term incentive is desired in comparison to market competitive levels.

## 12.12.2 Expressing the amount of short-term incentive

The amount of short-term incentive to be delivered can be expressed as:

- A monetary amount.
- A percentage of salary range midpoint.
- A percentage of salary.

Table 12.2 shows an example of target incentive awards using a salary range midpoint.

*Table 12.2: Salary range midpoint*

| Job level | Salary range midpoint | Target percentage | Target incentive award |
|:---:|:---:|:---:|:---:|
| A | 50,000 | 20% | 10,000 |
| B | 60,000 | 22.5% | 13,500 |
| C | 72,000 | 25% | 18,000 |

## 12.13  Performance measures

The business plan review should provide some good direction on appropriate performance measures. From building the total remuneration strategy plan, designers should know not only the business purpose of their short-term incentive plan, but also the business results it is intended to facilitate and the behaviour and/or results to be rewarded with an incentive remuneration plan payment. The final question is, "How can this performance be measured?"

The answer to the above question provides the right performance measure to use in the plan, however there are two important dimensions that can complicate the selection of a performance measure. These are:

- The organisation level to which the performance measure applies.
- The type of performance measure (financial or non-financial).

As shown in Figure 12.9, performance measures apply to corporate organisations and divisions as well as departments and individuals.

| Performance measures | Organisation level | | | |
|---|---|---|---|---|
| | Corporate | Business unit | Department | Individual |
| Financial | ✓ | ✓ | | |
| Quantitative | | ✓ | | |
| Non-financial | | | ✓ | ✓ |
| Qualitative | | | | ✓ |

*Figure 12.9: Common applications of performance measures*

## 12.13.1 Guidelines for selecting performance measures

The following guidelines apply when choosing the relevant performance measure for your programmes:

*Table 12.3: Guidelines for selecting performance measures*

| Type of performance measure | Examples | Applications |
|---|---|---|
| Financial performance measures | • Net earnings<br>• Net income<br>• ROE<br>• EPS<br>• ROA | Work best for corporate or division units |
| Quantitative performance measures | • Market share<br>• Unit volume<br>• Productivity goals | Work best for corporate or division units |
| Non-financial performance measures | • Implementing a new business system<br>• Completing a new facility | Work best for departments or individuals |
| Qualitative performance measures | • Successfully integrating two similar business functions<br>• Upgrading employee skill levels | Work best for departments or individuals |

## 12.13.2 Decisions about the performance measures to use

The decision regarding which performance measures to use must be made within individual organisations as a short-term incentive plan is designed.

Considering the current business climate and frequent reorganisations and restructurings, non-financial and qualitative performance measures can be valuable in achieving new managerial focus on new business results or different business methods.

### 12.13.3 Matching the performance measures to the plan

Performance measures may also vary based on the type of short-term incentive plan being utilised as follows:

- Sometimes qualitative data are most applicable when using a performance target plan.
- Formula plans, however, use a performance measure such as profit, and individual performance would rarely be a measure in a profit-sharing plan.

---

*Example:*

A typical profit-sharing plan may provide for 10 percent of the pre-tax profits above 8 percent of the organisation's employed capital. Individual awards for participants would then be a proportion of any total amount of the incentive fund.

---

### 12.13.4 Shareholder value as a performance measure

Some financial experts believe that traditional accounting measures, such as earnings per share (EPS) and return on equity (ROE), can be manipulated by executives and improved without having any positive effect on the value of shares held by shareholders.[9] For this reason, some companies use "shareholder value" measures in lieu of standard performance measures. Examples include:

- Discounted cash flow.
- Return on capital versus weighted average cost of capital (Economic Profit).
- Economic value added (EVA)
- Total shareholder return (TSR).

Using economic profit to illustrate the concept further, shareholder value advocates would say that executives should increase the ratio of return on capital versus the weighted average cost of capital because this drives a higher market value of organisation stock held by shareholders.

### 12.13.5 The best performance measure

What kind of performance measure is best? It would be ideal if there were a right answer for everyone, but there is not. The answer depends on what measures:

- Drive success in the business.
- Can be accurately measured.
- Fit the management style of the executive team.

---

9    Bussin, 2018; Bussin & Ncube, 2017; Maloa & Bussin, 2016.

## 12.14   Incentive award determination

Incentive award determination will vary according to the following factors:

- **Size of the organisation:** For smaller companies, this decision may be as simple as having the CEO decide, on a discretionary basis, who contributed the most. Where required, more precise methods are available.
- **Type of plan selected:** Under performance target plans, the initial incentive-fund decisions typically depend on designated performance measures.

Using these plans, companies must decide what will drive incentive awards, namely organisation performance, individual performance or both.

- Organisation performance, or
- Individual performance, or
- Both.

A decision will also have to be made whether to:

- Weight various levels of organisation performance, or
- Select one level of organisation performance to drive the decision on the short-term incentive award.

### 12.14.1 Weighted performance levels

This solution involves weighting the performance levels, for example, corporate performance, 20 percent; division performance, 40 percent; and individual performance, 40 percent. Therefore, the performance of each organisation level contributes to the amount of incentive funds available, as shown in the table below. Note that the corporate and division organisation level did not perform well, but the individual level did, so the total award came out slightly above the total target award.

*Table 12.4: Weighted performance levels*

| Size of target award | Organisation level | Weighting | Adjusted target award | Actual performance | Incentive funds available |
|---|---|---|---|---|---|
| 10,000 | Corporate | 20% | 2,000 | 80% | 1,600 |
|  | Division | 40% | 4,000 | 75% | 3,000 |
|  | Individual | 40% | 4,000 | 150% | 6,000 |
| TOTAL |  |  | 10,000 |  | 10,600 |

## 12.14.2 Organisational performance levels

In order to ensure that incentives are self-funded, many companies believe that one organisational level measure must drive the overall incentive award. This is known as the trigger. For example, exceeding budget net profit – if this is not achieved, then regardless of performance at the other levels, no incentives are paid.

## 12.15  Main features of various types of incentive schemes

This section outlines the main features of each type of scheme and, where possible, common market practice.

### 12.15.1 Individual awards

Individual awards can be allocated from this fund on the basis of individual or department performance, or both.

### 12.15.2 Profit-sharing plans

In profit-sharing plans, awards are allocated to individuals on a pro-rata basis. It is interesting to note that profit-sharing principles can be used in performance target plans. For example, an incentive fund can be determined by a profit-related formula such as the one shown in Figure 12.10.

Formula = 10% of pre-tax profit that exceeds
8% of the organisation's capital employed

| | |
|---|---|
| Capital employed | 100,000,000 |
| Pre-tax profit | 10,000,000 |
| 8% x capital employed | 8,000,000 |
| Amount of profit exceeding 8% | 2,000,000 |
| Amount of incentive fund (10% x 2,000,000) | 200,000 |

*Figure 12.10: Profit-related formula for an incentive fund*

Typically, a predefined percentage of profit before tax is paid into the bonus pool. This is usually done after the budgeted net profit is reached, and market practice ranges between 5 percent and 40 percent of the excess of budgeted net profit. These percentages vary depending on the number of people eligible for participation and the size of the potential pool. Sometimes schemes are designed in such a way that one has to achieve some personal goal(s) to qualify. Table 12.5 shows the main advantages and disadvantages of profit-sharing plans.

---

**Example:**

- Budgeted profit before tax is 10m.
- Bonus pool percentage is 10 percent of the excess.
- Actual achievement is 12m.
- The bonus pool is 10 percent of 2m, which equals 200,000.
- This is often split among participants proportionate to salary (provided that there is internal equity within the organisation's salaries).
- Say participants earn 1m in total.
- The calculation is the bonus pool (200,000) multiplied by 100 divided by the total salary cost (1m) = 20 percent of salary for each participant.

---

*Table 12.5: Main advantages and disadvantages of profit-sharing*

| Main advantages | Main disadvantages |
|---|---|
| • Ease of calculation<br>• It is an important measure | • Only one measure<br>• Poor line of sight for lower-level employees |

## 12.15.3 Gain-sharing

Gain-sharing is typically an organisation-wide formula-based scheme for lower-level staff aimed primarily at improving productivity. The most famous gain-sharing plan is the Scanlon Plan, but there are many different variations on the theme. It differs from profit-sharing in that it has measures which employees at a lower level can control, and excludes items in the income statement such as interest, tax, depreciation, bad debt, and other economic (e.g. foreign currency gains/losses) and accounting (e.g. provisions and amortisations) factors that may influence profit.

*Table 12.6: Main advantages and disadvantages of gain-sharing*

| Main advantages | Main disadvantages |
|---|---|
| • No budget setting; we work off prior period's actual results | • Can get complicated when one "backs out" of new technology that increases output and does not necessarily better productivity |
| • Line of sight and control over measures is good | • Caution against saving on maintenance cost, research and development or safety to reduce input to the detriment of future years |

## 12.15.4 Bonus schemes

Unlike profit-sharing and gain-sharing, bonus schemes are often not formula-driven, but targets are set that are typically quantitative and qualitative in nature. Bonus schemes usually have between four and seven measures, which are carefully chosen to drive business strategy. Targets are usually expressed as threshold (budget), target and stretch target (excellence level). Most organisations would choose a few targets related to the business as a whole (business targets), and then a few for each function or division.

*Table 12.7: Example of bonus scheme framework*

| Targets | Weight | Threshold (Budget) | Target (Budget+x%) | Stretch Target (Budget+y%) |
|---|---|---|---|---|
| **Business targets (organisation-wide)** | | | | |
| 1. EVA | 30% | 5,000,000 | 6,000,000 | 7,000,000 |
| 2. Market share | 20% | 40% | 42% | 44% |
| **Division targets** | | | | |
| 1. Net profit | 20% | 1,000,000 | 1,200,000 | 1,400,000 |
| 2. Implement new line | 10% | On time, in cost | Better | Even better |
| 3. Reduce debtor days | 10% | 60 days | 50 days | 30 days |
| 4. Achieve equity targets | 10% | 45% | 50% | 55% |

Actual performance is then measured against this table and gives a weighted performance score that determines the percentage bonus related to salary.

*Table 12.8: Main advantages and disadvantages of bonus schemes*

| Main advantages | Main disadvantages |
|---|---|
| • Can apply to the whole organisation and every functions or division | • Target-setting is up to management |
| • Having several measures increases the robustness of the scheme | • Achieving equivalence of stretch between divisions and functions |

The bonus scheme is common to all levels and is the most common corporate scheme globally. An example of how to implement a bonus scheme is set out in Table 12.9.

*Table 12.9: Steps to be taken to implement a bonus scheme*

| Step | Action |
|------|--------|
| 1 | Set the "incentive scheme base" as a percentage of salary |
| 2 | Set bonus scheme targets:<br>• Threshold (0-50% of incentive base can be earned)<br>• Target (100% of incentive base can be earned)<br>• Outstanding (150-300% of incentive base can be earned) |
| 3 | Calculate bonus based on performance against target |

## 12.15.5 Commission schemes

Commission schemes are typically applied to sales and business development staff, who earn a percentage of what they sell. The percentage is often set depending on the difficulty of selling, the level of guaranteed pay (mix) and the average lead time for the sale to happen. The diagram below sets out the principle on a scale of one to ten.

**(Easy sell/order taking)**          **(Average)**          **(Hard sell/cold calling)**

```
0                    3          5          7                    10
├─────────────────────┼──────────┼──────────┼─────────────────────┤
```

**Low percentage**                                    **High percentage**
**commission**                                        **commission**

General market practice is to provide enough base salary to attract and retain employees, and to provide an opportunity to earn another 30 percent to 200 percent in commissions. Commission schemes are usually:

* Uncapped.
* Linked to individual sales.
* Subject to a team target where one can earn a bonus on top of commission if the team, region or product achieves budget.

Table 12.10 illustrates the main advantages and disadvantages of commission schemes.

*Table 12.10: Main advantages and disadvantages of commission schemes*

| Main advantages | Main disadvantages |
|-----------------|--------------------|
| • Excellent line of sight | • Territory arguments (size and ease) |
| • Good control over earnings | • If too aggressive, may impact on customer perception |

> **Example:**
> - Commission can be earned at a rate of 5 percent from the start.
> - Base salary is, say, 8,000 per month.
> - Sales achieved for the month (minus bad debt) is 170,000.
> - Commission is 5 percent of 170,000 = 8,500.
> - Monthly earnings consist of base salary (8,000) plus commission (8,500) = 16,500.

### 12.15.6 Value-add schemes (VAS)

These schemes are a measure of the amount of economic profit made by the organisation in a year. The calculation is typically the profit (after a number of accounting adjustments) minus the cost of capital. The cost of capital, in a nutshell, is the weighted cost of debt plus equity. The formula is:

*Value-add = Profit – the Weighted Average Cost of Capital*

Table 12.11 shows the main advantages and disadvantages of value-add schemes.

*Table 12.11: Main advantages and disadvantages of value-add schemes*

| Main advantages | Main disadvantages |
|---|---|
| • Focus management on the cost of capital and return on assets | • They can be complex to calculate |
| • A good correlation to increase in share price | • The adjustments can be seen as arbitrary, especially where there is major long-term capital investment |

## 12.16  Conclusion

That which is rewarded gets done. Incentives are a powerful driver of behaviour, thus careful consideration is required when designing incentive schemes. In later chapters we look at long-term incentives and sales compensation schemes.

## 12.17  Summary

Organisations implement variable pay to tie the salary and wage bill to the fortunes of the company. Variable pay is split up into short-term incentives where the measurement period is up to one year, and long-term incentives where the measurement period is over one year. The reason to implement variable pay is to align employee performance with shareholder interests. The remuneration mix is mostly determined by the lifecycle of the business, the level you are in the organisation, the type of job you have and the country/region you are in. A global trend is to include more qualitative performance measures. It is now well-established that organisations that have implemented financial schemes outperform those that do not.

## 12.18  Self-evaluation questions

1. Name four main types of short-term incentives
2. Name three main types of long-term incentives
3. Why do organisations implement variable pay?
4. What are some of the principles of incentive schemes that would make them effective?

# CHAPTER 13

# How To Design An Incentive Scheme

There are various approaches to the design of incentive pay. A project approach is advocated because it is systematic, however the design process is only the vehicle used to ensure that certain characteristics of incentive pay are built into the incentive scheme. In this chapter we will discuss these characteristics (the requirements of a good incentive scheme) and the process (the project to design and implement the scheme) of embedding them in the incentive scheme.

## 13.1    Requirements of a functioning incentive scheme

Variable pay is not a creator of performance but rather a carrier of performance momentum. Variable pay creates value by communicating a business strategy that rewards employee performance. Variable pay strongly links the day-to-day efforts, behaviour and performance of plan participants and business objectives. The "momentum" is initiated by the organisation's clear move to create a performance culture. The variable pay plan makes this real to the employees and managers by meaningfully rewarding results.

> An enabling performance climate and sound performance management process in the business are essential preconditions to the introduction of variable pay. These performance practices must enable and be aligned to the variable pay plan(s) used by the business.

### 13.1.1   The "building blocks" of variable pay

There are 11 variable pay building blocks. These 11 building blocks represent the "DNA" of variable pay, and therefore should be part of any variable pay methodology. The "DNA" falls into three independent constructs, described as follows:

### 13.1.2   Congruency (Construct 1)

Congruency is the extent to which participants understand, believe in and practice the required behaviour that leads to the achievement of business and variable pay goals. The following five substructures make up congruency:

* *Alignment (or line of sight)*

Alignment is the extent to which the performance drivers of the plan align with the business strategy, performance objectives, interest of stakeholders and day-to-day activities of the participants. The performance measures are realistic in terms of opportunities and resources. The achievement of the plan goals is acceptable to stakeholders, and the business objectives are achievable.

- *Efficacy/Goal difficulty alignment*

Efficacy/Goal difficulty alignment is the self-belief of participants that they will be able to achieve the contracted goals. Efficacy is high if the participants have the competencies, authority and information to perform, they believe that they will earn more through the variable pay plan, there is sufficient scope to achieve the targets, and participants believe that they will achieve it.

- *Understanding*

Understanding is the level to which participants understand the rules, calculations, and purpose of the scheme. It also includes an understanding of the feedback on performance against the performance criteria. When the plan is well accepted by the participants, the participants know what to expect and are certain about their required contribution.

- *Transparency*

Transparency is the sharing of information with participants so that they know what to expect, and what they need to do, to receive feedback regularly on targets and hurdles and to know what benefits to expect. Where there is transparency, participants feel that they are treated fairly and that the rules of the scheme are applied consistently.

- *Continuous improvement*

Continuous improvement is the extent to which the plan is continuously reviewed and improved. In successful plans weaknesses are corrected and targets re-contracted. Plans do not become entitlements, and the targets are always regarded as relevant to the business objectives.

### 13.1.3  Instrumentality (Construct 2)

Instrumentality is the belief that if a person meets the performance expectations, he or she will receive a (greater) reward than if they do not meet the performance expectations. The reward could be monetary, promotion, recognition, or a sense of accomplishment. If all levels of performance (including low performance) lead to the same rewards, the instrumentality is low (for example, all performance levels lead to the same increase). In an "entitlement culture" as opposed to a "performance culture", the rewards of work are often distributed with little regard for differences in contribution to the organisation. In a "performance culture", those who perform are differentially rewarded. Success depends on how much variable pay plan participants trust those in charge of the plan. Employees are more likely to believe promises that good performance will be rewarded if they trust their leaders. When subordinates do not trust their leaders, they often attempt to influence the reward system through a control mechanism (for example, union involvement, detailed contracts, and so on). Where employees believe that they have some control over how, why and when rewards are distributed, instrumentality and motivation tend to increase. Instrumentality is made up of the following four sub-structures:

- *Certainty*

Certainty is the extent to which the plan's rules are established. In plans where high certainty exists, plan rules are not manipulated, the rules are clear, no unethical practices exist, and participants are unconcerned about job security. Additionally, the expected payouts are in line with the plan rules.

- *Trust*

Trust is an assured reliance on the strength, character, or truth of something. In this case, trust is the extent or degree to which a trusting relationship exists between the participants and the custodians of the plan. Where trust is high, the participants believe the promises made and accept them in good faith. Fair and equitable pay practices exist, and previous negative experiences with variable pay also do not affect participants' attitudes toward the plan.

- *Exclusivity*

Exclusivity is the extent to which participation in the plan is reserved only for people who make a material contribution to the outcome of the plan. In plans where participation is exclusive, the payout is not diluted by people who are not contributing, or people who cannot influence the plan outcome are excluded.

- *Business risk*

Business risk is the extent to which uncontrolled risks prevent desired plan outcomes. In plans with high business risks, conflict between a plan's objectives exists, and insufficient information is available to support the plan. The plan's purpose, design and outcome are unacceptable and unachievable to some or all of the different stakeholders.

### 13.1.4 Performing (Construct 3)

The third construct, performing, is the extent to which high-performing leadership and practices exist in the business. It is made up of the following sub-structures:

- *Performance management*

Performance management encompasses the extent to which performance management principles are practiced in the business. Whenever this dimension is strong, the processes of performance contracting, feedback and performance development are well entrenched. Managers assist employees by removing stumbling blocks in the way of performance. Performance management is associated with positive or negative consequences.

- *Performance culture*

Performance culture is defined as the extent to which the business is managed and led to deliver successful outcomes. Where there is a performance culture, leadership sets clear goals, communicates well, creates the opportunity to take risks, and ensures sufficient resources to enable performance. Strong, significant correlations exist among the constructs, in other words, if the value of a construct increases, the values of the other two constructs also increase in tandem, and vice versa. This implies that if any one of the constructs with its associated sub-structures is absent, the overall impact of the variable pay plan on the business reduces to zero. This leads to the conclusion that a systemic approach to variable pay is essential.

### 13.1.2   What role does participant influence play in funding and distribution?

The extent to which participants influence the funding and distribution of funds significantly affects the plan outcome. The more influence participants have, the more positive the plan outcome. Plan designers should use plan designs where the participants are able to influence the funding of the plan and control the distribution of funds. Participant influence is the extent to which participants are able to influence the funding of the variable pay plan (for example, increase the bonus pool) and the distribution of the funds to them (for example, determining participants' share).

### 13.1.3   Does the size of rewards play a role?

In terms of the expectancy theory, valence is the value that the individual personally places on rewards. This is a function of values, needs and goals. "Norms" regarding the size of variable pay develop amongst scheme participants. This is a function of internal and external parity expectations and is more a reflection of market practices than of performance. It is, however, important to provide rewards that employees want in exchange for achieving objectives. To manage that, internal and external benchmarking is important. Merely paying out more money does not repair a variable pay plan that does not meet the criteria required for a good incentive pay plan.

### 13.1.4   What are the most common reasons why variable pay plans fail?

The most common reason why variable pay plans fail appears to be the lack of a performance climate and the associated absence of proper performance management processes. The rest of the variable pay constructs are not functional if there is not a performance culture. The second reason that plans seem to fail is because of a lack of understanding among participants. If participants do not know what is expected, do not know what to do and have no feedback on their progress, they cannot perform. The third major reason for plan failure pertains to the inability of participants to influence outcomes, whether this stems from a lack of resources, ability, confidence, mandates or information. This goes hand-in-hand with the design of the plan and the structure of participants' work allowing them to create funding and be in control of the distribution. A fourth possible reason could be that participants do not trust the custodians of the plan. This is a less common reason for failure, but if mistrust is present, the plan owners should review the plan rules and investigate the reason for the lack of trust.

Variable pay has a significant and definitive role to play as a communicator of business strategy, as a motivator of employees, and as an employee retention instrument.[1] Unfortunately, variable pay has not always been managed effectively. The causes are many, but personal interest, unrealistic expectations, and poor methodologies are at the heart of the problem. The author proposes that an empirically-validated variable pay methodology will bring greater certainty to what needs to be addressed when designing plans; provide empirically-defined norms against which plan practices can be measured; and enable practitioners to predict if a plan will add value, or is adding value, to the business.

## 13.2 Designing and implementing an incentive scheme

### 13.2.1 The project approach

The incentive pay life cycle refers to the different phases during which incentive pay evolves from the business need to the business outcome. The phases are:

- Analysis of the need within the context in which the incentive pay solution will be implemented.
- Design of the incentive pay solution.
- Implementation of the incentive pay solution.
- Leveraging of the incentive pay scheme.
- Incentive pay scheme value-add.
- Feedback on the scheme performance.

The model is depicted in Figure 13.1 below.

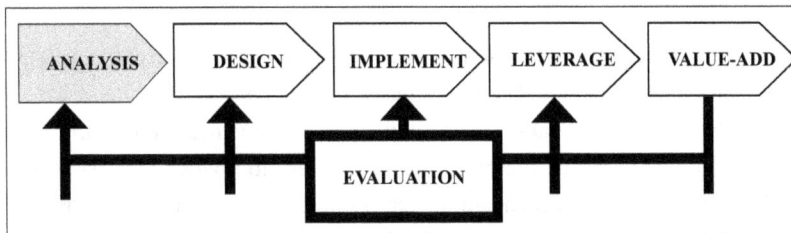

*Figure 13.1: The life cycle of incentive pay*

### 13.2.2 Opportunity to build the requirements into the incentive scheme

During the life cycle of the incentive scheme, various opportunities present themselves to embed the "requirements" in the scheme. In the table below, the most probable opportunities to embed requirements during the life cycle are depicted.

---

1   Sibangilizwe, Bussin & de Swardt, 2012.

*Table 13.1: Opportunities to embed the requirements of incentive schemes*

| Requirements | Project stages in the incentive scheme | | | | |
|---|---|---|---|---|---|
| | Analysis | Design | Implement | Leverage | Evaluate |
| Congruency | | | | | |
| • Alignment | X | X | X | X | |
| • Goal difficulty/efficacy alignment | X | | X | X | |
| • Understanding | | | X | X | |
| • Transparency | | | X | X | |
| • Continuous improvement | | X | | | X |
| Instrumentality | | | | | |
| • Trust | | | X | X | |
| • Certainty | | | X | X | |
| • Risk | X | X | | | |
| • Eligibility | X | X | | | |
| Performing | | | | | |
| • Performance culture | X | | | X | |
| • Performance management | X | X | | X | |

## 13.2.3   Phase 1: The analysis phase

During the analysis phase, designers determine the appropriateness of incentive pay as a solution to improve business performance. The outcome of the analysis is a business case that either supports or rejects the implementation of incentive pay as a business solution. A framework to analyse the environment in which the incentive scheme has to operate will assist the designers to gather information about the organisation's environment, organisational characteristics, and human resource and remuneration strategy. This information is then analysed and considered to determine alternative solutions and the viability of each solution. This investigation (analysis) is conducted before any firm commitment to continue with the design can be given.

•   *Collecting relevant information*

Collecting information based on the constructs of incentive pay requires a systematic process of information collection. Different data-gathering techniques can be used, such as interviews, surveys, observation, document analysis or a combination of all. Individual designers or teams can collect the information. The availability of resources and the complexity of the scheme under consideration determine the speed and accuracy with which the data will be collected.

- *Framework of issues to investigate during the analysis phase*

The analysis should include the external environment, the business characteristics, human resource and remuneration strategy, and appropriate incentive scheme design.

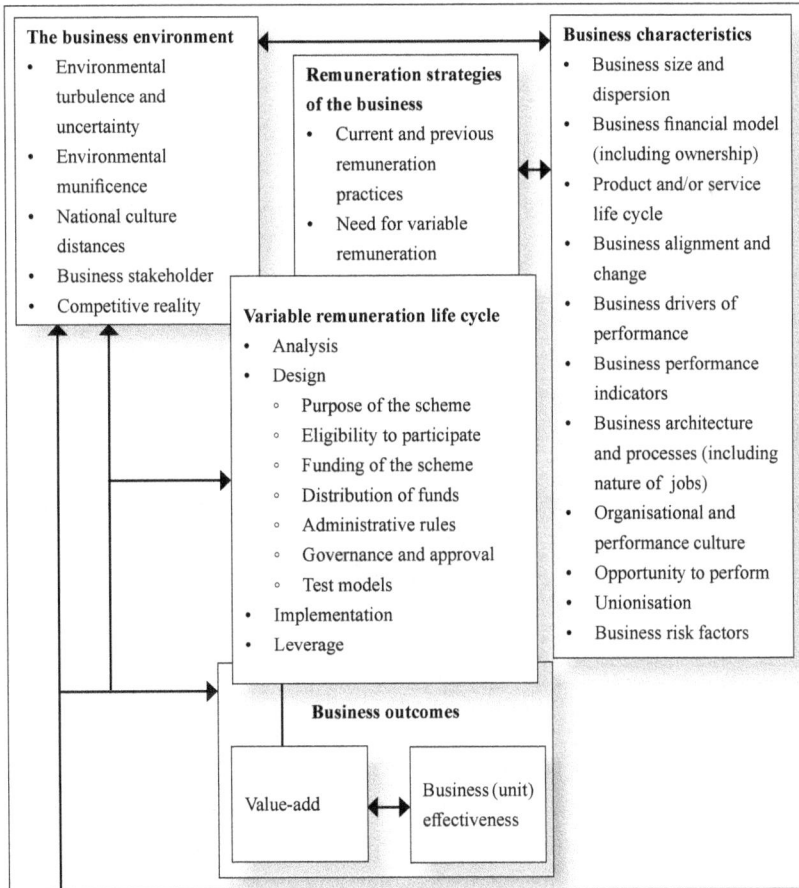

*Figure 13.2: Framework of issues to analyse*

The framework consists of five areas that influence incentive pay. As a result of the interaction between the areas, they influence each other. The elements of each area are discussed below.

### The business environment

The business environment refers to the social, political, economic and technological influences and resource availability in the environment.

## 1 Environmental turbulence and uncertainty

During periods of environmental turbulence and uncertainty, sharing the risk with the employees leverages remuneration, however it also affects employee engagement. It is not advisable to implement a scheme during major structural and system changes. Windfall or cyclical pay-outs are more probable and may be seen as poor governance.

## 2 Environmental munificence

If environmental munificence is high, resources are abundant. Greater environmental munificence allows more freedom to adopt different remuneration strategies and allows wider participation in incentive schemes, with a higher probability of achieving or exceeding targets.

## 3 National culture distances

Culture affects the behaviour of people. Applied to remuneration, culture may affect the attitude of participants from different cultures towards an incentive pay scheme differently. Companies operating "across borders" may have to adjust their incentive pay schemes to the local culture and conditions.

Geographical differences in the product or service provision provide important information to determine whether decentralised or centralised solutions will be required. Studies have found that the further the subsidiary is from the holding company, the more the incentive pay practices differ.

## 4 Business stakeholders

Business stakeholders' perceptions about the appropriateness of the scheme influence the success of the scheme. Shareholder activism could lead to the cancellation of, or changes to, a scheme. Customer resistance may lead to product deterioration and failure (for example, endowment policies lost ground because customers resisted the perceived high commissions paid to sales consultants). Community perceptions about the differentiation in income between top executives and workers influence the trading environment for businesses. The role of business stakeholders in incentive pay has been placed under the microscope, and the governance of incentives has been elevated to top priority for boards and shareholders. Scheme designers must analyse the impact of the interests and needs of the different stakeholders on incentive pay schemes and make recommendations that will include the views of stakeholders.

## 5 Competitive reality

The competitiveness of the business' trading and employment environments influences remuneration. If the trading conditions are very competitive, the business will not have the capacity to set high remuneration levels without becoming uncompetitive in delivering products to the market. This may facilitate a strategy to leverage the incentive pay by creating a higher ratio of variable to fixed remuneration and thereby sharing the risk with the employees. In the above situation, competitiveness leads to the business using a "follower" remuneration strategy, which provides less room for differentiation and exposes the business to the risk of becoming uncompetitive as an employer. An alternative approach could be to follow a "leading" remuneration strategy. This means that more resources would be employed to remunerate employees competitively and to attract the best talent to create a competitive edge under difficult conditions. While the business might become less competitive over the short term, the investment might pay dividends once the performance of the business started to improve because of superior individual contributions.

## Business characteristics

### 1 Business size and dispersion

Smaller companies will tend to have proportionally more participants in incentive schemes than larger companies. This is because the number of employees who can impact the goals of an incentive scheme will tend to be proportionally higher in smaller companies. The golden rule is that participants in incentive schemes should be chosen on the basis of their contribution to achieve the scheme's purpose. A typical problem arises where only employees who are directly involved in production or sales participate in a scheme, but their support teams are excluded. This often leads to discontent and poor morale among non-participants.

The company's operating model directly affects eligibility. Eligibility differs drastically in the case of centralised versus decentralised and capital-intensive versus labour-intensive business models. The aggregation level on which the incentive pay scheme is set also affects behaviour. If the level is too high, the participants may lose the line of sight and will not be motivated by the scheme. On the other hand, it may stimulate co-operation between the different business areas. If the aggregate level is too low, and important contributors are excluded because of the number of participants, dysfunctional behaviour may be stimulated or silo behaviour encouraged.

### 2 Business financial model (including ownership of the business)

Ownership of the business also plays a role in the choice of incentive pay schemes. In privately-owned companies, closely-held companies, joint ventures, co-operatives, mutual organisations, and autonomous subsidiaries of larger public companies, the choice of incentive pay plans differs materially from that of public companies. While the practices related to short-term incentive pay schemes are comparable, private companies set substantially different targets for long-term incentive pay schemes. Eligibility for long-term incentive pay schemes is not taken as deeply into the organisation as in the case of public companies. Privately-owned companies also do not use long-term incentive pay as frequently as public companies. "ownership" on an emotional level also influences participation. Commitment to the business rather than an incentive scheme may determine the behaviour of the participants.

## 3  Product and/or service

Client expectations of products and/or services make it either acceptable or unacceptable to incentivise products or services. Certain investment advice will be viewed with suspicion if it is incentivised. In other cases, the gap that exists between client expectations and the current service standards could be a legitimate reason to introduce incentive pay to focus the behaviour of participants and motivate them to improve business performance. Measurement of client expectations must, however, be credible in the eyes of the participants. This will avoid debates about the legitimacy of assessments. Where reliable client expectation measurements do not exist, the designers have to be extra careful to ensure buy-in to the scheme.

## 4  Business alignment and change

Incentive pay must be implemented in a well-managed business environment to make a difference to business performance. Incentive pay forms part of a larger business model and needs to be aligned with the business strategy, structure, resources and performance strategy. Incentive pay plays a role in supporting the implementation of strategy in an organisation. It is an enabler that motivates employees to achieve desired goals. The broader elements of a good business strategy, leadership, infrastructure, and performance management must exist for incentive pay to be successful. Incentive scheme design is a product of the organisation in which the scheme is located and the environment in which the organisation operates. There is no room for reflex reactions to introduce incentive pay as a cure for performance and organisational problems in a business.

The following questions will solicit information that will add to the understanding of the business alignment and leadership:

- *Do the managers of the business consistently demonstrate leadership?* The role of leaders is critical in the total process of incentive pay design and implementation. If the leaders do not take responsibility for remuneration and/or do not set targets and defend them, the possibility of a successful implementation decreases. Leaders also have to "sell" the stretch targets to the participants. Incentive pay is built on the premise that more has to be delivered with the same capacity. Leaders have to defend the inaccuracies that are often part of the compromises scheme designers have to make.
- *Is the culture of the organisation characterised by trust, mutual respect and a willingness to work towards common goals?* The lack or presence of the above will play a role in deciding on a design option and may even be a prerequisite for implementation.
- *Does the scheme have a sponsor and champion?* Lack of sponsorship could mean a scheme with no support in terms of design capacity, feedback on performance, and assurance of governance during implementation.
- *Are the current fixed remuneration levels internally equitable and externally competitive?*

Competitive does not mean higher than the market. What is important is the role of incentive pay in the total offer. If the incentive pay is going to be building on a perceived inequitable fixed remuneration basis, the risk of failure will increase. If the external market is much higher than the internal remuneration levels, the size of the incentive payment could be higher, and vice versa.

## 5    Business drivers and performance

Determining the drivers of performance is essential in incentive scheme design. In the model below, the integration between the business strategy, critical success targets, and performance management process is depicted. Performance measures are derived from the performance objectives, which are set at organisational, departmental, unit, team, and individual level. Evaluation of performance against the critical success targets (translated into performance measures) takes place to determine to what extent the targets and strategy were achieved. In the performance management system, the performance measures are used to contract performance expectations, which are then measured against the actual performance achieved. This result informs the incentive pay allocation.

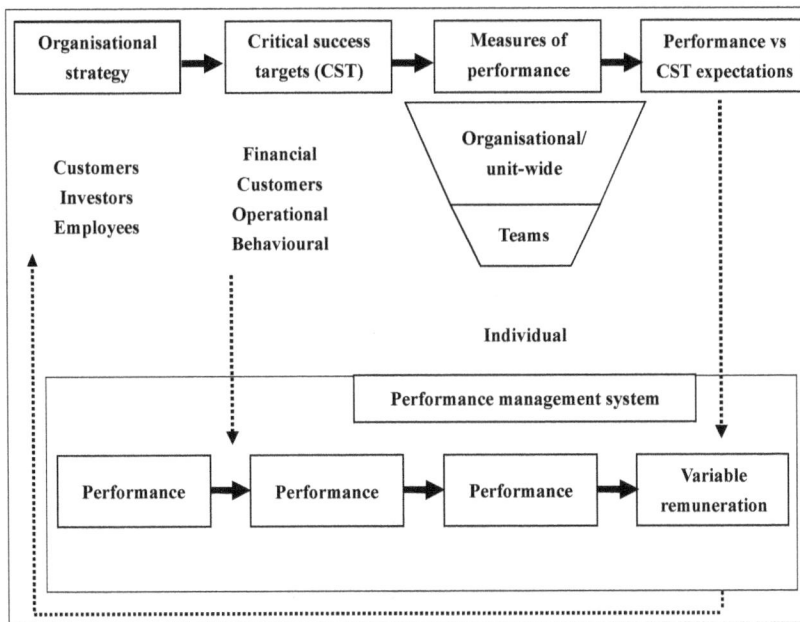

*Figure 13.3: The relationship between business performance and performance management*
*Source: WorldatWork[2]*

The relationship between performance management and incentive pay can be described as two dependent yet distinct business processes. Incentive pay is dependent upon some of the performance management elements but has distinctive elements and processes that differentiate it.

---

2    WorldatWork, 2003a.

---

**Incentive pay differs from performance management in the following ways:**

- Incentive pay has exclusive eligibility. Participation is confined to participants who can make a difference to the achievement of the purpose of the incentive pay scheme.
- Incentive pay has specific rules and governance criteria to determine the participation and the rewards paid by the scheme.
- Best practices in performance management allow for consistent feedback and adjustment to performance standards to allow for optimum performance. This is not possible with incentive pay because the funding fluctuates.
- In performance management, risk-taking is encouraged. and performance evaluation may be compromised, based on the effort that was put in. This is not possible in incentive pay because of funding constraints.
- There are no funding or cost implications associated with performance management.
- Performance management results may be used to determine eligibility and distribution of rewards.
- Leveraging of incentive pay is unique to remuneration management as a technique to optimise performance.
- Performance management has a developmental and a judgemental character and is in its own right designed to improve performance.
- It is therefore concluded that incentive pay should not substitute for performance management, as this will be detrimental to both business processes. It is important that both processes use the same methods to determine performance measures and that performance is assessed against the same criteria. This congruency is essential to participants in incentive pay schemes as it increases the expectations of success and reward, and therefore increases motivation.

**Business performance improves by more than 25 percent if the following are present:[3]**

- Fairness and accuracy of informal feedback.
- Risk-taking.
- Emphasis (in informal review) on performance strength.
- Employee understanding of performance standards.
- Internal communication.
- Manager knowledge about performance.
- Opportunity to work on the things the employee does best.
- Feedback that helps employees do their jobs better.
- The opportunity to work for a strong executive team.

---

These findings emphasise the role of human motivation in the performance management process and the importance of including these motivational principles in incentive pay. Human beings are not isolated from the factors that influence their personal motivation when they become participants in an incentive pay scheme.

Performance measures can be identified on three levels: organisation, group or team, and individual. On the organisational level, the following performance measures have been identified:

---

3    CLC, 2003.

*Table 13.2: Performance measures on the organisational level*

| **Financial/Economic considerations** | **Customer/Market position** |
|---|---|
| • Profit<br>• Return on equity or investment<br>• Revenue growth and mix<br>• Results versus budget or operating plan<br>• Stock price or market value<br>• Economic value<br>• Shareholder value<br>• Cost reduction/productivity improvement<br>• Asset utilisation/investment strategy | • Customer opinion of products<br>• Customer retention<br>• Stability or growth of customer base<br>• Market share<br>• Customer satisfaction<br>• Service<br>• Cross-selling<br>• Customer acquisition |
| **Operational/ Improvement/ Internal business process perspective**<br><br>• Productivity<br>• Quality of products<br>• Speed<br>• Innovation/organisational learning<br>• Information technology<br>• Work processes<br>• Innovation (identify the market and create a product and service offering)<br>• Operations (build the products/services and deliver the products or services)<br>• Post-sale service | **Learning and growth perspective**<br>• Employee capabilities<br>• Information systems<br>• Motivation, empowerment and alignment<br>• Return on human capital<br>• Leadership<br>• Human capital<br>• Research<br>• Image<br>• Culture |

Organisational performance criteria are used for organisation-wide or top management schemes. In the case of top management schemes, the accountability for organisational success shortens the line of sight, while the balanced scorecard provides a holistic perspective on the business performance. Where organisation-wide schemes are used, organisation-wide performance criteria become relevant.

Team performance can also be measured. Differentiation between teams based on their functions and purposes provides the designer with guidelines on how to design, implement and manage the team performance and incentive pay. During the analysis phase, designers will identify if the business has a need for team-based incentive pay. The classification in the table below provides an understanding of the implications of team-based incentive pay schemes.

*Table 13.3: Classification of types of team and incentive pay*

| Types of teams | Definition of team | Performance measure | Remuneration strategy |
|---|---|---|---|
| **Permanent (full-time)** | | | |
| **Pooled teams** | • Team members do the same work<br>• Typically narrow skills | • Individual contribution | • Same fixed remuneration<br>• Individual incentives |
| **Sequential teams** | • Teamwork in sequential order<br>• Work is handed over to next person with different skills and responsibilities<br>• Team members are interdependent for performance | • Team success | • Different fixed remuneration<br>• Team incentives |
| **Reciprocal teams** | • Team members have the same type of skills and support one another by helping to alleviate bottlenecks or with difficult problems | • Team success | • Same fixed remuneration<br>• Team incentives |
| **Temporary (Full-/part-time)** | | | |
| **Project team** | • Diverse skills in different subjects<br>• Work towards common project goal | • Project milestones | • Different fixed remuneration<br>• Team incentives |
| **Parallel team** | • Diverse skills working together to resolve a problem | • Problem-solving<br>• Focus on improvements | • Different fixed remuneration<br>• Financial and/ or non-financial recognition |

Individual performance measures can be classified into three broad groups: person-based, behaviour-based, and outcome-based. Single performance assessment systems or combinations of performance systems could be used, depending on the business needs.

*Table 13.4: Application of the individual performance measures in incentive pay*

| Performance measure | Characteristics | Remuneration strategy |
|---|---|---|
| **Person-based (What people are/can do)** | | |
| **Traits** | Personal traits related to the person | • Should not be used in remuneration<br>• May be supportive information to determine initial salary offer<br>• Not legally defensible in incentive pay |

| Performance measure | Characteristics | Remuneration strategy |
|---|---|---|
| **Knowledge/ Skills** | The person is assessed on their application of skills and knowledge. Useful in the case of skill building and multi-skilled environments. | • Useful to determine fixed remuneration<br>• Only ad hoc bonuses and incentives |
| **Competencies** | Competencies are displayed behaviour in a work context. Competencies enable performance and should be linked to strategy. (Could also be classified as behaviour-based individual performance measure, but varies if it is not tied to a job or role, but to business strategy.) Well-researched competency frameworks are available. It has become a relatively easy method of behaviour assessment. | • Useful in determining fixed remuneration<br>• Assesses the person and not the performance. Not tied to specific duties |
| **Behaviour-based (Activity- or input-focused: What people do)** | | |
| **Behaviour-anchored** | Specific behaviour that relates to the individual job. It is very appropriate if the employee has control over the correct behaviour and not necessarily the outcomes. It is complex and difficult to apply. | • Useful in incentive pay and fixed remuneration |
| **Critical incidents** | Critical incidents related to behaviour-based measures. Evidence of all positive and negative incidents is fed back the moment they occur. Records are kept for formal feedback. | • Useful in incentive pay and fixed remuneration |
| **Outcome-based (Output-focused: What people produce)** | | |
| Work planning and review (WPR) | Focuses on task completion and clear performance standards. It is often defined at task level. | • Useful in incentive pay and fixed remuneration |
| Management by objectives (MBO) | Sound, job specific and legally defensible. It is related to business strategy. It focuses on annual results and ignores routine tasks. It is sensitive to changing circumstances, but insensitive to goals that are dependent on others. | • Useful in incentive pay and fixed remuneration |

The designers will establish during the analysis phase what type or combinations of performance measures are in use in the business or are required for future use. If appropriate performance management systems exist, performance targets will be relatively easy to establish. If they do not exist, performance measurement systems will first have to be created. This may require a delay in the introduction of the incentive pay scheme. Reliable performance measures and a database of performance information are essential information for incentive pay schemes to be built on. This information must be shared with the participants if one is to be able to build trust and leverage behaviour.

## 6    Business performance indicators

Financial indicators, such as profitability, turnover, cost drivers and historical performance, are indicators of business competitiveness. However, if the organisation is operating in a fast-changing industry as a result of volatile markets or technological changes, historical measures become unreliable or may not even exist. Financial indicators can be analysed on a universal basis or more specifically benchmarked to the industry or specific peer groups within the industry. This analysis allows the designers to understand where possible opportunities for performance improvement could be located.[4] Through the use of specific comparisons, external influencing factors will be reduced and a more accurate assessment of the business performance can be made.

## 7    Business architecture and processes (including nature of jobs)

An understanding of how the business operates gives designers the opportunity to determine the viability of an incentive pay solution. There are several aspects of the business that need to be analysed. The products and services to be delivered determine the potential and nature of the incentive pay design to be used. Single product delivery versus multiple delivery dependence will change the design requirements. In the case of multiple delivery dependence, complex design options may be required. The business processes to deliver the products or services also influence scheme designs. An understanding of these business processes allows the designers to appreciate the complexity of the business processes and identify leverage points.

The organisation's structure and integration of roles play a role in the way incentive pay schemes will be designed. If the organisation is integrated so that performance is dependent on the integrated and collective effort of all or a large group of participants, the design will differ considerably from one where individual lines of contribution can be identified. Similarly, if larger groups of participants are eligible to participate, the design will be different from schemes where fewer people participate. The roles of participants vary between highly programmemable (jobs or tasks where behaviours are easily defined) and not programmemable. Incentive pay is attached more easily to highly programmemable jobs or roles. However, if turbulence and volatility exist in the business or if the programmemable jobs or roles are in support areas, the jobs do not lend themselves to incentive pay. The nature of work differs between jobs or roles.

---

4    Bussin & Blair, 2015.

Levels in the organisation typically affect line of sight. Jobs with more repetitive tasks are better suited for activity-based schemes, while jobs with a research character may not be suited for incentive pay at all. An analysis of the nature of the work performed will indicate whether it should be included in the scheme design.

## 8 Organisational and performance culture

The organisational culture determines largely whether a participative or an individualistic design alternative will be used. Organisations that are not ready for a participative approach to incentive pay schemes will experience dissonance if an integrated incentive pay solution is implemented. The preferences of the participants also play a role in determining whether an individualistic rather than a participative scheme design will be preferred. Schemes where distribution of the bonus pool is based on the discretion of management will require high levels of trust and communication from line management to legitimise the scheme among participants. Management's attitude towards the measurement of accountabilities plays an important role in the design solution. If management prefer individual accountabilities, they may not support integrated solutions. Where supervisory skills are limited, complex integrated solutions will be more difficult to implement than direct line of sight solutions.

A performance culture is supported by performance management practices. Where there is a performance culture, the probability that incentive pay will be successful is higher. The designer must therefore look for evidence that supports the following:

- Clear, reliable performance measures should exist for the business.
- Managers manage performance effectively and provide feedback to employees on the actual versus the desired levels of performance.
- Employees understand the performance measures and know how to improve performance.

Through the introduction of clear objectives and measurable criteria for performance, substantial improvement in performance can be achieved, without even introducing incentive pay. Feedback, corrective communication, coaching and training are essential building blocks upon which the success of incentive pay and performance improvement rests. Offering incentive pay to employees who are not competent or who do not know what is expected of them is unproductive and premature. If there is not a performance management culture, incentive pay should not be introduced.

## 9 Opportunity to perform

It is necessary to analyse whether the employees (potential participants) have the power, knowledge and information to influence important decisions. They must also have the organisational "right" to influence the outcomes. Empowerment of participants to influence business results should become part of the design and implementation of the incentive pay scheme if it does not already exist.

The potential for performance improvement must exist; the return on the investment is higher if a larger performance gap is closed through the introduction of incentive pay. Experience has shown that in closing the gap, designers stop incentivising the participants once the required performance levels have been achieved, thereby effectively penalising them for their higher performance. This problem must be anticipated and provisions should be created with regard to how the scheme will be adjusted to sustain the performance. A further variation of this performance penalisation is the retrenchment of participants because of redundancy. Careful planning is required to prevent dysfunctional behaviour and the maintenance of trust levels in the organisation if performance levels have reached optimum levels.

An important consideration is whether the business has substantial control over the factors that lead to performance. If uncontrollable factors determine the outcomes, the risks associated with incentive pay schemes could outweigh the benefits of introducing a scheme. The "transmission loss" between the business needs and expectations and the phases of the incentive pay life cycle is depicted in the figure below. Uncontrollable variables could redirect the outcomes of the incentive pay scheme.

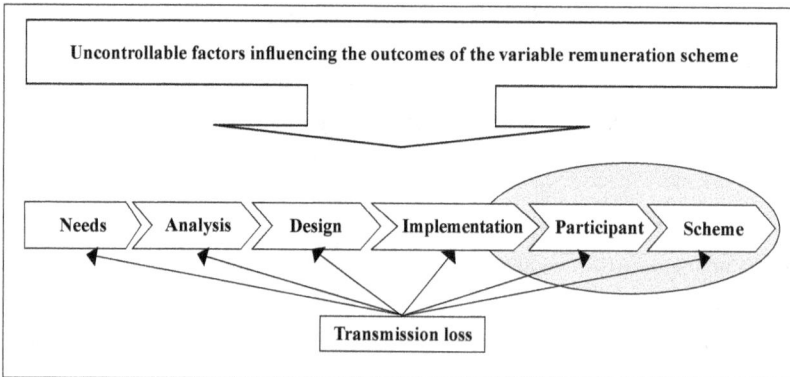

*Figure 13.4: The phenomenon of transmission loss in incentive pay*

## 10 Unionisation

The business relationship with the union could be adversarial or co-operative. Traditionally, unions do not support incentive pay. Unions represent the interests of their members and may be suspicious of any effort by management to alienate them from their members. Management may regard incentive pay as not being part of the formal contractual relationship and may like to keep it as part of their "managerial prerogative" area. Whatever the circumstances are, however, obtaining union buy-in or support for incentive pay remains an important element for the success of the incentive pay scheme.

Where more than one union is recognised in the business, complexity may increase if there is competition between the unions. Pro-active consultation and early involvement may reduce tension and allow for meaningful debate.

## 11 Business risk factors

Risk factors that could place the scheme at risk should be identified and evaluated, and conscious decisions made as to whether to continue with incentive pay under those conditions. It is important during the analysis phase to identify potential barriers to the successful design, implementation and leveraging of the scheme. These barriers could be serious enough to stop the design and implementation process or, at least, have design and implementation implications. Possible barriers could be:

- The readiness of employees to accept incentive pay.
- The current employee relations environment and employment contracts.
- Stakeholder misalignment.
- The volume of other changes in the business is overloading management.
- The inability to support effective measurements (for example, a lack of appropriate information systems).

### *Remuneration strategies of the business*

## 1 Current and previous remuneration practices

Current and previous remuneration practices set the climate in which incentive pay will be implemented and practiced. The remuneration strategy could be to follow, to match, or to lead market practices. There are benefits associated with leading market practices and paying more. Over time, the business should attract and retain better talent, however this may become unaffordable over a long period. Leveraging incentive pay to substitute fixed remuneration has an impact on the attitude of employees towards incentive pay. It has been found that a culture of entitlement grows (emotionally and legally) where this practice is followed. Where higher fixed remuneration is paid, the incentive pay tends to be higher because of the higher base.

## 2 Need for incentive pay

An understanding of the organisation's perceived need for incentive pay may be derived from the "pros" and "cons" of the current remuneration strategy. The effect of the remuneration strategy on the desired business goals should determine whether incentive pay schemes need a full design upgrade or whether they already suffice. It is possible that the organisation's need may not be for incentive pay but may be for a change in management practices.

Current remuneration practices mean that there are entrenched interests in the organisation. Some employees will not like to see any changes to their current dispensation. Others will be sceptical of changes. In a business where incentive pay practices were previously implemented, participants will have attitudes towards the existing scheme, which will influence any changes to the status quo. If there were changes to the fixed remuneration when the original incentive pay scheme was introduced, contractual obligations may have been created and adjustments to the fixed remuneration may be required. Where no incentive pay schemes existed before, challenges related to understanding and expectations will face the designers.

*Evaluating the viability of an incentive pay solution*

During the analysis phase, the viability of an incentive pay solution is assessed. The designers must determine to what extent the scheme will add value to the business outcomes and whether risks will be mitigated. These answers can be obtained through analysis of the information and predictions of the influence these factors will have on the successful implementation of the scheme.

At this stage, the designers can identify with a fair degree of accuracy the most appropriate scheme design to pursue during the design phase. A matrix to assist designers in evaluating the scheme is depicted in the figure below. The matrix provides a visual classification of the different solutions based on the information gathered during the analysis phase.

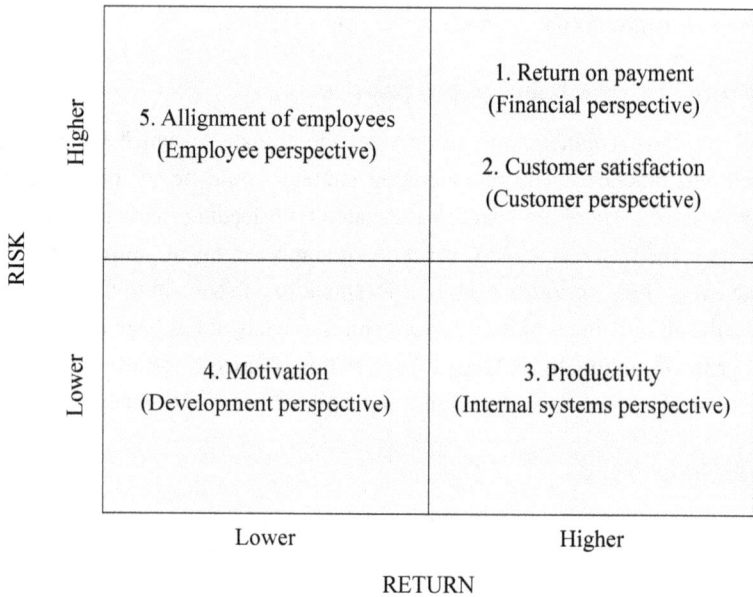

| | RISK | Lower RETURN | Higher RETURN |
|---|---|---|---|
| **Higher** | | 5. Allignment of employees (Employee perspective) | 1. Return on payment (Financial perspective)<br><br>2. Customer satisfaction (Customer perspective) |
| **Lower** | | 4. Motivation (Development perspective) | 3. Productivity (Internal systems perspective) |

*Figure 13.5: Matrix to classify the design options of incentive pay schemes*

The decision matrix will be revisited during later stages of the incentive pay life cycle to identify risks and for assessment of the scheme outcomes.

*Preparing a business case*

At the conclusion of the analysis process, a business case is prepared to determine the feasibility of going ahead with the design of the incentive pay scheme.

The business case should include the following aspects:

- The business environment.
- A brief overview of the business, the performance drivers identified from the business strategy, and the need for incentive pay.
- An assessment of the business' readiness for incentive pay.
- An assessment of the potential for business improvement.
- The current remuneration and performance management practices.
- Analysis of best-practice solutions that could be used during the scheme design.
- Calculation of the costs associated with the design and operation of the scheme.
- Investigation of the possible barriers and risks associated with the implementation of the proposed scheme.
- Recommendations for next steps.

The business case is submitted for approval for design of the scheme. At this stage only the resources to design a scheme are approved, and not the implementation. (For simpler designs, the analysis and design processes could be integrated.) If there is a clear need for the scheme and the implementation will hold no risk, the design of the incentive pay solution can go ahead. For sophisticated scheme designs, a clear distinction between the analysis and the design phase is recommended to ensure that risk and potential success could be assessed clearly after each phase.

### *Summary of the Analysis Phase*

The output of the analysis phase is an understanding of the business environment, the business' operating model, its performance measures, the drivers of success, the culture of the business, and its remuneration approach. Potential incentive pay schemes should be reviewed as possible solutions for the business. The analysis phase should determine whether:

- There is a reasonable expectation that the incentive pay solution will contribute to the performance of the business.
- There is congruency between the business model and the role of the incentive pay scheme.
- Incentive pay has an impact on the other stakeholders and, if necessary, what approach should be followed.

The analysis phase is a critical moment in the life cycle of incentive pay because the cost of continuing from here on becomes exponentially higher. In terms of the incentive pay life cycle, the analysis phase establishes the need for an incentive pay solution. The design phase that follows is about solution crafting. The investigations done during the analysis phase provide information, potential solutions and sponsorship for the design phase, which requires more resources and stronger mandates for the designers.

### 13.2.4   Phase 2: Design of incentive pay schemes

Once the business case proposal has been accepted, the designing of an incentive pay scheme commences. Good governance requires that the authority for approval will be at the highest levels in the organisation. The design process should produce a scheme document that will be used for approval and communication. Below, the design phase of an incentive pay scheme is depicted.

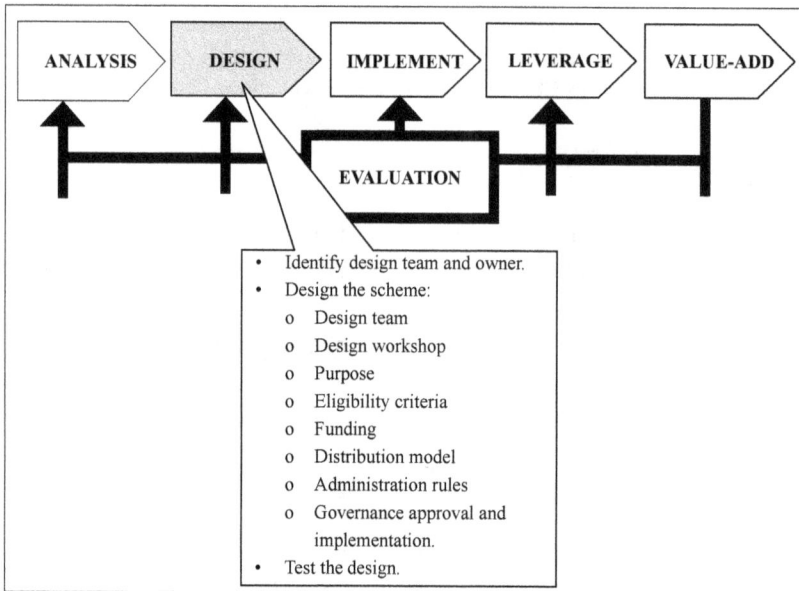

*Figure 13.6: The design phase*

A formal scheme design increases motivation as it strengthens the perceived relationship between performance and the expected reward (also referred to as instrumentality). In designing the incentive scheme, instrumentality is enhanced because of the structure and specific rules created for the scheme. An incentive scheme "contract" consists of the following:

- The scheme purpose is the description of why the scheme is developed. It includes the conditions that the plan should support and how the plan is linked to critical business objectives.
- Eligibility to participate in the scheme deals with the challenges of selecting a critical mass of participants who will influence the scheme outcome without diluting the rewards. The participants must perceive that their performance is in relation to the reward. If everyone receives the same reward irrespective of their performance, the motivation levels of the higher performers will go down.

- Funding of incentive pay is the method(s) followed by the designers to obtain funds to fund the scheme. Funding is influenced by the line of sight between the business objectives and the participants' behaviour. It is also a governance issue, as this is the driver of the cost of the scheme. The return on payment (ROP) is sensitive to the funding formula.
- Distribution of incentive pay is the emotional component of the incentive pay scheme design. Line of sight between the participant's performance and ultimate reward, as well as the relativity between the rewards of participants, are the design constructs that influence the levels of performance.
- Administration is important, as certainty about the expected rewards is key in order to increase motivation. Conflict, different interpretations about scheme rules and administrative overload could render the scheme ineffective.
- Sound governance must be built into schemes from the beginning. Incentive pay is a sensitive governance area for public companies. A broader stakeholder community requires incentive pay to be managed with great care.

During scheme design, the implementation and leveraging of the scheme should be anticipated and adjustments made to ensure that these phases are successful. The design of the scheme is informed by the analysis phase. A dedicated design team should work on the design to ensure the maximum participation and functional input. Ideally there should be a continuation of the team that worked on the analysis of the scheme viability, but as will be seen in the paragraph below, other considerations may change the design team composition.

### *Forming a design team*

The outcomes of the analysis process will guide the selection of the design team. The scheme designers should carefully select the design team members according to predetermined criteria. Most design team members will come from within the business, but external resources could be co-opted if the need for specific skills exists. The number of participants will depend on the complexity (and number) of schemes required, however a team of between six and 12 members representing all areas of the business seems to be a benchmark. The design team members should be selected against the following criteria:

- Knowledge of the business.
- An appreciation of the business drivers that the scheme should support.
- Ability to challenge traditional approaches and conceptualise new solutions.
- Ability to be respected in the business for their views and opinions.
- Ability to motivate a new scheme with peers and colleagues.
- Capacity to participate and deliver in researching and designing the scheme.
- Ability to design practical solutions.
- Ability to divorce themselves from personal gain.
- Union members, if it is a unionised environment.

The team must be representative of all the internal stakeholders and diverse enough to reflect all the different opinions of the participants. The competencies required in the design of incentive pay plans could come from different areas but are normally concentrated in a number of business functions. Apart from the probability that the competencies may be concentrated in these functions, co-ordination between these functions is critical to the outcome of the implementation.

The functions that should be consulted and/or co-opted in the design of incentive pay schemes are the following:

- **Scheme owner**

The scheme owner is the person who commissioned the incentive pay scheme as a business solution for his or her business. It is the person who has to convince the people with governance responsibility of the value of the scheme. The scheme owner is also the "champion" of the scheme and the driver behind the leveraging of it.

- **Line management**

Line management support is critical to the success of incentive pay schemes; line managers should take part in the development of the plans so that they will understand and support the scheme. Moreover, they can evaluate how the incentive pay scheme will be received and predict the probable success. Line managers can often point out potential flaws in the design of the incentive pay scheme that are not provided for in the technical design. An actively participative approach in the design of the scheme will take longer, but the scheme will be more effectively implemented and it will save time in the long run.

- **Strategic expertise**

The designers need to tap the expertise of planners and strategists so that appropriate performance goals and measures are included in the incentive pay plan. The purpose of incentive pay plans should be aligned with the objectives of the business plan so that the incentive pay scheme will drive the appropriate behaviour of the participants.

- **Motivational expertise**

Employee relations, performance management, rewards and personnel information systems must be co-ordinated with incentive pay schemes. For example, incentive pay schemes should be considered when negotiating employment contracts. The impact of changes to employment contracts as a result of changes in the incentive pay scheme should be kept in scope, as it may have legal implications. Similarly, collective agreements about incentive pay schemes will require intensive negotiations and consultations. It is also crucial to consider benefits and administrative issues when designing an incentive pay scheme. For example, the impact of the incentive pay scheme on salary and benefit administration should be taken into account. If pay-outs have to be made to large numbers of staff, or performance evaluation results are linked to the pay-out, the personnel system's ability to deliver the results must be taken into account.

- **Accounting expertise**

The cost of incentive pay schemes must be calculated accurately between the responsible accountants and the designers, as the objectives of the accountants and the remuneration experts are often in conflict. Where the purpose of the incentive pay scheme is not clear, conflict between motivational objectives and cost efficiency may surface. This is where the interaction between the different disciplines should provide synergistic solutions that best serve the interest of the business. Increased emphasis on corporate governance focuses the attention of the different stakeholders directly on the financial impact and implications of incentive pay design. Incentive pay should not create unpleasant surprises with regard to the financial performance of the business or lead to unjustified remuneration of individuals.[5] Furthermore, where incentive pay provisions and costs are included in financial plans, they are likely to become milestones rather than paving blocks to a successful scheme. Incentive pay schemes can cause periodic demands for cash when payments are made. Financial managers can anticipate such demands by reviewing remuneration programmes in advance. This is more applicable to larger incentive pay schemes or where more than one incentive pay scheme exists and serious impact on profit plans or cash flow may result.

- **Tax and legal advisors**

Tax experts and lawyers can add considerable value to incentive pay schemes, particularly if there is to be a deferral option provided for amounts earned from an incentive pay scheme. Where these options are considered, the risks to the business and the participants need to be analysed in full for the designers to evaluate, and the options should be mandated by the business. Scheme contracts are also legal contracts that bestow rights and obligations on the parties.

- **Information technology and/or information managers/consultants**

Information systems and access to information are critical components of incentive pay schemes; sophisticated activity-based schemes rely on information systems. Commission and productivity schemes are often dependent on the measurement of individual activities. Where more than 100 participants become eligible for participation in an activity-based scheme such as sales commission, it is recommended that specialist software be acquired. Systems developed in-house may not be sufficient to co-ordinate all the variables of a properly designed activity-based incentive scheme. During the first year of the scheme, in-house system development is justified because of the initial instability in schemes (especially sales commission schemes). However, if a scheme does not take all the risks into account or integrate with other systems in the business through proper system development, the scheme is at risk.

- **Prospective eligible participants**

A minimum requirement for a design team is to include people who are affected by the scheme and want to see the scheme succeed. The level of involvement of team members will vary

---

5    Bussin & Nel, 2015.

according to the level of change required and the experience and skill of the design team. Involving participants improves transparency and ownership.

### *Conducting a design workshop*

Members of the design team are selected against the criteria developed for the project. Their line manager(s) or the scheme owner must communicate their participation. Each design team member should know his or her responsibilities and the objectives he or she must achieve. This will ensure that design team members know that the project is sanctioned by their line management, that their contribution is a business requirement, and that the necessary resources should be allocated to the project.

The value of using design teams is that they provide a better fit to the organisation and the "buy-in" from the business is higher. This is offset by time constraints on the team members, which is a serious problem if the management does not support the project. Lack of creativity and "outside-the-box" thinking is also a risk when internal team members are used. Where the barriers exceed the benefits of using a design team, an advisory team could be created to facilitate solutions and support the design team. The advisory team could also play a role in guiding the work of several design teams if the business requires several incentive pay schemes.

After the mandates of the design team members have been authorised, a design workshop is organised. The length of the workshop will depend on several factors, most of which should be known because of the information gathered during the analysis phase. These include:

- The complexity of the envisaged incentive pay scheme:
  - If the scheme affects large groups.
  - If the line of sight between the required behaviour and performance measures and/or distribution criteria is clear.
  - If a governance problem looms.
- The complexity of the business (for example, a single product/business unit versus a multiple product or group of diverse business units).
- The existence of existing incentive pay scheme(s) versus situations where no scheme exists.
- The readiness of the business for incentive pay (for example, lack of a performance culture and information systems).
- Practical arrangements (for example, interference from the office during the design process, availability of information or people with whom to consult).

There is often a high level of emotionality around remuneration and incentive pay schemes, with people pursuing personal interests. These dynamics affect the functioning of the team.

The facilitation of the design workshop should start with the results of the analysis phase as input to the design phase. An agenda for the design workshop may include the following:

- Developing a charter for the design team. The charter should give direction to the purpose and objectives, authority and interaction with other interested parties, and the process or roadmap to guide their actions in designing the incentive programme.
- Define the goals that should be achieved.
- Specify the type of scheme or schemes that will be designed (it is possible that if a number of schemes are needed, smaller sub-teams should be formed).
- Creation of a risk register with steps to mitigate the risks.
- Outline for a process of approval.
- An implementation and evaluation plan.

Once a broad understanding about the design framework has been established, the design team begins to debate and investigate the structure of the incentive pay scheme systematically.

### Defining the purpose of the scheme

The first step in auditing or designing an incentive pay scheme is to define its scope, outcomes and benefits. A statement of how the incentive pay scheme will help the organisation to achieve its business goals should be formulated to guide the discussions. A distinguishing feature of a successful incentive pay plan is unmistakable clarity about what the plan is to accomplish. Employees must know why the company launched the plan in the first place, how success will be evaluated, and how they will contribute to the success of the business if the scheme purpose is achieved. The purpose describes the key attributes of the plan and the principles to which the plan should adhere.

The purpose statement often makes a distinction between financial (outcome-based or hard) measures and non-financial (operational, process or soft) measures. Financial measures include costs, profits and financial returns. Examples of non-financial measures are defect rates, cycle time and productivity measures. The focus of the incentive pay scheme also plays a role in determining the nature of the measures. If the scheme is aimed at eligibility at the top of the business, the measures are normally broader and influenced by more uncontrollable variables. In these cases the financial measures have the benefit that they measure the final accountability of the participants. The same criterion is not applicable to participants lower in the organisational structure because they do not have the same influence over the variables. Measurements with a direct line of sight such as the non-financial measures will be more applicable in these cases. Non- financial measures are often leading indicators of future financial performance, while financial measures are often historical. Performance measures are discussed in more detail under funding of the incentive pay scheme.

The choice of a purpose for an incentive pay scheme needs careful consideration as multiple objectives could be in conflict. If one purpose of a scheme is to attract and retain key skills and a second is the objective to transfer the risk of lowering remuneration in periods of poorer performance and better remuneration when performance is better, there may be two objectives in direct opposition. However, combining financial and non-financial measures may shorten the line of sight, which in turn improves motivation.

Where the scheme has a "people" purpose such as to achieve a more competitive remuneration programme, improve retention, or increase the ratio of variable to fixed remuneration, entitlement problems seem to emerge. Overall business performance improvement seems to be better if schemes with a financial purpose are used. Non-financial measures are better drivers of organisational change; financial measures such as profits and costs provide weak direction and make it difficult to communicate how the behaviour of employees on lower levels needs to affect the performance goals.

The purpose should be aligned with the rest of the design elements, for example, the definition of eligibility, the funding of the incentive pay scheme, and the distribution of the funds. Without alignment, the incentive pay scheme could confuse participants and implementation could be complicated.

The purpose statement should meet the following criteria:

- It must be specific enough to allow for the auditing of the outcomes of the plan.
- It should contain a statement on how the incentive pay scheme will support the overall business objectives and strategy.
- It must provide clear parameters of performance. Examples of such parameters could be the costs of the incentive pay programme expressed as a proportion of fixed remuneration or business performance, or in relation to overall company expenses.
- It should contain a statement of the required hurdle rates, either as minimum activity levels (non-financial criteria) or minimum financial-value creation (financial criteria).

The purpose of the incentive pay scheme acts as a guide to the designers for the rest of the scheme design. It forms the basis of the communication strategy for line managers who have to communicate the scheme. It is also the benchmark against which the results of the scheme are measured. Ultimately, the purpose is the starting-point from where changes will be made during the annual review of the incentive pay scheme.

### Eligibility

Scheme design requires a decision about the eligibility for inclusion in the incentive plan. The eligible participants are aligned with the purpose of the incentive pay scheme if their normal tasks or roles have a direct influence on the outcome of the scheme. One of the reasons for the failure of incentive pay schemes is that designs give employees little ability to influence results. Therefore, if the measurement of success is based on financial criteria, employees who do not have influence over financial criteria should be excluded. Participants should devote their time to the achievement of the purpose of the incentive pay scheme. They should also have the skills, competencies and opportunity to have a significant impact on the purpose. Designers must assess the participants against demographic factors such as average age, tenure and receptivity to change, the willingness to improve individual and/or group performance and to share information, and level of technical competence and ability to work as a team.

People will take actions in their own interest. It emphasises that people are motivated by the achievement of clearly defined goals and the expectation of payment of valued rewards for performance. This means that if a specific kind of behaviour is rewarded, the organisation will get more of that behaviour, and vice versa. If participants cannot identify with the objectives of the scheme, or will not be motivated by the rewards, they will not change their behaviour and may even have a negative effect on other participants. A more competitive incentive pay strategy can be developed if the designers acknowledge that different jobs and people have different effects on motivation.

The funding of the scheme and the distribution of the payouts also play a role in the identification of participants. If too many employees are eligible, the value of the payouts will be so diluted that it may not influence the behaviour of the participants, leaving the scheme ineffective. Participants should also have the skills, competencies and opportunity to have a significant impact on the purpose. The best results are achieved if a set payout schedule method is followed that will ensure that 90 percent of participants should benefit from the scheme. Between 50 percent and 60 percent should hit their goal and 10 percent should reach the excellence level that has been set. The total number of eligible participants in an incentive pay scheme can be expressed as a percentage of the workforce. Smaller companies will tend to have proportionally more participants than larger companies. This is because the number of employees who can impact on the goals of an incentive pay scheme will tend to be higher (on a percentage basis) in smaller companies where there are fewer organisational levels.

The organisation's operating model directly affects eligibility. Eligibility differs drastically in the case of centralised versus decentralised and capital-intensive versus labour- intensive business models. The level on which the incentive pay scheme targets are set up will affect behaviour. If the level is too high, the participants may lose the line of sight and not be motivated by the scheme. On the other hand, it may stimulate co-operation between the different business areas. If the level is too low, and important contributors are excluded, dysfunctional behaviour may be stimulated.

There is a trend for companies to increase the number of participants in incentive remuneration plans because these plans are forms of contingent remuneration – that means that no remuneration is paid unless performance warrants it. During times of high-cost consciousness/ low affordability, the use of incentive pay plans directly tied to company performance makes good business sense. Where incentive pay is used as contingent remuneration, a culture of entitlement is fostered.

Another technique used by companies to define the incentive pay scheme participants is to identify critical positions; those core organisational competencies that drive business success. Human Resources professionals and remuneration professionals should have a list of these positions, and they should further ensure that those employees whose efforts are critically important to company success are participants in the company's incentive pay scheme. Given the principle of line of sight, this criterion could become less relevant if the participants have no control over the outcome of the scheme.

Some organisations use specific eligibility requirements such as the following:

- Minimum salary. Salary levels are used as cut-off point for participation in the incentive pay scheme. This method is somewhat arbitrary, but objective.
- Salary grade. Experience shows that using salary grade as the primary requirement places pressure on the job evaluation system and few jobs end up being evaluated in the level below minimum bonus plan eligibility. This kind of dysfunctional behaviour impacts on the business performance.
- Reporting relationship. This has to be used with discretion to ensure that the correct people are included and that reporting lines are not abused.
- Ceilings. In these methods, the maximum amount available to pay as incentives is used to determine the cut-off number of participants.
- Discretionary invitations to participate.
- Remuneration committee approval.
- Employment status, for example, full-time versus part-time, employment status changes such as promotions and transfers, and interruptions of service.
- Performance rating to exclude certain employees.
- Eligibility for other plans.
- Initial plan eligibility, in other words, from when will a person qualify for participation?

The above specific eligibility requirements are objective but often irrelevant if they include participants who are not able to influence results. They are at best valuable if they are founded on utility criteria and form objective groupings of eligibility. For example, job grade may be used if the people in those jobs are a representative group of people who are able to influence the outcome of the scheme. Whatever combination is used, the eligibility criteria will erode over time. It is therefore better to be conservative at the outset and include fewer participants to provide for future inflation in participants.

Participants should not participate in more than one scheme with the same purpose. Where this happens, the designers should at least ensure that the participant does not get rewarded twice for the same effort. From a governance perspective, participation in more than one short-term incentive scheme raises suspicion. The eligibility to participate in the scheme plays a major role in determining the funding requirements. It is not, however, the only requirement, but it is certainly one of the most critical considerations.

## *Funding*

Funding the incentive pay scheme is central in any scheme design. It is often the focus of the business' stakeholders, especially if the cost is perceived as being too high, or if the corresponding value-add is not achieved. If the funding is too low, the participants may ignore the incentive pay scheme. The probability of achieving targets also plays a role. If participants perceive the target as impossible to achieve, there will be no motivation to pursue it. Volatility in payments (large and small payments with an element of unpredictability) also has an effect on behaviour. The expectancy theory determines that there should be an expectation that if certain behaviour is displayed, a specific reward will be received. The strength of the motivation will depend on the perceived ability of the person to achieve the performance, the strength of the instrumentality (trust) that the reward will be given, and the value that the person attaches to the reward.

A strong relationship exists between the funding of the incentive pay scheme and its purpose. The purpose of the incentive pay scheme should support the business plan and the performance objectives it is intended to facilitate, as well as the behaviour and/or results that should be rewarded with the payout. The selection of participants is also important for the funding decision, and participants must relate to the funding formula. The method of funding and the distribution of the funds are often interlinked in the same model. Examples can be found in commission schemes, piece-rate or productivity schemes and profit-share schemes, where fixed participation quotas drive individual participation.

Where funding and distribution are based on different models, a close relationship still exists between the participant's behaviour directed towards increasing the bonus pool and gaining the maximum share from the pool. If there is no relationship between funding and distribution, the outcome of the scheme is not optimal. Participants who see only a relationship between the distribution and their behaviour will concentrate only on gaining the maximum from the pool of funds. This emphasises individual contracting and performance management. Where a poor relationship exists between the funding model and the participants' behaviour, results may be achieved in spite of the existence of an incentive pay scheme, and payouts will have been wasted.

## *Selecting performance measures*
*(See also Tables 13.2, 13.3 and 13.4)*

With incentive pay scheme design, a central debate is always the process of target setting. This tends to be emotional and filled with personal interest. Unless it can be tied to objective processes that are defendable and fair to participants, suspicion is often raised about the targets to be achieved. In the figure below, the process to define the performance measures is described as a process where the critical success targets (CST) are informed by and integrated with the organisational strategy. The critical success targets are then translated into performance measures. Performance measures could be a single measure or a combination of measures and are defined at organisational, business unit, departmental, team, and/or individual level.

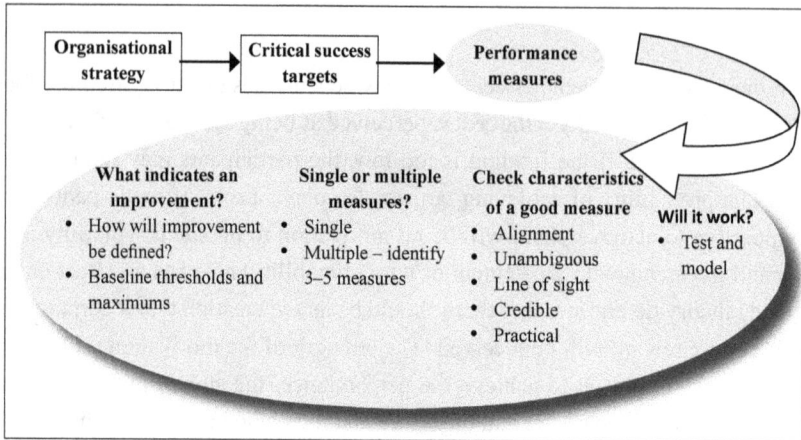

*Figure 13.7: Framework for selecting performance measures*

### Characteristics of performance measures

Performance measures are quantitative or qualitative objectives and standards against which performance is evaluated. The standards are derived from the organisational strategy and critical success targets, and should have the following characteristics:

- **Specific:** The tasks or activities to be done as well as the expected outcomes should be stated
- clearly.
- **Measurable:** Results must be quantifiable, observable or verifiable.
- **Attainable:** Are the targets, with a stretch, within the control of the participant to reach?
- **Relevance:** The performance measures must be related to the business objectives and the individual objectives of the participant.
- **Time-bound:** The objectives must be achieved within a clear timetable.

Performance measures are often set through business-specific criteria, including budget plans and management targets. The value of business-specific performance measures lies in the flexibility and analytical insight with which they are created. They are better suited to the unique circumstances of the business and are therefore useful. Business-specific performance measures are, however, viewed with suspicion by the different stakeholders. Shareholders will not accept them if they do not exceed market-expected returns; the community and customer base will not tolerate remuneration that they perceive as exploiting consumers or leading to the inequitable remuneration of selected individuals; and participants view targets as too difficult if they perceive them as unachievable, and may not even attempt to achieve the targets.

Universal/generic targets, or targets used across industries and continents, are defensible because they are used universally and all businesses can be valued against them. The use of universal/ generic performance criteria or hurdles aims to reward performance that comes from superior performance itself and not from macroeconomic or industry factors. However, uniqueness in the circumstances of a business creates problems where universal/generic methods are used.

Performance measures, and specifically the hurdles per performance measure, should ensure that a minimum return is achieved before any incentive is paid. A good example of a universal/generic financial measure with a built-in hurdle is value-based management (VBM). VBM is an approach to managing a business with the primary goal of maximising long-term, sustainable value for the business' shareholders. It is a process that focuses on maximising the value of the investments made by suppliers of debt and equity funding. VBM provides an expectation that managers will operate in a manner that will provide returns in excess of the cost of equity capital and debt.

Performance measures are commonly divided into financial and non-financial performance measures. Another classification is quantitative and operational measures. Financial performance measures (net earnings, net income, ROE, EPS, ROA) and quantitative measures (market share, unit volume, productivity goals) are more common in higher levels of the organisation. Non-financial measures (implementing a new business system, completing a new facility) and operational measures (successfully integrating two similar business functions, upgrading employee skill levels, producing $x$ units) are used lower in the organisation. The operational and non- financial criteria work best for departments or individuals, and are non-financial criteria are treated as leading indicators of ultimate business performance. A combination of financial and operational benchmarks is also popular. Performance measures relative to the organisational levels are depicted in the table below.

*Table 13.5: Performance measures relative to organisational levels*

| Performance measures | Organisation | Business unit | Team | Individual |
|---|---|---|---|---|
| Financial and quantitative criteria | • Self-funded<br>• Budget schemes<br>• Equity plans | • Self-funded<br>• Budget schemes | | |
| Non-financial and qualitative criteria | | | • Gain-share<br>• Activity-based schemes | • Gain-share<br>• Activity-based schemes |

The performance measure and level at which it is applied influence the funding models chosen by the designers. If the performance measure is financial, the funding model will be organisation- or business unit-wide. Typical funding models will include self-funded and budgeted schemes. Non- financial performance measures are normally used on a lower organisational level to distribute individual pay-outs. Typical funding models will include activity-based schemes and gain-share. Where performance is measured on more than one level in the organisation, the contribution on each level could be weighted to calculate the bonus distribution. For example, a participant working in a business unit that contributes to the total group results could share in the achievements of the business unit as well as those of the overall group. This will enhance co-operation between business units. If the measurements of an operational nature are done at the operational level, it could be required that measures of a financial nature should be achieved before full payouts will be made. This will affect line of sight, but may reduce the risk to the business.

The number of performance measures must remain manageable (between three and five measures). These include a combination of qualitative and quantitative measures. If not all the meaningful activities are included as performance measures, the non-measured activities may become neglected. An example of this is where sales are rewarded at the expense of long-term customer relations.

Including too many measures in a scheme has the following dangers:

- It makes the scheme unnecessarily complicated.
- It divides the pay-out into so many different areas that the accomplishment of any one does not provide sufficient economic gain to the participant.
- Having too many performance measures may lead participants to infer that anything not included is not important.

Specific considerations to take into account when performance measures are selected are listed below:

- Performance measures must be aligned with business objectives.
- Performance measures must be translated from the business strategy.
- Performance measures require credible competitive data.
- Management must ensure that performance measures will lead to the achievement of objectives.
- Performance measures must not lead to a waste of resources.
- Performance measures should include quality criteria (for example, increased sales should not create a debtor problem).
- Performance measures should be credible and unambiguous.
- Performance measures subject to uncontrollable factors should be avoided.
- Unreliable performance measures could set a wrong basis for performance hurdles:
  - Incentive pay schemes should ideally not be implemented in start-up businesses because of the volatility and lack of history and results.
  - Performance measures with a cycling risk should not be used.
  - If new production processes, substituting labour for capital, price changes, changes in the product design or raw material, or any factors beyond the control of the participants that could influence results are present, the performance measures should not be used.
  - Where new products that could erode profitability or add value beyond participant control influence the performance measures, the performance measure should be excluded.

- o    There must be a line of sight between participant behaviour and performance targets.
- o    Pay-out caps must be used with discretion.
- o    Manipulation of performance measures should be avoided or prevented.
- Performance measures must be practical or easy to administer.
- Performance measures should adhere to good governance principles.
- Performance measures must be transparent to all the stakeholders.

### *Funding models*

There is a certain amount of confusion among writers about the different categories of incentive pay schemes that exist. Incentive schemes and bonuses are often used as synonyms and sometimes as definitions to differentiate between scheme designs. There is a clear difference between the funding model and the incentive pay scheme type. Funding is the method by which money for awards is generated; funding models are described as the methods employed by designers to generate the necessary funds to finance the incentive pay scheme. Funding is based on the "line of sight" principle, which means that the behaviour of the participants is aligned with the mechanisms that will lead to the achievement and exceeding of the performance standards.

Funding models represent categories of incentive pay scheme types grouped together on the basis of the way they are funded and the funds are distributed. The four categories described below cover all the possible incentive pay scheme designs that could be produced. The categories identified are: self-funded incentive schemes; self-funded bonus schemes; budgeted incentive schemes; and budgeted bonus schemes. The term "incentive" refers to schemes where participants have pre-contracted certain targets to receive predetermined incentives, while "bonus" refers to schemes where payments are made without specific pre-contracted targets with participants. This is depicted in Figure 13.8 below.

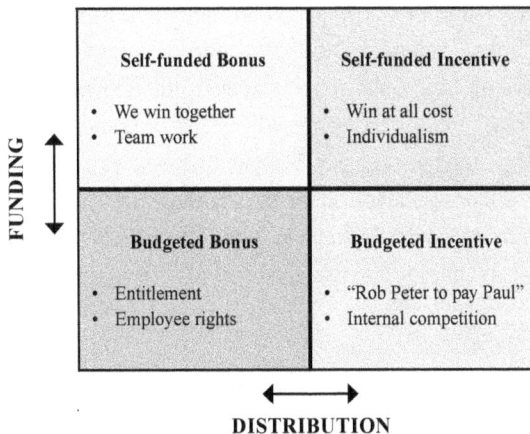

*Figure 13.8: The influence of the funding model on the business*

## *Size of the award*

The return on pay-out (ROP) is determined through a three-step calculation. The first step is to determine how much money is needed for pay-out if the target is 100 percent achieved on every measure. This calculation will give the cost of the scheme at target level and it could be calibrated for scenarios above and below the target. The second step is to calculate the value of the improvement for each measure of performance. The improvement caused by the introduction of the scheme can be divided into cash value and operational measures. Calculating the cash value is relatively simple, but in the case of value-added returns (for example, client loyalty and increase in intellectual capital), attaching a cash value becomes difficult. The solution is not to quantify qualitative improvements but to state them as qualitative improvements.

The third step in the calculation is to determine the financial ROP. The formula* is:

### Net ROP percentage = (gain – payout)/payout x 100

* Any qualitative gains from the scheme are listed as statements of qualitative gains. This is done to supplement the quantitative gains in the above calculation. The two sets of information provide the full value-add of the scheme.

Achieving a positive return on the scheme pay-out is one of several calculations that should be made. A positive return on the pay-out is, however, no guarantee that the scheme pay-out will be acceptable to the participants or motivate them. People are motivated if they believe that their effort will be "good enough" to achieve the objective(s) and that they will be rewarded when they achieve the objective(s). The third factor that drives motivation is the value that the individual attaches to the outcome.

Determining the ideal remuneration size depends on the expectations of the participants. This differs according to individual needs and different industry practices. Where targets are too high, participants will give up before the scheme is even implemented. If the targets are more challenging, the expectations of larger payments will be higher compared to situations where the difficulty level is lower. The ratio between pay-out and the business gains affects the expectations of participants. Similarly, job or role levels in the organisation influence expectations of pay-out. People higher in the hierarchy expect higher pay-outs. Participants' awareness of the external and internal incentive pay practices influences the level of satisfaction they will derive from the outcomes of the scheme.

The historical pay-outs also create an expected benchmark. Research indicates that there is a significant gap between what participants want to be paid for their performance and what they receive. These expectations must be moderated within the business' ability to remunerate and the value of the returns on the performance improvement. Awards could be financial and/or non-financial, but should be meaningful.

Designers may need to do surveys of the expectations and the current level of satisfaction among participants to determine what level of remuneration is necessary to satisfy their expectations. Where multiple measures of performance are used, the different performance measures should be weighted to determine their contribution to the final payment. If possible, the financial contribution of each measure should be calculated according to the contribution it made to the business outcome. This will not always be practical, and where qualitative measures are used, estimations or arbitrary values should be assigned to these measures.

### *The distribution model*

There is a close relationship between the funding of the scheme and the distribution of the funds. Both deal with the perceptual link between the expected performance and the reward from the scheme. The two design elements must be aligned to avoid conflict and confusion. It may happen that designers use the two design elements on an integrated basis, for example, where the funding and the distribution are actually the same process. Examples of this are commission schemes and activity-based productivity pay-out formulas. Examples can also be found in budgeted and self-funded incentive schemes, where the funding formula and the distribution formula are integrated, for example, where the incentive pool is created from "over-profits" and the individual's share is determined by the individual contribution to the "over-profit".

The funding element and the distribution element may also be used independently. This is where the funding is done independently from the distribution. The size of the pool is determined by the funding mechanism while the distribution is done using different criteria. For example, the funding is done using financial criteria, while the pool is divided on qualitative criteria. Where the independent method is used, care should be taken that the behaviour of the participants remains focused on the purpose of the scheme.

### *Perceived fairness of distribution*

Distribution of pay-outs is based on either behavioural or results measures. Behavioural measures are performance measures based on "how people do things". They deal with the process side of the business, workflows, values, and individual and group behaviour. Such measures are useful where a long line of sight exists between the participant's behaviour and the ultimate performance of the business. Behavioural measures are within the control of participants. On the negative side, behavioural performance measures are not directly linked to business outcomes, and payments may be made without any corresponding business achievement.

Results measures emphasise business achievements, which are either financial or operational. Results measures are useful when the line of sight is clear, for example, if the participant's performance is closely related to the business objectives. Operational performance measures are short-cycle measures that deal with the effectiveness of single and/or multiple performance measures. To identify operational performance measures, business processes are analysed to understand how they create results. Examples of operational performance measures are timely deliveries, cycle time, and defect rate. Financial performance measures include financial indicators and financial ratios, volumes, and end results (aggregate performance). Financial performance measures are not effective as leading indicators and tend to focus on past performance. Financial performance measures help participants to understand the business and their role in making it successful.

Performance measures could be either mechanistic or subjective. Mechanistic distribution measures are preferred by participants because they create certainty and therefore increase motivation, however designing these measures is complicated and not very reliable. For this reason, subjective measures are always considered a viable alternative. In certain situations, mechanistic formulas could become a burden to the business. If there are uncontrollable external events that influence the outcome of the incentive pay scheme, mechanistic formulas place a legalistic (or at least moral) obligation on the business to perform in terms of the scheme rules, which could be costly if the business cannot afford the windfall payouts. This is often mitigated by escape clauses in the scheme contract, but these create suspicion and lower motivation. Mechanistic formulas are better suited to huge populations or where financial and quantitative measures are used.

Assessment of participants' performance remains subject to management discretion. This is applied in output measurement instruments such as management by objectives (MBO) or work performance and review (WPR). The use of management discretion in these instruments is generally acceptable. However, the use of discretionary distribution criteria, which are not clearly defined, potentially runs the risk of sending indifferent messages to the participants, especially if the distribution is not aligned with the purpose and the funding formula. Where discretionary distribution criteria are defined after the fact, the line of sight is broken and the value of the scheme is reduced. Uncertainty about pay-outs, as in the case of discretionary pay-outs, reduces the levels of motivation.

The following factors contribute positively to the perception of fair distribution and participant satisfaction:

- Openness about the decision process.
- Having the "right" individuals involved in the distribution process.
- Clearly-stated criteria for distribution exist prior to the distribution.
- Involvement of the participants in the distribution process.
- The existence of an appeal process.

### *Design factors that influence pay-out*

During the designing of an incentive pay scheme, the designers have to make a number of critical decisions about the distribution of the payout. In this section, a list of these critical decisions is discussed:

- **Forms of payout**

Payout could be in cash, in a non-cash form, or in different forms of equity. The cash and equity forms of payout are generally understood, but this is not the case with non-cash payments. The term "scheme with a trophy value" is used as it explains the motivational theory behind it well. Not all participants prefer the non-cash method of incentive because they want to decide what they want to do with the incentive they have earned. Cash therefore has more universal appeal.

A "trophy" scheme normally has a shorter life span compared to other forms of incentive pay. Non-cash payouts or schemes with trophy value refer to incentives awarded to participants when they have achieved certain milestones. These could be items that the participant "wins", for example, a holiday or articles in a catalogue. Such an award has trophy value because it remains visible to the participant for a long period after it was awarded and has some "bragging" value to friends and family. As such, it has good retention and motivational value for a longer period. Cash, on the other hand, slips away without the participants being able to remember what it was used for.

A trophy value scheme implies that it is over and above fixed remuneration; it has a direct line of sight. If managed cleverly, it could involve the participant's support group (for example, their family). Non-cash payouts are associated with a high level of leveraging of motivational elements. They create excitement and are often associated with intensive communication support. Such an award is perceived as a celebration of success and has more commitment value than cash. Trophy schemes appeal to higher human needs, such as recognition, thus they have more impact than basic cash payouts. Appreciation is often more valued than the reward itself. In contrast to cash, which may create entitlement, trophy value schemes do not create obligations. In schemes with trophy awards, every participant could win.

Non-cash payouts are, however, very information and administration intensive. A large portion of the incentive budget goes into the administration of the scheme, which reduces the returns on the scheme (ROP). It also has more potential to be manipulated, and extra care should be devoted to managing the payout and the total scheme. In the author's experience, schemes with a trophy value (non-cash payout) work well in support of company-wide marketing campaigns because they create short-term excitement and focus among participants.

The authorities regard schemes with a trophy value as income, and any benefit is therefore taxable. This increases the complexity of managing these schemes. The infrastructure required to manage these schemes is considerable, and specialist companies often manage them.

- **Frequency of pay-outs**

The frequency of payout is influenced by two guidelines. The first is that the shorter the interval between the performance and the payout, the higher the motivation. The second is that the more frequent the payment of the incentive, the more pressure on administration and management time.

The scheme design could provide for bonus banks to encourage sustained performance. This means that future payments of the banked bonus will depend on continued performance levels. The frequency of payout has a direct impact on the behaviour it stimulates. If the reward is paid soon after the behaviour is displayed, the motivation levels will be higher because of increased awareness and the perceived line of sight. Short-term payouts tend to focus behaviour on short-term objectives and ignore the long-term objectives necessary for sustainability. Participants higher in the organisational hierarchy are accustomed to delayed rewards, while at the lower levels, the opposite applies. Because the frequency of payout is so diverse, there is a case for allowing multiple payout systems.

- **Cycling**

Cycling refers to the variation of performance above and below the baseline. Cycling could result in payouts being made during the overview period without an accumulated improvement over the total period. This typically happens when the phasing of the targets is incorrect or if external factors influence the outcomes. The principle of cycling is explained graphically in the figure below. In the example, the first two payments were made because the performance at the time was above the target, yet at the end of the overview period, performance dropped to below the accumulative target level and the annual target was not achieved.

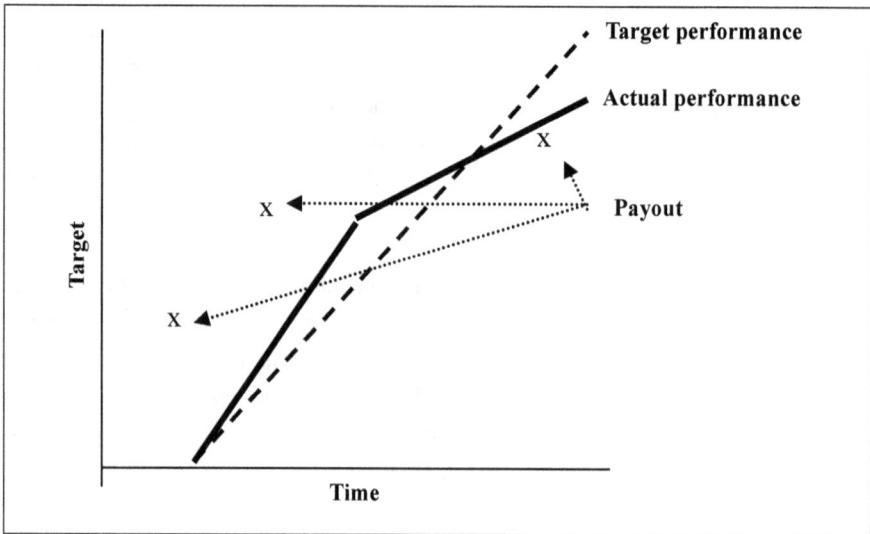

*Figure 13.9: The effect of cycling on cumulative performance*

Many "losses" caused by premature payouts occur if the cycle time of incentive schemes indicates that payouts are to be made before the end of the overview period. This leads to the concept of deferred payments referred to above in an attempt to smooth payments and avoid paying incentives, only to incur losses in the next accounting period.

- **Timing of payouts**

Timing of payouts influences the line of sight. The sooner after the event that payouts are made, the higher the motivation. Payouts can be immediate (spot bonus), short-term, tied to normal work cycle, annual, or according to project milestones and duration.

- **The threshold or minimum**

The threshold is the minimum level of performance at which a payout is earned. The threshold is determined by the scheme rules and could be on or below the target performance baseline.

- **Maximum or "cap"**

The "cap" is the level of performance at which the payouts stop. This ensures that the cost of the scheme is controlled and prevents windfalls. It also limits the upside earnings potential and may be a disincentive to performance after the maximum has been reached. However, if the interests of all stakeholders are analysed, good corporate governance requires that payouts must be limited. Benchmarking and peer comparison could provide guidelines to the level of capping. Capping could be absolute, for example, only 5,000 per person or 10 percent of salary, or it could be relative, for example, 20 percent of the over-profit or not more than 10 percent of the total profit before tax. Relative capping allows for growth in the bonus pool, although at a lower and more controlled rate.

Depending on the purpose of the scheme, differential rates of incentive could be used at different stages of the performance curve. In the figure below the different rates of incentive are depicted. The target is 100 percent but a threshold of 90 percent is set from which payments accumulate. The rate of payment increases after the target performance has been reached and is then absolutely capped at 105 percent of the performance.

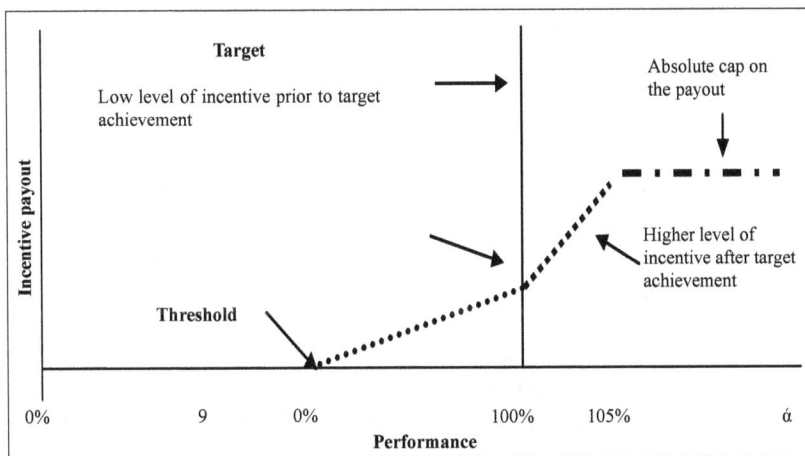

*Figure 13.10: Different levels of incentive against different performance achievement levels*

- **Windfalls and cave-ins**

A windfall is an incentive or bonus earned due to unplanned, extraordinary event(s) outside the participants' control. A cave-in is a lower-than-expected incentive award as a result of events outside the control of the participants. Scheme rules should provide for guidelines on how to manage windfalls and cave-ins. The governance rules dealing with management discretion and their authority to change rules in these events should be contracted upfront. This is necessary in order to maintain the trust relationships that exist between the participants and management, and not destroy motivation levels.

- **Effect on benefits**

Incentives paid in lieu of fixed remuneration erode the basis of benefits such as retirement planning and life and disability cover. Designers should make calculations of these effects and consider alternatives to avoid eroding these benefits.

- **Change in control**

Incentive pay schemes, especially equity-based schemes, provide for change in the control of the company. They could allow for the immediate payout of incentives or vesting of options/ shares. This flexibility is useful as governance policies may differ between management groups. The presence of these clauses in the scheme rules could spark speculation about poor governance.

*Methods of distribution*

Distribution methods are the methods by which payouts are distributed to individual participants in the scheme.

- **Equal percentage of fixed remuneration**

If the salary bill is 100 million and the incentive pool is five million (or 5 percent of the fixed remuneration bill), the distribution will be 5 percent of fixed remuneration.

- **Fixed amount to each employee**

If the total pool is five million with 1,000 participants, the incentive payout will be 5,000 per employee.

- **Graduated distribution**

Graduated distribution is the actual payout as a percentage of the targeted pool applied to individual target payouts. For example, each participant receives a different bonus based on his or her performance rating and current salary, but the size of the bonus pool remains fixed. In this example, the required incentive will be calculated and then divided into the available pool to determine the factor by which the required pool should be adjusted to ensure that the incentive pool is divided evenly.

- **Performance management**

Performance management processes are useful instruments to measure performance and distribute incentives. About 50 percent of companies use individual recognition awards, which help to hold participants accountable for achieving the purpose of the incentive pay scheme. However, if such awards do not have credibility or do not work well, it is better not to use them. Performance appraisals should ideally not be introduced as a distribution mechanism for the incentive pay system; they should exist on their own merit, with the incentive pay scheme benefiting from the existing performance appraisal system. Performance management is integrated into the business processes to create work value. It consists of the processes of selecting for success, defining role value, goal-setting, developing performance measurement criteria, counselling, and coaching.

There is a debate about whether businesses should pay for the "what" only, or whether the "how" is as important. If fixed remuneration is increased based on temporary performance, an unjustifiable burden is created for future remuneration. Therefore, a performance-based distribution model that links work value (referring to the high-level business processes of inputs, throughputs and outputs) with rewards will provide differentiation in the way funds are applied and show the relationship more accurately. The links between work value and rewards given in the figure below analytically ensure optimisation of the remuneration spending. For instance, the roles that require skills and competencies (the inputs) are better paid through base salary. These skills are also constantly subject to market changes and the personal role contribution of the individual. Linking the additional fixed remuneration to the person in these circumstances will create less of the annuity. In the case of roles associated with outputs, incentive pay is more appropriate, especially if it is associated with short-term performance.

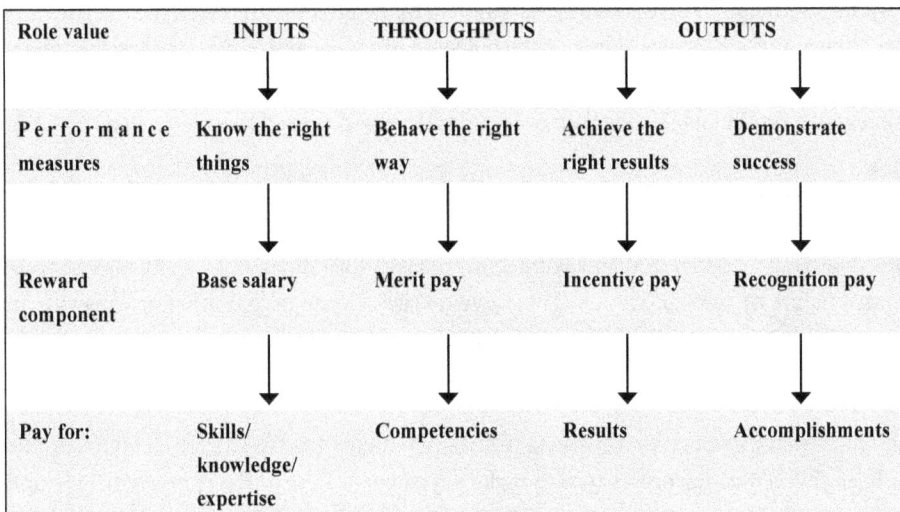

| Role value | INPUTS | THROUGHPUTS | OUTPUTS | |
|---|---|---|---|---|
| | ↓ | ↓ | ↓ | ↓ |
| Performance measures | Know the right things | Behave the right way | Achieve the right results | Demonstrate success |
| | ↓ | ↓ | ↓ | ↓ |
| Reward component | Base salary | Merit pay | Incentive pay | Recognition pay |
| | ↓ | ↓ | ↓ | ↓ |
| Pay for: | Skills/ knowledge/ expertise | Competencies | Results | Accomplishments |

*Figure 13.11: Linking work value with rewards*

Incentive pay must never be assessed in isolation. The effect of other forms of remuneration and the role in the organisation need to be taken into account to achieve a total picture of remuneration. The increased complexity and integrative nature of modern-day work reduce the importance of individual performance appraisals in incentive pay schemes and place more emphasis on total rewards. Performance appraisals deal with far more than objective measurements of performance; there is a whole area of ego involvement, prestige and fairness in terms of labour law that confuses the process. Furthermore, performance management in a business is utilised for a wide range of actions (such as career management, development needs, fixed remuneration, incentive pay, recognition schemes, retention programmes, and selection criteria for retrenchment). This means that the interaction between the appraiser and appraisee is often driven by other considerations.

Performance appraisal systems for use in incentive pay schemes should have the characteristics described below. If they do not, consideration should be given to using other performance measurements.

The work and job design must allow for individual appraisal; it is no good having a situation where the work is designed for (integrated) group performance and then individual performance is assessed. Where this happens, the potential for dysfunctional behaviour increases. Where individual performance appraisals are used, the individual (participant in the scheme) must be responsible for the whole job and not be dependent on other people for performance.

The communication between the appraiser and the appraisee must be open and regular, and the scheme participant must get regular feedback so that the final appraisal is not a surprise. Opportunity and support to improve the assessment rating must also be created. This will improve not only the appraisal scheme, but also the outcome of the incentive pay scheme. Collaboration must exist between the participants and the manager(s) to enable learning opportunities, sufficient resources, and continuous feedback in order to achieve and exceed stretch targets.

It may be necessary to measure and reward group or team performance. Team distribution amplifies the message that teamwork and group solutions are important and that those teams should take responsibility for managing the process under their control. It also reflects the integrated nature of work processes. The move towards lateral organisation process structuring to reduce costs and improve the quality and speed of decision-making requires team-based distribution practices.

On the other hand, critics of team-based distribution argue that for fear of losing team morale, it has been found that businesses tend to make payments in spite of the team not achieving their objectives. Group-based payments may lead to overpayment of average performers during good years and underpayment of good performers during periods of poor performance. The following are examples of different methods to evaluate team contribution:

- ○ Evaluate individuals in the group on their contribution to the group.
- ○ Evaluate the team's performance and base the total award on this assessment.
- ○ Award separate amounts for team and individual performance.
- ○ Evaluate the team's performance first and then use it as the basis for individual assessments, which could mean that these individual assessments could be moved up or down.
- ○ Distribute the funds equally among the team members or base the award on their fixed salary.

- **Peer assessments**

Peer assessment can add credibility to the distribution of funds. It is, however, a very emotional process that could easily go wrong. Peer assessments can take the form of completing assessment forms, discussion of performance with the participant present, or the use of 360-degree feedback questionnaires. Supervisor rating by subordinates is also a method of peer rating. Peer assessments do not work well unless an open culture prevails; if participants are not motivated to participate, this method will not work. The participants must also be in a situation where they could have observed the work of the peers that they are assessing. Peer assessments work better in areas of professional work, where standards are better known and documented. Where peer assessment works, information is brought into the open and adds to the credibility of the distribution process. To enhance the process, supportive business processes such as measurement criteria could be brought into the assessment. Peer assessment should be viewed only as information gathering about performance.

- **Multiple measures**

In multiple-measure plans, different weighting can be given to each measure. The weighting will be determined by the purpose of the scheme as it reflects the business strategy.

- **Step payout**

Step payout occurs where each incremental improvement is paid at a specified level. These intervals determine that if the performance levels have not reached the next level, the payout falls back to the previous level. This method could be used in schemes where the performance measures do not allow for simple continuous performance improvement, for example, behavioural measures.

- **Continuous payout**

Continuous payout means that the scheme is paying for every increment of improvement in the performance measure. The benefit of this approach is that it provides motivation to continue performing well once the threshold has been exceeded. The negative aspect of this approach is the open-ended risk to the business. This often leads to the introduction of a cap to prevent uncontrollable risks.

## *Summary*

Up to this point, the design of the purpose of the scheme, eligibility to participate, funding of the scheme and the distribution of funds has been discussed. These areas are traditionally the focus of incentive pay scheme design. However, failures of incentive pay are often caused by the administration or lack thereof. The administrative rules often provide the "look and feel" of the incentive pay scheme, which influences the perceptions about the scheme.

## *Scheme administration*

The administrative rules of the plan must as far as possible be standardised within group companies where more than one incentive pay scheme is deployed. This is necessary to simplify the administration and interpretation of the scheme rules. From a labour law and equity perspective, consistency is required in organisations and standardised rules are therefore better. Other considerations that need to be taken into account under plan administration are the following:

- Rules related to the continuation and termination of the scheme.
- Movement of staff between departments/divisions.
- Promotions of participants in and out of the scheme need to be covered in the rules.
- Payroll execution: In the case where regular payments are made to larger groups, a branded debit card could be used into which to pay the incentive monies. This will remind the participants about the scheme and the objectives every time they use the card, thereby enhancing the value of the scheme.
- Tenure of employment of the participants: This includes aspects such as death, retirement, disability, unpaid leave, termination, secondments to other areas of the business.
- Provision for expenses (before and after target achievement): This is an important process in the management of the schemes as "surprises" during payout, either from a cash flow or profitability perspective, could harm the business.
- Frequency of payments forms part of the distribution design and requires administration.
- More frequent payments affect the approval mandates. Processes to calculate the payments and the approvals must be defined.
- Recording of payments.
- Reporting of payments.
- Dealing with exceptional circumstances.
- Defining the responsibility for administrative tasks, which will ensure that misunderstanding and failure of delivery will be limited.

Incentive pay schemes have the potential to be manipulated, which leads to counter-productive behaviour and attempts to "beat the system". Measures need to be put in place, firstly, to prevent this kind of behaviour, and secondly, to cancel the scheme if this kind of behaviour occurs.

Manipulation of budgets or targets is well known and recorded. Similarly, if management unfairly changes the targets without explanation, the integrity of the scheme could also be destroyed. Complaints about the standards or targets could easily lead to unrealistic adjustments in the standards. In sales environments, targets for apparently similar sales areas are often very diverse because of client potential, profitability and different risk profiles. In these cases, target setting becomes very difficult as it depends on the ability of the sales manager to do proper territory planning and the ability to convince sales consultants that the sales plan needs to be changed and targets adjusted. These difficult planning variables are often manipulated in favour of the participant, which could leave the scheme dysfunctional.

Hiding information from management in an attempt to maximise income is another form of recorded dysfunctional behaviour. A production standard or sales target will not rise because the people do not reveal the true potential or solutions involved. The group then protects these standards, and people breaking the standard are sanctioned into staying within the norm. This situation often leads to a culture of non-performance.

In many cases it is not possible to measure the contribution of support staff, who are then excluded from the incentive pay scheme. This could lead to behaviour where the non- participants refuse to support the productive participants. This is often so counter-productive that management's time is taken up in solving internal conflict and there is not enough time to devote to optimising output. Cases have been reported where employees made career decisions based on the presence of incentive pay schemes in certain jobs, choices that could not be justified under other circumstances.

Higher production also leads to other fears among employees, such as loss of work opportunities. All the benefits of the scheme are ignored in these circumstances and behaviour is shifted towards protecting their work security. Trust (or the lack thereof) between management and participants could change the outcome of the scheme. In worst case situations, the workers (and their union) could harass management by overloading them with grievances and complaints and tying them up in paperwork until they concede to sub-standard targets.

Incentive pay schemes also create expectations of permanent income. It is possible that participants in the scheme may insist on remuneration if the scheme comes to an end. It is therefore important that the terms of the scheme should address the duration of the scheme.

The cost of administering incentive pay schemes increases the cost of remuneration administration. Time to design, implement and administer schemes is several times more than for fixed remuneration. System design and information networks are far more resource intensive. An incentive pay scheme also creates the opportunity for more disputes and management time spent on non-productive behaviour. The administrative rules of the incentive pay scheme are more than a set of rules to guide the day-to-day management of the scheme; they must also ensure that the scheme remains focused on its purpose. In addition, employee attitudes towards incentive pay have hardened. Modern-day employees will raise grievances and appeal to the legal channels if they feel unfairly treated. More managers are held accountable for their remuneration decisions than before.

An area of scheme design that is closely related to the scheme administration is that of the governance principles by which the scheme is managed. Governance issues about incentive pay are emotive and focus the attention of the different stakeholders on the scheme. Incentive pay schemes are perceived in many circles as perverse (see the references to failed schemes), or at least viewed with suspicion.

### Governance

Incentive pay is a primary focus area of corporate governance. Initially, incentive pay schemes drew attention when they were mainly used for executive remuneration. The perception that executives were overpaid compared to ordinary employees focused the attention of remuneration committees on this area of remuneration. Schemes should therefore provide for proper guidelines on how the scheme should be governed.

Since corporate scandals hit the United States some years ago, stringent measures have been introduced to discourage abuse of incentive pay schemes. Executives are now held accountable if the company does not succeed. In terms of new legislation, in the event of results that were overstated in terms of accounting standards, the Chief Executive Officer and Chief Financial Officer must repay the company for equity-based remuneration and incentives they received during the previous 12 months. Governance guidelines on the following aspects should be specified in the scheme rules:

- The powers of the role players who will approve the scheme within the organisation's levels of approval.
- The powers of the role players who will approve amendment to the rules or invoke escape clauses.
- The powers of the role players responsible for the approval of payouts.
- How reports about incentive payments will be structured and reported.
- Audits of schemes should take place after the overview periods. These audits need to be reported to the approvers of the schemes. Audits should provide an assessment of the value- add of the scheme and include an assessment of whether the scheme has achieved its purpose.
- Once the incentive pay scheme has been designed, prudent governance requires that the scheme be simulated to determine its functionality and the business implications of the scheme.

*Testing of the design*

During the funding design of the scheme, a validation/modulation of the proposed scheme through financial and business modulation helps to provide a realistic expectation of the cost and benefits, as well as employee reactions to the scheme. If necessary, changes are made to the design. It is likely that the design team will need to test the design with a wider spectrum of people or communicate it more widely. Consulting with a wider audience may lead to further adjustments or rejection of the proposed scheme. Once the designers have agreed on the final design, it should be documented in the prescribed format. A presentation should be prepared and presented as a detailed proposal to the management team, who will accept the proposal, reject it, or require further details or adaptations. If the scheme is accepted, it will be registered on a central database. Where a number of schemes are implemented in a group of companies, each scheme will be assigned a unique payout number to allow for future tracking of payouts made by the scheme.

*Summary of the design phase of the incentive pay scheme*

During the design phase, an incentive pay solution is crafted. The output of this phase is a scheme document that states the purpose of the scheme. There should be clarity about the purpose, and it must be comprehensive enough to justify the investment. The eligibility of participation and inclusion is defined. Funding is determined by selecting a funding approach that will ensure the maximum line of sight between participant behaviour and the purpose and funding of the scheme. Distribution of the funds to participants has been decided, again with a line of sight between participant behaviour and the distribution criteria as the determining factor. Scheme rules to provide clarity about the administration of the scheme have been drafted, and where more than one scheme is implemented, consistency between the scheme rules is ensured. The governance of the scheme is described, and matters such as approval and changes to the scheme rules documented.

Once the scheme has been designed, it is modelled to determine the potential cost and returns that will be achieved against possible outcomes. This is then presented to the authorities for approval. Approval of the design means that implementation planning will start. Implementation must ensure that awareness, understanding, acceptance and, ultimately, entrenchment of the incentive pay scheme take place. The investment in incentive pay is substantial. Failure to implement a well-designed scheme could mean that the resources invested in the design, and more importantly, the ultimate payout, will be wasted.

## 13.2.5 Phase 3: The implementation of incentive pay schemes

An incentive pay scheme has been implemented if all participants understand, accept and internalise the performance measures of the approved scheme. They must understand the behaviour that they will have to display to achieve the performance measures. Systems will be in place to measure the performance, regular feedback against the performance criteria will be given, and if targets are achieved, payments will be made on the set date. Where incentive pay schemes are implemented, understanding of the business and accountability for results are reinforced at all levels of participation. The implementation of incentive pay schemes can vary from a single memo to eligible employees to an extremely complex process involving stakeholder negotiations and substantial change management. The complexity of the schemes designed and their differences from traditional work practices substantially impact the ease of implementation. All implementations should be supported by a plan, which needs to be presented to management for support and approval. In terms of the methodology, the constructs of the implementation phase of incentive pay are depicted in the figure below.

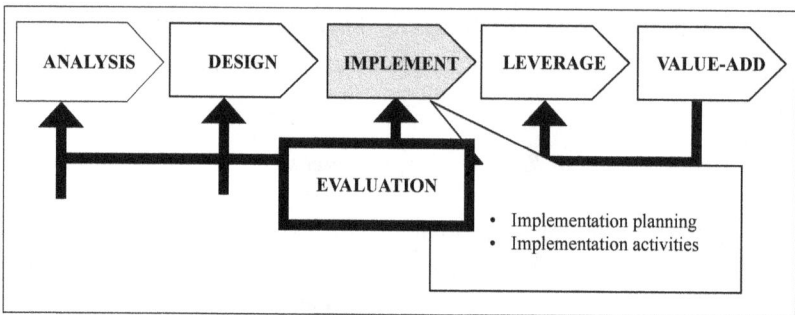

*Figure 13.12: The implementation phase*

### *Implementation planning*

Depending on the complexity of the implementation, a core team will suffice for low-level change interventions. However, for more complex implementations, the implementation team needs cross-functional representation (see Figure 13.13 below).

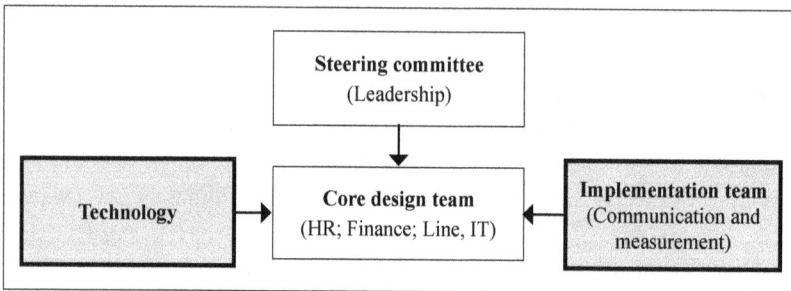

*Figure 13.13: Low-level versus complex implementations*

In the above model, the core team is used in all implementations, while the extended team (shaded, additional blocks) is used only in complex implementations. The level of change (low or high level) will determine the involvement of the role players (see the list below) and the cost of the implementation:

- The Steering Committee (leadership group), which must always be involved.
- Representatives from the design team (including line management), who form the core team.
- A representative from Human Resources if the person was not included in the design team.
- Communication/ change management expert (extended team).
- Technology representatives (extended team).
- Measurement and contracting representatives of the participants (extended team).

This team (either the core or core with the extended team) should review the implications of the scheme and agree on the actions that need to take place in order for the scheme to be implemented successfully. The activities that need to be resolved by the different role players and implementation team are described in the next section.

### *Implementation activities*

#### *Sign-off and approval*

Before the incentive pay scheme can be implemented, it has to be approved by the management team and/or the person identified as the authorised approver. Incentive pay schemes are part of the business model. Approvers must satisfy themselves that the scheme will enhance the business and performance, as well as be aligned with the expectations of the different stakeholders in the business. There must also be reasonable expectations that the scheme will improve the business results. The approval process is best served if the designers offer the approvers an analysis of the scheme in terms of the positioning in the business, the project cost/budget estimates, the scheme design, the administration of the programme, the roles of key participants and the risks identified. Plans to mitigate the risks should be submitted so that the approvers can make informed decisions.

#### *Appointing an implementation leader*

An implementation leader has to be appointed to guide the implementation process; he or she must have a sense of ownership of the scheme and must want to improve the business process. The implementation leader should also have credibility with the management team, the participants and the implementation team. Knowledge of the implementation process and the change requirements are further requirements.

#### *Business and management process adjustment*

Incentive pay schemes add the most value if they integrate with the business and management processes. Introducing incentive pay schemes could be very disruptive to the existing business and to management, who will be affected by the changes. They should be aware and involved in the proposed changes to the business processes.

*Changes to IT system*

In certain cases, changes to the IT system may be required. This could be in respect of the production system itself, or just the reporting of activities. Activity-based incentive pay schemes (for example, commission schemes) will in general require more extensive system development because of the need for different databases to interact with one another. Typically, a database with the participants' information and the funding and distribution rules has to be created and linked into the operational systems from where data will be imported. The system must perform calculations and provide management reports.

*Payment process*

A number of enterprise incentive management (EIM) systems have been developed recently; it is predicted that these will proliferate over the next few years. The new EIM software packages will reduce the dependence on legacy systems, and a part of the implementation process will be to investigate and implement the most appropriate software to do incentive pay payments.

The implementation team needs to take note of the many adjustments required to make the payment of incentive pay possible. Where the scheme was not implemented before the start of the overview period, it may be necessary to do calculations retrospectively. The payroll has to be informed of the scheme and the system configured to process payments. Payment dates and the procedures for payments must be agreed and payroll codes allocated to the scheme so that reporting on the scheme can be done. A system to monitor possible payments and a calculator to do "what if" scenarios are valuable instruments to calculate the business' obligation and to provide feedback to participants. The use of the calculator to give feedback will increase the levels of motivation during the duration of the scheme.

The cost of incentive pay schemes cannot be added to the business at the end of the overview period. Systematic accrual of the cost against the income statement should take place during the overview period. This requires the appointment of a responsible person and regular entries to the financial statements. The cost of incentive pay should always be pre-target (in other words, included as an expense prior to the target assessment).

*Scheme rules and documentation*

Following target setting and contracting with participants, the scheme rules, collective agreements and individual contracts should be developed, signed and stored. Any changes to the agreements should be documented, and if these cannot be implemented during the overview period, stored for reconsideration during the review phase.

*Communication and change management*

The change readiness of the business to introduce the scheme should be analysed (see Table 13.6 below), which will determine the cost and complexity of the change process. The change assessment factors are chosen from the specific environment in which the scheme will be implemented, and a determination of the change scales is made based on the designers' assessment of the complexity of the change risks.

*Table 13.6: Determining the level of change required by management*

| Change assessment | Change level | |
|---|---|---|
| | Low change | High change |
| How many people are affected? | <10 | >50 |
| How radical is the anticipated change to the current scheme? | Tweaking only | Very different |
| How critical is the performance of the participants? | Moderate | High |
| Are there tensions between HR, finance and line management with regard to the incentive pay scheme? | Low | High |
| Is the eligible group highly visible to the market, vocal, and difficult to retain? | No | Yes |

Where the change readiness results indicate that complicated change management processes need to be followed during the implementation process, more resources will be required. Communication will be the cornerstone of such a change plan and special communication tools will have to be developed. The components of the communication plan include communication drafts (executive presentations and scheme rules), which have been written and agreed to, and channels for communication delivery, which have been funded and approved. Managers who will communicate the scheme have been informed of the rules and implications of the scheme. The content of the communication is planned in detail so that line managers will be able to inform participants of when and why the incentive pay scheme will change; how it will benefit the participants; what behaviour changes are necessary; how the scheme differs from previous schemes; and how it works.

When incentive pay cheques are paid, line management has to play a leadership role. Incentive pay differentiates between individual participants, and the reaction to the differentiation has to be managed in such a way that the correct behaviour will be rewarded and repeated. The response of the unsuccessful participants should be turned into opportunities to encourage the correct behaviour and not become a breeding ground for discontent. The communication should be done with enthusiasm and credibility; participants need to understand rationally and emotionally that the incentive pay scheme will benefit people who demonstrate the correct behaviour. They should be able to explain the scheme rules and calculate the rewards. The way in which communication is done could itself have a greater impact than the amount paid. Some organisations have found that if they communicate the scheme poorly, they have to increase the amount of remuneration.

In studies it was found that among companies which reported significantly less successful incentive pay schemes, only 27 percent said that they had communication plans, while 70 percent of the companies who claimed successful incentive pay schemes reported that they had communication plans. Communication in the implementation of incentive pay should provide for general awareness of the scheme, and ensure regular reference to it during performance management discussions. The introduction of incentive pay should make a difference to the amount and quality of work produced, and encourage the satisfaction and retention of participants.

The quality of the communication documentation should reflect the commitment of the business. A typical communication document should include the scheme rules, the philosophy behind the scheme, a leader's guide for line management and a list of most frequently asked questions. There should be enough information, but not an overload that will discourage studying of the documentation. A helpline method for scheme queries can be useful if a large population has to be served. It will also provide an option if questions only arise later. Remuneration calculators, especially if they are self-help instruments, are useful communication tools that can enhance awareness and motivation. Regular updates on the progress against the scheme targets are part of the communication documentation.

Individuals who could feel aggrieved because they are not participating in the scheme should receive effective communication on why they are not participating and what the remuneration philosophy, if any, is with regard to them as a category of employees.

*Training*

In schemes where large populations are eligible for participation, the scheme content is best left to trainers to transfer. In the case of large populations, ongoing training of newcomers and follow-up training to ensure top-of-mind awareness are necessary. This requires training material to be prepared, trainers to be trained and training to be scheduled. Training is valuable if it contributes to learning retention and dialogue about the scheme. Training/education about the scheme affords line managers the opportunity to explain the scheme and motivate participants with regard to their role in terms of the business processes and performance drivers.

*Executive support*

Executive leadership and support should be building up during the different phases of the development of the scheme(s). This will ensure sustained support for the scheme(s) during the implementation and operational phases. Leadership provides the direction and finally accepts ownership of the scheme(s). Where strong leadership is shown throughout the design and implementation process, participants accept that the scheme(s) is/are not optional, but part of the business. Executive support contributes directly to building commitment to the organisational goals.

Executive support for the incentive pay scheme(s) could be directed through a set of governance rules for the implementation and management of the scheme(s). These rules should direct the design, implementation and control standards. With awareness levels about corporate governance at their highest ever, executives are under constant observation with regard to how they deal with the sensitive issues of remuneration, specifically incentive pay. The governance rules referred to above should be expanded to provide for guidance on design, approval and auditing of the schemes, both administratively and against the purpose of the scheme(s).

Executives or the remuneration committee cannot be expected to provide these guidelines themselves. The designers or remuneration experts employed by the company should engage with the executive or remuneration committee members and present to them drafts of governance rules and management interventions that ensure good corporate governance. The executives or the remuneration committee should also be able to rely on the designers to provide them with information that will enable them to make decisions about the right remuneration levels, the performance targets, and the performance against the targets. The education of the executive or members of the remuneration committee about remuneration terminology, philosophy and history, as well as new trends and legislative developments, is part of the corporate governance plan for the business. Sufficient time to consider proposals will allow the executive or remuneration committee the opportunity to ask the correct questions and consider the interests of all the stakeholders. The independence of the remuneration committee does not have to be compromised by the involvement of consultants appointed by management to advise them and the remuneration committee. If the remuneration committee members need a second opinion on remuneration matters, they should obtain advice that will enable them to fulfil their governance role.

### *Implementation plan and timelines*

Once a clear picture of the desired changes and the need for the changes has been developed and agreed upon, the format of the implementation approach (for example, "big bang" or incremental roll- out) should be decided upon. While the scheme implementation is being planned, provision can be made for the review of progress against the scheme purpose. Implementing the incentive pay scheme signals the commitment of line towards the operational goals and the scheme. If it is done with conviction, participants' confidence and commitment towards achieving the purpose of the scheme will increase.

## Implementing the incentive pay scheme

After all the analysis and preparations have been completed, the implementation of the scheme is done according to the rollout plan. This requires adherence to time frames for the milestones leading to a final implementation. Communication to affected employees during implementation ensures support and understanding; everyone needs to know what is happening, why it is happening, and when. In spite of all the precautions that have been taken, the new incentive pay scheme may not be appreciated. There could be many reasons for this, but to overcome it, a strong belief in and commitment to the new scheme will be necessary. Through constant reviewing and improving of the scheme, the necessary confidence in the scheme will be created. Many promising schemes have been shelved before they could make the contribution they had been intended to make.

## Evaluation of implementation

The quality of the implementation is a critical link in the chain of events that leads to an operational incentive pay scheme. While it is possible that a good design may lose its impact if it is not well implemented, it is only after implementation that the acceptance, understanding and potential value of a scheme can be assessed with some degree of certainty. It is therefore an opportune moment to evaluate the quality of the implementation after implementation to allow for adjustment or re-implementation if required.

The assessment should include an evaluation of the communication, understanding of the scheme purpose and the behaviour necessary to enhance performance. The designers and implementers of this quality measurement should ideally be outside the management line and independent from the implementation process. In conclusion, incentive pay schemes should be audited regularly and recalibrated to adjust for changes. Implementation audits should be qualitative to ensure that the scheme is implemented according to minimum standards, as well as quantitative to determine why it achieved or did not achieve targets.

## Summary of the implementation phase

Traditionally, the design of incentive pay schemes has received the most attention. There is, however, a growing awareness of the importance of proper scheme implementation. This includes planning, communication, training, change management, and adjustment to business processes and information systems to ensure a smooth-running scheme. During implementation, targets are negotiated and communicated. At the end of the implementation process, the implementation is evaluated to determine its success.

Failure to leverage the scheme to achieve its purpose after implementation is a common risk in the management of incentive pay. The tendency to "file away" the scheme after implementation is common. Management time, leadership and conflict management to remind participants constantly of the targets, their commitment to them and their progress against them are all necessary to make incentive pay schemes successful. The leadership challenge of incentive pay management to actively seek ways to support participants to achieve and exceed their targets. The process of leveraging incentive pay is discussed in the following section.

### 13.2.6 Phase 4: Leveraging the incentive pay scheme

Leveraging the incentive pay scheme is the process through which the ROP is optimised through communicating with the participants and by linking the incentive pay scheme to other business processes. In terms of the incentive pay life cycle, leveraging happens once the scheme has been implemented and evaluation against performance measures has commenced. This is depicted in the figure below.

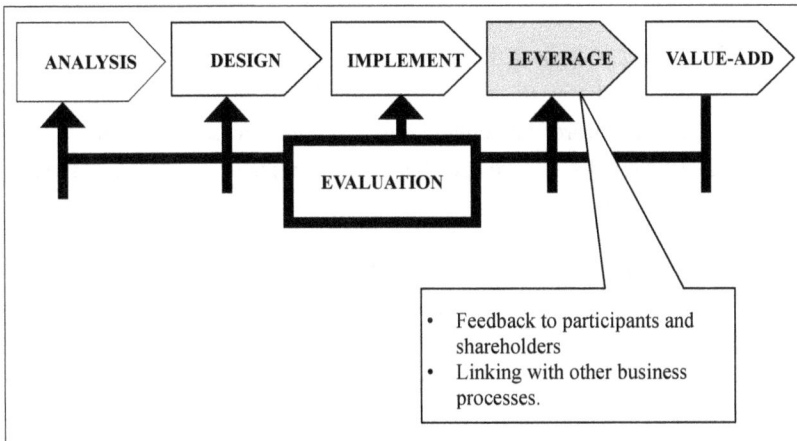

*Figure 13.14: The leveraging phase*

***Feedback to participants and shareholders***

For the scheme to be effective, continuous feedback needs to be given to the participants on their performance against the performance measures, both for the funding of the scheme and the distribution of payouts to individual participants. This is a line management function, and the success of the scheme depends on the quality with which the feedback programme is implemented. Steps must be planned to correct deviations from the stated objectives that may occur. These corrective actions will be done by line management as part of and during the normal course of business. While this information is objective, it does not carry a message. The value of reward as a feedback measure is that it goes beyond objective feedback and appeals to the emotions and intellect of the participants. Design of feedback is part of the scheme design and it should be offered systematically.

Reinforcement of line of sight is essential. The scheme must ideally be integrated with the daily work and the performance goals of the position/role. Feedback could be accompanied by the distribution of performance statements stating how the participant performs against the performance measures and what the participants can do to improve performance. Other specific information such as the current year's incentives compared to the previous year and year-to-date performance will provide a better perspective on the performance and encourage higher performance.

New participants need to be orientated in respect of the scheme purpose and rules to allow for ongoing support. Scheme rules and objectives are most reliably communicated through written communication; books, brochures, payout letters, individual contracts and question-and-answer information sheets are examples of communication instruments. Verbal communication could also be used, in particular where the visibility of line management needs to be increased and motivation to perform is required or enhanced. Electronic communication offers quick and comprehensive feedback, especially if it is derived directly from production or financial systems.

Feedback about the progress against the scheme is given to the shareholders to inform them about the progress against the goals, and also about the obligations building up. They need to know whether they can afford the scheme and whether forces outside the influence of the participants are affecting results. Where necessary, adjustments to the rules need to be made and communicated to the participants.

### Linking incentive pay with other business processes

Leveraging incentive pay implies that it should be linked to other business processes such as performance management, training, organisational development and job design. The benefit of this link is the additional focus of the scheme and the enabling that takes place through these business processes. It enables and creates consequences for performance, and also integrates all human resource interventions, which is necessary for a focused approach to optimising human effort.

### Summary of the leverage phase

Leveraging the incentive pay scheme is done through feedback and linking of the scheme results with other business processes. The principle of feedback is supported by several of the motivational theories. Incentive pay that is linked to other business improvement processes creates more opportunities for performance improvement and the achievement of incentive pay targets.

The incentive pay methodology provides for self-regulation. The assessment of the scheme is done during implementation and on review after the first cycle has been completed. This process is described in the following section.

The fifth phase in the incentive pay life cycle is the value-add of the scheme.

### 13.2.7  Phase 5: Value-add of the scheme

The outcome of the scheme is its result of the systematic implementation. In terms of the methodology, it is a defined phase because it defines what constitutes success and therefore determines whether the incentive pay solution has added value.

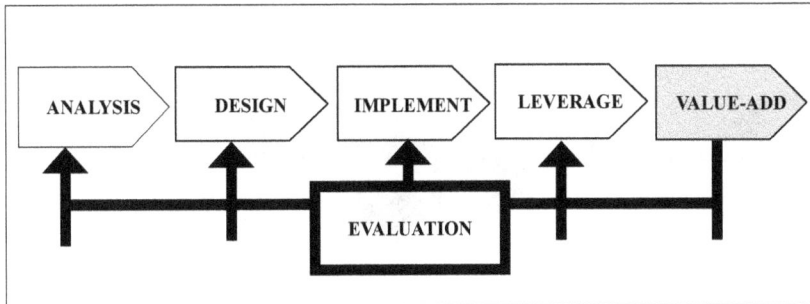

*Figure 13.15: Value-add in the incentive pay life cycle*

The value-add of the scheme is subject to all the transmission loss that takes place between the business need for incentive pay and the delivery of the outcome. Not all variables are within the control of the scheme designers, the business or the participants. The objective of the incentive pay methodology is to provide consistency and predictability with regard to the controllable variables and to mitigate the negative effect of the uncontrollable variables.

The outcome of the scheme is a combination of objective and subjective criteria (the ROP). The outcome of the scheme is described against the purpose of the scheme as viewed by the different stakeholders. An assessment of whether the scheme was successful is therefore a combination of objective calculations (with transmission loss discounted) and subjective criteria.

The outcome remains important as continued investment into the incentive pay scheme depends on the outcome. In the methodology, the constructs that drive the incentive pay scheme predict the outcome and become a standard against which the scheme(s) is/are developed, implemented and leveraged. The methodology of incentive pay is aimed at predicting, or if an *ex post facto* assessment is done, explaining, what the outcome will be or why the scheme was successful or not.

The incentive pay methodology provides for self-regulation. The assessment of the scheme is done during implementation and on review after the first cycle has been completed. This process is described in the following section.

### 13.2.8 Phase 6: Evaluating incentive pay schemes

Incentive pay schemes are monitored after implementation to assess whether they are achieving their purpose (the desired business targets). The ultimate goal of incentive pay, if the scheme is designed and implemented systematically, is to pay out substantial remuneration to participants. This requires significant business targets to have been achieved and participants to be highly motivated.

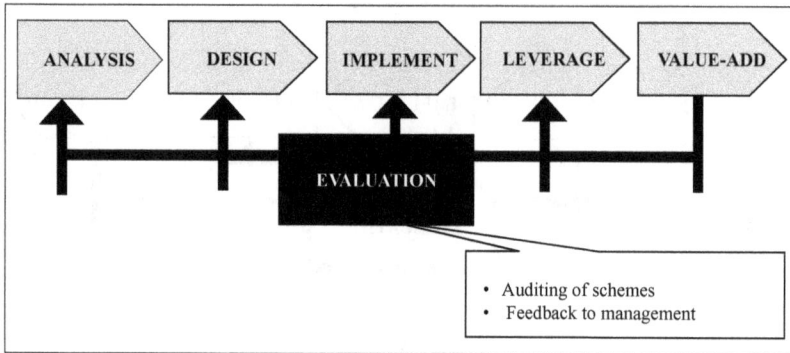

*Figure 13.16: The feedback process of the incentive pay life cycle*

It is recommended that assessments be done regularly during the life of the scheme and that the assessment feedback should be used to correct errors made during the design, implementation and leveraging of the scheme. Reviews using a validated questionnaire are recommended to assess whether the scheme has met the requirements for a well-functioning incentive pay scheme.

After payout, a final assessment must be done to determine if the scheme has in fact contributed to business results. This is important for continued application. Recommendations about improvements should also be made. As part of corporate governance, being able to state with certainty that the incentive scheme has contributed to business results is a tremendous benefit. Approvers of incentive schemes should be given enough assurance that the scheme has contributed to business results, allowing them to discharge their responsibilities in a defendable way.

## 13.3 Summary

The building blocks of variable pay are congruency, instrumentality and performing. Congruency refers to line of sight, difficulty of goal attainment, understanding and transparency, while instrumentality is the belief that if the person meets the performance expectations, s/he will receive a greater reward than if s/he does not meet the performance expectations. The sub-structures are certainty, trust and business risk. The third construct, performing, is the extent to which performing leadership and practices exist in the business. It is made up of two primary sub-contracts – performance management and performance culture.

## 13.4  Self-evaluation questions

1.  What are some of the main requirements of a good, functioning incentive scheme?
2.  Name the main phases of designing and implementing an incentive scheme.
3.  How can an incentive scheme add value to the organisation?
4.  What is the role of performance management in incentive schemes?
5.  How should one treat windfalls and cave-ins?

# CHAPTER 14

## Sales Force Incentives

### 14.1 Introduction and context

Winning and keeping customers is the ultimate competitive challenge. Organisations must serve customers effectively, and they must continually seek to improve their customer contact performance. Customers demand effective products, better service and quality, and competitive pricing. Organisations attempt to produce the right products for the right customers at the right price.

The sales force must deal with both the changing demands of customers and the developing competencies of the organisation. In most industries, the sales force is the primary customer contact resource, and the customer often sees the sales representative as the "face" of the organisation. Effectively managing sales personnel in today's competitive environment involves rethinking traditional assumptions about motivating and rewarding these individuals.

The sales force must satisfy customers' needs with the organisation's available products and services. However, as highlighted in Table 14.1, three factors continually change: products, buyers and competitors. Over time, complexity increases for each factor. Organisations respond to these changes by reshaping their sales organisation focus. As a result of these ongoing changes, organisations must continually examine the effectiveness of their sales forces in meeting customer expectations.

*Table 14.1: Changes in the marketplace and sales – organisation response*

| Factors | From ➡ | To |
|---|---|---|
| **Changes in the marketplace** | | |
| **Products** | • Few products<br>• Similar life cycles<br>• Similar products<br>• Simple products | • Many products<br>• Varying life cycles<br>• Dissimilar products<br>• Complex products |
| **Buyers** | • Few buyers<br>• General buyers<br>• Central decision-making<br>• Similar sized accounts<br>• Transactions | • Many buyers, functions<br>• End-users/specific specialised buyers<br>• Decentralised decision-making<br>• Varying account sizes<br>• Relationships |

| Factors | From    ➡ | To |
|---|---|---|
| **Competitors** | • Similar products<br>• Similar pricing<br>• Similar channels | • Dissimilar products<br>• Different pricing<br>• Dissimilar channels |

**Sales-organisation response**

| | | |
|---|---|---|
| **Organisation focus** | • Product focus<br>• Sales-driven<br>• Individual performance<br>• Slow to change<br>• Measure efficiency<br>• Activities | • Customer focus<br>• Customer-driven<br>• Team performance<br>• Quick to change<br>• Measure effectiveness<br>• Strategic direction |

## 14.2 Key sales remuneration definitions

Sales remuneration has a unique vocabulary to describe various programme characteristics. The following are some of the most prevalent terms:

**Mix:** The mix is the relationship between the base salary and incentive-opportunity component. Mix is expressed as a percentage of "target total remuneration", which is the pay level for achieving expected performance. The mix is realised when results are achieved at the "meets expectation" level. For example, a 90/10 plan reflects a mix of 90 percent base salary and 10 percent incentive opportunity.

**Leverage:** Leverage represents the upside earning opportunity. A common leverage amount for sales positions is a "triple", which means that three times the at-risk portion of the mix equals the upper earning opportunity for the top 10 percent of all performers. Note that leverage does not specify a "cap" – it sets an upper earning target only for the best performers.

To calculate triple leverage, multiply the at-risk portion by three and add the result to the base salary. For example, a sales job with a target total remuneration of 100,000, an 80/20 mix and triple leverage would have a base salary of 80,000 (100,000 x 0.8), target incentive earnings of 20,000 (100000 x 0.2), and a target upside leverage of 140,000 (20,000 x 3 plus the base salary of 80,000).

Whether a sales job calls for triple leverage, double leverage or some other leverage, is largely driven by three factors: (1) the degree of customer persuasion, (2) profitability associated with the products and services sold, and (3) labour-market pay data associated with top-performing salespeople and what it takes to retain the most successful salespeople.

**Commission:** A commission is a type of incentive. It can be expressed as a percentage of sales revenue, a percentage of gross margins (profit), or a monetary amount per unit sold. A commission-only remuneration plan is sometimes referred to as full commission or straight commission.

**Bonus:** A bonus is also a type of incentive. In most cases, a bonus payment is tied to actual performance compared to a goal (for example, a sales quota). The bonus payment may be expressed as a percentage of salary, a percentage of a defined target incentive award, or a flat monetary amount. For example, a bonus of 25 percent of base salary may be paid if 100 percent of the sales quota is achieved. Sales bonus plans are used most often when the earnings potential of different territories needs to be equalised through the quota allocation process.

**Formula:** An incentive formula relates the pay opportunity to performance achievement. Most sales-incentive plan formulas fall into one or more of the following three categories:

- *Unlinked incentive formula.* In a sense, each performance measure acts as its own incentive plan. Bonus or commission is earned by the sales representative for accomplishments against one measure, regardless of what occurs on the other performance measures. Too many unlinked performance measures may motivate sales representatives to "shop the plan" to attempt to maximise their earnings by doing what is easiest for them to accomplish, instead of what management prefers to have accomplished.
- *Adjusted-value incentive formula.* Values of performance measures vary to reflect their relative importance to the organisation. For example, with the use of point systems, values can be selected to underscore the importance of a desired sales result. Product A may be worth more for each dollar of sales than Product B. In such a case, the point value for each dollar of Product A sales may be worth 10 points, while each dollar of Product B sales may be worth only five points. As a result, sales representatives are paid more to sell Product A than Product B because of the greater strategic value of Product A to the organisation.
- *Linked-incentive formula.* Linking two or more performance measures in a defined manner can ensure that sales objectives are achieved in the order of importance as determined by management. In general, there are four types of linked-formula designs: hurdles, multipliers, modifiers and matrices. With hurdles, a stated level of performance must be achieved on one measure before another measure (and, therefore, a bonus or commission payment) can be activated. Multipliers are used to calculate a second commission or bonus payment based on incentive earnings from the primary performance measure. Modifiers are used to adjust a primary commission earned for non-performance of measures. With matrices, two competing performance measures are tied together so that payout rewards are highest when outstanding performance is achieved on both.

## 14.3    Designing a total remuneration strategy for sales executives

A sales force and commission incentive cannot exist in a vacuum. It should be designed and co-exist within an organisation's overall strategic objectives and its remuneration strategy. That said, it is possibly the most important factor in an organisation's variable pay armoury – if an organisation does not achieve its sales targets, there is a good chance that many other financial targets and incentives will not be achieved; any amount of profit starts with a sale.

The first step in designing a sales commission plan is to define its purpose. A strategy statement should define how the remuneration plan is to be utilised to help the organisation achieve its business goals. As illustrated in Figure 14.1, a number of factors drive a total remuneration strategy.

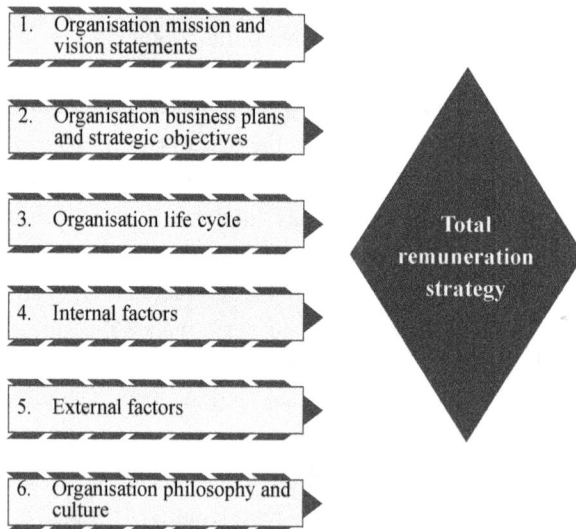

*Figure 14.1: Total remuneration strategy*

## 14.4    Basic design issues

When a suitable sales incentive scheme is designed, some key questions have to be answered, such as the following:

- Are the performance measures appropriate?
- Are the territories or targets properly equalised so that staff with "easy" sales territories or product lines do not have an unfair advantage over those working in more difficult areas or with less commercially attractive merchandise?
- Is the plan equitable between other people performing at the same level, and managed consistently?

Figure 14.2 sets out key design factors for sales remuneration plans.

| Factors | Decisions |
|---------|-----------|
| Eligibility | Which jobs will be included in the plan? |
| Target total remuneration | At what market percentiles should base salaries and incentive opportunities be set? |
| Mix and leverage | What is the salary/incentive ratio (mix)? What percentages over target pay are acceptable (that is, leverage)? |
| Performance measures | What is the desired level of production (for example, dollar sales, units)? What strategic measures must be met (for example, product mix, profit)? |
| Incentive formula | Will bonuses or commissions, or both, be used? |
| Formula features | What are the caps, thresholds, performance periods and payment periods? When should sales crediting occur? |
| Scheme rules | What are the rules of the scheme, for example, for retrenchment, death, organisation merger/buyout, and so on? |

*Figure 14.2: Key design factors*

Table 14.2 sets out the main performance measures associated with sales excellence.

*Table 14.2: Main performance measures*

| Performance measures | Benchmark metrics and definition | Specific illustrative performance measures |
|----------------------|----------------------------------|--------------------------------------------|
| Volume | Metrics to gauge "top line" results in either absolute or relative terms | • Revenue units<br>• Revenue as percentage of quota<br>• New product(s) revenue<br>• New customer(s) revenue |

| Performance measures | Benchmark metrics and definition | Specific illustrative performance measures |
|---|---|---|
| **Profitability** | Metrics to quantify the sale of profitable business | • Gross margin<br>• Gross margin percent<br>• Price realisation (that is, actual price to list)<br>• For annuity income, the term of the contract<br>• Product/Business "mix" (that is, applications or solutions that have profit advantage) |
| **Sales productivity** | Metrics to measure improvement in the return on sales investment | • Revenue by sales job<br>• Revenue by customer segment<br>• Revenue per first order |
| **Customer satisfaction** | Metrics to assess customer retention and loyalty | • Survey ratings of customer satisfaction (overall, year-to-year gains)<br>• Account or revenue retention (that is, "churn" measurement)<br>• Account share growth |

When considering metrics, it is wise to remember that the goals being set do not take the place of supervision. All too often, we would like the sales plan to serve as a "control mechanism" for the sales force to do or not do something. For example, a consumer goods salesman is expected to rotate the product, ensure pricing signs are up, and perform other operational and administrative duties related to their sales visit. By including these behaviours in the sales plan metrics, and then forgoing supervision, we invite non-compliance, or worse, perceived compliance, as salespeople are more likely to follow the money to the next sale rather than spend too much time in visiting a client who already placed the order. It is the sales supervisor's role to ensure compliance with the company's policies, and best not to have the plan act as a controller.

## 14.5 Types of sales remuneration plans

Before we discuss the types of remuneration plans, it is important to note that when benchmarking sales compensation to the market, we must keep in mind that we are not only trying to determine the rate of pay for the average performer, but also the rate of pay for the lowest performers as well as for the highest performers. This allows us to get a good market "feel" for the overall shape of the leverage curve. In practice, we can peg the company's lowest performers to the total cash 10th percentile of the market, the average performers to the market median, and the top performers to the 90th percentile of the market. Otherwise, we could run the risk of overpaying the lowest performers and underpaying the highest performers. This could lead to turnover at the higher performance level while the lowest performers have no incentive to leave. Exactly the opposite of what we want!

There are seven basic forms of sales remuneration plans:

**Salary only:** This form of remuneration is generally used where the product being sold does not lend itself to incentive payments, for example in some forms of capital equipment sales, where identifying the "seller" can be difficult. It is also used where the use of incentives could be construed as unethical, or where the organisation makes a decision that it will recruit and pay high basic salaries to exceptional salespeople, whose performance is subject to regular scrutiny and reward through the merit payment system. Where the "salary only" approach is used, organisations may, nevertheless, award non-cash incentives to reward success in short-term sales campaigns. They may also have other rewards, such as all-employee profit-sharing schemes, to reinforce the message of success.

**Salary and standard bonus:** This approach consists of basic salary plus a target-related bonus to be paid out at set levels in relation to the achievement of organisation sales targets. Bonus targets can be based on a formula related to sales or a range of agreed objectives, and they may contain a discretionary element.

**Salary and individual bonus:** This plan type is basically the same as for the salary and standard bonus, but is geared to the achievement of individual targets. They can be a mixture of sales and other factors such as retaining customers, achieving a given percentage of new business, numbers of sales visits made in relation to a plan, and so on.

**Salary with standard bonus and commission:** This is a situation where there is a bonus in relation to overall sales levels and other targets, plus commission paid as a percentage of sales revenue. As with executive and other incentives, commission payments can be subject to "accelerators" – higher percentage payments are made once a given sales threshold has been met – or "decelerators", to control maximum earnings levels and also to control sales where there are product supply constraints.

**Salary with individual bonus and commission:** This works in the same way as above, but the bonus element is related to the achievement of individual targets, both sales and non-sales.

**Salary plus commission:** With this form of remuneration, basic salary is set in relation to the market, and commission as a percentage of sales is paid in addition. In some cases, basic salary can be set very low as an incentive to stay on the road and generate sales. As with the commission-only approach described below, these schemes tend to rapidly to sort out good sales staff from poor sales staff and cause the latter to resign and leave this type of work.

**Commission only:** This is the really tough end of the sales remuneration spectrum. This means that, typically, after a brief training and induction phase, the individual is out on his or her own, dependent on maintaining a high level of sales for survival. This approach has been commonly used in the selling of insurance, for example, but organisations that use it expect, and get, a very high drop-out rate with new salespeople. A sales force paid commission only is typically self-employed.

A useful guide to help you decide on the mix between salary and commission is illustrated in Figure 14.3. You can rate the sales function on a scale of one to ten where order-taking or easy selling is scored 1, and really difficult or cold selling is scored 10. Another useful guide to setting the remuneration mix between basic salary and commission percentages is the value of the product. The mix guidelines are shown relative to the score.

| 1 | | 3 | 5 | 7 | | 10 |
|---|---|---|---|---|---|---|
| | | | Remuneration implication | | | |
| Selling | | Order taking | Medium sell | | Cold selling | |
| Product value | | High value | Medium value | | Low value | |
| | | • Higher salary<br>• Little or no commission | • Market related monthly salary<br>• Medium commission | | • Little or no salary<br>• High commission | |

Figure 14.3: Remuneration mix guideline

## 14.6    Sales roles as drivers

Another way to help you decide on the remuneration mix is to determine the predominant sales role of your sales force. Table 14.3 shows the most appropriate mix for each of the main roles.

Table 14.3: Main sales roles and remuneration mix

| Sales role/ Elements | Transaction | Solutions | Consultative | Partnership/ Alliance |
|---|---|---|---|---|
| Key elements of the value proposition | Product features, cost and availability | Product sets/ bundles Operating costs | Creativity Profitability Risk management | Strategic positioning Shared risks |
| Key focus of the role | Products | Solutions | Diagnostics advice | Business strategy integration |
| Key skills of the role | Product knowledge and pricing | Creativity to see alternatives | Business skills and acumen Value creation | Project, resource and budget expertise |

| Sales role/ Elements | Transaction | Solutions | Consultative | Partnership/ Alliance |
|---|---|---|---|---|
| Key measures of performance | Number of accounts Revenue | Product and services sales growth | Account profitability | Performance-based agreements |
| Base/variable pay mix | 0/100 – 50/50 | 50/50 – 70/30 | 70/30 – 80/20 | 80/20 – 100/0 |
| Variable pay vehicle | Commission | Commission/ incentive/bonus | Incentive/bonus/ commission | Incentive/bonus |

For example, in a "transaction"-type sales role the key focus is product sales volume. The key personnel requirements include product knowledge, pricing knowledge, and the persistence to maintain the focus required to "hit the numbers". For a transactional sales role, a commission plan based on the attainment of revenue and/or number of account targets is often appropriate.

This commission model would be highly inappropriate for a sales force consisting of consultative roles. Here, the key focus of the role is on diagnosing client problems and providing relevant advice and solutions in line with their business strategy. In this situation, key performance measures should be focused on account profitability and packaged solutions. The appropriate reward plan should encourage this focus.

## 14.7 Sales roles change focus over time

It is important to remember that as the business evolves and the strategy changes, the focus of the sales role also shifts. The process of alignment should be thought of as a continuous process rather than a one-off event.

Not only is it crucial to have a thorough understanding of the sales roles when designing a sales reward plan, but it is equally important to understand how the sales roles will change as the business changes, to ensure that the reward plan maintains its relevance. Figure 14.4 illustrates a common business or product life cycle and the most appropriate remuneration mix.

| Launch | Grow | Hold share Reap profit | Optimise | Realign for growth |
|---|---|---|---|---|
| **Sales approach and resources** | | | | |
| New product or solution<br><br>Self-directed market-makers | Best product or solution<br><br>Bigger, better market-makers | Lowest price<br><br>Account managers, administrative roles | Best value<br><br>Specialised skills, team sellers | Unique approach by segment<br><br>Adaptive sellers, new talent |
| **Typical sales remuneration practices** | | | | |
| Uncapped, flat commission, no or small base 0/100 – 50/50 | Base plus ramped commission, bonuses 40/60 – 60/40 | Base plus commission, and bonus capped 60/40 – 80/20 | Base plus bonus, recognition, capped, team plus personal 70/30 – 80/20 | Base plus commission or bonus, new metrics, no entitlements 40/60 – 80/20 |

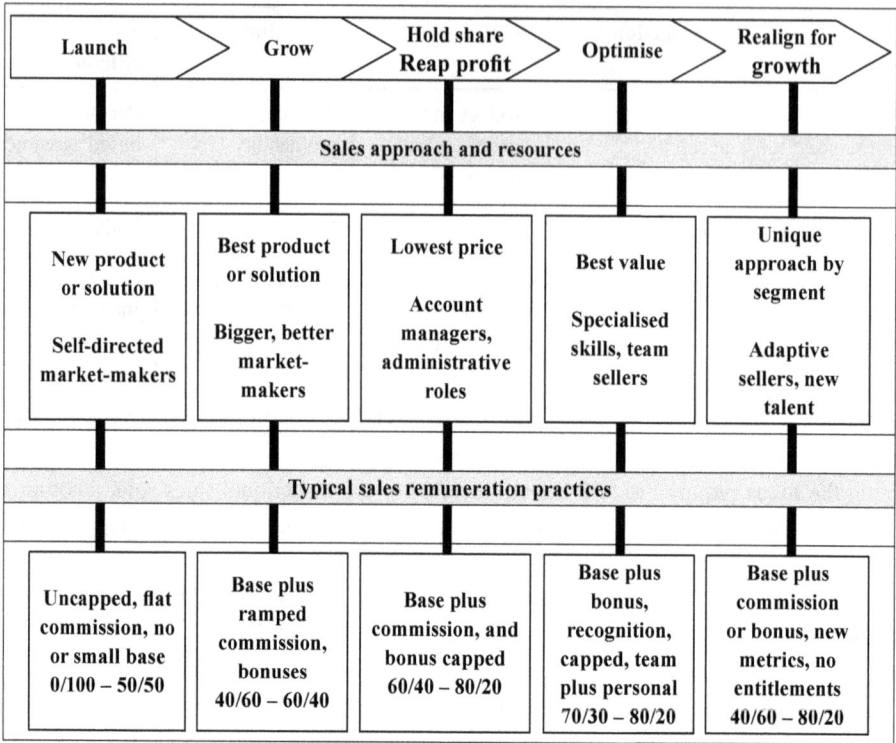

*Figure 14.4: Business life cycle and continuous re-alignment*

Each shift in a business life cycle phase requires a review of strategy to ensure maximum advantage is extracted from the existing market context. Adjustments to sales force structure, approach and resources should follow any fine-tuning of business strategy. Similarly, reward practices should be adapted to ensure they support and promote a new sales force structure. Table 14.4 sets out example incentive plans with some comments.

*Table 14.4: Sample incentive plan formulas for a sales representative job (commission %'s [*] are illustrative only – the sales value as well as profitability margins would need to be considered)*

| Straight commission | | |
|---|---|---|
| Base salary: none<br>Commission: monthly<br>Target pay: 120,000, uncapped | Percentage of quota | Percentage of sales revenue [*] |
| | 0–100% | 4% |
| | More than 100% | 7% |
| **Comments:** *The mix is 0/100 with a progressive ramp after 100 percent of quota is met. The strengths of the formula are its simplicity and its ability to drive volume. The weaknesses are that it can result in under- or overpayment, and it may lead to overselling to customers.* | | |

| Variable commission | | | | |
|---|---|---|---|---|
| Base salary: 60,000<br>Commission: monthly<br>Target pay: 120,000, uncapped | Percentage of quota | Percentage of sales revenue [*] | | |
| | | *Prod A* | *Prod B* | *Prod C* |
| | 0–100% | 3% | 5% | 9% |
| | More than 100% | 5% | 8% | 12% |

*Comments: The mix is 50/50 with a progressive ramp after 100 percent of quota. The strengths of this formula are its simplicity and the fact that it drives the "right" sales volume. The weaknesses are that, ultimately, sales representatives still can choose what – and what not – to sell.*

| Bonus plan | | |
|---|---|---|
| | Percentage of monthly quota | Percentage of monthly target incentive |
| Base salary: 84,000<br>Commission: monthly<br>Target pay: 120,000, capped | 70% | 0% |
| | 80% | 50% |
| | 90% | 75% |
| | 100% | 100% |
| | 140% | 120% |
| | 120% | 140% |
| | 130% | 160% |

*Comments: The mix is 70/30 with no ramping. The strength of this formula is it addresses multiple objectives by varying payout by product. The weakness is that including too many products can dilute the sales focus.*

| Adjusted-value commission point plan | | |
|---|---|---|
| | Product | Point Value/Unit<br>(each point equals some monetary amount of incentive) |
| Base salary: 60,000<br>Commission: monthly<br>Target pay: 120,000, uncapped | A | 5 |
| | B | 8 |
| | C | 6 |
| | D | 10 |
| | E | 2 |

*Comments: The mix is 70/30 with no ramping. The strength of this formula is it addresses multiple objectives by varying payout by product. The weakness is that including too many products can dilute the sales focus.*

| Linked plan | | |
|---|---|---|
| | Gross profit | Level of commission earned [*] |
| Base salary: 60,000<br>Commission: monthly<br>Target pay: 120,000, uncapped | 15% | 0% |
| | 20% | 10% |
| | 25% | 25% |

*Comments: The mix is 70/30 with no ramping of commission. The strength of this formula is that it links two measures – the payout of quarterly bonuses and commission earnings. The weakness is that it may be too complicated.*

After the formula type has been selected, the following elements of the plan must be determined:

**Capping:** Sales-incentive remuneration plans should be uncapped whenever possible in order to drive the strongest sales drive. In some cases, capping may be necessary to avoid overpayment owing to windfalls or inaccurate quota setting. Capping methods include a total cap on earnings; a percentage-limit bonus payment; a sales credit limit per order or account; and a regressive (declining rate) formula that limits earnings.

**Threshold:** A threshold is the minimum level of performance obtained before an incentive is paid. Thresholds help offset the cost of base salaries and provide performance standards. The level of threshold set is directly determined by the level of base salary e.g. a market-related base salary may have a 100% level of performance before an incentive is earned, while a base salary below market levels would have a lower threshold before incentives are earned.

**Performance and payment period:** Measurement periods can be weekly, monthly, quarterly or annual. If they happen less frequently than once a year, they are either "discrete" or "cumulative". A discrete period measures performance without reference to previous periods. A cumulative period considers year-to-date performance. A salesperson whose performance is measured quarterly but on a cumulative year-to-date basis must continue to achieve results that meet annual objectives. Each quarterly performance period reflects total performance from the beginning of the year, and the salesperson is held accountable for an annual quota while undergoing measurement and earning rewards each quarter. The most common payment periods are monthly, quarterly and annually. If the sales cycle is short, the base salary is low and the mix is high, payment is more frequent – perhaps monthly. If the sales cycle is long, the base salary is high and the mix is low, payment periods tend to be longer – quarterly or annual.

**Sales and crediting:** The time when an order is credited for sales remuneration purposes can vary because of an organisation's processes for bookings, invoicing, shipments and payments. As a general rule, a credit should be made for sales remuneration purposes at the time when the salesperson should stop thinking about the order.

## 14.8  Sales bonus or commission schemes: advantages and disadvantages

Bonus schemes related to targets, or commission schemes where the payment is calculated as a percentage of sales, each have their advantages and disadvantages, as described below.

### 14.8.1    Advantages of bonus schemes

The main advantages of bonuses over commission schemes are that they:

- Permit flexible design, thus enabling management to encourage and reward various types of individual or group behaviour.

- Provide for a basic salary element to cover basic needs and free the representative to attain higher remuneration needs through the bonus scheme.
- Enable payments to be timed to suit the business and its need to retain good staff.
- Provide some protection against fluctuations in third-party demand levels.
- Make the equalisation of rewards easier.
- Strictly underpin business strategy.

### 14.8.2    Disadvantages of bonus schemes

The main disadvantages of bonus schemes are the following:

- The link between effort and reward can be weakened.
- Objectives may be unattainable or difficult to appraise.
- A team bonus is paid when there was no team effort (interdependence of jobs) to achieve it.
- Bonus schemes can be more complicated than commission schemes.
- There can be a confusion between bonus and merit payments.
- Replacing one with the other can be demotivating unless the rationale for the change is properly communicated.

## 14.8.3    Advantages of commission schemes

Many problems can be removed by careful planning and monitoring of whichever type of scheme is chosen. Commission schemes have the following advantages:

- Pay is linked solely to sales volumes or profitability.
- There is maximum financial incentive, thereby driving sales behaviour the strongest (but this can lead to undesirable behaviour – see disadvantages).
- Only successful sales representatives will stay (as long as it is not too disruptive).
- Sales costs related to salaries vary with the measure of performance chosen.
- Where there is more than one product, they can offer greater flexibility by paying different commission rates to promote different products.
- Commission schemes are generally easy to understand and monitor.
- Payments can be closely linked to income received, avoiding the problem of tying up money in salaries in advance of receipts.
- From the sales representative's point of view, commission schemes keep up with inflation because payments generally increase in line with product price rises.
- They can allow the sales force to be truly self-employed.

### 14.8.4    Disadvantages of commission schemes

Despite the advantages of commission schemes mentioned above, there are some disadvantages:

- Uncertain and fluctuating earnings can be a demotivator.
- Sales representatives can be tempted to act unethically by overloading customers with stock and pushing goods they may not need, which is potentially damaging to customer relations and the long-term stability of the business.
- Management has little financial control over earnings.
- Management has little disciplinary control.
- Loyalty to the organisation can sometimes take second place to individual self-interest. For example, a self-employed representative may use the sales area set out by one organisation to sell the products of another to supplement their income.
- Schemes may emphasise sales at any price rather than profitable sales.
- Non-selling services (such as merchandising, stocking-up, and maintenance) are discouraged because they cost the individual money in terms of lost sales time.
- Income from commission schemes can exceed those of other higher-graded employees. If income exceeds that of sales managers, the problem can be compounded by promotion difficulties.
- The greater the commission element, the more likely sales representatives are to be inflexible about sales territory divisions, calls to be made, non-selling services, and so on.
- Lack of pay security can cause recruitment and retention problems, especially during an economic downturn when, ironically, companies need a high-calibre sales team.
- Where commission is linked to sales turnover, price rises are automatically built into sales force remuneration. Internal relativity problems can ensue where price increases exceed pay rises.
- Commission drives only one part of the balanced scorecard.

## 14.9    The use of decelerators

Faster or slower – which do you want? Although accelerators are used in commission schemes to reward additional sales, decelerators are also used. These produce a "regressive" commission line, which is one which pays out a lower percentage once a given sales threshold is reached. The reasons for using decelerators are as follows:

- To avoid "windfall" pay-outs.
- Where high sales are not directly attributable to extra sales effort.
- Where the correlation between "selling" the product to the customer and the size of the eventual order is low.
- If a maximum earnings level is thought necessary.
- To encourage new orders by reducing the commission value of repeat business.
- Where there is a danger of sales exceeding production capacity.

## 14.10   Elements of a sales remuneration plan

Figure 14.5 shows the various elements of a sales remuneration plan. These plans should be written in plain language so that everyone can understand them.

*Figure 14.5: Main elements of a sales plan*

| Factors | Description in plan |
|---|---|
| **Purpose** | Role of sales representatives; plan importance. |
| **Plan overview** | Brief summary of plan features. |
| **Eligibility** | List of jobs that are included in the plan. |
| **Plan components** | Description of remuneration elements: salary, bonus and/or commission. |
| **Plan qualifiers** | Presentation of all qualifiers, for example, threshold, definition of a sale, house accounts or split credits, windfalls/shortfalls, caps on incentive earnings, and others. |
| **Legal statement** | Relevant and/or organisation-specific statement indicating rights to change the plan.<br>Related to administrative arrangements, for example, joining, leaving, retirement, retrenchment, leave, maternity leave. |
| **Appendix** | Supporting documentation, for example, salary ranges, commission rates and product categories, incentive calculation illustration. |

## 14.11   Non-cash incentives

### 14.11.1   All that glitters is not gold

The provision of various kinds of non-cash incentives to meet the needs of sales campaigns and other reward policies is now a multi-million-dollar business operation in many parts of the world. It delivers everything from specially produced lapel badges and pens to holidays in exotic locations. Consider the tax implications of these plans prior to implementation and, if taxable, who bears the cost of such fringe benefit tax. The principal types of non-cash incentives available are:

- **Luxury consumer goods:** Available either directly or through catalogues catering for tastes from white goods to cut glass.

- **Holidays:** Of varying length and location, depending on the size of reward required, so that employees can find somewhere that suits them.
- **Car schemes:** Recognising exceptional performance by allowing top sales representatives to have, say, a more prestigious car.
- **Premium clubs:** Set up to provide special rewards for top sales representatives or a given number of high achievers at the end of a sales contest. Membership can be marked by anything from a special tie to a "conference" on the French Riviera.

### 14.11.2   When and how to use non-cash incentives

To get the maximum benefit from non-cash incentives, the following points may be useful:

- **Beneficiaries:** Decide whether it is better in terms of organisation practice and business needs to reward just the top performers, or to distribute rewards more evenly to recognise general achievement and reinforce the message that everyone has a chance to win an award.
- **Publicity:** Right from the outset, publicise the rewards and the means of achieving them, and at the end, give wide publicity to the "winners".
- **The award ceremony:** Make an occasion of it. For instance, plan a formal occasion where the chairperson or chief executive officer makes the presentation in front of the winners' colleagues. Local press coverage can be helpful, as well as coverage in organisation magazines. The prize winners should be given as much face time with the top leadership as possible and be made to feel in the centre of things

### 14.11.3   Considerations

Where non-cash incentives reward short-term effort, care is needed to ensure that the "prize-hunters" do not pursue the rewards to the detriment of longer-term objectives. Research in this area also suggests that it is unwise to let this approach overshadow the continuing need to have competitive basic salaries and cash incentives. Consumer goods should not replace pay to any serious extent; their role should be just to provide additional recognition.

Poor administration of schemes and unwise selection of prizes and options can also cause problems, as can tactless handling of those unable to reach the standards required to get a prize. Finally, and more importantly, the tax implications of all non-cash incentives should be considered. There is little motivation to be had from being awarded, say, a video machine, and then finding that tax is due on its purchase value with no organisation provision to cover the liability.

## 14.12   Sales remuneration and the e-world

### 14.12.1   Who owns the online sales?

With more customers ordering goods and services over the Web, questions are being raised regarding sales commissions, account ownership and quota allocation.

With the rise of e-commerce, the sales department appears to be slated for decommissioning. Why employ a salesperson when customers can use a mouse to point and click their way to purchases? While the volume of business that is sold through the internet will continue to soar, the death of the salesperson is a premature assumption. Even dot.com companies are finding they need to hire salespeople to help promote their products. In fact, one of the fastest growing sales employment segments is advertising sales representatives for web-portal companies. These companies have learned that when choice is available, uncertainty is present and risk is inherent, a salesperson can help guide customer decision-making. The two criteria for sales remuneration use are therefore customer contact and customer persuasion. Selling, as well as the use of sales remuneration, will continue in the 21st century, however employers need to be prepared for major challenges to sales pay programmes. Consider these issues:

- Should the salesperson receive sales credit and therefore incentive payment for orders put through the web?
- Who owns the customer – the salesperson or the webmaster?
- Should salespeople encourage their customers to use the web to order products?
- What sales remuneration practices should be avoided in a web-enabled environment?

These questions are currently being asked within sales departments. Remuneration managers can expect to have one of these issues land on their desks. Our rule of thumb in these cases is to start with the role of the salesperson and follow this simple strategy: pay for the point of persuasion.

### 14.12.2    How e-commerce affects the sales force

The primary role of the salesperson is to persuade. If other resources such as the company website can handle re-orders, then a salesperson should not be distracted by these duties. If a customer already knows what he or she wants to buy (a standard product with little uncertainty), then there is no need to involve and reward a salesperson. In such cases, it is appropriate for the customer to order the product via the web, thereby bypassing the involvement and reward of a salesperson. Here are some basic guidelines:

a) E-commerce is primarily for the fulfilment of orders of products sold by the salesperson. In such cases, the "account" belongs to the salesperson.
b) E-commerce is used primarily by buyers who do not need sales advice. These should not belong to the salesperson.
c) E-commerce is the primary sales link with the customer, but customers must be persuaded to "sign up". These accounts belong to the organisation, but the salesperson may get an incentive for "signing up" a new customer.

### 14.12.3    Errors to avoid

The following are noted sales remuneration design errors. Be on the lookout for the following two most common errors:

- **My territory:** There is a common, but mistaken, philosophy that promotes the view that the salesperson "owns" everything in his or her territory, and should thus receive sales credit for all sales in that area, whether or not they effect the sale. Such a mistaken perspective creates high payouts without corresponding effort or contribution. Unfortunately, the salesperson also spends excessive time auditing sales credit reports from various sales channels, which is a very ineffective use of the sales personnel's time.
- **Appeasement pay:** Many sales leaders believe that they must credit all sales generated through the website to the salesperson to ensure their co-operation. Known as "appeasement pay", such a practice avoids the inevitable. While some token reward system may be necessary to provide initial positive support for the website, the double cost of such a practice will prove prohibitive over time. Finally, employers should be prepared to help the sales management team make changes to these critical subsystems to ensure continued effective use of the sales remuneration plan.

## 14.13    Cross-selling incentives

Perhaps the most effective pay method available to support the desired types of sales behaviour is cross-selling incentives. This refers to remuneration for making multiple sales, usually of different product lines, to the same customer. Payments may be made for selling multiple products at the time of the initial sale or paid over a period of time, as the relationship with the customer is further developed. This method supports the fundamental principle that the more needs satisfied per customer, the greater the stability, retention, and profitability of the customer.

Supported by both anecdotal evidence and sporadic research, that principle seems rather obvious. Unfortunately, most companies have built their customer databases around product sales, not their customer, and they do not have complete customer information. Someone unfamiliar with the sales process would question why sales personnel need incentive remuneration to reinforce this behaviour. Why wouldn't a salesperson go back to sell a second product to customers they already know rather than experience the high level of rejection they typically experience while prospecting for new customers? There are four primary reasons:

- **New sales focus:** Most remuneration plans emphasise new sales or new customers. Many discount the remuneration paid on repeat customers. This approach is supported to a certain extent by the idea that a second sale to an existing customer is easier to make than the first sale to a new customer. However, it ignores the additional profitability that comes with a second sale. Most training programmes also focus on prospecting for new customers rather than retaining existing customers.

- **Greed factor:** The greed factor plays a role in discouraging cross-selling, particularly in selling to individuals. Sales personnel recognise that they already receive a portion of all available funds from those to whom they have already sold. They assume that those prospects to whom they have not sold have 100 percent of their funds available for that specific product need, particularly because the product they are selling may replace any product already owned by that individual. The logic is that someone you do not already know is a better prospect than someone you have sold to because they can afford a more expensive purchase.

- **Fear factor:** Although training and remuneration changes can usually overcome these assumptions, it takes time, as well as focused training, to overcome the fear factor. In the enthusiasm of the sale, the typical salesperson promises to keep in touch with the client and correct any problems that might arise. He or she may also make rather optimistic statements about his or her organisation's performance or products. Although there are plenty of exceptions, most sales personnel lose touch with their customers, because they do not perceive a sufficient financial incentive to maintain a close relationship. They are also afraid of being embarrassed over what they said or did not deliver if they were to go back to the customer to pursue additional sales opportunities. Rejection, which is part of prospecting, is easier to face than potential embarrassment over promises not kept.

- **Customer ownership:** A fourth factor which complicates the implementation of marketing strategies that encourage cross-selling is the feeling of ownership that the sales force has for its existing customers. In many sales environments, management has relied on its sales force to handle marketing, prospecting, and sales. Individuals in this environment often feel that because they found, wooed, and sold to the customer, they "own" this relationship. In some cases, they prove this by taking the customer with them when they change companies. Companies that actively pursue cross-selling frequently use several groups of sales personnel to make sales of different products. In those situations, the person who created the original relationship will feel that his or her relationship is being threatened.

Your current sales force will have difficulty accepting this new paradigm because it disturbs what is, from their perspective, a successful relationship and a source of continuing income. Particularly when remuneration is commission only, this belief will be difficult to change, at least until the remuneration system moves off commission only and the organisation gets serious about creating warm leads and maintaining customer relationships.

Cross-selling remuneration may not have the immediate impact one might expect because of these factors. Remuneration will eventually will lead to changes in cross-selling results, but changes in training and management tactics are also needed to reduce the impact of these historically prominent operating behaviours.

## 14.14    Sales manager incentives

Many organisations debate how to reward sales managers. Figure 14.6 sets out some guidelines.

*Figure 14.6: Guidelines for the design of an incentive plan for sales managers*

| Example A | Example B | Example C |
|---|---|---|
| ***Primary role:*** To act as a "seller" by growing revenue and/or unit volume because:<br>1. More volume equals more profit.<br>2. Market share is small and opportunity exists to grow.<br>3. All sales are "good" (that is, undifferentiated volume is acceptable). | ***Primary role:*** To maximise sales profitability by producing profitable sales because:<br>1. Profit flexibility exists (that is, prices can be negotiated and product mix will affect contribution).<br>2. Field sales costs are large (that is, the total value of products and related services is not fully recognised in the sales process and therefore profit contribution is a critical measure of business success). | ***Primary role:*** To develop HR by developing the sales personnel in the sales unit because:<br>1. The selling process is varied and complex.<br>2. On-the-job training has an immediate favourable impact on business results. |
| ***Performance measures***<br>Volume in money or units | ***Performance measures***<br>Volume (preferably compared to a goal) or profit contribution (for example, gross margin less controllable selling expenses) | ***Performance measures***<br>Volume and sales representative productivity |
| ***Plan concept:*** Use an override commission (for example, based either on a percentage of total sales produced by all sales representatives in the sales unit or on a percentage of sales representatives' earnings). | ***Plan concept:*** Use a target incentive remuneration opportunity (for example, a bonus). The bonus opportunity should be weighted equally between volume attainment and profit contribution performance. | ***Plan concept:*** Use a target incentive remuneration opportunity (for example, a bonus). The bonus opportunity should be weighted equally between volume attainments and, for example, the number of sales representatives reaching the sales quota. |

## 14.15    Incentives for relationship management

It is a common belief among sales organisations that happy customers buy more. As a result, to support relationship management activities, incentive remuneration should revolve around retaining and increasing the current buying levels for a group of customers. A close relative of cross-selling, relationship management is tied to increased income or profitability of the customers rather than the product mix attributable to the group. It is particularly well suited to those individuals who sell and manage relationships with institutions rather than individuals or households. Many larger companies actually house relationship managers from their principal suppliers to facilitate more rapid service and better understanding of their needs.

Designing incentives for relationship management shares many of the challenges of cross-selling incentives. It is often difficult to obtain supporting data on which to set performance standards and associated incentives.

## 14.16    New sales roles

The world is changing, and the next wave of new sales roles are here which need to be included in the remuneration design. Set out below are examples of new sales roles.

- **End-user sales specialists:** Virtually any organisation that sells its products through distributors faces the challenge of creating demand among end users. Organisation A, an international organisation which manufactures computer keyboards, printers and related supplies, found it had to work with the end users rather than focus exclusively on resellers. To meet this challenge, the organisation redefined the focus of its sales force. Instead of the salespeople spending 85 percent of their time working with Organisation A's resellers and 15 percent with end users, the organisation reversed the time allocations. Sales representatives became end-user specialists; within the first year of this change, Organisation A's revenues grew substantially.
- **Retention sales specialists:** Most companies realise between 80 and 90 percent of their annual revenue from current customers. Retaining customers and, more importantly, realising the same or more revenue from year to year, is critical to the business's profitable growth. To retain customers and protect revenue, some companies have implemented retention sales specialists. Organisation B, a large waste management organisation, recently redefined its sales process and the roles of its salespeople. One outcome of that work was a new sales job: core account retention specialist. Anyone holding this job is responsible for retaining current revenue with current customers.
- **New customer acquisition specialists:** Organisation C, specialising in closures for a variety of containers, was frustrated by not achieving its planned 15 percent sales growth, a reasonable target given industry conditions. Management divided the sales organisation into two teams: core business managers and new business development managers. The new business development managers were responsible for winning new customers through a focus on selling Organisation C's capabilities to companies that were in the early stages of a new package design. The first full quarter after implementing the new sales role, revenue was up 20 percent, and top management projected 30 percent revenue growth for the following year.

- **Telephonic account manager:** Increasingly, companies are learning that customers can be won and retained without deploying individual sales representatives. Organisation D implemented a specialised telephone account sales force that focused on converting accounts from a predetermined list of target prospects into customers. Not only were these accounts receptive to being contacted by telephone, they also proved to be the fastest-growing revenue division in the highly competitive small office/ home office segment of the office products industry.

- **Service consultant:** Recent surveys completed with several companies across industries show that salespeople spend 15 to 30 percent of their time on service-related activities – finding the status of orders, answering questions about shipments, resolving billing disputes, and the like. If some or all of this service work can be assigned to others, the amount of time available for selling increases. To test this idea, some companies are experimenting with a new sales role: service consultant. A service consultant typically supports three or four field-based sales representatives and addresses, and solves any customer problems that the sales representative or account manager cannot handle expediently.

Given the challenging conditions of today's business climate, the CEO has many obstacles to achieving business growth and success. New customers are more difficult to acquire; current customers are more difficult to retain. Therefore, it is imperative that the CEO creates and communicates an appropriate business strategy. One of these levers is sales rewards and remuneration.

In designing and implementing pay initiatives to improve sales organisation effectiveness, there is a lot at stake. Sales roles need to be aligned with the sales strategy in order to support the business in achieving its overall objectives. Sales roles drive key elements of the sales management process – particularly pay. Understanding sales roles – and how they contribute to the business strategy – is essential to making appropriate remuneration design decisions and helps ensure that you "fill the coffers" rather than "break the bank".

## 14.17  Summary

Without sales there is no profit. A global trend is to work out how to enhance sales through better sales force incentives. This is done via a combination of commission schemes and bonus schemes. An important debate is whether or not to cap the incentive scheme – most organisations prefer not to. The main performance measure has shifted from turnover/volume to gross profit and gross margin. When all members of the team have contributed to hitting the company goal, regardless of individual commissions, a trend is to pay them all a bonus. The remuneration mix between base pay and variable pay hinges strongly on how difficult it is to sell the product and the value of the product. All schemes should have a detailed set of rules.

## 14.18   Self-evaluation questions

1.   What is the difference between commission and bonus?
2.   Name the main types of sales force remuneration plans.
3.   What are the most common performance measures for the sales function?
4.   Name the primary elements of a sales remuneration plan.
5.   What are some of the sales remuneration complexities in the e-world?

# CHAPTER 15

# Long-term Incentive Schemes

The subject of long-term incentive schemes, which are commonly referred to as share schemes, causes debate and continues to receive attention in the media. Normally the public slant is the extent to which participants in share schemes are enriched and the tenuous correlation in many cases of their rewards with the company's performance and/or rewards offered by peer companies.

At the other end of the scale, shareholders and executives continue to regard share schemes as a valuable tool to leverage performance, align management and shareholder interests, and retain key employees. The subject is by no means exhausted, and a number of developing trends are evident.

## 15.1  What is a share scheme?

As part of the incentivisation of employees, particularly executives and senior management, companies would like employees to think and act like shareholders in the sense that their primary motivation should be to act in a manner that raises the value of the company's shares. This is normally achieved by devising short-term incentive schemes (which pay out annually or more frequently, such as a bonus scheme) and long-term incentive schemes (where the payout typically takes place over more than a year, such as a share scheme).

The use of share schemes as a long-term incentive is based on the premise that if employees own shares in the company, they will be more likely to think like shareholders (because they are shareholders).

Other reasons for the implementation of share schemes are the following:

- They are used as an attraction mechanism for scarce skills or hot talent (the prospective applicant is drawn by the prospect of future rewards from the share scheme).
- They are used as a retention mechanism for scarce skills or hot talent (the employee is dissuaded from leaving the company's employment because of the prospect of future rewards from the share scheme).
- Market forces dictate their use (other companies competing for scarce skills or hot talent have competing rival share schemes).

## 15.2  Share schemes defined

A share is a unit of ownership in a company. Share units must be settled for in cash except where listed shares are used, where transfer of ownership occurs on the vesting date.

### 15.2.1 Types of shares

The following are the types of shares typically used within long-term incentive schemes:

- Ordinary shares.
- Performance shares.
- Share options.
- Phantom shares/share appreciation rights.

The differentiating features of each type of share scheme are set out in Table 15.1.

*Table 15.1: Differentiating features of main long-term incentive schemes*

| | **Qualify for voting at the company's general meetings for members** | **Qualify for dividends** | **Value** | **Ranking\* upon liquidation** | **Convertible to ordinary shares** |
|---|---|---|---|---|---|
| Ordinary shares | Yes | Yes, as approved by the company in general meeting | Usually higher than preference shares | Lowest ranking | N/A |
| Performance shares | No | Usually at a specified rate of interest | Usually lower than ordinary shares | Higher than ordinary shares | Possible, depending on terms of issue. Usually at option of the shareholder, once specified conditions have been met |
| Share options | No | No | Usually defined as the growth in the value of full shares over a specified period | Lowest ranking | No (but options once exercised and paid for are settled with shares or via a cashless sale). |
| Phantom shares or share appreciation rights | No | No | Equivalent to ordinary shares or share options respectively, but without share ownership | Lowest ranking | No (but benefits can sometimes be settled with shares) |

\* *"Ranking" means the order in which shareholders' investment in share capital will be refunded upon liquidation of the company.*

- In the case of the full value share schemes, the value of the benefit at vesting is the full value of the shares, while in the case of the appreciation schemes, it is determined by the accrual in the increase of the value of the shares over the vesting period.
- The different scheme designs have different benefit and cost implications as well as different tax profiles that should be weighed up in the approval of share schemes by Boards and Remuneration Committees. In addition, the retention, performance and motivation profiles of the schemes need to be considered. During the vesting period, the value of dividends is sometimes added to the performance shares in the form of shares. These dividend equivalent shares will only be delivered to the extent that the award actually vests.

## 15.2.2    Trading of shares

If the shares are held in a listed public company, the shares may be traded on a securities exchange through a stockbroker. Shares in a non-listed public company or a private company must be traded privately. In practice, this amounts to a severe restriction on the trading of non-listed shares and their relative value to a prospective purchaser. The trading of scheme shares by participants is prohibited during the pre-determined "blackout" periods due to regulations aimed at preventing insider trading.

## 15.2.3    Value of shares

The value of listed shares is a function of the price buyers are willing to pay and sellers are willing to sell at on a securities exchange (that is, pure market function). This information is available online in real-time and is well publicised in the daily press. The value at which shares are traded may be influenced by many factors, such as the company's financial results (revenue, profit after taxes, cash flow, return on capital, earnings per share, etc.), and in particular its expected future trading results. Investors and traders take this information into account in comparison with peer companies (other similar companies), other sectors of the securities exchange, and other investment alternatives (for example, the bond market).

The most common valuation method of a listed company's shares used by independent valuators (such as auditors, investment analysts and actuaries) is to discount the company's expected future share price and dividends. The most popular valuation model at present, the Black and Scholes model, applies this basis of valuation. However, more sophisticated valuation models (the binomial method is fairly popular and accepted) are available.

By comparison, shares in a private or unlisted public company are typically valued lower. This is due in part to the restricted opportunity to trade such shares in the eyes of investors and traders, and in part to less stringent corporate governance measures (there is a perceived increase in investment risk).

A common way of valuing shares is to multiply the profit (e.g. EBITDA) by a price earnings (PE) ratio. This will generally range from five to, say, 30, depending on the profitability of the organisation and its perceived investment risk, as well as investor perceptions of the sector and market in general.

### 15.2.4 Conversions into shares

Companies sometimes raise cash by issuing loan instruments such as bonds (debentures). These instruments (like loans) are normally interest-bearing and sometimes have a conversion option into shares. Typically, conditions would apply to such a conversion, and the bond holders could have the option of whether to convert or not.

## 15.3 Features of share schemes

### 15.3.1 Elements of a share scheme

The following are the elements which must be considered when implementing a typical share scheme:

- Types of shares.
- Types of schemes.
- Allocation value.
- Offer price.
- Exercising options and rights.
- Vesting of shares.
- Topping up of shares.
- Release and payment of equity instruments.
- Stop or loss provisions.
- Re-pricing of share options.

### 15.3.2 Types of shares

Apart from shares or options to take up shares, and instruments that are convertible into shares (such as bonds), share schemes may issue phantom shares or share appreciation rights to employees.

In a phantom scheme, the terms, conditions and benefits to participants are similar to those in a "real" share scheme (the rules of a phantom scheme are drawn up to simulate a "real" share scheme). The reasons for adopting different share types are dealt with in subsequent sections, but we need to develop an understanding of a number of other issues first.

### 15.3.3 Types of schemes

Any of the following types of schemes may be implemented:

- **Share purchase scheme:** Paid-up shares are issued to each participant and generally held in trust until the vesting and other conditions have been met. A loan is issued to the participant for the issue value of the shares. Normally the loan is subject to interest, and dividends due to the participant are utilised as a set-off against the interest on the loan. The loan is normally repayable when the shares are released to the participant (once the performance and other conditions have been met).

- **Share option scheme:** Share options are usually issued to participants subject to vesting conditions. The options are exercisable at the participant's discretion but not before the vesting and other conditions have been met (in the standard share option arrangement). Exercising of options normally takes place simultaneously with payment for and release of the shares to the participants.
- **Convertible debenture scheme:** Convertible debentures are issued to participants in return for cash or a loan (as per the share purchase scheme). In the case of a loan, the interest due by the participant on the loan and the interest receivable by the participant on the debentures are normally offset. The debentures are normally convertible to shares once vesting conditions have been met and the participant elects to make the conversion. Once converted, the proceeds due to the company for issuing the shares are offset against the redemption value of the debenture.
- **Performance or restricted share schemes:** Full shares are issued to participants once performance and/or other criteria (such as elapsed time) have been achieved. No strike price is generally payable by the participants.
- **Phantom schemes:** Phantom shares are issued to participants subject to vesting conditions, in the same way as real shares. Once the conditions are met, the proceeds from the notional sale of the shares are remitted to the participants in cash. Phantom shares are typically used when insufficient real shares are available for issue to participants or if trading of real shares is severely limited (for example, shares in a small unlisted private company). The value of the phantom shares at vesting may be settled with shares if the company has elected the option to do so in the scheme rules, or otherwise in cash.
- **Share appreciation right (SAR):** A right, usually granted to an employee, to receive a bonus equal to the appreciation in the company's stock over a specified period. Like employee stock options, SARs benefit the holder if there is an increase in stock price; the difference is that the employee is not required to pay the exercise price (as with an employee stock option), but rather just receives the amount of the increase in cash or stock.

### 15.3.4 Allocation value

The total allocation value of a scheme is normally determined on the basis of allocation multiples. These are expressed as a multiple of the participant's annual guaranteed remuneration package (which is the annual base pay plus the annual value of fringe benefits and other payments of a fixed and regular nature). The allocation multiple multiplied by the annual guaranteed package gives the issue value of the equity instruments under the scheme (shares or share options and the like) to be granted in total to the participant (that is, the value of the sum of all issues to the participant). Equity instruments that have vested and/or been released to participants are normally deducted from the total allocation multiple in determining a new allocation.

### 15.3.5 Offer price

The offer price refers to the price at which an offer of shares, share options or phantom shares is made available to a participant in the scheme. Typically, this is the market price of the share at the time of the offer, as per the securities exchange, in the case of a listed share, or as per independent valuation in the case of an unlisted share.

In limited instances, the offer price may be lower than the market price. In such cases, an immediate benefit is conferred on the participant. For example, when shares, share options or phantom shares are granted in place of a cash bonus, they may be granted at a discount in market value equal to the gross bonus.

As stated above, in the case of performance shares, there is generally no offer price.

### 15.3.6    Exercising options and rights

Exercising an option is a legal term used to describe the point at which the offer of a share option or share appreciation right is accepted by a participant in a scheme. The participant becomes bound to pay the offer price at an agreed point in the future (possibly subject to certain agreed conditions), and it therefore represents the point at which ownership is transferred. Legally speaking, options can be exercised when they vest or are released to a participant to be sold or held. Furthermore, the exercise of options can be agreed to be contingent upon the fulfilment of conditions, for example, the participant must be employed by the employer at the point when vesting takes place, or the number of options that vest are determined according to the degree to which agreed performance conditions are met.

### 15.3.7    Vesting of shares

The vesting of shares to employees is normally subject to the achievement of specified conditions. These may be time-related and/or performance-related, as indicated in Table 15.2. Vesting means that shares may be released to a participant against payment of the issue price, or, in the case of share options or other equity instruments, these may be exercised, and the shares released against payment of the offer or strike price.

*Table 15.2: Vesting options*

| Vesting condition | Example | Purpose |
|---|---|---|
| **Time-related** | 25% of the shares vest if the participant is in service after three years, 25% after four years and 50% after five years. | As a retention mechanism and to motivate employees to maximise the value of the shares in the medium- to long-term |
| **Performance-related** | A performance schedule is drawn up whereby percentages of shares vest, dependent on the achievement of performance conditions. Examples are that profits should exceed the previous year's level by inflation plus a certain percentage, or return on assets should compare favourably within a peer group. | To establish a link between the level of reward and the level of performance owing to factors under the control of management that will serve to increase the share price |

Table 15.3 illustrates average vesting periods in Asia, the United States of America and Europe:

*Table 15.3: Comparison of typical vesting periods*

| Comparative vesting periods (year) | Asia | USA | Europe |
|---|---|---|---|
| Maximum | 10 | 10 | 10 |
| Average | 4 | 3 | 5 |
| Minimum | 2 | 1 | 3 |

The periods in Table 15.3 reflect the earliest vesting dates. Schemes also specify a maximum vesting period. The purpose of the maximum vesting period is to allow an additional period to elapse in cases when a share's value at the earliest vesting date is below the price at which the offer was made to, and accepted by, the participant. This is commonly referred to as shares that are "under water". The purpose is also to encourage holding the share or equity instrument longer in line with shareholder interests.

## 15.3.8 Topping up of shares

Most companies offer equity instruments to participants on a regular basis. The number of equity instruments to be offered to individuals is determined with reference to the difference between the number of equity instruments due in terms of the issue multiples referred to above, and the number of equity instruments issued. For purposes of calculating the latter, some companies subtract the number of equity instruments that have vested from the number of equity instruments issued (typically in Asia and the United States of America), while others do not (typically in Europe).

Companies that use their long-term incentive schemes as part of a retention strategy for scarce talent tend to argue in favour of the former practice (since equity instruments that have vested no longer constitute an effective retention lever).

## 15.3.9 Release and payment of equity instruments

Once the vesting terms and conditions have been met, the equity instruments become releasable to participants. This means that the shares or share options may be sold and the proceeds used to pay the issue or exercise price to the company (if applicable) and any taxes that may be due, or that the participant may take transfer of ownership of shares due for his or her own account against payment in cash.

## 15.3.10 Re-pricing of share options

This refers to a practice related to the stop/loss provisions mentioned above, and it means that a company issues new options to participants to replace those repurchased in terms of the stop/loss provisions. The new options are issued at current market prices (which in the circumstances will typically be lower than the original offer prices). Similar to the stop/loss provisions, this practice has been criticised publicly. Many securities exchanges around the world prohibit re-pricing of share options.

## 15.4  Taxation of participants

### 15.4.1  Phantom shares

Participants are generally taxed on any amounts received in cash and, in some tax jurisdictions, on any amounts accruing to them. Accrual means any amount that is unconditionally due and receivable by an employee, including amounts not yet received. Therefore, schemes should be structured so that payment to employees and accrual of benefits to employees occur simultaneously, so as to avoid participants having to pay tax on money they have not received (and may not end up receiving!).

---

*Example*

1,000 phantom shares are issued at a price of 10 each and vest at a price of 12 each. The employee's marginal tax rate is 40 percent. Tax payable by employee:

$$40\% \text{ x } (12 - 10) \text{ x } 1{,}000 = 800$$

---

### 15.4.2  Performance or restricted shares

Using the example above, except that the issue price is 0, the tax payable by the employee would be:

$$40\% \text{ x } (12 - 0) \text{ x } 1{,}000 = 4{,}800$$

### 15.4.3  Share purchase schemes

These schemes are typically structured as follows. Employees purchase shares offered to them by the company, but do not pay for them until the shares vest and are releasable to them. Therefore a loan exists until payment for the shares takes place. Normally, interest is charged on the loan. This is usually offset partially or in full by the value of dividends received on the shares. If the interest charged is at a rate lower than the official rate, it is likely that this will be considered a taxable fringe benefit. When the shares are sold, the participant is liable to capital gains tax on the difference between the selling price and the purchase price of the shares. In the case of share traders, the full proceeds may be taxable.

---

*Example*

1,000 shares are issued at 10 each. Dividends are payable at 1.20 per share. The official rate is 15 percent. The employee's marginal tax rate is 40 percent. Shares are sold for 15 each.

Annual tax payable by employee (until loan on shares is repaid):
      Taxable amount per share: $(10 \times 15\%) - 1.20 = 0.30$ per share
      Tax payable: $40\% \times 0{,}30 = 0.12$ per share, or 120 $(1{,}000 \times 0.12)$.

Tax sale of shares:

$$1{,}000 \times (15 - 10) \times 40\% = 2{,}000$$

---

### 15.4.4    Share option schemes

Usually share options are granted to participants subject to a vesting term, after which the options may be exercised and are released to participants upon payment of the option price. Participants are usually taxed on the difference between the option price and the market price at exercise.

---

*Example*

1,000 shares are offered at 10 each. The options are exercised and released when the market price is 12. The employee's marginal tax rate is 40 percent.

Tax payable:

$$40\% \times (12 - 10) \times 1{,}000 = 800$$

---

### 15.4.5    Other schemes

It may be possible to structure some schemes on the basis that capital gains tax (which is generally lower than the tax rate for individuals) is payable. Using the example for performance shares above, the capital gains tax payable would be:

$$25\% \times 40\% \times 12 \times 1{,}000 = 1{,}200$$

## 15.5    Factors affecting value to participants

Aside from the obvious, namely, the number of shares or share options issued to a participant and the issue price, the following factors can affect the value to participants:

- Growth in the share price.
- Whether the scheme is structured tax effectively.
- Whether performance hurdles are in place.
- How soon the equity instruments vest.
- Whether top-up occurs at each vesting point

It is possible to construct a model to simulate the combined effects of all the factors when evaluating a scheme from a participant's – and the company's – perspective, and compare the costs and benefits of different schemes.

## 15.6 Real shares or phantom shares for listed companies?

All share schemes around the world have impacted the profit line since January 2005 in terms of IFRS 2 (International Accounting Rules for share-based payments). They also dilute the shareholders' interest (if the shares are issued and payment is delayed until vesting takes place). In some countries, the tax law does not permit deductions for many schemes where new shares are issued for a scheme.

Complex financial modelling is required to determine the answer to the above, as well as to determine which scheme type is most favourable and whether the equity instruments should be purchased in the market or issued. Hedging alternatives also need to be taken into consideration to reduce the impact of share price movements on scheme expenses.

## 15.7 Accounting for share-based payments (IFRS 2)

Share-based payments to employees are accounted for by companies as an expense and credited to capital. A number of aspects are critical in determining the "value" to be accounted:

- Whether settlement is in cash or in equity.
- Whether performance conditions apply, and whether they are market related or not.
- The expected attrition rate.
- The model to be used to value the equity instruments.
- The minimum and maximum vesting periods.

In summary, share-based payments should be accounted for at fair value at date of grant of the share-based benefit. In general, this can be done with reference to either the value of the assets or services received by the company, or the value of the equity interests granted. In the case of employee benefits, the value of the latter is presumed to be more readily determinable than the value of services rendered.

The fair value of equity interests granted and settled in equity is determined by applying an option valuation model (such as Black/Scholes, although the specific method is not prescribed). The following may be taken into account in the valuation:

- Exercise price.
- Market price.
- Expected volatility.
- Expected dividends (if applicable).

- Rate of interest in the market.
- Expected term of the option.
- Probability of forfeiture.
- Probability of meeting specified vesting conditions (such as financial performance hurdles).

Equity interests granted and settled in cash are determined by the cost of settlement.

Differences between the initial valuation of the equity instruments at date of grant and the eventual realised value are accounted for (trued up), except in cases where benefits are settled with equity and the performance conditions are market-based. However, in all cases, the number of instruments that vest is trued up.

In the case of employee benefits, the services are presumed to be received over the period of vesting if the vesting terms specify that employees must complete a specified period(s) of service. Accounting for the value of equity instruments is therefore normally spread over the vesting period. However, if vesting is unconditional, the benefits are deemed to accrue upon granting.

## 15.8    Topping-up practice

Shares and share options are typically issued to participants on an annual basis until the target issue multiple is reached and/or to top up shares or share options that have vested. The basis for the argument to issue shares or share options regularly is particularly relevant in the case of volatile shares.

Investors argue that management is in the best position to determine when the share price is likely to spike or increase dramatically. Consequently, they are in a position to benefit themselves (and other scheme participants) simply by timing the issue of shares or share options opportunistically. Rewards gained from share or share option schemes in this manner have no correlation with efforts by management to increase the share price. To counter practices of this nature, best practice from a corporate governance perspective suggests that shares or share options should be issued annually.

## 15.9    Performance conditions

Institutional investors in the United Kingdom have argued that the correlation between the performance of management and the performance of the share price is often tenuous. This is because many factors apart from management's performance affect the share price (for example, the future earnings prospects for the company and the sector within which it operates; how future economic fundamentals are expected to affect the business; and the future competitive ability of the business versus its peers locally and internationally). Consequently, investors argue that external factors favouring a company may give rise to an increase in its share price, while management may not have performed up to expectation. They argue further that rewards gained by management under such conditions have not been properly earned. Performance conditions or hurdles have been conceived as an attempt to align rewards from equity-based schemes with management performance.

Typically, the performance conditions may be that the company's earnings should exceed those of the previous year, plus inflation, plus a percentage, and/or that the company's earnings growth and/or return on capital employed (or a similar ratio) must compare favourably with that of peer companies. The performance hurdles are typically measured at the vesting points, and depending on the score achieved, a percentage of the possible shares or share options may vest.

---

*Example*

1,000 shares are issued that vest 40 percent after two years and 60 percent after three years. After two years, the score achieved for the performance hurdle is 80 percent. The number of shares vesting after two years is:

$$80\% \times 40\% \times 1,000 = 320 \text{ shares.}$$

---

Some schemes have catch-up terms whereby the qualifying terms for vesting, if not achieved, may be extended to the next vesting point. In the example above, this would mean that 80 shares ((1,000 x 40%) – 320) would be carried forward to the vesting point after three years. This is a controversial practice and not always considered to be acceptable, as it falls under a principle of allowance for possible "re-testing" against targets and giving participants a second bite at the cherry which investors do not have.

## 15.10 Legal aspects

Most regulatory and tax jurisdictions restrict a company from providing financial assistance for the purchase of its shares other than if an approved scheme exists for salaried employees to participate in the company's shareholding. Such an employee share participation scheme must be approved in the company's constitution, the company must be solvent, and the scheme must be approved by a clear majority of the members (shareholders) present in a general meeting.

If the company is listed, further regulations are typically required by the stock exchange where the share is listed. These generally include:

- The rules of the scheme must be approved by the listing stock exchange.
- Not more than 15 percent of the company's issued share capital may be held by participants in the share scheme and by the share trust (in respect of shares held by a trust but not yet allocated to participants).
- Not more than 3 percent of the issued share capital of the company may be held by a single participant or his or her appointed nominee.

## 15.11 Design trends

The terminology associated with share schemes has been described in the preceding sections. In this section, we summarise current design trends:

- Companies have been moving away from share option schemes to a number of other scheme types, mainly because of the negative views around the risk disparity of stock options and the additional cost impact of share options compared to other schemes.
- Target issue multiples have been increasing steadily.
- No meaningful share participation is evident to date for employees below job level C-2 (CEO minus 2) to date.
- Performance conditions are common in schemes applying in the United Kingdom and United States of America, and are expected to increase further in other parts of the world.
- Increased disclosure requirements are expected to lead to greater uniformity in schemes and more stringent corporate governance measures for schemes in future.
- The implementation of IFRS 2 has led to alterations in scheme design to reduce the effects of the proposed accounting guidelines on company earnings and to deal with the effects of the tax changes.

## 15.12 Stakeholder requirements

The criteria shown in Table 15.4 are used by stakeholders to evaluate share schemes.

*Table 15.4: Strategic, financial and detail considerations*

| Strategic considerations | Shareholders | Company | Executives |
|---|---|---|---|
| Maximum alignment with shareholder interests: | Y | Y | Y |
| • Gearing implications of schemes (full share value versus differential growth in share value, i.e. options) | | | |
| • Share dilution implications | | | |
| • Retention (share options have a lower perceived value when they are under water, i.e. the exercise price is lower than the issue price at vesting) | | | |
| • Performance motivation (high gearing from schemes based on differential growth versus tax and strike prices payable at vesting) | | | |
| • Risk/reward relationship | | | |

| Strategic considerations | Shareholders | Company | Executives |
|---|:---:|:---:|:---:|
| • Dividends accrue to participants from inception | | | |
| Minimum cost implications to company arising from risk profile (as a result of varying share prices over vesting periods) | Y | Y | |
| Issuing shares versus acquiring shares (market timing, and cash versus loan financing for acquisitions) | Y | Y | |
| Alignment with market remuneration levels: embedded full share value for retention (especially in bear markets) versus geared value increase for performance (especially in bull markets) | Y | Y | Y |
| Best practice and sound governance | Y | Y | Y |
| **Financial considerations** | **Shareholders** | **Company** | **Executives** |
| Minimised cash flow to company | Y | Y | |
| Immediate cash flow implications to company – can be designed to be positive if shares are to be issued | Y | Y | |
| Maximised ratio of benefits to economic cost (discounted cash flow (DCF) after tax) | Y | Y | |
| Maximised benefits (DCF after tax) | | | Y |
| Maximised earnings per share (EPS) (efficient combination of accounting cost and share dilution over time) | Y | Y | |
| Maximised share retention by executives after vesting (especially after payment of taxes and strike prices at vesting) even if share price growth is negative | Y | Y | Y |
| Most appropriate constitution of assets: | Y | Y | Y |
| • Tradability/switching | | | |
| • Asset spread, hedging, gearing, derivatives | | | |
| **Detail considerations** | **Shareholders** | **Company** | **Executives** |
| Shareholder approval requirements | | Y | |
| Legal risk, especially section 38 of the Companies Act 71 of 2008 | Y | Y | |

| | | | |
|---|---|---|---|
| Tax risk, especially section 8C and 24B of the Income Tax Act 58 of 1962 | Y | Y | Y |
| Adherence to IFRS 2 requirements | | Y | |
| Shares awarded as part of employee schemes as a percentage of overall issued share capital | | Y | |
| Implications regarding trading during closed periods | Y | Y | Y |
| Disclosure requirements (e.g. regarding directors) | | Y | Y |
| Administration implications | | Y | Y |

In line with good corporate governance and shareholder requirements, it is the duty of any company to adopt a share scheme that has the most favourable impact on earnings per share (EPS) (shareholder driver), is tax compliant for the company and participants (tax driver), has a favourable accounting cost to the company (IFRS 2 driver), and results in full ownership of shares by the employee by meeting performance criteria (employee driver).

A scheme that meets these criteria is a win–win for all stakeholders, namely, the employee, the company and the shareholders.

## 15.13 Role of the remuneration committee (RemCo)

The role of the remuneration committee is outlined in the guidelines below.

### 15.13.1 Remuneration committee guidelines

*Establishment of a remuneration committee:* A remuneration committee is established with the powers and duties set out in the following paragraphs. This committee will report to and derive its powers from the board of directors and conduct all of its proceedings subject to the authority of the board of directors.

*Membership of committee:* The members of the committee, including the chairperson, will be appointed by the board of directors, and will continue to act until they resign or are removed from office. The committee will comprise not fewer than three serving directors of the organisation, of whom the majority, including the chairperson, will be non-executive directors. In some jurisdictions, all members must be non-executive directors. The CEO, Executive: HR and the Reward Head typically attend RemCo meetings by invitation, but should excuse themselves from any deliberations that may affect their own remuneration and/ or where they would have a conflict of interest. The scope of the remuneration committee is mostly on prescribed officers, executive committee members of listed executive officers (depending on the minimum statutory requirements). However, their scope should include oversight and approval of the remuneration policy applicable to all employees within an organisation, and they should be familiar with the details of how this policy is applied to lower-level employees.

***Role of the committee:*** The committee observes the following guidelines and procedures:

- The organisation will use all components of the remuneration system to leverage performance.
- In order to achieve an appropriate balance in the remuneration package, the committee will determine fixed pay.
- A performance bonus or incentive will be awarded and paid annually in arrears for achievement of agreed performance levels.
- The proportionality of the different elements of remuneration may be compared at annual intervals with the remuneration policies of selected peer companies or an approved salary survey.
- The investigations and research to be conducted by the committee will allow sufficient time for final recommendations to be submitted to the board.
- The committee will engage with investors and stakeholders on the remuneration policy and request support therefor from shareholders.

***Powers of committee:*** The members of the committee will have full access to all financial information contained in the books and records of the organisation, including the personnel records of an employee for whom the committee will be making pay recommendations. The committee may appoint external consultants for the purpose of obtaining salary survey information, to provide an independent review of proposals tabled by management, and for assisting in the conduct of the peer review. The committee may also consult with the organisation's attorneys and its auditors where necessary. In addition, the committee is empowered to obtain the assistance of the HR executive or department in obtaining the relevant information.

***Proceedings of committee:*** The chairperson will be responsible for the convening of the committee, maintaining minutes and copies of all reports and data which have been utilised by the committee in reaching its decisions, as well as the communication of decisions to the board, where applicable.

## 15.14   CEO pay

Remuneration of the CEO is more complex than meets the eye, and a strategic perspective on remuneration requires research that looks beyond how much CEOs earn. This dichotomy of attraction, motivation and retention of good executives versus tough corporate governance and media attention places remuneration decision-makers in a difficult position.

Generally, the international trend is to link CEO pay more strongly to performance. Table 15.5 sets out the most common determinants of CEO pay.

*Table 15.5: Determinants for executive pay*

| 1. | **Organisation size** | Turnover, number of employees, value of assets |
|----|----------------------|------------------------------------------------|
| 2. | **Organisation performance** | Profitability, return on investment, value added |

| 3. | **Executive-specific factors** | Age, experience, tenure, career path |
|----|-------------------------------|---------------------------------------|
| 4. | **Organisation structure** | Holding, subsidiary or single-unit organisation, capital or labour-intensive |
| 5. | **Job- or position-specific factors** | Level of decision-making, consequence of error, organisation level |
| 6. | **Job complexity** | Job-sizing instruments are used to determine job size |

Because CEO pay is the "cork in the bottle" and all other employee pay depends on this directly or indirectly, particularly at the executive level, it is critical to set CEO pay correctly. Some organisations only benchmark CEO pay and then all other levels of pay are set relative to this.

When considering proposals for CEO pay, RemCos are presented with benchmark information from salary surveys or request information of their own. Although at first it appears relatively easy, executive management are often accused of cherry-picking survey data to promote their case. The most commonly used definition of "the market" is "a place from where you recruit or to which you lose people".

However, for CEO positions, the definition of the market is problematic, especially in industry sectors where there are few comparable players. Consider, for example, unique state-owned entities and regulators, a new bank, a small mine, or an asset management organisation – the definition of comparator becomes more difficult. A robust methodology needs to be adopted to select organisations that provide a direct and relevant comparison of CEO pay.

It is important, when defining the market, to consider a number of factors apart from financial components. These include a full assessment of the organisation, based on the following criteria:

- Holding, subsidiary or single-unit organisation.
- Private, public or state-owned enterprise.
- Complexity of industry or market.
- Listed or not.
- Local stock exchange listing only, overseas listing (for example, LSE, NYSE) or both.
- Organisation size in terms of turnover, operating budget, capital employed, profit, assets, market cap, number of employees.
- Job content, not just position title.
- Job size – not all CEO job sizes are the same.

Once the comparator group has been selected, pay can be easily determined for guaranteed pay, short-term incentives, long-term incentives and retention schemes. The results are presented as percentiles, as shown in Table 15.6.

*Table 15.6: Elements of CEO pay*

| Chief executive officer[1] | | | | | |
|---|---|---|---|---|---|
| Job code | EM0045 | | | | |
| County code | | | | | |
| Country name | | | | | |
| Currency | | | | | |
| National data source | Live survey data | | | | |
| Modal grade (Paterson) | F3 | | | | |
| Company size | 8 | | | | |
| | **10th** | **25th** | **50th** | **75th** | **90th** |
| Basic salary | 2,263,362 | 2,547,697 | 3,021,588 | 3,495,479 | 3,779,814 |
| Fixed bonus/13th cheque | 134,938 | 151,889 | 180,142 | 208,395 | 225,346 |
| Total base salary | 2,221,236 | 2,500,279 | 2,965,350 | 3,430,421 | 3,709,464 |
| Car allowance | 188,764 | 212,478 | 252,000 | 291,522 | 315,236 |
| Housing benefit | 224,719 | 252,949 | 300,000 | 347,051 | 375,281 |
| Sundry benefits | 67,416 | 75,885 | 90,000 | 104,115 | 112,584 |
| Pension/Provident fund contribution | 198,622 | 223,574 | 265,161 | 306,748 | 331,700 |
| Medical contribution | 65,151 | 73,335 | 86,976 | 100,617 | 108,801 |
| Total guaranteed package | 2,445,816 | 2,753,071 | 3,265,164 | 3,777,257 | 4,084,512 |
| Short term incentive | 1,104,070 | 1,242,768 | 1,473,933 | 1,705,098 | 1,843,796 |
| Total annual remuneration | 2,805,528 | 3,157,973 | 3,745,380 | 4,332,787 | 4,685,232 |
| Realisable long term incentive | 1,447,994 | 2,805,488 | 5,067,979 | 7,330,468 | 8,687,963 |

Realisable Long-Term Incentive - the total realisable value for the current year, which describes the value of the LTI component of remuneration/compensation held in the current year, which would be realisable into the future at vesting points. It is the portion that the Executive would be walking away from.

Assigning a value to the long-term incentive portion of a CEO's pay has become complex since recent developments in the design of long-term incentives for executives. The most important of these recent developments are:

- Expensing of employee share schemes became mandatory from 1 January 2005 in terms of the new International Accounting Statement (IFRS 2) regarding accounting standards for share-based payments.
- The expenses in terms of IFRS 2 for share options are generally not tax deductible.
- Recent changes have been introduced in many tax jurisdictions with the aim of taxing all gains under employee equity schemes as normal earnings. This has been in reaction to certain scheme constructions in the past in terms of which capital gains tax (CGT) was payable on gains made.

---

1    21st Century, 2021.

Proper governance emphasises the reporting of a single figure of remuneration at executive level and details the methodology for this reporting line. In simplest terms, it is important to note that when one considers the benchmarks of long-term incentives, one differentiates between the award, the vehicle type, the vesting conditions, and how this combination translates to an annual value of total guaranteed package (the realisable value).

There are many possible ways of resolving the frustration and conflict between RemCos, boards and executive management. Some of the more important ones are:

- A clear definition of the market.
- A robust and defensible anchor for the CEO's package.
- Well-trained RemCos.
- Ensuring that the RemCo has access to top remuneration experts for advice and to validate executive proposals.
- Comprehensive RemCo packs showing all the components of the remuneration structure and how the proposal will affect the total earnings.

Listing requirements from stock exchanges generally set out many guidelines for good RemCo governance.

### 15.14.1    Guidelines for setting CEO and executive pay

The key guidelines that should be followed in setting CEO and executive pay are:

- "Defensible" is the key word, in terms of pay.
- Tie pay directly to the value delivered.
- Market norms are a useful parameter but not an absolute guide.
- Robust remuneration policies and strategies are a must.
- Impeccable governance is mandatory.

It is important for the CEO's remuneration programme to be reviewed periodically. The purpose of this review is to assess and evaluate the overall programme design, the appropriateness of its competitiveness in the general market, and the effect of the linkages with performance.[2] This evaluation, sponsored by the board remuneration committee and undertaken by independent external specialists, ought to be undertaken every two to three years to ensure the integrity of the organisation's total board and executive remuneration structure processes and impact on corporate performance.

### 15.14.2    Selecting comparators for remuneration benchmarking

When presenting remuneration benchmarking reports to EXCOs, Boards, RemCos or any other stakeholder, one of the first questions they will ask is, "Who did you compare us to?" You

---

2    Diez, 2018; Bussin & Modau, 2015.

will probably say the right things in reply, such as: "This is the market we use for our general employee population", "Everyone does it this way", or "The CEO told us which companies to use for comparison". This is often followed by a heated debate.

It stands to reason that there are different, often conflicting, views which depend on through whose eyes you are looking. The employees would want to "upgrade" comparators, the shareholders would want to "downplay" comparators, and the RemCo is stuck in the middle, genuinely trying to select ones that are fair to all.[3] How should they do it?

Here are some scenarios for consideration. When trying to answer these, look at each situation from an impartial RemCo point of view.

- How would you benchmark, or which comparators would you pick, for an organisation where there may only be one in the country, for example, the central bank or your national airline?
- How would you benchmark or pick comparators for an organisation that is far bigger than the other local comparators in its industry sector, for example, an airline or a power utility?
- How would you benchmark or pick comparators where there are only a few similar organisations in the industry sector, for example, mainstream banks?
- From which level up is organisation size relevant and to what extent?
- If you have an executive who covers two portfolios, how should you benchmark that person, and where should you pitch his or her pay? As an example, your finance executive is a certified accountant and a master's degree in law, and covers both the finance and legal departments for the organisation.
- Your independent non-executive director is the organisation's biggest deal maker – how would you benchmark their salary?
- You have a job description and a job grade, and want to fill the post with someone who will develop into the position in a few years' time. Where do you pitch the pay?
- You have a small business unit in your portfolio that is not performing well, and you want to put your best executive in there to turn it around. Where do you pitch the pay?
- What percentage of employees could be outside the pay scales and still be considered acceptable?
- A small organisation employs about 20 people to manage buildings and properties worth over two billion. Where do you pitch their pay?
- Does an overseas listing make a difference to local pay?
- Finally, the person closest to you (child, partner, or parent) needs to fly overseas. The pilot has about 300 people on board. How do you value that job?

There are many more vexing questions that the authors have come across, but these will suffice for now. How did you do in determining possible answers for these? Could you present a robust methodology and answers confidently to your RemCo? Here are some guidelines to improve your chances of success.

---

3    Diez, 2018.

### 15.14.3 Guidelines on selecting comparators

There have been many lessons learnt over the years. Some of the more important ones relating to remuneration are set out below.

- Once you have sufficient participants in a niche survey, the information becomes repetitive and does not alter materially if you get more participants. This starts at between six and eight comparators.
- One or two swallows do not make a summer. You will always find an exception or two, and most people have almost certainly heard only of the higher exception.
- If you have a sticky situation with a particular job's benchmark, never go to war on a benchmark done only on title, grade and capsule job description. In this instance, one needs a more comprehensive appreciation of the job and perhaps a personal visit to the comparator organisation.
- For key positions, always use more than one method of comparing the jobs to the market, and try comparing the job to several markets.
- Find a robust "peg" for the CEO; it gives a good anchor.
- Select comparators for different reasons. Find ones that are not necessarily only in your industry sector. Try some of the following, or find ones more applicable to you, where there may be some similarity in the following features:
  - Complexity and type – for example, single or multiple products, processes, capital or labour-intensive.
  - Market or customer – who do you compete with for share of purse?
  - Organisation structure – for example, another organisation with two large, dominant divisions.
  - Location of business – for example, hotels, banks and cell phone companies operate throughout the world.
  - Ownership structure – for example, global owners or family-owned listings.
  - Geographic location – it is often wiser to compare with organisations in the region, even though they are not in your industry sector.
  - Competing for the same resources or customers – operating a business model.

Using these metrics opens the debate on which job deserves to be paid more – the executive in charge of A or the executive in charge of B? (A is labour intensive, and B is capital intensive.)

- A employs 10,000 full-time staff and makes a profit of 10 million.
- B employs 500 full-time staff and makes a profit of 50 million.

There are compelling arguments for both A and B. The main point is that there are many considerations and variables. In this case, only two are presented. It is not a simple matter, and a lot of passion is spent on convincing the other party on the complexity of the situation.

It is important to have a good feel for who the organisation's competitors and comparators are. Selecting the comparators should be done against agreed criteria. Use several different criteria and be sure to understand exactly what the job entails. After all, we would not want apples to be compared with oranges.

## 15.15  Summary

Share schemes are implemented to align executive thinking with that of the shareholders'. The second reason is that when they are implemented more widely to all employees, they share the wealth of the organisation. Whilst it is easier to implement share schemes for listed companies, non-listed companies can implement phantom shares or rolling incentive schemes. An increasingly common approach to issuing shares is the implementation of performance hurdles (both individual and company). The vesting periods range across countries with a common time frame of between three and five years. Huge wealth can be generated via top-performing shares which can create havoc with pay gap ratio analyses. RemCos have oversight of this process, including the determination of CEO pay.

## 15.16  Self-evaluation questions

1.  What is a share?
2.  Name the different types of shares
3.  What is a share scheme?
4.  What is a phantom share scheme?
5.  What are some of the critical aspects when accounting for share-based payments under IFRS2?
6.  What are the guidelines regarding share top-ups?
7.  What is the role of the RemCo?
8.  What are the key determinants in setting CEO pay?

# CHAPTER 16

## Employee Benefits

### 16.1 Introduction

The topic of benefits in remuneration circles is often fraught with contradiction. On the one hand, it is difficult to ascertain how much exactly they contribute to attracting, retaining and motivating employees. On the other hand, benefits costs are getting higher all around the world, which makes companies pay closer attention to them. From the market perspective, benefits tend to be fairly uniform and thus it is hard to differentiate one company's benefits from the next. And from the employees' perspective, benefits have more or less importance depending on the stage of the life cycle in which each employee finds themselves. Plus, employees often perceive benefits as a given, regardless of company performance, and thus any efforts to reduce costs by reducing benefits would be viewed negatively by staff.

As total remuneration practitioners, it is important to understand the value of benefits both as perceived by employees as well as a company expense. Armed with this knowledge we can create a benefits plan, understand benefits choices and trade-offs, design benefits programmes, and address benefits administration. All the benefits provided can then be summarised in a Benefits Policy Statement. Such a document would include:

- the objectives of the policy including any differences by geography, level, etc.,
- the role benefits play in the company's total rewards strategy including the competitive positioning,
- the philosophy behind employer and employee cost sharing,
- the types of benefits offered along with the choices provided, and
- the administrative guidelines and processes, including compliance statements.

As an aside, the concept of benefits, as others in the remuneration arena, has plenty of its own terms. At the end of the chapter we have included a brief glossary of commonly used terms which are not described elsewhere.

### 16.1.1 The need for employee benefits

Employee benefits around the world vary considerably, but in most cases have their origins in three main causes, one of which is legislation. For the most part, labour laws protect the rights of employees and their families. One consistent way in which governments around the world do so is by providing a minimum level of coverage for medical needs, short and long-term disability, time off, unemployment, retirement and survivor benefits. Legislation gives rise to statutory benefits, which we will discuss at length below.

Unions have also contributed to the rise of additional, company-provided employee benefits, as it is often easier to negotiate additional benefits above those provided by law than to negotiate for salary increases. Of course, once a benefit was added to the collective agreement, it would not be taken out, and other unions in different industries could then copy the benefits gained elsewhere.

Employers see in benefits the opportunity to increase employee engagement at presumably a lower cost than wages or bonuses. The emphasis is on management showing their concern for employees while, at the same time, seeking a better return on their people investment via presumably increased retention and productivity. The cost advantage to employees should be easy to ascertain; for one, benefits are often not taxed. Additionally, by purchasing in bulk, companies can buy benefits at a lower cost than employees can buy benefits for themselves (and with lower restrictions). As a result of both of these, each dollar of company spend in benefits should represent more than a dollar of value to the employee. However, the data on the effectiveness of the ROI of benefits is inconclusive, and they are often perceived as a fixed cost of doing business rather than as a strategic remuneration tool.

As benefits are linked to local legislation, it is difficult to create a global programme. However, many companies want to ensure that at least a minimum level of benefits is provided in each location where they operate, in line with the corporation's values and culture. As we explain below, in some cases, such as multinational pooling of health insurance policies, having a single plan in many locations may provide savings in plan costs.

### 16.1.2  The difficulty in assessing the value of employee benefits

Part of the difficulty in assessing the value of employee benefits stems from the fact that different employees value benefits differently. For instance, to a fresh university graduate, benefits may be the last of the criteria used when selecting a company to work for. To a single male below 25, medical benefits are only a passing thought, retirement is too far away, and life insurance may appear unnecessary. Instead, he may value more time off or even a higher salary. To a married female in her early 30s with two young children, medical coverage is indispensable and life insurance becomes an issue – not only to cover her children but also to ensure her parents are looked after, and even to help pay the mortgage when her income is gone. Retirement is still too far away and additional time off could be nice. To an employee in their late 50s, retirement is very important, as is medical coverage. Life insurance is less of an issue as the children are likely past college age and able to fend for themselves, and the mortgage is mostly paid up. Time off is also less of a concern. In other words, the exact same plan would have a different perceived value by each of these employees, despite the fact that the company spends the same amount to provide the benefit to each of them. While the company may see an average ROI for the whole programme, individual employees would not agree necessarily on it. Most employees do not know what percentage of their total remuneration package goes into employee benefits, thus adding to the perception that benefits are an entitlement. As a consequence, it is not enough to roll out good benefits plans – care must be taken to communicate their value as well.

## 16.2   Types of benefits

Before looking into the planning, design and administration of benefits, we should first understand the various types of employee benefits. Generally, they are categorised as:

- Statutory benefits.
- Medical benefits.
- Life insurance.
- Retirement benefits.
- Other benefits.

### 16.2.1 Statutory benefits

Statutory benefits are those that are required by law. They go by different names in different countries, but can generally be grouped under four rubrics: workers' compensation, social security, unemployment compensation and medical benefits continuation.

- **Workers' Compensation:** Workers' compensation is intended to provide for injuries or diseases incurred at work. Benefits are typically provided for:
  a. Medical care for work-related injuries.
  b. Short-term disability while recovering.
  c. Permanent partial or total disability benefits stemming from injuries received while on the job.
  d. Survivor benefits.
  e. Rehabilitation.

  The increase of employee safety programmes around the world contributes to keep workers' compensation costs under control.

- **Social Security:** When an employee becomes disabled, retires or dies, Social Security partially replaces the lost income. These benefits are funded from taxation – in the form of contributions – of both employees and employers. In countries where the population is aging, a large proportion of these contributions are used to pay for benefits to older beneficiaries creating a two-sided problem: the first is that there are more beneficiaries than there are younger contributors, and the second is that when the younger contributors age, there will be fewer reserves to help cover their costs. This has led to an increase in taxation for both employees and employers, as well as an increase in the retirement age in order to maintain contributions.

  Although the amounts paid for Social Security benefits usually vary according to the amounts contributed, generally these programmes provide benefits for:

a. Old age or disability.
b. Dependent benefits (for retired or disabled employees).
c. Survivor benefits (for the family of deceased employees.

- **Unemployment Compensation:** Unemployment compensation exists in many countries to provide some level of security for those individuals who are willing to work but are not currently employed. For the most part, these programmes are funded via a tax to employers. In most cases, the programmes pay a percentage of last wages, up to a cap. Unemployment compensation has limits as well on the length of time it will be paid (often between six months up to 18 months of benefits). Their aim is to ease the transition until a new job is found, especially for those who were laid off as part of a corporate reorganisation. Typically, to be eligible, individuals must fulfil certain requirements.
- **Medical Benefits Continuation:** Many countries require that health insurance be provided for up to three years (or until the employee has found a new job) to employees who have been laid off. Some countries also require employers to provide paid or unpaid leave to employees for up to 12 weeks for various medical or family reasons, including caregiving for family members, or child adoption. Maternity and paternity leave also falls into this category.

## 16.2.2 Medical benefits

Medical benefits are those which relate to coverage for employees' health, disabilities, dental and vision care.

- **Health Care:** Health care benefits are the most prevalent kind of benefits provided to employees. They typically include coverage for doctor visits, hospitalisation and surgery, prescription medicines, laboratory/x-ray fees and other related expenses. Less often coverage is extended to mental health and Employee Assistance Programmes.
- **Short- and Long-Term Disability:** In addition to statutory worker's compensation, employers generally provide short-term and long-term disability plans. A short-term disability plan pays out a percentage of the person's income for up to six months for medical conditions which prevent the employee from working beyond the period covered by sick leave. A smaller number of companies provide long-term disability plans covered by a policy from an insurance company. These plans generally provide 40 to 60 percent of the last drawn salary for individuals who are no longer able to work. Coverage starts from the time short-term disability coverage ends. Long-term programmes can pay for a period varying between two years and life.
- **Dental Insurance:** Dental care is becoming a more common benefit, typically covering preventive and curative treatment, and exclude most cosmetic and orthodontic treatments.
- **Vision Care:** Many employers offer a vision plan, usually covering the costs of eye examinations, eyeglasses and contact lenses.

Many employers prefer that employees use their Health Savings Accounts (see below) to cover dental and vision benefits, even if group coverage policies are involved.

### 16.2.3  How benefits are paid for and delivered

In most countries, there are at least five ways in which health benefits are delivered:

- *National Health Systems* typically provide subsidised health care through specified government-sponsored facilities and doctors.
- *Health maintenance organisations (HMOs)* provide health care for a fixed fee. Employees pay for guaranteed medical services at specific clinics.
- *Preferred provider organisations (PPOs)* provide medical services via a series of contracts between the employers who select a panel of health-care providers who agree to cost of service provisions in exchange for minimum usage. Employees pay lower premiums while agreeing to use the panel of providers.
- *Point-of-service plans (POSs)* combine HMO and PPO benefits by allowing the employee to choose the modality they wish to use in each case. The employee can even choose an out-of-panel provider at a higher cost/deductible.
- *Health insurance plans* are contracts between employers and insurance companies to provide coverage for the cost of services in exchange for premiums which are paid by the employees. The employers buy these group policies at a lower cost than what each employee would have to pay to purchase the same amount of coverage.

It should be noted that in some countries, notably the USA, medical benefits are extended beyond employees and their immediate families to company retirees. The cost of maintaining this practice is generally high which may account for its limited expansion, even if there is a clear need for it.

Another trend related to payment and delivery refers to tax-effective Health Savings Accounts (HSAs), which can be used to pay for medical expenses which are not covered by any other plan. Usually these are capped.

## 16.3  Health care costs

Health care costs have been increasing around the world at a rate faster than cost of living inflation.[1] The drivers of health care costs include the aging of populations coupled with longer life expectancy around the world, increases in chronic disease driven by lifestyle changes, expensive new drugs and medical technologies, governments shifting health costs to the private sector, and rising demand and expectations from employees.

---

1   Lock, 2014.

Japan has one of the highest percentages of elderly in the world, with 23.3% of the population categorised as elderly in 2000 and predictions of up to 42.3% of the population in 2050.[2] Similar projections suggest that elderly to working-age population ratios already go beyond 33% in Hong Kong and China.[3] In Singapore, the growing proportion of elderly is expected to rise from 6% in 1990 to over 30% in 2025.[4] As such, the ability for governments to meet the health care needs of the their older populations, as well as for companies to provide suitable benefits for elderly employees, is crucial on both the local and global fronts.

Employers are reacting by increasing deductibles and co-insurance amounts, reducing maximum benefits, and tightening controls on pre-authorisations, second opinions and the coordination of benefits. There is also a trend towards more panel doctors and clinics. In addition, many MNCs make use of the multinational pooling approach. Multinational pooling is a contract between a company and an insurance provider to group together a number of local insurance policies into a single contract. Savings can accrue from an improvement in experience, better return on investments, and better pricing from lower risk due to better ability to predict mortality and morbidity rates with larger number of employees and dependents in the plans.

Cost containment is best accomplished with a combination of short- to long-term approaches to address the drivers of health care costs. Much money is spent on unnecessary diagnostics, prescription drugs and even specialist visits. In the short-term, costs can be controlled by increasing the portion of the premium and the benefits which the employee pays via increasing deductibles and co-insurance amounts and reducing maximum benefits. This strategy can help to increase responsible use of health care services. Companies can also redesign their plans to minimise programme inefficiencies, and look into tightening controls on pre-authorisations, second opinions and the coordination of benefits.

Yet cost cutting is not the only solution. After years of insurance premium rate shopping, companies are finding that this strategy no longer has the same impact. For companies, too much cost sharing or continually making benefit cuts at every insurance plan renewal is not sustainable. Over time, aggressive cost shifting to employees can make the health benefit programmes uncompetitive and may diminish the perceived value of the benefit.

Long-term, employers can reduce health risks in their employee and dependent populations by providing incentives to employees for healthy behaviours.[5] Employees can be encouraged to take personal ownership for responsible utilisation of, and spending on, health care services. One approach is to incentivise employees by using flex points or different tiers of cost sharing to use preferred provider networks, government versus private hospitals, generic versus brand name

---

2    United Nations, 2015.

3    Park & Shin. 2011.

4    Mei & Zhiwei, 2011.

5    Trust for America's Health, 2013.

drugs, seeing a generalist before visiting a specialist ,or taking proactive measures to improve their health (e.g. smoking cessation or weight loss).[6] Another approach is to educate employees about the risks associated with their decisions and choices. A Caesarean birth, for example, creates a risk to the mother's health and increases the cost of childbirth. Lifestyle decisions, such as smoking or poor food choices, can lead to life-threatening illnesses.[7] Information can also help employees make better decisions about their choice of hospitals and the cost of their services.

Cost containment solutions typically fall into four categories, which tend to be market-specific (see Figure 16.1 below):

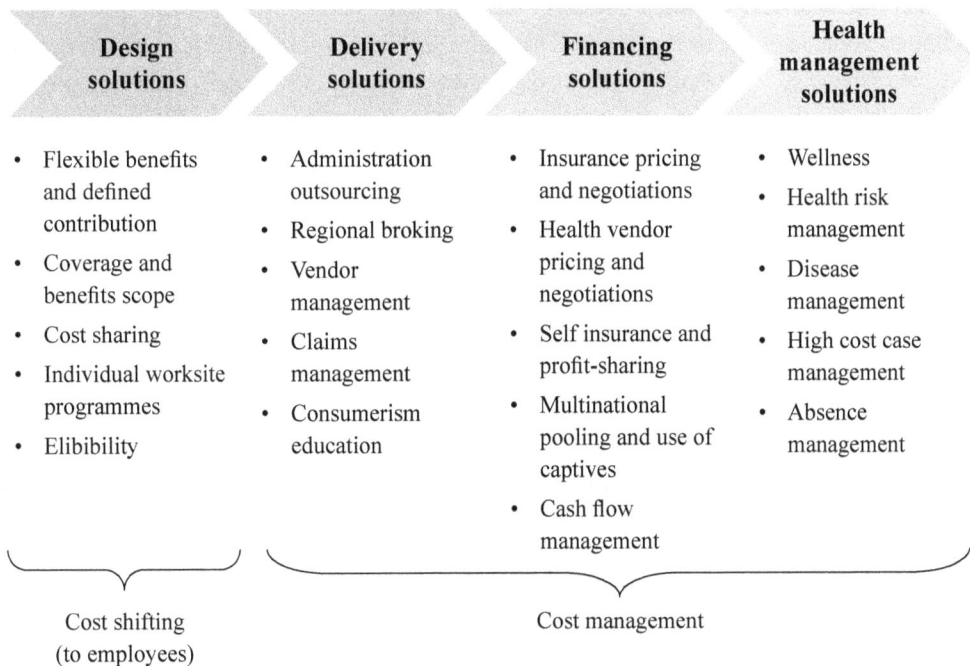

| Design solutions | Delivery solutions | Financing solutions | Health management solutions |
|---|---|---|---|
| • Flexible benefits and defined contribution<br>• Coverage and benefits scope<br>• Cost sharing<br>• Individual worksite programmes<br>• Elibibility | • Administration outsourcing<br>• Regional broking<br>• Vendor management<br>• Claims management<br>• Consumerism education | • Insurance pricing and negotiations<br>• Health vendor pricing and negotiations<br>• Self insurance and profit-sharing<br>• Multinational pooling and use of captives<br>• Cash flow management | • Wellness<br>• Health risk management<br>• Disease management<br>• High cost case management<br>• Absence management |

Cost shifting (to employees)      Cost management

*Figure 16.1: Categories of health cost containment solutions*

- **Benefits Design:** benefits structure such as traditional or innovative defined contribution and flexible benefits; eligibility requirements; determination of what should and should not be covered; and premium and claim cost-sharing arrangements.
- **Benefits Delivery:** vendor contracts; outsourcing employee administrative workload to a single regional broker; and claims management to reduce fraud and ensure payment of only reasonable, customary and medically necessary expenses.
- **Benefits Financing:** negotiating better pricing with insurers for profit-sharing or with networks for multinational pooling; volume purchasing; and in-house captives to transfer risks or self-funding instead of insurance.

---

6    Centres for Disease Control (CDC), 2010.

7    County of San Diego Health and Human Services Agency (HHSA), 2013.

- **Health Management:** prevention programmes that will keep healthy employees healthy; at-risk management to identify and manage individuals with health risks; disease management to manage the progression of illness; case management to manage high-cost claims; and absence management that includes effective return-to-work programmes.

A specific design solution that has become more prevalent is flexible benefits, or Flex, which encompasses a menu of benefits and cost-shifting mechanisms. For companies that do not currently offer Flex, it will involve implementation costs, but can save significant costs in the long term. Flex allows employees to choose a mix of health insurance and other benefits that suits their personal needs, while it increases the employer's control over total benefit spending. Additional voluntary benefits can be added as part of the Flex programme without incurring extra costs, and can include individual insurance programmes which can financially protect employees between jobs by allowing them to buy insurance for hospitalization, accidents or loss of income at highly discounted rates.

Controlling claims and reaping the benefit of an improved claims experience requires proactive steps on the part of organisations, including a fiscal responsibility to audit insurers, third party administrators and other claims payers. Employers need to know what kind of quality controls their vendors apply to verifying eligibility, paying the right type of benefit, applying cost sharing accurately, and ensuring that the provider has submitted an accurate bill. A best practice to consider is auditing the vendor prior to the "live" date to ensure the plan is set up accurately, thereby avoiding errors at a later time. Employers also need to know that they will get credit for any savings that come from audits or recovering funds that another carrier should have paid. It is also vital to assess whether your providers will offer rate guarantees, and if it is possible to consolidate vendors for economies of scale.

Large companies are turning to multinational pooling networks to reduce premium pricing and provide for dividend refunds from favourable claims experiences. Some employers are also reducing their HR and benefits costs by consolidating their insurance with a single broker who negotiates all or a portion of their insurance plans and provides full outsourcing to handle their employee administration needs. Other financing opportunities include renegotiating vendor and insurance fees and volume purchasing deals with preferred provider networks for large employee populations.

Best practices in health management are emerging as well:

- In China, for example, where manufacturing is pervasive and construction projects are innumerable, employers are proactively undertaking ergonomic assessments to reduce the costs associated with worker injury.[8]

---

8　Sussmuth-Dyckerhoff & Wang, 2010.

- In India, 60 percent of employee health insurance costs are attributed to parental medical claims, so MNCs are considering providing such proactive measures as diabetes coaching to decrease hospitalisation costs of chronic diseases that typically affect elder populations.[9]
- And in Australia, companies are negotiating group health premium discounts contingent on the establishment of health risk management programmes.[10]

In addition, such value-added features as Employee Assistance Plans (EAPs), health portals and Health Risk Assessments (HRAs) can differentiate health plans and serve as attraction/retention tools, as well as help to drive wellness and attendance up and costs down. HRAs allow individuals to assess their own level of health risk by answering questions related to medical/health history, lifestyle, occupational history and biometrics (e.g., blood pressure, cholesterol levels). Best practice would involve having a health professional follow up directly with an individual to provide health coaching or encouraging them to participate in a care management programme.

## 16.4  Life insurance

One of the most prevalent benefits provided to employees is life insurance, which is typically coverage in the form of a group term policy valued at 12 to 36 months of the employee's basic pay. In most countries, the plan premiums are wholly paid by the company. In some cases, employees can choose to have greater coverage (usually incremented by an additional 12 months' basic pay up to ten years of coverage), at the employee's cost. It is also customary to find an accident provision in the policy whereby the benefits received are doubled in the case of death due to an accident.

## 16.5  Retirement benefits

Retirement plans are a means to allow employees to accumulate wealth while employed so they can have enough money to be able to retire when the time comes. To employees, especially those above the age of 50, retirement plans rank very highly in terms of importance.

It is important to note that, in many countries, local legislation includes termination indemnities which apply to retirement as well as death. Thus, the prevalence of retirement plans is related to the government-mandated benefits. If the latter are substantial, there will tend to be less of the former as usually termination indemnities can be considered as a substitute for retirement plans.

There are generally two types of pension plans across the world: defined benefit plans and defined contribution plans.

---

9   Luthra, 2012.

10   OECD, 2011.

### 16.5.1 Defined benefit plans

An employee receives a pre-determined level of pension payment which is calculated as either a fixed amount or as a percentage of earnings. This amount is also a function of years of seniority in the company. The most common approach to calculate the pension amount is to use the employee's average earnings over the last three to five years of service for a prospective retiree, and provide a pension that is about 30-80 percent, adjusted for years of service. Companies fund this liability by using an actuarial formula and making deposits that will allow for full pension payments for all retiring employees.

The final payout depends on the probability of retirement in the company, the amount of pay the employee is likely to be receiving at that point, and the volatility of the markets in terms of the returns on the fund. Because these three parameters are all probabilistic and independent from each other, it is hard to predict how much money will be needed in the future to pay the liability. Since the plans require funding, they are also negative in terms of cash flow to the company. Around the world, accounting and tax rules tend to not be favourable towards this type of plan.

### 16.5.2 Defined contribution plans

Under a defined contribution plan, also called savings plans, employers and employees make predetermined contributions – often between 6-10 percent of monthly pay. In most countries, but not all, employees are able to defer pre-tax income, and employers typically match 50 percent of employee contributions. The final payout to be received upon retirement is unknown as it depends on the investment returns of the pension funds in which the employee's money is invested. These plans are affected by low contribution rates from employees as well as by insufficient returns on the funds, due both to market volatility as well as by poor investment choices by employees. This final payout may be in the form of a lump sum or an annuity (which usually has survivor benefits).

Defined contribution plans require a great deal of governance and administration. Often, companies name a plan administrator to manage all aspects of a plan. There is usually a fiduciary committee that sets plan guidelines to be followed by the administrator. The plan would normally engage a variety of professionals as well, including accountants, trustees, investment managers, actuaries and attorneys.

### 16.5.3 Cash balance plans

Cash balance plans are a hybrid of defined benefit and defined contribution plans. More precisely, they are defined benefit plans that look like defined contribution plans. Employees have an account into which a percentage of remuneration is deposited. This amount grows, both from contributions by the employer and from a predefined interest rate. In some cases, the employee contribution varies as a function of profit.

In some countries, there are other variations on the savings plan approach. These can be Provident Fund Plans such as in India and Singapore, and Superannuation plans such as in Australia and New Zealand. In all cases, there are tax and accounting rules that sponsor the use of these plans.

## 16.6 Other benefits

There are a variety of other benefits, some of which are legally required, and others which are commonly provided. The list below, while comprehensive, is not exhaustive:

- **Paid Time Off During Working Hours:** This benefit includes payment for rest periods, wash-up time, travel time, lunch, clothes-change time, and get-ready time.
- **Payment for Time Not Worked:** Many companies apply the paid-time-off (PTO) approach, where all time off is grouped into one total amount and any day off is reduced from this bank. Benefits in this category include:
  a. Paid vacation and payments in lieu of vacation.
  b. Pay for holidays not worked.
  c. Paid sick leave.
  d. Others: pay for military duty, jury duty, time lost due to a death in the family or other personal reasons, volunteering time, maternity and paternity leave, caregiving leave, adoption leave, sabbaticals.
- **Child Care:** Many companies offer child care services to their employees as a benefit. Sometimes they provide this benefit in the company's premises. In other cases, employees can be refunded when they pay selected local child care providers.
- **Elder Care:** An increasingly important benefit is support for elder care assistance due to the longer life expectancy and aging of their parents.
- **Domestic Partner Benefits:** These benefits are provided by employers to an employee's unmarried partner. Often, they are extended for either same gender or opposite gender couples. The major difficulty lies in the definition of domestic partner in a way that insurance companies will extend group coverage.
- **Financial Advice:** A recent addition to the benefits arsenal. Some companies provide subsidised financial advice services provided by third parties. This is a particularly important benefit when employees are free to choose from a broad array of savings plans fund options.
- **Legal Insurance:** A less common benefit whereby companies provide access to legal services. In most cases, coverage includes routine legal services but exclude provisions covering felonies. For the most part fees are paid by the employee, not the employer.
- **Perquisites:** In a few countries there are still tax-effective benefits which are still prevalent. Often referred to as 'perqs' or 'perks', these include policies such as use of company cars and drivers, use of company holiday facilities, appointment of household staff or security staff, and concierge services. Perks can also include the provision of items such as corporate credit cards, mobile phones, personal computers, admission to sporting events, subsidised meals and uniforms, social club/gym memberships, education allowance, housing/utilities allowance, additional paid time off, company loans, etc.

## 16.7  Benefits for contingent workers

A recent trend around the world is the use of contingent workers (sometimes called "gig" workers). Partly this is due to companies wanting to have flexibility to contract and expand the workforce on short notice to adapt to ever changing market conditions. In addition, there is a growing segment of the workforce (perhaps as high as one third) of employees that prefer the freedom of contingent work.

Contingent workers are defined as those working through temporary help agencies, working for a contract company, working on call, and working as an independent contractor. The main difference is that the employment relationship is contractual as a third-party vendor.

Companies can reduce employee benefits' costs by using a contingent workforce. This is mainly due to the fact that the benefits provided to contingent workers are usually lower than those offered to regular employees. More specifically, they are normally only offered basic life and health benefits.

## 16.8  Planning, design and administration of benefits plans

The total reward strategy of an organisation aims to support the goals of attraction, retention and motivation of employees. Within this strategy, the first step in the planning and design of the benefits plan is to determine how it will be used to help support these three goals. This is balanced with an assessment of the competitiveness of the benefits plan vis-à-vis the cost of providing and the perceived value the employees place on the programme. Ideally, employers should avail themselves with a local benefits survey as the data therein can help in making the decisions implied below.

There are four key issues in the administration of employee benefits:

- Who should be covered?
- How much choice of benefits to offer employees?
- How should benefits be funded?
- Are the benefits in compliance with local legal and taxation regulations?

We explore these issues next.

### 16.8.1  Who should be covered?

The question of who should be covered by the benefits plan is not so straightforward.

- As mentioned earlier, organisations have different types of employees, including retirees. Should coverage be restricted to active full-time employees only? If not, should all employees be treated the same regarding benefits coverage?

- Will all employees be eligible to all benefits upon joining the organisation? Or should there be a probation period for different employee types and/or benefit types?
- Which employee dependents to cover?
- Should survivors of employees and/or retirees be covered? For which benefits?
- What disability coverage should be offered to employees?
- Should coverage be extended to employees during layoffs, leaves of absence, and/or other times away from work?

The answers to these questions will help in making decisions regarding who the beneficiaries are.

### 16.8.2  What choice of benefits to offer employees?

- Should all employees be offered a standard benefits package designed for an average employee?
- Should the company implement a flexible benefit plan to allow employees flexibility in choosing the benefits of greatest value to them?
- Another approach is to offer a basic benefits package and give the employees the option of buying additional coverage.
- An in-between approach is to limit choice to a smaller number of options, including:
  a.  Additional levels of life insurance.
  b.  The inclusion of death or disability benefits under retirement plans.
  c.  Choices of dependents to be covered under the medical plans.
  d.  Choice of disbursement method under the retirement plans.
  e.  A tiered network approach to medical coverage.
  f.  Health savings accounts also provide choice of coverage.

As stated earlier, ideally, data from a local benefits survey can help in making the decisions implied below.

### 16.8.3  How should benefits be funded?

There are several ways in which benefits can be financed. The main ones are:

- Non-contributory: the employer pays all costs.
- Contributory: employer and employee share the costs.
- Employee financed: the employee pays total costs for some benefits.

Companies often keep benefit options contributory, under the premise that if employees pay for a portion of the benefits, they will perceive them as more valuable and will also have more reason to help control benefits costs.

### 16.8.4  Are benefits in compliance with local legal and taxation regulations?

Different countries have different legal and tax regulations concerning benefits. For instance, in some cases, benefits, including retirement plans, are tax-free, whereas in others they are partially or fully taxable. Similarly, some jurisdictions make a minimal medical plan mandatory, whereas in others there are no regulations in this respect.

Due to the variety of rules and regulations around the world regarding benefits, it is common for organisations to set local – rather than global – policies regarding benefits.

It is also important to ensure compliance with all local regulations via checklists, audits and other appropriate tools.

### 16.8.5  Benefits plan administration

There are three main tasks when administering benefits plans: employee communication, claims processing, and cost control.

To ensure employees completely understand their benefits and the value of each, companies must be careful in crafting a solid employee benefits communication plan. ***Employee benefits communications*** is no different than communication about other aspects of employee remuneration, however care must be exercised in that benefits can be a very technical subject. Therefore, benefits issues must be communicated primarily in writing to allow employees enough time to digest the information and consult if necessary. Keeping an Employee Benefits Handbook permanently updated in the company's intranet is perhaps the most common way to do so. The Employee Benefits Handbook contains detailed descriptions of all benefits, including levels of coverage and eligibility requirements, written in simple language that any employee can understand. Other approaches include individual or group meetings with the benefit specialists and/or the vendors. Another approach sometimes used is Employee Benefit Statements. In these statements, employees receive an individualised report on the cost of all the various benefit options the employee receives. A benefits page in the intranet also allows for the employee to sign up for various options, calculate their cost, verify coverage and update their own data, thus saving time and increasing accuracy of this information.

***Claims processing*** refers to an event occurring (e.g., disability, hospitalisation, birth of a child, etc.) which triggers a request for payment. To process a claim, first there is need to confirm that the cause for the request has occurred and that the employee is eligible for the benefit plan they are claiming from. If the cause and eligibility are confirmed, the administrator then proceeds to calculate the payout. This may involve an assessment of the amount being claimed, as well as any coordination of benefits with other plans covering the same claim (e.g., a claim on child hospitalisation which can be separately covered by the insurance plan of both parents' health plans).

*Cost control* in administration is mostly related to ensuring payouts are carried out as per plan provisions. In addition, administrators are responsible for finding a competitive bid among various vendors, including brokers and plan administration providers.

## 16.9 Role of benefits in attraction, retention and motivation

Some benefits are better geared to retaining employees, particularly when linked to seniority. These include retirement plans and paid time off. Medical plans that are better than the average of the market also help with retention. For example, in Asia it is very effective to include coverage for parents of the employee in health plans. The assumption is that it is difficult for an employee working in a company where the parents have their health insurance covered to leave for another where there is no such plan. Employees would often rather stay with the company than to have to explain to their parents that they are no longer covered for health insurance.

Employee engagement surveys and conjoint analysis can provide clues as to employee preferences. However, whereas many engagement surveys are able to answer the question of which plan modality is preferred, there is little evidence to support that employee motivation is linked to benefit improvements.

As to attraction, it is unclear if employees are attracted to a company due to benefits alone. Anecdotally, above-market benefits appear to help in attraction and retention, but each company needs to run the numbers to ascertain if the additional costs are justified, or if the improved benefits need to be offset by reductions elsewhere in the total rewards package.

There is also insufficient evidence to determine if benefits can help improve business results. Some elements, such as stock ownership and team incentives[11], are linked to improved company results. Other benefits have also been found to be linked to individual employee productivity.

## 16.10 Current issues in health care

### 16.10.1 Rise in chronic diseases

As populations live longer and become more affluent, the prevalence of chronic disease invariably rises. Chronic diseases contribute significantly to the disease burden of families, individuals and communities, and share similar features, some of which are explained below.

*Epidemics of chronic disease* start at young ages and take decades to become fully established. Because chronic disease takes a long period of time to fully develop, there are many opportunities for prevention and intervention. A systematic and sustainable long-term treatment plan is required to effectively manage chronic disease. For instance, in Singapore, the incidence of chronic disease (e.g., diabetes) has increased national health care expenditure by an additional 11% per year.

---

11  Centre for Disease Control and Prevention, 2010.

While it is undoubtedly important to allocate resources to manage chronic conditions, recent studies have shown that investing in *preventive care* is the solution to bringing down health care costs in the long run. Three main lifestyle habits (physical inactivity, poor nutrition and tobacco use) contribute to four chronic diseases that account for half of all deaths worldwide. Other notable modifiable habits include alcohol consumption, sleep and stress. Tackling these modifiable behaviours treats these problems at its source and would go a long way in getting populations healthier and health care costs lower.

*Preventive screening*, alongside behaviour modification, has also been proven to be a cost-effective way of detecting latent disease such as pre-diabetes, and offering an opportunity for intervention before further progression.

## 16.10.2 Limitations of public health care

Health care is an expensive government investment and becoming an even greater burden on developing countries, particularly on those with rapidly aging populations. Governments will not be able to afford their current level of health care spending, necessitating a growth in private health care, especially in the less-developed countries. Already many governments spend less of their total expenditure on health care in comparison to the emerging private sector. It is also important to note that a large portion of private health care spending is out-of-pocket (OOP) rather than private pre-paid, where private pre-paid refers to expenditure by private insurance institutions. Since OOP payments are expenditures borne directly by a patient (where insurance does not fully cover the cost of the health good or service), it is entirely reliant on the individual's ability to pay. When the financing of health care is highly dependent on OOP payments, the burden is then shifted towards those who utilise more health care services and possibly from high- to low-income earners where health care needs are greater. This is unsustainable and will likely exacerbate the already existing impoverishing effect seen in low-income nations. A solution could be to supplement basic government health care by encouraging the private sector to grow in a way that lends itself to private pre-paid operations over OOP spending.

A case in point is illustrated by stories from China, India and the Philippines, which over the past few decades have grown rapidly to house the world's factories, BPOs and call centres. Unfortunately, this massive growth has resulted in health care deterioration. China has aimed to expand its biomedical industry and provide more universal health care, yet case studies have revealed that despite some progress, health reforms in China have not been completely successful. The worrisome case of Qin Jinpei, who was discharged from a hospital despite suffering from the final stages of lung cancer, is not uncommon, and reflects the loopholes in the current Chinese health care system. Patients like Qin Jinpei, who suffer from chronic diseases, are being discharged despite the seriousness of their conditions to prevent the hospitals from incurring extra costs — costs that exceed government insurance.

In India, private health care spending takes its toll on households as government insurance has very low coverage or is unable to properly fund itself to offer quality health care service. This becomes a more pertinent concern with the rise in "rich country" and work-related chronic diseases — a product of the gradual transition from an active agrarian culture to one that is more sedentary as it urbanises. A prominent example of this is the growing risk of developing diabetes. Nearly 70 million people are reported to have diabetes, with predictions estimating a growth to 101 million by 2030. Although diabetes is still a greater problem in cities, the fact that it is rapidly spreading to the countryside is indicative of the necessity for increased health insurance for the entire working population.

The Philippines is rapidly becoming the epicentre for Asia's call centres due to its inexpensive labour pool, English language proficiency and accent, and low turnover rate. However, whilst this shift is positive for the economy, it has negative ramifications in terms of health care. 24/7 shift work, which has become more common to support the West, is especially disruptive to sleep cycles, and may lead to musculoskeletal disorders as well as low immune resistance to disease. Other effects span from acute health problems, like digestive disturbances, to more chronic and social effects, like increased cancer risk. Most significantly, shift work may also lead to a lack of productivity and efficiency in the workplace as worker wellbeing and health is compromised.

An examination of all three case studies suggests an increasing prevalence of chronic disease in emerging economies and a resulting impact on the productivity and health of the workforce population. Since modifiable health risk behaviours such as lack of physical activity, poor nutrition and tobacco use are responsible for much of the illness, suffering and early deaths from chronic diseases, it is therefore wise to focus on combating these risk factors to improve workforce health. The WHO estimates that if the major risk factors for chronic disease were eliminated, at least 80% of all heart disease, stroke and type 2 diabetes would be prevented, and more than 40% of cancer cases would be prevented.

Let us also look at the Singapore case. The Singapore health care financing system was premised on the philosophy of shared responsibility, i.e. that while the Singapore government will continue to subsidise health care to bring down prices to affordable levels, the people must contribute to the cost of services they consume. Over the years, Singapore, like many other countries globally, has seen a gradual rise in health care costs as the population ages, public expectations rise and advances in medical technology lead to an increasing number of possible interventions. While established programmes such as Medisave, MediShield, Medifund and government subsidies have long formed the centrepiece of health care financing and have brought about a drop in government health care spending from 50% in 1965 to 39% in 2017, they have also resulted in a level of out-of-pocket spending that is twice as high as other developed Asian economies. This is largely because when the subsidies system was designed, they would not have been able to anticipate that long term elderly care needs and health care costs would rise faster than national income. As the population demographic of Singapore changes and GDP growth slows, the refinement of existing health care financing and provision policies is taking place to ensure efficiencies and affordability in the health care system. The government has also been working on a series of technology reforms to revamp the health care industry. The Ministry of Health is putting forth various initiatives aimed at empowering individuals to take control of their own health and increasing participation in health promotion. Examples of such initiatives include the national Personal Health Management (PHM) platform and National Electronic Health Records. The national electronic health platform allows every citizen to access personal health records, laboratory test results, medical reports and scheduled appointments with health care professionals. Citizens will also be able to set goals for the optimisation of health and/or disease management and, chart progress via electronic devices such as smartphones, tablets, PCs and even gaming consoles. In line with the last medium, a gamification system will also be established to appeal to the individual's competitive streak as well as increase the fun quotient in an otherwise mundane undertaking. By providing citizens with the technology to self-monitor health, actively manage disease and access information, Singapore will be taking the next step forward in health care innovations.

### 16.10.3 Strategies for the future

Below are areas that employers should consider when developing a benefits and wellness strategy for their workforce:

A current innovation in health care is the concept of a *private exchange*, a marketplace of health insurance and related products. Private exchanges allow for the option of a defined contribution system. With this model, employers decide how much money they would like to spend on employee benefits and put aside designated funds for their employees to spend on the insurance products of their choice. This 'defined contribution' model, as opposed to the 'defined benefits' model, allows employees to self-select the insurance and wellness products most appropriate for them with the help of decision support tools. This approach is in many ways the best of all worlds, enabling employers to continue supplying insurance at a capped premium, and giving employees the opportunity to pick their benefits accordingly.

The International Data Corporation (IDC) Health Insights predicted three innovation areas: citizen-centric focus (including greater spending on health care IT and more public-private partnerships), organisational agility (including increased investments in cloud and virtualisation), and collaborative health care (including an increase in popularity of wearable devices use and digital hospitals). All three areas, despite different loci of focus, share similar themes, especially in their emphasis on a shift from public to privatised health care. Such a shift would not only lead to a greater collaboration between the various components of the health care industry, but would also promote a greater focus on personal health management.

When employees access the private exchange, they are asked a series of questions that determines their "profile". Relying on "decision-support technology", the most suitable benefits plan is then offered to the employees based on their life stage and health preferences. Utilising the same "decision-support technology", the platform also generates a list of wellness products and services that are targeted towards the employees' risk factors once they have completed the health risk assessment (HRA) and biometric screening. This product feed is personalised to each employee and is further refined as employees browse and make purchases via the platform. Selecting from among an assortment of insurance packages and wellness products, the employee can utilise the private exchange system to meet their personal needs and are thus more likely to appreciate the value of the benefits provided. A MetLife survey showed that on average, employees estimate the cost of their employee benefit plans at 55% the true cost, but fully 28% of those surveyed estimated that cost at only 25%. A particularly important facilitator for this interaction is the use of a powerful and interactive platform that has the necessary technology to not only guide users through the process of selecting benefits that best suit them, but also offer end-to-end transactional services and ensure that the buying experience is a seamless one.

One of several issues with the current defined benefits plans is that companies bear the entire burden for the rising cost of health care benefits that may, in the end, not meet the individual needs of the employee population. With defined contribution plans, companies can cap benefits budgets and in doing so, establish more fixed and predictable budgets for their employees while allowing for employee choice. Co-pays and deductibles encourage employees to think twice before going to doctors for trivial concerns and to take more personal responsibility for their health and wellbeing.

One of the key sources of inefficiency is the sheer number of intermediaries between the disparate providers and the workplace employees. This inefficiency is further exacerbated by paper-intensive claims administration that leads to redundancies and bottlenecks. Aggregation of the selected providers into a single marketplace where employees can shop and perform transactions online will go a long way in relieving HR of the administrative burden.

Learning about *cost drivers analysis* of inpatient and outpatient medical claims data from a disease management perspective can help employers better understand cost drivers and implement targeted interventions designed to optimise risk factors and bring down health care costs. Understanding the utilisation rates of benefits will also enable companies to objectively assess the suitability of current benefits plans for the workforce, and whether the adoption of a structurally different programme, such as Flex, is required.

*Preventive screening health risk assessments and biometric screenings* provide employers with baseline data of their workforce health and help employees identify their personal health risks. Early detection of chronic diseases before they progress unfavourably with age offers an opportunity for intervention and leads to better outcomes.

Another trend is to ***assist employees in their decision to become healthier*** by guiding them towards establishing health goals (based on their individual HRA and biometric screening results), and providing them with recommendations for relevant products and services. Targeted content and products will help employees better understand their health status and, with this understanding, bring about an impetus for change.

Investing in employee wellbeing may increase engagement and productivity, and lower health care costs. Employers can utilise Flex dollars to ***incentivise healthy behaviour*** in their employees, encourage participation in health promotion programmes, and reward improved health outcomes such as reduced BMI. Studies have shown that employee participation in programmes aimed at controlling body weight, improving nutrition, or increasing exercise is associated with a significant decrease in BMI. Current-year participation in a weight control programme is significantly associated with a reduction in BMI of about 0.15 in the same year, and the effect persists for two subsequent years. Additional studies on workplace wellness initiatives have also shown that medical costs fall by roughly $3.75 and absenteeism costs by $2.73 for every dollar spent on a wellness programme. Johnson & Johnson estimates that wellness programmes saved them over $250 million on health care costs from 2000-2010.

The performance of workplace interventions needs to be judged by ROI data, without which it is difficult to justify the continuance of such activities. The ***ability to collect accurate and reliable data sets*** from employees is, therefore, a crucial aspect of the overall wellness strategy. Effective and seamless data collection can be done through tracking of all electronic transactions done via the private exchange, as well as platform integration of popular activity trackers such as Fitbit and Garmin.

## 16.11  Summary

Health care is a complex subject which is often given only a side glimpse by remuneration professionals as it is deemed to be non-strategic, not clearly helpful to attract, retain and motivate employees, and largely driven by legal and tax regulations. However, it represents an important, and growing, part of total remuneration costs. Deteriorating employee health and the increasing prevalence of chronic disease caused by poor lifestyle choices are problems of aging populations that are also becoming more affluent. The establishment of a private exchange and shifting the focus from treatment to prevention may not necessarily solve all the current issues, but will assist employers in the move from a defined benefits model to a defined contribution one, and encourage employees to take a more active role in their health care and benefits decisions.

## 16.12  Self-evaluation questions

1.  What can account for the difference in employee benefits costs between two companies? List as many reasons as you can.

2.  Which factors about your employee demographics should you consider when designing an employee benefits programme?
3.  What strategies can be pursued to reduce employee benefit costs without negatively impacting employees?
4.  How can employee benefit programmes be used to attract, retain and motivate employees?
5.  Can you explain the concept of experience rating and the role it plays in insurance costs?
6.  Which benefits may you want to emphasise to increase employee retention?
7.  Explain the difference between defined benefits and defined contribution.
8.  What approaches would you use to ensure that your employees understand the value of their benefits?

## *Glossary of Commonly Used Benefits Terms*

| Term | Definition |
| --- | --- |
| Benefits Administration | The process of managing the benefits of the organisation. Involves enrolling employees into the programmes, interacting with the insurance companies and managing the claims. |
| Broker | The individual or company that contracts for insurance policies with insurance companies on behalf of their client. |
| Claims | A request from a policyholder to the insurance company for payment related to an event covered in the policy. |
| Co-Insurance | The portion the employee pays for a health care service covered in the policy, after the deductible. |
| Coordination of Benefits | The process of determining which insurance policy will pay for which portion of a claim when the employee is covered by more than one policy. |
| Co-Pay | The amount the employee is obligated to pay the provider for certain covered services. |
| Deductible | The amount of money the employee must pay for claims submitted to the benefits administrator before the insurance policy will cover any expense. |
| Experience | The history of gains or losses the insurance company has when comparing premiums collected vs. claims paid for a specific policy. |
| Generic Drugs | A pharmaceutical that contains the same chemical components as another that was previously protected by a patent. Generally cheaper than the original drug. |
| Morbidity Rate | In the context of benefits administration, it is the frequency with which a specific type of claim for a certain covered event actually occurs in the population covered by the policy. |

| Term | Definition |
|------|------------|
| Mortality Rate | In the context of benefits administration, it is the number of actual deaths in a year, as a percent of the population covered by the policy. |
| Policy | A contract stating that, in exchange for a premium, the insurance company will pay the insured a specific amount if a certain event occurs. |
| Premium | The amount paid for the insurance policy coverage. |
| Provider Networks | The doctors, clinics, hospitals and other health care providers that have been contracted to provide services under a specific policy. |
| Reasonable and Customary | The general prevailing cost of a health service within a specific location. |
| Wellness Programmes | These are initiatives aimed at improving the overall health of individuals covered by a policy, with the ultimate objective of reducing morbidity, thus improving experience and lowering premiums. |

## Additional reading

### What a benefits administrator and broker should do to help you manage your benefits

Ideally, a benefits administrator addresses employer pain points of worsening workplace health; spiralling health care costs; lack of ROI data, unappreciated one-size-fits-all benefits; and manual, paper-intensive administration. In addition, the large amounts of out-of-pocket payments, paper claims and manual reimbursements are a huge administrative burden on employers who struggle to cope with a disparate supply chain including insurers, brokers, third party administrators and health care providers.

Companies should use the benefits administrator's platform to incentivise employees to get healthier and have access to valued insurance coverage. The money firms spend on their employees' insurance typically only benefits those who are sickly and require treatment. In a more logical approach, employees who are healthy, or those already covered by the benefits of their working spouses, can convert the insurance dollars they do not need into "spending dollars." Employees can maximise these dollars on discounted health, insurance and wellness services from the benefits administrator's online marketplace, or other company approved flexible benefits.

The benefits administrator can help companies unlock wellness in the workplace without spending more, by shifting existing health care expenditure from treatment to prevention. Employees are rewarded with additional spending dollars for making measurable lifestyle improvements to achieve better health. In addition to enjoying lower health care costs, companies are able to reduce their administrative costs and workload. The benefits administrator platform can serve as a customisable one-stop shop to consolidate and manage existing insurance, health care and wellness benefits vendors, data and activities.

The goal of the benefits broker is to help companies improve their workforce health while capping premium inflation, enabling personalised benefits and significantly reducing HR's benefits administration burden. The administrator and broker can leverage technology and health care big data. Technology helps companies combat rising premiums while reducing administrative costs. For instance, to make operationalising a defined contribution benefits programme easy, the administrator can aggregate all the players in the employee benefits value chain into a private marketplace, and automate all the paper, data and payment flows between employees, companies, insurers, hospitals, clinics, health screeners and wellness providers.

The administrator can also significantly improve the user experience by digitising all the paperwork and eliminating manual processes. They can create an HR portal containing invoices and reports and allow for the company's HR to upload the employee listing and additions, deletions and work life events. The provider portal enables product uploads. The broker's insurer portal transforms quotation, placement, underwriting, claims and invoicing data into online content. The administrator's employee portal should include benefits enrolment and summary, claims submission/tracking and the education, rewards and range of services they need to better manage their personal health. Decision support tools recommend the most relevant mix of insurance and wellness services for each employee's life stage, lifestyle and health needs.

The administrator can also add a wellness shop where transactions are cashless and paperless; the system generated QR code on the e-voucher should be accepted by vendors at the point-of-sale and be reflected on the portal in real-time. This eliminates the need for out-of-pocket spend and waiting for reimbursement. For insured, self-funded or Flex purchases outside the benefits panel, employees should be able to conveniently use the administrator's mobile app for claims submission/tracking.

The analytics capabilities should allow employers to measure the ROI effectiveness of their wellness initiatives and benefits plans. The administrator can capture and analyse data from medical claims, health screening results, activity tracking, lifestyle risk assessments, and employee browsing and purchasing behaviour. Companies can then use this data to prioritise the wellness interventions with the greatest impact on claims and to streamline their benefits offering the following year. This iterative process is aimed at ensuring that the benefits and wellness plan design for every firm will always be relevant, appropriate and cost-efficient. Technology and analytics can support data-driven insights and decision making for HR, perform risks versus costs analyses, and aggregate key health metrics.

To address the issue of worsening health in the workplace due to ageing, sedentariness and the advent of chronic diseases, technology can provide employers and employees with an easy and affordable way to access wellness at work. Face-ageing technology can help employees visualise the future impact of their current lifestyle habits. Risk assessment tools can provide every employee with an evaluation of their health status along with personalised health and wellness tips, tele-video consultations, fitness activity suggestions and electronic activity sign-ups. Employees can be encouraged to set targets and track progress against lifestyle improvement goals, with prompts guiding them towards establishing sustainable action plans with quantifiable milestones and incentives. Progress can be tracked using integrated apps, wearable devices or surveys. Biometrics should be able to be uploaded from the labs onto the administrator's platform and tracked year-on-year, at both the individual and organisational levels. An engaging and interactive user interface can lead to higher employee participation rates, including lifestyle risk questionnaires and health screenings.

Many companies that would like to offer flexible benefits cite prohibitive cost and administrative burden as the main obstacles. The administrator's platform should reduce the implementation time and associated costs, making flexible benefits affordable and accessible to all companies.

Companies can provide employees a wellness spending account, funded by Flex by opting down from unnecessary benefits, trading unused annual leave, or allowing employees to make purchases using credit cards. The administrator's platform can enable cost-effective electronic worksite marketing via insurer bancassurance or direct and agency channels. The administrator can also activate a mobile app with instant quotations and pre-packaged Flex-in-a box offerings to allow insurers to promote and cross-sell relevant group and voluntary benefits to a captive workforce, increasing penetration rates, profitability and sales performance.

Employees with specific health risk factors may be offered differentiated coverage through either voluntary individual or group top-up policies. Portable products such as critical illness, hospital cash or travel insurance can be offered in the portal and promoted to employees when they undergo their annual group insurance enrolment process.

# CHAPTER 17

## Retention and Engagement

### 17.1 Retention strategy framework

According to global research done by the Corporate Leadership Council Advisory Board, about 25 percent of an employee's decision to "stay" in a company relates to remuneration. 25 percent. This may not seem much, but in a world where keeping good employees is important, every little bit helps. In this chapter, we discuss the remuneration trends that relate to retention.

In our view, employees join companies and leave bosses. Thus, the best spend may well be on the training and development of bosses to be better and more inspiring leaders. Once this is done, remuneration options can be considered. The number of organisations implementing specially designed retention mechanisms is increasing.[1] There is a wide range of options, each with their own advantages and disadvantages, which need to be considered on a case-by-case basis.

As a result, the need for organisations to adopt a purposeful attraction, retention and engagement strategy is becoming imperative for organisations to introduce effective staff engagement tactics.[2] Market indicators suggest the cost to an organisation of losing a valued staff member is probably between 50 and 100 percent of the person's annual wage, usually the result of both direct and indirect costs of unplanned employee turnover. Direct costs include recruitment, training new people, and the cost of mistakes they make before settling in. Indirect costs include reduced performance, the effect of increased stress, and reduced job satisfaction.

### 17.2 Remuneration options for retention

Market trends on the remuneration options for retention are set out below. This gives an indication of how to spend vis-à-vis the 25 percent due to compensation.

- **Market positioning:** Organisations using this strategy pitch their guaranteed package at the upper quartile (Q3) of the market for key or scarce resources. Sometimes a different pay scale is created for specific scarce or critical job families, for example engineering.
- **Restraint-of-trade payments:** These payments are often one to five times the annual total guaranteed package (TGP). Conditions are attached to the payment, which is fully taxable to the employee and deductible by the employer over the period of restraint. When enforcing the restraint, the courts look at how severe the restraint is in terms of area, time and damage

---

1 Botha, Bussin & De Swardt, 2011; Bussin & Toerien, 2015; Nienaber, Bussin & Henn, 2011; Nzukuma, 2011; Pregnolato, Bussin & Schlechter, 2017.

2 Moore & Bussin, 2009; Motaung, Bussin & Joseph, 2009.

in relation to the loss of earnings and the inability of the employee to participate in economic activities. Restraints that are unreasonable or too onerous are often not enforced.

- **Sign-on payment/Retention payment:** A payment is promised when an employee joins an organisation. Practices differ somewhat, but the two most common approaches are:
  - Pay the bonus on day one, and the employee has to repay if he or she leaves within a period of time, often one to three years.
  - Promise the payment in, say, two to three years, on condition that the employee stays and accomplishes certain performance targets.

  These payments are fully taxable to the employee when received and fully deductible to the company when paid. The quanta are often up to one to two times the annual salary on the level of the appointment and the amount forfeited with the previous employer upon resignation, i.e. in the form of previous retention awards, long-term and short-term incentives.

- **Sign-on loans:** In this instance, the employee is guaranteed a loan, typically to cover costs related to studies or relocation, and the debt is written off if the employee is still employed by the company after a period of time, for example, three years. There are tax implications up front, as it is generally taxable and not deductible. There is typically a fringe benefit tax due if the interest on the loan is less than the prescribed rate. It is taxable to the employee when the debt is written off. Deductibility is uncertain for the employer since it was never included in "income" (and taxed). Deductibility would hinge on whether it is in the production of income.

- **Rolling or banking of incentives earned:** This is a popular approach for non-listed organisations that do not offer long-term incentives in the form of shares or share equivalents because of its ease and efficacy. Typically, organisations will target a guaranteed pay (GP) to variable pay (VP) ratio based on salary surveys and niche benchmarking. For example, consider the market data for a CEO in a business of similar size and complexity:

| Position | Median GP | Median STI | Median LTI |
| --- | --- | --- | --- |
| CEO | 1,000,000 | 500,000 | 750,000 |

An incentive scheme is designed where the bonus payout for achievement is 1,250,000 (500,000 STI and 750,000 LTI quanta). This is then paid out over, say, three years, typically in one of the following ratios:

- 50 percent in year one, 30 percent in year two and 20 percent in year three (provided still in the organisation's employ).
- 34 percent in year one, 33 percent in year two, and 33 percent in year three (provided still in the organisation's employ).

Another approach is to put all the incentive money in an accrual account and pay out from it one third of the value each year. That is to say, if the executive earns a bonus of 600,000, the payout would be 200,000 and the rest is "banked". If on the following year the executive earns 500,000, this amount goes into the "bank" where now there are 400,000 left from last year plus the 500,000 from this year = 900,000. One third is paid (300,000) and the remainder (600,000) is "banked" again.

On payment, this is fully taxable to the employee and deductible to the organisation. A major advantage of this approach is that it links the incentive targets to the organisation strategy and line of sight.

- **Flexible work arrangements:** The employment contract is driven by mass customisation of remuneration, benefits, employment conditions, working hours, leave, and supplementary business-related expenditure. Work-life balance and catering for the specific needs of the generations (veterans, boomers, generations X and Y) is growing in importance. High-performing organisations have grasped the "administrative nettle" in order to facilitate retention.

- **Post-retirement benefits:** This approach is more effective for those employees close to retirement. One could consider retirement at 62 years of age, and the organisation elects to continue paying into the retirement and medical funds until, say, 67 years of age. The value of employer contributions to these funds on behalf of the ex-employee would be taxable as a benefit to the retired employee, while they should be deductible by the employer.

- **Group-wide bonus with car:** In this instance, organisations typically select a single measure or factor that triggers the bonus payout, for example, "sales" in a retail organisation, and "on-time arrivals and departures" in an airline. If the target is met, a nominal bonus is paid of, say, 100. Should the target be hit for six months in a row, and the employee has not been absent once, he or she qualifies for a ticket for the draw of, say, a small car. All employees receive the same amount of 100, and all eligible employees have a shot at winning the car. This scheme is particularly effective in improving an important measure to the organisation and creating teamwork, and in our experience is relatively cheap. Both the 100 and the value of the car would be taxable to the employee and deductible by the employer, assuming that the employer purchased the car at full value.

- **Long-term incentives (LTI):** With recent changes to section tax codes around the world, organisations are redesigning their share and long-term incentive schemes. This vehicle is still an important one, though, and the benchmarks for quanta are not expected to change radically. Generally, where it used to be possible to tax gains on shares at capital gains tax (CGT) rates (10 percent), these gains are now taxed at marginal tax rates (usually 40 percent). The IFRS 2 charge to the income statement is not deductible. It is too soon to comment and to survey trends, as most organisations are either in investigative, design or obtaining approval phase. Some unlisted organisations have implemented phantom (shadow) share schemes. A more popular approach is a combination of various approaches, for example restraint of trade and rolling incentives.

- **Short-term incentives (STI):** The global trend for the past ten years has been to ratchet up the variable pay portion in the remuneration mix. This ties the onerous salary and wage bill to the fortunes of the business and drives awareness of the strategy. Well-designed schemes motivate and retain employees over the period of the incentive plan, typically up to 12 months.

- **Deferred remuneration:** The most recent trend is for companies to defer a portion of the STI to a future date linked to continued employment of the employee. Deferred incentives were introduced as a measure to create longer-term focus in incentive plans without the onerous requirement to tie the long-term incentives to corporate performance targets. Holding periods post-vesting of long-term incentives create the same result, but over a period of up to three years post-vesting of the LTIs. Unfortunately, there is no silver bullet that addresses the needs and preferences of all employees and employers. Strategies and trends vary, and the most appropriate solution should be selected ending up in a balanced package which supports the short- and long-term business objectives, line of sight for employees and alignment with shareholder interests. Remuneration may not be the most important consideration to the organisation, but is a lot more important than whatever comes third or fourth.

## 17.3  Engagement

Organisations implement attraction and retention strategies and schemes. Some work, but many do not.[3] The unintended consequence is that employers may be fuelling the frenzy and driving pay costs higher. Perhaps the time has come to implement robust employee engagement strategies. After all, there is a high correlation between engaged employees and the bottom line.

One of the characteristics of the knowledge economy is the high level of mobility of knowledge workers. This cost, in both financial and non-financial terms, is high. Staff turnover is expensive and finding replacement skills can be a difficult task. The era of the knowledge worker is here, and with an individual skills base, workers have the intellectual clout to move themselves to whatever attractive offer may arise. What challenge does this leave for the employer?

The definition of "retain" has two meanings: "to hold or keep in possession" and "to engage the services of". The traditional focus in many HR practices has been to hold or keep rather than to engage a service, yet high-value employees and those with "hot" skills want to be "engaged", and not "kept". Organisations need to shift their thinking and focus on what they need to do to help these employees become fully engaged in the organisation. Perhaps the focus then is to engage people for as long as possible, rather than trying to retain them for as long as possible.

---

3    Schlechter, Faught & Bussin, 2014; Schlechter, Hung & Bussin, 2014.

An innovative retention strategy and an organisation reward strategy would certainly aid this process.

Part of engaging knowledge workers means providing an environment where skills transfer and knowledge sharing are easily facilitated. After an organisation brings new employees in through the door and has filled all of its hot skills positions, it cannot rest. The reality is that someone is going to leave relatively soon. What should be done is to transfer that knowledge immediately – almost the second that new employees walk through the door.

### 17.3.1 Conceptualisation of employee engagement

Research has shown that engagement is not something that happens overnight; it is something that needs to be built into the corporate culture. It is a matter of keeping one's ear to the ground, understanding and monitoring engagement, and dealing with issues as quickly as they emerge, including instantaneous recognition of top employees.[4] What engages employees is the feeling that they are making a difference in the work that they care about, that they are working with people who share their mission and values, and that their organisation respects them as adults.

Engagement can make a huge difference to performance.[5] Improving employee engagement is not exceptionally difficult or expensive.[6] A lot of the drivers of engagement are subtle issues and do not require a large amount of capital outlay.

### 17.3.2 Comparative studies on drivers of engagement, attraction and retention

Towers Perrin carried out two sets of research, one in the United States of America and one across six countries in Europe. They asked both groups questions on a variety of workplace factors in their organisation – practices, processes, culture, leadership style, and development opportunities. In other words, they probed all the key elements typically seen to be the drivers of workforce behaviour.

They found a "top 10" list of drivers of attraction, retention and engagement. While there were some similarities between the European and America reports, the key factors were quite widely divergent in each list. The results of the comparative studies are shown in Tables 17.1 and 17.2.

---

4    Schlechter, Thompson & Bussin, 2015; Smit, Stanz & Bussin, 2015.

5    Van Rooy & Bussin, 2014.

6    Bussin & Mouton, 2019.

*Table 17.1: Top 10 drivers in Europe*

| Top 10 Drivers in Europe | | |
|---|---|---|
| **Top 10 attraction drivers** | **Top 10 engagement drivers** | **Top 10 retention drivers** |
| 1 Work-life balance | Senior management interest in employees | Manager inspires enthusiasm for work |
| 2 Recognition for work | Ability to improve skills | Career advancement opportunities |
| 3 Career advancement opportunities | Senior management to demonstrate values | Company reputation as a good employer |
| 4 Challenging work | Challenging work | Fair and consistent pay determination |
| 5 Competitive pay | Decision-making authority | Intention of working after retirement in another field |
| 6 Learning/development opportunities | Company reputation as a good employer | Decision-making authority |
| 7 Job autonomy | Ability to influence company decisions | Overall work environment |
| 8 Variety of work | Company focus on customer satisfaction | Intention of working after retirement to stay active |
| 9 Pay rises linked to individual performance | Fair and consistent pay determination | Manager provides access to learning opportunities |
| 10 Company reputation as a good employer | Overall work environment | Senior management demonstrates values |

*Table 17.2: Top 10 drivers in the United States of America*

| Top 10 Drivers in the USA | | |
|---|---|---|
| **Top 10 attraction drivers** | **Top 10 engagement drivers** | **Top 10 retention drivers** |
| 1 Competitive healthcare benefits | Senior management interest in employees | Career advancement opportunities |
| 2 Competitive pay | Challenging work | Retention of high-calibre people |
| 3 Work-life balance | Decision-making authority | Overall work environment |
| 4 Competitive retirement benefits | Company focus on customer satisfaction | Ability to improve skills |
| 5 Career advancement opportunities | Career advancement opportunities | Resources to get job done |
| 6 Challenging work | Company reputation as a good employer | Competitive pay |

| Top 10 Drivers in the USA | | |
|---|---|---|
| | **Top 10 attraction drivers** | **Top 10 engagement drivers** | **Top 10 retention drivers** |
| 7 | Calibre of co-workers | Collaboration with co-workers | Clear goals from manager |
| 8 | Pay rises linked to individual performance | Resources to get job done | Challenging work |
| 9 | Recognition for work | Ability to influence company decisions | Manager inspires enthusiasm for work |
| 10 | Company reputation as a good employer | Senior management vision | Overall satisfaction with benefits |

## 17.4  Hot skills

A shortage of staff with "hot skills" is unlikely to be quickly alleviated. An organisation's success may increasingly depend on these workers and its ability to attract and retain key talent critical to organisational competency.

The following questions could serve as a template:

- What are the hot skills critical to the organisation?
- Who possesses those skills?
- What is important to the people who have these skills?
- What is needed to develop and transfer these skills continuously?

### 17.4.1  Hot skills categories

Cognisance should be taken of these prevailing categories and skill levels. Attraction and retention options are suggested for each category.

*Critical skills:* These skills are categorised as essential for the sustainability and effective service delivery of an organisation's mandates, and are based on core business requirements. Should the employees holding down these skilled positions leave the organisation, it would be significantly affected because of the considerable impact on the operations of the organisation should the position remain vacant for any period of time

*Scarce skills:* These skills are based on market demand-and-supply factors. In many instances, scarce skills are also critical to the organisation and may receive the remuneration treatment for both categories. This is particularly apparent in highly technically advanced areas. It is therefore important to determine whether the scarce skills as determined by the market are also critical enough within their organisation to warrant special remuneration treatment.

*High-fliers:* These skills reflect a very high level of consistent competence and performance over a long period of time and tend to attract the attention of an organisation's executive management.

### 17.4.2  Skills premiums and specific remuneration treatment

*Critical skills:* Since this category of skills is critical for organisations to sustain their business objectives, the most appropriate strategy must be sought and applied to suit specific objectives. These interventions will ensure that the organisation is able to retain skills essential for business continuity. Attraction and retention options include:

- **Higher basic salary:** To stay competitive, payment for employees with critical skills will usually focus on the 75th market percentile (upper quartile). This will enable managers of these staff members to ensure that the guaranteed portion of their packages is compatible, both to attract and motivate skills identified as critical. To this end, it is crucial that the organisation subscribes to a robust remuneration survey so that accurate market quartiles can be determined.
- **Variable pay:** This part of the employee's total remuneration includes variable pay components such as a performance incentive scheme or a reward and recognition scheme. Measurable targets should be in place, and the payouts of these schemes should be targeted at a competitive market quartile.

**Market premiums and allowances:** As per the base pay description above, critical skills are usually catered for within the organisation's pay scales and do not attract premiums or allowances based on external market comparisons. There are, however, cases where job family-specific pay scales are created to reflect the market should the current scales (by grade) not sufficiently cater for these skills. This method is, however, often an administrative burden and is driven by scarcity in the market. In these cases, both the critical skills and scarce skill remuneration treatments are applied to the position, thereby not increasing the organisation's fixed costs. This is illustrated in Figure 17.1.

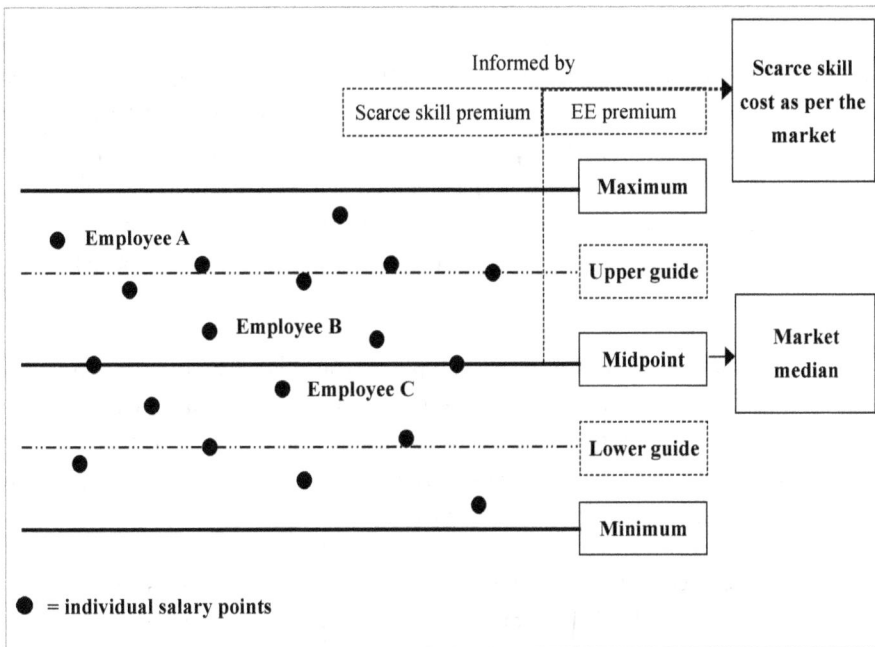

*Figure 17.1: Hot skills remuneration treatment*

**Scarce skills:** These skills reflect the demand and supply of a particular skill at a particular time. The skill requirement may not necessarily mean it is complex, but could imply that, owing to circumstances, only a few people in the market have these specific skills. The situation changes over time when skill pipelining or the completion of large national projects facilitates more people acquiring this level of skills, negating their "hot skills" status.

- **Base pay (guaranteed pay):** In order not to distort the salary scales within an organisation, these employees would be paid within the applicable grade range. It should be ensured that the guaranteed portion is in line with the appropriate levels of employees within the same grade.
- **Variable pay:** This part of the employee's total remuneration includes variable pay components such as a performance incentive scheme or a reward and recognition scheme. Measurable targets should be in place, and the payouts of these schemes should be in line with the rest of the organisation's remuneration policy.
- **Market premiums and allowances:** A scarce skills premium may be placed over and above guaranteed pay (GP). By keeping GP constant, the incumbent can be brought back to the appropriate base pay should demand-and-supply factors change. The scarce skills premium is a market premium over and above the base pay. The premium will be on top of guaranteed pay as a "bonus premium" and can be removed once the demand-and-supply situation has changed. Market premiums are not guaranteed, and the quantum should be

in line with the market rate to complement a guaranteed basic pay. These premiums are not regarded as part of the employee's guaranteed portion of pay, but should be taken into account when comparisons are done on total cost to company per employee. It is important to note that not all scarce skills are equal, therefore suggesting a standard market premium would be the wrong approach. Each position should be assessed, and the size of the premium determined by the gap in the market. The premium is usually expressed as a percentage of the midpoint of the organisation's pay scale, and the same level of premium is paid to individuals irrespective of their position within that scale. This concept is also illustrated in Figure 17.1 above.

***High-fliers (consistent high performance):*** Employees in this category consistently display improvement in performance and skills level over a long period. They may be innovative, have wisdom, and command authority over their areas of influence by virtue of their wisdom and expertise. They also command respect among peers in the field. Their market value increases over time and they will command relatively higher pay.

- Base pay (guaranteed pay): Pay should be gradually moved towards the market upper quartile. Pay scales will adjust according to the market and consequently, employees can be maintained on upper quartile level or higher, depending on the consistency and level of superior performance.
- Variable pay: These employees would generally earn larger performance incentives than their peers based on the attainment of robust performance measures.
- Market premiums and allowances: Once these employees are paid on the upper quartile, a premium above this level may be considered to retain their services. This is, however, not common practice, and any variable pay is usually catered for in the bonus scheme where the employee, because he or she is a top performer, usually achieves the stretch targets and resultant relatively high level of bonus.

### 17.4.3  Pay scale design

In the example shown in Figure 17.1, the organisation's pay scales have been aligned to the market median, and the midpoint of the above scale has been anchored at this market quartile. A spread has then been applied to either side of this midpoint to create the minimum and maximum salary levels for the scale. This would be done for every grade level within the organisation and employees paid within this range.

### 17.4.4  Remuneration options

Employee A could be a critical skill or a high-flier. This is evident by the employee's position in the pay scale in relation to his or her peers. Because Employee A is paid above the upper guide of the pay scale, he or she is effectively being paid at a higher market point than Employee C. As salary scales move in line with the market, the only way that an employee should be able to get to that point would be through consistently good performance. The employee would move through the scales more quickly than his or her peers (high-fliers) as a result of higher increases, or if the skill were deemed critical and paid around the upper guide or maximum of the pay scale to reflect a different market quartile (the upper quartile, if the pay scale is wide enough).

Let us assume that both Employee B and Employee C have scarce skills. Their scarce skill premium would be determined by the cost of that scarce skill in the market, or an agreed premium would be applied.

In the first scenario, the difference between the midpoint of the salary scale and the "market cost" of the scarce skill is what would determine the level of premium payable. This premium would then apply to both Employee B and Employee C even though their salary levels are different. In other words, it applies to the skill category and not the employee.

Another approach that is often used is to apply an agreed premium to certain levels of skill. An example of how this could work can be seen in Table 17.3. Let us assume that at this particular company not all skill categories are equal. It is possible to pay different premiums to the technical, engineering and IT skills categories.

*Table 17.3: An approach to premiums for skills shortages*

| Description | Percentage premium |
| --- | --- |
| *Most extreme shortage of skills.* At least 25% or more of these posts have been vacant in the past year. Offers have been made, but the pay scales alone cannot attract the required skills to join the organisation due to scarcity premiums or evidence exists of high turnover in the order of 25% or more. | 10% of the applicable pay scale midpoint |
| *Extreme shortage of skills.* At least 10 to 25% of these posts have been vacant in the past year. Offers have been made, but the pay scales alone cannot attract the required skills to join the organisation due to scarcity premiums or evidence exists of high turnover in the order of 10 to 25%. | 7.5% of the applicable pay scale midpoint |
| *Shortage of skills.* At least 5 to 10% of these posts have been vacant in the past year. Offers have been made, but the pay scales alone cannot attract the required skills to join the organisation due to scarcity premiums or evidence exists of high turnover in the order of 5 to 10%. | 5% of the applicable pay scale midpoint |

## 17.5  Business case for investing in employee engagement

### 17.5.1  Justification

It is critical for the organisation to spell out the reasons for following the route of employee engagement. The business case for employee engagement becomes an imperative benefit in order to increase the proportion of engaged employees. The importance of engagement to employee retention and total shareholder return (TSR), as well as organisation branding, cannot be underestimated.

According to Towers Perrin, research shows that companies with higher levels of employee engagement outperform their competitors in terms of profitability. Managers must first understand what engages their employees and what factors drive engagement in their companies. Employees will be happier and more productive, which ultimately leads to a positive impact on business results.

Employee engagement also acts as a catalyst for the retention of staff and is critical to any organisation that seeks not only to retain valued employees, but also to increase its levels of performance. One of the most important drivers of an employee's intention to leave is his or her level of commitment to the organisation.

## 17.5.2   Work-life balance

Business has recognised that employees live in a society and the balance between work and home life is also important in order to obtain a more engaged workforce. A lack of interest or neglect by corporate management in this area leads to high cases of burnout resulting from increasing stress, and a resultant drop in productivity.

Research recently defined "burnout" as the erosion of work engagement. Data from the Gallup Employee Engagement Index offers insight into the degree to which engagement levels at work may affect employees' attitudes and behaviour away from the office.

## 17.5.3   The cost of disengagement in America and the United Kingdom

The Gallup Organisation's employee engagement survey, using the results of its engagement index and national average for productivity and salary as a base, estimates that actively disengaged employees cost American businesses between $270 and $343 billion a year. This includes high rates of absenteeism and staff turnover from this sector of employees.

In the United Kingdom, using similar census data on the number of working adults, their average salary and productivity, Gallup also estimated that the productivity gap among actively disengaged employees costs somewhere between £43 and £44 billion a year.

In their research, they used responses to seven core statements as the parameters for defining "engagement":

- I understand how my work contributes to the organisation's overall success.
- I am personally motivated to help the organisation succeed.

- I am willing to put in a great deal of effort beyond what is normally expected.
- I have a sense of personal accomplishment from my job.
- I would recommend the organisation to a friend as a good place to work.
- The organisation inspires me to do my best work.
- The organisation values are aligned with my personal values.

### 17.5.4   The link between engagement and financial performance

In the US study, Towers Perrin moved this data one step further. They collected financial data for respondents' companies (where they were publicly listed – a sample of about 5,000 companies) and began to calculate links between those respondents' scores on certain engagement factors with their companies' overall financial performance.

It is interesting to note that the analysis showed a direct correlation between employee engagement itself and revenue growth. The implications of the study are quite apparent. The power of discretionary effort by highly engaged employees on multiple levels can be seen, for example, in the service business, where an engaged employee has been proven to focus on customer service and excellence, and by doing so has improved customer loyalty and retention. Business indirectly benefits as revenue grows and behaviour modelling and performance culture improve.

### 17.5.5   Engagement's effect on total shareholder return

Hewitt also conducted a different financial analysis in its full database of 2,000 "Best Employer" companies in over 50 countries worldwide – client and former client companies and those who had taken part in Hewitt's "Best Employer" listings – to measure the correlation between high engagement levels among their employees and total shareholder return (TSR) to the organisation. Tracking the results of Hewitt's engagement surveys over a period of four years with the TSR of those companies, they found a positive correlation between the two. In short, companies that had between 60 to 100 percent of employees engaged (in Hewitt's classification system, where the average organisation has 49 percent of employees engaged) showed an impressive average TSR of 20.2 percent for the period. Meanwhile, those companies with moderate levels of engagement (49 to 60 percent engaged employees) had an average TSR of 5.6 percent, and companies with fewer than 40 percent engaged employees saw a negative TSR (–9.6 percent).

Although this is a straight correlation, Hewitt contends that their individual client work shows that engagement has a causal relationship with business performance and not vice versa. This conclusion is based on the number of companies they have seen improve results after specifically focusing on engagement.

One of the most practical models of engagement, the Five Pillars of Engagement, was developed by Accenture. The five pillars are shown in Figure 17.2.

| 1 RECOGNISE AND REWARD SUPERIOR PERFORMANCE | 2 ESTABLISH A LEARNING ENVIRONMENT | 3 CREATE KNOWLEDGE-SHARING COMMUNITIES | 4 MANAGE THE CULTURE OF CHANGE | 5 PROVIDE OPPORTUNITIES TO GROW AND DEVELOP |
|---|---|---|---|---|
| Organisations can foster a culture of belonging by rewarding and recognising employees based on both individual and business performance. Individual performance should be judged not only on financial contributions (such as meeting sales targets), but on other contributions as well, such as superior customer service or innovative process improvements. Make sure rewards are not only financial; consistent recognition for a job well done through frequent informal praise, organisation award programmes, perks, parties or other means will go far towards establishing a culture that values individuals' contributions. | Organisations with the most engaged workforces provide a significant number of learning opportunities for employees to excel. To establish a learning culture, offer plenty of formal learning opportunities (such as classroom or online courses), but also provide lots of informal learning experiences (eg mentoring programmes, "lunch and learns", observational feedback or specific assignments designed to sketch a person's capabilities). Additionally, provide employees with managers who are capable and willing to review an employee's learning needs frequently, to ensure that they align with career plans and goals. | Engaged employees feel supported by a culture in which knowledge, information and resources are easily shared. Many organisations try to achieve this culture by providing web-based tools that enable employees to access knowledge capital. However, knowledge databases can become unwieldy and littered with excessive, irrelevant information. Organisations can address this problem by providing information based on employees' roles in the organisation or by providing training on effective use of such tools. In addition, encourage other forms of knowledge sharing, such as communities of practice that enable employees to share insights and experience. | Workforces committed to an organisation's goals must understand both what the goals are and how they are being affected or executed through changes such as mergers, acquisitions, or the outsourcing of key business processes. Communicating details about major organisational changes in a timely fashion will foster a culture of trust and belonging, and help employees pursue organisational goals more effectively. Programmes designed to reduce any negative impact of such changes on morale and productivity (such as assigning "buddies" to newly acquired employees) will also ensure that engagement levels remain high. | Few employees feel committed if they are not given opportunities for career development. Our research suggests that to foster such cultures, companies should ensure that employees have career development plans addressing training activities and work experience in possible future roles. Assigning career counsellors to provide personalised attention ensures that employees have realistic plans. Organisations with high employee engagement scores gave counselling sessions at least twice a year; low scores gave sessions less than once a year. |

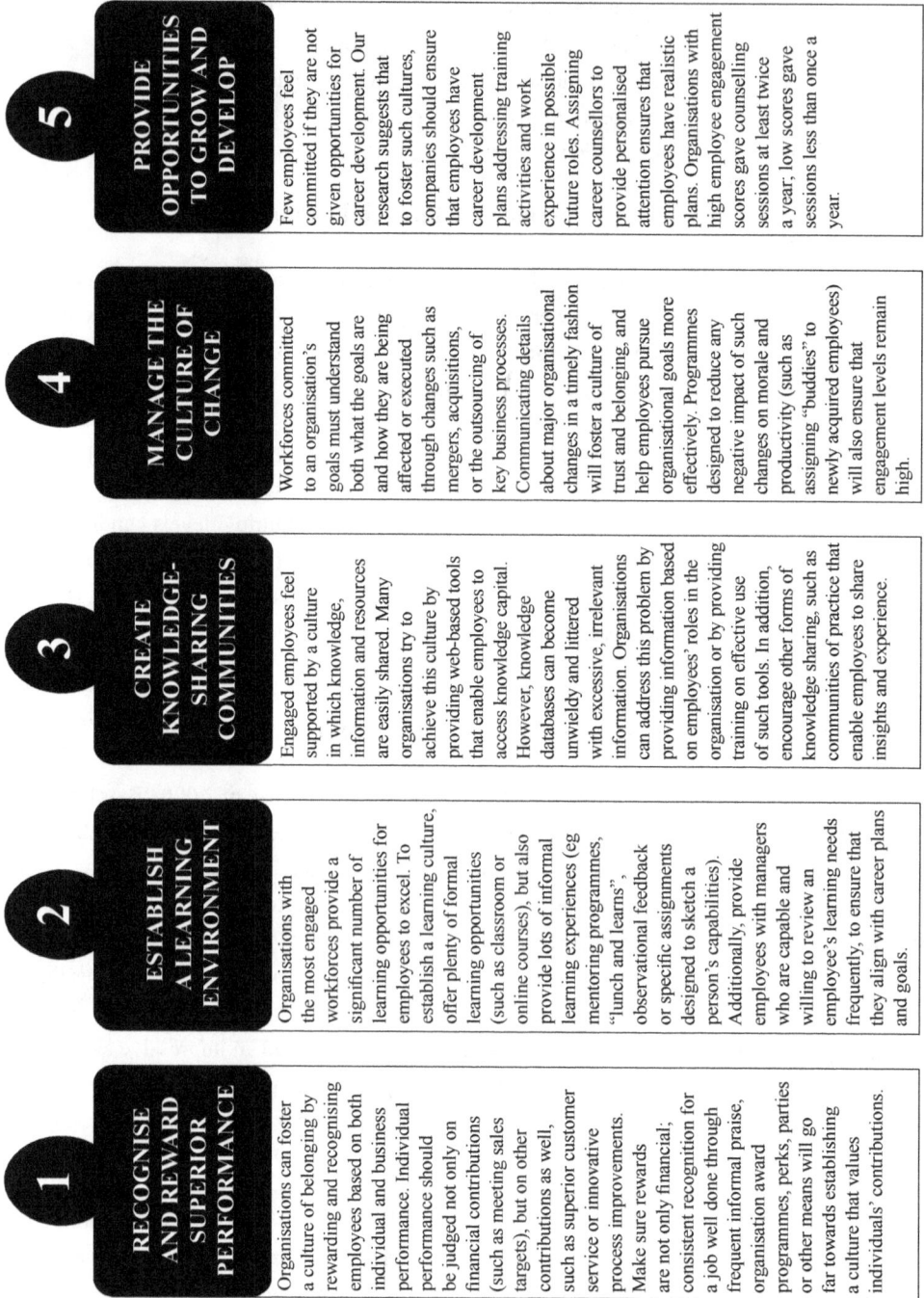

*Figure 16.2: The five pillars of engagement*
*Source: Cawe[7]*

---

7  Cawe, 2006

## 17.5.6 Key drivers of employee engagement

Shaffer[8] stated that achieving employee engagement is about getting to think and act like business leaders and about creating a work environment that causes people to perform at exceedingly high levels – a place where employees want to use their discretionary effort on behalf of the organisation. According to his research, the four dimensions to creating engagement are:

- **Line of sight:** I know how what I do contributes to business goals and outcomes.
- **Involvement:** I know I can make decisions which will influence business results.
- **Share information:** I have the information I need to guide my decisions.
- **Reward and recognition:** I know I will be rewarded for my contributions.

On the other hand, Development Dimensions International's (DDI) value proposition includes four sequential components. In DDI's model of engagement drivers (see Figure 17.3), organisations need to hire people who fit the job profile, develop leaders with the right skills, and provide support through strong strategies. More specifically, an engaged environment builds loyalty in employees by meeting their personal and practical needs, thereby encouraging them in stay in the organisation. An engaged working environment also leads to greater employee motivation, which can make the distinction from the organisation's competitors.

Finally, long-term benefits appear on the bottom line, which shows that the organisation has more satisfied and loyal customers, increased profits, better quality products or services, and greater growth potential.

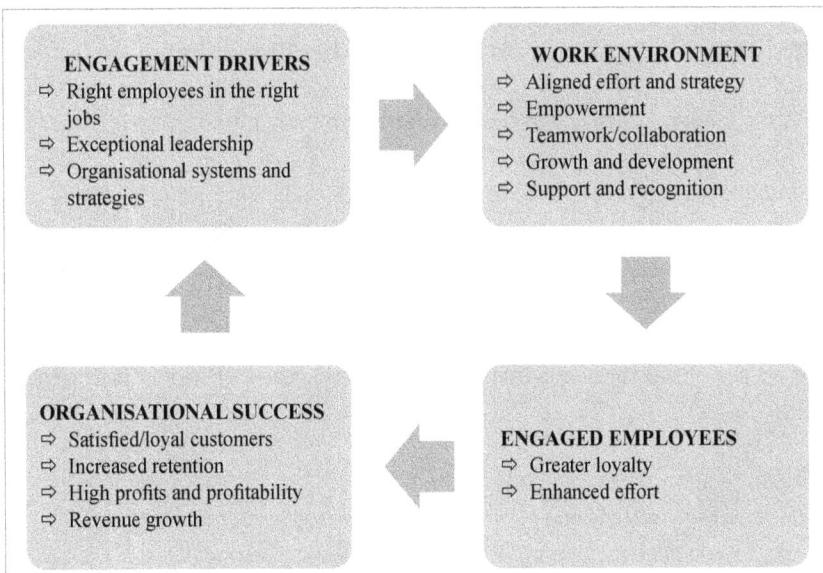

*Figure 17.3: DDI's engagement value proposition*

---

8    Shaffer, 2005.

As seen in the model, organisations can drive engagement by proactively leveraging three sources of influence for change: employees, leaders and organisational systems. These three drivers work together to create an engaged working environment, but the ultimate ownership of engagement rests with the employee.

In order for engagement to occur, organisations must tap into employees' passion, commitment and identification with the organisation. In order to do this, organisations must ensure that the right employee is in the right job. In other words, employees who have the skills to do the job, as well as the personal motivation and willingness, must be correctly placed in the organisation.

DDI's research draws the following conclusions:

- Additional studies have shown that changes in leader behaviours can have a real impact on employee engagement. Engaging leaders understand that their role is not to take charge of all the decisions; it is about recognition for a job well done and giving people the room and encouragement to grow. It is also about being tough when necessary and holding people accountable for their performance.
- Organisations need strong systems and strategies that support and foster engagement. Examples of these are hiring, promotion, performance management, recognition, remuneration, training, and career development.
- Together, these systems provide an organisation with a foundation upon which to accelerate engagement. A shaky or incomplete foundation will make an organisation's efforts to build engagement more difficult, if not impossible.

## 17.6 The importance of measurement and benchmarks

Since 1997, the Gallup Organisation has surveyed over three million employees in more than 300,000 work units within companies. This survey consists of 12 questions – called the Q12 – to measure employee engagement on a five-point scale indicating weak or strong agreement. Results have shown that companies with high Q12 scores experience lower turnover, higher sales growth, better productivity, better customer loyalty, and other manifestations of superior performance.

The following are the 12 questions that the Gallup Organisation uses in measuring employee engagement:

- Do you know what is expected of you at work?
- Do you have the materials and equipment you need to do your work right?
- At work, do you have the opportunity to do what is best every day?
- In the last seven days, have you received recognition or praise for doing good work?
- Does your supervisor, or someone at work, seem to care about you as a person?

- Is there someone at work who encourages your development?
- At work, do your opinions seem to count?
- Does the mission/purpose of your organisation make you feel your job is important?
- Are your associates (fellow employees) committed to doing quality work?
- Do you have a best friend at work?
- In the last six months, has someone at work talked to you about your progress?
- In the last year, have you had the opportunities at work to learn and grow?

The question is, what are the remuneration implications for retention strategies? A shift in the organisation mindset may involve some of the following points:

- Pay for contribution rather than job duty adherence or service.
- Reward requires competence development and application.
- Rely on performance-related pay as a means of conveying messages about organisation values, critical success factors and how people are expected to contribute.
- Include both input (competence) and output (results) in performance reviews.
- Introduce robust broad-band pay structures where lateral development, and acquisition and use of competence are rewarded.
- Develop team reward systems which support flexible work practices, multi-skilling and teamwork.
- Introduce gain-sharing, profit-sharing or any bonus scheme that shares the added value of
- employee efforts.
- Communicate reward innovations to employees.
- Involve, as far as practical, employees in the design of reward processes.
- Provide training to everyone on the application and implications of the reward policies and practices.

## 17.7 Conclusion

Remuneration-based retention strategies are critical, but simply throwing money at the problem will not make retention issues go away in the long term. The focus in retention strategies has shifted from a one-size-fits-all to customisation. Each employee is motivated by different factors depending on their age, status, career goals, and so on. Therefore, retention strategies must be targeted at individual employees or groups of employees.

The main reason why retention is such an issue for organisations is that retaining valued workers helps keep companies successful. When star performers leave, they take their knowledge with them. Organisations need to learn how to engage talent competently to ensure the continuous transfer and encoding of knowledge, so that in the event of knowledge workers leaving, their knowledge is retained by the organisation. Through successful engagement with knowledge employees, a high level of commitment can be achieved during their tenure at the organisation, thereby maximising the return to the employer as well as the employee.

## 17.8 Summary

Organisations struggle to find top talent, and once they have, they struggle to keep it. Remuneration is only 25 percent of the decision to stay. The other 75 percent boils down to inspirational leadership, challenging work, and performance and career opportunities. World trends on engagement depict that work-life balance and career advancement opportunities are increasingly important. Cutting down on staff turnover can save the equivalent of an employee's annual remuneration package. With the mix of generations in a workforce, a global trend is to tailor-make the reward offering according to employee needs.

## 17.9 Self-evaluation questions

1. Name a few remuneration options available to retain staff.
2. What is meant by engagement?
3. How should you reward for scarce skills?
4. How should you reward high-fliers?
5. What is the business case for investing in employee engagement?

# CHAPTER 18

# Recognition

## 18.1 Context and linkage

Recognition tends to be an afterthought; something to address after the "important rewards", such as base pay and incentives, have been implemented. Not nearly enough leadership time is spent on creating well-designed recognition strategies and policies, which is a dangerous area to neglect given the latest research linking it to financial performance and share price.

Few organisations have established clear definitions for recognition plans, therefore, a clear and consistent understanding of what to expect from these plans generally does not exist. This is starting to change, and hopefully this chapter will contribute to that change.

High-performing organisations understand the value placed on and received from recognition plans, along with the role of human capital in an organisation's success. Recognition plans are no longer allocated to an HR assistant, but are becoming critical elements in a total reward system and in reinforcing employees' commitment to organisation objectives. Today's competitive business climate demands that leaders understand and use all the tools available to ensure success. Recognition has become one of these powerful tools.

## 18.2 Definitions and differences clearly understood

A major reason for the difficulty in understanding the value of recognition plans, and in viewing the plans as part of the organisational reward system, is the lack of consistent definitions of recognition plans and a list of expectations.

### 18.2.1 Incentive

Incentive plans reward specific results or criteria that are announced at the beginning of the performance cycle; they are retrospective awards at the end of a period once the targets have been met or exceeded. Awards tend to be formula-driven and timed to pre-announced targets. The emphasis is more on the financial or tangible value earned than on the psychological value of the achievement. (Note: Psychological value is not absent from incentive plans, but it is not the primary focus.)

### 18.2.2 Recognition

Recognition plans typically reward employee contributions in non-financial ways and drive ongoing, on-the-spot type recognition of behaviour, projects completed, or very short-term targets having been met. The emphasis is generally on the psychological value provided to the recipient versus the financial value of the award. Although there are organisations that award overseas trips to the top winners of their recognition programmes, the most general type of reward includes recognition points which can be exchanged for products at a retail store, movie tickets, a weekend away, a day off, a pat on the back or a nice letter to the employee's family citing the reasons why the employee is being recognised.

Any discussion of an organisation's reward system must include recognition plans for at least two reasons:

- Recognition plans are now considered a component of current reward systems models.
- Recognition plans provide, in the reward system, an element that targets designed organisational behaviours and cultural values, and should not duplicate measures which have already been included in the other incentive plans within the organisation.

## 18.3  Positioning recognition in the total reward system

Figure 18.1 shows a typical positioning of recognition programmes in the total rewards strategy of organisations.

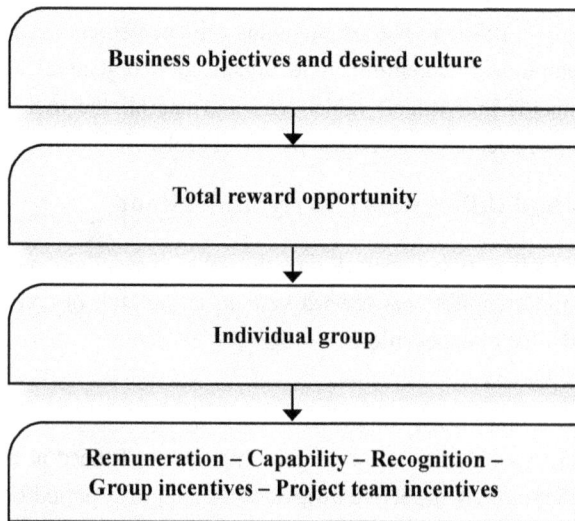

*Figure 18.1: Positioning recognition in the total reward system*

Cultural implications need to be incorporated into the design of recognition plans, especially regarding: (1) team rewards, (2) "peer-to-peer" nominations, and (3) organisational values.

**Team rewards** have become important in many organisations, yet individual achievement is promoted through recognition plans. As part of a total reward system, recognition plans must incorporate a team structure, if reinforcing teamwork is part of the organisation's desired culture. A typical example of disconnect between a plan and the team culture is an "employee of the month" programme.

**Peer-to-peer nominations** greatly increase the perception of fairness in these plans. Organisations need to ensure robust systems and rules, and provide sufficient training to ensure a high enough EQ (emotional quotient) to accommodate this approach.

**Organisational values** need to be considered as well as the organisation's culture.

## 18.4 The business case for implementing a recognition system

### 18.4.1 Increased profits

Research data have shown a causal pathway relationship between employee attitudes, customer impressions and profit.[1] The findings are that improvements in employee attitudes drive higher customer satisfaction, which results in higher profits. Recognition, if measured by feeling appreciated, being acknowledged, and having contributions recognised on the job, can be viewed as a key element of employees' attitudes.

The growing body of data and the inter-relationships between the measures of attitudes (soft) and financials (hard) demonstrate the significance of recognition as an organisational performance issue.

### 18.4.2 Communication vehicle

The total reward system, along with its recognition component, is a powerful communication vehicle. The organisation directs and energises employees through its reward system, which tells employees what is important to the organisation and, specifically, how employees are to perform if they are to be rewarded. Recognition plans are powerful in this regard because of their flexibility in combining objective and subjective criteria, periodic and event-driven nominations, and employee and management selection processes.

## 18.5 Design considerations

Formal organisation recognition plans differ, and there are many different types. There are, however, four main characteristics that can be used for classification:

- Participants.
- Criteria.
- Nomination and selection process.
- Awards.

---

1   Rucci, Kirn & Quinn 1998.

### 18.5.1  Participants

Traditionally, recognition plans involved individuals at lower levels,but there has been a shift towards teams and all levels. Another trend has been to recognise a work group or an entire organisation. The emphasis on organisational objectives and the need for everyone to feel part of the group has driven group-wide recognition plans.

A balance needs to be created between individual and group, and this can be done only if the recognition plan is incorporated into the total reward system.

### 18.5.2  Criteria

The current trends for developing criteria for recognition plans are much more strongly aligned with specific organisational strategies and objectives than ever before. Just as competencies and performance have become part of the remuneration plan, learning and results are now being reflected in the recognition plan.

Both hard and soft measures are being used in recognition plans, and these multi-factor criteria options are being applied to teams or groups.

### 18.5.3  Nomination and selection process

The nomination and selection process has evolved from a management-only process to one that includes peers and joint (employee–management) selection committees. Employee education and empowerment provide additional value to the organisation.

### 18.5.4  Awards

Awards can be classified into two main categories, namely:

- Symbols or utilities.
- Points.

*Symbols or utilities:* Symbols or utilities are often "worth" more than the money because they last longer and have some "trophy" value. Examples of utilities are sporting equipment, white appliances, cameras and electronic equipment, while symbol examples are trophies and statues.

*Points awards:* There are many variations of points awards, which include:

- Leaders and managers awarding points to employees.
- Peers awarding points to colleagues.
- Companies awarding "loyalty" points to customers.

These points are "converted" to gifts or more of the product or service bought in the first place. In some large corporations, there are extensive catalogues showing a wide range of gifts and giving the points value of each gift. External organisations are often used to administer these schemes, given the large volumes of people and points traded.

There are excellent examples of huge "events" arranged, where the CEO presents awards at gala dinners. The awards are often substantial amounts of money, overseas trips, and extended study tours.

## 18.6  Recognition schemes: The lottery

One of the most effective recognition schemes is called the "lottery scheme". In a nutshell, the process can be described as follows:

### 18.6.1  Eligibility

All employees are eligible, unless they are in a disciplinary process.

### 18.6.2  Criteria

Usually a single-strike factor that is a group-wide measure is used. It is often the single most important measure for that organisation and is the top item on the business strategy for that year. Examples are:

- Airline – "on-time" landing and departure.
- Food chain – shrinkage reduction.
- Insurance – sales volume.
- Consulting organisation – quality.
- Manufacturing – safe operations.

Sometimes there are two or even three measures, but ideally there should only be one.

### 18.6.3  Awards

If the organisation achieves the strike factor goal, then every employee receives a cash bonus that is nominal in amount, say, 500. If the goal is achieved for six months in a row, and the employee has not been absent during this period, all employees who are eligible then receive a lottery ticket which goes into a big draw of a significant prize. The prize has to be large enough to create interest.

## 18.7  Critical success factors

As important as recognition is to an organisation, management continues to undervalue the impact it has on employees' satisfaction and financial performance. The critical success factors of good scheme design involve at least seven steps:

- Forming and mandating the design team.
- Securing measures, research information and current best practice.
- Establishing the plan objectives, desired outcomes, and a framework for evaluating the plan.
- Creating the plan structure (rules, criteria, awards, and so on).
- Determining the plan support requirements.
- Selecting the award vehicle.
- Project planning the overall plan, including the financial rationale and business case.

### 18.7.1  Benchmark findings

When doing the research on best-of-breed schemes, one often comes across the following typical benchmark findings. This could serve as a checklist for design:

- The plan is aligned with the desired culture.
- High level of commitment by executives.
- Participants can impact criteria (good line of sight).
- Criteria are more objective than subjective.
- Both individuals and teams are recognised.
- Recipients are recognised in public before their peers.
- Both behaviours and achievements are recognised.
- Goals are clear and the plan is well communicated.
- Management understands and uses the plan.
- Plan design and operation involves employees.

Other important design issues include:

- The process for deciding awards (subjective or objective).
- The subjective award decision-maker (management, peer, committee, other).
- The percentage of population receiving an award.
- The median award value and total award budget.
- The budget for plan support.
- The date of the previous reassessment and next assessments.

## 18.8 "Virtual scorecard" approach

In many organisations, certain departments are far less in the spotlight than others, despite the fact that their individual contributions may be every bit as important to the overall goals of the organisation. The customer service employee who retains a major account for a specific duration should receive comparable recognition to the sales employee who lands the next big account.

The idea of running a programme throughout an entire organisation may sound like a logistical nightmare for the person who has to administer it, which is why many organisations are using computer software that handles the administration, creates an "intelligent" database that can be interrogated, and helps maximise the return on investment (ROI). It can give a snapshot of not only individual and departmental performance, but the progress of the organisation as a whole, effectively demonstrating ROI. This "virtual scorecard" approach shows CEOs which team members are meeting or exceeding goals at any given time, so they can calculate immediate returns on human investment.

## 18.9 Case study: Guidelines to management

### 18.9.1 Recognition at organisation X

It is generally accepted that managers are not always good, timely and consistent in recognising and rewarding people. Inconsistent application of recognition and rewards creates a lot of unhappiness. Our hope is that this chapter provides specific, uniform guidelines.

### 18.9.2 Principles of celebration

What are the best ways to celebrate accomplishments and provide recognition to innovative employees? The following "Seven Celebration Principles" should be followed in order to make effective use of recognition systems:[2]

- **Emphasise success rather than failure:** We tend to miss the positives if we are always too busy searching for the negatives.
- **Deliver recognition and reward in an open and publicised way:** If not made public, recognition loses much of its impact and defeats much of its purpose. "Reward in public; discipline in private."
- **Deliver recognition in a personal and honest manner:** Avoid recognition that is too "slick" or overproduced.
- **Tailor your recognition and reward to the unique needs of the people involved:** Having many recognition and reward options will enable managers to acknowledge accomplishments in ways appropriate to the particulars of a given situation. Therefore, it is important to consider possibilities from a larger menu. Also ensure that the value of the

---

2   Jossey-Bass & Pfeiffer, 2009.

reward is calibrated to ensure consistency. "Reward what you value with something they value."

- **Timing is crucial:** Recognise contribution throughout a project. Reward contribution close to the time that an achievement is realised. Time delays weaken the impact of most rewards. "Achievement occurs only if there is a chance of failure."
- **Strive for a clear, unambiguous and well-communicated connection between accomplishments and rewards:** Make sure people understand why they are recognised and the criteria that are being used. "Use all types of rewards as vehicles of communication."
- **Recognise recognition:** Recognise people who recognise others for doing what is best for the organisation. "Good managers manage; but good leaders lead."

"The Seven Celebration Principles" form a good basis from which to start, and also make it possible to compare some of our reward and recognition systems against these principles.

### 18.9.3 Rewarding high-quality outputs: standard, formal rewards

The following rewards are conditions of employment but can still be used as vehicles to recognise good performance:

- **Annual performance-related salary increments for staff employees:** The annual performance appraisal, and the intermediate review at half-year, allow managers to assess individuals' contributions and recognise efforts made towards achieving the organisation's goals. These sessions can be used to congratulate individuals and to recommend an appropriate performance rating. (Performance ratings are cross levelled by the leadership team and often change. Therefore, be careful not to create expectations and use the recommended rating as recognition per se.)
- **Increment letters** provide an opportunity for heads of department to write a personal thank-you to their staff for the individual contribution made through the year.
- **Incentive bonus scheme:** Separate out a maximum percentage or absolute amount (say, 4% or 6,000, whichever is higher) that can be earned. The scheme can be output-based and focus on production (uptime), cost (with special emphasis on variable cost), product quality, revenue and EBIT (earnings before interest and taxation). It is even more important to recognise and reward the behaviours, individual contributions and performances (inputs) that contribute to our achieving goals or results, such as profit (outputs). Ways to achieve this are described later.
- **Long service awards:** In addition to the financial award (cash or gift) and long service award function, it is important to recognise and celebrate long service in an open and public manner, as close as possible to the date of the actual event. Individual staff members should not have to collect their cheques and certificates for their service award from the HR administration section; these should be handed to them in an open forum. Long service is also recognised when people with 30 or more years' service retire. A ceremony is held and

a gift presented. Department heads should also arrange for a farewell for any employee who leaves the organisation with more than five years' service.

### 18.9.4  Recognising high-quality inputs

The individual actions, desired competencies and behaviours (inputs) which contribute to the achievement of the organisation's goals need to be recognised and when appropriate, rewarded on an ongoing basis. Three avenues exist by which this can be achieved:

*Informal recognition*

It is not necessarily only cash or a gift that will leave a lasting impression on the achiever or their peers and colleagues; various though highly effective ways can be used to recognise individual and team achievements.

If a set menu of awards is in place for any particular achievement, the chances of one department giving a reward to its people versus another department not giving an award for the same achievement are slim. There is nothing more demotivating than doing a good job and then seeing other people being rewarded for the same well-done job while receiving no recognition oneself. For example, why should one department be rewarded for coming to work, while other departments are expected to be at work?

The following should be considered, although the list is certainly not exhaustive:

- A verbal "thank you" or "well done".
- A thank-you card.
- A letter of recognition on the achiever's personal file.
- A congratulations card (for example, an achievement at work, or marriage, birth of a child, sporting achievement).
- Achievements published in the newsflash, organisation magazine, or even the local newspaper, if appropriate.
- "Thank you" and "congratulations" cards distributed to all section heads.

Examples of physical gifts are:

- A cap.
- A key ring or key case.
- A tie or scarf
- A calculator.
- A wallet.
- An umbrella.
- A pair of sunglasses.

- An engraved pen and pencil set.
- A golf shirt or ladies' blouse.
- A jacket.
- A clock or watch.
- A tablet or similar device
- A voucher (always a safe choice).
- A sponsored dinner for the employee and his or her family.
- Time off.

### MD's discretionary recognition payment

The managing director may authorise special monetary awards up to a maximum amount (perhaps up to the equivalent of two weeks or even one month of basic pay). The bonus is used to recognise certain achievements or completion of a specific project. There are excellent examples of companies recognising innovation through a once-off recognition payment. An award may also be recommended in instances where outstanding performance, commitment, and exceptional results are achieved over a number of years. Typically, this could be considered when performance is no longer adequately rewarded via the performance management system (that is, where the salary has moved beyond the midpoint).

Recommendations should be made to the relevant head of department for discussion with the other leadership team members.

The importance of timing is vital. The longer the delay in recognising success, the less impact the reward will have. Countdowns to target dates are excellent communication vehicles for the involvement of all employees. Use awards to communicate what you hold important.

Recognition must ideally be given in public to ensure maximum impact and ongoing motivation. Managers must take the lead in the area of recognition and regard this as part of their job. Paying attention to the negative and not reinforcing the positive with their team is a recipe for disaster. Use rewards as a way to provide feedback.

## 18.10  Recognising employees

There is an essential principle that is often overlooked when managing a department, division or, i.e. one should consider what motivates people the most. Statistics show that recognition improves the quality of work as well as commitment does.

### 18.10.1  Advantages of monetary recognition

The advantages of monetary rewards are that they are:

- Desirable.
- Easy to administer and handle.
- Understood by an employee.
- Able to provide an extra boost to a long-term programme.

### 18.10.2 Disadvantages of monetary recognition

Disadvantages of monetary rewards are that they:

- Have no lasting value.
- Are not exotic.
- Cannot be enhanced.
- May become an expected reward.

### 18.10.3 Non-financial ways to recognise employees

The best-of-breed remuneration practices have both financial and non-financial recognition schemes. Some ways of rewarding employees using non-financial methods are:

- Give a one-minute praising.
- Praise employees immediately for a job well done.
- Be specific regarding recognition.
- Boost an individual's self-esteem by encouragement.
- Use the person's first name.
- Greet employees.
- Give credit where credit is due.
- Acknowledge individual achievement.
- Implement recognition awards, such as naming an award after an employee.
- Create a "Hall of Fame".
- Start a yearbook with the names and photographs of outstanding employees.
- Give individuals a sense of appreciation with "Out-to-Dinner" programmes.
- Make a "Behind the scenes" award for those whose actions are not usually in the limelight.
- Invite employees to your home for a special celebration of public recognition or social awards.
- Recognise employees in front of their colleagues and spouses.
- Offer a deserving employee a change in job responsibility.
- Time off is always an effective form of rewarding employees.
- Let the employee choose the reward to his or her liking.
- Organise a "Team Lunch".
- Allow staff to display their organisation name and logo on their clothes. They usually take great pride in doing so.
- Co-ordinate a surprise celebration of the achievement of an employee or group of employees.

- In one organisation, each employee is given a Mickey Mouse watch after three months of employment as a reminder to always have fun while working for the organisation. On the 10th anniversary, an employee is given a gold Mickey Mouse watch. Providing a fun working environment always accomplishes good results in productivity and commitment.
- Make awards for specific achievement and activities such as "Outstanding Employee Awards".
- Offer incentives as a positive way to reward achievement of goals, improvement of services and development of cost-saving programmes.
- Encourage employee suggestion rewards – there is nothing wrong with a cash award, but it is soon spent. Seemingly small gestures (such as a plaque, or bulletin boards with pictures of employees) can be as effective as banqueting and travel.
- Thank employees for their initiative.
- Make people feel good about themselves – it builds strong motivation.
- Recognise employees all the time.
- Make group or team awards a part of the decision-making process. This allows staff to share in ownership.
- Give attendance awards. One organisation gave production workers 100 shares each for one year for achieving one year of perfect attendance.
- One way to build anticipation and momentum and obtain certain desired behaviour is to reward employees in a contest of some sort.
- Introduce a field trip, special events, or travel rewards for high performers, for example, send the person to a health spa for a day or weekend.
- Give share ownership to foster empowerment and feelings of ownership.
- Acknowledge a long relationship between an organisation and an individual.

## 18.11   Conclusion

Every employee must understand that the recognition plan is to recognise achievements in relation to the demands of the job. That is why offering employees a wide range of types of recognition is recommended. Once employees are recognised for their hard work and realise that they do make a difference to the organisation and are valued, they will perform at higher levels.[3]

Recognition is food for the soul and often costs nothing. The power of carefully implemented, high-leverage recognition is probably the least-developed area in our reward strategies basket.

## 18.12   Summary

Recognition is probably the most under-utilised reward element. Recognition can be formal or informal, financial or non-financial. Good recognition policies ensure that similar behaviour is recognised similarly. Well-designed recognition programmes are often worth several times the value of the money invested in them.

---

3   People Dynamic Magazine, 2000.

## 18.13 Self-evaluation questions

1. What is the difference between incentives and recognition?
2. What is the business case for implementing a total reward system?
3. What are the critical success factors for recognition schemes?
4. Give examples of formal and informal recognition.

**An Example to Emulate: Dave Novak at Yum!**

Dave Novak was CEO at Yum! brands from 1998 until 2015, where he was recognised as one of the world's top CEOs by **Fortune** and *Harvard Business Review*. He attained this by providing unparalleled growth for all three of the main Yum! Brands: KFC, Pizza Hut and Taco Bell.

In his book *Taking People With You: The Only Way to Make Big Things Happen*, he explains how, when he was in charge of KFC, he implemented a recognition programme based on rubber chickens. You know, those rubber toys that looked like a plucked chicken. He made sure to know when truly outstanding things happened in the company, and when they did, he would personally fly to meet the person who had done the outstanding thing. The usual form was to get the person's supervisor involved in organising the equivalent of a "surprise party", so that the person would be caught unaware of the fact that the CEO himself was coming down to congratulate him or her and give them their very own rubber chicken. These rubber chickens became a source of immense pride and a mark of honour among those that received them. They often took them home to show their families and displayed them prominently in their workspace. Immense motivation by a master motivator!

# CHAPTER 19

# International Assignment Remuneration

## 19.1 Context and linkage

The focus of this chapter is on international assignments. Employees sent on international assignments are referred to as international assignees or expatriates.

The remuneration of international assignees tends to be a rushed, last-minute negotiated decision where urgent business needs justify nearly any cost. Someone with needed expertise or ability is sent to another location and the business assumes an obligation to "do what's fair" and keep the employee whole, even sending the employee's entire family overseas. The implications often arise only after the assignee arrives in the host country, and when the assignment comes to an end, the new position in the home country, for example, pays less than the employee earned on assignment.

Few organisations spend sufficient time creating a well-designed global mobility strategy and related remuneration policies. This is a dangerous area to neglect, given the latest research which indicates very high employee turnover at the beginning and end of international assignments.

Most large global organisations have established a clear policy for remunerating international assignees, however it is a complex area of remuneration fraught with issues such as volatile exchange rates, weak and strong currencies, differences in cost of living between countries, family considerations, and attractive and less attractive countries to work in. This is an area where clear principles and policies are required to ensure fairness, consistency, equity and retention. International assignments, after the one-time costs of expatriation, typically cost up to three times annual salary and twice (or more) the cost of local talent; ensuring a return on this investment is critical for the company and the overall employee value proposition.[1] This chapter will assist in the management of international assignment remuneration.

Global, and increasingly regional, organisations understand the value of effective international assignment remuneration, along with the role of human capital in an organisation's success. International assignment remuneration is no longer left in the hands of a sole HR administrator, but is becoming a critical element in a total reward and talent management system; in reinforcing employees' commitment to organisation objectives and as part of performance development plans strengthening the talent pipeline and building global experience and mind-set.

---

1 Trompetter, Bussin & Nienaber, 2016.

## 19.2 Types of international assignments

The question of what constitutes an international assignment is one of the first issues to be established. Based on the purpose, duration and the company's intent to repatriate, five common types of international employment are distinguished.

### 19.2.1 Business trip

A business trip has the following characteristics:

- The purpose is to meet face to face with others, attend an event, make a presentation, solve a problem, etc.
- Duration is typically from one day to 30 days in one location.
- Unaccompanied by family.
- No change in tax or remuneration position.

Typically, a daily allowance or per diem is paid to cover meals and incidental expenses; alternatively, actual costs are covered via an expense report. Hotel accommodation is the norm.

### 19.2.2 Short-term assignment

A short-term assignment has the following characteristics:

- The purpose is to complete a specific project or solve a problem, requiring a specific expertise or ability; it could be a developmental assignment as well and staffed with someone possessing the necessary project-related expertise, who lacks global experience.
- The assignee remains responsible for his or her "normal" job duties in the home country; the home position is not backfilled.
- From 1-12 months in the host location.
- Unaccompanied by family. Home leave may be granted monthly or every quarter.
- Normally, no change in tax position. Company pays excess tax.
- A daily allowance or "per diem" is paid covering the cost of food (at home and away from home), laundry, personal care and transportation (unless transport is provided separately).
- Accommodation is provided by the employer, usually a serviced apartment or extended-stay hotel or dormitory (for non-office workers) with kitchen and laundry facilities within the unit.

### 19.2.3 Fly-in, fly-out or rotational assignment

A fly-in, fly-out assignment has the following characteristics:

- Pattern of ongoing/open-ended employment in a foreign location with limited local accommodation. The assignee returns home each evening or each weekend or alternates (rotates) between a period at home and a period at the work site. Reasons for physically returning home frequently can include host location hardship, host location cost or host location tax rules.

- Unaccompanied by family.
- Change in tax position.

Typically, rotation schedules are either 14 days on 14 days off or 30 days on 30 days off, depending on the duration of travel to the home country. Accommodation and meals are provided by the employer. There is often a rotation allowance which can include an inconvenience allowance, country allowance (depending where the host country is and the level of development, e.g. a rotation allowance to Afghanistan will be higher than a rotation allowance to Germany), and often partial replacement for overtime and other allowances if they are paid on a regular basis in the home country on normal work schedule rules.

### 19.2.4  Long-term international assignment

A long-term international assignment has the following characteristics:

- The purpose is to establish or manage a function, business unit or product line; hire local staff, or fulfil other objectives which require an extended full-time presence. Often the assignee's job in the home country is backfilled, even though the assignee remains employed by the home country entity. International assignments are sometimes referred to as secondments, because the primary employment relationship is maintained in the home country for salary, tax and social security purposes, while a secondary assignment letter is signed stating the terms and conditions in effect for the duration of the international assignment only.
- Duration is between one and three years, extendable to five years. Normally the assignee must be localised upon five years if they wish to remain in location at a sustainable cost, and because social security totalisation agreements between countries normally require foreigners to join (and contribute to) the local social security or provident fund system. If assignees do not wish to localise, they are repatriated or reassigned. If the company has not planned a next role the expatriate may resign from the company, giving their next employer the benefit of the global experience they gained at the former company's expense.
- Normally accompanied by family members, except for adult children.
- Change in tax position.
- Substantial change in reward package which would include dependent education at a suitable international school (if local schools are not compatible in terms of home country language or curriculum), tax equalisation, company-subsidised housing and, cost of living allowance (see section on cost of living calculation below.)
- Typically retain links to home country compensation systems, social security and any company-sponsored retirement benefits.

- Annual home leave provided for the assignee and accompanying family members with the purpose of maintaining both personal and work-related contacts, which are essential at time of repatriation. Some employers allow expatriates to use their home leave to visit alternate locations as long as the cost does not exceed home country airfare, but many employers are moving away from these policies to ensure the assignee is maintaining home country ties and avoid the perception of "company-paid vacations."

### 19.2.5 Permanent transfer

A permanent transfer has the following characteristics:

- Indefinite international change in place of work, within the same company. There is no intention of repatriation at the time of the move, and the home country duties are immediately passed to others or the role is backfilled.
- Accompanied by family.
- Change in tax position occurs when the former and new countries have different tax rates.
- Employed on terms and conditions of the host country employing company.
- No COLA, tax equalisation, company-lease, hardship or currency protections are provided, therefore it is essential to identify a permanent transfer as such from the start, to avoid the cost and complexity of an international assignment. Employees strongly prefer an expatriate remuneration package, so the local compensation package for a permanent transferee is normally based on a net-to-net calculation which determines the local gross salary requirement (in local currency) necessary to maintain the same net income after tax, housing and cost of living.

## 19.3 Philosophy, key concepts and definitions

Today's competitive global business climate means that employees increasingly have to work in various countries and return to the home base. Business leaders have to understand and use all of the tools available to ensure success. An effective, equitable approach to internal assignment remuneration is one of these powerful tools.

The first challenge when establishing an international assignment remuneration policy is deciding the proper place of international mobility within the overall business plan and within the talent management process. Some global organisations conduct extensive workforce planning, first to determine talent requirements by function and location, then to assess their ability to meet talent requirements through local hiring and promotion from within. Any remaining gap would then need to be filled through contract talent or global mobility. Without a deliberate workforce planning process, an organisation may find itself with a large number of costly expatriates and frustrated local staff who see the top jobs filled with non-local talent.

In terms of philosophy, some organisations view international assignments as part of the overall employment value proposition, and they use such opportunities to appeal to those seeking adventure, or perhaps as a necessary part of career development. Other organisations assume people do not want to leave home, and therefore include generous incentives to entice people to uproot and move.

Another common challenge when establishing an international assignment remuneration policy is the lack of consistent definitions of each element of international assignment remuneration and the underlying philosophy. The following definitions are all key elements of an international assignment policy.

- **Home-based salary:** This is the contractual salary the assignee is paid for performing the job. It is consistent with the home country market and the home-organisation pay scales.
- **Home net salary:** This is the home-based salary less hypothetical tax (the tax that the assignee would ordinarily have paid in the home country).
- **Cost of living index:** This is a figure that represents the difference in the cost of goods and services between a home and host location, exclusive of housing. For example, the COL index for an assignee sent to Paris, France from South Africa may be 160 or 1.6, meaning a defined market basket of goods and services would cost 1.6 times more in France than in South Africa. COL indices can be purchased from mobility data providers who conduct ongoing local pricing and analysis of cost of goods and services.
- **Cost of living allowance:** The cost of living allowance paid to an expatriate on a long-term assignment is intended to bridge the difference between the cost of goods and services between the home and host locations. It is calculated by multiplying the cost of living index by the home country spendable income. The home country spendable income refers to portion of a person's after-tax salary that is normally spent on goods and services based on their home location, family size and income.
- **Exchange rate:** This is the currency exchange rate between the two countries involved in the assignment (home country and host country). If an assignee is paid in one currency only, the exchange rate is normally set at the beginning of the assignment and reviewed annually or when there is a change in the rate which is greater than an agreed range, for example ±5% or ±10%. Some companies avoid the need to reconcile currency movements by using a split payroll whereby some compensation is paid at home and the "spendable" portion is paid locally in the host location.
- **Hardship or location allowance:** This is an allowance paid by most organisations when sending an employee into a location that has adverse living conditions in terms of political stability, infrastructure, communication, education, air and water quality, corruption, etc. Some organisations provide a standard allowance for all expatriates in a location (for example, 15% for all people posted to Mumbai, India), while others base the allowance on the difference in conditions between the home and host locations. In such case, an employee

transferring from a city similar to Mumbai may receive no allowance, while an employee from London or another less adverse location would receive an allowance.

- **Employee currency election:** This is the percentage split of the total assignment remuneration package which is paid in the host country and the home country, if the employer is willing to accommodate a split currency. The home country portion is typically to ensure that the expatriate is able to continue to meet home country commitments such as retirement fund contributions, home loans, university fees etc. Employers that allow split currency arrangements are less likely to agree to year-end currency reconciliation, since they are already allowing the employee to hedge against currency risk through split payroll.

A company's specific policies on international assignment remuneration will be aligned to its philosophy, as well as consideration of the following objectives:

- Provide consistent, equitable treatment for all international assignees, worldwide.
- Protect purchasing power.
- Recognise job level globally.
- Attract talent to take an assignment.
- Retain talent upon repatriation or localisation.
- Offer flexibility within limits and especially where tax effective.
- Be competitive.
- Address spouse support issues.
- Have a simple structure to provide seamless coverage for different scenarios.

## 19.4 Approaches to international assignment remuneration

The application of the above philosophies has resulted in the emergence of three broad approaches to international assignment remuneration:

- **Build-up method:** This method is also known as the "balance sheet method". It uses the home basic salary as a base salary, minus hypothetical tax, and builds on this by adding an international premium, a cost of living index and the exchange rate to deliver a net assignment package. The build-up method is used to maintain internal equity and to equalise the impact of host country tax.
- **Local market approach:** This approach uses the principle of applying the better of build-up or local market. It is used where a strong local market exists in the host country, and where the build-up method delivers less than the local market remuneration levels (for example, an assignee sent to a major first world country such as the United Kingdom or United States).
- **Internationally mobile expatriate:** This approach is used by large global multinational organisations, which often have a large pool of permanent expatriates who move from one country to the next on assignments. The internationally mobile expatriate approach is used

to put all expatriates on an equal footing, regardless of nationality as well as countries to where they are expatriate.

## 19.5 Positioning international assignment remuneration in the total reward system

The following figure shows a typical positioning of the build-up method:

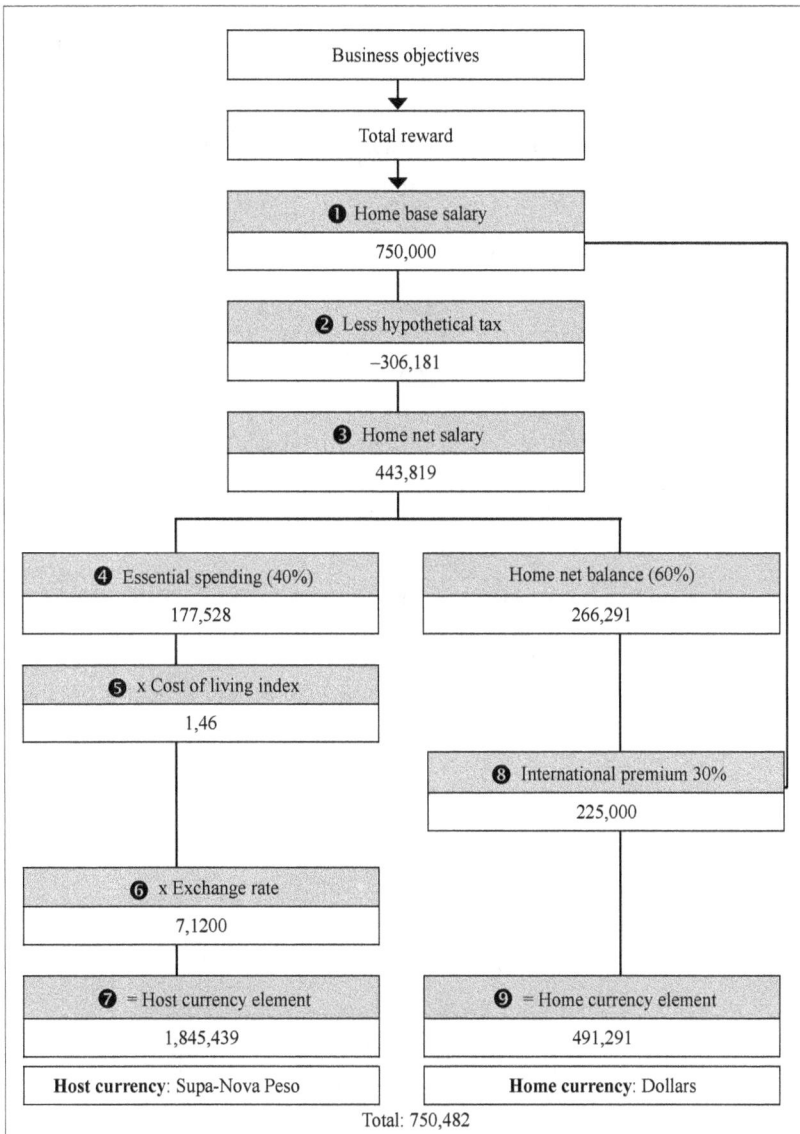

*Figure 19.1: Build-up method*

## 19.6  Design considerations

The approach to expatriate remuneration differs from one organisation to another, and even within a single organisation, depending on a number of factors:

- Purpose of assignment.
- Length of assignment.
- Home and host location.
- Job level.

Designing an international assignment remuneration policy should include the organisation's position on each of the elements reflected in Table 19.1 below. Typical applications of each element are shown for each of the three broad approaches.

*Table 19.1: Comparison of approaches for international assignments*

| Remuneration | Build-up method | Local market approach | Internationally mobile expatriate |
|---|---|---|---|
| **Purpose and prevalence** | Used to keep the employee economically whole, neutralising differences in taxes, housing cost and other living costs.<br><br>Used by a majority of organisations for long-term assignments. | Where local talent is available, repatriation is not business critical and where the employee has an interest or desire to live and work in the new location. The overriding principle and purpose of local market-based packages is local internal equity, followed by cost control, as it is nearly always less expensive than a build-up approach. Used by a growing number of organisations for long-term assignments, and by a majority of organisations for locally hired foreigners, permanent transfers and localised expatriates. | Used to put all group expatriates on an equal footing regardless of nationality. Employees resign from home country and re-locate to group organisation, usually in a tax-free country.<br><br>Used by few large global groups with significant numbers of assignees. Also referred to as career expatriates. |

| Remuneration | Build-up method | Local market approach | Internationally mobile expatriate |
|---|---|---|---|
| **Market relationship** | Contractual base salary is stated in home currency and maintained at home country competitive levels, under home country salary policies and structures. | Salary is established and maintained according to local (host) country pay structures and policies. Some foreigners may be paid at the high or low end of local structures depending on their origin, but local pay equity is the eventual goal. | International base salary typically in US$ or Euro, based on an average "country basket" of competitive salary levels. Some organisations establish a global employment company (GEC) in a designated country, and all expatriates are employed by this GEC, subject to a common pay scale, set of allowances, and hypothetical tax rate. |
| **Tax philosophy** | Assignees neither lose nor gain as a result of the assignment, in terms of home and host taxes. | Taxed in host country, and potentially by home country if the home country taxes worldwide income (e.g., American or Chinese citizens). Net pay depends on tax laws and structure of package. | Taxed in host country, taking advantage of tax-free home country status. |
| **Hypothetical tax** | Tax deduction applied to the expatriate's salary based on the hypothetical "stay at home" tax rate. | N/A | Generic model used to calculate home net salary. |
| **Home net salary** | Result of home base salary less hypothetical tax. | N/A | Result of home base salary less hypothetical tax. |
| **Cost of living allowance (COLA)** | COLAs are used to neutralise the effects of differences between the cost of goods and services between the home and host country, based on the expatriate's salary level and accompanying family size.<br><br>Applied to essential spending only (typically 40% of home net salary). | N/A | Since a common home country is assumed, a "location allowance" may be given to all career expatriates working at the same location, regardless of the individual's origin. The allowance may be based on relative cost of living only, or may be based on differences.<br><br>Applied to essential spending only (typically 40% of home net salary). |

| Remuneration | Build-up method | Local market approach | Internationally mobile expatriate |
|---|---|---|---|
| **Exchange rate** | Fluctuations in exchange rates are neutralised by paying the "local spendable" portion of salary (which includes the COLA) in the host location in local currency. The remainder of the salary is paid in the home country in the home country currency. This requires a split payroll arrangement. Alternatively, all compensation is paid in either home or host currency, and a year-end reconciliation is prepared to correct for currency movements.<br><br>COL is linked to exchange rate, which is used to deliver local amount of assignment salary. | Paid in local currency where possible but may be paid in US$ or home currency for locations where local currency is considered volatile. | Paid in local currency, HQ or designated home currency, split currency or US$ if allowed. COL is linked to exchange rate. COL exchange rate is used to deliver local amount of assignment salary. |
| **Mobility premium** | May include a hazard allowance based on 3rd party location ratings (measuring such things as pollution, quality of healthcare, schools, transportation infrastructure, communications, etc.) May also include a mobility premium of 10-15% to compensate for the disruption of relocating and living in a foreign country. | N/A | Less prevalent for internationally mobile (career) expatriates, as they have "signed up" for a mobile career and therefore do not need additional incentives to leave home.<br><br>A hazard pay component may be included in a location allowance. |

| Remuneration | Build-up method | Local market approach | Internationally mobile expatriate |
|---|---|---|---|
| **Car benefit** | Excluded from assignment salary calculation and provided in host country in line with local host policy where appropriate. | In line with host country policy. | Excluded from assignment salary calculation and provided in host country in line with local host policy where appropriate. |
| **Housing** | Housing typically provided in host country, often furnished, and includes utilities, water, lights and housekeeper, depending on host country policy.<br><br>No involvement by organisation in home country housing arrangement, but caution against selling. | Housing typically provided in lesser developed host locations. In more developed locations, housing is the employee's responsibility, unless having the company lease is more advantageous from a tax or legal perspective.<br><br>No involvement by organisation in home country housing arrangement, but caution against selling. | Housing typically provided in host country, often furnished, and includes utilities, water, lights and housekeeper, depending on host country policy.<br><br>No involvement by organisation in home country housing arrangement, but caution against selling. |
| **Employee currency election** | May allow assignee to elect a mix of how much in host and home once a year. | Assignee elects a mix of how much in host and home once a year. | Assignee elects a mix of how much in host and home once a year. |
| **Variable incentive bonus** | Remain on home country scheme based on home base, but in line with host country and individual performance.<br><br>Variable pay is designed to ensure that total reward (TR) is competitive within home country. Often tax equalised. | Participate in host country scheme. Based on host base in line with host country and individual performance.<br><br>Variable pay is designed to ensure that TR is competitive within host country. | Remain on home country scheme based on home base, but in line with host country and individual performance.<br><br>Variable pay is designed to ensure that TR is competitive within home country/international market. Often tax equalised. |

| Remuneration | Build-up method | Local market approach | Internationally mobile expatriate |
|---|---|---|---|
| **Retirement benefits** | Remain on home country retirement scheme (most prevalent). Basis of retirement funding is home base as assignee is expected to return and retire in home country. | Remain on home country retirement scheme, where possible. Basis of retirement funding is home base as assignee is expected to return and retire in home country. If the assignee converts to local by resigning from the home organisation, retirement funding reverts to the host country. | Remain on home country retirement scheme. Basis of retirement funding is home base as assignee is expected to return and retire in home country. |
| **Medical benefits** | Some organisations allow assignees to remain on home country medical scheme, and others provide offshore medical cover. If in there is a difference in medical costs between what the home country provides and the costs in the host country, this is settled by a claim.<br><br>The majority of organisations provide assignees with emergency evacuation cover. | Medical cover and benefits are provided locally in line with host country policy.<br><br>The majority of organisations provide assignees with emergency evacuation cover. | Most organisations provide offshore medical cover.<br><br>The majority of organisations provide assignees with emergency evacuation cover. |
| **Guaranteed 13th month pay** | 13th month is paid if it is part of the home salary policy. If paid, it is based on the gross home country base salary and tax equalised. | 13th month is paid if it is part of the host salary policy. If paid, it is based on the gross host country base salary. | 13th month is paid if it is part of the home salary policy. If paid, it is based on the gross home country base salary. |
| **Relocation allowance** | Relocation is generally paid for household effects and personal items, but only some organisations pay for the removal of luxury/general items. | Relocation is generally paid for household effects and personal items, but only some organisations pay for the removal of luxury/general items. | Relocation is generally paid for household effects and personal items, but only some organisations pay for the removal of luxury/general items. |

| Remuneration | Build-up method | Local market approach | Internationally mobile expatriate |
|---|---|---|---|
| **Disturbance allowance** | Outward disturbance allowance of one month's net home base salary.<br><br>Return disturbance allowance of one month's net home base salary. | Outward disturbance allowance of one month's net home base salary.<br><br>Return disturbance allowance of one month's net home base salary. | Outward disturbance allowance of one month's net home base salary.<br><br>Return disturbance allowance of one month's net home base salary. |
| **Education policy** | Provide appropriate education support for assignees' children in order to minimise the disruption to their education caused by an international assignment. Employer carries tax cost. | Local education policy applies. | Provide appropriate education support for assignees' children in order to minimise the disruption to their education caused by an international assignment. Employer carries tax cost. |
| **Partner support policy** | No attempt to compensate for loss of income of spouse. May provide partner support, e.g. budget to study or find a new job or an allowance to take up a hobby. | N/A | No attempt to compensate for loss of income of spouse. May provide partner support, e.g. budget to study or find a new job. |
| **Flights** | Two flights per year for unaccompanied assignees. One flight per year for accompanied assignees. Additional flights are provided on compassionate grounds, typically on the death of a family member or next of kin. | Two flights per year for unaccompanied assignees. One flight per year for accompanied assignees. Additional flights are provided on compassionate grounds, typically on the death of a family member or next of kin. | Two flights per year for unaccompanied assignees. One flight per year for accompanied assignees. Additional flights are provided on compassionate grounds, typically on the death of a family member or next of kin. |

The above table presents prevalent practices associated with the three approaches. Rigorous and careful benchmarking is often required in advance to ensure your practices are properly aligned to business needs, your industry and for the locations involved. Further, it is important to be aware that the "expat community" is often well connected and assignees are known to compare details about their remuneration packages.

## 19.7 Critical success factors

As important as international assignment remuneration is to an organisation, management often continues to undervalue the impact it has on assignees' family lives, careers and personal finances. The critical success factors to good international assignment package design involve the following:

- Seek input from current and former assignees in the design process.
- Make use of research information and current best practice.
- Make use of tax experts regarding tax in both host and home countries (reciprocal tax agreements make this essential).
- Candidates' soft-skill abilities (EQ) should be assessed before the candidates are assigned.
- Typically utilise international assignments as developmental opportunities for high-potential employees.
- Companies should invest time and effort in managing employee and spouse expectations.
- Companies should track employee career development over the long-term (more than five years) time horizon.
- Ensure all expatriates understand the policies and guidelines for calculating each element of their pay package.
- Secure a good provider for the international assignment administration function.
- Review assignments annually and plan ahead, as assignees have an incentive to stay longer than required due to the high levels of assignment remuneration.

## 19.7.1   Benchmark findings and lessons learned

The following are typical benchmark findings for best practices in international assignment remuneration. This could serve as a lessons learnt checklist for an expatriate pay scheme design:

- Companies generally assist with tax compliance.
- Companies strive to put international assignee on equal footing with what they had at home.
- Most companies use external consultants for overall design, COL data and parity.
- Many companies ask the international assignees or accompanying spouse to complete a readiness assessment to ensure they have the necessary attitudes and cultural skills and adaptability to succeed in the new location.
- Successful localisation of expatriates who wish to remain in the host location (i.e. make it their new home location) requires at least two conditions: the option of localisation must be stated in their original assignment contract or in a written policy, and the expatriate must be interested in remaining in the location indefinitely.

Other important design considerations include:

- Soft issues such as the spouse's loss of employment, repatriation and re-skilling.
- Volatile currency against the major currencies in the past.
- Selling houses and cars in the home country at a loss.
- Provision of a car benefit and social club membership in the host country.

- Communication with expatriates about tax, cost of living, currency or other complex matters.
- Children or dependant parents staying behind in the home country.

## 19.8 Current issues

Any international assignment remuneration policy must always take into account the fact that there is a greater number of dynamics involved with expatriate pay than with that of local employees. Many issues are still being grappled with by organisations that have been managing international assignees for many years. Some of the current issues being debated are the following:

- Hard-currency trend is on the decline (used only in highly unstable markets). Open-ended local-based packages assume local currency, local taxes, etc.
- Assignees from low cost of living/low-paying countries will always tend to earn less than assignees doing the same job in a host country and who come from higher cost of living/ higher-paying countries, using the build-up model.

A few solutions to "trailing spouse" issues are the following:

- Help the spouse to find a job.
- Assist with the choice of a career by:
  ○ Preparing a resumé/CV.
  ○ Obtaining a work permit.
  ○ Organising career counselling.
  ○ Reimbursing for tuition.

In addition, the following continue to cause problems:

- There is a significant trend towards a dual or hybrid approach to international remuneration.
- Home needs (to cover commitments in home country currency) are often overlooked or neglected.
- Host needs (to cover local day-to-day living costs and fixed currency in local situations) are often not adequately covered.
- Expatriate remuneration continues to be in a state of flux in response to the changing world in which we work.

The statistics of expatriates returning home and leaving the organisation within a few years is high. Organisations often do not take the time to focus on a repatriation programme. It is assumed that because the person used to live in a certain place, "he (or she) will be fine". Suggestions to ensure a smoother repatriation and secure longer tenure include the following:

- Ensure that the person reintegrates into a real job of equal or higher complexity and status than was the situation when the person left.
- Ensure that the spouse and family are thoughtfully integrated back into the community.

- Avoid saying anything such as: "Things here are different now. Where have you been?"
- Be open to new thoughts and ideas the person may have learnt while away.
- Induction back into the organisation, focusing on what has changed, new strategies and new focus areas is of the utmost importance.

Many methods of paying expatriates exist, and this issue is a huge debate within remuneration committees. Whether to pay them in home-based pay or host-based pay must be decided on, however a combination is often best. How to pay them often depends on their job, status and personal commitments. As a rule of thumb, expatriates should be neither better nor worse off.

## 19.9  Summary

The main types of international assignments are business trips, project assignments, fly-in fly-out assignments and permanent transfers. Arguably this is one of the most complex areas of remuneration. In addition to all the normal remuneration considerations, one also needs to consider the cost of living indices, exchange rates, international premium indices and the ability to ensure that the employee is no worse off. A build-up (balance sheet) approach has traditionally been the most common methodology to setting expatriate compensation, and the overwhelming trend is to localise employees as fast as possible due to exorbitant costs.

## 19.10  Self-evaluation questions

1  Name the main types of international employment.
2  What are some of the key elements of an international assignment policy?
3  Name three approaches to international assignment remuneration?
4  What are some of the main issues with international assignees/ expatriates?
5  Describe the balance sheet approach of building up an equalised remuneration package.

---

**Case study: Guidelines to management – reward and recognition at ABC Group**

The following example will help understand international assignment policy. The name ABC Group and the issues are not those of an actual organisation, but represent the typical issues organisations have to deal with and what the main elements of the policy are to satisfy the difficulties experienced.

**Introduction**

The remuneration of international assignees at ABC Group has long been a point of discussion. Increasing numbers of assignees have been sent to various countries in the past few years. No formal policy has been established. The typical practice was to make the potential assignee an attractive enough net salary, offered in hard currency (usually US dollars), and converted into local currency on a monthly basis. This worked for a while, but lately the group has experienced several difficulties:

---

- Assignees complain that their buying power is being eroded by the weakening US dollar (they are getting poorer each month in the local currency).
- Assignees are given an organisation car in the host country, but they often get transferred back home just months before the vehicle is to become their own in terms of the organisation car scheme rules.
- A shortage of US dollars and high currency conversion costs makes it difficult to repatriate funds out of the host country.
- Assignees decline internal job postings back in the home country as they feel the salary is too low and they cannot move back for less pay.

### *What we mean by international assignment remuneration policy*

ABC Group's response to the difficulties it was experiencing was to establish principles to guide the remuneration of international assignees. These principles are outlined below.

The ABC Group assignment reward package aims to:

- Provide consistent equitable treatment for all international assignees, worldwide.
- Protect purchasing power against changed spending patterns.
- Recognise job size.
- Provide "reasonable gain".
- Offer flexibility within limits and where tax effective.
- Be competitive.
- Address spouse support issues.
- Have a simple structure to provide seamless coverage for different scenarios

The principles set out in this document provide the framework for international assignment remuneration and benefits for the typical expatriate assignment of two to three years duration.

## The ABC group assignment remuneration system

ABC Group will use a dual approach to international assignment remuneration, based on the "better of home or host" principle. For the majority of assignments, a standard ABC Group build-up methodology will apply. This model is explained in the following pages of this document. However, where a clearly established market rate exists for the Group's local employees and where this would typically deliver higher net salaries to assignees than the Group's build-up methodology, ABC Group will seek to position assignment salaries around this market rate.

For assignments into the United States of America and the United Kingdom, the local market rate will be applied only to assignees from countries for which the Group build-up methodology typically delivers less than the market-rate salary. The framework of the build-up methodology is as shown in Figure 19.2.

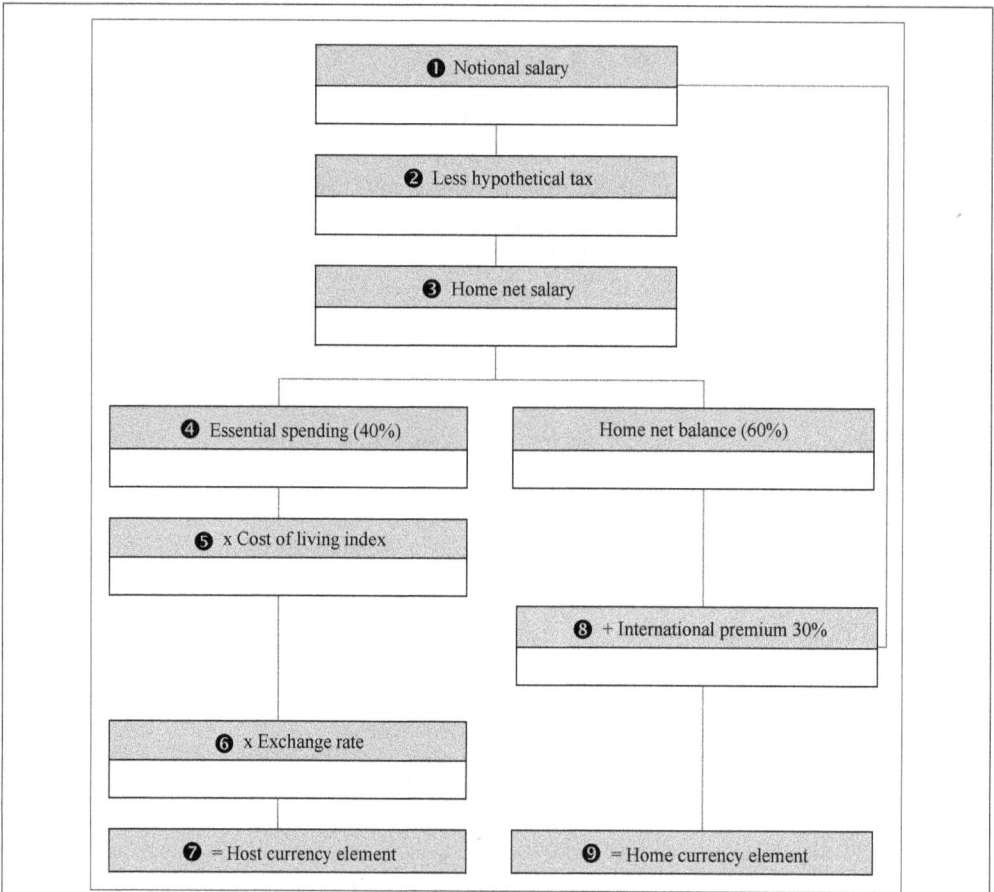

*Figure 19.2: Framework of the build-up methodology*

- **Notional salary:** This is the current home country base salary. Where appropriate, this figure may include the value of any flexible benefits which are forfeited in the home country as the result of the assignment.

- **Hypothetical tax:** This represents the tax for which the assignee would have been responsible in their home country. Where appropriate, the calculation of this figure will take into account tax dispensations that would have applied to standard organisation contributions and the value of any standard home country benefits which are "lost" as a result of the assignment. Tax dispensations which could arise from additional contributions to the organisation or personal benefit plans will not normally be included in the calculation.

- **Home net salary:** This is the notional salary less hypothetical tax.

- **Essential spending and home net balance:** This split has been determined based upon consultant and government data.

- **Essential spending:** The 40 percent essential spending amount reflects the proportion of income typically spent on essential day-to-day living, for example, groceries, household goods, clothing and entertainment. While an employee is on assignment, ABC Group's policy is to protect the assignee's purchasing power of these essential daily living costs. ABC Group specifically does not include in this figure spending on items such as utilities, furnishings and medical treatment, which are typically provided by the host organisation.

- **Home net balance:** This is the balance of the home country net salary after the split for essential spending. The 60 percent home net balance includes discretionary spending, which is the amount the assignee chooses to spend on home country housing, savings, investments, holidays, and so on.

- **Cost of living (COL) index:** In order to protect the assignee's daily spending power from cost of living differences, ABC Group applies a COL index to the essential spending proportion of the assignee's income. The index measures the relative cost of the same basket of goods and services in the home and host countries. This data are obtained from independent consultants and will normally be adjusted annually. Interim adjustments may be applied if the index changes by more than 15 percent.

- **Exchange rate:** This is normally a "fixed" exchange rate which is set annually at the beginning of the organisation's fiscal year. In countries where interim cost of living adjustments are made, ABC Group will use the appropriate exchange rate at the time the adjustment is made. The rate used will apply to any proportion of the assignment salary the assignee chooses to have paid in the local currency.

- **Host currency element:** This is the value in local currency of the assignee's essential spending after the cost of living index and exchange rate have been applied. While the assignee may elect to draw more or less than this amount in local currency, ABC Group believes this is a reasonable guide to how much the assignee may need to spend on day-to-day living in the assignment location.

- **International premium:** This is calculated as a percentage of the assignee's notional salary. Many assignments involve significant disruption to the pattern of life to which assignees and their families are accustomed in their "home" country. If this is the case, ABC Group recognises the disruption by including an international premium as part of the assignment salary build-up. The international premium is intended to provide both remuneration for the social and domestic disruption and a reasonable financial incentive for the assignment. It is based on consultants' data and competitive market practice, and takes account of factors such as security, educational facilities, health care, language and cultural differences.

- **Home currency element:** This is the net value in home currency of the balance of the assignment salary (that is, home net balance plus international premium).

- *Salary delivery:* ABC Group recommends that assignees elect to split their salary payments between home and host currency in accordance with the figures quoted in their assignment salary build-up (subject to local legislation and payroll facilities). However, they may elect a different split, subject to any minimum required in their home country, to meet ongoing commitments to organisation benefit programmes.
- *Exchange rate:* The ABC Group exchange rate quoted in the salary build-up will apply to any proportion of the assignment salary the assignee chooses to have paid the local currency.

## Sample expatriate philosophy for ABC group

### *General principles*

- Rewards will ensure that ABC Group remains globally competitive and consequently is able to attract and retain competent staff.
- Rewards will be structured to facilitate the deployment of staff to different locations while ensuring that local requirements are met (for example, pay within local citizen scales).
- Rewards will be able to recognise the differences between individuals concerning country of origin, current location deployed to, and future career plans in terms of deployment against a logical and justifiable framework.
- ABC Group will meet all the statutory requirements of the country/location of the operation, for example, tax and labour legislation.
- Rewards will include conditions of employment which facilitate individual focus on the work, such as:
  - Recognition of expatriate/temporary nature.
  - Ease of settling into new location.
  - Organisation-provided or -facilitated medical aid or health care.
- Practices will be aligned on a global basis.
- Rewards will be justifiable to a large employee body in order to maintain a sense of internal equity.
- Reward will support business strategy and be aligned to the organisation's values.

### *Philosophy*

*"In ABC Group we manage rewards to best practice standards in support of the organisation's strategic objectives."*

### *Strategy*

The expatriate reward strategy states the corporate values in terms of rewards and emphasises the connection between rewards and employee behaviour by creating an environment that is conducive to performance and ensures the integrity and legitimacy of the total deployment process. This is accomplished by:

- Differentiating appropriately between employees through reward methods thereby rewarding on the basis of value and contribution.
- A commitment to attract, assign and deploy appropriately qualified and experienced expatriates in an efficient and effective manner.

### Principles of expatriate reward

ABC Group's HR values provide the foundation for the following nine principles of expatriate remuneration:

### Relative worth

The relative worth of one job to another will be determined by a job evaluation system.

### Market relatedness

ABC Group pays on market median. In countries or locations where ABC Group has a significant presence and/or where a well-defined skills market exists, local market data will guide local expatriate remuneration to align payments in those locations to that of citizen employees. In countries where the skills market is less developed or where no market information is available, expatriate rates of pay will be benchmarked against expatriate rates of pay in the country/location or a similar country/location.

### Taxation

ABC Group will ensure compliance with the tax legislation of the countries where we operate. In some economies, it may be necessary for remuneration to be quoted as net of tax to the employee, with the organisation ensuring that the appropriate tax is paid.

### Cost of living

Differences in cost of living are accounted for on a "no benefit, no loss" principle when compared to a home base. Expatriate cost equalisation is provided for through standard cost of living indices reported by organisations that specialise in this field.

### Performance

Expatriate performance is recognised during the annual salary review in both the basic/monthly salary review as well as bonus payments provided for in the salary review mandate.

### Quality of living or hardship

Differences in quality of living or hardship caused by, for example, climatic conditions, availability of goods and services, education standards and work conditions, are measured by a hardship rating instrument. A premium has to be paid to continue to attract employees to these bodies.

### Assignment intent

The reason for the particular assignment influences certain terms and conditions of expatriate remuneration. The duration, future or past skills deployment and role at the location influences the terms and conditions of an individual employee. Different assignment intents may therefore lead to different reward structures at the same location (even for the same work). These are justifiable against a pre-defined framework.

### Benefits

The organisation will provide employees with benefits where practical and where such benefits are commonly provided to expatriate employees (i.e. aligned to market practices). The reward structures will, however, reflect the value of such benefits as part of total remuneration. Retirement funding is considered to be an integral part of the organisation's benefit structure, aimed at long-term career and retention.

### Ease of administration

Expatriate remuneration is complex and highly differentiated due to locations, tax legislation and assignments. Where at all possible, cash will be provided in lieu of benefits. Systems must be supplied and streamlined to ease administration.

# CHAPTER 20

# Remuneration Committee and Boardroom Fees

## 20.1 Background and context

At a time when hunting for the "next Enron" is an international sport, shareholders and institutional investors are hyper-sensitive about the governance decisions taken by governing bodies. Enhanced levels of transparency are demanded and there are intense levels of scrutiny on any form of what is considered to be insider selling, detailed financial disclosure, or any type of reward given to directors and especially the chief executive officer (CEO) – all issues that feed the image of corporate corruption and executive greed. Many stakeholders and the media are also baying for blood and newspaper headlines like "The fat cats are still grabbing all the cream" hit sensitive nerves. There is a rising tide of resistance against executives who accept large incentives and receive huge pay rises despite poor financial performance being declared.

Executive remuneration is more complex than meets the eye, thus a strategic perspective on remuneration requires research that looks beyond how much executives earn. This dichotomy of attraction, motivation and retention of good executives versus tough corporate governance, shareholder scrutiny and media spotlights, places remuneration decision-makers in a difficult position.

An organisation's ability to understand the "drivers" of remuneration policy and CEO pay is therefore a critical component in determining its present and future success in good remuneration governance. Table 20.1 below summarises these drivers of remuneration levels.

*Table 20.1: Drivers of Remuneration Levels*

| 1. | **Organisation size** | Turnover, number of employees, value of assets |
|----|----------------------|-----------------------------------------------|
| 2. | **Organisation performance** | Profitability, return on investment, value added |
| 3. | **Executive-specific factors** | Age, experience, tenure, career path |
| 4. | **Organisation structure** | Holding, subsidiary or single-unit organisation; capital or labour intensive |
| 5. | **Job-specific factors** | Level of decision-making, consequence of error, organisation level |
| 6. | **Job complexity** | Job-sizing instruments are used to determine job size |
| 7. | **Strategy** | Remuneration philosophy, salary surveys, geographic footprint, extent of regulation and competition |

## 20.2  Impact of pay policy on organisations

Well-designed remuneration systems play a strategic role by promoting organisational success in highly competitive markets in which technological change constantly influences how employees perform their jobs. Indeed, some go so far as to argue that there are strong links between remuneration system design and organisational performance.

There are many examples of pay systems that have gone wrong and unhitching from them is difficult. To alleviate this, more information is needed to understand the impact of pay policy changes in organisations. In its simplest form, remuneration policy has positive and negative effects on organisations. There is solid evidence that remuneration decisions affect business performance. Strategic differences do matter and governing bodies need to make well-informed decisions without fearing a backlash from investors or having to deal with unintended consequences.

Corporate image and governance have a large influence on the market price and perceived value of an organisation. The collapse of Lehman Brothers, Enron, Wells Fargo and many other corporations has highlighted the need for good corporate governance with regard to remuneration and CEO pay.[1] Investors, analysts and stakeholders are nervous, and it can cost organisations dearly if they get the slightest sniff of something untoward.

Members of the committees making remuneration policy decisions are under the spotlight, and there is nothing more important than restoring investor confidence in the governance of executive and board member pay. In today's best-performing companies, the role of the remuneration committee is vital.[2] The committee is responsible for designing remuneration schemes that are understandable by its employees, defensible to its stakeholders and strongly tied to meeting the business objectives. A well-designed incentive remuneration programme provides a sustainable, strategic advantage for an organisation. With "say on pay" giving investors more and more leverage to influence the remuneration policy, a good relationship between the Chairperson of the Remuneration Committee and those investors are critical in order to solicit support for the remuneration policy vote.

## 20.3  Remuneration frameworks and models

Remuneration committee members need a good appreciation of remuneration systems and the organisation's context. Generally, a remuneration model or framework is adopted. Table 20.2 highlights the different remuneration elements.

---

1    Bussin & Blair, 2015; Bussin & Nel, 2015; Bussin & Modau, 2015.

2    Bezuidenhout, Bussin & Coetzee, 2018.

*Table 20.2: Primary Purpose of Remuneration Elements*

| Remuneration element | Purpose |
|---|---|
| Base salary | Pays for overall job requirements, accountability, complexity of tasks, and diversity of tasks. |
| Short-term incentive | Variable component to reward contribution to annual business plan. The most effective measures are revenue growth, earnings, earnings growth, and measures of profitability. Some portion of this bonus is also contingent on individual performance and division or group performance. |
| Long-term incentive | Used to focus attention on longer-term strategic imperatives, as well as to identify more closely with strategic goals, particularly an increase in shareholder value. This element is crucial in retaining employees. |
| Benefits or perquisites | Provides special payments and programmes that may set the organisation apart from others (may include items such as first class air travel, organisation car, enhanced medical care, and supplemental retirement programmes). |

In line with current trends, many companies are moving towards output-based pay, that is, paying for completed tasks and results produced as opposed to paying for activities or inputs. Remuneration committees (RemCos) need to decide whether the emphasis is on inputs or outputs and ensure alignment of all HR systems. For example, if you have an output-based incentive scheme, you would do well to have an output- based performance management system.

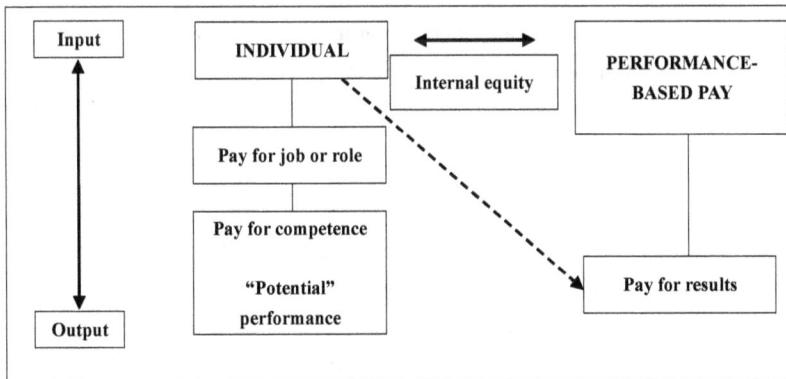

*Figure 20.1: Remuneration model: Input and output*

## 20.4 Structure of executive pay

Executive remuneration refers to the fixed pay, short- and long-term incentives, and related benefits awarded to those who occupy the most senior decision-making positions in private and public sector enterprises.[3] This normally includes the CEO and executives in the direct reporting

3    Mmolaeng & Bussin, 2012.

line. In larger corporations, the executive group may include two or even three levels below the CEO as the group that defines and implements the broad business strategy of the organisation.[4]

We start from the position that the determination of aggregate remuneration paid to people at these levels is required to meet several objectives:

- It needs to reflect the unique capabilities required for the leadership roles they fill, and their individual worth and value in the executive labour market.
- It must recognise their individual contribution to the financial success and growth of their respective organisations.
- It must take account of the uncertainty of employment in a business environment increasingly characterised by shorter-term appointments and the impact of mergers and acquisitions on executive tenure.
- More specifically, this very senior group of employees is accountable for safeguarding and growing the funds that shareholders invest. In this respect, there is a growing expectation that their own remuneration will, in some significant way, reflect the financial outcomes they provide for the enterprise owners.

There is general agreement that some of the larger corporations need to provide internationally competitive remuneration levels for their corporate leaders to compete successfully in a global marketplace. This is reinforced by the growing practice of opening the recruitment process for leadership positions in major companies to international talent. A growing number of large corporations draw more than half of their revenue from offshore operations, exposing their executives to a more international labour market, including remuneration packages. The significant issue is that although Asian and African remuneration levels are generally below those of Western economies, all are increasingly influenced by international trends in both the structure and quantum of executive remuneration.

The last 15 years have seen a significant shift in the mix of executive pay. Many corporations around the world now largely follow the United States of America's model of pay, with a growing emphasis on short- and long-term incentive payments, and a corresponding reduction in the proportion of fixed pay. Each component is typically expressed as a percentage of the total or aggregate reward when describing the executive remuneration structure within an organisation. The mix of fixed to variable, and within the variable components the mix of short- and long-term incentives, will generally differ depending on the level of the individual executive. The clear trend is for more senior executives to have a larger proportion of their total remuneration in variable pay.

---

4    Bussin, Hewitt & Wufflers, 2016; Coetzer, Bussin & Geldenhuys, 2017; Naidoo, Hewitt & Bussin, 2019.

## 20.4.1 Key issues in executive pay determination

Executive pay is a sensitive issue, particularly as companies issue their annual reports complete with remuneration details of the top executives. There are three key issues that consistently inform public comment on executive pay. First, do executives deserve the amounts they are paid? Secondly, are the variable components linked to appropriate measures of performance? And finally, is the overall remuneration structured and determined in a way that is defensible and credible to shareholders, the business media, and the community in general?

*Do executives deserve the amounts they are paid?*

There are many perspectives in this regard, and it is an area that is often exaggerated. The first concerns the essential issue of supply and demand. There is general agreement that there are unique competencies and skills required to succeed in organisational leadership roles. This clearly means that the available talent pool is select and limited. Not only is this pool small, but various business situations require highly specific skill sets. For example, the start-up phase of a business will require leadership capabilities and characteristics different from dynamic growth, turnaround or divestiture stages. National organisations are very different from multinational organisations, listed from non-listed, etc. In the executive labour market, the bar for success has been set higher as a result of the growing levels of competition (and related performance requirements) following the rapid extension of global markets and ongoing deregulation of industries (for example, utilities and telecommunications).

The logical consequence of this approach suggests executive labour-market segmentation based on supply and demand of specific experiences, skills and leadership capacities. Within this implicit market, executives who demonstrate a track record attract an individual premium based on their individual past record of success. The share market demonstrates this notion of "individual market value" through upward share price movements following news of the appointment of a high-profile and successful CEO.

The second perspective has to do with whether or not executives have a measurable impact on the organisation's business performance. Certainly, in the mind of some critics, the emphasis on executives and their impact on term performance is dominated by external circumstances, while managerial actions (such as quality of strategic planning) are important for the longer term. On this basis, executives clearly shape the future progress and success of their enterprises.

*Is performance pay linked to appropriate performance measures?*

There are strong and growing demands worldwide to make a significant proportion of executive pay contingent on performance. But which performance measures ought to relate to executive reward? The majority of short-term (annual) incentive pay plans are based around performance against traditional financial indices (for example, operating income, earnings before interest and tax, operating profit after tax). Clearly, these are important in tracking an organisation's success, however they tend to emphasise singular aspects of performance and ignore the capital invested in the organisation. For this reason, a growing number of organisations use financial measures that relate to capital investment, typically return on equity and return on capital employed. Companies are also increasingly rewarding executives for achievement of non-financial performance measures related to customers, market share, employees, corporate social responsibility, innovation, and operational effectiveness.

The investment community sees the primary role of management as the creation of wealth for the shareholders, thereby creating the need for a more direct correlation between shareholder returns and executive rewards. This emphasis leads to remuneration plans that measure performance against gains in share price or total shareholder return. Many organisations index their share price or total shareholder returns against a select comparator group of companies. These approaches aim to link the interests of executives with those of shareholders, but they too have limitations. First, the share prices are open to a range of influences outside the control of management (for example, cyclical economic swings, general business environment, international trends, and government actions). Second, share price targets measured over a specific period do not necessarily reflect sustained changes in fundamental shareholder value. Similarly, where share price gains against a comparator group are used, the end result is a relative, rather than an absolute, measure of performance. That is, organisation A's share price may fall, but the decline is less than the comparison benchmark and the performance target is met. On the one hand, we reward management for relative value preservation. However, from a shareholder's perspective, absolute value has declined, thereby defeating the objectives of providing a direct link between executive pay and shareholder returns. The issue is that executive incentive plans need to have an equal focus on the development and execution of business strategy, not just measurement of the annual financial or economic outcomes.

Some see the traditional value add-style value measurement as a secondary issue. While shareholder value is measured in the capital market, it is created in the product market. To create value for shareholders, the focus first needs to be on creating value for customers. The value-based management approach places the emphasis for executive performance on the allocation of capital to agreed strategic initiatives, translation of these initiatives into key performance indicators with clear and measurable goals, and assessing performance against those value creation targets. Therefore, executive rewards are linked to the creation of customer value, which in turn increases the value of the business.

### Design, structure and determination of executive pay

In the context used here, the remuneration structure refers to the relationship between fixed pay and the performance-based, variable components of pay. But an effective structure requires an equally effective design to ensure that variable pay is not simply used or regarded as deferred pay. Poorly designed plans may well have a structure that provides for a significant percentage of variable pay, but in practice the issue is how much of an incentive will be awarded, rather than whether or not any incentive payment at all has been earned. The implication is clear: executive pay plans need to have both a structure and design that promotes the variability and performance-related nature of short- and long-term incentives.

With regard to the determination of pay, there is always a concern among shareholders (and the community in general) that directors and executives are in a position to influence their own remuneration significantly. This is the reason for the widespread introduction of independent board remuneration committees as an integral part of corporate governance. Nevertheless, this form of self-regulation requires some degree of transparency to protect shareholder interests and maintain the credibility of corporate law. The governance models of most countries promote committee membership consisting only of non-executive directors. This reinforces and supports the required probity and independence of remuneration decision-making as the remuneration process is a critical aspect of people management.

## 20.5  Current trends and issues in linking executive pay to performance

### 20.5.1  Short-term incentives

There has been a clear shift in the preferred style of short-term incentive (STI) plans adopted by companies over the past years. A major feature of this change has been a movement away from discretionary bonus plans which are determined by the board after the fact, to target-based plans where specific performance requirements and contingent reward outcomes are set in advance, and after the financial year, subject to having met the targets, payment is made.

Discretionary bonus plans have fallen out of favour because of their inherent subjectivity and uncertainty. Payments typically depended on the judgement of the board or CEO with few, if any, guidelines defined for determining individual amounts. While the bonus may be received – and valued – as recognition for a job well done, there is usually no link to specific achievements related to the recipient. As a result, bonus plans are increasingly viewed as weak in influencing future behaviour.

Target-based plans define the required performance criteria, and amount of payment at varying levels of achievement against those criteria, prior to commencement of the year. This requires quantifiable targets and, for obvious business measurement reasons, financial results such as revenue growth, profit, return on investment, return on net assets and the like have been the most typical basis for setting annual performance targets. This is consistent with the trend through the 1980s and early 1990s to focus on outputs and end results as being perceived under the immediate influence – if not direct control – of line executives.

Many organisations have found the need to redefine the measures and formulae of their target-based plans during the course of the plan's life. What was seen as an appropriate relationship between the target performance and reward at the start of the period can be inappropriate at year-end. Where the formula-derived payment seemed unreasonably low as a result of changed external factors outside executive control, boards often exercised their discretion to make payments in excess of the formula. Similarly, where payments seemed unreasonably high as a result of windfall gains which were not due to executive actions, approving bodies generally felt obliged to honour the agreement but often changed the formula for the coming year.

Shareholders and the business press also have strong views on what feels fair and reasonable in terms of annual incentives paid to executives. Increased disclosure requirements mean that boards are under increasing pressure to justify STI payments seen as excessive or out of line with corporate results and shareholder returns. Several factors result in adverse publicity for individual companies in the area of annual incentive payments.

- **Competitive pressure:** The increased emphasis on at-risk pay for senior executives has forced individual companies to increase annual incentive opportunities to remain competitive in attracting and retaining executive talent. In some instances, this has led to significantly greater payments over time for consistent levels of performance.
- **Timing mismatch:** There is often a lag between the results achieved and public disclosure of incentive payments. This sometimes leads to large incentives paid only being disclosed at a time when corporate performance has deteriorated. This receives far more media attention than when modest payments are disclosed at periods of enhanced corporate performance.
- **Wrong measures:** Incentives are sometimes linked to measures that were appropriate at the start of the period, but not appropriate regarding critical aspects of the business results at the end of the year.
- **Poor calibration:** Formula-linked performance rewards are typically established within a framework of expected outcomes. Incentive payments can reach levels well above the range of acceptable if the results achieved are substantially beyond those initially contemplated. Typically, a major change in expected financial performance is a result of extraneous factors, rather than executive actions, and this increases shareholder (and general community) concerns about extraordinary incentive payments.

Apart from concern with the level of payments received under target-based plans, there are also questions about the extent to which annual incentive plans encourage an overemphasis on short-term outcomes at the expense of sustained performance over time. The danger is that business unit managers, in pursuit of narrowly defined annual financial objectives, may under-invest in infrastructure and development. This could render the business unable to grow – or even survive – in the medium to longer term.

Alternative approaches allow that performance is a function not just of achieving results, but also of the management behaviour used to achieve those results. This approach is consistent with the adoption of the "balanced scorecard" concept of planning, managing and measuring organisation performance. The balanced scorecard, together with variations that companies have built around the original model (for example, "triple bottom line"), formalises the view that management jobs have several areas of activity to control. These jobs are faced with a multitude of objectives, sometimes in direct conflict, and the need to optimise the balance of these competing objectives. Balanced scorecards document the specific objectives for an individual in areas such as financial performance, customer satisfaction, employee satisfaction and motivation, process improvement, corporate reputation, and strategic development.

Once the scorecard framework and individual objectives have been determined, it is relatively straightforward, although not always easy, to assign performance targets and weightings to the objectives as a link to reward payments. At the end of the period, reward payments are determined on the basis of actual outcomes relative to the predefined targets. This model appeals to many corporations because it provides high-level organisational clarity over a variety of process and outcome objectives. It also provides a consistent corporate approach and is tailored to the specifics of individual executive roles.

Short-term incentive design continues to evolve, and the trend is to move further from being a discretionary share in success, to being a significant tool for managing business outcomes. This change provides the opportunity to maximise the value and impact of the cost of the incentive plan by focusing on the business priorities and setting a framework for cascading these priorities through the organisation. However, this requires the board to make and defend judgements about non-financial short-term initiatives required to promote longer-term shareholder value. In this context, it is often easier to relate annual incentive payments to traditional financial and accounting results so that there is a direct link between STI payments and annual corporate performance. However, there is growing recognition that this is not necessarily the best link for creating sustained shareholder value.

## 20.5.2 Long-term incentives

Long-term incentives (LTIs) have, in recent years, been the growth element of executive remuneration packages in listed companies all over the world. Although there has been a constant progression in the value of equity based LTIs provided by major companies, there has also been a series of changes in the preferred form of equity used. Options became the overwhelmingly preferred mechanism for the delivery for LTIs since the mid-1990s. More recently there has been a growing use of performance share awards. This provides for the vesting of share grants to executives when specified performance hurdles are met. Performance and retention shares have mostly replaced the previously prevalent share option plans. Some organisations without – or unwilling to provide – access to shares for executives have used cash-based incentives.

As practitioners, we believe there are three issues affecting LTIs that require resolution: taxation, relative performance hurdles, and accounting requirements.

- **Taxation:** as vehicles for Executive Pay are often taxed differently to a bonus, practitioners must be aware of these differences and their impact on the pay programmes they wish to implement.
- **Performance hurdles:** these build the link between shareholders' and management's expectations as to what the business can produce in the way of returns.
- **Accounting requirements:** as these guide, in many jurisdictions, how these programmes affect the profitability of the company.

Further disclosure of executive remuneration can provide some measure of shareholder and general business community confidence. However, disclosure alone is insufficient to protect shareholders' interests, and those of directors and executives of companies who strive for legally correct and socially ethical dealings.

Corporate governance is about the way in which organisations are directed and controlled within the established legislation, rules and guiding principles that apply. At one level, disclosure refers to conformance in this context, but at another level, there are far broader social issues at stake. Institutional investors in Western economies draw their funds from the investment and retirement savings of their respective workforces and general public. The vast majority of these people depend on these investments for their post-employment security, and very few have earnings anywhere near those of the executives who manage the companies in which their funds are invested. In this respect, there is a need to go beyond simple conformance in annual reports to provide a credible and defensible rationale, supported by openness and transparency in how this rationale is applied to determining executive remuneration.

## 20.6 Definition of philosophy underlying executive remuneration programmes

Few companies have a clear statement of the philosophy and rationale underlying their executive remuneration programme and what they aim to achieve through their reward structure. The fact is that the remuneration programmes typically evolve, usually through management of individual components (fixed pay, retirement funds, annual bonus and long-term incentives), without full consideration of how each element fits within the total structure. As a result, the programme is often only loosely related to the organisation's business objectives, operating environment, culture and values.

A clear statement of philosophy involves high-level agreement on issues such as:

- The relationship between fixed and variable pay.

- The extent to which variable pay relates to individual, business unit and corporate performance.
- What performance indicators are used and how they are measured.
- How sustainable performance over the long term is rewarded.
- How total pay levels are benchmarked, and against which organisations.
- What expectations there are about share ownership by directors and executives
- How this is managed (for example, performance-based share plans, share purchase loan plans).

An important aspect of the philosophy is a statement about the conditions under which the board may revise performance targets and any other aspects of the programme.

## 20.7  Why do we need a remuneration committee?

### 20.7.1  Governance

Remuneration committees, as well as their non-executive director members, are playing an increasingly important role as companies focus on issues of corporate governance, especially when it comes to executive remuneration. Companies that fail to comply with the stock exchange listing requirements may face censure and possible fines. Depending on the breach, an organisation could be suspended or have its listing terminated.

Throughout the 1990s, especially with the emergence of a new economy, proponents of the alleged virtues of shareholder value as the primary objective of companies largely drowned out other voices. In just a few years since then, scandals have abounded, scoundrels are being rooted out, and the hunt for the scapegoat is on. Rules and practices in remuneration and disclosure can facilitate or inhibit the effective operation of governance.

### 20.7.2  Restoring investor confidence

On 2 December 2001, Enron Corporation, then the seventh largest publicly traded corporation in the United States of America, declared bankruptcy. This bankruptcy, the largest in American history at that time, sent shock waves throughout the world. Thousands of Enron employees lost not only their jobs, but a significant part of their retirement savings. Enron shareholders saw the value of their investment plummet. Hundreds, if not thousands, of businesses around the world were turned into Enron creditors in bankruptcy courts and are likely to receive only a small portion of the dollars owed to them. Following the global financial crisis in 2008, some companies received substantially large bailouts from governments yet continued to award large incentives off a very low base. This has rocked investor confidence and there has been a proliferation in governance frameworks in an attempt to improve governance.

The implications for directors, managers, board committees, consultants, investment analysts, asset managers, pension funds, the accounting profession, regulators, politicians, and the person on the street have been enormous. Remuneration policies are now being questioned far more frequently and closely. Common suggestions include:

- Are there enduring ethical principles that can be applied to executive remuneration, or is any action "right" if it meets those business objectives?
- Are executive pay levels escalating so far above the rank and file as to threaten organisational cohesion?
- Should remuneration professionals be advocates for employees or for shareholders?

The collapse of major organisations has posed certain ethical dilemmas regarding executive pay practices, with the misuse of surveys and statistics, repricing underwater share options, executive benefit enhancements, the size of executive pay packages, incentives and share allocations, exorbitant retention, backdated awards, and severance packages or golden handshakes in the spotlight.

To restore investor confidence, good remuneration governance is important, and this is where the remuneration committee comes in. Generally speaking, high-level credible remuneration committees provide stakeholders with a measure of comfort when it comes to good remuneration governance. It is also widely believed that the combined knowledge and experience of a diverse group of remuneration committee members leads to better solutions, too.

## 20.8 Non-executive directors' fees

Setting an appropriate level of fees for non-executive directors (NEDs) is a challenge. This is often a case of the police, judge and jury being the same person. Being a matter for shareholders to vote on, the policy underlying the setting of fees needs to be clearly determined, implemented and communicated.

### 20.8.1 Context and definitions

It may appear strange that one would have to define the concept of what a NED is. Given the need for flat, fast, nimble and flexible structures, the line has blurred a bit between the various categories of director. It used to be easy – you were either an executive (you had an office and employment contract, made daily decisions in the organisation, and played a role in the daily running of the organisation), or a non-executive (you attended board meetings every so often, made longer-term decisions, did not have your own office, and so on). But what if you are a non-executive, have an office at the organisation you serve, and work, say, eight hours a day, for, say, three to four days a week? Which set of principles should one use to set the fee structure – those for executives or those for NEDs?

Alternatively, consider a NED who brings in big contracts for the organisation on a regular basis, and quite rightly wishes to be remunerated for this. Which set of principles should one use to set this remuneration? Introduce the "independent" non-executive director, and once again, one is confronted with the definition differences between a non-independent NED and an independent NED. An example of a NED who is not independent may be a director from a holding organisation who sits on the subsidiary board. They may be non-executive – not involved in the daily running of the business – but they may not be independent. Some NEDs are not independent because they hold large shares in the company where they serve on the board; should their pay be calculated on the same basis as that of an independent NED? If one receives shares or a performance bonus in the organisation one serves, is one still considered independent?

Previously, we have set out the principles for setting executive director pay and the dilemmas of remuneration committees. In the next section, we set out the principles for setting NED fees.

### 20.8.2   Factors to consider when setting NED fees

A NED is contracted to provide a service to the organisation – to provide strategic direction and ensure wise, sustainable decisions. The contract is much like the contract with a service provider providing a service at your home. You get a quote, and if you think it is fair, you accept the quote and pay the fee when the job is done. You may not have selected the cheapest quote. It could have been the middle out of three quotes, or the highest. When the service provider finishes the job, they are paid against the quote – very rarely would you decide to pay the plumber or electrician a bonus for a job well done. You expected it in the first place. There is nothing stopping you from putting a clause in the quote to pay a bonus, but how would you agree on what a job well done is? At home, how did you choose that quote out of three quotes? Similar factors are considered when agreeing NED fees. Some of the most important factors to consider when selecting and setting NED fees are set out below:

- **From an individual's point of view:** Reputation, track record, experience, specific knowledge and skill, industry understanding, network reach.
- **Role played:** Chairperson or committee member, main board, audit committee, remuneration or HR committee, nominations and governance, or other committees such as risk, career and succession. Sometimes NEDs are even used to assist with the planning or execution of projects, but this is less common to avoid a situation where their independence becomes jeopardised. Lead independent directors (LIDs) also earn an additional fee in relation to their role.
- **Organisation type:** Organisation size – assets, turnover/sales, number of employees, market capitalisation, complexity of work/industry – single or multi-product or service, impact on sector, industry, national economy or international impact and footprint (impact on one sector versus the impact on the national and/or international economy), competitors (which can range from monopolies to cut-throat global competition).

We therefore have to consider the individual, the role and the type of organisation when setting NED pay.

### 20.8.3 A NED fee model

There are very few pay models available for NED pay because up until now, for the most part the trend has typically been for NEDs to all receive the same board fee and then additional fees in relation to their involvement in committees, serving as chairman etc.

With transparency comes the need for explaining why fees are different or the same for different directors – of late though, very few companies differentiate in the fees payable to different directors unless they assume a Chair or Lead Independent Director role. Robust models considering the most important factors have been developed, supported by remuneration databases. An example of a NED fee structure that takes into account role, individual and organisation is shown in Table 20.3.

*Table 20.3: A typical NED fee structure*

| Market remuneration data | | | | |
|---|---|---|---|---|
| Organisation size/ complexity/Impact/ strategic level | Lower quartile/ 25th percentile | Median/ 50th percentile | Upper quartile/ 75th percentile | 90th percentile |
| A | 900,000 | 1,000,000 | 1,100,000 | 1,200,000 |
| B | 700,000 | 800,000 | 900,000 | 1,000,000 |
| C | 500,000 | 600,000 | 700,000 | 800,000 |
| D | 300,000 | 400,000 | 500,000 | 600,000 |
| E | 100,000 | 200,000 | 300,000 | 400,000 |

### 20.8.4 NED performance

The concept of performance-related pay (PRP) is sweeping the globe. Why exempt NEDs? As an illustration, a PRP model for NED pay might look like the one shown in Table 20.4 below.

*Table 20.4: NED performance matrix*

| Transfer of knowledge Mentoring | 1 | 2 | 3 |
|---|---|---|---|
| 1 | 1 | 2 | 2 |
| 2 | 2 | 2 | 3 |
| 3 | 2 | 3 | 3 |

The performance ratings are:

- Exceeded expectations = 3.
- Met expectations = 2.
- Did not meet expectations = 1.

The results would feed into the payment structure for the NED, however this is not yet common practice. The evaluation of committees in how they perform relative to their Terms of Reference is common practice, but it has not yet filtered through to their fees.

### 20.8.5   Executive factors

Judgement is still required when identifying the correct executive-specific factor and level. We unfortunately cannot leave the entire process to a model. A model does, however, assist in making the decision more defensible.

In addition, because this is a negotiation with an individual, there is sometimes the case of: "100,000 is my fee – take it or leave it …"

### 20.8.6   Structure of NED fees

The structure of NED fees takes four main forms:

- Fees for attending meetings.
- Retainer for serving on the board (for example, annually).
- Combination of fees and retainer.
- Earn your money (payment in shares – a typical American structure).

Note that the fees and retainers can be paid in cash, shares or both.

By and large, companies either pay fees for membership of the board, irrespective of attendance at meetings as they are considered to be available not only during board cycles but also outside of board cycles.  There are still many organisations that follow the approach of splitting fees between retainers and attendance fees, however in addition to this, travel and subsistence allowances are disbursed, and travel and preparation time are compensated at 50 percent of the rate for the meeting, with caps on both. The norm internationally is for all directors to earn the same board fee and then committee fees in terms of their membership. Sometimes, although this is dwindling, a travel allowance is paid to those travelling long distances. A common currency is the norm regardless of the home country.

With the increase in fiduciary and legal responsibility, in-depth knowledge required, and hours spent on inadequate board submissions, we must expect these NED fees to increase over the coming years.

## 20.9  Remuneration committees (RemCos)

### 20.9.1  Who sits on remuneration committees?

Companies should appoint a remuneration committee or other such appropriate board committee, consisting mainly of independent non-executive directors, to make recommendations regarding executive and CEO pay. This committee is often chaired by an independent non-executive director who is not the chairperson of the governing body.

Boards should preferably consist of a majority of non-executive members as well as several independent-minded ones.

### 20.9.2  Size of the committee

There is generally no legal maximum or minimum. Depending on the size and the complexity of the organisation, the range typically is from three to seven members. RemCos generally meet on average four times per year but can meet from three times up to six times per year.

### 20.9.3  Selection criteria for remuneration committee members

A single RemCo member may likely not possess all the characteristics of the recommended profile to be used in the selection criteria. However, the RemCo chair is encouraged to appoint members with diverse backgrounds, experience and skill sets to enable the RemCo, as a collective, to efficiently discharge its fiduciary duties.

The following are guidelines that may be used when selecting RemCo members:

- **Availability:** The candidate's ability to help your committee versus availability for service is an issue worth considering.
- **Reputation:** Usually there is a trade-off between reputation and availability.
- **Communication skills:** It is sometimes dangerous to assume that because someone is a polished public speaker, he or she will be an effective communicator.
- **Experience:** This usually cuts down the training time if the members have the right experience.
- **Leverage:** This refers to the ability of a director to expand the relationships of the board and provide additional management expertise.
- **Remuneration expertise:** This is a desirable quality, which will reduce the need for training and enhance the quality of deliberations by the committee.

Appropriate use of external consultants (acting independently from management), consultations with the organisation's legal counsel, governance specialists, HR and finance teams, together with cross-board committee collaboration, will assist the RemCo in the execution of its duties.

## 20.9.4  RemCo dilemmas

RemCos are meant to prevent dilemmas from becoming impasses. Management, who are conflicted, want to offer the best possible reward package for their staff, but often find RemCos very frustrating as they do not get their support. This is a matter that requires a lot of patience and time to be invested so that all parties can understand the different perspectives and reach common ground for the greater good of all employees and the company at large.

## 20.9.5  RemCo architecture

Major factors contribute to the success of RemCos, including their composition, size and experience in remuneration matters. Selecting RemCo members is normally left to the board chairperson, the HR Director, the Company Secretary, the CEO and the CFO, depending on the size of the organisation.

They would typically follow the global benchmark as set out in Table 20.5.

*Table 20..5: Anatomy of a typical RemCo*

|   | Item | Global practice |
|---|------|-----------------|
| 1. | Authority | RemCo is mandated by the board to debate and investigate issues of remuneration, to set policy and create oversight of its implementation, and to provide the board with regular feedback on decisions taken. |
| 2. | Members | Members should be independent, external to the organisation. By implication, the chairperson should be external to the organisation and should preferably not be the Chairperson of the board. |
| 3. | RemCo size | This depends on the size of the organisation, but typically three to five members. |
| 4. | Scope of work | This depends on the maturity of management, but typically includes determination of reward for executives (CEO and first-line reports, or top, say, 50), approval of share schemes, incentive schemes, group benefit schemes, succession plans (if there is no separate HR Committee), pay increase percentages, non-executive director fee proposals, and oversight of the implementation of the remuneration policy across the organisation. |
| 5. | Frequency of meetings | Typically, three to four times a year. |
| 6. | Payment | Common alternatives include:<br>1.  Fees for attending<br>2.  Retainer<br>3.  Combination of fees and retainer; the combination approach seems to be the trend.<br>There is a premium for chairing the committee, in the order of 40% to 100% of the committee members' fees. |

| | Item | Global practice |
|---|---|---|
| 7. | Performance Payment | This is an area of considerable debate following Warren Buffet's article on how he has made the board of Coca Cola® "earn" their pay by removing their fixed fees and giving them shares only. In a number of countries, there are a few reported bonus schemes for non-executive directors, and there are organisations who allow NEDs to select whether they prefer cash or unrestricted shares. |
| 8. | Reporting | The chairperson of the RemCo would normally provide an executive summary, together with the remuneration policy, for inclusion into the annual financial statements. The names of RemCo members are normally published in the annual financial statements for listed organisations. In many countries, organisations need to report details about the RemCo and who their remuneration advisers are. In most developed economies, detailed disclosures regarding incentive schemes – targets, formulae, and payouts are required. |

Given this anatomy, RemCo members need to have a good appreciation of a host of things, the primary ones being:

- The industry norms and external environment.
- Remuneration theory and practice.
- The organisation's strategy and operations.

In addition to this, RemCo members should have good commercial skills and experience in remuneration. The trend will be for the fee paid to members to depend on their reputation, skills, and experience.

## 20.9.6 Executive process

To be successful, RemCo relies heavily on the executive management to prepare board packs in advance for pre-reading. Too much or too little information wastes a lot of time. Often, executive management expects RemCo to make vital decisions but provides insufficient information on the full remuneration picture. The full picture should include information on:

- Salaries and the cost to the employer of benefit schemes.
- STIs.
- LTIs and/or shares.
- Retention arrangements.

Any proposal submitted for RemCo's consideration should include information on where it fits and how it measures up relative to:

- Total earnings and total cost to organisation, and all the components of remuneration.
- Remuneration mix, i.e. the ratio between fixed and variable pay.

## 20.9.7   The market

When considering proposals from executive management, RemCos are presented with benchmark information from salary surveys or may request information of their own. Although at first it appears relatively easy, executive management are often accused of cherry-picking survey data to promote their case. Benchmark groups should be reliable, consistent and valid to ensure proper comparisons. The most commonly used definition of "the market" is "the organisations from where you recruit or to which you lose people".

For positions such as finance and HR, local market survey data could be used if it is a national company. For international companies, a global survey will be required to provide appropriate data for executive positions. For specialist positions or industries, a niche or club survey may be required. This is where the definition of market becomes problematic, especially in industry sectors where there are few comparable players. Consider, for example, a national airline, a new local bank, a small mine, a stock brokerage or an asset management organisation – the definition of comparator becomes more difficult. A robust methodology needs to be adopted to select organisations that provide a direct and relevant comparison of CEO pay.

It is important, when defining the market, to consider a number of factors apart from financial components. These include a full assessment of the organisation, based on the following criteria:

* Holding, subsidiary or single-unit organisations.
* Private, public or state-owned enterprise.
* Monopoly or many competitors.
* Complexity of industry or market.
* Listed or not.
* Local listing only or overseas listing (for example, LSE, NYSE), or a combination.
* Organisation size in terms of turnover, budget, profit, assets, market cap, number of employees. A good rule of thumb to use is half to two times market cap or revenue.
* Job content, not just position title.
* Job size – not all CEO job sizes are the same.
* Performance of organisation in terms of financials, shareholder return, strategic vision and people management practices.

## 20.9.8   Possible solutions and way forward

There are many possible ways of resolving the frustration and conflict between RemCos, boards and executive management. Some of the more important ones are:

* Well-defined Charter or Terms of Reference
* Well-trained RemCo members

- Comprehensive RemCo packs showing all the components of the remuneration structure, the total cost and how the proposal will affect the total staff costs whilst benefiting the organisation.
- A clear definition of the market and peer groups used for benchmarking purposes.
- A good anchor for the CEO's package.
- RemCo has access to top remuneration experts for advice and to validate executive proposals.
- Codes of good practice assist with delineation of responsibilities.

## 20.10    The high-level duties of RemCos

Scope-creep and searching too deeply into the organisation sometimes hamper the effectiveness of RemCos.  RemCos have several high-level duties:

- Adherence to good corporate procedures policies and processes.
- Knowledge of the organisational strategy and culture and how this translates into the remuneration policy.
- Decisions on remuneration outcomes given the performance of the organisation.
- Engagement with large institutional investors and shareholders, particularly when concerns are raised by these bodies on the remuneration policies and outcomes.
- Approval of remuneration plans.

Performance-related elements should constitute a substantial proportion of total remuneration, with consequences for non-performance being harsh. Companies should establish a formal and transparent procedure for developing a policy on executive remuneration, which should be supported by a statement of remuneration philosophy in the Annual Report. There should be an overriding principle of full disclosure by directors on an individual basis in terms of all areas of remuneration, including share schemes and other incentives.

The following checklist serves as a useful guideline for RemCos in carrying out their duties:

- Clarify authority delegated by the board.
- Ensure independence from organisation.
- Retain and maintain direct access to outside experts and consultants.
- Review and approve the organisation's remuneration policy.
- Give special attention to CEO and executive pay in the context of the remuneration paid to all employees in the organisation.
- Pay attention to fair remuneration, with specific reference to the minimum wage, the pay gap, and race and gender distribution of remuneration.
- Develop a remuneration committee report (for the annual proxy statement) which consists of a background statement, the remuneration policy and the remuneration outcomes.
- Understand the purpose of various pay elements.

- Consider the timeframe associated with pay elements.
- Be sensitive to external pressures.
- Pay special attention to areas of controversy.
- Compare pay programmes with relevant pay groups.
- Evaluate executive calibre, degree of difficulty of performance objectives and risk exposure, and tap executive potential.
- Assess the real value or cost of the executive total pay package.
- Ensure that owner and corporate economic values are prime drivers of the executive pay programme.
- Co-ordinate payments with performance goals.
- Balance fixed versus variable rewards.
- Define equity (share option) participation strategy.
- Make full and required disclosures.
- Deliberate and resolve, with special consideration, items that will have to be stated in the remuneration committee report.
- Review and revise remuneration philosophy and policy.
- Carefully select recognised industry index and/or an appropriate peer group for the performance group.

Table 20.6 gives an indication of the typical accountability of the board and remuneration committee. Setting up such a table for the organisation may alleviate confusion over authority levels and scope.

*Table 20.6: Split of accountability: An example*

|  | Approval/Review required | |
| --- | --- | --- |
|  | **Full board** | **Committee** |
| **Corporate organisation** | | |
| • Corporate bylaws (adoption or amendment) | X | |
| • Certificate of incorporation/amendments | X | |
| • Shares: all authorisation to issue or buy back shares | X | |
| **Board organisation** | | |
| • Board membership qualification | | Nomination |
| • Board committee memberships | | Nomination |
| • New member selection | | Nomination |
| **Remuneration** | | |
| • Salaries of CEO and corporate or prescribed officers | | Remuneration |
| **Executive employment agreements** | | |
| • Severance agreements | X | |
| • Retention agreements | X | |
| • Change in control agreements | X | |

| | Approval/Review required | |
|---|---|---|
| | **Full board** | **Committee** |
| **Fringe benefits** | | |
| • Establishment of new plans or amendments to existing plans | | Remuneration |
| **Incentive plans** | | |
| • All arrangements for corporate officers | | Remuneration |
| • Approval of specific financial targets | X | |
| • Determination of award funds | X | |
| **Long-term (cash) incentive plans** | | |
| • Approval of all plans (shareholders to vote on equity settled plans) | X | |
| • Establishment of performance targets | | Remuneration |
| • Award sizing | | Remuneration |
| **LTI plans** | | |
| • Establishment or amendment of share plans | X | |
| • Administration of share plans | | Remuneration |
| • Grants of all share plans | | Remuneration |

*Source: Adapted from Reda[5]*

## 20.11   Critical success factors for good corporate governance

The following are pivotal to enforcing good corporate governance:

- Enhanced disclosure.
- Shareholder activism.
- Strong financial means.
- RemCo comprised of independent non-executive directors.

Greater disclosure would deter organisation directors from accepting excessive rewards. Levels of remuneration should be sufficient to attract, retain and motivate executives of the quality required by the board. So, there needs to be a balance between excessive rewards and the responsibility of attracting the best to run the organisation.

## 20.12   Where the CEO fits in

The question here is: where do the most senior management (for example, the CEO) fit into RemCo? How much influence do they have?

---

5    Reda, 2002.

World trends are as follows:

- RemCo is a committee of the full board and is answerable to the full board.
- It is good practice for the RemCo chairperson to provide the full board with feedback regarding key decisions taken. Typically, the remuneration of executive directors is approved by the full board upon recommendation by the RemCo.
- The CEO attends RemCo by invitation.
- The CEO does not have a vote on RemCo.
- When RemCo discusses CEO pay, the CEO is excused. Typically, the company secretary taking the RemCo minutes would also be excused when discussing the CEO's pay.

## 20.13 Remuneration policy

One of the RemCo's duties is to design the remuneration policy that will lay the framework for remuneration practices within the organisation. Some of the headings that may be expected to appear in that policy are:

- Purpose.
- Rewards vision/philosophy.
- Remuneration framework/model.
- What we seek to accomplish with each of the components of remuneration.
- Assumptions.
- Scope.
- Guiding principles.
- Pay and benefits framework.
- Comparative benchmarking.
- Annual remuneration reviews.
- Remuneration mix.
- Variable pay.
  - short-term incentives; and
  - long-term incentives.
- Recognition plans.
- Link to performance management – guiding principles.
- Communication.
- RemCo scope and mandate.

This policy should reflect the current growth stage of the organisation or product and its remuneration strategies need to underpin the business strategies. These strategies may differ according to where the business currently is in its growth cycle. Typically, these are built into the remuneration policy. Table 20.7 may be used as a guide for RemCos:

*Table 20.7: Life cycle and remuneration options*

| Life cycle stage | Base salary | Formal annual incentives | Benefits | Perquisites and special benefits | Capital and wealth accumulation |
|---|---|---|---|---|---|
| Start-up | Substantially below market | Unusual | Basic medical insurance only | None | Founders' shares |
| Initial public offering | Somewhat below market | "Boilerplate" plans | Minimal | Significantly below average | Share options |
| Growth | At market | More formal and more closely tied to business plan | Average | Average | Combination share programmes (2 to 3 plans) |
| Emerging | At/Above market | Total cash concept with unit variations | Average to above average | Average | Equity and cash plans (options and PUPs) |
| Mature | Above market | Layered plans | Rich | Above average | Overlapping programmes |

## 20.14  Committee meeting guidelines

Typical agenda items are shown below but are a guideline only. Each organisation needs to set its own agenda. The RemCo's calendar is based on the timing of board meetings, year-end, timing of increases, and the size and complexity of the organisation.

**Event:** End of the year
**Meeting date:** Late February
**Recurring agenda items:**

- Approve minutes of prior meeting.
- Review prior year results of bonus plan.
- Evaluate performance of CEO, and review and approve proposed bonus plans.
- Review bonus plan targets for organisational units.
- Review and approve personal goals of CEO for current year.
- Review draft of Remuneration Committee responsibilities for inclusion in proxy statement report.
- Review draft of explanation of CEO remuneration for inclusion in proxy statement report.

**Event:** After annual shareholders' meeting and approval of share-related plans
**Meeting date:** June/July or September/October
**Recurring agenda items:**

- Approve minutes of prior meetings.
- Review and approve recommendations for share schemes.
- Review and approve mid-year promotions and new hires.
- Receive consultants' report on fringe benefits and benefit costs. The report must include:
  - competitive practices
  - recommended changes and costs.
- Receive annual management development and succession planning overview from CEO.
- Engage outside studies for various matters.
- Review performance of outside consultants.
- Consider approval of officer for nomination to the board.

**Event:** Late in year
**Meeting date:** November/early December
**Recurring agenda items:**

- Approve minutes of prior meeting.
- Receive consultant reports on remuneration levels, current levels, and competitive pay practices.
- Review and approve recommended changes in salary structure and bonus plan provisions.
- Approve additions to and removals from bonus plan participation.
- Review executive remuneration budget, and approve salary increases for next year.
- New ideas session (planning session for new ideas, plans and programmes).
- Discuss incentive measures for upcoming year.
- Annual review of executive severance plans.
- Review corporate remuneration philosophy and pay strategies.

## 20.15  Independent determination

The RemCo charter should acknowledge responsibility for setting the framework and reviewing administration of the total programme as it applies to executives. Specifically, the committee should have accountability for all aspects of the CEO's pay. This requires all committee members to be aware of general issues regarding board and executive pay, and fully conversant with their own organisation's programme. In turn, this requires regularly scheduled meetings and access to expert advice, other than that used by management.

### 20.15.1 Open communication

Board and executive remuneration are a vital and topical issue in corporate governance. It is important that shareholders understand the structure and processes for determination of pay at these levels. It is the direct accountability of the board remuneration committee that its organisation complies with the letter and spirit of the legislation, rules and accepted principles relating to all aspects of remuneration.

### 20.15.2  Periodic evaluation

It is best practice that the remuneration programme be reviewed periodically. The purpose of this review is to assess and evaluate the overall programme design, the appropriateness of its competitiveness in the general market, and the effect of the linkages with performance. This evaluation, sponsored by the board remuneration committee and undertaken by independent external specialists, ought to be undertaken every two to three years to ensure the integrity of the organisation's total board and executive remuneration structure processes and impact on corporate performance.

## 20.16  Summary

Organisations implement remuneration committees to improve the governance of remuneration and improve investor confidence. The structure of executive pay is different from non-executive director fees. The scope of the remuneration committee sometimes depends on the strength of the management team. Remuneration committee members should be independent.

## 20.17  Self-evaluation questions

1.  What is the primary purpose of the four main remuneration elements?
2.  Why do we need a remuneration committee?
3.  What factors do you consider when setting non-executive director pay?
4.  What are good selection criteria for remuneration committee membership?
5.  Name the key high-level duties of remuneration committees.

# CHAPTER 21

## Remuneration Governance

### 21.1  Corporate governance

"When a company's employees go to work in the morning, they ought to do so with a sense of purpose beyond that of simply making money for the owners. The motivation that comes from a shared sense of purpose and a determination to deliver value to others is a vital ingredient of long-term success. Instilling it is now the task of governance. It is more difficult than before, but it is also more interesting — and, in the long run, more rewarding."[1]

Corporate governance is a set of processes, systems, policies, laws and codes that influence or affect the way an organisation is directed, administered or controlled. Corporate governance also includes relationships with all stakeholders. Principal stakeholders include the shareholders, management, regulators, suppliers, board of directors, employees and the community. An important theme in corporate governance is that individuals are accountable for certain organisational outputs achieved in a manner that does not prejudice any stakeholders.

Remuneration governance is driven largely by international governance frameworks such as Sarbanes-Oxley, Basel, King IV and various stock exchange requirements. Most governance frameworks comprise recommended practices, implications of remuneration practice management, and regulations that describe how remuneration should be implemented. Almost every country with a stock exchange will have an existing Code of Corporate Governance. Generally, these codes follow similar principles, regardless of the size or form of the organisations covered. As an example, we will take a closer look at the King IV™ Report on Corporate Governance in South Africa, 2016. King IV follows many other international governance codes that have been made public during the last few years, especially following the implosion of the global economy and the number of large corporate failures that have caught investors completely off-guard. Many people believe that the design of incentive plans, and the results thereof, have had a significant influence on the behaviour of executives, and that these corporate failures could have been avoided if there were earlier interventions by shareholders. However, when shareholders see good results and receive high dividends, they are unlikely to start to ask too many questions, which is probably where they should have been more suspicious and less confident.

### 21.2  The King IV report

Reward governance refers to the promotion of the highest standard of corporate governance, transparency and consistency in the disclosure and decision making of remuneration-related matters; the adherence to minimum standards in the composition of remuneration committees

---

1    Montagnon, 2019.

and the finalisation of mandates for these committees; and ensuring that all remuneration related decisions are governed by well documented policies to prevent ad hoc decisions.

The remuneration of executives is one of the most debated topics in the corporate governance arena, due to the tension between stakeholders demanding to understand how remuneration decisions are made, and specifically how incentives align with performance, and views held by executives and board members that remuneration decisions are not for public comment but a matter for the governing body. In line with international developments, remuneration has great prominence in King IV.

The King IV report includes a code, with additional, separate sector supplements for SMEs, NPOs, State-Owned Entities, Municipalities and Retirement Funds. The King IV Code™ contains both principles and recommended practices aimed at achieving governance outcomes.

King IV has 17 principles, 208 recommended practices. The last principle, principle 17, only applies to institutional investors. The application of all 16 (or 17 as appropriate) principles are required to substantiate a claim that good governance is being practices. Organisations are required to explain in their annual reports how principles have been applied and what the outcome was. These explanations allow stakeholders to make informed decisions as to whether good governance outcomes have been achieved.

King IV fosters enhanced accountability on remuneration through:

- Definitive disclosure requirements.
- Separating non-binding votes on the policy and the implementation report.
- Stakeholder inclusion.
- The use of performance measures that support positive outcomes to be disclosed.
- A requirement for fair, transparent and responsible remuneration for executive management in the context of overall employee remuneration.
- An acknowledgement of the need to address the gap between the remuneration of executives and lower paid workers.

Principle 14 is devoted to remuneration and states: "The governing body should ensure that the organisation remunerates fairly, responsibly and transparently so as to promote the achievement of strategic objectives and positive outcomes in the short, medium and long term."[2] It is categorised into three sections: Remuneration Policy, Remuneration Report, and Voting on Remuneration.

Table 21.1 provides a summary of the recommended practices and some of the potential implications thereof for remuneration management practices contained in the Code.

---

2    Institute of Directors in Southern Africa, 2016.

*Table 20.1 King IV recommended practices and implications of remuneration management practices*

| Remuneration Policy | |
|---|---|
| The governing body should:<br><br>• Set direction of how remuneration should be approached on an organisation-wide basis.<br>• Approve the policy that gives effect to its direction on fair, responsible and transparent remuneration. | The policy should be designed to achieve the following objectives:<br><br>• Attract, motivate, reward and retain human capital.<br>• Promote the achievement of strategic objectives within the organisation's risk appetite.<br>• Promote positive outcomes.<br>• Promote an ethical culture and responsible corporate citizenship. |
| • The policy should address organisation-wide remuneration, and include provision.<br>• The governing body should oversee the implementation and execution of the policy: | • Remuneration to executive management that is fair and responsible in the context of overall employee remuneration.<br>• The use of performance measures that support positive outcomes across the economic, social and environmental context in which the organisation operates.<br>• A vote on the policy and implementation report.<br>• All elements of remuneration and the mix of these. |
| Remuneration Report | |
| • The governing body should ensure that remuneration is disclosed by means of a remuneration report in three parts: | • A background statement.<br>• An overview of the main provisions of the policy.<br>• An implementation report containing details of remuneration awarded during the reporting period. |
| Remuneration Report \| Background Statement | |
| • Provide the context for remuneration considerations and decisions, with reference to: | • Internal and external factors that influenced remuneration.<br>• Most recent results of votes on policy & report.<br>• Key areas of focus and decisions taken including substantial changes to the policy.<br>• Whether remuneration consultants have been used and whether the committee is satisfied that they were independent and objective.<br>• The view of the remuneration committee on whether the policy achieved its stated objectives.<br>• Future areas of focus. |
| Remuneration Report \| Remuneration Policy | |
| • Overview of main policy provisions and objectives: | • Remuneration elements and design principles for executive management and at a high level for other employees.<br>• Obligations under executive contracts. |

| | |
|---|---|
| • Overview of main policy provisions and objectives: (continued) | • Performance measures used to assess the achievement of strategic objectives and positive outcomes including the weighting and period of time over which measured.<br>• An illustration of potential consequences on the total remuneration on a single, total figure basis – minimum, targets and maximum performance outcomes.<br>• An explanation of how the policy addresses fair and responsible executive remuneration in the context of overall employee rem.<br>• The use and justification of benchmarks<br>• The basis of setting NED fees. |
| • Remuneration Report \| Implementation Report | |
| • Remuneration of each member of exec management, in separate tables (also refer to the Companies Act requirements if appropriate): | • A single, total figure of remuneration, received and receivable for the reporting period, all the remuneration elements, disclosed at fair value.<br>• Details of unvested variable remuneration awards in current and prior years including the number of awards, the values at date of grant, vesting and expiry dates and the fair value at the end of the reporting period.<br>• Cash value of all awards that were settled during the reporting period.<br>• Performance measures, weighting, results.<br>• Reasons for any payments made on termination of office.<br>• A statement regarding compliance with, and any deviations from, the remuneration policy. |
| Voting | |
| • Voting on remuneration | • NED fees by special resolution within the two years' preceding payment (as per the Companies Act).<br>• Remuneration policy and implementation report every year for a separate non-binding vote at the AGM.<br>• The policy should record measures that the board commits to take in the event that either the remuneration policy, or the implementation report, or both, have been voted against by 25% or more of votes exercised.<br>• An engagement process to ascertain reasons for dissenting votes. |

| • Voting on remuneration (continued) | • Appropriately address legitimate and reasonable objections and concerns raised which may include amending the policy, or clarifying or adjusting governance/processes. |
| --- | --- |
| | • If less than 75% votes are in favour, the following should be disclosed in the background statement of the following year's report: |
| | ○ With whom the company engaged and the manner and form of engagement to ascertain the reasons for dissenting votes. |
| | ○ The nature of steps taken to address legitimate and reasonable objections and concerns. |

## 21.3 How to improve remuneration governance and the consequences of non-compliance

King IV is a set of voluntary principles and good practices of corporate governance. If King IV conflicts with any legislation, the legislation will prevail. However, for entities with a primary listing on the South African Securities Exchange (JSE), certain aspects of King IV are binding by virtue of the listing requirements. The fact that Codes of Governance internationally tend not to be legally binding in themselves does not mean that there are no legal consequences arising from non-compliance. A court will consider King IV when evaluating what is regarded as practice in a particular situation, especially where governance duties are involved. Failure to meet corporate governance practice, and by implication the principles set out in the relevant code of governance, may imply liability of the board in certain circumstances.

Improved remuneration governance will protect all stakeholders. To improve remuneration governance, organisations will have to ensure that they invest time in developing a comprehensive remuneration philosophy, strategy and policies. All decisions taken by the authoritative body (the Remuneration Committee or another body) need to be tested against the strategy and policy. An authoritative body consisting of independent members, who are not conflicted in terms of the matters deliberated and decided upon, needs to be established for purposes of considering remuneration-related decisions for senior employees. Organisations are required to disclose information relating to the implementation of their policies in much more detail. Disclosure must be done comprehensively to enable all stakeholders to form an objective opinion of the quality of decisions taken by the authoritative body. Promoting the highest standard of corporate governance, transparency and consistency in the disclosure of remuneration for executive and non-executive directors as well as the highest-paid employees in the organisation is considered to be the norm.

The aim of remuneration governance in organisations is to provide an integrated approach for corporate governance through fundamental principles of sound remuneration practices and policies. Remuneration specialists need to refer to local governance codes and statutory requirements pertaining to the countries within which organisations have a legal presence to ensure that their organisations are compliant.

Most of the companies that had corporate governance failures did subscribe to principles of good corporate governance and had certain measures in place. This raises the question: does the drafting of codes of good governance really make companies healthier and more sustainable, and will they reduce the likelihood of corporate collapses? This question is linked to the concept of 'box-ticking', referring to the practice of ticking off certain areas/boxes to indicate that there was compliance with specific aspects. To merely tick boxes is clearly not ideal as there must be compliance with the rule and not just with the form.

## 21.4 Summary

Corporate governance is about the way in which organisations are directed and controlled within the established legislation, rules and guiding principles that apply. At one level, disclosure refers to conformance in this context, but at another level, there are far broader social issues at stake. Institutional investors in western economies draw their funds from the investment and retirement savings of their respective workforces and general public. The vast majority of these people depend on their investments for their post-employment security, and very few have earnings anywhere near those of the executives who manage the companies in which their funds are invested. In this respect, there is a need to go beyond simple conformance in annual reports to provide a credible and defensible rationale, supported by openness and transparency, in how this rationale is applied to determining executive remuneration.

There are numerous other international governance frameworks, statutes and stock exchange listing requirements that are important for global organisations. We looked at the King IV Code for South African companies as an example of one such framework. It comprises recommended practices, implications of remuneration practice management, and regulations that describe how it should be implemented.

## 21.5 Self-evaluation questions

1. What is corporate governance?
2. Name some methods of improving remuneration governance.
3. Describe some principles of remuneration disclosure.
4. Describe some principles of the remuneration philosophy, strategy and policy.

# CHAPTER 22

# Reward Trends

The field of compensation and benefits is on the verge of big changes. Of the Human Resources functions, it is one which, to date, has received little attention from HR Tech and HR Analytics tools. What we see most commonly today are tools designed to make administration easier, along with a new stream of 24/7 performance appraisals and some online salary surveys. But this situation is due to change soon.

Having a good idea of the global remuneration trends can be very helpful in setting one's own remuneration strategy and prepares one for the landscape ahead. The sources of these trends are a product of what leading organisations are doing or have on their radar screens.

A trend does not necessarily mean that it is good or a best practice; it means that more and more organisations are considering it. The following trends could be used to guide your remuneration strategy if they are appropriate and underpin the organisational operation strategy.

Below are our best 'guesstimates' of where the profession is going, as seen through our own 'Crystal Ball', in no particular order.

## 22.1 Pay for retention

Retention and engagement of employees has been one of the single biggest drivers of remuneration policy for the past number of years. There are many critical areas of skills shortage at the moment and, given the speed of change we are living through, the shortages may not end any time soon. Organisations have explored and implemented many different retention mechanisms from a remuneration point of view, and the results so far are mixed, yet the need is there and must be attended to. Companies will certainly pay a premium (say 90th percentile) to retain any individual with these skills, including leadership! Note that companies may choose to do this by paying a higher base salary with no variable pay to these employees. Certainly, there is bound to be differences between those with scarce skills (e.g. sophisticated technology) and those with skills which are easier to replace (e.g. accountants).

## 22.2 Pay for development

Stemming from the above argument, it is not a far-fetched idea that pay for development will also make a lot of sense for the future of work. The fast pace of change will make some of the skills that are useful today obsolete by tomorrow. Thus, individuals who can continue to grow their expertise and keep pace with change will be more highly prized, and thus more highly compensated.

## 22.3  Pay for productivity

One of the biggest challenges in remuneration management stems from aligning the diverse views that are always present in any compensation strategy discussion.

The first is the shareholder view: they are less concerned with the amount paid than with the return received. In other words, they are less concerned with internal equity and external competitiveness, and more with the performance part of the pay-for-performance model.

The second view is that of the market: there is a "price" for each type of employee and for the skills they bring. This is the external competitiveness model.

Then there is the HR function view: the function needs to balance attraction with retention and with motivation. Thus, market competitiveness serves to attract, but immediately attention turns to internal competitiveness to retain, and somewhere in the middle we find variable pay as a motivator, but only as long as it doesn't affect the other two; a difficult balancing act.

The fourth view is that of the company: overall KPIs are usually measured in a rather un-balanced scorecard where revenue growth and profitability dominate. If the pay package aims to increase productivity by driving revenue and profitability, all is well and good. But if HR cannot prove (not just imply but prove!) the link between higher pay and higher productivity, the company view will default to control of this cost as a means to seek productivity gains.

The final view is that of the employees: to an employee, reaction to pay is often emotional; akin to thinking "the amount in my pay check is the exact amount my company loves me!", which quickly devolves into "they love somebody else more!", or "that company loves their employees more than my company loves me!" This emotional reaction to pay makes it hard for Compensation & Benefits (C&B) professionals to then discuss "facts" and "data" (e.g. how often has the argument: "we pay at the 50th percentile and build our salary grades around the market data from our consulting vendors; you are paid within the salary band", really worked when trying to convince an employee that they are competitively paid?). Balancing these differing views certainly is one of the most difficult parts of the C&B job.

A consequence of this trend is that there will be more team-based incentives, as individual productivity for executives is practically impossible to measure.

## 22.4  Pay for location

A fairly recent trend based on an old concept is the idea that people are paid according to the labour market they are in. However, with the increased ability to work remotely, this concept of which market individuals are in becomes blurred. Should they be paid according to where the office is located, or according to where they choose to live? The answer may lie somewhere in between, with companies making allowances for internal equity but including discounts where an employee chooses to work remotely in a lower-cost location.

## 22.5 Gig workers/project-based pay

A possible compensation-related answer to the future of work, which encompasses gig employees and project-based employees, is to derive pay schemes especially suited for these types of employees, while at the same time retaining the essence of the organisation's compensation philosophy and corporate culture. This may include skill-based pay, gain-sharing pay for outcomes, and even the idea of benefits for performance. The gig worker has a hard time securing benefits like health insurance. Benefits for performance basically means that coverage is extended or expanded based on hours worked and/or results achieved.

## 22.6 Specialist career tracks

A fairly significant trend is evolving, linked to the points made above about skills shortages and various pay models, where organisations are acknowledging that employees do not have to get onto the management track to advance up the corporate or salary ladder. Dual career paths, one for management and one for technical staff, can be designed, where it is possible for specialist staff to be promoted into the upper echelons of the organisation. The benefits of this are that the best technical people (who need to continue developing their skills!) are not lost into management, and it does sometimes happen that the best technical people make the worst managers. High-performing organisations should not allow poor people managers into the top 100 most senior positions.[1]

## 22.7 More flexibility

In our own experience, when employees are asked the question: "Would you rather have a pay increase next year or more flexibility?", more than three-quarters of them respond that they would prefer more flexibility. The trend is that, beyond Flex benefits, which are a well-established practice, organisations can also introduce the notion of flexible pay via the design of total guaranteed remuneration packages.

Total guaranteed remuneration packages rest on three fundamental pillars: internal equity, structural flexibility, and external market competitiveness. The total package concept is exciting and flexible in that employees can choose, from a number of different options offered to them, the structure of their total remuneration package that is most suitable to their preferences, risk appetites and lifestyles. The advantage of total package to the employer is that it contains and defines the total fixed cost of employment and empowers its employees to structure more compensation packages more aligned with pay for development and pay for retention.

---

1    Van der Vyver & Bussin, 2013.

## 22.8  Intense focus on the wage gaps

This trend is going to be around for a while. The inequality debate is a global issue for which at this stage there are few sustainable answers that are backed by political will.[2] The gap between highest and lowest wages within a company is perhaps the most visible because organisations have been required to disclose it in their annual reports, and because, in spite of this, it is currently widening. The lowest paid employees are particularly vulnerable to the impact of artificial intelligence and robotics as the so-called fourth industrial revolution gathers pace.

The only way to counter this is to greatly increase the effectiveness of the educational system. Some commentators argue that in fact the fourth industrial revolution will likely create more jobs than it destroys, but only for those with the right level of skill and for those who continue with life-long education.

The gender pay gap is the gap between what men and women in the same role, and on the same performance and competence level, are paid.[3] The same definition applies to race pay gap. In the EU and UK, the disclosure of pay gaps, and specifically gender pay gaps, is becoming compulsory. There is legislation that forbids discrimination, and the practices in this book should guide companies to a fair compensation system of similar pay for similar work, regardless of the demographics. And yet, it is a gap that still persists. Artificial intelligence tools for recruiting and determining pay offers may make it easier to deal with this issue, coupled with government legislation, particularly around using prior salaries to determine pay package offers. At some point, companies may be legally required to disclose this data point as well.

Corporate governance guidelines often require that performance measures that support positive outcomes across the triple context in which the organisation operates, and/or all the capitals that the organisation uses or affects, should be used when crafting remuneration policies. This will hopefully in time also have an effect on these trends.

## 22.9  Media scrutiny

Exorbitant remuneration has always made striking headlines in the press. Organisations thus need to ensure that their processes are extremely robust and can withstand any stakeholder scrutiny.

## 22.10  Optimising rewards

Perhaps one of the biggest difficulties C&B professionals face is the changing expectations of employees, given the non-changing expectations of shareholders. How to balance these two certainly qualifies as the "horns of a dilemma"! However, the answer lies in applying analytics

---

2    Bussin, 2015a; Bussin & Barrett, 2016.

3    Adelekan & Bussin, 2018.

to employee preferences that, at the same time, either produce higher performance, or reduce overall cost at the same perceived value.

Let's look at these two possibilities: on the one hand, assume employees prefer a lower-risk pay mix (say 90/10) over a higher-risk pay mix (say 75/25). If the company, through analytics, can demonstrate that this new pay package actually reduces turnover (and the cost associated with it), with no material loss of performance, then it can build a business case to make this change. The second example would be to use conjoint analysis to explore which combination of benefits has the highest perceived value at a given cost point. Or conversely, which combination of benefits can provide the same current perceived value at the lowest cost.

Analytics will be a great tool to derive pay packages that are best suited to attract, retain and motivate employees. We have already discussed the notion of flexible pay, which could be supported via analytics. An important area where organisations should spend considerable HR analytics time is in the determination of which incentive mechanism works best.[4] It is possible to use analytics to look into the question, "Do incentives work?" If so, which ones deliver more bang for the buck? STI? Higher pay mix? Team vs. Individual Incentives? Performance Shares vs. Stock Options? These are questions for which everyone has an answer but on which analytics can provide an evidence-based answer.

Another trend is the number of companies that choose to base their reward strategies on employee feedback. Hence, the cost invested in remuneration is optimised when companies realise which aspects of the reward plans their employees value more. Companies make their reward programmes more cost efficient through offering more value for a given cost or achieving cost savings by delivering value for less. An example of such technology is in EY's methodology named TRiO, which is able to establish a quantitative view of how employees perceive value (see Figure 22.1 below). This is then analysed with information on the cost of each reward element. Other factors, such as strategic alignment, risk and competitiveness can be included to quantify overall reward effectiveness. Combinations of reward elements yielding the maximum effectiveness at various levels of cost – the 'efficient frontier' of the Total Reward investment – can then be identified.

---

4    Diez, 2018.

**Increase total reward effectiveness**

**Efficient frontier**

**Decrease cost**

**Increase cost**

**Current package**

**Decrease total reward effectiveness**

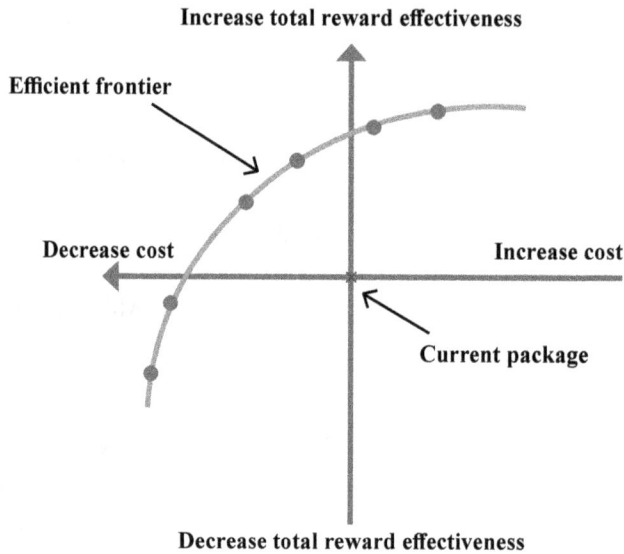

*Figure 22.1: Building an Efficient Rewards Frontier*

## 22.11 Crypto-pay

With the creation of crypto-currencies comes the opportunity of crypto-pay. On the one hand, organisations involved in this industry could "put their money where their mouth is" and use their own product to pay employees, both salary and incentives. This creates an interesting possibility, but also fraught with risk, as crypto currencies are more volatile than other currencies.

At the same time, crypto-pay creates a tool for developing international pay systems based on a single currency.

## 22.12  Salary surveys

An area ripe for disruption is salary surveys: the day is not far where the likes of LinkedIn and other recruiting platforms can supply data, both to individuals and organisations, on salaries worldwide. They already capture data from employers as they post their job offers and can easily capture data from employees and package it to protect confidentiality. One aspect where this approach can be seen as an opportunity is that it could become easier to assign a market price to various degrees of depth of knowledge of a skill, as well as a price for combinations of skills. Access to such data could permanently change the outlook from paying for the job to paying for the individual. The Blockchain can also be used in this respect to ensure the data is accurate.

A by-product of such a trend would be that candidates/employees would have access to the data, thus ending the confidentiality mindset that currently prevails. This change could bring yet more equity to our overall remuneration practices.

## 22.13  Conclusion

Many of these trends have been on the radar screen for a few years now and some have become more pronounced than others. The order has changed, and some are more important in specific industries. Well-informed remuneration professionals should become know with these trends and start thinking about deciding which ones are appropriate for the organisations they serve.

A winning rewards strategy that fits all cases does not exist. Which strategy a company can deploy will depend on a number of factors, including business strategy, the type of people the company wishes to attract, company culture, stage of business growth, strength of competitors, the company's employee value proposition, and the state of the labour market, among others. A well-designed strategy can positively affect results, whereas a poorly designed strategy can actually cause the company to lose value, as we have seen in recently publicised cases where incentive systems led to improper behaviours.

Organisations realise that a personalised, agile, holistic rewards system is essential to attracting, motivating and developing talent. So why are so many companies falling short, even as they know that their rewards programmes are outdated?

This is a good question that deserves collective thought. Our view is that organisations have been very dogmatic about the notions surrounding pay-for-performance as the only model to follow. Shareholders expect a return on their compensation investment; the CFO prefers costs to be variable and thus likes the idea of higher variable pay; senior management pursues profitability as a KPI; and the HR function often aids and abets these arguments by managing the cost side of the equation more than the revenue side when it comes to looking at ways to enhance productivity. Also, many companies still base their compensation decisions on market practice ("If my competitor does it, we should do it too!"). And the theoretical constructs around agency theory and expectancy theory (that is to say extrinsic motivation) have yet to change to a different mode of thinking (e.g. prospect theory) in the general HR community. Old loves die hard! It will take time for a few insightful companies to start using their data to analyse compensation packages and outcomes, for the new models to debunk old paradigms, and for the rest of the world to notice and start changing. A case in point: it has been extensively promoted in the business press that companies like AB InBev and Netflix remunerate their employees at the top of the market and, at the same time, that they are incredibly successful in their business results, yet few companies are willing to emulate these two. This will change in due course.

## 22.14  Summary

Globally, reward trends are relatively similar on each continent. The top trends concern the introduction of new pay models, developing more flexible approaches to remuneration, the application of analytics to the work of remuneration professionals, and the possible disruption that may come from new currencies, platforms and technologies. We will also see more scrutiny on pay equity.

It is recognised that these trends will continually impact as the future of work evolves. Which trends will become more prominent may be dependent on the maturity of the market, the industry and governance requirements.

## 22.15  Self-evaluation questions

1. Name at least five remuneration trends.
2. How does media scrutiny and governance impact executive pay?
3. How does flexibility impact the retention and engagement of employees?
4. What are the implications of not linking pay to performance?
5. Describe the flexibility trend.
6. What are the pros and cons of having more transparency regarding remuneration?
7. How will technology change the future of work? How will pay practices evolve to meet this trend?

# Toolkit 1

# Sample Remuneration Policy and Philosophy

## Introduction

How we remunerate employees reflects the dynamics of the market and context in which we operate. It aligns at all times to the strategic direction and specific value drivers of the businesses within which our organisation operates. Remuneration plays a critical role in attracting, motivating and retaining high-performing individuals. Remuneration also reinforces, encourages and promotes superior performance.

Through variable remuneration linked to value drivers, superior performance is recognised and rewarded, while poor performance and underachievement are penalised. Remuneration is never a stand-alone management process, but is rather fully integrated into other management processes, such as the performance management process and the overall HR policies.

## Rewards vision

The rewards component focuses on providing simple, integrated, holistic solutions, common messages, and a package that is differentiated from the market in order to attract, retain and energise talented, high-performing people.

## Remuneration/reward philosophy

Recognition and reward is one of our key strategies to foster a high-performance culture with engaged employees. Performance-related Pay (PRP) forms the cornerstone of our reward philosophy, supported by a robust performance management system.

The hallmark features of our reward philosophy are as follows:

- Our reward philosophy strives to set its overall remuneration package at a competitive level, by benchmarking to the market and, in addition, to provide incentives geared to performance.
- Our reward philosophy also strives to enable maximum flexibility in terms of the utilisation and reward of the workforce, and to provide maximum choice for individuals in respect of the structuring and application of their reward.
- Our reward philosophy creates an environment that is conducive to performance through the reward structure by enabling growth and development, and by differentiating appropriately between people through the various reward methods provided and through the reward process, on the basis of their contribution only.

- Our reward philosophy establishes accountability and ownership of the reward process with line management by enabling them to link the total reward process to their business objectives and manage it in a fair and equitable way, ensuring a balance between affordability and quality of life for employees.

*Table 1: Remuneration and Reward Philosophy*

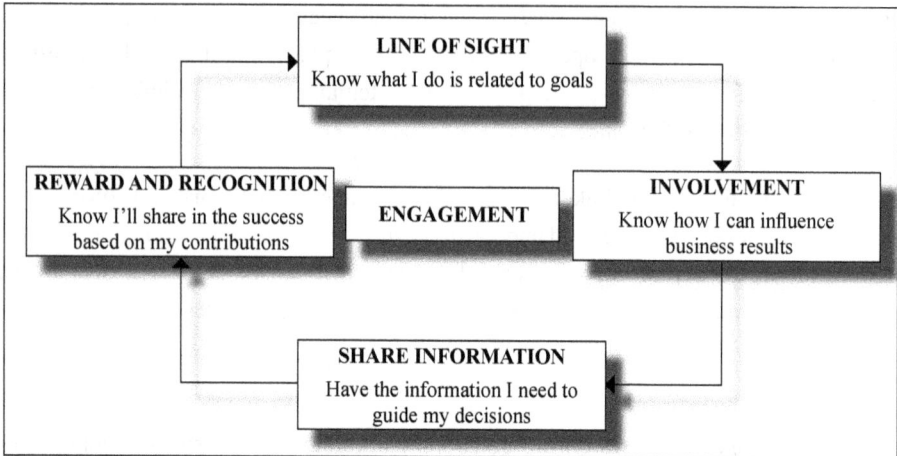

## Framework

The reward strategy is designed to be aligned with the organisation strategy and the execution of that strategy, along with an emphasis on value-based management. This in turn will maximise the performance and effectiveness of the organisation, thereby increasing shareholder returns.

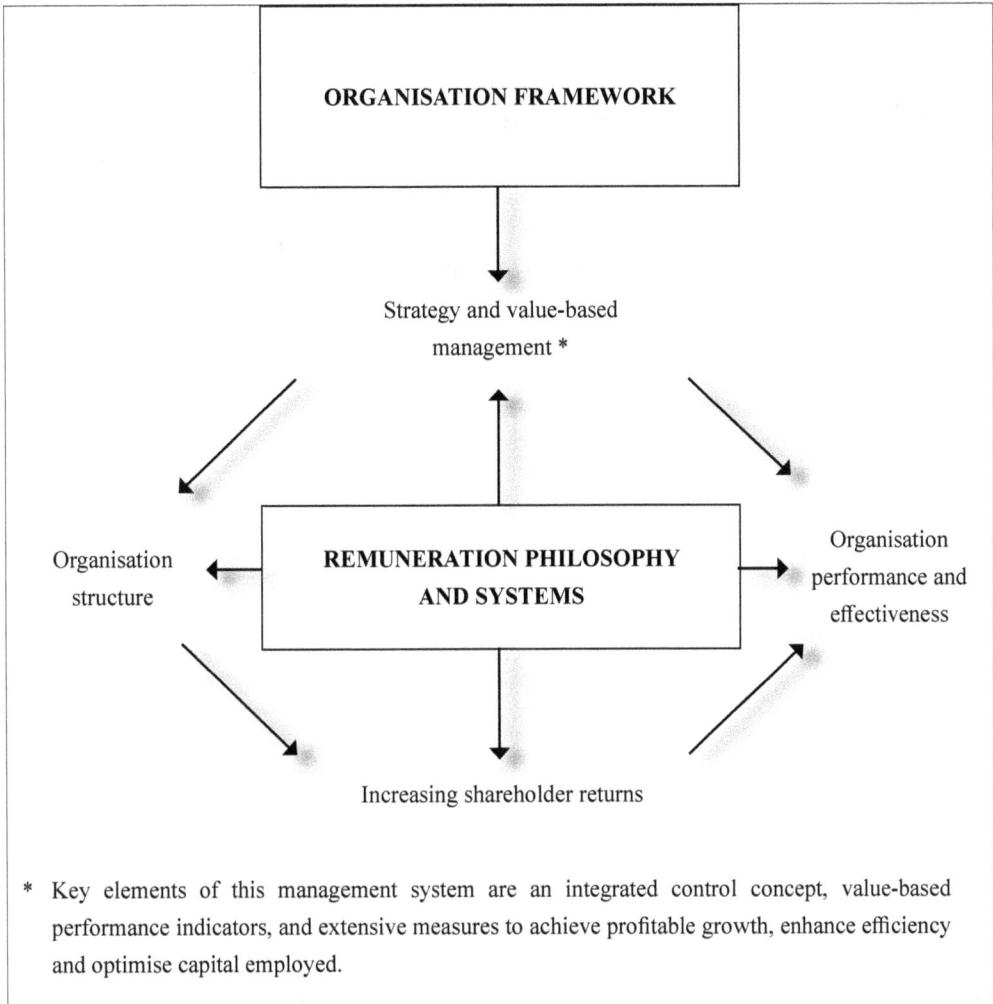

*Figure 1: Remuneration framework*

Based on the existing organisation's strategy, the objectives of the remuneration policy are to:

- Influence the organisation's employer brand positively in order to attract and retain excellent people.
- Assist in creating and enforcing a high-performance culture where sufficient differentiation is made between excellent and poor performers.
- Motivate and challenge staff to achieve more than just satisfactory performance levels.
- Simplify salary structures and related matters.
- Ensure that all employees are recognised and rewarded for their performance in a fair and equitable way.
- Conduct job evaluation and grading to ensure that employees are remunerated equitably according to the value they are contributing to the company.

## *Objectives*

- **Pay and benefits:** Attraction and retention of talented, high-performing people.
- **Performance bonuses and short-term incentives (STIs):** Support and reinforcement of desired behaviour and delivery at all levels.
- **Long-term incentives (LTIs):** Attraction, retention and alignment with shareholder thinking.
- **Recognition:** Support and reinforcement of a culture of belonging, performance and affinity.

The above points are summarised in Table 2.

*Table 2: Remuneration Elements*

| Remuneration element | Purpose |
|---|---|
| **Basic pay** | • Fair pay for a day's work<br>• Pays for overall job requirements, accountability, complexity of tasks, and diversity of tasks |
| **Benefits/Perquisites** | • Safety net for emergencies<br>• Provides special payments and programmes that may set the organisation apart from others |
| **Short-term and medium-term incentive** | • Gets results and ensures successful execution of the strategic plan<br>• Variable component to reward contribution to business plan |
| **Long-term incentive** | • Crucial in retaining employees<br>• Focuses attention on longer-term strategic imperatives |

## *Assumptions*

The following assumptions are an integral part of the philosophy:

- It is aligned with corporate values.
- It is based on a total rewards philosophy and approach.
- Leadership provides the context – rewards complement the culture.
- It places emphasis on developing a collaborative, highly-motivating and energised culture – it is focused on delivery.
- There is a strong focus on customer value, customer partnering and unique competitive advantage.
- The human qualities of entrepreneurship and innovation are balanced by a disciplined and collaborative way of working.
- It reinforces employees' self-reliance.

## *Scope*

Remuneration policy is applicable to all employees who are permanent or contract employees who are on the payroll and whose contracts with the company are for more than six months in a financial year. It is not applicable to temporary personnel from third-party employers.

## *Guiding principles*

- Alignment with business strategy.
- Integration with other people management solutions and initiatives.
- Fit for purpose, not one-size-fits-all.
- Flexible and adaptable.
- Manage risk and liability.
- Optimise investment in people.
- Performance-based reward.
- Fair and equitable, and supportive of diverse needs.
- Reinforce teamwork and a high commitment, belonging, high-performance culture.
- Legislative compliance.
- Embraces more than just money – it's the whole work experience.
- Stands up to scrutiny by stakeholders.
- Education and feedback are the cornerstones.
- Utilises experts.
- Shift from entitlement and bargaining to culture of earned and belonging.
- Open and transparent communication.
- Non-discriminatory practices.
- Internal and external parity.
- Affordability.

## Remuneration policy

### *Pay and benefits framework*

Guaranteed remuneration is determined by a number of factors:

- **Job evaluation – a job-complexity and job-sizing tool**
  The level of guaranteed pay for an individual is based on his or her level of responsibility in the organisation and the size of his or her grade.
- **Remuneration surveys/benchmarking – skills scarcity premiums**
  Where market surveys indicate that a particular job grouping is significantly out of line with the market, a market premium percentage may be allocated. The percentages are covered in the retention submission.

- **Market position**

  Our defined market position is the median (50th percentile), however the movement for entrants to sustain superior performance ranges from the lower quartile (25th percentile) to the upper quartile (75th percentile). This movement is based on performance, track record, market benchmarking and affordability.

- **Individual performance and contribution**

  Guaranteed remuneration will be modified in relation to performance of individuals or teams to create a clear differentiation between low, acceptable and high performance.

- **Job family-pay scales**

  Remuneration bands will be determined for each job family, based on prevailing market forces, which will determine the ranges of remuneration applicable to each employee grouping.

*Appointment and promotion*

Appointments and promotions, internally and externally, will be done on the minimum, as per the range. Exceptions will be motivated within the relevant delegation framework.

*Successor*

Employees appointed on a development plan may be appointed at 7.5 to 20 percent less than the minimum of the range.

*Variable remuneration – incentive schemes*

Variable remuneration programmes will be established within the organisation and its operations to support the achievement of its objectives and in accordance with its approach to value-based management. These programmes will seek to enable participants to retain a clear view of their remuneration opportunities.

Since variable pay should be self-funding, payout is dependent on the company achieving its overall performance targets (individual, business unit and company targets must all be met).

*Comparative benchmarking*

- Targeting remuneration to market levels will generally be on the basis of total guaranteed package, to provide the organisation with guidance.
- In order to compare the variable remuneration component, market practices with regard to typical remuneration mixes and principles of long-term incentive will serve as the basis for the recommendations. Local and international best practice may inform the designs employed by the organisation.
- The organisations selected for the purposes of providing benchmark data will focus on, but may not be restricted to, our industry sector, as well as national remuneration data.

- There may be discretionary elements of pay beyond benchmarked levels for scarcity, attraction or retention, as appropriate.
- Expert remuneration consultancies will be used to provide us with market data to assist us in our remuneration decisions.

### *Annual remuneration reviews*

In order to maintain appropriate remuneration competitiveness *vis-à-vis* the labour market, remuneration will be reviewed annually.

Annual remuneration reviews will be informed by:

- Projected inflation.
- Internal equity.
- External market.
- Performance.
- Contribution of each operation.
- Affordability.

### *Salary management – guiding principles*

- Consider the overall pay history of the individual.
- The most important aspect to consider is the individual's unique market worth.
- Actively manage the remuneration of good performers who are considerably underpaid.
- "Slow down" the pay of overpaid people (underperformers who are paid at the top of the pay scale).
- Give poor performers no increases.
- Avoid creating expectations of interim increases.
- Pay ranges are guidelines only.

### *Benefits – guiding principles*

- The organisation will implement benefit solutions that meet the aggregated needs of employees, while at the same time being sufficiently flexible to cope with a rapidly changing environment.
- The organisation will endeavour to provide flexible and portable benefits options, however will not entertain benefit structures that require extensive infrastructure and unnecessary administrative support.
- Access to benefits will be open to all.

This will be achieved by individuals being allowed choice in the type and level of benefits (within the rules and legislation governing the benefits), in order to:

- Limit the organisation's exposure to open-ended benefit liabilities.
- Give employees the flexibility to optimise individual benefit and cash flow needs.
- Offer easy access to benefit schemes that are affordable and/or tax-efficient.
- Require individuals to take responsibility for their own tax compliance.

### Guiding principles for variable pay – short-term

- Superior individual performance will be recognised even if corporate performance targets are not met.
- Variable remuneration will be pitched at the median quartile (50th percentile) of the market.
- Defensible differentiation: This means that where employees stand to gain differing amounts, these are based on clearly evident, predetermined performance measures and contribution levels.
- Good governance: The scheme design reflects good corporate governance principles.
- Reinforce entrepreneurial spirit: The scheme lets individuals decide how to achieve targets.
- Frequent review: Design of performance targets needs to be reviewed annually to effect continuous improvement in line with market conditions and organisation strategy.
- Equity: There will be equity of treatment and access to relevant information will be provided.
- Clarity of performance contract: There needs to be clarity around which performance targets and measures need to be managed as part of the day-to-day performance contracts of teams and individuals, and which performance targets and measures are those against which performance bonuses will be paid (standard performance goals versus stretch goals).

### Guiding principles for long-term incentives

The LTI adopted is the rolling or banked incentive scheme. The payment will be in the proportion of:

- 50 percent in year 1.
- 30 percent in year 2.
- 20 percent in year 3.

The scheme rules are contained in the Incentive Scheme Rules document.

### Linkage to performance management – guiding principles

- Performance-related pay (PRP) will be institutionalised as the norm in our organisation.
- All employees will have a portion of their pay determined by their individual or team performance.

- Performance outputs will be developed for all employees in support of the organisation strategy.
- Performance outputs will be "smart" and customer-focused:
  o Specific.
  o Measurable.
  o Achievable.
  o Relevant.
  o Time-based.

## Communication and implementation considerations

At the executive level, and as far as it is practical down the organisation, employees will be involved in the design, implementation and modification of remuneration programmes. We are committed to open communication with all internal stakeholders about the design and launching of remuneration programmes, and ongoing changes to them, with clear statements of what remuneration is designed to achieve.

## Remuneration Committee

The composition of each remuneration committee is at the discretion of the local board. The role of the Group remuneration committee is to:

- Determine the basis for allocation of share options and to grant options to executives.
- Investigate, recommend and approve the remuneration of the chief executive officer and other executive directors and senior management.
- Consider and make recommendations to the board concerning an incentive scheme and thereafter monitor the implementation.
- Make other general recommendations to the board regarding the remuneration strategy and policy guidelines of the organisation affecting its executives.
- Provide management with a mandate to negotiate pay increases for staff.

### *Non-executive director fees – guidelines*

As part of achieving and maintaining reasonable, acceptable levels of remuneration, the committee is encouraged to consider the following guidelines.

### *Base fees*

- The base fee is the general level of fee earned by directors in their professional capacities (for example, as lawyers, accountants, executives, management consultants).

- Travel time and preparation for meetings, as well as actual attendance, are taken into consideration.
- A comparison can be made with the level of the chief executive officer's remuneration, disregarding any incentive package.
- Company performance (that is, profit, dividends and share price) is not considered to be of special significance for the purpose of setting a base fee.
- The fee must be fair.

*Supplementary fees*

- Supplementary work resulting from the membership of subcommittees should be spread as evenly as possible among board members and recognised in the level of the base fee.

*Reimbursement of expenses*

- The organisation will reimburse the directors for all direct and indirect expenses reasonably and properly incurred.
- Accommodation and travelling expenses should include those incurred in attending all meetings in connection with company business.
- The organisation will reimburse directors where they have used personal transport, but travelling expenses should be realistic.

*Directors' and officers' liability insurance*

- Directors should arrange for such insurance to be taken out, and to be paid by the company.

*Payments on termination*

- The payment of retirement benefits to executive directors is an accepted practice in many companies and should be determined as is needed. Alternatively, a termination payment can be negotiated as part of the overall remuneration package.
- The committee should ensure that payments of benefits of any nature on termination are not restricted by the company's articles of association, but are fair to the company and can be adequately justified to shareholders if the company is called on to do so.

### Flexibility

All the components of remuneration are, in the normal course, a matter of negotiated commercial contract and, accordingly, should be sufficiently flexible to suit each individual circumstance.

### Roles and responsibilities

Table 3 sets out the roles and responsibilities regarding remuneration issues.

*Table 3: Roles and responsibilities regarding remuneration*

| Who | Responsibility |
|---|---|
| **Board** | • Approves remuneration philosophy policy and executive remuneration. |
| **RemCo** | • Recommends remuneration philosophy, policy and executive remuneration to board. |
| **CEO/EXCO** | • Recommends remuneration philosophy, policy and executive remuneration to RemCo.<br>• Develops remuneration strategy and implements remuneration in the organisation. |
| **HR** | • Develops remuneration strategies that underpin the HR strategy and organisation strategy. |
| **Group remuneration committee** | • Develop best-practice remuneration solutions.<br>• Ensure uniform implementation.<br>• Provide advice and strategic direction. |
| **Divisional remuneration committee** | • Implement remuneration practices and tactics.<br>• Provide advice and practical application. |
| **Line managers** | • Understand the remuneration policies, strategy and systems, for example, job evaluation, performance appraisals, bonus schemes, benefit structures.<br>• Apply them to staff and resolve queries.<br>• Provide HR with constructive feedback that will assist in improvement. |
| **Payroll/HRIS** | • Process payroll and handle queries.<br>• Ensure database integrity.<br>• Form part of HR and remuneration team to resolve remuneration issues. |
| **Job evaluation committee** | • Grades jobs submitted to the committee. |
| **Unions** | • Conduct negotiations or discussions regarding remuneration. in good faith. |

# Toolkit 2

## Definitions of Remuneration Terms

### General remuneration terms

**External equity** is the perceived fairness of pay relative to what other employers are paying for the same type of work.

**Internal equity** is the perceived equity of a pay system in an organisation.

**Job evaluation** is the systematic process of assessing job content and ranking jobs according to a consistent set of job characteristics and market-related remuneration.

**Job grading** is a form of job evaluation that assigns jobs to predetermined job classifications according to their relative worth to the organisation.

**Performance-based increases** are pay increases given to individual workers according to an evaluation of their performance and the organisation's performance.

**Salary band** is a pay range for each job grade including a minimum, median and maximum point.

**Red-circled rate** is a rate of pay higher than the contractual, or formally established, rate for the job.

**Salary surveys** are studies made of salaries paid by other organisations within the employer's labour market.

### Definition of specific remuneration terms in build up to total earnings

a)  For countries that have the total guaranteed package approach to structuring remuneration:

**Base or basic salary** is the fixed guaranteed cash payment made to an employee. This includes a fixed bonus, a 13th cheque, and foreign earnings.

**+ Car benefit** is the fully inclusive cost of the annual car benefit. This is either the full car allowance inclusive of all amounts paid (that is, a fixed car allowance but excluding reimbursements) or in the case of a company car, the fully inclusive actual cost to company of providing the company car.

**+ Other benefits** (other than operational costs) include the cost of additional guaranteed perquisite benefits (perks) and allowances such as housing, low-cost loans, club fees, professional fees, subscriptions, cell phone allowance, computer allowance, or any other similar benefits. In the case of housing benefits, the cost is defined as either the amount of subsidy paid or the rental paid on the employee's behalf. In the case of a subsidised home loan, the cost is the difference between the interest rate charged to the company and the interest rate charged to the employee.

= **Total flexible remuneration or cash package** is the basic salary plus total car benefit and other perquisite benefits (for example, cost of housing benefits, club fees + professional association fees + subscriptions, cost of low-interest personal loans) **but excluding employee benefits**.

+ **Employee benefits/cost of employee benefits** include the cost of the employer's contribution to pension and/or provident fund (including both retirement and insured benefits), group life benefits and medical aid.

= **Guaranteed package** is the total annual guaranteed cost to a company of employing an incumbent. The cost includes the total annual salary, plus non-cash fringe benefits. Typically these include company car, company pension or provident fund and medical aid contributions, group life and accident insurance, company assistance or subsidies, low-interest loans, and any other recreational or other benefits. This excludes any form of variable pay.

+ **Short-term incentive** is an annual bonus tied to the performance of the company, team and/ or individual performance. Short-term incentives refer to incentives that are applicable for up to one year, such as incentive target, discretionary bonus, and profit share.

- **Incentive target**: The bonus is related to the achievement typically of a financial target such as turnover or profit, as well as other objectives. The incentive bonus is typically a percentage of the total guaranteed package.
- **Discretionary bonus**: The bonus is a discretionary amount that bears some relationship to the individual's performance.
- **Profit share**: The bonus is a predetermined percentage of the organisation's profits, usually also dependent on the achievement of other objectives as well.

= **Total remuneration** is the total all-inclusive annual cost to a company of employing an incumbent. This cost includes base salary, guaranteed benefits and short-term incentives.

+ **Long-term incentive** refers to incentives that are applicable for over one year, such as long-term cash incentive schemes.

- **Long-term cash incentive scheme**: The incumbent participates in a bonus incentive scheme in which the incentive is paid out over several years. Usually a portion (for example, one-third) is paid each year; the remaining "banked" amount can be increased or decreased depending on performance from one year to the next.

= **Total earnings** include total remuneration (base salary + benefits + short-term incentives) plus payments resulting from long-term incentives paid in the past year.

b)   For countries that have the total compensation approach to structuring remuneration:

Base Salary (Including 13th Month) Allowances

1.   Total Fixed Pay
     Annual Incentives

2.   Total Cash (a + Annual Incentives)
     Long-Term Incentives

3.   Total Compensation (b + LTI)
     Life/Health Plans
     Pension/CPF Contribution
     Other Benefits

4.   Total Benefits (Sum of three above)
5.   Total Package (c + d)

"Forced curve" – where there is a desired distribution of performance scores.

"Line of sight" – refers to being able to control the measures that are being used.

# Toolkit 3

# Sample Job Description Form

| | |
|---|---|
| Job title: | Job grade: |
| Department: | |
| Location/site: | |
| Section: | |
| Date: | |
| Position in the organisation:<br>*(use job title only)*<br>Supervisor (2nd level) | |
| Immediate supervisor | |
| **This position:** | |
| Subordinates | |
| Comments (for example, is there anything unusual about the organogram?): | |
| Other important contacts (on work-related issues, excluding the supervisor):<br>Internal: | |
| External: | |

1. **Primary purpose of the job**

   *(One sentence, explaining why the job exists. This should be unique to this job and <u>not</u> generic so that it fits other jobs in the organisation.)*

2. **Major task headings/Key Performance Areas (KPAs)**

   *(KPA headings should match the headings in section 5, the detailed description of KPAs.)*

3. **Other special requirements**

4. **Salient information/Parameters of work environment**

   *(This is optional, but is useful in showing parameters, for example, budget size, sales, units serviced, billing, turnover, tonnes per annum, and so on. It is important for this section to be filled in for director or senior management positions.)*

5. **Detailed description**

   *(Describe each KPA as set out in section 2 above. Start with a verb and avoid describing trivial or incidental tasks.)*

6. **Job specification**

   *(NOTE: This is a requirement that is set by the company and is to be completed by top management. It is generally used for recruitment purposes.)*

### 6.1 Education

*(Formal education)*

Min: _____

Ideal: _____

### 6.2 Legal

*(For example, driver's licence, blasting certificate)*

Min: _____

Ideal: _____

### 6.3 Training

*(On-the-job-training, should the present incumbent leave)*

Min: _____

Ideal: _____

### 6.4 Experience

*(Career path that should ideally be followed before attaining this position)*

|  | Job title | Minimum time spent |
|---|---|---|
| 1. |  |  |
| 2. |  |  |
| 3. |  |  |

Job analyst's name: _____

Job analyst's position title: Consultant

Seen by incumbent:_____

Signature: _____

Date: _____

Agreed by supervisor (1st level):

Signature: _____

Date: _____

Agreed by supervisor (2nd level):

Signature: _____

Date: _____

# Toolkit 4

# Common Systems of Job Evaluation

Many systems of job evaluation are used. Set out below in alphabetical order are some of the more common ones. Please contact Dr. Mark Bussin at drbussin@mweb.co.za to make suggestions, amendments and inclusions.

## 1.   Calibr8 (Keith Roxburgh©)

*Table 1: Calibr8 System*

| KNOWLEDGE | |
|---|---|
| Professional knowledge | This factor looks at the required knowledge, gained through study, courses, experience and mentoring, that the position holder needs in order to be equipped to manage his/her job effectively.  It also takes into account specialised skills and highly developed attributes that will add substantially to the ability to achieve end results. |
| Leadership/Influence | This refers to the use of knowledge in setting direction in business situations. |
| Interaction skills | This refers to the need to influence others through the use of knowledge and abilities in order to achieve end results. In other words, how does one use knowledge in order to get the co-operation and buy-in of others? |
| **COMPLEXITY** | |
| Judgement | This factor considers the judgements and recommendations the position holder has to make in the course of his or her work, and the level of the business upon which such judgements or recommendations will impact. |
| Process complexity | This factor considers the complexity in which the position has to operate. To an extent this is similar to the levels of work concept, but also takes into account diversification factors. |
| **CONTRIBUTION** | |
| Decision-making | What decisions is the individual expected to make in order for the role to be effective in achieving its goals, and what level in the company will these impact? At the higher end, this factor considers the difference in divisional, company or group strategic decision-making. |
| Strategic impact | This factor looks at the extent to which decisions described above will impact the company as a whole.  All position impacts are considered in relation to the extent that they affect the company as a whole, right down to convenience-type impacts provided by indirect support staff. |
| Impact type | Simply, given the level of decisions or recommendations of the incumbent, is the impact of this decision direct or indirect (or co-ordinative and direction-giving versus advisory or specialised)? |

## 2. Equate (South African Government)

**Equate**

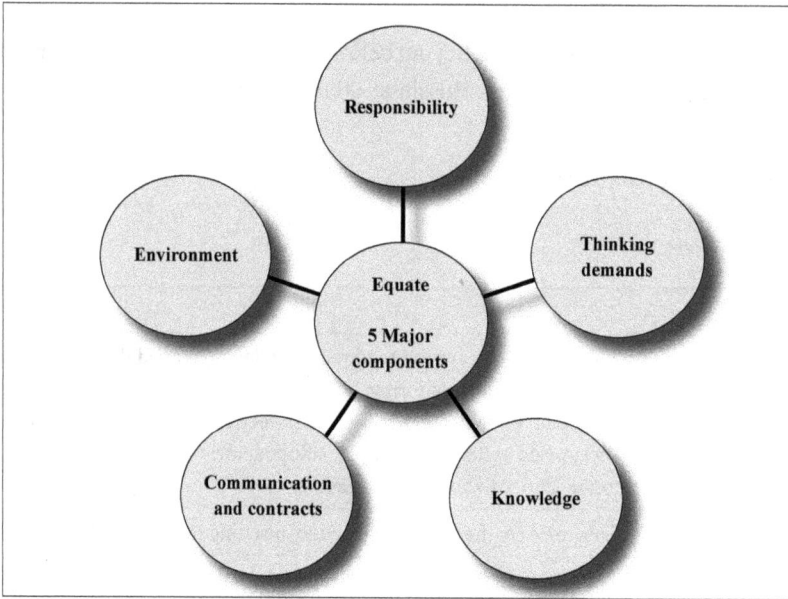

*Figure 1: Equate's five major components*

## 3. Execu-Measure (21st Century Pay Solutions Group©)

**Execu-Measure**

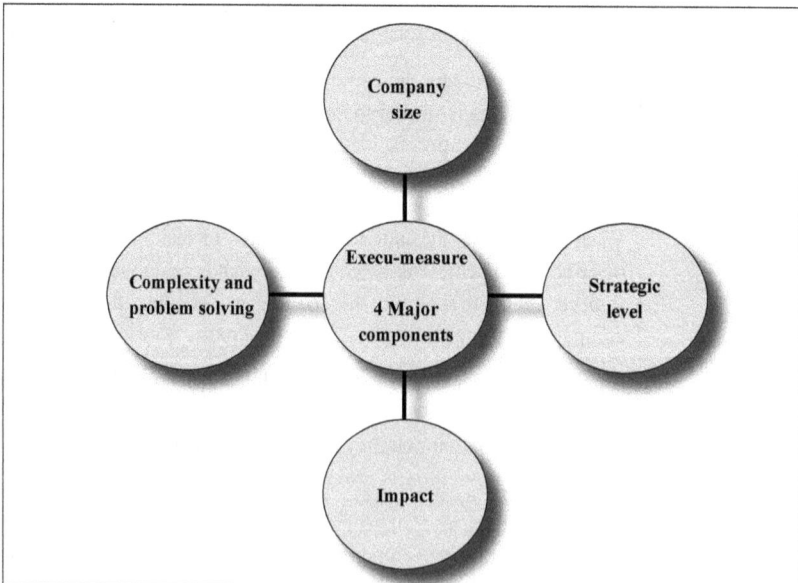

*Figure 2: Execu-Measure's four major components*

## 4. HAY job evaluation system (HAY Management Consultants©)

*Table 2: Evaluation model of Hay systems theory*

| HAY | |
|---|---|
| **Know-how** | • Technical – specialised depth and breadth<br>• Managerial requirements – plan, organise, staff, direct and control resources for results<br>• Human relations skills – influence, motivate, change behaviour and build relationships |
| **Problem-solving** | • Environment – the context of the job and its focus<br>• Challenge – the availability of guides and the complexity of analysis required |
| **Accountability** | • Freedom to act – focus on decision-making authority vested in position to achieve results<br>• Scope – focus on magnitude of the results expected, relative to the enterprise<br>• Impact – focus on relevant scope |

## 5. JEasy-web based (21ˢᵗ Century Pay Solutions Group©)

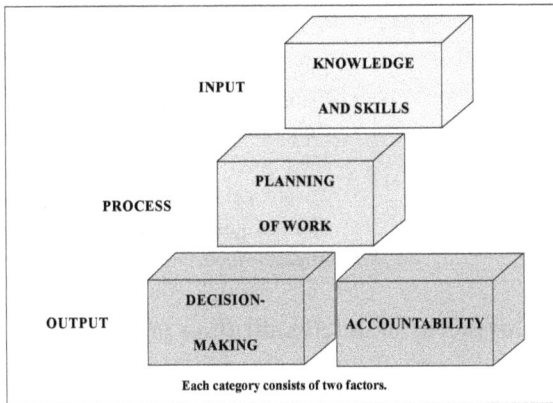

*Figure 3: JEasy Factors*

# 6. JE Paterson Points (21ˢᵗ Century Pay Solutions Group©)

Paterson Points is a web-based points grading evaluation system which was designed to fully align with any equal pay legislation. The factors are:

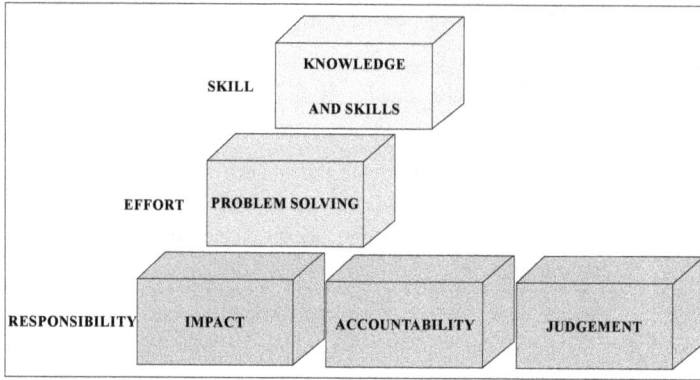

*Figure 4: Paterson points factors*

## 7. JE Manager job evaluation system (Hay©)

*Table 3: Factors of JE Manager*

| JE Manager | |
|---|---|
| Main factors | • Judgement<br>• Planning and leadership<br>• Communication<br>• Job Impact<br>• Theoretical knowledge and application<br>• Skills acquisition and practice<br>• Impact – focus has on relevant scope |

## 8. Paterson job evaluation system (classification method)

*Table 4: Grading factors of Paterson*

| Paterson | | |
|---|---|---|
| **Factor/Dimension** | **Description** | **Used For** |
| Factor 1 | Decision-making, responsibility, and judgement | Banding |
| Factor 2 | Supervision, co-ordination of people and work, or sapiential authority | Subbanding |
| Factor 3 | Complexity of tasks | Subgrading |
| Factor 4 | Variety of tasks | Subgrading |
| Factor 5 | Degree of precision required | Subgrading |
| Factor 6 | Work pressure and physical effort | Subgrading |

*Table 5: Paterson evaluation model*

| Band | Kind of decision | Title/Level | Sub-band | Kind of grade | Typical titles |
|------|------------------|-------------|----------|---------------|----------------|
| F | Policy-making | Top management | FU | Co-ordinating or supervisory (policy) | Managing director |
|   | | International expert | FL | Policy | Executive director |
| E | Programming/ long-term strategy | Senior management | EU | Co-ordinating or supervisory (programmes) | General manager, business manager |
|   | | Specialist | EL | Programming, long-term | Senior manager, business area manager |
| D | Interpretive/ probabilistic | Middle management | DU | Supervisory (interpretive) | Department manager |
|   | | Professional | DL | Interpretive/ probabilistic | Section manager |
| C | Process/system | Skilled | CU | Supervisory (skilled) | Supervisor/ foreman |
|   | | Advanced operational | CL | Process/system | Artisan, sales rep |
| B | Automatic/ operative/ subsystem | Semi-skilled/ operational | BU | Supervisory (semi-skilled) | Charge hand, bookkeeper |
|   | | | BL | Operational/ subsystem | Operator, driver, clerical |
| A | Primary | Basic skills | A | Defined | Trainee, basic skills |

## 9.   Peromnes job evaluation system (Deloitte©)

*Table 6: Peromnes factors*

| Peromnes factors | |
|------------------|--|
| Factor 1: Problem-solving | The nature and complexity of the decisions, judgements and recommendations made in the job |
| Factor 2: Consequences of judgements | The impact or results of legitimate decisions, judgements and recommendations |
| Factor 3: Pressure of work | The volume, variety and type of work required within the time available in which to do it |

| Peromnes factors | |
|---|---|
| Factor 4: Knowledge | The level of knowledge required to perform the job competently |
| Factor 5: Job impact | The influence that the job has on other activities, both within and outside the organisation |
| Factor 6: Comprehension | The level of understanding required of spoken and written communications |
| Factor 7: Educational qualifications | The minimum essential qualifications required to perform the job |
| Factor 8: Training and experience | The typical period of training and experience to achieve competence, after achieving the required minimum qualifications |

## 10. REMeasure job evaluation system (Web-based) (Remchannel©)

*Table 7: Evaluation model of REMeasure*

| Input factors | |
|---|---|
| **Factor** | **Weighting** |
| Qualification, knowledge and skills | 50 |
| Experience and training | 50 |
| Weighting A – D | 25% |
| Weighting E – F + | 20% |
| **Process factors** | |
| Problem-solving | 50 |
| Communication | 50 |
| Weighting A – D | 40% |
| Weighting E – F + | 20% |
| **Output factors** | |
| Financial impact | 70 |
| Influence | 50 |
| Weighting A – D | 35% |
| Weighting E – F + | 60% |

## 11.  Stratified Systems Theory (SST) – adapted

*Table 8: Comparison of the Paterson and SST job evaluation systems*

| PATERSON | SST | LINE | SPECIALIST | DESCRIPTIONS |
|---|---|---|---|---|
| F | 5 | TOP MANAGEMENT | | Corporate strategic direction and policy sign-off |
| E | 4 | SENIOR MANAGEMENT | GROUP/ FUNCTIONAL / ADVISOR | Translation of corporate direction into organisation planning and management |
| D | 3 | MIDDLE MANAGEMENT | PROFESSIONAL / SPECIALIST | Translation of organisation plans into functional plans and best-practice systems |
| C Upper | 2 | FIRST LINE SUPERVISORS | TECHNICIAN / PRACTITIONER | Optimising a given system to achieve plans |
| C Lower | 1 | SKILLED WORKERS | | Solving a range of technical problems within a recognised technical discipline through the appropriate use of tools |
| B | 1 | OPERATIONAL SKILLS | | Routine application of industry-specific tools and equipment which require training but not discipline: apprenticeship |
| A | 1 | PRIMARY SKILLS | | Routine task orientation using simple tools and equipment normally of a manual nature |

*Table 9: Evaluation model of Stratified Systems Theory (SST)*

| Pure SST band | SST-derived band | Short title | Short description |
|---|---|---|---|
| 7 | G CCS | Global corporate governance/ Global multinational | Construct complex systems (G CCS) Global strategy and direction formulation Global multinational Income mostly from other companies |
| 6 | G OCS | Global corporate governance/ Multinational | Oversee complex systems cross-national and global-regional (G OCS) Strategies and direction formulation Income mostly from one organisation |
| 5 | SI | Strategic intent (SI) | Corporate strategic direction and policy sign-off |

| Pure SST band | SST-derived band | Short title | Short description |
|---|---|---|---|
| 4 | SE | Strategy execution (SE) Senior management/Senior professional/Specialist | Translation of corporate direction into organisation planning and management |
| 3 | MP | Management/ Professional/ Consultant (MP) | Translation of organisation plans into functional plans and tactics |
| 2 | SP | Supervisory/ Technician/ Practitioner (SP) | Optimising a given functional system to achieve plans |
| 1 | AO | Advanced operational (AO) | Solving a range of technical problems within a recognised technical discipline through the appropriate use of a range of tools |
| 1 | O | Operational (O) Clerical/Operator | Routine application of industry-specific tools and equipment which require training but not discipline apprenticeship |
| 1 | P | Primary (P) | Routine task orientation using simple tools and equipment normally of a manual nature |

## 12. TASK job evaluation system (Deloitte©)

*Table 10: Evaluation model of the TASK*

| Stage 1 | Assessment of overall skill level of job |
|---|---|
| Stage 2 | Assessment of complexity of job content and relationships Assessment of requisite level of knowledge and understanding |
| Stage 3 | Assessment of job influence Assessment of work pressure. This fine-tunes assessments of stage 2 |
| Stage 4 | Establishment of job grade by converting the sum of the scores to a TASK grade using a standard conversion table |

A cross-correlation table showing all the types of job evaluation system has been provided in Table 16.

Tables 11 to 15 give an indication of typical job titles by grade or level. Obviously this is indicative because the appropriate method of grading is to use the full job description to grade jobs.

*Table 11: Generic titles by typical Paterson grade*

| Paterson Grade | Typical grades for typical jobs |
|---|---|
| A 1 | Cleaner, Tea Maker |
| A 2 | Security Guard, Packer |
| A 3 | Cook, Boiler Operator |
| B 1 | Receptionist, Fireman, Crane Driver, Apprentice, Cashier |
| B 2 | Medical Aid Assessor, Inventory Control Clerk, Driver |
| B 3 | Secretary, Wages Clerk |
| B 4 | Operations Supervisor, Shift Supervisor |
| B 5 | Customer Services Consultant, Telesales Consultant, PA |
| C 1 | Bookkeeper, HR Assistant, Canteen Supervisor, Bricklayer, Microbiologist |
| C 2 | Programmer, Safety Officer, Assistant Foreman, Welder, Fitter and Turner |
| C 3 | Credit Controller, Senior Buyer, Service Engineer Technician |
| C 4 | Site Foreman/Supervisor, Chemist, Geologist |
| C 5 | Chief Safety Officer, Production Superintendent |
| D 1 | Financial Analyst, Industrial Relations Manager, Transport Manager |
| D 2 | Legal Officer, Quality Control Manager, Project Manager, |
| D 3 | Medical Doctor, Production Manager, Senior Scientist |
| D 4 | Financial Manager, Logistics Manager, Marketing Manager, Civil Engineer |
| D 5 | Group Manager, Senior Actuary, Chief Chemist |
| E 1 | Business Area Manager, Business Unit EXCO, Group or National Expert |
| E 2 | Business Unit Manager, General Manager of Major Corporate Function |
| E 3 | Subsidiary Director |
| F 1 | Subsidiary MD/CEO, Head of major Strategic Business Unit, International Expert |
| F 2 | Group Executive Director, COO, Main Board Member |
| F 3 | Group Managing Director, Chairperson, Group CEO |

*Table 12: Typical titles by SST Grades*

| Derived SST Grade | Typical grades for typical jobs |
|---|---|
| P1 | Tea Maker, Gardener, Picking Clerk, Manual labour |
| P2 | Messenger, Easy Operator or Clerical |
| O1 | Operator, Driver, Clerk, Telephonist |
| O2 | Operator (multi-machines), Clerk (multi-function), Secretary |
| O3 | Process operator, PA, Bookkeeper, Administration Officer |
| AO1 | Artisan single trade, Executive Assistant, Sales representative (General) |

| Derived SST Grade | Typical grades for typical jobs |
|---|---|
| AO2 | Artisan multiple trade, Sales representative (Senior or Technical) |
| AO3 | Mechanician, Accountant |
| SP1 | First line Manager/Supervisor, Practitioner, Technician |
| MP1 | Professional, Discipline Expert |
| MP2 | Head of a Sub-Department or Discipline, Seasoned Professional |
| MP3 | Head of Departments or Discipline, Business Unit Expert |
| SE1 | Business Area Manager, Chief Researcher or Adviser, Business Unit EXCO, Group or National Expert |
| SE2 | Business Unit Manager, General Manager of Major Corporate Function, Subsidiary Director |
| SI1 | Subsidiary MD, Head of Major Strategic Business Unit, International Expert |
| SI2 | Group Executive Director, COO, Main Board Member |
| SI3 | Chairperson, Group CEO, Group Managing Director |
| G | Global CEO, Global Chairperson, Global Executive Director |

*Table 13: Typical school titles by level*

| Level | High School | Primary School | Support |
|---|---|---|---|
| 1/Eu | | | CEO/Rector |
| | Head of school | | |
| | | Head of school | |
| 2/El | EXCO | | EXCO |
| | | EXCO | |
| 3/D | HOD | | Senior manager |
| | | HOD | |
| 4/Cu | Subject leader | | Manager |
| | | Subject leader | |
| 5 /Cm | Senior experienced teacher | | Supervisor |
| | | Senior experienced teacher | |
| 6/Cl | Teacher | | Advanced or specialist admin |
| | | Teacher | |
| 7/Bu | New teacher | | General admin |
| | | New teacher | |
| 8/Bl | Trainee teacher | | |
| | | Trainee teacher | |
| 9/A | | | General worker |
| | | | |

*Table 14: Typical university titles by level*

| Title | Paterson | Peromnes | Equate |
|---|---|---|---|
| Professor | D5 | 4 | 14 |
| Associate Professor | D3 | 5 | 13 |
| Senior Lecturer | D2 | 6 | 12 |
| Lecturer | C5/D1 | 7 | 11 |

*Table 15: Typical senior government official titles by level*

| Typical Level | Title | Generic title |
|---|---|---|
| 13 – D3/D4 | Director | Manager |
| 14 – D5/E1 | Chief Director | Senior Manager |
| 15 – E2/E3 | Deputy Director General/ Deputy Permanent Secretary | Executive Manager |
| 16 – Eu/Fl | Director General/Permanent Secretary | Head of Department |

*Table 16: 21st Century job evaluation – cross correlation table*

| 21st CENTURY 7 LEVEL BROAD-BAND | 21st CENTURY 7 levels with sub-grades | 21st CENTURY JE^asy LEVELS | 21st CENTURY EXECU-MEASURE | SST | PATERSON BROAD-BAND | PATERSON | PATERSON POINTS | PEROMNES | TASK | HAY (typical application) | REWARD LEVELS | REMEASURE | JE MANAGER (typical application) | EQUATE | Mercer IPE Position Class | Towers Watson Grading Application | EMPLOYMENT EQUITY - OCCUPATIONAL LEVELS | DESCRIPTION |
|---|---|---|---|---|---|---|---|---|---|---|---|---|---|---|---|---|---|---|
| **P (Primary Skills)** | | | | | | | | | | | | | | | | | | |
| Unskilled | P1 | 1a | | | | A1 | 5 | 19/18 | 1 | 54 – 62 (57) | 4 | 20 - 29 | 1 – 7 | 1 | 40 | 1 | Unskilled and defined decision making | Steps to accomplish work or processes are clearly defined and understood. Tasks are sometimes repetitive and uncomplicated and the work cycle is short. |
| Basic Skilled | | 1b | | Low 1 | | A2 | 6 | 17 | 2 | 63 – 72 (66) | 5 | 30 - 39 | 8 – 16 | 2 | 41 | 1 | | |
| Higher Skilled | P2 | 1c | | | A | A3 | 7 | 16 | 3 | 73 – 84 (75) | 6 | 40 - 49 | 17 – 24 | 3 | | 1 | | |
| **O (Operational)** | | | | | | | | | | | | | | | | | | |
| Basic Operational Skills | O1 | 2a | | | B Lower | B1 | 8 | 15 | 4 | 85 – 97 (90) | 7 | 50 - 59 | 25 – 34 | 4 | 42 | 2 | Semi-skilled and discretionary decision making | Accountable for direct product, process or service quality. Incremental improvement of existing processes and procedures according to clear guidelines. Choosing of correct action on the basis of set standards, training procedures and past experience. |
| | | 2b | | | | B2 | 9 | 14 | 5 | 98 – 113 (104) | 8 | 60 - 69 | 35 – 44 | 5 | 43 | 3 | | |
| Mid Level Operational Skills | O2 | 2c | | Mid 1 | B Mid | B3 | 10 | 13 | 6 | 114 – 134 (125) | 9 | 70 - 79 | 45 – 54 | 5 | 44 | 4 | | |
| | | 2d | | | B Upper | B4 | 11 | 12 | 7 | 135 – 160 (151) | 10 | 80 - 89 | 55 – 64 | 6 | 45 | 5 | | |
| High Level Operational Skills | O3 | 2e | | | | B5 | 12 | 11 | 8 | 161 – 191 (173) | 11 | 90 - 99 | 65 – 74 | 7 | | 6 | | |
| **AO (Advanced Operational)** / AOS (Advanced Operational Specialist) | | | | | | | | | | | | | | | | | | |
| Advanced Skills | AO1 | 3a | | High 1 | C Lower | C1 | 13 | 11 | 9 | 192 – 227 (208) | 12 | 100 - 109 | 75 – 84 | 7 | 46 | 7 | Skilled technical and academically qualified workers, junior management, supervisors, foremen and superintendents | Applies broad knowledge of products, techniques and processes. Evaluates procedures and applies previous experience. A good solution can usually be found. Determines own priorities. What has to be done is stipulated, but may require initiative in terms of how it should be done. |
| Advanced Operational Skills | AO2 | 3b | | | | C2 | 14 | 10 | 10 | 228 – 268 (252) | 13 | 110 - 119 | 85 – 94 | 8 | 47 | 8 | | |
| Advanced Operational Checking | AO3 | 3c | | Low 2 | C Mid | C3 | 15 | 9 | 11 | 269 – 313 (291) | 14 | 120 - 129 | 95 – 104 | 9 | 48/49 | 9 | | |
| **L (Leader)** / S (Specialist) | | | | | | | | | | | | | | | | | | |
| Certified Specialist / Supervisory/Team Leader Single Team | SP | 3d | | Mid 2 | C Upper | C4 | 16 | 8 | 12 | 314 – 370 (342) | 15 | 130 - 139 | 105 – 114 | 10 | 50 | 10 | | |
| Practitioner | | 3e | | High 2 | | C5 | 17 | 7 | 13 | 314 – 370 (342) | 15 | 140 - 149 | 115 – 124 | 11 | 51/52 | 11 | | |
| **24** / P (Professional/Consultant) | | | | | | | | | | | | | | | | | | |
| Technician/Team Leader Multiple Teams; Entry Level Cons/High Level Technician | MP1 | 4a | | Low 3 | D Lower | D1 | 18 | 7 | 14 | 371 – 438 (406) | 16 | 150 - 159 | 125 – 134 | 11 | 53 | 12 | Professionally qualified and experienced specialists and mid-management | Professional knowledge of sub-discipline or discipline. Provide input in the formulation of Organisational/Functional Unit business plans. Formulate and implement departmental/team plans that will support the BU business plans. Optimisation of resources (finances, people, material, information and technology) to achieve given objectives in most productive and cost effective way. |
| Middle Management; Professional | | 4b | | | | D2 | 19 | 6 | 15 | 439 – 518 (479) | 17 | 160 - 169 | 135 – 144 | 12 | 54 | 13 | | |
| Tactical Optimisation; "Qualified" Consultant | MP2 | 4c | | Mid 3 | D Mid | D3 | 20 | 5 | 16 | 519 – 613 (571) | 18 | 170 - 179 | 145 – 154 | 13 | 55/56 | 14 | | |
| 3rd Level Specialist; Highest Level Consultant | MP3 | 4d | | High 3 | D Upper | D4 | 21 | 5 | 17 | 614 – 734 (677) | 19 | 180 - 189 | 155 – 164 | 13 | 57/58 | 15 | | |
| | | 4e | | | | D5 | 22 | 4 | 18 | 614 – 734 (677) | 19 | 190 - 199 | 165 – 174 | 14 | 59 | 15 | | |

| 21st CENTURY 7 LEVEL BROAD-BAND | 21st CENTURY 7 levels with sub-grades | 21st CENTURY JE^asv LEVELS | 21st CENTURY EXECU-MEASURE | SST | PATERSON BROAD-BAND | PATERSON | PATERSON POINTS | PEROMNES | TASK | HAY (typical application) | REWARD LEVELS | REMEASURE | JE MANAGER (typical application) | EQUATE | Mercer IPE Position Class | Towers Watson Grading Application | EMPLOYMENT EQUITY - OCCUPATIONAL LEVELS | DESCRIPTION |
|---|---|---|---|---|---|---|---|---|---|---|---|---|---|---|---|---|---|---|
| **SE (Strategic Execution)** / **SE (Professional)** | | | | | | | | | | | | | | | | | | Knowledge of entire business area/BU/ company or group. Provide inputs for/ formulation of the overall organisational strategy. Translates the overall strategy into business plans for BU/Functional Unit, thereby operationalising organisational strategy. Implements and manages business plan, goals and objectives and ensures the achievement of overall key Organisational/ BU/Functional outputs. Manages the development of innovation and change. |
| Organisation/ Distinctive Authority | SE1 | 5a | 22 | Low 4 | E Lower | E1 | 23 | 4 | 18 | 735 – 879 (805) | 20 | 200 – 209 | 175 – 184 | 14 | 60/61 | 16 | | |
| Abstract/ Strategic Research | | | | | | | | | | | | | | | | | | |
| Senior Management / Experienced Professional | | 5b | 23 | Mid 4 | | E2 | 24 | 3 | 19 | 880 – 1055 (954) | 21 | 210 – 219 | 185 – 194 | 15 | 62 | 17 | | |
| Strategy Execution / Recog authority in industry/ specialist field | SE2 | 5c | 24 | High 4 | E Mid | E3 | 25 | 3 | 20 | 1056 – 1260 (1142) | 22 | 220 – 229 | 195 – 204 | 15 | 63/64 | 18 | Senior Management | |
| **SI (Strategic Intent)** | | | | | | | | | | | | | | | | | | |
| National Authority/Rare Authority | SI1 | 5d | 25 | Low 5 | E Upper | E4 | 26 | 2 | 21 | 1261 – 1507 (1372) | 23 | 230 – 239 | 205 – 214 | 16 | 65 | 19 | | |
| | | 5e | 26 | | | E5 | 27 | 2 | 22 | 1508 – 1800 (1628) | 24 | 240 – 249 | 215 – 224 | 16 | 66/67 | 20 | | |
| Sometimes International | | 6a | 27 | | F Lower | F1 | 28 | 1 | 23 | 1801 – 2140 (1960) | 25 | 250 – 259 | 225 – 234 | 16 | 68 | 21 | Top Management/ Executives | Controls the functional integration of the business. Determines the overall strategy and objectives of the business. Directs the company into the future. The nature of the work and focus is long-term. Sign-off on policy or strategy. |
| | | 6b | 28 | | | F2 | 29 | 1 | 24 | 2141 – 2550 (2328) | 26 | 260 – 269 | 235 – 244 | 16 | 69 | | | |
| Top Management (usually Board level), strategic intent and policy making decisions | SI2 | 6c | 29 | Mid 5 | F Mid | F3 | 30 | 1+ | 25 | 2141 – 2550 (2328) | 26 | 270 – 279 | 245 – 254 | | 70 | | | |
| | SI3 | 6d | 30 | High 5 | F Upper | F4 | 31 | 1+ | 26 | 2551 – 3020 (2812) | 27 | 280 – 298 | 255 – 264 | | 71 and above | | | |
| | | 6e | 31 | | | F5 | 32 | 1+ | | 3021 – 3580 (3232) | 28 | 290 – 299 | 265 – 275 | | | | | |
| **G-Global Corporate Governance** | | | | | | | | | | | | | | | | | | |

| 21st CENTURY 7 LEVEL BROAD-BAND | 21st CENTURY 7-levels with sub-grades | 21st CENTURY JE^asy LEVELS | 21st CENTURY EXECU-MEASURE | SST | PATERSON BROAD-BAND | PATERSON | PATERSON POINTS | PEROMNES | TASK | HAY (typical application) | REWARD LEVELS | REMEASURE | JE MANAGER (typical application) | EQUATE | Mercer IPE Position Class | Towers Watson Grading Application | EMPLOYMENT EQUITY - OCCUPATIONAL LEVELS | DESCRIPTION |
|---|---|---|---|---|---|---|---|---|---|---|---|---|---|---|---|---|---|---|
| Global Corporate Governance (Minimal Board Influence) - Oversee Complex Systems: Cross-national and global-regional strategy and direction formulation. There is minimal board influence | GOCS1 | | 32 | Low 6 | | G1 | | | | 3581 - 5060 (4321) | | | | | 74 | 22 | | |
| | GOCS2 | | | Mid 6 | G Lower | G2 | | | | | | | | | | | | |
| | GOCS3 | | 33 | High 6 | | G3 | | | | 5061 - 6020 (5541) | | | | | 76 | 23 | | |
| Global Corporate Governance - Construct Complex Systems: Cross-national and global strategy and direction formulation. Determining of overall multi-national organisations strategy and direction. Often owns a major share of the group. No other influence other than legal and public interest | GOCS4 | | 34 | Low 7 | G Upper | G4 | | | | 6021 - 9640 (7831) | | | | | 78 | 24 | | |
| | GOCS5 | | | Mid 7 | | G5 | | | | | | | | | | | | |
| | GOCS6 | | | High 7 | | G6 | | | | | | | | | | | | |

**\*\*\*Copyright acknowledgements**

Execumeasure Paterson Points, JEasy – ©21st Century

HAY and JE Manager – ©HAY Management Consultants

Peromnes and Task – ©Deloitte

Remeasure – ©PWC

Mercer IPE Position class — ©Mercer

Towers Watson Grading application — ©Towers Watson

# Toolkit 5

# Preparation for Broad-Banding

| Broad-banding workshop | |
|---|---|
| Creating innovative broad-band structures | |
| Session 1 | Understanding the drivers |
| Session 2 | Preparing the business case – are you ready? |
| Session 3 | Practical example – case study |
| Session 4 | Implications, implementation, and selling the concept to stakeholders |

| Session 1: Understanding the drivers | |
|---|---|
| Current situation | Problems with current situation |
| | |
| | |
| | |
| | |
| | |
| | |
| | |
| Why broad-banding? | |
| Why will broad-banding help overcome current problems? | Implications |
| | |
| | |
| | |
| | |
| | |
| | |
| Drivers and barriers to implementing broad-banding | |
| Drivers | Barriers |
| | |
| | |
| | |
| | |
| | |
| | |
| | |

| Drivers and barriers to implementing broad-banding ||
| Driver | Plan to harness the driver |
|---|---|
|  |  |
|  |  |
|  |  |
|  |  |
|  |  |
|  |  |
|  |  |
| Overcoming the barriers ||
| Barrier | Plan to overcome barrier |
|  |  |
|  |  |
|  |  |
|  |  |
|  |  |
|  |  |
|  |  |

| Session 2: Preparing the business case – are you ready? <br> Broad-banding – the business case ||
| Benefits of implementation | Cost-saving/implication |
|---|---|
|  |  |
|  |  |
|  |  |
|  |  |
|  |  |

| Session 3: Practical example – case study |
|---|
| This needs to be developed for your organisation based on the metrics provided in this textbook. |

| Session 4: Implications, implementation, and selling the concept <br> to the stakeholders <br> Implications of implementing broad-banding ||
|---|---|
| Career paths |  |
| Communication |  |
| Costs |  |

| Fringe benefit admin | |
|---|---|
| Interface with IT | |
| Organisation structure | |
| Pay policy | |
| Pay scales | |
| Timing | |
| Training | |
| Understanding | |
| Union negotiations | |

**Implementation framework**

| Activity | Timing | Responsibility |
|---|---|---|
| Phase 1 | | |
| Phase 2 | | |
| Phase 3 | | |
| Phase 4 | | |

**EXCO presentation headings**

| | |
|---|---|
| 1. | |
| 2. | |
| 3. | |
| 4. | |
| 5. | |
| 6. | |
| 7. | |
| 8. | |
| 9. | |
| 10. | |

# Toolkit 6

# Article – Reward for Good Governance

You may have the perfect organisational strategy and marketing plan, as well as sound financial results, but the market can still penalise you for poor remuneration governance. In this article, we set out some thoughts on how to go about improving the analyst's views of your remuneration approach.

**Are the basics in place?**

As a bare minimum, the basics need to be in place before you can be rewarded for good remuneration governance. There are many variations, but the key themes are:

1. Remuneration **philosophy.**
2. Remuneration **policy.**
3. Remuneration **strategy.**
4. Remuneration **procedures.**
5. Remuneration **committee (RemCo).**

The following guidelines may help in getting these basics in place. As a rule of thumb, fewer words – short and to the point – are better than long-winded documents. Less is better.

**Remuneration philosophy**

The remuneration philosophy usually consists of a paragraph or two. It tells the analyst in a nutshell what you reward in your organisation. For example, do you reward:

- Performance? Individual, team or organisation performance?
- Outputs?
- Complexity of work performed?
- Scarcity of skill?
- Track record?
- Quality?
- Qualifications?
- Experience?
- Years in the job/length of service?
- Loyalty?
- Not sure?

Every employee should know exactly what is rewarded in your organisation. Some cadres prefer length of service, others reward performance, and the rest reward a mixture of the above.

Analysts prefer the top two. Some trade unions prefer the bottom two. The philosophy should be stated in your financial report for everyone to see, and you should stick as closely to it in the application as possible.

**Remuneration policy**

The remuneration policy should cover important points such as:

1. How do you set your remuneration levels?
2. How do you use job evaluation?
3. How do you do remuneration benchmarking?
4. How did you select your comparators?
5. What is your position on fringe benefits and tax structuring?
6. What is your short-term incentive (STI) formula?
7. What is your long-term incentive (LTI) formula?
8. What is your desired remuneration mix?
9. What are your RemCo's scope and powers?
10. What provisions do you have for recognition?

The policy should be no longer than about 15 pages, written in plain English, and unambiguous.

**Remuneration strategy**

It is often the case that you are not where you want to be from a remuneration point of view. The strategy sets out:

- Where you want to be.
- How you are going to get there.
- Over what time period.
- Who will be doing which part of the strategy.

When developing the strategy, it is recommended that you use one of the remuneration strategy frameworks that consultants typically use to design a strategy. It needs to underpin and support the organisation strategy. It is no use implementing a remuneration strategy that does not support your business strategy.

**Remuneration procedures**

This is the file that tells you step by step which forms to fill in. Procedures should not go to RemCo. Ideally, these should be placed on the intranet for easy access and employee self-service.

The remuneration procedure policy document should also set out how things in the policy are done, for example, the detailed benchmarking procedure. This allows for continuity and replication from year to year. It also allows for an audit, should this be required.

## Remuneration committee

The credibility of the remuneration committee (RemCo) is important. RemCos need to put the basics in place, appoint reputable advisers, and be sure that they can answer any question put to them at an annual general meeting by analysts, journalists, trade unions, executives and all other stakeholders. This means that the remuneration approach needs to be **robust** and well-understood by all RemCo members.

The table below sets out a typical RemCo structure.

*Table 1: Anatomy of a typical RemCo*

|   | Item | Global practice |
|---|------|-----------------|
| 1 | Authority | RemCo is a subcommittee of the main board, mandated by the board to debate and investigate issues of remuneration and bring proposals back to the board for approval. |
| 2 | Members | Members should be independent and external to the organisation. By implication, the chairperson should be external to the organisation. |
| 3 | RemCo size | This depends on the size of the organisation, but is typically three to five members. |
| 4 | Scope of work | This depends on the maturity of management, but typically executive remuneration (CEO and first line reports, or top, say, 50), share schemes, incentive schemes, group benefit schemes, succession plans, mandated pay increase percentages, and payment of non-executive directors. |
| 5 | Frequency of meetings | Two to Three times a year |
| 6 | Payment | Common alternatives include: <br> 1. Fees for attending. <br> 2. Retainer. <br> 3. Combination of fees and retainer. <br><br> The combination approach seems to be the trend. There is a premium for chairing the committee, in the order of 40% to 100% of the committee member's fees. |

| | Item | Global practice |
|---|---|---|
| 7 | Performance payment | This is an area of considerable recent debate, following Warren Buffet's article on how he has made the board of Coca Cola® "earn" their pay by removing their fixed fees and giving them shares only. There are no reported bonus schemes for non-executive directors, but a minority of organisations allow shares or share purchase schemes. |
| 8 | Reporting | The chairperson of RemCo would normally provide an executive summary for inclusion into the annual financial statements. The names of RemCo members are normally published in the annual financial statements for listed organisations. In the United Kingdom, for example, organisations need to report details about the RemCo and who their remuneration advisers are. They also go a step further in the United Kingdom, where organisations are compelled to describe the incentive schemes – targets, formulae and payouts. |

Given this anatomy, RemCo members need to have a good appreciation of a host of things, the primary ones being:

- The industry norms and external environment.
- Remuneration theory and practice.
- The organisation strategy and operations.

In addition to this, RemCo members should have good commercial skills and experience in remuneration. The fee paid to members should depend on their reputation, track record, skill, experience, and performance or contribution.

**What next?**

To be rewarded by the market, these basics need to be in place and everyone must know them. Transparency and good communication are required, especially if there are historical practices that need to be rectified. A plan for rectifying these historical practices needs to be developed and communicated. Once this has been done, the premium placed on your business will have made the effort worthwhile.

# Toolkit 7

## Article – The impact of Recession on Global Pay

### Introduction

Remuneration packages during a recession are often challenging and complicated to put together. Many things have to be taken into consideration, such as total cost to company of an employee's payment package. However, this must be looked at in the context of the company's financial situation. Two distinct groups present themselves when examining remuneration during a recession, the first group being blue-collar workers and lower management (Paterson job grades A to C), with directors and senior employees composing the second group (Paterson job grades D to F).

The remuneration of each group is handled in distinct ways, based on their pay systems and rewards over base pay. The first group is usually paid on an hourly basis with company contributions to pension funds and short-term incentives such as 13th cheques.[1]

The second group is paid according to experience and the complexity of their jobs, which usually involve running departments, divisions and companies. Consequently, their pay packages are much higher. The remuneration they receive is based on substantial salaries with large perks and benefits.

Handling the pay of each group during a recession presents some interesting challenges for payroll consultants. The blue-collar group has to live with reduced working hours and cut salaries, and over and above this, company contributions to long-term incentives, such as pension plans, are suspended or reduced. The second group suffers the reduction of salaries and the termination of benefits and performance targets. The savings on remuneration of both groups are among the many ways payroll and employee benefits can be handled during a recession without reducing staff numbers.

### Blue-collar unskilled/skilled and lower management
(Paterson pay grades A to C)

#### *Pay cuts*
Currently pay cuts, both voluntary and enforced, are a popular method of dealing with remuneration during a recession. Across the board, companies are using pay cuts to reduce salary and wage costs to companies. Lower management, new engineers and blue-collar workers are on average receiving pay cuts of 5 to 10 percent.

By doing so, companies are attempting to maintain staff levels and avoid unpleasant layoffs and retrenchments. Skill retention is the primary motive behind this. Companies are fully aware

---

1    Grigoriadis & Bussin, 2007.

that economies go through "boom and bust" cycles. Retaining skills during a recession so as to capitalise on the consequent economic upswing is an important consideration. Firing staff only to attempt to re-hire them in an environment of high competition would slow the growth of production in an environment of growing consumer demand.

### Hour and working-day reduction

In the more labour-intensive industries such as motor manufacturing and shipbuilding, actual working hours have been reduced. Instead of working full days or whole weeks, companies have been cutting back to 35 hours a week or assigning a 3- or 4-day working week. By doing so, they are able to keep workers on but at a reduced wage or salary. Skilled workers are kept in practice at their respective tasks and up-to-date on any developments that may occur within their respective industry, but at diminished remuneration burden to the company.

### Voluntary leave

Employees are being encouraged to take voluntary unpaid leave or spread working weeks between departments and work groups. That is to say, one department will work for a week then stop; the following week the next department will work for that week. This is done so that everyone is kept in work and pay, but reduces overall salary and wage costs.

### Short-term incentives

All short-term incentives are suspended. Production-target and cost-saving bonuses are considered unnecessary expenses in such financially tight times and will resume only when consumer consumption increases. Other short-term benefits, such as a 13th cheque and shift allowances, are on hold until company profitability has been restored.

### Long-term incentives

Pay increases have been put on hold. In tight financial times, corporations are not in any position to offer pay raises, adding to variable costs. Instead, pay increases are being deferred or simply not considered until company profitability has been restored.

Pension benefits have been frozen or reduced. Companies are not offering annual pension contribution increases, or in extreme cases are reducing or stopping the amounts companies are paying into company and private medical aid schemes.

### Upper and middle management

(Paterson pay grades D to F)

### Short-term incentives

Director and upper management bonuses have been reduced in a number of industries, while in other industries they have been deferred until economic conditions improve and company profitability has been restored or substantially improved.

### *Performance incentives*

Performance incentives are also being reduced in many industries as a result of the global financial crisis. Before the crisis hit, many directors and senior management would receive large performance incentives based on various accounting and company performance targets. These incentives have been cut in order to save on remuneration costs and as moral examples to lower-level employees.

### *Long-term incentives*

The global financial crisis has negatively affected many companies' long-term incentive schemes. This has led to salary cuts, as directors and senior management have traditionally received large annual salaries. In terms of remuneration, these salaries have been drastically reduced as both cost-saving measures and motivational tools to junior employees.

### *Pension benefits*

The reduction of pension benefits is also used as a common remuneration cost-reduction tool. By limiting the amount of money the company spends on the accumulated benefits of senior employees, corporations can save large amounts, reducing cost-to-company figures.

### *Voluntary retirement*

Some senior employees retire voluntarily; senior employees often do this because they are much older and are closer to retirement age, but some companies offer them re-employment at a later stage, when the economy has improved, because they want to retain those people with the ability, experience and skill to deliver the company's strategy.

### Blue-collar unskilled/skilled and lower management

(Paterson pay grades A – C)

Blue-collar workers and junior employees are experiencing remuneration cost-saving measures as their international counterparts. Working hours are being reduced and workdays are being cut short. However, pay cuts are not being used. Unfortunately, job cuts of unskilled workers appear to be the favoured method of cost saving during recession.

### Upper and middle management

(Paterson pay grades D to F)

Global trends show that executive pay is, in fact, being cut, and all benefits and bonuses withheld or cancelled.

### *Alternative remuneration methods*

Some interesting and innovative methods of employee remuneration have been developed.

### *Commission*

Employees previously on pure salary have had their salaries cut and have been placed on a partially commission-based earning related to the amount of work they manage to produce.

### *Emotional rewards (psychological rewards)*

Emotional rewards are being used to motivate employees who have had salaries reduced. For example, paid visits to theme parks and family centres are offered by companies to employees on reduced work hours and who have families.

### *Personal development*

Employees are being offered extended training and personal development courses in everything from business management to childcare.

### *Financial assistance and advice*

Employees facing reduced work hours and cut salaries are being sent on financial management courses and being allowed to see a personal financial management consultant at company expense.

### *Payroll consultant/manager responsibilities*

The function of payroll consultants during an economic recession is to manage the cost to company of employees so as to save both money and jobs.

The first group, blue-collar workers and lower management, need to have their hours and wages or salaries reduced and managed in such a way as to retain their employment, give them a living wage, and save the company as much money as possible.[2] It is beneficial to retain these experienced workers as they will be needed in the future when economic conditions improve and production is ramped up to meet new demand.

Upper and middle management present a special set of challenges. Firstly, they are highly-skilled and experienced people. They will be in demand, and the company is under threat of their being headhunted by other organisations. If their salaries and benefits are trimmed too much, they will most likely be happy to move on to superficially better offers or offers with only short-term benefits. What the payroll consultant or manager must do is balance the need of the organisation to save on variable costs during a recession with the employees' needs and desires for good salaries and large bonuses. With carefully-managed short-term pay cuts, it should be possible to retain these employees.

---

2   Mmolaeng & Bussin, 2012.

# Toolkit 8

## Remuneration in a Downturn

The impact of the economic downturn is now being felt by most companies. We cannot do what we always used to do, even if it was smarter, if our company has been affected. It calls for careful consideration of the various options. This article focuses on what organisations are doing from an HR and remuneration point of view.

There is no need to over-react or be alarmist, but there is a need to consider your options carefully when the downturn bites your organisation. First prize is usually to hold on to jobs, avoid retrenchment, and keep the ship sailing. If all of that is not possible, then several remuneration options are being considered and implemented in organisations.

### Please can I keep my job?

Keeping a job is important for many reasons. Medical aid and retirement benefits keep going, the mind keeps going, dignity and esteem are upheld, and most importantly, if the job is lost, finding one again will be difficult. Based on a recent survey conducted by 21st Century Pay Solutions Group, organisations are implementing many innovative practices in order to save jobs. Table 1 sets out the 10 most commonly implemented solutions.

*Table 1: Summary of job-saving practices*

|  | Remuneration | Work |
|---|---|---|
| 1. | Freeze pay increases. | Short work week. |
| 2. | Predicted increases are lower. | Reduced over time. |
| 3. | Merit increases are lower. | Reduced use of contractors. |
| 4. | Every employee agrees to take a pay cut of, for example, 15 percent. | Unpaid leave. |
| 5. | STIs are not paid out while retrenchments are being made. | Job-sharing. |
| 6. | STI targets are revisited. | Unpaid sabbatical. |
| 7. | Payouts are held back for the moment or being deferred. | Employees' innovation ideas, money-saving ideas taken more seriously. |
| 8. | Performance contracts and targets are revisited. | Take a year off to study at your own expense. |
| 9. | Performance-related pay is being strengthened. | Freeze on hiring new employees. |

| | Remuneration | Work |
|---|---|---|
| 10. | LTI plans are being revisited, for example, lowering grants and performance criteria. | Share your job with someone |

**Future focus areas**

Organisations are focusing more strongly on the following themes to reposition for the future:

- Flatter, faster, more responsive structures.
- Strengthening the link between performance and pay.
- Defensible differentiation in terms of the remuneration approach and spend.
- More efficient salary administration systems and processes, including web-enabled remuneration tools.

The call here is for "mass customisation", where return on reward is maximised. Big across-the-board pay increases are a thing of the past, and we need to get better at spending money more wisely. Many boards are saying, "Don't come to us with a blunt instrument; come with a sharp instrument". That is, be a lot more focused. The implications of this are paying according to:

- Scarcity of skill.
- Performance.
- Market positioning.
- Track record.
- Value-add.

Differentiation according to these factors needs to be done in a defensible way, but done more aggressively and in a more targeted way, based on company-specific objectives. This implies robust salary survey information and performance management systems.

Even though there has been an economic crisis, there are still some common themes:

- There is a scarcity of company-specific key skills to drive business strategy.
- It is an employer's market, but when it turns, retention will be high on the agenda.
- Build teams for the upswing, and hold on to them when it does swing.

These themes are almost global in their prevalence, but give organisations an opportunity to "re-group" from a remuneration point of view. The emphasis has shifted from attraction in order to ensure short-term deliverables are being met, to retention of core teams to ensure long-term business sustainability.

**Suggestions**

There are some golden do's and don'ts that high-performing organisations are adhering to in these tight times:

- There should be on-the-level feedback and communication to employees on the state of the organisation, financial health, future plans and importance of people.
- Engage employees – engaged employees are less likely to leave, are happier, and serve customers better, all of which improve the bottom line.
- Don't stop training and development.
- Don't cut into the muscle and memory of the organisation as a preventative measure.
- Co-agree across-the-board pay cuts before retrenching. Ask everyone to think like an owner: innovate.
- Be concerned with systems and processes and how to improve them.
- Clean up your act – notice the stain on the carpet, cigarette stubs lying around, and weeds growing on the property. Make it pleasant for the customer to visit.
- Speed up turn-around times.
- Produce more for less, while improving quality.
- Institutionalise, delighting the customer.

**Concluding thoughts**

Remuneration in organisations has shifted from an egalitarian approach to a very specific targeted approach for core teams that will take the organisation into the future. Building sustainable structures and rewarding them appropriately will emphasise the difference between employers that have an average employee value proposition (EVP) versus those with a really good EVP.

We are entering a new era that doesn't tolerate bureaucracy, inefficiency, poor quality, poor customer service, arrogance or complacency. The financial shake-up is a good reminder to be grateful for what we have, strive for more, and above all, get our house in order. All this, while remembering work-life balance.

# Toolkit 9

## Article – What are Your Labour Turnover Figures Telling You?

### What is your labour turnover?

Labour turnover (LTO) is usually defined as the total movement of people in and out of an organisation. A reasonable amount of turnover is healthy as it brings in new blood, techniques, ideas and energy. However, should the turnover rate get out of hand, it becomes problematic, because it often involves losing people who are disproportionately expensive and time-consuming to replace.

### Which circle are you in?

Sheila Rothwell makes reference to two circles, namely a vicious circle and a virtuous circle. These are shown in Figures 1 and 2.

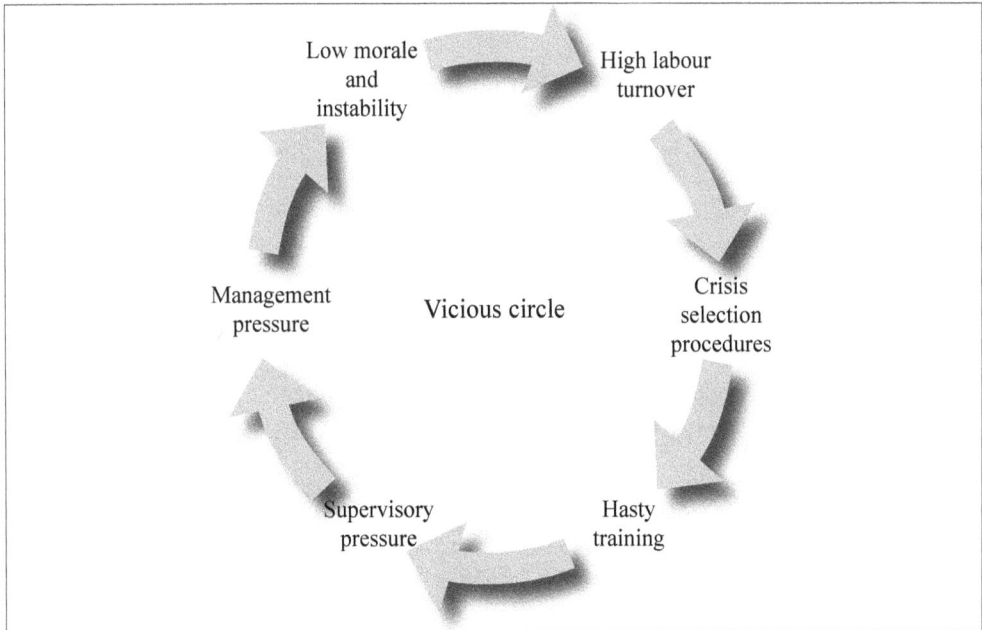

*Figure 1: The self-reinforcing nature of LTO – vicious circle*

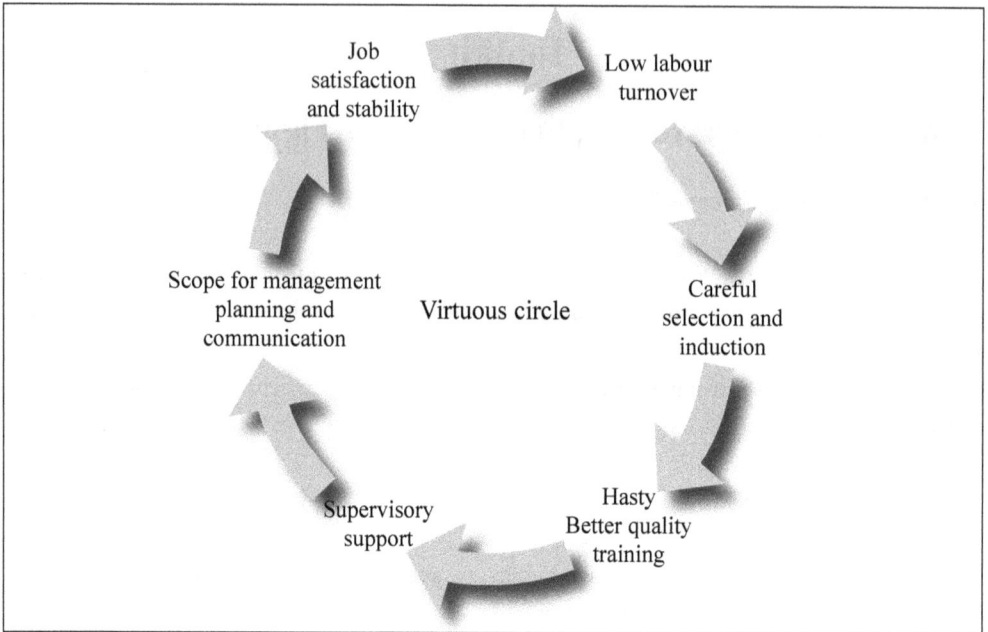

*Figure 2: The self-reinforcing nature of LTO – virtuous circle*

## Different types of labour turnover and their interpretation

LTO can be analysed by four broad categories, namely:

- Dismissal.
- Voluntary separation.
- Retrenchment.
- Other (for example, retirement, pregnancy, and so on).

With high LTO, it is important to note into which of these categories most separations primarily fall. For example, consider two companies with a high LTO (see Table A).

| Table A | | | |
|---|---|---|---|
| | **% LTO** | **% Voluntary** | **% Dismissal** |
| **Company A** | 37 | 30 | 70 |
| **Company B** | 38 | 70 | 30 |
| | | | |

In Company A, 70 percent of the workers are fired, which may indicate supervisor problems, training, problematic company systems and procedures, or selection and induction problems.

In Company B, there may be problems with pay, future prospects and promotion opportunities. Median length of service (MLS) within an organisation adds even more insight to the matter. If people leave voluntarily after three years, they are more likely to be in Company B, where the prospects are poor.

This could be more serious than in Company A, as the company has already invested considerable time and money in training and developing these people. These costs will have to be re-incurred to replace the lost staff.

**How do we calculate LTO?**

A widely-accepted formula for the calculation of LTO is:

$$\text{Labour turnover rate} = \frac{\text{Number of leavers during a period}}{\text{Number of employees for that period}} \times \frac{100}{1}$$

**How much is too much?**

One must realise that labour turnover is not always bad; it is either good or bad depending on the consequences for the organisation, which may be either economic or behavioural.

Allen Bluedorn presents an interesting way of looking at LTO. He proposes that a "specific turnover rate should be thought of as a purchasable commodity". If you are thinking of changing the turnover rate in your organisation, you should think in terms of "acquiring" the change; the greater the changes, the greater the benefits will have to be in order to outweigh the cost.

Since the marginal utility of a commodity decreases as more of it is obtained, a point will be reached when one more unit will not be worthwhile to the buyer. The optimal turnover rate then is the rate at which "the marginal cost equals the marginal utility of the turnover rate".

**What does it cost to lose staff?**

The cost of loss of staff involved can be analysed in three distinct phases:
- **Separation costs:** These include the cost of separation pay, the loss of efficiency prior to separation, and the effects of any period of vacancy during the replacement search period.
- **Acquisition costs:** These include the costs of recruitment, selection and replacement, or alternatively, the cost of promotion or internal transfer.
- **Learning costs:** These include the costs of the new incumbent formally or informally acquiring the knowledge, skills and attitudes required to perform the job and to integrate into a team. Included here is the cost as a result of any errors that one may make during the period of learning.

The cost for an executive earning 60,000 basic salary, assuming the recruitment is done from outside the company, can be expected to be:

| Separation | Cost |
|---|---|
| Three months' period of notice at below-average effectiveness | 9 000 |
| Administration cost | 500 |
| **Acquisition of new employee** | |
| Recruitment expenses (20% of employee's salary) | 12 000 |
| Cost of advertisement | 2 500 |
| One day's interviewing time for two executives | 3 000 |
| Learning cost | |
| Three months at below-average effectiveness | 9 000 |
| **TOTAL COST** | **36 000** |

As can be seen, the costs of losing an employee are high, and there is a considerable amount of wastage.

**How do you reduce unwanted labour turnover?**

One can control labour turnover successfully, but since it usually has more than one cause, action in more than one area may be necessary to control it effectively. Most organisations will need to look at some of the basics or "hygiene factors" (to use Herzberg's terminology) and one or more of the "motivating factors". This will mean examining the terms and conditions of employment and other employment practices, as well as at least one of the factors relating to environment or personal circumstances.

Factors identified by Rothwell that need to be considered in order to reduce avoidable job-related turnover are as follows:

- **Improve pay:** Consider pay systems, differentials of skilled and professional employees, and fringe benefits.
- **Change hours:** Scrutinise recruitment and selection procedures, plan induction and training, select and develop supervisors, and improve working conditions and facilities (for example, heat, light, ventilation, dirt and noise, canteen, restroom and toilet facilities, and childcare facilities).
- **Develop management functions and procedures.**
- **Plan manpower:** Make opportunities for promotion and train existing staff.
- **Redesign jobs.**

- **Communicate:** To reduce "avoidable turnover", such as turnover which is home-related, communicate with the employee and provide measures that will assist him or her to overcome the personal crisis. For example, provide transport; help with housing; assist with adjustments to domestic responsibilities; recognise personal and marital problems; plan for "outside commitments" to minimise dismissal, layoff and redundancy; prevent ill health; and phase retirement.

There is an old proverb which says: "A person must be very brave who attempts to kill a porcupine by sitting on it." Too many managers have been sitting on their "turnover porcupines" for too long. However, one must bear in mind that less is not necessarily better. Companies may actually profit from labour turnover by carefully selecting their turnover reduction targets.

# Toolkit 10

## Total Rewards and the Employee Value Proposition (EVP)

### Introduction

"What's in it for me?" is probably the simplest description of the employee value proposition (EVP). Minchington[3] defined an EVP more broadly as a set of associations and offerings provided by an organisation in return for the skills, capabilities and experiences an employee brings to the organisation. According to the Corporate Leadership Council,[4] the EVP is the total employment experience and therefore the differentiated total compelling employment offer.

Even though many organisations are not currently focused on the attraction and retention of key talent due to the economic meltdown, it remains important for organisations to have a unique, relevant and compelling EVP for it to act as a key driver of talent attraction, engagement and retention in the long term. The EVP should identify the unique people policies, processes and programmes that demonstrate the organisation's commitment to, for example, employee growth, management development, ongoing employee recognition, community service, etc. The EVP contains the reasons why employees will choose to commit themselves to a specific organisation.[5]

The EVP is an employee-centred approach that is aligned to integrated talent management strategies. An organisation's EVP is typically informed by existing and prospective employees, therefore an organisation needs to understand what talent it needs to attract and retain currently and in the future, and how it will differentiate its offering in the labour markets. The challenge for organisations therefore is to:

- Clearly articulate the EVP and package or brand it (also referred to as employer branding).
- Link the proposition to business strategy, talent needs and business results.
- Integrate the different components of the EVP with financial and non-financial reward elements.

### EVP and Total Rewards

The term EVP is often incorrectly used to mean the same as TR. Confusion is then created in terms of what EVP stands for versus what total rewards refers to. Although rewards are critical to an organisation's EVP, it is only a subset of the EVP. Authors have different opinions of what components should be included in the ambit of an organisation's EVP. For example, Lamoureux[6] stated that the key components of the EVP are:

---

3   Minchington, 2010.

4   Corporate Leadership Council, 2007.

5   Tandehill, 2006.

6   Erickson, 2009.

- **Remuneration** - salary, incentives, cash recognition, pay process.
- **Benefits** – healthcare, retirement, insurances, recognition programmes.
- **Affiliation** – work environment, trust, transparency, organisational commitment.
- **Career** – advancement opportunities, personal growth and development, training, job security.
- **Work Content** – challenge, autonomy, meaningfulness, variety.

Towers Perrin[7] explained that the EVP complements total rewards by adding components such as market benchmarking, leadership research and organisational performance. Black[8] identified four components that form the foundation of an organisation's EVP, namely:

- Strong leadership.
- Organisational reputation, which includes reputation, culture, contribution to the community and the world, stability and core values.
- Interesting and compelling job and career opportunities.
- Tangible and intangible rewards.

The 21st Century Pay Solutions Group uses the following diagram in explaining the concept of an EVP:

| Employee value proposition | | | | |
|---|---|---|---|---|
| **Remuneration** | **Performance feedback** | **Career and Development** | **Work environment** | **Inspirational leadership** |
| • Ticket to the game <br> • Has to be right <br> • Flexible <br> • Internal and external equity | • How am I doing? <br> • Development <br> • Control over performance <br> • Link to pay | • I know where I am going <br> • Growth of portable skills <br> • Vertical and horizontal | • Stimulating <br> • Telecommuting <br> • Work/life balance <br> • HR policies | • Leading and managing <br> • Training <br> • Development <br> • Dual career paths |
| **Attract** | **Motivate** | **Retain** | **Enjoy** | **Enthuse/Inspire** |

Rewards are therefore clearly a component that contributes to the overall EVP, but the EVP also includes the intangible experience and reputation of the organisation as well as, inter alia, culture, organisational brand and success, transformation initiatives, environmental concern and job security.[9]

---

7   Towers Perrin, 2007.

8   Black, 2007.

9   Armstrong & Brown, 2006.

**Some Examples of Organisations' Employee Value Propositions**

Organisations clearly differentiate themselves in terms of their EVPs. Some examples of how organisations define their EVP are listed below:

- Working at **Starbucks** is a lot like working with your friends. We understand, respect, appreciate and include different people. And we believe in keeping each other informed, so our senior leaders regularly hold Open Forum events to answer your questions. Starbucks refers to their EVP as "Your Special Blend", which includes a wide range of perquisites if one works for the organisation, i.e.:
  - Competitive pay.
  - Insurance: medical, prescription drug, dental, vision, life, disability.
  - Bonuses.
  - Paid time off .
  - Retirement savings plan.
  - Equity in the form of Starbucks stock and a discounted stock purchase plan.
  - Adoption assistance.
  - Domestic partner benefits.
  - Emergency financial aid.
  - Referral and support resources for child and elder care.
  - A free pound of coffee each week.
- At **Google,** the EVP includes a culture that drives a fun place to work, subsidised broadband for all employees, pool tables in the tea room, on-site dental care, free T-shirts twice a week, free meals, and the opportunity to bring your dog to work.
- **Nedbank's** employer brand of "great things begin with great people" is supported by the nine elements of the Nedbank EVP, namely:
  - Performance is recognised and rewarded.
  - An organisation that truly cares.
  - A place where you can thrive.
  - We have a community of leaders with a clear vision.
  - A values-based organisation with a high performance culture.
  - An organisation that is proudly South African.
  - People that are bright and amazing to work with.
  - A role with a sense of purpose and true value-add.
  - People's individual needs are respected.
- **Allstate** includes the below in their EVP three components:
  - A company that is innovative, successful and community-minded.
  - Leaders who inspire, build trust and empower employees to achieve optimal performance.
  - An environment where employees feel valued and rewarded.

- The **Sasol** EVP consists of the following five themes:
  - Flexible work practices.
  - Rewards and benefits.
  - Learning and development and career opportunities.
  - Organisational reputation and leadership.
  - Relationship with my line manager.
- The **Sodexho** EVP themes are summarised as follows:
  - We care about our employees in the same way that we care about our clients and we strive to provide each and every employee with a wide range of professional and personal opportunities to improve the quality of their daily life.
  - Our employees are able to develop their careers both locally and globally across all of our service areas. They have the flexibility to align the pace of their career with their various life stages.
  - By living the Sodexho values and ethical principles, and actively fostering diversity and inclusion, our people make Sodexho a company of the future.

## Conclusion

The EVP is the unique and proprietary way in which organisations attract, retain and motivate employees. Increasingly more organisations are citing "culture" as a challenge to attract and retain talent, therefore forward-thinking organisations are revisiting their employee value propositions to ensure that the components that make up their EVPs remain relevant and in step with what employees require when they search for an organisation to work for. Organisations have also started to differentiate their EVPs on the basis of the different needs that employees have in the generational segments. For example, career opportunities are much more important for younger employees than older employees, and therefore a stronger emphasis is placed on career opportunities when organisations recruit for younger employees. The CLC[10] also found that engineering and research employees place a premium on innovative work, IT employees place a premium on organisational technology, and marketing employees value product brand awareness – these areas of interest can be very effectively integrated into the organisation EVP, with minor adjustments for different areas of the workforce.

The integration of total rewards and the EVP is the key to obtaining optimal effectiveness of both systems. By using an EVP effectively, organisations distinguish themselves in the marketplace to both attract and retain critically skilled employees. In order to do this, organisations should communicate to both potential and current employees a compelling and unique EVP, of which total rewards is a critical part.

---

10  CLC, 2007.

# References

21st Century Pay Solutions. 26 September 2011. *SAICA CFO executive remuneration seminar.* Rosebank: Johannesburg.

21st Century Pay Solutions. 2021. Paterson Training Course. Rosebank: Johannesburg.

Abosch, K.S. 1998. Variable pay: do we have the basics in place? *Compensation & Benefits Review, 30*(4):12–22.

Armstrong, M. & Brown, D. 2006. *Strategic reward: making it happen.* London: Kogan Page Publishers.

Armstrong, M. & Murlis, H. 2004. *Reward management: a handbook of remuneration strategy and practice.* 5th ed. London: Kogan Page Polishers.

Armstrong, M. & Thompson, P. 2005. E-Reward Fact Sheets, no. 31. *E-Reward.co.uk. research report.* [Online]. Available at: http://www.sara.co.za [Accessed 10 October 2007].

Armstrong, M. 2014. *A handbook of personnel management practice.* 13th ed. Cambridge: Cambridge University Press.

Bannister, R.J. & Gentry, W. 1999. *Aligning executive pay and company performance. Aligning pay and results.* New York: American Compensation Association.

Barksdale, D. 1998. Leading employees through the variable pay jungle. *HRMagazine,* 111–118, July.

Begbie, C., Bussin, M. & Schurink, W. 2011. A food-manufacturing manager's experiences and perceptions of the implementation of an incentive scheme. *South African Journal of Human Resource Management/ SA Tydskrif vir Menslikehulpbronbestuur, 9*(1): Art #323. doi:10.4102/sajhrm.v9i1.32

Black, S. 2007. *The employee value proposition: how to be an employer of choice.* Available at: https://knowledge.insead.edu/career/the-employee-value-proposition-2127

Bluedorn, A.C. 1978. A taxonomy of turnover. *Academy of Management Review, 3*(3):647–651.

Botha, A., Bussin, M. & De Swardt, L. 2011. An employer brand predictive model for talent attraction and retention. *SA Journal of Human Resource Management/SA Tydskrif vir Menslikehulpbronbestuur, 9*(1): Art. #388. http://dx.doi.org/10.4102/sajhrm.

Bowers, J.R. 2003a. *How to ensure return on your reward investment.* Working paper. Philadelphia, Pennsylvania: HayGroup.

Bowers, J.R. 2003b. Valuing work: an integrated approach. *WorldatWork® Journal, 12*(2):28–39.

Broderick, R. & Mitchell, D.J.B. 1988. Who has flexible wage plans and why aren't there more of them? In C.H. Fay & R.W. Beatty (eds.). *The compensation sourcebook.* Amherst, MA: Human Resource Development Press, pp.144–148.

Burkholder, B. 2002. Orchestrating a finely tuned incentive plan. *Workspan, 08*(02):16–23.

Bussin, M.H. 2004. *The factors driving change to remuneration policy and outcomes.* Doctoral thesis. Faculty of Industrial Psychology and People Management, University of Johannesburg.

Bussin, M.H. 2009. *The remuneration nuts and bolts series.* Johannesburg: Knowledge Resources.

Bussin, M. & Blair, C. 2015. Financial indicators of Company Performance in different industries that affect CEO Remuneration in South Africa. *South African Journal of Economic and Management Sciences, 18*(4):1-13 DOI: http://dx.doi.org/10.17159/2222-3436/2015/v18n4a7.

Bussin, M. & Nel, M. 2015. Relationship between CEO remuneration and company financial performance in the South African retail and consumer goods sector, *Acta Commercii, 15*(1): Art. #240. http://dx.doi. org/10.4102/ac.v15i1.240.

Bussin, M. & Toerien, W.C. 2015. Influence of reward preferences in attracting, retaining, and motivating knowledge workers in South African information technology companies. *Acta Commercii, 15*(1): Art. #290. http://dx.doi. org/10.4102/ac.v15i1.290.

Bussin, M. 2015a. CEO Pay performance sensitivity in the South African context. *South African Journal of Economic and Management Sciences, 18*(2):1-13.

Bussin, M. 2015b. Factors driving changes to remuneration policies in South Africa. *South African Journal of Labour Relations, 39*(2):15-29.

Bussin, M. & Huysamen, D. 2003. The factors driving change to remuneration policy and outcomes. *South African Journal of Human Resource Management/SA Tydskrif vir Menslikehulpbronbestuur, 2*(2):45-54.

Bussin, M. & Modau, M.F. 2015. The relationship between Chief Executive Officer (CEO) remuneration and financial performance in South Africa between 2006 and 2012. *SA Journal of Human Resource Management, 13*(1): Art. #668.

Cawe, M. 2006. *Factors contributing to employee engagement in South Africa.* Master's thesis. Faculty of Industrial Psychology and People Management, University of Johannesburg.

Centers for Disease Control. (CDC). 2009. *The power of prevention: Chronic disease...the public health challenge of the 21st century.* [Online]. Available at: http://www.cdc.gov/chronicdisease/pdf/2009-power-of-prevention.pdf [Accessed 14 November 2016].

Centers for Disease Control. (CDC). 2010. Selected Preventative Screening Recommendations. [Online]. Available at: https://www.cdc.gov/nccdphp/dnpao/ [Accessed 14 November 2016].

Chiang, F. 2005. A critical examination of Hofstede's thesis and its application to international reward management. *International Journal of Human Resource Management, 16*:1545–1563.

Cliffe Dekker Hofmeyr. 2009. *King III in a nutshell.* Johannesburg: Cliffe Dekker Hofmeyr.

Codrington, G. & Grant-Marshall, S. 2004. *Mind the gap.* Johannesburg: Penguin Books.

Corporate Leadership Council. (CLC). 1999. *The compelling offer: a quantitative analysis of the career preferences and decisions of high-value employees.* Workforce Commitment Series 3. Washington, DC: Corporate Leadership Council.

Corporate Leadership Council (CLC). 2001a. *Global executive stock option plans.* Washington DC: The Corporate Adviser's Board.

Corporate Leadership Council (CLC). 2001b. *Legal responsibilities of compensation committees.* Washington DC: The Corporate Adviser's Board.

Corporate Leadership Council (CLC). 2001c. *Executive compensation administration.* Washington DC: The Corporate Adviser's Board.

Corporate Leadership Council (CLC). 2001d. *Executive compensation administration.* Washington DC: The Corporate Adviser's Board.

Corporate Leadership Council (CLC). 2002. *Executive compensation metrics and selection.* Washington DC: The Corporate Adviser's Board.

Corporate Leadership Council (CLC). 2003. *Benchmarking the high-performance organisation: a quantitative analysis of the implementation of high-impact performance management strategies.* Washington DC: The Corporate Adviser's Board.

Corporate Leadership Council (CLC). 2007. *Building and Managing a Competitive Employment Value Proposition in the United Kingdom.* Washington DC: The Corporate Adviser's Board.

Corsello, J. 2006. *Compensation as the foundation to a talent management strategy.* [Online]. Available at: http://www.yankeegroup.com [Accessed 1 February 2008].

Covey, S.R. 1998. Variable pay. *Executive Excellence*, June: 5–6.

County of San Diego, Health and Human Services Agency (HHSA). 2010. *3-4-50: Chronic disease deaths in San Diego County.* [Online]. Available at: http://www.sandiegocounty.gov/hhsa/programs/phs/documents/CHS-3-4-50SanDiegoCounty2010.pdf [Accessed 28 May 2013]

Delves, D. 2000. Balancing the cost and benefits of options: how to solve the stock option bind. *Compensation & Benefits Review, 32*(2):51–56.

Diez, F. 2018. Pay for Performance: What pay scheme is best for achieving results? Latvia, European Union: Lap Lambert Academic Publishing.

Du Toit, G.E., Erasmus, B.J. & Strydom, J.W. 2007. *Introduction to business management*. 7th ed. Cape Town: Oxford University Press.

Ellig, B.R. 2003. Executive pay: a primer. *Compensation & Benefits Review, 35*(1):44–50.

Engel, M.M. 2002. Long-term incentives. In P.T. Chingos et al. (eds.). *Paying for performance: a guide to compensation management*. 2nd ed. New York: John Wiley, pp.187–204.

Encyclopaedia Britannica. *Cost of living*. [Online]. Available at: http://global.britannica.com/EBchecked/topic/139483/cost-of-living. [Accessed 17 December 2014].

England, J.D. & Barrett, A. 2003. To protect and serve: how the compensation professional can help the compensation committee. *Workspan, 05*(03):25–30.

Erickson, R. (2009). *Back to Basics: The Employee Value Proposition During Tough Economic Times*. Available at: www.bersin.com.

Freher, E.W. 2002. Designing the annual management incentive plan. In P.T. Chingos et al. (eds.). *Paying for performance: a guide to compensation management*. 2nd ed. New York: John Wiley, pp.153–168.

Furnham, A. 2003. Personality, individual differences and incentive schemes. *North American Journal of Psychology, 5*(3):325–334.

Gallo, D.D., Hellerman, M. & Jones, M. 2003. Behind the scenes: compensation's role in corporate governance. *Workspan, 05*(03):33–38.

Gauthier, B. 2002. The sales compensation challenge: Meeting the diverse needs of multiple business units. *Workspan, 03*(02):34–38.

Gerhart, B. & Rynes, S.L. 2003. *Compensation: theory, evidence and strategic implications*. Thousand Oaks, CA: Sage Publications, Inc.

Gerhart, B. 2000. Compensation strategy and organisational performance. In S. Rynes & B. Gerhart (eds.). *Compensation in organizations*. San Francisco, CA: Jossey-Bass, pp.151–194.

Giancola, F. 2008. Should generation profiles influence reward strategy? *Employee Relations Law Journal, 34*(1):56–68.

Gilles, P.L. 2000. A fresh look at incentive plans for privately held companies. *Compensation & Benefits Review, 32*(6):61–72.

Grant Thornton. 2008. *Recruitment and retention: the quest for the right talent*. [Online]. Available at: http://www.gt.co.za [Accessed 3 April 2008].

Greenhill, R. 1988. *Performance related pay*. Cambridge UK: Director Books.

Grigoriadis, C. & Bussin, M. 2007. Current Practice with Regard to Short Term Incentives for Middle Managers. *South African Journal of Human Resource Management/SA Tydskrif vir Menslikehulpbronbestuur, 5*(1):45-53.

Gross, S.E. & Edelsten, M. 2006. Paying the price of global expansion. *Workspan, 09*(06):42–46. Scottsdale, AZ: WorldatWork Press.

Gross, S.E. & Friedman, H.E. 2007. Creating an effective total rewards strategy: holistic approach better supports business success. *Mercer Human Resources Consulting CD – Your guide to the age of talent*. New York, United States: Mercer.

Gross, S.E. & Nalbantian, H.R. 2002. Looking at rewards holistically. In P.T. Chingos et al. (eds.). *Paying for performance: a guide to compensation management*. 2nd ed. New York: John Wiley, pp.1–19.

Gunkel, M. 2006. *Country-Compatible Incentive Design: A Comparison of Employees' Performance Reward Preferences in Germany and the USA*. Wiesbaden, Germany: Deutscher Universitats-Verlag.

Hansen, F., Smith, M. & Hansen, R.B. 2002. Rewards and recognition in employee motivation. *Compensation & Benefits Review, 34*(5):64 –72.

Harris, R. 2002. Designing incentive compensation programs to support value-based management. In P.T. Chingos et al. (eds.). *Paying for performance: a guide to compensation management*. 2nd ed. New York: John Wiley, pp.169–185.

Harris, S. & Clements, L. 2007. What's the perceived value of your incentives? *Workspan*, *02*(07):21–25. Scottsdale, AZ: WorldatWork Press.

Hastings, R. 2009. *Netflix Culture: Freedom & Responsibility*. [Online]. Available at: https://www.slideshare.net/reed2001/culture-1798664/2-Netflix_CultureFreedom_Responsibility2 [Accessed 2 December 2020].

HayGroup. 2001. *The impact of current economic conditions on reward programs*. Philadelphia, Pennsylvania: Hay Viewpoint.

Heneman, R.L. 2001. Corporate business strategies and compensation strategies. In R.L. Heneman (ed.). *Strategic reward management. Design, implementation and evaluation*. Greenwich, CT: Information Age Publishing Inc, pp.189 – 211.

Hill, B. & Tande, C. 2006. *Total Rewards: The Employment Value Proposition*. Available at: https://tandehill.com/wp-content/uploads/2019/12/Total-Rewards.pdf

Hofstede, G. 2004. *A summary of my ideas about national culture differences*. [Online]. Available at: http://spitswww.uvt.nl/web/iric/hofstede/page3.htm [Accessed 2 December 2004].

Hutson, D. 2000. New incentives are on the rise. *Compensation & Benefits Review*, *32*(5):40–46.

Ittner, C.D. & Larcker, D.F. 2002. Determinants of performance measure choices in worker incentive plans. *Journal of Labour Economics*, *20*(2): pp. S58–S90.

Jesuthasan, R. 2003. Business performance management: improving returns on rewards investments. *WorldatWork® Journal*, *12*(4):55–64.

Jossey–Bass & Pfeiffer. 2009. *Knowledge, motivation, rewards and incentives*. [Online]. Available at: http://209.85.129.132/search?q=cache:V6R3fz-isngJ:www.undercurrent.co.za/Knowledge/Motivation%2520theory%2520and%2520Incentives.htm+%22emphasise+succ ess+rather+than+failure%22&cd=1&hl=en&ct=clnk&gl=za [Accessed 23 February 2010].

Kaplan, R. & Norton, R. 1996. *The balanced scorecard*. Boston: Harvard Business School Press.

Kerr, S. 1995. On the folly of rewarding A, while hoping for B. *The Academy of Management Executive, 9(1)*:7-14.

King, M.E. 2001. *King report on corporate governance in South Africa – 2001*. Johannesburg: Institute of Directors.

King, M.E. 2009. *King III code on corporate governance for South Africa*. Johannesburg: Institute of Directors.

Kurlander, P. & Barton, S. 2004. Improving your odds: successful incentive compensation automation. *Workspan*, 01(04):30–33.

Lawler, E.E. 1990. *Strategic pay: aligning organisational strategies and pay systems*. San Francisco, CA: Jossey-Bass.

Lawler, E.E. 1983. *Pay and organisation development*. Reading, MA: Addison-Wesley.

Lawler, E.E. 2000. *Rewarding excellence: pay strategies for the new economy*. San Francisco, CA: Jossey-Bass.

Lawler, E.E., Nadler, D.A. & Cammann, C. 1980. *Organisational assessment*. New York: Wiley & Sons.

Lock, S. 2014. The State of Healthcare in South East Asia. *The Economist Intelligence Unit Perspectives*. [Online]. Available at: https://www.eiuperspectives.economist.com/healthcare/state-healthcare-southeast-asia [Accessed 14 November 2016].

Locke, E.A., & Latham, G.P. 1990. *A theory of goal setting & task performance*. Englewood Cliffs, NJ: Prentice Hall College Division, p. 544.

Locke, E.A. & Latham, G.P. 2002. Building a Practically Useful Theory of Goal Setting and Task Motivation: A 35-year odyssey. *American Psychologist, 57*(9):705–717.

Luo, S. 2003. Does your sales incentive plan pay for performance? *Compensation & Benefits Review, 35*(1):18–24.

Luthra, S. 2012. Healthcare in India: A call for innovative reform, an interview with Victoria Fan. *The National Bureau of Asian Research.* Available at: http://www.nbr.org/research/activity.aspx?id=298#. UaRKF0Awd8E. [Accessed 28 May, 2013].

Malambe, L. & Bussin, M. 2013. Short-term incentive schemes for hospital managers. *SA Journal of Human Resource Management/SA Tydskrif vir Menslikehulpbronbestuur,* *11*(1): Art. #487. http://dx.doi. org/10.4102/sajhrm.v11i1.487

Martin, T. 2004. Can compensation impact the bottom line? *Workspan, 02*(04):26–29.

Martocchio, J. 1998. *Strategic compensation.* Upper Saddle River, NJ: Prentice-Hall, Inc.

McAfee, R.B. & Anderson, C.J. 1995. Compensation dilemmas: an exercise in ethical decision making. *Development in Business Simulation and Experiential Exercises, 22*(1): 156–159.

McCord, P. 2014. *How Netflix Reinvented HR.* [Online]. Available at: https://hbr.org/2014/01/how-netflix-reinvented-hr [Accessed 7 November 2016].

McGorion, I. 2010. *African trends.* Johannesburg: 21st Century Pay Solutions Group.

Menefee, J.A. & Murphy, R.O. 2004. Rewarding and retaining the best. *Benefits Quarterly, 20*(3), 13-20.

Mei, W.Y. & Zhiwei, T. 2011. *The Elderly in Singapore.* Available at: http://www.singstat.gov.sg/publications/ publications_and_papers/population_and_population_structure/ssnsep11-pg1-9.pdf. [Accessed 13 May 2013].

Miceli, M.P. & Heneman, R.L. 2002. Contextual determinants of variable pay plan design: a proposed research framework. In R.L. Heneman (ed.). *Strategic reward management: design, implementation, and evaluation.* Greenwich: Information Age Publishing.

Milkovich, G. & Newman, J. 2014. *Compensation.* 11th ed. Boston: Irwin McGraw-Hill.

Minchington, B. 2010. *Employer Brand Leadership – A Global Perspective.* Newstead, Australia: Collective Learning Australia.

Mmolaeng, M. & Bussin, M. 2012. Drivers of public sector unions' wage demands in a low-inflation and recessionary environment in South Africa. *South African Labour Relations, 36*(1): 1–17. http://hdl.handle. net/10520/EJC120857.

Modise, J. 1993. *Executive compensation and corporate performance.* Unpublished MBA report. Johannesburg: University of the Witwatersrand.

Moen, P. 2000. Effective work/life strategies: working couples, work conditions, gender and life quality. *Social Problems, 47*(3):291–327.

Monster. 2020. *Accounting Supervisor Job Description.* Available at: https://hiring.monster.com/employer-resources/job-description-templates/accounting-supervisor-job-description/ [Accessed 30 March 2016].

Montagnon, P. 2019. *Focus on corporate culture to prevent the next scandal.* Available at: https://www.strategy-business.com/article/Focus-on-corporate-culture-to-prevent-the-next-scandal? [Accessed 28 October 2019].

Moore, A. & Bussin, M. 2009. Reward preferences for generations in the information technology industry. *South African Journal of Human Resource Management/ SA Tydskrif vir Menslikehulpbronbestuur, 10*(1):1-9. http://dx.doi.org/10.4102/sajhrm.v10i1.325.

Moynahan, J.K. 1981. *Incentive compensation workbook.* Chicago, IL: Bank Marketing Association.

Nel, A.C. 2002. *Performance management and reward – an integrated approach.* Unpublished master's thesis, University of Pretoria.

Nienaber, N. 2009. *The relationship between personality types and reward preferences.* Published Doctoral thesis. Johannesburg: University of Johannesburg.

Nienaber, R., Bussin, M. & Henn, C. 2011. The relationship between personality types and reward preferences. *Acta Commercii, 1*: 1-21.

Novak, D. 2013. *Taking People With You: The Only Way to Make Big Things Happen.* New York, NY: Portfolio and Penguin.

Nzukuma, K. & Bussin, M. 2010. Job hopping among Senior Black African managers in South Africa. *South African Journal of Human Resource Management/SA Tydskrif vir Menslikehulpbronbestuur, 9*(1): Art #360. http://dx.doi.org/10.4102.

Ochurub, M., Bussin, M., Goosen, X. 2012. Organisational readiness for introducing a performance management system. *SA Journal of Human Resource Management/SA Tydskrif vir Menslikehulpbronbestuur, 10*(1): Art #389. http/dx.doi.org/10.4102/sajhrm.v10i1.389.

OECD Library. 2011. Burden of out-of-pocket health expenditure. *Health at a Glance,* OECD Indicators, pp134-135. Retrieved from: https://www.oecd-ilibrary.org/docserver/health_glance-2011-en.pdf?expires=161526 2853&id=id&accname=guest&checksum=0336E4C3919A0DE37E6B892C43CD267F

Orens, R.M. & Elliott, V.J. 2002. Variable pay programs: pay for results. In P.T. Chingos et al. (eds.). *Paying for performance: a guide to compensation management.* 2nd ed. New York: John Wiley and Sons, Inc, pp.20–42.

Park, D. & Shin, K. 2011. *Impact of Population Aging on Asia's Future Growth.* [Online]. Available at: http://www.adb.org/sites/default/files/economics-wp281.pdf. [Accessed 27 May 2013].

Reda, J. 2002. *Compensation committee handbook.* New York: John Wiley and Sons, Inc.

Reynolds, L. 1998. Variable pay laws may benefit employers. *HRFOCUS,* Article 9987, December.

Rock, D. & Jones, B. 2015. Why more and more companies are ditching performance ratings. *Harvard Business Review.* [Online]. Available at: https://hbr.org/2015/11/what-really-happens-when-companies-nix-performance-ratings

Rodgers, C. 1999. *Managers' perceptions of a total package compensation system.* Unpublished Master of Management Research Report. Johannesburg: University of the Witwatersrand.

Romweber, J.T. 2003. The effects of good compensation committee governance. *Workspan, 05*(03):41–43.

Ross, T.L. & Ross, R.A. 1988. Productivity gainsharing: resolving some of the measurement issues. In C.H. Fay & R.W. Beatty (eds.). *The compensation sourcebook.* Amherst, MA: Human Resource Development Press, pp.157–166.

Rothwell, S. 1982. Productivity improvement through reduced labour turnover. *Long Range Planning, 15*(2):67–76.

Rynes, S. & Gerhart, B. 2000. *Compensation in organisations.* San Francisco, CA: Jossey-Bass.

Schlechter, A., Faught, C. & Bussin. M. 2014. Total Rewards: A study of artisan attraction and retention within a South African context. *SA Journal of Human Resource Management/SA Tydskrif vir Menslikehulbron bestuur, 12*(1): Art # 648. http://dx.doi.org/10.4102/sajhrm.v12i1.648.

Schlechter, A., Hung A. & Bussin M. 2014. Understanding talent attraction- the perceived attractiveness of financial reward elements for knowledge workers. *SA Journal of Human Resource Management/SA Tydskrif vir Menslikehulpbronbestuur, 12*(1): 647.

Schlechter, A., Thompson, N. & Bussin, M. 2015. Investigating the Perceived Attractiveness of Non-financial Reward Elements by means of an Experimental Design. *Employee Relations Emerald, 37*(3):274 –295. http://dx.doi.org/10.1108/ER-06-2014-0077.

Schlechter, A.F., Syce, C. & Bussin, M. 2015. Predicting voluntary turnover in employees using demographic characteristics: a South African case study. *Acta Commercii 15*(1): Art. #274. http://dx.doi. org/10.4102/ac.v15i1.274.

Scholl, R.W. 2002. *Motivational processes – expectancy theory.* [Online]. Available at: http://www.cba.uri.edu/scholl/notes/motivation.Expectancy.html [Accessed 1 December 2003].

Schuster, M. 1988. Gainsharing: the state of the art. In C.H. Fay & R.W. Beatty (eds.). *The compensation sourcebook.* Amherst, MA: Human Resource Development Press, pp.148–153.

Serino, B. 2002. Non-cash awards boost sales compensation plans. *Workspan, 08*(02):25–31.

Sibangilizwe, N., Bussin, M. & de Swardt, L. 2013. Confirming a theoretical pay constructs of a variable pay scheme. *SA Journal of Human Resource Management/ SA Tydskrif vir Menslikehulpbronbestuur, 11*(1): Art# 464. http://dx.doi.org/10.4102/sajhrm.v11i1.464.

Smit, W., Stanz, K. & Bussin, M. 2015. Retention preferences and the relationship between total rewards, perceived organisational support and perceived supervisor support. *SA Journal of Human Resource Management/SA Tydskrif vir Menslikehulpbronbestuur, 13*(1): Art. #665. http://dx.doi.org/10.4102/sajhrm.v13i1.665.

Snelgar, R.J., Renard, M. & Venter, D. 2013. An empirical study of the reward preferences of South African employees. *SA Journal of Human Resource Management/ SA Tydskrif vir Menslikehulpbronbestuur, 11*(1): Art. #351.

South African Reward Association. 2009. *SARA practice notes.* [Online]. Available at: http://www.sara.co.za [Accessed 1 October 2009].

Stein, S.J. 2007. *Make your workplace great.* Mississauga, Canada: John Wiley & Sons, Ltd.

Tauber, Y.D. 2003. Gaining independence. *Workspan, 05*(03):10–14.

Sussmuth-Dyckerhoff, C. & Wang, J. 2010. *China's health care reforms.* [Online]. Available at: http://www.mckinsey.com/~/media/mckinsey/dotcom/client_service/healthcare%20systems%20and%20services/health%20international/hi10_china_healthcare_reform.ashx [Accessed 14 November 2016].

Thomas, H., Smith, R. & Diez, F. 2013. *Human Capital and Global Business Strategy.* Cambridge: Cambridge University Press.

Towers Perrin. 2007. *Using total rewards to build an effective employee value proposition.* [Online]. Available at: http://www.towersperrin.com [Accessed 15 May 2008].

Tropman, J.E. 2001. *The compensation solution.* San Francisco: Jossey-Bass.

Trust for America's Health. 2013. *Strategies to move from sick care to health care in four years.* [Online]. Available at: http://healthyamericans.org/assets/files/TFAH2013HealthierAmericaFnlRv.pdf [Accessed 13 May 2013].

United Nations. 2002. *World population ageing 1950-2050.* [Online]. Available at: http://www.un.org/esa/population/publications/worldageing19502050/countriesorareas.htm. [Accessed 28 May 2013].

Van der Merwe, S. & Bussin, M. 2005. An evaluation of a communication, facilitation, and project management tool to enhance the effectiveness of project execution. *South African Journal of Human Resource Management/ SA Tydskrif vir Menslikehulpbronbestuur, 4*(3):48-54.

Van der Vyver, D. & Bussin, M. 2013. Performance-Related Pay in Government: Lessons from South Africa. Compensation & Benefits Review. *SAGE Journals, 45*: 8-20. Doi:10.1177/0886368713485038.

Van Neck, K.H. & Smilko, J.E. 2002. Variable pay plans: creating a financial partnership with the work force. *WorldatWork® Journal, 11*(4):74–79.

Van Putten, S.M. & Graskamp, E.D. 2002. End of an era? The future of stock options. *Compensation & Benefits Review, 34*(5):29–36.

Van Rooy, R. & Bussin M. 2014. Total rewards strategy for a multi-generational workforce in a financial institution. *SA Journal of Human Resource Management/SA Tydskrif vir Menslikehulpbronbestuur, 12*(1): Art. #606. http://dx.doi.org/10.4102/sajhrm.v12i1.606

Williams, V. 2001. Making performance management relevant. *Compensation & Benefits Review, 33*(4):47–51.

Wilson, T.B. 1999. *Rewards that drive high performance: success stories from leading organizations.* New York: AMACOM.

WorldatWork. 2003a. *GR5 performance management: strategy, design and implementation.* Scottsdale, AZ: WorldatWork Press.

WorldatWork. 2003b. *GR6 Variable pay: incentives, recognition and bonuses.* Scottsdale, AZ: WorldatWork Press.

WorldatWork. 2003c. *GR1 Total remuneration management.* Scottsdale, AZ: WorldatWork Press.

WorldatWork. 2003d. *GR7 International remuneration: an overview of global rewards*. Scottsdale, AZ: WorldatWork Press.

WorldatWork. 2007. *The WorldatWork handbook of compensation, benefits & total rewards*. Hoboken, NJ: John Wiley & Sons, Inc.

WorldatWork. 2020. The Total Rewards Model. [Online]. Available at: [Online]. Available at: https://www.worldatwork.org/total-rewards-model/ [Accessed 17 October 2020].

Xpatulator.com. 2014. *International Cost of Living Calculators*. [Online]. Available at: http://www.xpatulator.com/. [Accessed 17 December 2014].

Young, W. 2002. *A post-mortem of corporate failure – an analysis of the effect that remuneration policy has on directors and consequent corporate failure*. Unpublished MBA research report. Pretoria: Gordon Institute of Business Science.

Zillmann, M. 2000. *Motivation*. [Online]. Available at: http://www.academic.emporia.edu/smithwil/00fallmg443/eja/zillman.html [Accessed 1 December 2003].

Zingheim, P.K. & Schuster, J.R. 2003. Getting back to basics. *Workspan*, *05*(03):55–58.

# Index

www.ingramcontent.com/pod-product-compliance
Lightning Source LLC
Chambersburg PA
CBHW082120210326
41599CB00031B/5821